challenge and
e idea and/rhapsody of the
seize the day and opportunity
less opportunity to/found

an dreams both of
... One was the
... on forever
... and innocent, hardship
... challenge. In
... them, starved them
... was the
... limitless opportunity
... found
... could
... a road, ever
... and

A FAIR

By ISAAC BASHEVIS SINGER

Among those who ran away from Hitler and managed to reach America was the poet Getzele Tertziver, a tiny, dark-complexioned man with a small head, shoulder-length hair, and on his chin a wisp of a beard. He had a crooked nose, a mouth with small, widely-spaced teeth as black as lead, and large black wandering eyes--the right one looked up, the left one down. The humorists in the Warsaw Yiddish Press often printed jokes about Getzele Tertziver, his wild appearance and his poems which no one understood, not even the critics who believed in modernism. Getzele Tertziver had published one book, a mixture of poems, aphorisms and miniatures, titled "The World History of My Future."

Getzele Tertziver, as did his grandfather the Tertziver Rabbi Alterel, reversed everything. He slept in the daytime and was awake at night. Only one typesetter in Warsaw could decipher Getzele's handwriting. Years after pelerines for men went out of fashion, Getzele's apparel was a pelerine hanging to his ankles, a flowing tie, and a black, wide-brimmed hat. He smoked a long pipe. Even though the Tertziver Chassidim considered him a ~~non-believer~~ heretic who shamed his pious ancestors in Paradise, they surreptitiously sustained him. Old Chassidim who remembered Rabbi Alterel when he was young swore that Getzele resembled him like two drops of water--the same face, the same way of walking, the same mannerisms. True, Rabbi Alterel ascended to the highest spheres while Getzele had fallen into abyss of apostasy. Still, they would not allow his grandson to starve.

How strange that wild-eyed Getzele, who could not make himself understood either in his writing or in his speech, using a gibberish of Yiddish, Hebrew, Aramaic, which he spewed forth quickly and in a chassidic sing-song, had married three times, and each time with a beauty. When the writers in the Yiddish Writers Club in Warsaw tired of discussing literature and reviling one another, it was enough to mention the name Getzele Tertziver to revive the conversation. Everyone asked the same question: "What had those women seen in him?"

Dictionary of Literary Biography

American Novelists Since World War II

Second Series

Dictionary of Literary Biography • Volume Six

American Novelists Since World War II

Second Series

Edited by James E. Kibler, Jr.
University of Georgia

Foreword by William Targ

A Bruccoli Clark Book
Gale Research Company • Book Tower • Detroit, Michigan 48226
1980

Matthew J. Bruccoli, *Editorial Director*
C. E. Frazer Clark, Jr., *Managing Editor*
Richard Layman, *Project Editor*

Printed in the United States of America

Library of Congress Cataloging in Publication Data

Main entry under title:

American novelists since World War II.

(Dictionary of literary biography ; v. 6)
"A Bruccoli Clark book."
Includes indexes.
1. American fiction--20th century--Bio-bibliography.
2. Novelists, American--20th century--Biography.
3. American fiction--20th century--History and criticism. I. Kibler, James E. II. Series.
PS379.A554 1980 813'.54'09 [B] 80-22495
ISBN 0-8103-0908-4

10 9 8 7 6 5 4

For
James B. Meriwether

Contents

Contents

Foreword

Several years ago a common expression uttered in literary journals and public places was, mournfully: "The novel is dead." There were editors and writers in high places and low who believed this to be a fact. But they proved to be myopic. Because, while they solemnly declared that the novel had expired, exciting new novelists were emerging with healthy regularity. And publishers, even the larger conglomerates, were continuing to publish novels, and first novels, too—in both hard and soft covers.

The predecessor of the present volume together with the present work combine to offer ample evidence that the American novel and novelists are alive and thriving. There are problems, yes—industry and trade problems, market problems and distribution problems and cost problems. But the novelists are still alive and thousands of new novels—some first rate—are being published. Did not William Styron and Norman Mailer prove this just recently? Obviously they were not aware that the "novel is dead."

There is an abundance of creative ferment in the atmosphere. Small, new presses are proliferating; interesting new talents—first novelists—are blossoming on these frail but living trees. And while it is true that America has not produced a Grass, a Sartre, a Camus or Beckett, we do have Joan Didion, Toni Morrison, Elizabeth Hardwick, Isaac Bashevis Singer, and many others of striking quality. We also have in these pages ample assurance of a new body of risk-takers, stylists, nontraditionalists. Indeed, in the seventy biographies presented here we have the whole spectrum of writing talent.

Yet, despite all claims or wishful thinking, post-World War II in America has shown no signs of a genuine literary renaissance. It is regrettable that some of our leading major novelists are not as productive as one would like—not productive as was, say, William Faulkner. Nor alas, do we have anyone with Faulkner's immense gifts. Some of our star writers of fiction publish far too infrequently so as to almost vanish from the scene. One notable example is Paul Bowles. Henry Roth (*Call It Sleep*) is the prime case. Nor has any Melville or Hawthorne emerged in our time. But a renaissance (in reverse!) has come upon us, alas. The "product" consists of a low-level brand of writing, and an intense productivity unique in America. The vitality of the publishers who promote the stuff, joined by the motion picture and TV producers, is unparalleled in our history. Scores of novels, pure and homogenized, are pouring forth; fiction sordid and rancid; sex and sorcery-obsessed, sub-naturalistic, romantic, spaced-out, high and low schlock, horror and fright-wig fiction—all of these kinds of books are being written and published brazenly, but, in the main, by nonwriters. The audience for these books is not the literate reader; the books are espoused by the film and TV industry and foisted, with huge promotion budgets, on the sub-genre reader looking for ersatz romantic raw sex and space adventure, as well as terror and violence. Of course, none of these books has validity in terms of literature, any more than do the comic strips in newspapers. But they are books nevertheless, and they do affect the publishing statistics and appear on best-seller lists.

There are books of high distinction among the works in our post-World War II omnium-gatherum; some are downright masterpieces. Harriette Simpson Arnow's *The Dollmaker* might be so considered. Likewise Eleanor Clark's *Baldur's Gate*. Paul Bowles, author of four excellent novels and numerous other works, has as yet to garner the readership he merits, especially in view of the remarkable novel *The Sheltering Sky*, published many years ago but still a shining star in his bibliography. And then there is *Ratner's Star* by Don DeLillo, certainly deserving of pause and consideration. It is called, properly, "a red giant of a book." Mary Gordon's first novel, *Final Payments*, published in 1978, is a moving, powerful study, in part, of guilt and self-punishment. Mario Puzo's historic blockbuster of a novel, *The Godfather*, one of this century's most popular novels, has been both reviled and lavishly praised. There is little question in my mind (I was the publisher's editor of that novel) that it presents one of the most successfully realized central characters in all modern

American fiction, a figure who has already had an enormous impact and influence on our literature and culture. Another sensational and shock-ridden book, a novel of high merit and importance, is Judith Rossner's fourth novel, *Looking for Mr. Goodbar,* which Pat McAlexander says "will have a place in American literary history because of its convincing, finely drawn portrait of the sexual and moral confusion of its time." Other remarkable and enduring novels by authors included in our pages here are from the pens of J. P. Donleavy, John Irving, and Jessamyn West.

The statistics in *Variety* will show that *entertainment,* inspired and supported and stimulated by the film/TV tycoons, is the genre most frequently seen in the best-seller lists. America, in its "cottages," flats, penthouses, and seashore mansions, is literally now a factory, a General Motors of fiction. But all the numerous seven-figure sales made from these books, books bearing shock, eroticism, and terror in bronze, silver, or gold embossed paper covers, have not spelled death to the Serious Novel, which continues to be published and recognized and respected in the main. These men and women of authentic literary talent and intent are continuing in the tradition of Literature.

—*William Targ*

Preface

This volume supplements *American Novelists Since World War II*, First Series, further documenting the growth of a body of literature still in the making. It was noted in the foreword to the earlier volume that the years since the second world war have been extremely active ones for American novelists. The seventy entries published here demonstrate further just how active these years have been and how vital the novel form remains. Series one gathered most of the novelists best known by the general public and literary critics. Many of the novelists included here have not yet been accorded extensive public recognition; but there has never been a firm correlation between literary merit and contemporary public acceptance, and authors included here may be more deserving of acclaim than certain of those championed by the literary establishment. Most of these writers are still alive and writing, some of them only beginning promising careers. A knowledge of their work is integral to an appreciation of our living contemporary literature.

The purpose of the entries in *Dictionary of Literary Biography* is to provide reliable information about the professional careers of literary people. Emphasis is placed on biography and a synthesis of the critical reception of authors' works. Bibliographies of the authors' writings and the critical writings about them are selected. The lists of books at the beginnings of entries are intended to give an overview of the subjects' book-length work in all genres; major books are included, but ephemeral works such as chapbooks or pamphlets are normally omitted. Primary bibliographies at the ends of entries are selected to include works other than original book-length writings, such as screenplays, translations, and contributions to books and periodicals. The most useful books and articles about the authors are selected for the secondary bibliographies. If there are significant public collections of an author's papers, the information is listed at the end of the entry.

Acknowledgments

This book was produced by BC Research.

Nadia Rasheed was the in-house editor.

The production staff inluded Mary Bruccoli, Joyce Fowler, Timna Gainey, Sharon K. Kirkland, Cynthia H. Rogers, Karen L. Rood, Robin Sumner, Cheryl A. Swartzentruber, Theodora J. Thompson, and Lynne C. Zeigler.

The editor would like to thank the following individuals who have been particularly helpful in forming this book: Ernest Bufkin, James Colvert, Warren French, George Garrett, Martha Hale, Evans Harrington, Bert Hitchcock, William Koon, Warren Leamon, Stanley W. Lindberg, and Louis Rubin. Jacquelyn Price and Walter W. Ross III did the necessary library research with the valuable assistance of the following librarians at the Thomas Cooper Library: Michael Havener, Donna Nance, Jean Rhyne, Ellen Tillett, Gary Treadway, Joyce Werner, and Beth Woodard. Photographic copy work for this volume was done by Pat Crawford; and assistance in locating photographs and other illustration material was provided by the *Louisville Courier Journal & Times*, the University of Denver Office of Institutional Advancement, the University of Georgia Libraries, and the University of Kentucky Libraries.

The following photographers generously allowed us the use of their photos: Peggy Bach, Wally Bowen, Geraldine Brooks, Richard Byrd, Charne, Robert T. Coleman III, Nancy Crampton, Richard De Combray, Dana Durst, Joel Gardner, Bernard Gotfryd, Erich Hartmann, John Hubbard, Shyla Irving, Jill Krementz, John LeBaron, Jacqueline McCord, Rollie McKenna, Dan Moore, Mark Morrow, J. S. Peck, Antoinette W. Roades, Matthew Rolston, Robert Satter, Max Schaible, Larry B. Stevenson, Angus Stewart, Thomas Victor, and Gabriel Penn Warren.

Finally, grateful acknowledgment is due the subjects of entries in this book who were kind enough to read their entries for accuracy. Without the assistance of all these people, this book would not have been possible.

Dictionary of Literary Biography

American Novelists Since World War II

Second Series

Dictionary of Literary Biography

HARRIETTE SIMPSON ARNOW
(7 July 1908-)

SELECTED BOOKS: *Mountain Path*, as Harriette Simpson (New York: Covici-Friede, 1936);

Hunter's Horn (New York: Macmillan, 1949; London: Collins, 1950);

The Dollmaker (New York: Macmillan, 1954; London: Heinemann, 1955);

Seedtime on the Cumberland (New York: Macmillan, 1960; London: Collier-Macmillan, 1960);

Flowering of the Cumberland (New York: Macmillan / London: Collier-Macmillan, 1963);

The Weedkiller's Daughter (New York: Knopf, 1970);

The Kentucky Trace: A Novel of the American Revolution (New York: Knopf, 1974);

Old Burnside (Lexington: University Press of Kentucky, 1977).

Harriette Simpson Arnow is best known for her novel, *The Dollmaker*, in print almost continuously since its publication in 1954. Few novels so movingly and unsparingly dramatize the anguish of the dispossessed rural poor trying to retain their values and integrity in a violent urban environment. Without the sentimentality that mars some other novels about forced migration, *The Dollmaker* chronicles the attempts of its heroine, Gertie Nevels, a hulking Kentucky hill woman, to preserve her family, her creativity, and her pride in her hill heritage. An acknowledged masterpiece, *The Dollmaker* has overshadowed Arnow's other fiction, which is yet to be assessed as fully.

A masterful storyteller who uses traditional narrative form, Arnow feels that her desire to tell stories, or write fiction, was kindled as a child, when she heard her parents and grandmothers spin tales about her forebears from before the Revolutionary War. In her parents' strict, religious home in rural Kentucky, writing was considered frivolous and impractical; Arnow was expected to follow family tradition and become a teacher. Secretly she wrote short stories during high school and college—two years (1924-1926) at Berea College and two years at the University of Louisville, where she received a B.S. degree in 1930. Two years of teaching after graduation persuaded Arnow that the profession was not for her. She quit and decided to devote more of her time and energy to writing. In 1934, at twenty-six, she scandalized her family by moving to a furnished room near the main library in Cincinnati, where she could read the "great novels" and try to write fiction. She supported herself with odd jobs and worked for the Federal Writers' Project. Her first publications, "A Mess of Pork" and "Marigolds and Mules," were short stories that appeared in 1935 in the little magazines of the 1930s. Written in terse, evocative prose revealing a perfectly attuned eye and ear, both stories demonstrate the skill at characterization and at depicting shocking violence that distinguish her later novels. National recognition came in winter 1936 when the prestigious *Southern Review* published "The Washerwoman's Day," a story that foreshadows *Hunter's Horn* (1949) and *The Dollmaker* in its searing criticism of narrow piousness.

In March 1939 Arnow married newspaperman Harold Arnow. Tired of city living, they turned to farm life in southern Kentucky. A daughter, Marcella, was born to them in 1941. In 1944 they moved to Detroit, where Harold Arnow took a job with the *Detroit Times*. A son, Thomas, was born in 1946. They settled in their current Ann Arbor, Michigan, homestead in 1950.

Arnow's early years were shaped by the small town of Burnside in Pulaski County, Kentucky. There she attended school and watched the steamboats and railroad transport passengers to or from Cincinnati, New Orleans, and Miami. The other world that attracted Arnow most, though, was not the cities, but the primitive hills east of her home. Her first prolonged stay with the hill people who were to become the primary subjects of her fiction occurred in 1926. To earn enough money to resume college she boarded with a family in a remote corner of Pulaski County and taught in their one-room schoolhouse for seven months. In her first novel, *Mountain Path* (published in 1936 under her maiden name, Simpson), she tells the story of Louisa (Arnow's middle name) Sheridan, a college student-teacher who finds herself similarly situated in feud country. The full-bodied characters and Arnow's acute portrayal of their harsh yet emotionally rich lives reveal the depth of her bond with the hill people and their effect on her imagination.

More than merely providing a privileged look at life deep in the backwoods, *Mountain Path* dramatizes a universal struggle central to Arnow's more distinguished, later fiction: the confrontation between the individual conscience and society, whether it be family, community, or the wider political, social, economic world. *Mountain Path* asks whether Louisa can overcome her upbringing, and begin a life in tune with her deepest instincts and values.

Enthusiastically received by reviewers and readers alike, *Mountain Path* established Arnow as a writer of considerable talent. Alfred Kazin called *Mountain Path* a superb book "of its type"—a regional novel about Southern mountaineers. He praised Arnow's authentic characterizations and her "spiritual indignation," congratulating her for resisting the "spurious lyricism" and complacency that characterize many novels about Southern highlanders. He perceived that Arnow's novel departs from the overused literary conventions of "mountain fiction" established in the nineteenth century. Like many of these earlier novels, *Mountain Path* does depict backwoods Kentuckians feuding and moonshining, and a young city woman teaching school in the mountains. But while the heroines of earlier, popular novels by Lucy Furman and Charles Neville Buck try to uplift the ignorant "hillbillies," reasoning them out of their feuds, Louisa learns to appreciate her hosts' values and even considers eschewing her career plans to begin life anew among them. By insisting on the tag "Kentucky" or "regional," Kazin had implied that Arnow's novel has a limited appeal. Arnow's focus on her characters' freedom of choice and moral responsibility, however, seems to surpass the limits of any provincial literature.

Hunter's Horn persuaded most critics that Arnow was more than a "regional novelist." A best-seller, it also won best novel of 1949 in the *Saturday Review* national critics' poll amid such formidable competition as Orwell's *1984*. Critics consistently lauded Arnow's characters, her artful, "effortless" prose, and what Malcolm Cowley calls her "poetry of earth" in describing her characters' connection to their land.

The story of a hill farmer's stalking of an elusive red fox, *Hunter's Horn* dramatizes a compulsion as consuming and as mythic as Ahab's hunt for Moby-Dick. Nunn Ballew's chase after King Devil, the fox who depletes the community's livestock and runs the families' hounds to death, begins as a combination of sport and expediency but grows into a frightening obsession that causes Nunn to wonder who is the hunter and who the hunted. His farm falls into disrepair, his debts mount as he spends all his money on two pedigreed foxhounds, and he risks losing the respect of his wife, his children, his neighbors, his preacher, and, he fears, God.

Harriette Simpson Arnow

In *Hunter's Horn* Arnow further develops the theme she had explored in *Mountain Path*: the battle to resist external pressures and make choices based on one's deepest instincts and beliefs. As Nunn ignores his detractors and continues to chase King Devil, he appears to demonstrate a stalwart independence. But the true test of his self-reliance comes not with his obsessive pursuit of King Devil, but rather with the decision he faces when his spirited fourteen-year-old daughter, Suse, becomes pregnant.

The novel's absorbing subplot focuses on Suse's dreams of getting an education and going north, thereby escaping the fate of most mountain women: having more children than they can feed. In a scene that illustrates Arnow's remarkable ability to sustain suspense and to cement the reader's sympathies with her characters, Nunn must decide Suse's fate before the assembled community. Almost against his will, the reader shares Nunn's anguish. Assured that her irreverent father will not bow to the prevailing notions of decency he has always scorned, an unashamed Suse is stunned and angered when he proclaims that his fire will warm no bastard: she must marry the baby's father. Nunn, nearly frozen with ambivalence and grief, wins back the neighbors' approval in exchange for his daughter's back and heart being "broke to the plow." Arnow's portrait of Nunn's conflicting loyalties demonstrates her ability to create male characters as palpable and as complex as her most arresting heroines. Few American novelists so genuinely dramatize the entangled bonds among family members, the joy and anguish of being born into a group.

The Dollmaker firmly established Arnow as a major American (not Kentucky or regional) novelist. Another best-seller, it too earned critical accolades, tying for best novel of the year in the *Saturday Review*'s national critics' poll, topping Eudora Welty's *The Ponder Heart* and Faulkner's *A Fable*; it was a runner-up to *A Fable* for the National Book Award. Perhaps partly because most of the novel is set outside Kentucky, critics were less tempted to call the book "regional." But the power of Arnow's dramatization of the corrosive effects of living in a modern industrial society makes arguing over labels patently petty. "One is convinced, part way through the book," says Joyce Carol Oates, "that it is a masterpiece. . . . Critical examination seems almost irrelevant."

This riveting story of a family's migration during World War II from the Kentucky hills to a crowded housing project in Detroit centers on Gertie Nevels's efforts to hold her family together before and after she joins her husband in Detroit, where he has gone to work in a defense plant. An intimidating, self-reliant, inarticulate six-foot-four-inch craggy mountain of flesh, Gertie has an effect on the reader that matches her size. Heaped with details of how city life befuddles and splinters the uprooted family, the novel re-creates Gertie's overbearing world with claustrophobic precision. Gertie's grappling with religious and social prejudice, labor strikes, economic insecurity, family strife, and her own faintheartedness raises questions about the ability of the human spirit to resist defilement and malaise in a modern industrial society.

More than just a naturalistic account of a family's disintegration, *The Dollmaker* is a richly symbolic, innately moral work of art. Gertie's wavering strength is reflected in the novel's central symbol, the man-sized block of cherry wood she whittles. Her deepest hope is that the man "hidden" in the wood will be the laughing Christ in overalls she has envisaged since childhood. But Detroit often forces her to choose between defending her artistic / spiritual integrity and feeding or protecting her family. Falteringly, guiltily, she advises two of her children to relinquish evidence of the "hillbilly" in them in order to "get along" with their Northern neighbors; she stops whittling for pleasure and agrees to carve tortured, blood-dripping Christ figures for grocery money. Later, a jigsaw replaces her knife as she churns out ugly, painted dolls on a family assembly line. Horrified, she discerns the shamed, repentant Judas lurking in the sweet-smelling, pure-grained cherry wood. Gertie discovers her own identity and destiny as the man in the wood betrays his.

The scene describing the death of Gertie's five-year-old daughter, Cassie Marie, best illustrates Arnow's power and distinctiveness as a writer. An innocent, disarming, creative character, Cassie has a bit of Huckleberry Finn in her and demonstrates Arnow's unusual ability to render children authentically. Mistakenly Gertie believes that Cassie's playmates' cries of "cuckoo" as they hear her talking aloud to her imaginary friend Callie Lou will harm Cassie more than the loss of Callie Lou. The novel's most memorable line is Gertie's telling the desperate, disbelieving Cassie, "There ain't no Callie Lou." But aware on some level that Callie Lou represents Cassie's pride in Kentucky, where Callie Lou was born, and Cassie's refusal to become assimilated, Gertie belatedly decides to let Cassie revive Callie Lou. As the immobilized child sits cradling Callie Lou on the railroad tracks, where she can avoid Gertie's rebuke, Gertie watches a train sever Cassie's outstretched legs. Gertie's hysterical search for Cassie as she runs to tell her forlorn child that it is all right to keep Callie Lou—"a body's gotta have somethen all their own"—her horror at watching the train lurch forward, and her descent into near madness afterward draw the reader unconditionally into Gertie's blurred, truncated world. Arnow's fluid prose, her precise, startling details (especially Cassie's bloodied, dangling boot), and the horrific punch of her violence bespeak a master's command.

However profoundly depressing are Gertie's gradual debility and defeat, *The Dollmaker*'s world is not without hope. Nature, art, and a parent's bond with a child provide solace and meaning. But more encouraging is Arnow's conviction that other people are one's best resource. Arnow's belief that art is "for the masses . . . a mirror in which man sees his own image or that of his neighbor" is embodied in Gertie's belated, anguished realization at novel's end that she could have carved Christ in the cherry wood if only she had perceived her Detroit neighbors as models. Christ can live in the common man even in Detroit, a place Gertie imagined was hell on earth. The dirty, howling project children even keep Callie Lou alive after Cassie is buried beneath the Northern cemetery's artificial grass.

Arnow's talent for dramatizing Southern highlanders struggling against a recalcitrant, hostile environment finds rich expression in her two social histories of the settling of southeastern Kentucky and northern Tennessee, *Seedtime on the Cumberland* (1960) and *Flowering of the Cumberland* (1963). Often as gripping as her best fiction, they established her as a reputable historian. Her most recent book, *Old Burnside* (1977), combines a history of her home community with family memories.

Arnow's return to fiction in 1970 with *The Weedkiller's Daughter*, her only novel not focusing on the lives of Kentucky mountaineers, was inauspicious. Set in a Detroit suburb in the 1960s, the novel dramatizes the attempts of fifteen-year-old Susie Schnitzer to preserve whatever rudiments of uncorrupted nature remain in her seemingly plastic world and to keep her mind free of the racial and ethnic prejudice and hate that infest her home and community. *The Weedkiller's Daughter* is as potent a condemnation of postindustrial American values as *The Dollmaker*, but it lacks the captivating characters of Arnow's earlier fiction. An exception is an older woman who keeps a farm on the outskirts of town. Regarded as weird, she is dubbed "The Primitive." Her name is Gertie Nevels.

The Kentucky Trace: A Novel of the American Revolution (1974) comes closer to the power and immediacy of Arnow's earlier fiction. The hero, Leslie Collins, a backwoods rebel, is engaged in a struggle as demanding as his fight against British and Loyalist soldiers: he plans to rescue, then adopt, an abused, neglected infant. His plot to get the child is intricate, ingenious, and hilarious, demonstrating Arnow's gleeful appreciation of that era's customs, rituals, and language.

Though Arnow has always had a modest, fervent following, she has only recently begun to receive consideration in the popular and academic presses. The essay that won her the most notice was Joyce Carol Oates's appreciation of *The Dollmaker*, first published in the *New York Times Book Review* in 1971 and later as the afterword to the Avon paperback edition. Oates's hailing it as "our most unpretentious American masterpiece" may have accelerated its republication. A volume on Arnow appeared in the Twayne United States Authors Series in 1974, and several essays have appeared during the 1970s in academic journals and popular magazines. Avon reprinted *Hunter's Horn* in paperback in 1979. But Arnow has yet to receive attention commensurate with her achievements.

A partial explanation is that she is often pigeonholed as a regionalist. "Regional" suggests to many that an author is preoccupied with documenting an area's dialect, customs, and picturesque landscape. Arnow accurately evokes her region; but like Faulkner, she dramatizes moral dilemmas that transcend geographical boundaries. Unlike Faulkner, Arnow has not been included in literary histories chronicling the literature of the South, for Kentucky, which did not secede from the Union during the Civil War, is rarely considered southern. Lately she has been noted as an Appalachian writer. She should be seen as an American writer with uncircumscribed appeal. *Hunter's Horn* and *The Dollmaker* have been translated into several foreign languages and have sold briskly.

Naturalism is another unfortunate label that may have stunted Arnow's reputation. Applied to *Hunter's Horn* and *The Dollmaker*, it suggests a doctrinaire narrowness. There was some justification for critics' labeling *Hunter's Horn* a naturalistic work illustrating "biological determinism." Like Suse, the fox Nunn chases is trapped by her body: King Devil turns out to be a female, caught because a belly swollen with pups slows down her flight. But Arnow's novels cannot accurately be termed examples of literary naturalism. Throughout her career she has been drawn to stories involving a character's struggle against political, biological, economic, and religious forces that threaten one's freedom or life. But her novels begin with characters rather than with theories, and her people are too strong and too individualized to fade insignificantly into the novel's background. Arnow acknowledges admiration for Zola's *Germinal*; but her characters

RACK LBB 64
ARNOW—219L—GAL. 64

middle room, so that Gertie and Clovis were alone in the room beside the kitchen. Still, she was conscious of the restless sleep of the children on the other side of the thin walls. They were all so close together it didn't seem decent. The whole place wasn't as big as either of the two main rooms at the Tipton Place.

She shut her eyes and tried to think that she was there when Clovis fell quickly into a deep, satisfied sleep. She drowsed and dreamed of pines talking. The talking rose, became the roar of a fast through train, its screeching whistle rising above the roar as it neared the through street. This was followed at once by the tumultuous sound of its passing, so clos it seemed in the very house. Amos and Cassie screamed out in fright, then as the sounds subsided they sank gradually into a whimpering half-sleep. There remained only the quiverings—the windows, the steel springs of the bed, the dishes, a chair touching the wall.

There came at last a silence so complete she could hear the ticking of the clock under the bed, and the snoring of Sophronie's children behind the wall of the girls' bedroom. The feeling that had followed her at times since she had got on the train came back in the silence —she had forgotten something, something very important. But what? She was sorting out the things she'd left behind when she found herself lifted on one elbow, listening.

Someone was moving about on the other side of the wall. She heard running water, the soft thud of a pot going over the gas flame, the creak and slam of an icebox door—breakfast getting sounds. Soon she heard the opening and closing of the outside door, and whoever it was did not come back. He had not taken time to eat his breakfast. He was most likely the husband of that Sophronie in the sleazy nightgown. She was too lazy to get up and cook breakfast.

She drowsed, but sleep enough never came to drown the strangeness of the bed or the closeness of the air. It seemed only a little while before she found herself listening again. A singing it was, in the alley now. Tipsy he was, and a tenor, "They'll be pie in a sky—" A woman's voice cut him off, something like the girl Maggie's, but near crying, "Please, Joseph, please. Du neighbors—"

"Quitcha tucken," the man said, and a door on the other side of the alley slammed.

"Tucken." What was "tucken," she wondered. Then the door next her own was opened quietly, but slammed shut so loudly that Clovis turned in his sleep. She heard the opening of the oven door, the little whoosh of the lighting gas, then the opening and closing of the icebox door. A chair was pulled out followed by the hissing sound of the cap jerked off a bottle of something fizzy like pop. She heard a chair tip back against the wall, so close through the thinness seemed like she could feel it. She could see the man's chair leaning against the wall, warming his cold feet in the oven, as he drank from the bottle. She heard the soft clink of glass on steel as he put it down. But where had be been and why, at this time of night? She sat straight up in bed with wonder and surprise when the voice came, low, more like a sigh than a voice, "Oh, Lord, that moven line," for the voice was a woman's voice, Sophronie's.

The sounds on the other side of the wall or her own abrupt movement awakened Clovis enough that he mumbled sleepily: "Don't be afeared, Gert. Th doors locks good."

"Oh, I ain't afeared," she whispered. "It's that Sophronie. Why, she's jist got in home."

He clamped one ear against the pillow, put an arm over the other. "When else would a woman on th three-tu-twelve shift git home?"

pickle

The Dollmaker, *galley proof*

dwarf his,who are incapable of saying, as Gertie does in *The Dollmaker*, that she "caused it all."

In *Hunter's Horn* and *The Dollmaker* Arnow achieves the raw power of Dreiser's *Sister Carrie* (1900), but without sacrificing style. At times in these long novels her meticulous reconstruction of a character's world is so detailed, so complete, that the reader can feel inundated and yearn for streamlining. These novels, however, can generate massive emotional power. Some episodes are forceful enough to be short stories: the riotous religious revival in *Hunter's Horn* recalls Twain's pointed satire of evangelical Protestantism in *Adventures of Huckleberry Finn*. The astonishing opening chapter of *The Dollmaker*, in which Gertie performs a tracheotomy on her baby with a twig and a knife as surgical instruments, has indeed been printed as a short story.

Arnow alone has rendered Kentucky highlanders fully and fairly, rescuing them from the literary stereotype of the lazy, suspicious, ignorant, manically violent hillbilly. Taking their dignity for granted, Arnow also avoids the passionate yearning for identification with the rural poor that betrays insecurity and condescension. In her long manuscript now in progress, she writes of a Kentucky farming family living near the Tennessee border, just southwest of the hills that spawned Gertie Nevels and her hardy, sinewy breed. Arnow's unique, obstinate characters, even in the face of economic ruin and spiritual exhaustion, will endure and prevail. With luck and justice, so should Arnow's place in American literature.

—*Glenda Hobbs*

Other:

Introduction to *Mountain Path* (Berea, Ky.: Council of the Southern Mountains, 1963);

"Some Musings on the Nature of History," *Historical Society of Michigan Publication: The Clarence M. Burton Memorial Lecture*, 1968;

"Personal Recollections," *Appalachian Heritage*, 1 (Fall 1973): 11-14.

Periodical Publications:

FICTION:

"Marigolds and Mules," *Kosmos*, 3 (February-March 1935): 3-6;

"A Mess of Pork," *New Talent*, 10 (October-December 1935): 4-11;

"The Washerwoman's Day," *Southern Review*, 1 (Winter 1936): 522-527;

"The Two Hunters," *Esquire*, 18 (July 1942): 74-75, 96;

"The Hunter," *Atlantic Monthly*, 174 (November 1944): 79-84;

"Love?," *Twigs*, 8 (Fall 1971): 1-15;

"Fra Lippi and Me," *Georgia Review*, 33 (Winter 1979): 867-875.

NONFICTION:

"Language—the Key That Unlocks All the Boxes," *Wilson Library Bulletin*, 30 (May 1956): 683-685;

"Reading without a purpose," *American Library Association*, 53 (November 1959): 837-839;

"Progress Reached Our Valley," *Nation*, 211 (3 August 1970): 71-77;

"Gray Woman of Appalachia," *Nation*, 211 (28 December 1970): 684-687;

"No Rats in the Mines," *Nation*, 213 (25 October 1971): 401-404.

References:

Barbara L. Baer, "Harriette Arnow's Chronicles of Destruction," *Nation*, 222 (31 January 1976): 117-120;

Wilton Eckley, *Harriette Arnow* (New York: Twayne, 1974);

Glenda Hobbs, "Harriette Arnow's Kentucky Novels: Beyond Local Color," *Kate Chopin Newsletter*, 2 (Fall 1976): 27-33;

Hobbs, "A Portrait of the Artist as Mother: Harriette Arnow and *The Dollmaker*," *Georgia Review*, 33 (Winter 1979): 851-867;

Joyce Carol Oates, "Joyce Carol Oates on Harriette Arnow's *The Dollmaker*," in *Rediscoveries*, ed. David Madden (New York: Crown, 1971), pp. 57-67; reprinted as "The Nightmare of Naturalism," in Oates's *New Heaven, New Earth: Visionary Experience in Literature* (New York: Vanguard, 1974), pp. 99-110;

Arline R. Thorn, "Harriette Arnow's Mountain Women," *Bulletin of the West Virginia Association of College English Teachers*, 4 (1977): 1-9.

Papers:

The Harriette Arnow Special Collection at the University of Kentucky in Lexington includes typescripts of eighteen unpublished short stories, an unpublished novel, "Between the Flowers," an early version of *Mountain Path*, near complete typescripts of *Hunter's Horn* and *Seedtime on the Cumberland*, a holograph of *The Dollmaker*, and correspondence.

WENDELL BERRY
(5 August 1934-)

SELECTED BOOKS: *Nathan Coulter* (Boston: Houghton Mifflin, 1960);

The Broken Ground (New York: Harcourt, Brace, 1964; London: Cape, 1966);

A Place on Earth (New York: Harcourt, Brace & World, 1967);

Openings (New York: Harcourt, Brace & World, 1968);

Findings (Iowa City: Prairie Press, 1969);

The Long-Legged House (New York: Harcourt, Brace & World, 1969);

Farming: A Handbook (New York: Harcourt Brace Jovanovich, 1970);

The Hidden Wound (Boston: Houghton Mifflin, 1970);

The Unforeseen Wilderness: An Essay on Kentucky's Red River Gorge, text by Berry with photographs by Eugene Meatyard (Lexington: University Press of Kentucky, 1971);

A Continuous Harmony: Essays Cultural and Agricultural (New York: Harcourt Brace Jovanovich, 1972);

The Country of Marriage (New York: Harcourt Brace Jovanovich, 1973);

The Memory of Old Jack (New York: Harcourt Brace Jovanovich, 1974);

To What Listens (Crete, Nebr.: Best Cellar Press, 1975);

Sayings and Doings (Lexington, Ky.: Gnomon Press, 1975);

Clearing (New York: Harcourt Brace Jovanovich, 1977);

Three Memorial Poems (Berkeley: Sand Dollar Press, 1977);

The Unsettling of America: Culture and Agriculture (San Francisco: Sierra Club Books, 1977).

Wendell Berry is a poet, novelist, and essayist whose steady literary achievement has earned him wide recognition both as an artist and as a spokesman for contemporary environmental concerns. Amid the more frequent and more widely ranging poetry and essays, his fiction has sustained a constant center, a native ground, where he explores the rich dramatic possibilities latent within the history of his singular subject—the small-farming tradition in America. Berry is preeminently a philosopher-poet who has wedged in the path of inexorable Progress the ancient, stable traditions of agrarian societies, based on an understanding of agriculture-as-*culture*, of farming as art and religion. His designs are equally ancient and traditional as he engages both the *dulce* and *utile*. Indeed his novels are at times both lyrical and instructive as they explore a way of life less encumbered (though in its way no less complex) than that of modern society, while at the same time reclaiming the clear values and orderly disciplines of the older ways. Counseling mankind in the responsible ethics capable of forming a healing suture between man and nature, Berry's fiction reenters the moral tradition which brings together the interests of art with the evocation of right action in the world. By his own action, Berry contests the wisdom of America's westering impulse (which he describes as the "unsettling of America") and reminds his readers of the necessity for staying in place, for nurturing the resources others have often used and walked away from. "I am at home," his poetry declares. "Don't come with me. / You stay at home too." In both life and art, his constant search has been to find adequate expression for man's responsible relationship with a chosen place. Consequently, though America has had and continues to have its spokesmen for wilderness, Berry is distinctive for his formidable and unyielding literature of settlement.

Berry works and lives in his native Henry County on a small farm that rises steeply from the banks of the Kentucky River and stretches high on to rough hill country. The son of an attorney, who himself chose to practice just a few miles from his native farm, Berry also has returned home, but by a circuitous route, to Port Royal in north central Kentucky, some fifty miles from Louisville. Having studied at the University of Kentucky (A.B., 1956; M.A., 1957) and taught at Georgetown College in the late 1950s, he spent several years in California (1958-1960) at Stanford, first as a recipient of a Wallace Stegner fellowship for fiction and then as a lecturer (he returned as a visiting professor, 1968-1969). A Guggenheim Fellowship took him to Italy and France (1961-1962), and then followed two years of teaching at New York University (1962-1964). But in 1964 he returned to Lexington to become a member of the faculty of the University of Kentucky. The logical conclusion of this homeward movement, however, occurred the following year, when in 1965 he reentered his family's long history and association with the land (a tradition that began five generations earlier with his distant great-grandfather who had settled at Port Royal about 1803) by moving from Lexington with his wife, Tanya, and two children to the small farm he had bought at Port Royal, the Lanes Landing Farm.

Having chosen to return to Port Royal, Berry chose as well the constant subject of his poetry and fiction—his native community. There he had served an early apprenticeship on and around the family farms of his father and grandfathers, where he learned the values and disciplines that would later come to fruition as the moral imperatives of his contemporary land ethic. Within his close circle of family and friends, Berry writes, he learned the "two halves of a whole relationship to the earth." Particularly from his grandfather and father came the sense of continuity with and responsibility for the land; and from Nick, a patron black farm worker, a sense of intimacy, the pleasure of "*being* there." (Old Nick and Aunt Georgie are the focus of *The Hidden Wound,* 1970, a study of the impact of slavery on his native culture and of the contemporary attitudes toward working the land that it has fostered; Berry writes that his memory of these two respected members of the farm has been "one of the persistent forces" in his mental growth.) Berry's formative education, then, was no less communal than institutional, drawn—as is his art—from the historical and perceptual unity of past, present, and future. Linked by this inseparable thread of descent, the resulting body of work—whose "moral vision of man in harmony with the land" has been described as "rare and attractive to our times"—is unusually coherent, unified, and consistent: at its core lie a primary humility before the mystery of the world, a belief in the dignity of physical work, and an inevitable, personal responsibility for one's actions in the world.

In the tradition of Faulkner and others, Berry creates a fictional mythos from his historical place. The literary locus of Port William is the home of seven generations of farming families whose consciousness reaches back to the early 1800s. The major narratives, however, occur sometime within the early decades of the century and up to the early 1950s. This represents the final days of America's traditional farm communities just prior to the historically critical period when they began to break apart under the influence of technological and economic forces at the end of World War II. Berry's characters—he focuses on three distantly related families: the Coulters, the Feltners, and the Beechums—farm the rolling hills and bottomlands west of the Appalachians in the lower part of the Kentucky River shed. Farming here requires special care and attention if it is to remain productive. And from this necessity grows his major unifying theme of stewardship, often symbolized as interlocking marriages between a man and his family, his community, and the land.

Berry's interest in preserving the character and identity of his native culture generates a rich mixture in his fiction of autobiography and imaginative history. While incidents and dialogue in the novels are often recognizable from his autobiographical essays in *The Long-Legged House* (1969) and *The Hidden Wound,* the larger history of Port William is the product of an enduring oral tradition, and Berry writes largely from its collective memory. His fiction then is both an exploration and a discovery of the meaning of his own place in his native land and a reconstruction of the mythos of a community kept alive in the consciousness of its inheritors. Finding this effort in some ways satisfying, and in others limiting, Berry has described his novels as a record of what he considers to be only a partially successful attempt to find, in the words of Edwin Muir, a "pure image of temporal life."

In *The Long-Legged House* he explains that the decision to write about his native place offered a mixed blessing. From his point of view as a young writer Port Royal was "undiscovered country" and brought with it certain opportunity; yet, "naked of associations and assigned values," free to be what he would make of it, the literary Port William was fraught with grave obligation. For Berry had consciously to reject a literary inheritance he describes as "corrupt and crippling," a tradition steeped in "local colorism" and rooted in the worn cliches of the Romantic South. Free from this distorted regionalism, with "everything . . . yet to be done," Berry was faced with solving the formal problems—for which he believed were no adequate or "authentic" local precedents—that would allow him to present the true significance of his native land and its people.

Berry's first novel, *Nathan Coulter* (1960), provoked little fanfare, though it was favorably received; at the age of twenty-six he was acknowledged by one reviewer as "a natural born writer," while his small but finely executed novel was lauded for its careful craftsmanship and its rich undertones. Only four years later did he first gain national attention, resulting from prestigious illustrator Ben Shan's edition of "November 26, 1963." Written in response to the assassination of John F. Kennedy, Berry's short poem became a minor best-seller for 1964, just at the critical, and thus difficult, time when he was preparing to leave New York for what his colleagues believed would be his unfortunate return to Kentucky. "My literary friends [thought] that I had worked my ruin." On the contrary, he later wrote, "I had grown more alive and more conscious than I had ever been."

Nathan Coulter is a spare but engaging

Bildungsroman, a novel of education and initiation. Completed at Stanford under the direction of Wallace Stegner, the novel was begun as many as five years earlier in a writing course at the University of Kentucky taught by poet and novelist Hollis Summers. The product of careful, academic scrutiny, Berry's fiction at this early date falls comfortably into the prevalent formal tradition of the late 1950s: the prose is highly crafted, pared to its essentials and stylized in its economy, while the narrative is embellished with carefully chosen symbolic figures and actions.

Written from the first-person point of view of its young eponymous narrator, *Nathan Coulter* sensitively portrays the working lives of the Coulter family, who perform the labor of farming by hand, aided by mule-drawn equipment and by fellow members of the community. Here, each man's value is known by the quantity and quality of his work, and the difficulty of the labor becomes the measure of manhood. Nathan and his brother Tom are slowly ushered into this tradition by their elders, and the rhythms of the novel follow from the sometimes mischievous insousiance of youth to the demanding disciplines of adulthood.

Compelling for its combination of innocence and latent agrarian violence, the novel traces Nathan's growth from early childhood through his departure from home as a young man. The principal characters determining the major agrarian themes of the novel, however, are Nathan's father, Jarrat, and uncle, Burley. Through them, Berry defines the nature and quality of the land ethic that had become, by the turn of the century, Kentucky's legacy.

In his portrait of Jarrat Coulter, Berry reveals a man ironically crippled by his own strength, limited by his attempt to stand as an unassailable figure in the landscape. His passion for rigid control and dominance in the matters of family and farm has resulted in a "severe and isolated manhood," a psychological wound (a recurrent emblem for Berry) that afflicts all of Jarrat's relationships. In Berry's view, a man merely holds his land in trust; no one really possesses it as Jarrat has attempted to do, and to try to dominate it by sheer will is to invite disaster. Consequently, Jarrat has alienated himself from the healing relationship of farming and has generated a deep emotional rift between himself and his family. In contrast, there is Burley, who cares nothing for the competitive Coulter tradition. His gentler nature allows him to be a surrogate father for Nathan; but by refusing to own land he has dismissed the importance of accepting a personal commitment to the land—the farmer's quintessential "marriage." The opposing, seemingly irreconcilable positions of Jarrat and Burley are in fact resolved in the course of Berry's later novels. But here the possibility of articulating a viable land ethic remains in situ, and the reader is left with a moving portrait of agrarian tragedy as seen through the eyes of youth.

By January 1960, Berry had already begun his second and much more ambitious novel, *A Place on Earth* (1967). In what he has described as a liberating "assault on the confines of *Nathan Coulter,*" he continued the work while in Florence the following year, and while in New York the year thereafter. In the summer of 1963 he returned to Port Royal where he found himself "deep into the writing" of the novel, while simultaneously reconstructing his writing sanctuary, a family cabin of long-standing on the bank of the Kentucky River. Berry had spent what he describes as "probably the most important months in my life" at this cabin during the first summer of his marriage (1957), reading the poetry—ranging from William Carlos Williams to Andrew Marvel and the Chinese translations of Kenneth Rexroth—that has had a shaping influence on his thought and work. Deeply immersed in writing and rebuilding, he produced a long, brooding, episodic novel whose range and vision bear testimony to the richness of his sources but whose form and execution reveal the excess of its possibilities. The cabin was soon finished, but the labor of fiction continued nearly five more years.

A Place on Earth is more a document of consciousness than a conventional novel. Berry views the world of Port William through the troubled mind of Mat Feltner, a gentle, stoical, sixty-one-year-old farmer who, in contrast to Jarrat Coulter, wants desperately to share his farm with his only son, Virgil. Ironically, however, his hopes are destroyed when Virgil is killed in World War II. Time and action in the novel are nicely framed by the length of one full growing season, concurrent with the closing months of the war. The entire work is dominated by the almost palpable emptiness and sterility resulting from Virgil's absence and by the long process of rebirth in Mat's coming to terms with his loss. This drama of understanding constitutes all there is of a conventional plot, and the remainder of the novel explores the rich texture and drama of the other lives in Port William.

In the course of the novel Berry engages nearly half a dozen stories with equally attentive treatment. Though Mat's story finally emerges as the thread central to the novel, Burley Coulter shares both the narrator's perspective and Mat's sense of loss, owing to the death of his nephew Tom. Also there are the tragic tales of Mat's brother-in-law, who has been physically and emotionally wounaed in World War I, and of Giddeon Crop who abandons his wife and farm in a long hegira of despair. Among the most engaging tales is that of Old Jack Beechum (the subject of the third novel, as well) who appears as the cantankerous and indomitable patriarch of the community; in addition, there are the disreputable Roger Merchant, a Harvard graduate turned alcoholic, and Whacker Spradlin, an indolent bootlegger who, like Merchant, is a model of irresponsibility. Yet all is buoyed by Berry's brilliant sense of the comic incident and masterful gift of storytelling. Here pathos and humor remain refreshingly complementary as Berry re-creates the mood and temper of this mid-century farming community.

The novel's multiple designs, however, result in goals that may seem if not at odds, then at least rather mixed. While dramatizing the impact of the war on one small community, and on the life of one decent, innocent man, Mat Feltner, it reveals at the same time Mat's culpability in accentuating his loss. What follows is a broadly educative narration which orchestrates both Mat's and the reader's understanding of man's proper "place on earth." Through Mat, Berry reminds the reader of the simple yet discomforting truth that man is merely an impermanent fixture on the earth. For Mat this means that stewardship requires his faithful presence, but guarantees neither recognition for nor perpetuity of his designs. Mat has defined his future in terms of his son, his responsible apprentice. But amid the vagaries of the world, Virgil vanishes and all that remains is an empty dream. Virgil's name, of course, is appropriately symbolic, and what Berry accomplishes here is the destruction of the very simplistic, pastoral vision he is sometimes accused by his critics of perpetuating. Through Mat, we learn a hard lesson in mutability—the only certainty on earth is change (a lesson taught to Berry by his respected Aunt Georgie, whose graphic folklore appears in the novel through her fictional identity, Aunt Fanny). Mat has become rigid in his response to the world, at the cost of those around him—his wife, daughter-in-law, and future grandchild. Only when he learns to abandon his hostility to the world's inconstancy and to accept the restorative, transcendent consolation of Nature does he resolve his internal conflict and return to patient stewardship of the land.

A Place on Earth was not widely reviewed and was only moderately well received. Robert Hazel, who read the unrevised manuscript and the finished novel, noted that Berry's extended narration creates "an anti-novelistic tendency in the book, as if Berry were moving towards fictionalized essay as a form," but commended the novel for its particularly skillful rendering of the interior lives of its characters. Eminent modernist critic Guy Davenport reviewed the novel approvingly, speaking of its musical qualities, its sense of elegy, and its evocation in structure and movement of the changing rhythms of Berry's native Kentucky River setting. So despite Berry's reputation as a highly traditional writer, this second novel is in many ways a very innovative and personalized work, unified, as Jack Hicks has noted, by Berry's special understanding of the role of husbandry and by each character's ability or inability to fulfill it.

During the seven years intervening between the publication of this and the third novel, Berry firmly established his literary identity with the publication of four poetry collections, two collections of essays, and a distinguished book-length essay in behalf of the preservation of Kentucky's Red River Gorge. By 1975, then, he had for a decade been refining and deepening both the understanding and expression of his special land ethic while living on and actively restoring his own small farm. *The Memory of Old Jack* (1974) reflects this period of maturity and settlement in its confident style and orderly vision.

Part agrarian tragedy and part celebration, Berry's third novel is a lyrical elegy for a man who learns the lesson of his history, who is restored by his return from moral exile to his proper role as husband to the land. The novel was widely reviewed and generally praised for its finely crafted prose and eloquent treatment of agrarian themes. Given Chicago's Friends of American Writers Award for 1975—"for encouraging and promoting high standards and ideals among American writers"—*The Memory of Old Jack* is the embodiment of Berry's agrarian ideals and is at once elegiac, didactic, and exhortatory.

The novel takes place in the course of a single day in September 1952. Born in 1860, Jack is a fiercely independent man whose memory reaches beyond the Civil War and so spans a great portion of Kentucky's agricultural history. As "Old Jack," he is the respected patriarch of Port William, and his memory of its history provides the structural framework for the novel as his mind wanders from the opacity of the present into the clarity of his past. Through Jack's life, Berry chronicles the demise of the once respected small-farming tradition in America and writes this novel as a requiem for the passing of a way of life, while at the same time frankly condemning the attitudes responsible for its death.

But once again, Berry's protagonists are potentially their own worst enemies. Unlike many other strictly agrarian novelists who traditionally have pitted man against the harsh forces of nature or repressive economic systems, Berry places his characters in classic conflict with themselves. Jack Beechum, for a time, becomes the victim of his own pride, hubris (which in Berry's view has been a principal nemesis in man's relationship with nature). Jack's wife belongs to the mercantile class; and her designs for his "improvement" bring to the novel the central opposition of Berry's land ethic, where land is viewed either as a spiritual resource or merely as a commodity for self-enhancement. Having succumbed to the latter choice, Jack attempts to fulfill his wife's ideal of the acquisitive, gentleman farmer—but with tragic results; only when he recovers, in the tradition of his predecessors, a "willingness to live within the limits of his own fate" does he find peaceful reconciliation with himself and his land. Unfortunately Jack's only child is, like her mother, of the mercantile view. Divorced from the land, she and her husband, a banker, have sentimentalized the idea of farming, and so falsified it. And with the destruction of the ideal follows the death of its possibility. Consequently, Berry here completes the solution to the problem of continuity by handing Jack's farm into the care of his responsible tenant, who has earned his new ownership by years of attentive stewardship. Though there is some suggested optimism for the continuance of a family tradition in the portrait of Andy Catlett, the novel's young apprentice, the general thrust of this work makes it clear that "Old Jack's death has raised anew and more starkly than ever the possibility that men of his kind are a race doomed to extinction."

Berry's continuing search for avenues of reentry into a proper state of harmony with the natural world has earned him increasing attention and respect. His traditional stance—he counsels the wisdom of rhyme and narrative in poetry, and of exemplary action in fiction—whether in literary or cultural matters, redirects our attention to enduring and intrinsic values that are not easily dismissed. Constantly in a state of exploration of his own personal, moral, and ethical understanding of the world, Berry remains a leading spiritual descendent

Louisville Courier Journal & Times

Wendell Berry

of Jefferson's agrarian vision and Thoreau's radical farmer. Environmental essayist and novelist Edward Abbey and Ken Kesey, Berry's fellow classmate at Stanford, have both lauded him with encomiums attesting to the vatic import of his work, while poet Gary Snyder has offered quieter though no less admiring praise. And yet, though for Berry the consequences of contemporary society's disregarding his message may ultimately seem perilous, to suggest he courts an apostolic role would be misleading. On the contrary, preferring to command attention by the quiet discourse of his literature, Berry is a reserved, thoughtful observer of the human condition who offers a qualified hope and vision for the future that lies in the essentially inseparable character of man and nature.

Berry has cultivated both his life and work with great discipline, and his judicious sensibilities have been received by a broad and appreciative readership. Though he early gained the admiration of the alternative culture of the 1960s with publication of his writing in small West Coast journals, the *Whole Earth Catalogue*, and the *Mother Earth News*, his pervasive interest in the culture evolving around him comfortably transcends and defies easy categorization. His work appears in publications as diverse as the *Hudson Review*, *Harper's*, and the *Nation*, on the one hand; and in *Organic Gardening* and *Blair and Ketchum's Country Journal*, on the other. Consistently, however, Berry is of one mind as he ranges from a discussion of "the ecological crisis as a crisis of culture" to the practical summation of using draft horses on hilly farm land. Among the works central to a study of his thought are "The Specialization of Poetry," a discussion of the proper role of the artist in society; "Discipline and Hope," which represents the core of his moral and ethical position; and *The Unsettling of America* (1977), a broad summary critique of American cultural and agrarian values. The last of these provoked national attention immediately following its publication by the Sierra Club Press.

Berry's commitment to large social and broadly cultural issues has drawn him increasingly away from the writing of fiction and poetry. Having left academics and teaching in 1978, he accepted a position as a contributing editor for *New Farm Magazine*, a Rodale Press publication dedicated to the interests of small-farming, a subject he learns through experience at Lanes Landing Farm.

—Gary Tolliver

Periodical Publications:

"The Specialization of Poetry," *Hudson Review*, 28 (Spring 1975): 11-27;

"The Gift of Good Land: A Biblical Argument for Ecological Responsibility," *Sierra Club Bulletin*, 64 (November/December 1979): 20-26.

References:

John Ditsky, "Wendell Berry: Homage to the Apple Tree," *Modern Poetry Studies*, 2, no. 1 (1971): 7-15;

Robert Hass, "Wendell Berry: Finding the Land," *Modern Poetry Studies*, 2, no. 1 (1971): 16-38;

Jack Hicks, "Wendell Berry's Husband to the World: *A Place on Earth*," *American Literature*, 50 (May 1979): 238-254;

Speer Morgan, "Wendell Berry: A Fatal Singing," *Southern Review*, 10 (October 1974): 865-877;

Gary Tolliver, "Beyond Pastoral: Wendell Berry and a Literature of Commitment," Ph.D. dissertation, Ohio University, 1978;

Bruce Williamson, "The Plowboy Interview: Wendell Berry," *Mother Earth News*, no. 20 (March 1973): 6-12.

PAUL BOWLES

(30 December 1910-)

SELECTED BOOKS: *Two Poems* (New York: Modern Editions Press, 1933?);

The Sheltering Sky (London: Lehmann, 1949; New York: New Directions, 1949);

A Little Stone: Stories (London: Lehmann, 1950);

The Delicate Prey and Other Stories (New York: Random House, 1950);

Let It Come Down (New York: Random House, 1952; London: Lehmann, 1952);

The Spider's House (New York: Random House, 1955; London: Macdonald, 1957);

Yallah (New York: McDowell, Obolensky, 1957; London: Merlin, 1957);

The Hours after Noon: Short Stories (London: Heinemann, 1959);

A Hundred Camels in the Courtyard (San Francisco: City Lights Books, 1962);

Their Heads Are Green and Their Hands Are Blue (New York: Random House, 1963);

Their Heads Are Green (London: Owen, 1963);

Up Above the World: A Novel (New York: Simon & Schuster, 1966; London: Owen, 1967);

The Time of Friendship: A Volume of Short Stories (New York: Holt, Rinehart & Winston, 1967);

Pages from Cold Point and Other Stories (London: Owen, 1968);
Scenes (Los Angeles: Black Sparrow Press, 1968);
The Thicket of Spring: Poems 1926-1969 (Los Angeles: Black Sparrow Press, 1972);
Without Stopping: An Autobiography (New York: Putnam's, 1972; London: Owen, 1972);
Three Tales (New York: Hallman, 1975);
Next to Nothing (Kathmandu, Nepal: Starstreams Poetry Series, 1976);
Things Gone and Things Still Here (Santa Barbara: Black Sparrow Press, 1977);
Collected Stories 1939-1976 (Santa Barbara: Black Sparrow Press, 1979).

Paul Bowles has never fit well into a single category; he is intensely private, preferring to display his life only in art and variously as poet, short-story writer, novelist, translator, journalist, musicologist, and composer (operas, film and theatre scores, and art songs). There was even an early period when he tried being a painter. In the 1930s he was thought of as a composer of theatre music; in the 1940s as music reviewer, journalist and translator, and writer of remarkable short stories; in the 1950s as America's preeminent existential novelist; and in the past two decades as one who has worked with his young Moroccan friends to create, in his English translations, a Moghrebi literature of novels, short stories, and folk tales. His own four novels reflect a multitude of interests, and he conceived of *The Sheltering Sky* (1949), his most famous novel, as having musical structure. Though his circle of admirers is too large to be called a coterie, it cannot be said that he has received much critical attention or that he has widely influenced literature. His employment, especially in his short stories, of sensational materials ("their foolish Gothic violence," in Alice Toklas's phrase, which his publishers had commercially stressed) has been employment in his own manner, emphasis falling not on an act itself or even the thought it generates but shifting to an interior sense of dead detachment, the realization that life is nothingness and that even brutality means little compared to the horror of vacuity.

Born in Jamaica, New York City, the only child of a disapproving dentist and a mother who had been a schoolteacher, Bowles started at the age of four to write short stories. In grade school he composed music (his early *An Opera in Nine Chapters* apparently fused both literary and musical interests; as he was later to note, "I had always felt extremely circumscribed in music," having many things to say "that were too precise to express in musical terms"). The publication of his poem, "Spire Song," in *transition* when he was sixteen gave him immediate entree to intellectual circles and little magazines. Graduating from high school in January 1928, he studied briefly at the School of Design and Liberal Arts before he enrolled, that September, at the University of Virginia ("what is good enow for edgar allen poe is good enow for me"). The following March he ran away to Paris and returned in September to take a job at Dutton's, a bookshop, and to begin writing, in his spare time at work, a first novel, *Without Stopping*. "It was the application of automatic writing to the general subject of my trip to Europe, scenes put together, but not in a very coherent fashion, I'm afraid. I was very influenced by *Finnegans Wake*." Over forty years later, Bowles was to assign the title of this aborted work to his autobiography.

In the spring of 1930 Bowles returned to the University of Virginia for another semester; that was the extent of his college education. He preferred his private instruction from the composer, Aaron Copland, whom he had met in 1929 and who soon recommended that Bowles return to Paris and study with Nadia Boulanger. The March 1931 trip to Paris really began Bowles' literary life, for it was then that he met Gertrude Stein and fell under her influence. "So you're Paul Frederic Bowles!" she exclaimed, having known him only as a correspondent who had solicited an example of her work for a little magazine he guest-edited. "I thought you were at least in your seventies." Bowles remembers: "Of course I always looked younger than I was—like a kid, really—though I was already twenty, but I could have passed for seventeen." (More likely it was the correspondence, finely phrased and variously signed with some form of his triple name, that had confused Stein.) Disliking the name Paul, which she thought romantic ("and I didn't have one ounce of romanticism in me"), she rechristened him Freddy. More alarmingly, she told him he was not a poet, and she was not even certain that his was her kind of music—she decided he had problems with "attentuation." "Now Bravig Imbs, for instance, he's just a very bad poet," said Stein. "But you—you're not a poet at all!" Years later, Bowles confessed: "Poetry was a thing which I wrote very very quickly; it was never a product of thought or work, it was right off the top of my head. They [the poems] were not profound.... In fact most of them were surrealist and weren't about anything ... just words and phrases as they came into my head.... Stories involve ... more time, more work. I don't believe that anything you don't have to work on at all can possibly be very good."

(18) There are two young Englishmen in town who run a bar known as the Right On Inn. Upstairs are eight bedrooms, where tourists live in the summer. The two are also joint owners of a garage not far away in Emsallah. Americans and English car-owners patronize the place because the men speak English, although they have no mechanic working for them, only Moroccan boys who must be told at each moment what to do. I took the car in two days ago with a radiator problem, but while it was there they ran the battery down to zero. Today they sent Abdelouahaïd back to report that I must buy a new battery. When evening came I thought I would pay a visit to the bar and see what they had to tell me in person. I set out on foot about twenty after ten. The streets were damp, but the sky was very clear and black and starry, with patches of fast-flying vaporous clouds. Absolutely no one was out: only the night-watchman in the park in front of the Immeuble San Francisco. When I got to the roundabout at the Boulevard de

Manuscript

Both Stein and Toklas took immediately to the young Bowles and invited him and Copland, who had now joined his protege abroad, to visit them that summer in Bilignin. If Bowles had once had reservations about Stein's oeuvre (he had been known to call her "gertrude stain"), he now felt that everything she wrote made sense; never again was he to doubt the validity of her achievement or her right to criticize him and direct his work. In her *Autobiography of Alice B. Toklas* (1933) Stein characterized Bowles as "delightful and sensible in summer but neither delightful nor sensible in the winter.... Bowles told Gertrude Stein and it pleased her that Copeland [*sic*] said threateningly to him when as usual in the winter he was neither delightful nor sensible, if you do not work now when you are twenty when you are thirty, nobody will love you." To ensure that he *did* work and avoid surrealistic writing, which she distrusted, she now considered where he should go next. Alice Toklas had a talent for putting people in a proper setting, and she suggested Morocco. Stein agreed. It was the land of summer where he could be delightful and especially sensible. The advice taken, Bowles and Copland rented a house in Tangier. Thus was Bowles introduced to the pleasures of expatriate life in North Africa. Although he had gone to Morocco ostensibly to work on his music, he evidently sent some of his prose to Stein, and again she gave him new direction. "I like your story, I like your descriptions, go on with them . . . you are not so bad in description and I always think there is a future in description." A decade later he seriously applied himself to writing stories. And just as his subject matter would frequently turn out to be North Africa—particularly the foreigner's uneasy, often fatal, encounter with an alien culture—so too would his theory of composition owe much to Gertrude Stein and her notion of description.

Bowles himself believes he thought seriously of becoming a writer only after watching Jane Bowles, whom he married in 1938, at work on her novel, *Two Serious Ladies* (1943): "It seemed to be a new way to write, or a new approach, psychologically, which I found very interesting. Perhaps I would not have had the desire to write had I not read the manuscript . . . when she wrote it—and loved it. I'm sure that that was the thing that detonated the original explosion." If, as he later said, Jane wrote like Daisy Ashford, grown-up, he too was ever to aim at achieving an artful simplicity: "Little by little the desire came to me to invent my own myths, adopting the point of view of the primitive mind." He first wrote animal legends "and then tales of animals disguised as 'basic human' beings." And he always called Jane Bowles his ideal audience.

The Sheltering Sky, Bowles' first novel and the work on which his reputation is grounded, commenced in a dream of Tangier that Bowles, then in New York, had in the spring of 1947. ("Dreams do clarify your life completely . . . they tell you much more than anything else could possibly tell you, about what you really want and how much you're willing to sacrifice to have it and what it entails.") The vision of Tangier impelled him to secure from Doubleday a contract for a novel and to embark for North Africa. By the time he sailed he thought he knew precisely what his book would be about and do: "It was going to be basically the story of the professor in 'A Distant Episode.' It was an autobiographical novel, a novel of memory, that is . . . a working out of the professor's story.... I wanted to tell . . . the story of what the desert can do to us. That was all. The desert is the protagonist." Enroute to Tangier he wrote a short story about another professor, "Pages from Cold Point," that obviously explores some of the problems (proscribed sexual relationships, self-delusion, alienation in "the Atomic Age") that would be basic to his novel.

The Sheltering Sky was to be "a long long long story instead of a short story," said Bowles. "If I'd begun plotting it and saying to myself, 'I'm writing a novel' . . . I wouldn't have been able to do it. I just had to live it, and write what I lived in my head—just as if I were doing a short story." The novel tells of three New Yorkers, Port and Kit Moresby and their friend Tunner who, presumably in 1947, go to North Africa, "this distant and unconnected part of the world." They land in Oran, Algeria, and slowly move south through a fantasy landscape into the reality of the Sahara; separated first by chance or whim, they are separated ultimately by death and self-willed abandonment. Nothing changes their characters: they merely confirm the natures they had brought with them.

As Bowles once noted, "The only effort worth making is the one it takes to learn the geography of one's own nature. . . . The act of dying must be longed for as the ultimate attainment.... By striving with every facet of the imagination to conceive of chaos, one manages only to explore a little more carefully the terrain of order." Bowles devised a three-part structure for his novel; and while the same sun shines on all, it burns into clarity only the Moresbys and seldom more than silhouettes their uncomprehending shadow, Tunner. An obsessive belief with Bowles is that the relationship between generations—parent and child, adult and youth—is invariably destructive. "Pages from Cold Point" demonstrated this in an overtly homosexual context. In *The Sheltering Sky* a curious mother and son, Mrs. Lyle and Eric, have an incestuous relationship. Though he later dismissed them as mere caricatures, based on real people he had encountered in his North African travels, they are plausible monsters.

Port tells his wife, "We've never managed, either one of us, to get all the way into life." The novel charts that journey, into the "famous silence of the Sahara," which itself becomes the epitome of sought isolation, of "solitude and the proximity to infinite things." Bowles wrote his publisher, "Really it is an adventure story in which the adventures take place on two planes simultaneously: in the actual desert, and in the inner desert of the spirit. The sexual adventures are like the oases, the shade is insufficient, the glare is always brighter as the journey continues. And the journey must continue—there is no oasis in which one can remain." The final quarter of the book, which takes Kit, after Port's death, into Arab captivity and madness, has bothered many readers. Bowles himself appreciated the reaction of Alice Toklas: "No novel since The Great Gatsby has impressed me as having the force, precision, delicacy that the best of Fitzgerald has until yours. Limiting yourself as you have in the number of your characters has not prevented you from completely portraying an epoch. I find one blemish . . . Kit in the Sahara—my wish to compress it puts me in what Gertrude called the banal majority." Doubleday evidently found more than that to object to; they rejected the book as not being a novel and eventually recovered their advance. New Directions took the book and had a hardcover sale of 39,000 copies.

In December 1949, the month of the novel's New York publication, Bowles was sailing to Ceylon when, the ship passing Tangier, he was overcome with nostalgia for North Africa: "I decided to write about the very part of the land that I was going by. . . . So I started *Let It Come Down*." He drew charts, plotted alliances, decided upon his characters, "How each one can manipulate the other, and then the others, in order to bring it to the situation that I want: the high point. . . . The idea was to plan it all up to the beginning of an inevitable denouement and write *that* section automatically." The novel took two years to complete: "It was an adventure story . . . in which the details had to be realistic. . . . It's a completely unreal story, and the entire book is constructed in order to lead to this impossible situation at the end."

The scene is contemporary Tangier, a city that "appeals particularly to those with a strong residue of infantilism in their character." Into this fantasy world comes Nelson Dyar, a New York bank clerk who, wishing to break out from the cell of his past, has been promised a job with a Tangier travel agency. When he meets the expatriate Daisy de Valverde she introduces him to hashish, the means that eventually unleashes his self-destructive impulses. It is a novel of endless conspiracy, Bowles having taken his title from *Macbeth*, a quotation that "shows the exact kind of treachery that we find in Tangier (in the book) on the part of the people. Everyone's working behind everyone else's back. . . . The worst act of treachery is not committed against [Dyar] at all—he commits it." Perhaps it is this novel which best illustrates his theory that "The character *as character* is not important. The character is acting out a situational drama in a given setting, and the whole thing is one thing—that is, the character, the setting, the mood, the action, the situation. The character's not apart from his situation (in that sense it's existentialist)."

Angus Stewart

Paul Bowles

The Spider's House (1955), begun in 1954, is the most conventional of Bowles' novels, both in subject matter and technique. It is also his longest book, the one written most quickly. The story tells of Stenham, an American expatriate novelist who has lived for several years in Fez; Polly (Lee) Veyron, an American tourist; and Amar, a Moroccan youth, all of whom meet in the autumn of 1954 in a Fez that is torn with the beginnings of civil war. Amar is looking for "the possible friend . . . in whom he could confide, who could understand him"; and presumably he finds this man in Stenham, a man whose experience occasionally so parallels Bowles' that the unwary reader is inclined to believe the book autobiographical. The novel takes its title from the Koran: "The likeness of those who choose other patrons than Allah is as the likeness of the spider when she taketh unto herself a house, and lo! the frailest of all houses is the spider's house, if they but knew." Bridging cultures would concern Bowles in all his subsequent stories set in North Africa: the possibility of a permanent and meaningful juncture between Moslem and Nazarene. Of all the Moroccans he has depicted, Amar remains the most appealing, the most comprehensible to the Western mind.

In 1956 the tape recorder reached Morocco and profoundly altered the course of Bowles' creativity. He now began to record the improvised stories of his young Moroccan friends and to turn them into English, accounts produced only when the narrators were high on kif. Kif, tape recorders, exotic locales, the unleashing of primitive impulses—these all coalesced in 1961 when he began *Up Above the World* (1966). Although this, his fourth novel, is his shortest, he was to have great problems with the plot, and the book would be the longest "in work." The novel tells the story of a retired doctor, Taylor Slade, and his second wife, Day—thirty years his junior—who travel from San Francisco to some Latin American country. On shipboard they meet a tiresome clubwoman, Mrs. Rainmantle, who is enroute to visit her son, Grover. When the three shipmates disembark they spend the night together in a run-down hotel. Early the next morning the Slades slip away, unaware that their companion has been murdered in her sleep. In the capital city, to which the Slades have now gone, they encounter a seemingly affable young man, Vero Soto, who prevails upon them to become his guests. Thus commences a series of adventures in which the Slades are kidnapped and given treatment (via drugs and tape recorders) to alter their memory, to eradicate the memory of Mrs. Rainmantle. (Vero is Grover; it was he who had had his mother killed.) Bowles recognized from the start that this would be an uncharacteristic novel for him, and he wondered if it should not appear under a pseudonym. For him it was to be "a light novel, an entertainment, as opposed to a novel—what Gide would have called a *sotie* as opposed to a *roman*." When he started work he thought, "Now I'm going to write a suspense story, not a serious novel—something else, something that I haven't tried. . . . That's another category—that's not really a literary category."

Although Bowles has a detailed knowledge of North Africa and most of the places he sets his stories—the land, the customs, the characteristics of the people—his books are never political, sociological, or geographical in focus. His concern is the mystery of human consciousness, and his fiction is not the elucidation, but the delineation, of mystery. We read his books to follow a mind moving against a de-emphasized, albeit exotic, background, as that mind becomes conscious of itself and establishes its own reality by attitude and action. Bowles insists that the writer knows no meaning other than what is encased in his vision: "We do no thinking, give no reasons, have no sensations, make no apologies. This is our behavior, and it impresses them," he has said in *Next to Nothing* (1976), one of his most substantial poems.

"*What* a devious young man you are!" complained Muriel Draper in the 1930s. Bowles was startled but he never forgot the remark: "I can only think she was referring to my manner of relating a story. When I begin to recount an incident, my first intention is to give a bare report of the principal events and nothing more and eventually allow extensions of that material. It must become increasingly obvious to the listener that I am withholding information; this can hardly be an endearing characteristic to observe in a friend." It is this element of mystery which has made many readers suspicious of the role that Bowles plays in the composition of the Moghrebi works; they would prefer to believe, erroneously, that these works are his own pseudonymous productions.

This baffling novelist remains, nonetheless, Gertrude Stein's protege. She herself believed that if you knew you could do something, then why bother trying? To be creative is to struggle against the unknown and make something that is often inevitably ugly. Bowles' productions are too finely fashioned ever to be thought ugly—no matter what his subject and materials. His struggle has always been to get further into human consciousness and to explore its manifestations, especially for himself. The world is welcome to look over his shoulder and make of these writings what the world will. "I am the wrong direction, the dead nerve-end, the unfinished scream. One day my words may comfort you, as yours can never comfort me," he concludes in *Next to Nothing*.

—*Lawrence D. Stewart*

Screenplays:

Paul Bowles in the Land of the Jumblies, text and narration by Bowles, Gary Conklin, 1969;
Senso, by Lucchino Visconti, additional dialogue in English by Bowles and Tennessee Williams, Domenico Forges Davanzati, 1954.

Other:

Scenes from the Door [two songs], music by Bowles and words by Gertrude Stein (Fez, Morocco: Éditions de la Vipère, 1934);
Jean-Paul Sartre, *No Exit*, translated by Bowles (New York: French, 1946);
Roger Frison-Roche, *The Lost Trail of the Sahara*, translated by Bowles (Englewood Cliffs: Prentice-Hall, 1952);
"Majoun Keddane," in *The Artists' & Writers' Cookbook*, ed. Beryl Barr and Barbara Turner Sachs, with introduction by Alice B. Toklas (Sausalito, Cal.: Contact, 1961), pp. 285-287;
Larbi Layachi (Driss ben Hamed Charhadi), *A Life Full of Holes*, taped and translated from the Moghrebi by Bowles (New York: Grove, 1964; London: Weidenfeld & Nicolson, 1964);
Mohammed Mrabet, *Love with a Few Hairs*, taped and translated from the Moghrebi by Bowles (London: Owen, 1967; New York: Braziller, 1968);
Mrabet, *M'Hashish*, taped and translated from the Moghrebi by Bowles (San Francisco: City Lights Books, 1969);
Mrabet, *The Lemon*, translated from the Moghrebi and edited by Bowles and Mrabet (London: Owen, 1969; New York: McGraw-Hill, 1972);
"Mohammed Mrabet, Talking to Daniel Halpern," translated by Bowles, *Transatlantic Review*, 39 (Spring 1971): 125-129;
David Herbert, *Second Son: An Autobiography*, foreword by Bowles (London: Owen, 1972);
"A Secret," in *Hotzarouli* (Allentown, Pa.: Cedar Crest College, 1972), p. 11;
"Etiquette," in *The Mystery & Detection Annual* (Beverly Hills: Donald Adams, 1972), p. 198;
Mohamed Choukri, *For Bread Alone*, translated with an introduction by Bowles (London: Owen, 1973);
Bowles and Mrabet, *The Boy Who Set the Fire & Other Stories*, taped and translated from the Moghrebi by Bowles (Los Angeles: Black Sparrow Press, 1974);
Choukri, *Jean Genet in Tangier*, translated by Bowles (New York: Ecco, 1974);
Isabelle Eberhardt, *The Oblivion Seekers & Other Writings*, translated by Bowles (San Francisco: City Lights Books, 1975);
"About Jane Bowles," in *Feminine Wiles*, by Jane Bowles (Santa Barbara: Black Sparrow Press, 1976), p. 87;
Mrabet, *Look & Move On*, taped and translated from the Moghrebi by Bowles (Santa Barbara: Black Sparrow Press, 1976);
Mrabet, *Harmless Poisons, Blameless Sins*, taped and translated from the Moghrebi by Bowles (Santa Barbara: Black Sparrow Press, 1976);
Mrabet, *The Big Mirror*, taped and translated from the Moghrebi by Bowles (Santa Barbara: Black Sparrow Press, 1977);
Choukri, *Tennessee Williams in Tangier*, translated by Bowles (Santa Barbara: Cadmus Editions, 1979);
Abdeslam Boulaich, Choukri, Layachi, Mrabet, and Ahmed Yacoubi, *Five Eyes: Stories*, edited and translated by Bowles (Santa Barbara: Black Sparrow Press, 1979);
The Beach Café & The Voice, taped and translated from the Moghrebi by Bowles (Santa Barbara: Black Sparrow Press, 1980).

Periodical Publications:

FICTION:
"A White Goat's Shadow: A Story," *Argo*, 1 (December 1930): 50-51;
"Bluey, Pages from an Imaginary Diary (1919)," *View*, 3 (October 1943): 81-82;
"Midnight Mass," *Antaeus*, no. 32 (Winter 1979): 24-31;
"Here to Learn," *Antaeus*, no. 34 (Summer 1979): 7-42.
NONFICTION:
"Fez," *Holiday*, 8 (July 1950): 13-22;
"The Secret Sahara," *Holiday*, 13 (January 1953): 71-75, 87-88;
"Paris! City of the Arts," *Holiday*, 13 (April 1953): 111-121;
"Europe's Most Exotic City," *Holiday*, 17 (May 1955): 49-52, 120-126,
"The Incredible Arab," *Holiday*, 20 (August 1956): 48-51, 58-61;
"The Worlds of Tangier," *Holiday*, 23 (March 1958): 66-70, 157-159;
"The Moslems," *Holiday*, 25 (April 1959): 77-81, 97-108;
"Casablanca," *Holiday*, 40 (September 1966): 75-78,

108-111, 120-122;
"Café in Morocco," *Holiday*, 44 (August 1968): 50-51, 62;
"What's So Different about Marrakesh?," *Travel and Leisure*, 1 (June-July 1971): 35-40;
"Morocco Perceived," *Esquire*, 83 (March 1975): 71-78.

Interviews:

Harvey Breit, "Talk with Paul Bowles," *New York Times Book Review*, 9 March 1952, p. 19;
John Bainbridge, *Another Way of Living: A Gallery of Americans Who Choose to Live in Europe* (New York: Holt, Rinehart & Winston, 1968), pp. 236-245; 249-250;
Mike Steen, *A Look at Tennessee Williams* (New York: Hawthorn, 1969), pp. 141-156;
Oliver Evans, "An Interview with Paul Bowles," *Mediterranean Review*, 1 (Winter 1971): 3-15;
Michael Rogers, "Conversations in Morocco. The Rolling Stone Interview: Paul Bowles," *Rolling Stone*, 23 May 1974, pp. 48-58.

References:

John W. Aldridge, *After the Lost Generation: A Critical Study of the Writers of Two Wars* (New York: McGraw-Hill, 1951), pp. 184-193;
Hans Bertens, *The Fiction of Paul Bowles: The Soul Is the Weariest Part of the Body* (Amsterdam: Rodopi, 1979; Atlantic Highlands, N.J.: Humanities Press, 1979);
Bernard Faÿ, *Les Précieux* (Paris: Librairie Académique Perrin, 1966), p. 149;
Richard Rumbold, "An Evening with Paul Bowles," *London Magazine*, 7 (November 1960): 65-73;
Lawrence D. Stewart, *Paul Bowles: The Illumination of North Africa* (Carbondale: Southern Illinois University Press, 1974; London: Feffer & Simons, 1974);
Stewart, "Paul Bowles: *Up Above the World* So High," in *The Mystery & Detection Annual* (Beverly Hills: Donald Adams, 1973), pp. 244-270.

Papers:

The papers of Paul and Jane Bowles are in the Humanities Research Center, University of Texas at Austin. Bowles' letters to Gertrude Stein are in the Beinecke Rare Book and Manuscript Library of Yale University.

JANET BURROWAY

(21 September 1936-)

SELECTED BOOKS: *Descend Again* (London: Faber & Faber, 1960);
But to the Season (Newcastle, U.K.: Keele University Press, 1961);
The Dancer from the Dance (London: Faber & Faber, 1965; Boston: Little, Brown, 1968);
Eyes (Boston: Little, Brown, 1966; London: Faber & Faber, 1966);
The Buzzards (Boston: Little, Brown, 1969; London: Faber & Faber, 1970);
Raw Silk (Boston: Little, Brown, 1977; London: Gollancz, 1977);
Material Goods (Gainesville: University Presses of Florida, 1980).

Janet Burroway is a writer of wide range and many voices. In part because she has consciously avoided current trends, and in part because she lived abroad for eleven years, during which time her first four novels were published, her reputation has only recently begun to catch up with the consistently high quality of her work. Burroway's themes are universal—love, death, the implications of choice, human culpability—and in the broadest sense, her novels are profoundly moral. She creates a determinedly realistic world, a *comédie humaine* with tragic implications, where evil is most often the result of blindness.

Born in Tucson, Arizona, and raised in Phoenix, Burroway began writing early, evincing enough talent even in elementary school that one teacher began tutoring her after school in poetry. After a year of study (1954-1955) at the University of Arizona, she entered *Mademoiselle*'s College Board contest—which Sylvia Plath had won the year before and was later to depict in *The Bell Jar*—and served as a guest editor in the summer of 1955, along with Gael Greene and Joan Didion. That fall she entered Barnard College, from which she was graduated in 1958. On a Marshall scholarship, she attended Cambridge University, taking a B.A. with first class honors in 1960. She continued to publish poems and stories while in England, and in 1960 her first novel, *Descend Again*, appeared there.

Burroway began *Descend Again* at Barnard, and its intellectual structure reflects the formal study in which she was engaged while writing it. The novel is set during World War II in Sintiempo, Arizona, a place modeled on the town in which her grandparents had lived. The war, which shakes the world lying beyond the rim of mountains that surround Sintiempo, has no effect on the town. Like the cave in Plato's myth which provides a structuring metaphor for the novel, the town remains outside of time.

As the story opens, protagonist Millie Delaney is twenty-three, teaching doggedly, drinking coffee every Saturday morning at 10:15 with school superintendent Duncan Angleberger and his wife, reading Plato's *Republic* as well as *Paradise Lost* and *Great Expectations*. The townspeople regard her as a young woman "both self-sufficient and quaint" and so leave her alone. She invests all of her hope in the young Miguel Laureado, a gifted student whom she tutors in secret. But at the moment when Miguel needs her most, she fails him because she has fallen in love and ignores the child—the first of many abandonments in Burroway's fiction. Millie's lover, arriving like an apparition across the desert, offers her the same enlightenment that she has given Miguel. Millie, though, lacks the courage and receptivity of her pupil. Rejecting her lover, she encloses herself, now pregnant, in her tiny house and dreams elaborate dreams of isolation. At the novel's close, Miguel climbs over the crest of the mountains. He will escape the cave; Millie will descend into it once more.

This first novel, despite its fairy-tale quality and occasional blurring of tone, suggests strongly the talent of its author, her humorous eye for detail, her command of arresting images and her inventive and sometimes daring use of what in dramatic terms would be called *business*: the gestures and unconscious actions which reveal character.

The dramatic elements in her writing became increasingly important as Burroway came to view herself as a potential dramatist. Returning from England, she spent 1960-1961 at the Yale School of Drama and saw her second play, *The Fantasy Level*, produced and her first book of poetry, *But to the Season*, published, both in 1961. The same year she married Walter Eysselinck, a young Belgian director; after teaching English at Harpur College from 1961 to 1962 in Binghamton, New York, directing a regional theatre program from 1962-1963, and designing costumes for Eysselinck's productions, she moved with her husband to Belgium. In the next three years, Burroway had two sons, completed a Master's degree (1965) at Cambridge, published two novels, served as costume designer for the Belgium National Theatre at Ghent and for the Gardner Center for the Arts in Sussex, and began to teach at the University of Sussex.

The increased complexity of Burroway's life and the multiple directions in which she turned during this period manifest themselves in a richness of setting and in a distinct sense of theatre in her second novel, *The Dancer from the Dance* (1965). In keeping with her conviction that she, as writer, must never repeat herself, must "earn [her] stripes" by trying widely different voices and narrative techniques, Burroway employs as narrator Stanford Powers, a sixtyish second-level administrator in the Paris office of UNICEF, who prides himself on his grooming and urbanity. Powers is certain of his objectivity, his sagacity, his credentials as humanist, but in fact he plays a Pandarus and then a voyeur, oblivious to his need to mold and manipulate, and unaware finally of the depths of his own longings. The novel opens after the fact; thus, throughout *The Dancer from the Dance* the reader knows that the narrator has emerged unscathed, yet unenlightened, from the tangle of love, pain, and death over which he has presided.

Burroway's third novel, *Eyes* (1966), is very different from her previous books. Set in a fictional New Orleans, the story is told in the third person, shifting point of view from character to character in a series of interlocking events which cover scarcely more than twenty-four hours. Pivotal figures in the novel are Angus Rugg, a middle-aged optic surgeon, and Jadeen Spatch, a substitute teacher in love with Angus's son Hilary. The novel opens shrouded in death: Angus remembers the long, carefully orchestrated death of his mother; he has just been told he has a serious heart condition; and before the day is over he must tell a patient that he is going blind.

The comfortable rhythms of life are jarred, and in the jarring, most of the characters in the novel lose that innocence which manifests itself as complacency. As events unfold, each examines himself without regard for public opinion, to see what substance lies beneath the surface. Thus, Rugg abandons the detachment of science and faces clearly the human implications of his career. Jadeen confronts the probable costs, among them the loss of her teaching position, of upholding liberal racial views, which she adopted without serious commitment in the first place.

The Dancer from the Dance and *Eyes* both received positive reviews but on the whole attracted little notice. (Granville Hicks perceptively singled out *Eyes* in the *Saturday Review* as a rewarding, well-written book readers were unfortunately very likely to miss.) *The Buzzards* (1969), nominated for a Pulitzer Prize, began to draw critical attention to Burroway.

Her personal favorite among her works, *The Buzzards* is a political novel of unusual artistry. Its controlling metaphor is adopted from the first chorus of the *Oresteia*, describing Agamemnon's yielding to Calchus ten years before. Calchus had observed warrior-birds swoop upon a pregnant hare, tearing out the unborn brood. From this omen, he had pronounced that Agamemnon must sacrifice his daughter Iphegenia before favorable winds would carry the Greek fleet to Troy. In *The Buzzards*, the irony of Agamemnon's choice hangs heavily over the novel. Alex, a conservative senator from Arizona, is clearly a great politician, perhaps great enough to win the Presidency itself. As the novel opens, the prize seems almost within his grasp; but by courting a national constituency, he has angered the good old boys back home, and his bid for reelection to his senate seat is in danger. All relationships, all actions must now be measured in terms of their effect on the campaign.

In *The Buzzards*, Burroway employs a variety of narrative techniques. Claudia, the senator's wife, speaks in an impressionistic style, her tense voice reflecting the riot of emotions and uncertainties within her which somehow forms the brittle strength she projects. Galcher (Calchus), political seer and campaign manager, speaks to the reader only through his journal; he is the cold thinker, the calculator. An amateur ornithologist, Galcher records in latinate clarity his sightings of birds, extrapolating from them a behavioristic view of mankind. Alex's oldest daughter, Eleanor, married and thus removed from the immediate family, is also removed from herself, struggling to maintain her identity in a quicksand of diapers and garbage. Chapters centering on Eleanor are in the third person, written with acerbic fidelity to the trivial routines of her life. Alex's character is revealed only through his speeches. Even as he confronts his public after the murder of his youngest daughter, he is unconsciously elated by its political possibilities.

Burroway's best-known novel, *Raw Silk* (1977), took seven years to write. When she began the book, she thought of it as a comedy about a young woman who is both squirming in an uncomfortable marriage and struggling to make it work. Narrator Virginia Marbalestier, the daughter of a California jobbing carpenter, has moved from her trailer park origins to a genuine Tudor manor with formal gardens. Her husband has transmogriphied from a charming young scientist (with a face so expressive that "people remembered being *listened* to" by him) to a stuffy, absolutely proper administrator in a British textile company. As Burroway envisioned the novel, while in college Virginia had lacked the courage to run away from California to Japan with a middle-aged history professor; now, twelve years later, she will finally go to Japan by traveling across Europe. She "saw the invisible line from Japan and back again, around the world, as the warp threads of Virginia's existence." As the novel grew its comedy became darkened and complicated by the very serious nature of Virginia's self-discovery: preservation entails abandonment; submission is a sin which must be committed over and over again.

The narrator of *Raw Silk* is an engaging character; she speaks with wry intelligence and rare honesty, and she fastens onto the details of her life with a characteristic humor even when she is suffering most deeply. A talented textile designer, she thinks in terms of pattern and texture. Her affinity for texture, for the *feel* of things, extends instinctively to people—to her daughter Jill, to Frances Kean who feels only the unspeakable pain of severe clinical depression, to Warren Montgolfier, the unconventional minister she meets and falls in love with in Japan, who wants her to return with him to California. But even in her relationships, she must discern patterns. Twelve years before, she chose not to fly the Pacific to the Far East. Now, she sees, she must make the same choice in reverse. In returning to pick up the loose threads of her life, she is affirming the patterns she has chosen all along: work, friends, marriage.

Raw Silk received excellent reviews both in England and America. Critics praised it not only for its maturity and technical skill, but also because it eschews feminist rhetoric and strongly asserts that individual freedom is, ultimately, an ideal state, not a real one. W. T. Lhamon, writing in the *New Republic,* noted that in "some ways . . . *Raw Silk* provokes women's novels today as surely as Ralph Ellison's *Invisible Man* challenged the black novel a quarter century ago. To re-enter social institutions which one has demonstrated as irremediably cruel is for both Burroway and Ellison the sign of full responsibility."

In 1971 the writing of *Raw Silk* was interrupted by Burroway's divorce and return to the United States. By the time the book was finally completed, its author had settled in Tallahassee, where she is now a professor of English at Florida State University. She has recently finished a sixth novel, "Opening Nights," which spans the seven weeks necessary to rehearse and produce a play for the summer opening of a small college theatre in southern Georgia. Shaara Soole, a theatre professor in the college, will costume the play; her ex-husband, Boyd, will come from New York to direct it; and Boyd's second wife, Wendy, will arrive for opening night. The play under production serves to comment in complex ways upon the lives of the characters in the novel, examining the androgynous within each person, the nature of human strength and weakness, the relationships between reality, artifice, and art. One strand of action, Shaara's decision to marry again, confronts by analogy many of the concerns Burroway herself faced prior to her second marriage, to William Dean Humphries, in 1978.

Characteristic of all Burroway's novels is the meticulous detail with which she renders the professions of her protagonists. "I feel bitterly cheated when an author tells me that somebody is a doctor and I can't feel it in the texture of the prose," she says. Thus, in the manner of James Gould Cozzens, Burroway does extensive research for her novels. (Because she was living in Belgium while working on *Eyes,* she did ophthalmic research in Flemish.) Her conviction that a person's work is a significant part of him is closely related to a similar belief in the importance of setting. Place is an integral element within the novel, just as each character is reflected in and influenced by the landscape he sees and the rooms through which he walks.

Thus, the visual quality of Burroway's work is very strong. Not surprisingly, Burroway is intrigued by the possibility of film and would like to try writing screenplays, which she feels can combine the immediacy of effect—writer to audience—of the conventional drama with the control of the narrative voice in fiction. Too, she continues to write poetry; her second collection, *Material Goods,* was published in 1980.

Whatever her determination to master other forms, Burroway remains quintessentially a novelist. As Jadeen Spatch tells her restless class in *Eyes,* "Thoughts are complex. Actions are not." It is precisely her ability to weigh the internal voices of her characters against the chilling simplicity of their actions and her skill at dramatizing the tension between the two that constitute Burroway's greatest talents. To achieve that tension, her novels are intricately patterned. But they are also strikingly clean. In the final analysis, they compel the reader to judge, finding, after all, the old verities.

—Elisabeth Muhlenfeld

Plays:

Garden Party, Barnard College, 1955;

The Fantasy Level, Yale School of Drama, 1961; Belgian National Television (in Flemish translation), 1965; Sussex: Gardner Center for the Arts, 1968;

The Beauty Operators, Sussex: Gardner Center for the Arts, 1968; London: Armchair Theatre, Thames Television, 1970; Belgian National Television (in Flemish translation), 1971.

Other:

"Poenulus, or The Little Carthaginian," adapted by Burroway, in *Five Roman Comedies,* ed. Palmer Bovie (New York: Dutton, 1970).

Periodical Publications:

POETRY:

"Song," *Atlantic,* 200 (August 1957): 45;

"Nuns at Birth," *New Statesman*, 80 (31 July 1970): 125;
"Separation," *New Statesman*, 89 (16 May 1975): 667; *MS.*, 4 (November 1975): 87.
FICTION:
"I Do Not Love You, Wesley," *Seventeen*, 16 (January 1957): 52-53, 102, 104;
"Extra Days," *Story Quarterly*, no. 2/3 (Winter 1976): 2-10.
NONFICTION:
"Poetry and the Primitive," in *Primitivism, Folk and The Primitive* (Binghamton, N.Y.: Harpur College Press, 1962): 53-59;
"The Irony of the Insufferable Prig: *Mansfield Park*," *Critical Quarterly*, 9 (Summer 1967): 127-138;
"Does Genius Have a Gender?," *MS.*, 6 (December 1977): 57, 83-84;
"*Opening Nights*: The Opening Days," *Women Writers on Their Work*, ed. Janet Sternberg (New York: Norton, forthcoming 1980).

Papers:

There is a collection of Burroway's manuscripts and important working papers in the Strozier Library, Florida State University in Tallahassee.

FREDERICK BUSCH
(1 August 1941-)

BOOKS: *I Wanted a Year Without Fall* (London: Calder & Boyars, 1971);
Hawkes: A Guide to His Fictions (Syracuse: Syracuse University Press, 1973);
Breathing Trouble and Other Stories (London: Calder & Boyars, 1973);
Manual Labor (New York: New Directions, 1974);
Domestic Particulars: A Family Chronicle (New York: New Directions, 1976);
The Mutual Friend (New York: Harper & Row, 1978; London: Harvester, 1978);
Hardwater Country (New York: Knopf, 1979);
Rounds (New York: Farrar, Straus & Giroux, 1979).

A great bear of a man with beard and laughing face, Frederick Busch has earned his reputation as one of the finest young novelists in America. He is also a short-story writer, literary critic, and teacher, but these pursuits are secondary to his primary concern with the novel. Writing about family love in a time of general domestic strife, controlling his experiments with form and voice in an era of gratuitous innovation, and urging the reader to feel in a time when emotion is suspect, Busch expands the limits of fiction and humanity.

He was born in the Midwood section of Brooklyn to Phyllis and Benjamin Busch. After attending local schools, he entered Muhlenberg College (Allentown, Pennsylvania) from which he received the A.B. degree in English in 1962. He then went to Columbia University as a Woodrow Wilson National Fellow to study for a master's degree in seventeenth-century English literature, but he left without completing the program. His life since then has been involved with writing of all kinds and at all levels of sophistication. Married to Judith Burroughs in November 1963 (they have two sons), Busch worked from 1963 through 1965 as a clerk in market-research firms and as a writer and editor, first for a public relations feature-article syndicate and then for *School Management*, a controlled-circulation magazine. In 1966, he was hired by Colgate University to teach and then to study for the Ph.D. in English. Although he never achieved the doctorate, he did earn the M.A. degree in 1967, writing a thesis on the fiction of John Hawkes while continuing to teach at Colgate. In 1977, Busch was visiting lecturer at the program in creative writing, University of Iowa; and in 1978-1979, he was acting director of the Iowa program and a visiting professor of English. During fall 1979, he taught at Columbia University as an adjunct professor of writing, but he simultaneously maintained his current position as a professor of English at Colgate.

His story "Is Anyone Left this Time of Year?" was included in *Prize Stories 1974: The O. Henry Awards*; and other stories have appeared in various editions of *Best American Short Stories*. In 1974-1975, he was poetry editor for the *Carleton Miscellany*. He was awarded a fellowship in 1976 from the National Endowment for the Arts, and in 1978-1979, he was fiction editor for the *Iowa Review*.

Through all of these stints as teacher and editor, through all of the busywork as director and clerk, Busch has written fiction of power and style. Having never gone through a period of publishing imitative fiction or first-person tales of growing up, Busch has already mastered various points of view from bewildered children, overworked doctors, and unhappy mothers to George Dolby and his "Chief," Charles Dickens. Doris Grumbach is correct when she remarks, "Busch has no single 'style' or voice. Instead he adopts a new *persona*, a new voice, for every story. The result is characters and events of great originality."

As might be expected, Busch's first novel, *I*

Wanted a Year Without Fall (published in London in 1971), is his weakest. He tends now to disown it despite his guarded approval of some of the pacing and dialogue. The novel was published when he sent the manuscript to a friend then living in Wales. All he asked for was an opinion, but without telling Busch, the friend submitted the book to his own publisher, Calder and Boyars, who then cabled Busch a surprise offer to publish *I Wanted a Year Without Fall*. He had written two novels before *I Wanted a Year Without Fall* (and one immediately after), which he says will never be released.

The ambiguities of *I Wanted a Year Without Fall* begin with the title: does the hero want to avoid a fall from grace, or the fortunate fall, or the season of fall with its promise of rain and death, or falling in love? These questions hover around the tale that is shaped by the classic structure of the journey, except that Ben and Leo are running from rather than questing toward: Ben from destitution in the city and the echo of a dead woman's voice, Leo from destitution in the country and the threats of an angry cuckold's violence. This literal level is grounded in a mythic foundation as Busch begins the novel with a quote from John Bunyan's *Pilgrim's Progress* and a lay from *Beowulf* which suggest a universal, pervading theme: men on the road grappling with unforeseen and unfamiliar enemies. The epigraph from Bunyan points to the "similitude of dream" and, indeed, surrounding all of the outrageous adventures is the outer frame of Ben silently telling the story to his sleeping son. The chant of the modern bard diminishes when compared to the rollicking heroics of *Beowulf*, but the clamor of absurdity echoes in both.

A delightful sense of the comic grins throughout the novel's elaborate and not entirely successful framework. A Boy Scout patrol, for example, pursues the questers; and gangsters on the trail of a secret detergent formula kidnap them. The humor is apparent from the beginning, not only in the absurdity of the unexpected action but also in the funny descriptions of daily routine, as in this account of Ben's joust with unwavering ranks of cockroaches: "I crunched a few—I heard them break—as I thumped to the sink and, when the water was foaming in, watched a cockroach midnight picnic party slip up and down on the enamel walls. . . ."

Ben's first-person narration has long sentences with many clauses held together by commas to suggest a quick pace and a sense of urgency. Some of the dialogue goes on too long, and some of it is too flippant, but generally the narration is convincing and rhythmical. More important is that Busch's eye for detail, a characteristic which is extraordinary in his later fictions and which joins his knowledge of how things work (a water pump, a roofing job, a hospital emergency room), is already evident in *I Wanted a Year Without Fall*. Busch knows that routine chores permit momentary order in chaotic lives.

For a short novel (156 pages), the pacing is too slow until Ben and Leo hit the road, but once on the lam they scurry from a fire escape to a train to the Staten Island Ferry while references to the Statue of Liberty and the river Styx float by, references which Ben treats with appropriate sarcasm: "That's very theological of you." Similarly, Leo wonders if they are part of an epic. He is associated, for example, with the alliteration which one expects in an Old English lay as he goes up "the last shallow snow-packed pitch of his path"; but for the most part Busch lets the tale unfold naturally even as he gives evidence this early in his career of a man who enjoys the texture of words. Indeed, he achieves many of his effects by playing off one style against another. The reader can only guffaw, for instance, at the leader of the gangsters, known as His Cousin, who speaks in clipped, correct sentences, and whose formality contrasts so vividly with the offbeat narrative that a sense of the grotesque results: "This is a matter of detergent. I will tell you that. Bodily health, alleged improvements of cleanliness, these are the issues. We do not deal in matters of defense." Laughter leers behind the clear and present dangers that loom all around Ben and Leo when they take to the road.

The conclusion is violent and death-ridden as Ben ends his old-time song for his sleeping son with words which suggest that he will have to tell the tale again in order to come to grips with the experience: "Once upon a time." *I Wanted a Year Without Fall* lacks the sense of pace and, most of all, the skill with character which show to such advantage in Busch's later novels, but with the mixture of violence and comedy and variations of language, it is an acceptable beginning.

After publishing a critical study of John Hawkes and a collection of stories, *Breathing Trouble*, in 1973, Busch took a giant step forward with *Manual Labor* (1974). A novel of marital pain so credible as to seem impossible for such a young writer, *Manual Labor* is the first of Busch's explorations of little people surviving unspectacular but numbing crises. The crisis in this instance is specific and full of dread: how can love survive when it is wracked by the deaths of children through miscarriage? This spiritually draining novel is about

John Hubbard

rebuilding a marriage, about the sheer effort involved in renovating two lives, as Anne and Phil Sorenson engage in physical work and emotional energy to turn the manual labor of reconstructing a nearly ruined house into a metaphor for their gamble to salvage love. As Phil says, "You forget with your hands."

They have a lot to forget. Busch reveals that he "loved" creating Annie, that he was "heartsick" when he finished with her character, and that he was interested in how "dogged, soft, gentle, pained, domestic, real heroism can be." The novel is both powerful and convincing because the Sorensons work literally to form their future lives out of the bloody losses of their immediate past. The soul-wrenching demands of their effort are suggested when Phil accidentally causes a crack in, appropriately, the living room wall while trying to jack up the house in order to level a slanting floor. Their despair, which shapes the general tone of trying to communicate through a barrier of domestic fear, is established early when Annie says, "Last time I was a mother I died."

By this point in his career, Busch is sure enough of his genius to show that character is action. As in *I Wanted a Year Without Fall,* a journey of sorts suggests structure: the Sorensons retreat from house to run-down house across the bleak New England landscape, but unlike *I Wanted a Year Without Fall* the journey in *Manual Labor* indicates not picaresque action but developed character. As Busch moves the Sorensons toward their last stand on the rocky coast of Maine, he shows how Annie's terror of death and Phil's fear for the death of their marriage is the crucial distinction that directs both the novel and their attitudes toward metaphorical labor. Anne says that work is a duty, but Phil insists that it is for "us." Yet even Phil begins to doubt. When he loses his thumb in a lawn mower accident, a mishap with sexual connotations, the blood which soaks his groin recalls Anne's first miscarriage. His futile search in the grass for the "orphaned" thumb affects his dream of the missing baby he longs to have:

> He is tiny on the snow. I stand breathless in his tracks. They are shallow, less in the snow than upon it. . . . I lumber through it, lifting it, lifting and kicking free, being clutched and tearing free to catch him, who by at least the snow is still uncaught. He skates on the surface and I sink. I stand and he diminishes. I see his future elude me. . . . He is vanishing.

Busch develops the distinctions in character with two sustained points of view: Anne's is an interior monologue couched in the form of a never-sent letter to her mother; Phil's is a journal in which he sets down and thereby orders their efforts to hold on to love and thus survive. The tension is never overtly stated, but their communication begins to drown in the accumulating despair of mental anguish and physical loss. While Anne writes letters she will not mail, and Phil composes poems he will not send out, they lose the ability even to talk: "How could we say what couldn't be said?"

Yet Busch is interested in not the melodrama of suicide but the heroism of hanging on. Although Anne now fears creativity in all forms, even literature, because she thinks that it produces only corpses, she nevertheless rejects suicide as something that "sounds like medicine. Something you clean clogged drains with." When she wonders if she is changing things in her letter in order to make her mother love her more, she indicates a self-consciousness and an awareness of narrative reliability which suggest the beginning of her surfacing from the obsession with introspection. Her scribbling to explain despair contrasts with Phil's writing to sustain life. His journal is an act of faith, a heroic effort to create order in the midst of grievous losses. The difference between Anne's fear of the past and Phil's confidence in the future, a difference between character which defines the novel, is shown in her emphasis on "I" and his on "we": "narrative leads to sanity. . . . We'll survive." Regeneration will come from the blood of their dead babies. Hoping to construct their future even as he constructs their house, Phil rearranges their past while he writes his narrative. Art is a means of cleansing.

His efforts pay off until the world begins to intrude, primarily in the guise of Abe, a sixty-year-old flower child who has dropped out to pursue extinction because of the deaths of his wife and son. Phil resents Anne's attentions to the old man, but he also realizes that Abe is a personification of death that his wife must exorcise. Busch's simile, which describes what Anne really sees when she finds Abe's body, specifies the choices she must finally make: "flabby Abe, all tensions relaxed like a baby asleep, his blood on the stones, born to peace." She chooses life and has the last word, speaking, significantly, not of herself but of their love: "We'll live."

The affirmation of the ending is earned. Following the discovery of Abe's body, Anne returns to the house and faces a room full of debris: the milk is sour; the lettuce is spoiled; the beer cans are beaded with oil; the light is flickering. Manual labor will always be a necessity in the Sorenson household, in the Sorenson marriage, in the Sorenson future, but they will live.

In 1976 Busch published *Domestic Particulars: A Family Chronicle*. Although concerned with its own lives and crises, it is a companion to *Manual Labor* in the sense that it focuses upon small acts of courage amid the despair of family turmoil. Parts of the novel were reworked from the stories in *Breathing Trouble*; and Busch struggled with one of the chapters, "Tax," for more than a decade, beginning it in college and continuing in graduate school before finishing it during a trip to England. Such painstaking care has paid off, for *Domestic Particulars* is a triumph of different voices, each one individualized and sustained in a cycle of love, loss, and the heroics of hanging on. One does not worry about the dilution of classical standards of heroism when reading of a mother tying herself to a crib with venetian blind cords for three days in order to stay awake and care for a sick child. The characters' struggles to affirm life is part of the vision of the novel. As one of them says, "Art should make a reparation and *not* a death."

This novel is also a gathering of domestic details, of smells in the kosher shops, furniture in the college inn, tentative conversations with a reluctant son, and how the weather was. Many of the details define characters who start out believing that life can be touched, only to end in wonder at where the dreams went. What happened, a mother asks, to their plans to live "an intelligent life of excitement. . . . high hopes and big talk and the sureness we were right?" Snuffed out by domestic particulars, answers Busch, by the trials of simply trying to love.

Composed of thirteen chapters, the novel spans a period from 1919 to 1976 as Busch parallels the many decades of war, genocide, depression, and political hysteria to the long years of pain and doubt in one family. These people are surely on a smaller scale than the historical events, but they are nevertheless devastated. The heart of this moving novel may be in Harry's explanation about "the flesh tearing away, the language less than adequate, the madness of continuing." They try to love one another because they care.

Busch begins with a portrait of Claire (Mac's wife and Harry's mother), recalling her youth in New York when food is scarce and maternal affection limited. Another version of Anne Sorenson, she suffers two miscarriages before Harry's birth. Claire's dilemma, however, is defined not by physical loss but by spiritual despair. Abandoning her dream of living an "intelligent life of excitement," she must learn to survive in what she calls an age of disgust, exchanging her stimulating life as an editor for existence with a sulking son and an unimaginative college professor who gives up ideas in order to watch the Colgate Comedy Hour. His primary hope is to keep his family safe.

The reader can only ask, safe from what, for Mac's fear of an external threat to his family during the Red Scare of the 1950s is groundless. Showing how all that matters are the internal tensions and the struggling at cross purposes, Busch so effectively differentiates narrative voices that he soon encourages sympathy for both Mac, who fears his son's birth, and Harry, whom Mac cannot touch: "I put a hand out for him and miss, and the hand is back at my side by the time he shuffles closer to be touched." Years later, Mac's hand is still at his side.

The transition to Harry's point of view occurs when Mac and Claire try but fail to touch him at his college graduation. No family battles have been waged, and no dissolution of family love has been declared, but damage has been done. How do they define a change that is not quite tangible? Busch's maturation as a novelist is evident in his mastery of tone, for he shows how parents accept their gradual separation from one another even while they watch bewildered as their child suddenly separates from them. The crucial point is that they all love each other with an intensity that hovers in the background of domestic pain, gliding behind the bedroom wall and generating emotion in the reader. Busch is superb as he delineates the awkwardness, the loose ends, the sheer embarrassment when Claire, Mac, and Harry have to sit down together for a moment at the graduation, acting out the role of a family.

Harry steps into adulthood as Busch illustrates what it means to care and yet lose. In the most effective chapter, "The Trouble with Being Food," Harry finds himself forced first to give up Katherine, the woman on whom he stakes his recovery, and later wife Anna, whose concern for a future of possibility and hope recalls Claire's once bright dreams. But if Harry lives with the guilt of leaving his parents, Anna lives with the pain and threat of breast cancer. Watching the surgeon walk toward him to explain the diagnosis, Harry voices the terrified but affirmative tone of the novel: "I watch the surgeon come. I will speak before he does. I will tell him we continue."

But they do not continue, at least not together. Divorced from Anna, separated from his past, and fearful of the future, Harry drifts into the bewilderment that has already numbed Mac and Claire. Only Claire's hysterical but determined insistence upon defining the inevitable separation of parent and child as Harry's "abandonment" enables her to continue. She understands that to accept the leaving is to invite despair, so she fights against the night in what is clearly a misguided but nevertheless specific instance of courage. One only hopes that Harry learns the same lessson at the end of the novel. There is little sense of reconciliation and no hint of catharsis in this narrative of the doggedness of love amid the agony of loss. *Domestic Particulars* ends with a glance toward the future but with the pain intact.

In 1978, Busch's career took an astonishing turn with the publication of *The Mutual Friend*. Stepping away, for the moment, from his emotionally searing probes into the intimacies of family life, he wrote a historical novel set in Victorian England. *The Mutual Friend* began as a play about Charles Dickens, but Busch had to change genres when he felt compelled to respond to what he calls the "force of my character's 'life.' " Described by Busch as the "bitchiest novel to do, and I still can't be certain whether I love or hate it," *The Mutual Friend* was named by the *Manchester Guardian* as one of the ten best novels published in England in 1978.

The successful creation of multiple voices in *Domestic Particulars* is carried over to this novel which, along with William Styron's *The Confessions of Nat Turner* and George Garrett's *Death of the Fox*, is one of the outstanding historical novels written by an American. An imaginative reconstruction of Dickens's last years as largely told by his factotum George Dolby, *The Mutual Friend* weaves Busch's painstaking research into the Victorian Age and his insights into the human heart and its dilemma. Dolby, Ellen Ternan, long-suffering Kate, and Dickens himself—they are all here bursting with language and life. The result is an elegant consideration of the challenges that fame and vanity pose to one's humanity as well as an inquiry into the nature of narrative itself.

The dominant voice, which Busch imagines with fidelity to the period and sympathy for the character, is George Dolby, Dickens's long-time secretary, who, while dying in a charity ward, is writing his memoirs of life with the Chief. His flesh decaying but his memory strong, he asks the reader to attend to the voices of the past. And attend the reader does to this extraordinary plunge into another time, to watch Dickens cater to his reputation as perhaps the greatest writer since Shakespeare with such energy and invention that he confuses the role with the man. He makes fictions out of nearly every step he takes in reality. Busch's portrait via Dolby is unforgettable: "Because he was the whore of self-pity, and also brave. He was the Chief. . . . The stage was his mind."

Much of Dolby's reminiscence is concerned with Dickens's last reading tour of America, a journey that the Chief finds at times unbearable: "Really, Dolby, I don't *want* to sleep in any more towns named Utica. Utica. *Utica*. Doesn't it sound like an herb you take for your health? . . . My God, Dolby, they don't breathe *air*! They live in steam . . . and spit tobacco juice." This finely honed sense of humor is an undercurrent throughout. Busch's Dickens is a man who changes everything with his pen to what he thinks it should be, but he fails to alter American fondness for bourbon and tobacco. Still, his imagination gets him through nearly every encounter until reputation and man merge. In essence, Busch suggests, Dickens creates himself: "He was a pirate, he stole the living world. . . . His voice rose and fell, muttered, yelped, screamed, whined, declaimed; he had as many faces and voices and tones as a church-choir in their highest public ecstasies, and I, too, was once again encircled, made his prisoner." Dolby admits that even he is probably one

72

Waking is easy, and Silver does it. He stands beside his bed, shivering not ~~with~~ from the early September chill, but from inside, ~~with a boyish anticipation, subcutaneous excitement that makes him feel his muscles ripple, as the flesh of~~ as boys quake ~~can crawl with happiness on birthday mornings~~ on the first uneasily glad ~~XXXXXXX~~ day of school. For Silver, it is another ~~day~~ 14 hours of work, of hospital rounds and then clinic practice, of seeming well--~~.....~~ sometimes, even to himself--by doing at least (with some luck) little harm.

The house is the same, though neater than when they lived in it as a family. His bedclothes seem flatter and less disturbed by his presence, clothing in the closet hangs in plastic laundry wrappers, towels in the hallway clost like in taped brown ~~packages,~~ paper, there are fewer hairs in the shower drain. The blinds on most windows are drawn, and the house has its own temperature, its own brown and black tones, separate from whatever happens outside. ~~in the world of upper New York State.~~ When he is standing silently, head-down, receiving the hot shower like a punishment, Silver understands: his house--its thirteen rooms, its walls of prints, its fine~~ly~~-tuned kitchen, garage with automatic door, the annex with his clinic--his house is a now a hotel. He leaves his towel on

Rounds, *revised typescript*

of the Chief's imaginings.

Like Busch, like the reader, and finally like Dickens himself, Dolby wonders when the Chief tells the truth. Yet Dickens has an answer to that query, an answer which is a key to both his life and this novel: truth gives way before invention. Both Dickens and Busch make up their worlds: the interminable train rides, the hotel fires, the food, and most of all the language. Perhaps Dickens even invents the resolution of his troubles with Ellen Ternan. The details of their affair may never be known, but Dolby suggests: "he was drawn to Ternan. . . . He needed love. . . . but he needed more to live forever in his mind. Ternan didn't want to live there." Touches like this which probe the motivations of a complex man are at the heart of *The Mutual Friend.*

Busch's success with the demanding genre of historical fiction testifies to his ability to unite language and imagination. He creates a fictional Dolby who will quote from a real Dickens letter describing a historically documented event, and then he lets Dolby describe the event himself. Dolby's account may be more accurate even though Busch has made it up. The contrast between descriptions is nearly always comic as well as revelatory about Dickens's need to massage his ego while inventing his world. The double focus allows Busch to capture a historical period as it was and as Dickens claims it was. An example of this technique is Dolby's letter to Georgina, which describes an incident involving the Chief and which Georgina reads to the Dickens household assembled especially for the occasion. Then, in a later chapter which Dolby narrates, Dolby retells the incident in words much less flattering to the Chief. The truth likely resides in the latter description. But, Busch suggests, the truth does not matter; the larger point is that Dolby helps to create the myth of Charles Dickens for the public much as the Chief seems to form the entire world for himself. Yet even then the reader is not sure, for Dolby always hedges: "I think I have got this part right." History and giants will not be pinned down.

Dickens himself may learn this lesson. In a small but sensitive scene, the Chief, now old and failing, takes a final tour of London, seeing, as it were, glimmers of his own immortality. A stranger on the train ignores, insults, and enrages him, but the stranger is nevertheless reading *David Copperfield.* Since Dickens has created his posthumous reputation with his books, he might as well depart the earth and the train.

Busch stresses the fictitiousness of all fiction, his as well as Dickens's, in the final chapter as the narration slides from Dickens to Dolby to Moon, the servant who sneaks in gin for Dolby while the dying factotum struggles to complete his tale. This point is crucial to Busch's concept of historical fiction, for Moon not only cares for Dolby's papers but also narrates the end of the novel after Dolby dies. The reader immediately wonders, what if Moon has controlled *The Mutual Friend,* not Dickens and not Dolby but Moon the Asian servant? Busch lets the suspicion linger when he has Moon say, "I will bloody well change it all. Rewrite the lives old Dolby set down, his and his Chief's and my own. . . . One wants something, after all, with a happy ending to it. I will make changes." Dickens creates the world, Dolby creates Dickens, Moon creates Dolby, and Busch and the reader create the shadowy Moon in their imaginations. History is all version and vision, dependent upon the whims of its storytellers. As the dust jacket notes, *The Mutual Friend* is a novel in which Dickens "has the honor to be variously portrayed." Perhaps the maid Barbara knows him best when she says of his novels: "No, a book is no more than a voice. There are many voices. All of them in time are lost."

Years before starting *The Mutual Friend,* Busch began doing research for an essay on a local pediatrician whom he admires. An early fictional version of the doctor is Dr. Hebner of *Domestic Particulars.* He explains, "I kept my research notes, the product of weeks of work, and when I started *R*, I went back to do more research—walking and standing through hour after hour, and day after day, of hospital and clinic rounds." The result is *Rounds* (1979; he also published a volume of short stories, *Hardwater Country,* in 1979), one of the finest American novels of the 1970s, and a novel which caps a decade of extraordinary achievement. *Rounds* is a book about love. It is also Busch's strongest novel because it combines the emotional intensity of *Manual Labor* and *Domestic Particulars,* the astonishingly accurate detail of *The Mutual Friend,* and the convincing fleshing out of voices with characters whose determination to come to grips with the confrontation of love and death endows them with dignity and grace. The title refers not only to a pediatrician's rounds through the hospital hallways of pain and hope but also to Busch's method of constructing the novel as voices and lives circle around each other, tentatively reaching out, touching, and finally establishing relationships for future possibilities.

Creation of character has more and more emerged as Busch's concern in fiction: "I wanted a book chock-ful of story here, of people. . . . And each book is an 'experiment' of its own—in a kind of language, mode of telling, nature of plotting.... For me, what 'experimental' fiction deals with are now givens; I want to work from them, not toward them, and what I want to do is make the seamless connection, no stitches at all in sight, between what we've learned about the art and what we need to experience about people whose flesh we want made word." One reason why the reader is moved by the predicaments facing the flesh made word in this novel is that so much is at stake in their lives. Busch controls the intense emotion by balancing feeling with detail, and the result is a splendid blend of character and action. Thus while Dr. Eli Silver, a pediatrician who has inadvertently let his only child die, copes with guilt and a shattered home, he also tries to keep his equilibrium by insisting upon the discipline of medicine as he intersects with the broken health of patients and strangers. As he says, taking care of babies is not fair. Similarly, Anne and Phil Sorenson, still in search of a child and thus their future, as they are in *Manual Labor*, rebuild old houses and cheap furniture while hoping to mend their lives; and Elizabeth Bean, a school psychologist, attempts to juggle her skills in guiding college students who need help with her own potentially destructive problems as an unmarried pregnant woman who rejects abortion.

In each case, the detail of work is a clue to character. Blessed with an eye for how things operate, Busch shows that one's handling of the little demands of the daily routine determines one's coping with the large questions of emotional turmoil. A fine example of the way he intersects private despair with professional duty occurs when Silver ponders a request from his runaway wife to return home:

> He had witnessed parents giving permission for possible radical surgery before probably routine exploratories on their children. They had seen only the small unconscious victim on the table, and surgeons busy with procedure—not *their* person—and nurses not knowing their baby's name. They had looked beyond that image into darkness and no control whatever, the hugeness of loss just out of sight but felt nevertheless; and, fearing to say no, they had given their powerless consent. Eli said, "Sure, Gwen. Of course."

Busch's feel for the interaction of form and content is evident in the way he handles tenses: past for Anne and Phil; present for the first part of Silver's tale. The novel begins with an ironic manger scene. Standing in a graveyard surrounded by grazing cattle, Silver stares not at a manger and birth but at his son's coffin and death. Gwen falls to her knees not in reverence but in despair. Busch renders this shattering opening scene in past tense and then switches to present tense as he begins the difficult process of developing Silver's near emotional collapse while avoiding the pitfalls of simplicity and sentimentality. Eli Silver cannot heal himself—love from Elizabeth Bean and concern for the Sorensons will help—but he must try. Anne's desire to watch a television program where "everybody cries except the doctors" suggests by contrast the extremity of Silver's condition. The healing of his love is the story of the novel.

The process toward recovery starts when Silver forces himself on Halloween—All Saints Eve—to differentiate his life between past and present. He distributes candy to healthy children significantly dressed as deformed monsters, recalls his son's death, and makes the terrifying decision to ease by mercy killing a dying child's long glide into oblivion. The tense shift from present to past is intentionally designed to slide into place at this crucial point where Silver must cope with the relationship of events which insist upon the reality of past happenings, their impingement on the present, and their shaping of the future: "Dolores was dying, now she dies more, she is closer to death, his only available gift, and it grows harder to think of her in the present tense. The present tense is always more dangerous. Dolores *was* dying this morning at the hospital when Silver fed her drugs and solution and helped her body start to stop."

Accepting the mandate to acknowledge the influence of past events upon present decisions, Silver finds himself once again inside the lives of other people. The rest of the novel details with sympathy and perception his halting efforts to connect his own past and present with the futures of himself and those who try, who need his help, and whom he comes to love. As he says, his is a tale worth telling.

All of Busch's novels are worth telling. Not yet forty years old, Frederick Busch is ready to begin the period of his greatest achievement. His last four novels are by no means apprentice work; they are finely constructed, emotionally true fictions which have already earned him the status of an artist who counts, a writer who matters to the cultural health of the nation. It is not at all outrageous to say that he will achieve major stature in the next decade. Readers who do not yet know him may ask, "Is he *that* good?" The answer is quick and definite: he is.

—Donald J. Greiner

Periodical Publications:

"But This Is What It Is to Live in Hell: 'In the Heart of the Heart of the Country' and *Under the Volcano*," *Modern Fiction Studies*, 19 (Spring 1973): 97-108;

"The Whale as Shaggy Dog: Melville and the Man Who Studied Yoga," *Modern Fiction Studies*, 19 (Summer 1973): 193-206;

"The Friction of Fiction: A *Ulysses* Omnirandum," *Chicago Review*, 26 (Winter 1975): 5-17;

"James Laughlin, A Man of Taste," *Harper's Bookletter*, 12 April 1976, p. 16;

"The Language of Starvation," *Ohio Review*, 17 (Spring-Summer 1976): 26-37;

"Charles Dickens: The Smile on the Face of the Dead," *Mosaic*, 9 (Summer 1976): 149-156;

"Icebergs, Islands, Ships Beneath the Sea," in *A John Hawkes Symposium: Design and Debris*, ed. Anthony C. Santore and Michael Pocalyko (New York: New Directions, 1977), pp. 50-63;

"Thoreau and Melville as Cellmates," *Modern Fiction Studies*, 23 (Summer 1977): 239-242;

"When People Publish," *Ohio Review*, 20 (Spring-Summer 1979): 41-62.

References:

Samuel R. Crowl, "Manual Labor," *Ohio Review*, 16 (Winter 1975): 123-124;

Richard Elman, "Specific Instances of Pain," *Nation*, 223 (6 November 1976): 468-469;

Donald J. Greiner, "After Great Pain: The Fiction of Frederick Busch," *Critique: Studies in Modern Fiction*, 19 (August 1977): 101-111;

Doris Grumbach, " 'Light' Reading for Late Spring," *Chronicle of Higher Education*, 14 May 1979, p. R10;

Mitchell Marks, "Manual Labor," *Chicago Review*, 26, no. 3 (1974): 192-193;

Joyce Carol Oates, "Manual Labor: A Family Haunted by Death," *New York Times Book Review*, 3 November 1974, p. 66.

R. V. CASSILL

(17 May 1919-)

SELECTED BOOKS: *The Eagle on the Coin* (New York: Random House, 1950);

The Wound of Love (New York: Avon, 1956);

Fifteen by Three, by Cassill, Herbert Gold, and James B. Hall (New York: New Directions, 1957);

Night School (New York: Dell, 1961);

Clem Anderson (New York: Simon & Schuster, 1961);

Pretty Leslie (New York: Simon & Schuster, 1963; London: Muller, 1964);

Writing Fiction (New York: Pocket Books, 1963);

The President (New York: Simon & Schuster, 1964);

The Father and Other Stories (New York: Simon & Schuster, 1965);

The Happy Marriage and Other Stories (West Lafayette, Ind.: Purdue University Studies, 1966);

La Vie Passionée of Rodney Buckthorne: A Tale of the Great American's Last Rally and Curious Death (New York: Geis, 1968);

In An Iron Time (West Lafayette, Ind.: Purdue University Studies, 1969);

Doctor Cobb's Game (New York: Geis, 1970);

The Goss Women (Garden City: Doubleday, 1974; Dunton Green, Sevenoaks, Kent, U.K.: Hodder & Stoughton, 1975);

Hoyt's Child (Garden City: Doubleday, 1976);

Labors of Love (New York: Arbor House, 1980).

Almost all writers would like critical appraisals of their work to consider the corpus, not the individual book. In the case of R. V. Cassill there is some difficulty in this approach. The texture of his literary interests and accomplishments is uneven; yet, like the work of Faulkner and Fitzgerald, even in his less illuminated moments his fiction challenges the intellect and imagination of his readers. In such paperback originals as *The Wound of Love* (1956) and *Night School* (1961) there is the unmistakable mark of the sensitive mind playing with the blatantly commercial requirement of erotic fiction. These two early paperback novels, plus some ten others published by Lion, Ace, Avon, Gold Medal, and the New American Library, constitute one side of Cassill—the professional craftsman—and for the genre, they are well done. But if this genre were all, Cassill would indeed be mere craftsman. He is, in fact, much more than that.

Ronald Verlin Cassill was born in Cedar Falls, Iowa, while his parents were attending Iowa State Teachers College. This stamp of the midwesterner has both delineated and obstructed his work. Like Joyce, he has impugned his connection with his time and place of birth, and he has even called himself an "exile" from his original environment. In his essay, "Why I Left the Midwest" (*In An Iron Time*, 1969), he says: "It seems to me I am speaking of reality when I say that I was born into the ethical life in and of the midwest. . . . I admit that all my notions of love and justice, the shape as well as the limitations of my sensibility were graven and determined for me by the midwest that preceded them." The key phrase is "limitations of my sensibility," suggesting a rather consistent motif in Cassill's fiction: the dichotomized nature of the midwesterner—especially the midwesterner who is also an artist.

This dichotomy of the isolated sensibility opposed and threatened by the social, artistic, and political power structure around and beyond it is the core theme of Cassill's serious fiction, even in those works that do not have as characters midwestern types. Cassill has said: "From my first novel onward I have explored the correspondences between the interior world—of desire and anxiety—and the public world of power—extra-social violences and politics," and elsewhere he cites as a basic trait of his nature "a kind of inertia of the heart." This inertia is a positive element in his fiction because it suggests less a lack of emotional movement than an unwillingness to succumb to the trite apothegms of what he calls "the indoctrinating forces that spoil our good lives." One other key to his work may be found in the Thomas Mann quotation Cassill has called his favorite by a fellow writer: "I was born to bear witness in tranquility."

In a sense, Cassill's life has been tranquil. He grew up in Iowa farm communities, hitchhiked the country as a teenager during the Depression, went to the University of Iowa where he received a B.A. in 1939, and then to the army where he became a first lieutenant in the Medical Corps, traveled in Europe, and studied at the Sorbonne. In 1947, he won an *Atlantic* "Firsts" for the short story, "The Conditions of Justice"; this same year he received an M.A. from the University of Iowa. He lectured at Columbia University (1957-1959), instructed in the Writers Workshop at the University of Iowa (1960-1965), and was writer in residence at Purdue University (1965-1966). Since 1966 he has been an associate professor of English (and from 1967 to 1971 president of the Associated Writing Programs) at Brown University. He received an O. Henry short-story award for "The Prize" in 1956. He has been the recipient of both Rockefeller Foundation (1954) and Guggenheim (1968) grants. During this basically academic life, he has produced the bulk of his many novels, short story collections, and nonfiction books.

In another sense, tranquility has been missing from the thematic impact of Cassill's fiction. He comments: "The circumstances of my life show one fracture of relationship after another and a very great deal of moving from one place to another. And between these external circumstances and my rooted emotions there has always been a bitter tension. My simple emotional patriotism and identification of myself as a midwesterner have been in conflict throughout my adult life with the swift historic alterations I have lived through."

Cassill's first novel, *The Eagle on the Coin* (1950), deals with alterations of social consciousness consistent with, if not ahead of, the time. The hero of this novel, Andrew Cameron—a liberal young professor caught up in a racial-sexual-political dilemma in a small industrial town in the Midwest—reacts in character and fights through to an ambiguous moral victory in his attempt to help elect a black to a local school board. The critical reception of this first novel ranged from the comment, "dull and unconvincing," in the *Library Journal* to "a powerful statement of what ails democracy at its grass roots," as voiced by Charles Roberts in the *Chicago Sun*. Cassill himself has said the novel "flopped," but the blueprint for subsequent fictional constructions of human corruption and probity is set down in this early work.

Pretty Leslie (1963) is a novel that successfully explores the sexual disorientation and degeneration of three characters, the pitiable masochist Leslie, her kind but murder-haunted physician husband, and the brilliantly conceived sadistic painter who exploits the weaknesses of others. While Freudian in tone, the novel is not a casebook analysis of tormented characters, but a subtle delineation of moral transference. Dark, sometimes sensational, the novel is a modern *Madame Bovary* of psychogenetic midwestern values turned sour by virtue masquerading as violence.

La Vie Passionée of Rodney Buckthorne (1968) reveals another side of Cassill's talent, one unfortunately not developed enough in the whole of his work to the present. In this comic satire, the midwesterner—a partial self-loather and a partial mountebank of ego—escapes the confines of academe (a Wyoming university) and rockets to the improbable but deadly liberating atmosphere of a Greenwich Village apartment. Here, like Pangloss intellectualizing his erotic needs, Buckthorne enmeshes himself in confusing webs of art and sex gone mad. While some critics saw Buckthorne's confusion at the end of the novel as Cassill's inability to make a cohesive statement through the prototype of his hero, perhaps a fairer view is to see Buckthorne as simply another aspect of what might be called "the Cassill man," the sojourner in the maelstrom of American moral waters. Cassill prefaces the novel with this quotation from Whitman:

> With all thy gifts America . . .
> What if one gift thou lackest (the ultimate human problem never solving),
> The gift of perfect women fit for thee—what if that gift of gifts thou lackest?
> The towering feminine of thee? The beauty, health, completion fit for thee?

The quotation suggests to the careful reader that no ultimate statement about meaning is yet possible in a value system which can only question itself with increasing ferocity and bitter humor.

Two later novels of interest are *Doctor Cobb's Game* (1970) and *The Goss Women* (1974). Of the former, loosely based on the Profumo scandal in England, critical reception was mixed, but most favorable comments were directed toward the skillful manner in which Cassill combined the ingredients of occultism, sexual explicitness, and political subversion in a highly readable work. *The Goss Women*, a reworking of some of the same ingredients with an American background, was less well received by critics.

Clem Anderson (1961) remains Cassill's best work. Critics of the 1960s largely minimized the worth of this large, ambitious, often brilliant novel which took Cassill five years to write. Of it Cassill says, "I took the silhouette of Dylan Thomas's life and within that composed the story of an American poet's self-destructive triumph. It probably is and always will be my most embattled work, simply because in its considerable extent it replaces most of the comfortable or profitable cliches about an artist's life with tougher and more painful diagrams." The novel is an account of the rise and fall of a prominent American poet (Anderson) as viewed by his good friend (Richard Hartsell), who is the narrator. Like Zietblom nervously and sympathetically recalling the destructive pattern of Adrian Leverkühn in Thomas Mann's *Doktor Faustus* (1947), Hartsell both wryly and compassionately compels himself and the reader to follow what "painful diagrams" are discernible in the mythic rituals of the artist in America. Few writers would dare undertake what Cassill does in this book—to communicate the essence of myth by extrapolating the vagaries of genius from raw, personal sources: whole sections of the novel are verbatim passages from an unpublished novel by the fictional poet. Granville Hicks called this "a clumsy device," and a *Time* critic said: "Novelist Cassill quotes a quantity of Anderson prose and verse, all of it unimpressive." While there may be some truth to the latter criticism only, the technique of incorporating Anderson's own prose is not only a courageously inventive technique, but a fascinating one as well for the reader.

Toward the end of the novel, Anderson experiences a "vision" in a moonlit game preserve in Kansas, where he is attending a writer's conference. It is a chilling, mystifying experience in which not only the small animals indigenous to the area—coons, jackrabbits, badgers—come marching out of the "fabulous velvet of the woods," but also "lions with goat heads, dragon-winged horses . . . unicorns . . . figures like Egyptian statuary . . . "; and then, to an amazed but cynical Anderson ("Disney could have done most of this") there appears an ultimate mythic figure: the Great Bride. There is the tension of waiting for the poet as he views the spectacle—as if the group were anticipating the arrival of the King. Anderson escapes the vision only when he realizes "he was not going to be able to volunteer as King." He snaps back to the real world on his knees, as if in prayer, holding "a knife-sized shard of flint" which has mysteriously gravitated to his hand. This curious vision is central to understanding the mythic nature of the novel. The wondrous embellishments of man-the-poet's imagination make demands on his spirit (and talent) that are impossible, even dangerous by comparison with demands on less percipient natures. The poet—a primitive loser in a highly sophisticated world—is fortunate enough to *hold* the vision, if only briefly, although he is finally denied union with it. This is the poet's magic, his contact with a chimera most men only vaguely sense. But it is also a deadly encounter for the most ambitious and the best. Life outside the chimera is too pale and real to be endured. This may be what Cassill meant when he described Anderson as a figure of "self-destructive triumph."

Cassill's latest novel, *Labors of Love* (1980), is another example of his competence in writing intelligent and often witty fiction with an erotic angst. One of the book's characters, a writer-editor named Tony Slater, even says as much in a moment of cynical or desperate introspection: "*angst* is the spice of spicy stories written in a serious literary manner." The novel concerns Tony's nervous passage through several worlds—serious literary ambitions versus the practical, debilitating demands of editorship; the safe haven of a home, wife, and children versus the exhilaration of a rather cabalistic young mistress named Margaret who seeks, then cheerfully fails, to wreck his marriage; and finally, but most interestingly, the interior nightmare Tony must face in sorting out his own psyche apart from love, sex, and responsibility of any kind. Although Cassill does not pursue—perhaps prudently—the alter ego image of Tony's "accusing Angel" introduced in the first chapter of the novel, the implication is clear throughout: the rewards of love come laboriously—not always as rewards, but very often as punishments.

Cassill's short stories, including such fine stories as "The Father," "Larchmoor Is Not the World," "This Hand, These Talons," and the often anthologized "The Biggest Band," have received high critical acclaim. In addition to his fiction, Cassill has written a textbook on creative writing, *Writing Fiction* (1963), and served as the critical editor of *The Norton Anthology of Short Fiction* (1977). Cassill remains a writer of unusual sensitivity and diversified talent. Although much of his work suggests the supreme craftsman without deep conviction, his best art—the stories and the novel *Clem Anderson*—deserve far more attention than they have yet received.

—*Charles Harmon Cagle*

Other:

Intro #1, edited by Cassill (New York: Bantam, 1968);
Intro #2, edited by Cassill (New York: Bantam, 1969);
Intro #3, edited by Cassill (New York: McCall, 1970);
The Norton Anthology of Short Fiction, edited by Cassill and others (New York: Norton, 1977).

FRED CHAPPELL
(28 May 1936-)

BOOKS: *It Is Time, Lord* (New York: Atheneum, 1963; London: Dent, 1965);
The Inkling (New York: Harcourt, Brace & World, 1965; London: Chapman & Hall, 1966);
Dagon (New York: Harcourt, Brace & World, 1968);
The World Between the Eyes (Baton Rouge: Louisiana State University Press, 1971);
The Gaudy Place (New York: Harcourt Brace Jovanovich, 1973);
River: A Poem (Baton Rouge: Louisiana State University Press, 1975);
The Man Twice Married to Fire (Greensboro, N.C.: Unicorn Press, 1977);
Bloodfire: A Poem (Baton Rouge: Louisiana State University Press, 1978);
Wind Mountain: A Poem (Baton Rouge: Louisiana State University Press, 1979);
Awakening to Music (Davidson, N.C.: Briarpatch Press, 1979);
Earthsleep: A Poem (Baton Rouge: Louisiana State University Press, 1980);
Moments of Light (Newport Beach, Cal.: New South, 1980);
How I Lost It (Athens, Ohio: Rosetta Press, 1980);
Midquest (Baton Rouge: Louisiana State University Press, forthcoming 1981).

The dust jacket of Fred Chappell's novel *The Gaudy Place* (1973) proclaims him "one of the most gifted of the younger North Carolina writers," a designation which tends to underrate his achievements. While it is true that his four novels have attracted little critical attention in this country and that only *The Gaudy Place* has entered a second edition, Chappell's work has won reviewers' praise and the respect of fellow writers, among them George Garrett, R. H. W. Dillard, and Reynolds Price. Perhaps an even more important gauge of Chappell's significance is the strength of his international reputation: *It Is Time, Lord* (1963) and *The Inkling* (1965) were published in England to rave reviews, and in France translations of *It Is Time, Lord* and *Dagon* (1968) by Maurice-Edgar Coindreau and of *The Inkling* by Claude Levy brought Chappell both critical and commercial success. The warmth of his French reception recalls that of William Faulkner, whose reputation as a novelist was very high in France while his work was being virtually ignored in this country. Chappell, however, remains unperturbed by his lack of popular recognition in the United States, maintaining that his career has been "just exactly what I could have handled. If I'd been more successful, I'd be dead somewhere."

The humorous detachment with which Chappell views his career is typical of the man. He was born in Canton, a small industrial town in the mountains of North Carolina. His parents, James Taylor and Anne Davis Chappell, were schoolteachers who had been reared in the region. The author's ties with his native area are close; the mountains and the people of western North Carolina figure prominently in both his novels and poetry. Although the region is conservative, it enabled Chappell to become acquainted with people from wide ranging social and economic levels. As Chappell grew up, he observed a culture undergoing a transition from a primarily agrarian economy to a society in which men's ties with the land and the stability this connection instills became more and more distant. This upheaval underlies all of Chappell's work. Thus, the author's native region not only provided him with characters and locale for much of his art but also suggested many of the moral and philosophical foundations of that art as well.

As an undergraduate at Duke University, Chappell gave serious attention to the composition of poetry. He became friends with other students—among them Reynolds Price—who had come to Duke to study with William Blackburn, a remarkably successful teacher of creative writing who had taught William Styron and Mac Hyman, among others. Chappell describes Blackburn's influence as "complete and total," though it often did not take the form of specific criticism of Chappell's work. Chappell recalls: "He never seriously criticized a piece of writing I turned in to him. . . . When I turned in something he didn't like, he just never said anything about it. And that was the end of it. If I turned in something he liked, he would say it was the best goddamned thing since, you know, Homer. . . ." In addition to encouragement, Blackburn suggested authors his students should read, and, perhaps more importantly, he provided outlets for their work in print. The anthology *Under Twenty-Five* (1963), a collection of pieces done by Blackburn's Duke undergraduates, included two short stories and ten poems written by Chappell.

In 1961 Chappell was awarded a National Defense Education Act fellowship. After completion of his undergraduate studies that same year, Chappell remained at Duke to work on his master's degree. He continued his friendships with both Blackburn and Price, who had returned from study at Oxford University to teach at Duke. During a literary festival on campus, Blackburn introduced Chappell to Hiram Haydn, an editor at Atheneum who had read one of Chappell's stories in *The Archive*, Duke's student literary publication. Haydn later wrote asking if Chappell would be interested in submitting a novel; but the young writer, considering himself primarily a poet, declined. The financial pressures of summer unemployment, however, soon made Haydn's offer more attractive, and Chappell sent him the manuscript of *It Is Time, Lord* in the summer of 1962. The publication of the novel the following year was quite encouraging to the young graduate student who was still struggling with an enormous master's thesis: a concordance to the English poetry of Samuel Johnson. Despite the pressures of graduate school, Chappell continued to submit both poetry and short fiction to a variety of publications.

When Chappell completed work for his M.A. degree in 1964, he moved with his wife, the former Susan Nichols, and son, Christopher Heath, to Greensboro, where he became writer in residence at what is now the University of North Carolina at Greensboro. The following year his second novel, *The Inkling*, appeared. A 1966 Rockefeller Foundation grant enabled Chappell to live abroad in 1967; he and his family stayed in Florence, where the author read proofs on his third book, *Dagon*, published in 1968. The year in Italy was a productive one artistically; he completed the first draft of his book of poems, *The World Between the Eyes*—which did not appear until 1971—and of his fourth novel, *The Gaudy Place*. A grant from the National Institute of Arts and Letters in 1967 provided funds for his return home, where Chappell again resumed his duties at Greensboro.

Other honors and awards Chappell has received include the Prix de Meilleur des Lettres Etrangères (French Academy) for *Dagon* in 1971; the Roanoke-Chowan Poetry Cup for *The World Between the Eyes* in 1972, for *River* in 1978, and for *Bloodfire* in 1979; and the Sir Walter Raleigh Award for *The Gaudy Place* in 1973.

Following the publication of *The Gaudy Place*, Chappell turned his attention once again to poetry, but the project which he undertook employed elements of the novel as well. *Midquest* (forthcoming 1981) is a long poem incorporating both autobiographical and fictional elements drawn in part from the same materials he had used in *It Is Time, Lord*. The completed work includes four book-length poems which combine narrative, lyric, and dramatic verse; each volume has been individually published: *River* (1975), *Bloodfire* (1978), *Wind*

Mountain (1979), and *Earthsleep* (1980). However, this ambitious project has not completely absorbed Chappell's time during the last seven years; he has managed to contribute short stories, poetry, and criticism to various anthologies and periodicals. At present, in addition to teaching classes in creative writing, science fiction, and film at the University of North Carolina at Greensboro, Chappell is engaged in several writing projects.

In many ways Chappell is an experimental novelist, a designation he himself has acknowledged. This aspect of his work explains in part the difficulties readers often encounter with his books. As R. H. W. Dillard has pointed out, Chappell is a difficult writer, not because of the complexities of his prose, but because of the philosophical nature of his perceptions. What is more, he approaches his craft with the sensibilities and often with the techniques of the poet. This orientation provides his fiction with much of its imaginative power, but it also places greater demands upon the reader. All four of Chappell's novels are short, and each one creates a minutely detailed world in which image and symbol unite to form a densely woven fabric of meaning. They exhibit the sort of condensation and economy of language associated with poetry, along with much of the poet's symbolic method.

Chappell himself has recognized the importance of symbolism to his work, but he draws a distinction between his own use of symbolic techniques and those employed by such authors as Faulkner and Thomas Pynchon: his is "more like a poet's symbolism, in which the intellectual structure is outside and behind, and the narrative takes place . . . in its own terms. And so you can figure out the novel; if you have a little information you can figure out symbolic structures . . . but you don't need it to enjoy the book."

A complicated foundation of symbolic meaning requires that Chappell's books be tightly structured, as indeed they are. Each novel creates its own universe in which actions arise from a complex relationship between characters and a generally hostile environment. The narrative structure of each book is shaped by the interplay between man and his world. Thus, a protagonist's perception serves a dual function: it is a central device for the presentation of character, and it determines the way his story will unfold. In *Dagon* and *The Gaudy Place* this technique offers little difficulty; both books employ a rather simple, straightforward narrative progression, leaving the complexities to be discerned in the moral and philosophical implications of the action. In Chappell's first two novels, however, the structural devices are much more complicated, challenging the reader to distinguish between fact and fancy, to question the nature of time and its effects upon characters' motivations and beliefs. In *It Is Time, Lord* Chappell juxtaposes chapters set in present time against a spurious view of the past, written in a journal by the novel's main character, James Christopher. The reader finds that he must sort out the events of the protagonist's life in much the same way the character himself does. *The Inkling* provides fewer narrative difficulties, but the cyclical structure of the book and its shifting narrative perspective require a similar involvement on the part of the reader.

Despite the fact that Chappell's novels achieve an impressive variety in character presentation, setting, and plot development, certain ideas and attitudes underlie all his fiction. Chappell himself has pointed out some of these concepts: all of the books share the theme of original sin, which Chappell defines as "a condition of things that exist before the character shows up." The first responsibility of the characters is to establish for themselves the nature of the world they must cope with. Chappell frequently symbolizes this initial responsibility through an inheritance—of property, as in *Dagon*, or of personality traits and attitudes, as in *It Is Time, Lord* and *The Inkling*. This problem is compounded by the influence of other characters. Chappell continually explores the effects of a single individual's actions upon those around him; none of his characters exists alone, and thus their problems have far-reaching implications. The main characters in each novel find their positions complicated by factors over which they can exert no control, and yet the protagonist must continue to struggle, superficially because of his responsibilities to those who depend upon him, but finally because of his need to understand himself.

Ultimately, then, the characters find themselves faced with moral crises which they must try to understand and resolve. But as Chappell explains, "their first imperative, their first duty, is to straighten out what actually happened in the past. All the books, to some degree . . . are predicated—and this is the dilemma that makes the books go at all—on the fact that you can't find out what happened in the past. There's no way to know; the past changes just as readily as the present is changing." A central concern of all the books, then, is the nature of time, how it is altered by human perceptions. To a certain extent, all Chappell's important characters find themselves paralyzed by an inability to understand the movement of time; this puzzle becomes a controlling metaphor in his fiction, though it is less pronounced in *The Gaudy Place* than in the three earlier novels. The inability of a character to cope with his position in time becomes emblematic of his incapacity to function within the context of human society.

A factor which influences a character's understanding of the nature of time is the implementation of the human will, or, more generally, the dichotomy between will and appetite. This duality motivates the symbolic structure of *The Inkling,* but it is important in the other novels as well. In *It Is Time, Lord* James Christopher ponders the Army Code of Conduct and concludes that the crucial directive is "*I will never surrender of my own free will.*" A paralysis of will and an accompanying increase of appetite signal the destruction of Peter Leland in *Dagon,* and Andrew Harper ruminates upon the extent to which he should impose his will upon his son in the final chapter of *The Gaudy Place.* Thus, in the world of Chappell's fiction, character action arises only from the engagement of will in facing a particular problem, and motivations must be interpreted in terms of the dichotomy between will and appetite. The complication in each novel, however, develops from the inability of the major characters to act, a condition which results from a combination of personality traits and exterior influences. For whatever reasons, the will becomes paralyzed, and the characters drift through a series of events they can neither understand nor control.

The major themes of Chappell's work as a whole are clearly delineated in his first novel, *It Is Time, Lord.* The first draft of the book was completed in five weeks during the summer of 1962, though the first chapter had been published the previous year. This story, which had first convinced Haydn of Chappell's talent, was itself an expansion of a sketch which Blackburn had included in his anthology *Under Twenty-Five,* a sketch which presents the reminiscence of a young boy called James who had been misunderstood by his father when he and his sister were frightened by some strangers in their barn. In the sketch Chappell not only establishes three of the novel's main characters—James, his father, and sister—but also suggests the nature of their relationship.

In the first chapter of the novel, James Christopher refers to the incident in the barn as "a single memory which has gathered such patina of usage that it seems much further distant than it is." James's attitude toward this memory signals both a central theme, the effect of past experiences on the present, and an important structural technique, the juxtaposition of material from several periods of time. James is a young man forced by his present situation to confront his past. Reared in the North Carolina mountains, he has moved to the piedmont town of Winton, where he lives with his wife, Sylvia, and their two children. An acute spiritual crisis causes James to lose all sense of direction, to resign his job, withdraw completely from life, and drift carelessly into the lives of the superficial people he meets through his lascivious friend Preacher. James's loss of purpose forces him to examine past experience, and he constantly ponders such memories of childhood as the incident with his father and sister. He is dismayed, though, to discover that the past is not fixed and constant. Rather, its outlines alter and dim, approach and recede. When the situation with Preacher and his friends builds to a violent climax, James attempts to escape into the past, to confront his sources, particularly as represented by his father. But he finds that no easy solutions exist, that realities, like memories, constantly change. This discovery leads James toward his goal; he reaches out toward his wife in an

Fred Chappell

attempt to reenter the world of human action and responsibility. But, realistically, Chappell does not allow James to achieve his potential within the framework of the novel. He senses a means, and he embraces an affirmative attitude, but nothing more.

The struggle for James to achieve a connection with the vital universe is not an easy one, and the nature of this struggle itself defines the complicated structural techniques. In his essay "Six Propositions about Literature and History," Chappell explains how James's dilemma gives rise to the novel's narrative development: "One of the major themes in my first novel . . . was that the human will is as helpless as a foetus under the ruthless pressure of time itself. Time, especially past time, presented itself to the protagonist as an always changing, always dangerous, force. To illuminate this point, I caused him to keep a journal of his past and present life which, though he momentarily thought it true, was in reality stuffed with lies." The first three chapters of *It Is Time, Lord* comprise part of this journal, though the reader is not immediately aware of that fact. The protagonist recalls his grandparents and his life in their house, but his memory particularly fixes upon two reminiscences—the events in the barn described in the early sketch and James's burning of his grandparents' house. The third chapter presents a sermon delivered by the Reverend James Christopher, one of the personae James assumes in his journal. Here the themes of the novel are codified: "This is the kind of thing the past is: it is not unchanging. It grows up soon with weeds and underbrush like a dangerous trail. It sours and rots like old meat in the mind." At the end of the sermon, the mask directs a challenge to the real James Christopher: "Take yourself up."

Only with the fourth chapter does the novel switch from James's narrative to the present level of time, and the reader is confronted with the problem of distinguishing reality from James's warped memories and lies. The process is not easy, and in the final analysis the reader can be no more sure that he understands the significance of James's past than the protagonist himself can be. An indication of the complexity of the problem is provided in the three separate accounts of the burning of the grandparents' house: James records one version in his journal of the first chapter; his father constructs a quite plausible myth of the event to explain to himself the boy's actions; and James presents an entirely different account later in the novel. The narrative structure, then, reinforces the theme that the past cannot be ascertained. James cannot begin the slow process of maturation and acceptance until he learns that the key to his present difficulties does not lie in this single event from his childhood.

Much of the richness and complexity of the novel lies in James's memories, however; and in outlining James's past Chappell draws upon his own reminiscences of childhood. Some of the characters are based upon members of his own family: James's father, for instance, loses his job teaching in the same way Chappell's father had lost his. Furthermore, certain of James's character traits are based upon aspects of Chappell's own personality. But the novel is not simply autobiographical; the materials Chappell draws upon are completely assimilated into the book's artistic design. A series of recurring images links the journal chapters with events in the present; there are frequent allusions to the zodiac, to the passage of time, and to games such as chess and checkers, allusions which underline the nature of James's disability. The novel is punctuated by literary references which link together the various masks assumed by the main character. In many ways, James Christopher is Chappell's Prufrock, the ineffectual dreamer who has allowed philosophical considerations to replace responsible action. Finally, he is a man who has severed all ties with humanity, who has lost himself in his attempt to define his world within a limited framework.

In the final chapter of *It Is Time, Lord,* Chappell attempts to unify the various strands of reality which have evolved from James's ruminations about the past and his present situation. He presents three dreams which embody the major themes of the novel and bring together the various patterns of imagery. Although this device is too weak to resolve all the complications suggested by the involved narrative technique, it does provide a successful resolution to the novel's considerations of time and its effect upon the human will. In the first dream, Preacher warns James against trying to solve his predicament through focusing on a single event from his past. The second dream, however, indicates that James remains obsessed with his interpretation of events. Only in the third dream is a resolution hinted at: James escapes from all the people who wish him harm by following a map provided by Sylvia. He discovers a sort of cave containing a sleeping giant which he recognizes as himself: "I have come the long way about, and now my task is to arouse him." As the novel closes, James turns instinctively to Sylvia, who sleeps beside him. For the first time, he seeks the strength of someone else; he begins to take himself up by reaching out.

It Is Time, Lord is a remarkable achievement for a first novel, but it is not the work of a mature talent.

Reviews of the book praised Chappell's ability to provide vivid descriptions and scintillating dialogue. The central weakness identified by critics—and one recognized by the author himself—is the overabundance of thematic material not adequately explored within the narrative framework. Although the structural experimentation is bold and adds to the novel's dramatic power, the juxtaposition of material is sometimes awkward. For instance, James becomes obsessed with having burned his grandparents' house; this action acquires the status of the central issue of his life, but he also ponders the incident in the barn. Chappell recalls that at one point in the composition of the book the rape of a child had been more clearly intimated in the barn scene; he excised this material because it would "lessen the impact of the work by having everything come down to one simple cause." But the significance of this seemingly crucial event remains unclear for the reader. Generally, however, Chappell controls the sprawling implications of James's story with remarkable ability. And if he failed to exhaust all the thematic implications of the material in *It Is Time, Lord,* he had at least outlined directions which his later fiction could pursue.

In *The Inkling,* his second novel, Chappell explores some of the issues suggested by *It Is Time, Lord* within a more limited, tightly organized structure. The novel opens with a scene which the author based upon a sonnet in Rimbaud's prose poem "Alchemy of the Word." A young man with a wounded hand sits drinking in a field of sage grass. He watches a boy playing with his sister in a neighboring yard until a baseball rolls nearby and leads him to accost the children with: "Hanh, you goddam kids! . . . What if you was to die? What if you was to die one day?" The reaction of the children recalls the experience of James Christopher and his sister, and as in the earlier novel, the relationship between brother and sister becomes a central concern of the plot. Jan Anderson, the brother, lives with his mother, his Uncle Hake, and his retarded sister, Timmie. As a small boy, Jan begins to discipline his will in an effort to bring control to his world. Initially he is successful; but a series of events—his sister's growing insanity, his uncle's marriage, his mother's death, and, finally, his own emotions as he matures—conspire to defeat his will and to bring about his eventual destruction. His sister stands in opposition to Jan's purpose; she seeks to sublimate his will to her own desires. But Timmie is not the only force which works against Jan's design. His mother depends upon his strength to counteract the destructive influence of Uncle Hake, a character who personifies Chappell's concept of the fallen state: "As long as Uncle Hake was around you knew the universe was still identical with the one you had always known: it had not suddenly been cleansed overnight."

The ultimate insult to Jan's scheme of self-control is his inability to deal with his developing sexuality. Lora, Hake's young wife, seduces Jan after the death of his mother, and he discovers that his will is no match for her sexual appetite; she dominates him, and he blindly submits to her until they are caught, first by Timmie and then by Hake himself. When Hake attempts to kill Jan, the boy responds by shooting his uncle. He has now become the young man of the opening scene, and crouched drinking in the field of sage grass, he sees the young boy he had once been, playing with his sister in the yard. He wishes he could warn this Jan of what awaits him—hence the novel's title—but he can only mutter the cryptic line, "What if you was to die one day?" Thus, as R. H. W. Dillard has pointed out, the opening scene and the novel's conclusion occur at the same moment; instead of escaping time, Jan finds himself inexorably trapped by it.

The Inkling is a stringently organized novel; the author deliberately attempted to create a work which was "consciously shaped from the beginning" as *It Is Time, Lord* had not been. To accomplish this goal, Chappell posited two levels of metaphorical or symbolic meaning which serve as a foundation for the narrative structure, though their presence is completely unobtrusive. In his essay "Two Modes: A Plea for Tolerance," Chappell wrote that the book was "about Will and Appetite as possible visions of reality, and the narrative structure was an allegory of the relationship between the French Symbolist poets, Arthur Rimbaud and Paul Verlaine." Jan, whose character reflects Rimbaud's, is of course the figure motivated by pure will. He is completely without appetite as the novel begins; his mother notices his lack of desire for anything. Even at mealtimes he does not seem to enjoy his food: "he merely chewed and swallowed whatever was on his plate, dutifully, as if he had been told to put more faggots on a blazing bonfire." Fire imagery is associated with Jan throughout *The Inkling.* Chappell hints at the reason for this association in the poem "Burning the Frankenstein Monster: Elegiac Letter to Richard Dillard" from *Bloodfire*: "What I mostly ripped off from Rimbaud was the notion of fire / As symbolic of tortured, transcendent-striving will."

The force of appetite is represented by both Hake and Lora, but its supreme exponent is

Timmie. Her desire to control others begins with her efforts to manipulate only Jan's actions, but eventually she sees herself as allowing all events to transpire. She grows progressively more powerful as Jan's will weakens. Her feverish interior monologues—which contain what Chappell refers to as "my wild translations of Rimbaud and Verlaine"—predict events at the conclusion of the novel and mingle her strange mystic visions with her obsessive need to master and wound her brother. She forces him to mask his eyes, the physical manifestation of his will, with nonmagnifying glasses. She coerces him into kissing her stuffed giraffe, the toy she calls Jannie and which she uses in the masturbation rituals which precipitate her feverish dreams. Within her mind she has fixed time, and she alone allows the other characters to act: "Time did not drip away any longer; had frozen it solid, like a block of glass around the house. She had trapped the others in unmoving." Timmie, then, opposes Jan's need to shape his world, and her obsessive, even incestuous, desire to possess him frustrates his will.

The other allegorical foundation upon which *The Inkling* is built also concerns the relationship between Jan and Timmie. Chappell explains that "The novel is finally about the marriage that doesn't come off between sulphur and quicksilver, the great thing that would produce a philosopher's stone, cause time to stand still." Jan is constantly identified with yellow, the color of sulphur. It is the color of his hair and of the sage grass he crouches in as the novel opens; it is also the color associated with fire, one of the symbols of his will. Timmie, on the other hand, is described in images of whiteness throughout the book. But this wedding does not take place; Jan discovers that time does not stand still; rather, it warps and twists. The final effect of this volatile combination of personalities is disastrous. At the end of the novel Jan walks away from the children he cannot warn, and the imagery underlines the nature of his tragedy: "Beneath his confused feet the earth ebbed and swayed, as it might ebb and sway below the feet of a man who had been hanged."

The symbolic superstructures provide Chappell with a series of interconnections between the characters, and they control the imagery of the novel, but they are not absolutely required to understand the central issues of *The Inkling*. Jan's dilemma is similar to that of James Christopher: he seeks to confront existence on his own terms. But whereas James's problem arises from a loss of will, Jan's is precipitated by his attempt to shape the world through the exercise of will. His effort is inevitably futile. At the end of the novel he understands only that his design has failed. He cannot fathom Timmie's motives in perversely attempting to wound him, nor can he warn the children of the fate which awaits them. In his final vision the entire effort is a sort of joke: "it bloomed before him in incredible brilliance and variegation, held unnumbered light shadows; and at last he laughed. He was laughing and shouting. *Hanh.*"

Most reviews of *The Inkling* acknowledged the book's simple power and the author's ability as a narrative stylist. The novel was criticized, however, for its subject matter. Insanity, hints of incest, and violence in a rural Southern setting became the basis for unfavorable comparisons with Faulkner, O'Connor, and McCullers. Richard Dillard has pointed out similarities between *The Inkling* and *The Sound and the Fury*, and Chappell himself recognizes certain structural and thematic parallels with *As I Lay Dying*, though he denies that Faulkner's novel consciously influenced the composition of his book. The fact that *The Inkling* makes use of materials which have become associated with certain aspects of the modern Southern novel does not mean, however, that Chappell's book is imitative or lacks originality. On the contrary, Chappell instills into his subject his own intellectual and moral concerns; and his structural experiments, though similar to those employed by Faulkner and Joyce, become the vehicle for these concerns in a way which reflects the evolution of an independent artistic consciousness.

The critical reception of *Dagon* reveals a similar misunderstanding of the author's intentions. The novel's setting and themes prompted reviewers to interpret it as another contribution to a worn-out and vaguely defined tradition of Southern gothicism. Clearly there are gothic elements in the novel. The central character, Peter Leland, is a minister who has taken off a year to complete a book he calls "Remnant Pagan Forces In American Puritanism." He goes to a large old house in the mountains which he has inherited from his grandparents. Once he arrives, his interest in the book declines as he explores the dark rooms and the oppressive attic. During a picnic with his wife, Sheila, he encounters Morgan, a tenant farmer. Immediately Peter becomes trapped in an inexorable chain of occurrences which lead him to murder his wife, surrender his will to Mina, the tenant farmer's daughter, and begin a process of moral and physical degeneration which culminates in his sacrifice at the altar of the god Dagon.

Both the characters and the themes of *Dagon* reflect concerns in *It Is Time, Lord* and *The Inkling*. Chappell discovered that in the first novel he had

-2-

"They must of kilt it and cut it up in little bits and throwed it in the river." He was wild with the thought of it. "It was some girl got knocked up and her boy friend made her do it."

She shrugged.

"Ain't that awful to think about? A poor little baby... Come on and show it to me, I got to see that baby foot."

"What'll you give me?"

They marched along, and he struck a mournful air. "Nothing," he said at last. "I ain't got nothing to give."

She stopped and looked at him, surveyed him head to toe with a weary satisfaction. "No, I guess you ain't," she said. "You ain't got a thing."

"Well then, what you got? You ain't got nothing but a poor little dead baby's foot which I don't believe you've got anyhow."

Slowly she reached into her pocket and produced it, held it toward him in her open palm, and he leaned forward, breathless, peering. He shivered, almost imperceptibly. Then his face darkened and his eyes went brighter and he slapped her hand. The foot jumped out of her hand and fell among the grasses.

"Shit, that ain't nothing. It's a doll, it's just a doll-baby's foot." She could tell that he was disappointed, but feeling smug too because, after all, he had caught her in the expectable lie. "I never told you it was real." She stooped and retrieved it. It lay pink and soiled in her soiled palm. Bulbous ankle and foot, little toes like beads of water. It looked too small and too separate from the rest of the world to be anything at all.

He took it from her. "I knew it wasn't no real baby." Became thoughtful, turning it in his fingers. "Hey, look here at this."

"I don't see nothing."

He held the tubular stub of it toward her. "Look how smooth it's cut off. It's been cut with a knife."

She touched it and the amputation was as smooth as the mouth of a shotgun barrel. "What's that got to do with anything?"

It had got darker now, drawing on toward the supper hour. Fitkinville grew gloomier behind them, though most of the lights were on in the kitchens of the houses.

"Means that somebody went and cut it on purpose..." Another flushed fantasy overcame him. "Say, what if it was a Crazy Silas? What if it was a man practicing up before he went and kilt a real baby?"

"It's just some little kid messing around," she said.

"No. Ain't no kid would have a knife like that." He ran his thumb over the edge of the cut. "Had to be a real sharp knife. Or an axe. Maybe it was a meat chopper!"

"Kid might get a knife anywhere."

He shook his head firmly. "No. Look how even it is and ain't hacked up. Kid would rag it up. A man went and done it, being real careful."

At last she nodded assent. Now at the same moment they turned and looked up the river back into Fitkinville, the squat darkening houses where the fathers and mothers and older sons now wore strained strange faces. The men didn't shave everyday now and the women cried sometimes. They had all turned into strangers, and among them at night in the houses were real strangers from far-off places saying hard wild sentences and often shouting and banging tabletops. In the oversheeted rooms both the light and the shadows loomed with an unguessable violence.

From Moments of Light, *manuscript*

"found out all kinds of moral questions, moral situations that interested me. And the two following novels develop the kind of questions that are raised at one point or another in the first novel." Peter Leland is a minister, as James Christopher had pretended to be; both characters work on books which are thinly disguised efforts to come to terms with their own moral gropings. In both *It Is Time, Lord* and *Dagon*, inheritance becomes a major symbol for an obsessive preoccupation with events in the past. In both books, a house is the physical manifestation of this obsession.

Parallels with *The Inkling* are less obvious but perhaps even more significant. Peter Leland, like Jan, is victimized by circumstances he can neither control nor understand; and as their dilemmas are similar, so are various situations in which the two characters find themselves. Elements of Jan's affair with Lora in *The Inkling* are explored in greater detail as Mina drains Peter of psychic and sexual energy. On a more pervasive level, *Dagon* continues the consideration of the relationship between will and appetite in *The Inkling*. Peter Leland is an intellectual, ill equipped to withstand a confrontation with evil as personified in Mina, who suggests the apotheosis of paralyzing appetite. When Peter first sees her, she greets him with: "You're awful good-looking. . . . You're so good-looking I could eat you up. I bet I could just eat you up." As Peter's identification with Mina becomes stronger, this prophecy is fulfilled. His will becomes impotent, and his own appetite, which takes the form of constant drinking, begins to control his responses to the world around him.

Mina is the priestess of the god Dagon, a maimed deity which figures in one of Peter's sermons and is central to his study of American Puritanism. As the title indicates, the presence of this god is the dominating symbol in the book. In "Six Propositions about Literature and History," Chappell explains the genesis of his use of the Dagon myth: "For my third novel . . . I discovered a literal event in Bradford's *History of the Plymouth Colony* [*sic*] which seemed to me metaphorically true of our own times. To drag Bradford's reported event into the present I posited a secret religious cult which had survived unseen for two centuries." The religious cult is the snake-handling group dedicated to the worship of this crippled god and directed by Mina. The ritual trappings of the cult are drawn from "an artificial mythology" created by H. P. Lovecraft, but the emphasis in Chappell's use of Dagon is entirely different from Lovecraft's. Chappell approaches the material "as a means of moral discovery," and Peter Leland becomes the central embodiment of that discovery.

One of Peter's sermons outlines the relevance of Dagon to contemporary American culture, thereby hinting at the god's importance to the design of the novel. Peter quotes the First Book of Samuel, in which Samson destroys the temple of the god; he goes on to trace the derivation of the name Dagon, which was initially associated with a Semitic term meaning "fish," and provides other allusions from Renaissance historians, *Paradise Lost*, and Bradford's *History*. Peter links the worship of Dagon to crippled sexuality and to the lust for money. He concludes that "Dagon was symbol both of fertility and infertility; he represented the fault in mankind to act without reflecting, to *do* without knowing why, to go, without knowing where."

By the time Peter arrives at his grandparents' house, he has accepted his inheritance and become an instrument of this god, and he begins to act according to the precepts his sermon had cautioned against. He wanders aimlessly from room to room examining objects, reading inexplicable old letters, perusing photographs of judging ancestors. The chapters describing these explorations convey a powerful sense of foreboding which culminates when Peter enters the attic. There he discovers a set of manacles suspended from the ceiling. When he finds that one fits his wrist exactly, his physical imprisonment parallels the increasing paralysis of his will.

Events following Peter's imprisonment take on an eerie, surrealistic quality. When Sheila comes to rescue him, he thinks at first that she is Mina. Relations between husband and wife grow increasingly tense, culminating in a scene in which Sheila is frightened by a snake in the yard behind the house. She demands that Peter kill it, and when he refuses she injures it and curses him. The symbolic applications are obvious, as is Peter's course of action. Several nights later, he kills Sheila with a poker and goes to Mina's house. There his isolation from his former life is complete; he enters a new bondage, surrendering his will to the relentless Mina. Throughout the novel, however, Chappell insists that Peter directs his own actions; he is not a helpless victim: "He was not a prisoner, not held by force. He was simply bound to Mina wholly; he was his own prisoner, he could escape by dying, by no other way." Like both James Christopher and Jan Anderson, he is incapable of directing the course of events. But unlike the two earlier characters, Peter comes eventually to both understanding and transcendence.

The road to understanding and acceptance is far from easy; it involves both spiritual and physical degradation. Mina commands Peter as she would a child, and when he is threatened by another of Mina's conquests, his reaction is presented in pitifully comic terms, recalling exaggerated battles between small boys. Eventually, Peter must seize upon a physical symbol of his lost manhood—he chooses a pump handle—to assert his humanity. He questions how far this degeneration could go before he loses all vestiges of his former identity: "At what point was this machine no longer recognizable as himself?"

Such a moment never comes. Mina moves Peter to a small coastal town where she directs his preparation for sacrifice. He suffers an ultimate indignity as his body is covered with bizarre tattoos. This ritual serves not only as the lowest point in Peter's degradation, but also as the first step toward his renewal: "his old self . . . was being obliterated; it was almost as if he were being reborn, inch by inch. . . ." Once again, Peter's world undergoes a transformation. His pump handle loses its authority; he is kept in chains, suggesting his imprisonment in the attic. Finally, he is granted a vision of the god itself, and he realizes its limitations: "The god was omnipotent but did not possess intelligence. Dagon embodied a naked will uncontrollable. The omnipotent god was merely stupid." Peter maintains his own identity throughout the vision, indeed, throughout his entire ordeal. Confident of his identity when Mina returns, he is happy to bare his throat to the sacrificial blade.

The final chapter of the novel presents the transformation of Peter Leland into "a new mode of existence." He gains an understanding of the purpose of the universe and the unity of all things. Time becomes fluid, and Peter realizes that the meaning of suffering is "charging with human meaning each separate moment of time." In this new realm, metaphor and substance become one; significantly, after extensive experimentation, he assumes the form of Leviathan: "He was filled with calm; and joyfully bellowing, he wallowed and sported upon the rich darkness that flows between the stars."

This transcendent vision makes the conclusion of *Dagon* unique among Chappell's novels, and the author admits that friends including Peter Taylor had advised him to remove it. Of all the books, though, *Dagon* had proved the most difficult to write, occupying three years while the others had taken only a matter of weeks for the completion of a first draft. Part of the reason for the difficulty was the overwhelming darkness of the subject matter, the unrelieved suffering; and the conclusion, according to Chappell, was a conscious effort "to alleviate the agony of it." Once he had foreseen this ending, he directed the action of the novel toward this resolution. But Chappell's explanation of the construction of the book may not completely explain the unusual final chapter. Perhaps a more significant reason is the author's unwillingness to accept "the triumph of evil in that way in the world." Such an attitude is present in each of Chappell's novels; but *Dagon* provides the most direct statement of it, a fact which perhaps influences the author's opinion that *Dagon* is "the best of the novels in that it's the most adventurous and most courageous."

Following the completion of *Dagon*, Chappell resolved to create a kind of novel different from any of the first three. He remembers wanting to construct a book "in which all the pieces fitted together, and that had a latitude of characterization in it." Furthermore, he wished to draw "a larger social picture" within a framework which was somewhat lighter, less ponderous in tone. The result was *The Gaudy Place*, a book which Chappell recalls writing in Florence over a period of three weeks on the back of the *Dagon* galleys. The novel presented several problems of revision, particularly regarding the point of view in the final chapter, and it remained unpublished for nearly five years. Chappell has described it as the most "plotted" of all the novels, "because everything depends on a few seconds of time."

Even a casual acquaintance with *The Gaudy Place* reveals the differences between it and its predecessors. Though all but the last chapter are told in third person, the narrator is less detached, more immediate than in either *The Inkling* or *Dagon*, and the narrative style is less complicated and philosophical. Few of the characters are given to metaphysical reflections; most are too completely involved in the demands of living from day to day. This is not to say, however, that the dominating issues of Chappell's earlier fiction are absent from *The Gaudy Place*; on the contrary, the novel provides a penetrating exploration of the nature of individual responsibility, the progression of time, and the impact of the human will upon motivation and action.

The Gaudy Place is divided into five chapters, each representing the point of view of one of the major participants in the drama. Arkie is a fourteen-year-old hustler in the town of Braceboro, North Carolina, a fictionalized depiction of Asheville. He moves from bar to bar down Gimlet Street, matching farmers for dimes and nickels and dreaming of the big con which will someday set him up permanently. Two other characters are linked with Arkie by association with Gimlet Street: Clemmie, nineteen, a prostitute who fights with the other whores when she is not entertaining a customer, and Oxie, her pimp, who has moved beyond the confines of Gimlet Street into a more lucrative position as bondsman and small-time racketeer. The crucial event of the Gimlet Street chapters is Oxie's abandonment of Clemmie, leaving her without protection from harassment by police and bar owners. Clemmie's reaction is violent. In a conversation with Arkie, she manufactures the lie that Oxie had arranged a new man to look out for her: "An old kind of guy. White hair. Looks like your grandaddy. But he's one of them bad kind, you know? Likes to knock you around. That's how he gets his goodies." This news upsets Arkie for two reasons; he had hoped to replace Oxie as the girl's "stringer" for purely financial gain, but more important, he loves Clemmie and resolves to eliminate the "per-vert."

Throughout the chapters dealing with Gimlet Street, Chappell emphasizes the connections between this area and the world beyond. Gimlet Street is the gaudy place, but it is also a microcosm of the universe. Arkie muses on the significance of his locale at the end of the first chapter: "Suddenly it occurred to him that this street . . . could take you anywhere in the world, it was joined to all the other streets there were." But he also realizes that Gimlet Street is the only world he knows, that he is trapped there by bonds of familiarity and by his obsessive love for Clemmie.

Just as Gimlet Street is connected with all the other streets in the world, so are the people who inhabit it part of a larger social picture. Chappell presents this idea by contrasting the Gimlet Street characters with the Harper family. Linn Harper is the son of history professor Andrew Harper. The boy's interest in science fiction leads him to other types of modern literature and eventually to the work of Camus. In a naive attempt to duplicate Mersault's gratuitous act in *The Stranger* (1942), Linn tries to break into a feed warehouse, but he is apprehended by the police and taken to jail, where he foolishly refuses to divulge his identity. The situation is indeed comic, but the reader cannot ignore the contrast between Linn's situation and Arkie's. Linn toys with existential philosophy during a weekend outing with friends at a mountain cabin. But for Arkie the question of existence is by no means academic; it plays itself out in a genuine struggle for survival which leaves little time or inclination for philosophical debate. Chappell establishes this juxtaposition in a subtly ironic manner. At no time does the comparison become obvious or heavy-handed, yet it is crucial to understanding the climax of the book.

Linn's predicament connects the lives of the Harpers and the characters on Gimlet Street when Oxie identifies the boy from a newspaper story and contacts his parents. Linn's mother calls upon her Uncle Zeb, a corrupt local politician, to use his influence in securing the boy's release. But when Uncle Zeb, Andrew, and Oxie all meet at the police station, Arkie appears. Mistaking Uncle Zeb for Clemmie's new pimp, he shoots the old man in the shoulder. This wildly chaotic climax hints at poetic justice, but like so many other comic scenes in the novel, there remains an underlying seriousness only barely concealed by the detached humor. For Uncle Zeb, the event is "just something he could tell later to his nieces and nephews and grandchildren," but for Arkie the consequences will be considerably graver. Oxie had referred to Arkie earlier as "a guy that might probably be needing me one of these first days but that I probably wouldn't be able to do him any good." The boy's action at the end of the novel makes Oxie's prediction reality.

The ending of *The Gaudy Place* is comic because Andrew Harper, the narrator of this section, is ignorant of the circumstances which led up to the event. Musing on Linn's predicament, Andrew thinks: "For though I demand in personal dilemmas emotional singleness, I also demand latitude of action, wider possibilities of solution than generally offer themselves. One of the horrors of reading history is to watch those reported events march upon the pages, strident, martial, antlike, as if there were some absolutely compelling reason for things to have taken place in the stupid manner they have done." This "latitude of action" is the perpetual limitation for the characters in *The Gaudy Place*. Each is bound, like Arkie, to the world he knows, and each is unable to function outside the world. Linn is thoroughly intimidated by his arrest and experiences in jail; Oxie is out of his milieu in the library and in the Harper's home. The differences between these particular characters and the worlds they represent are revealed in their attitudes toward their respective environments: with youthful arrogance Linn concludes that "the universe is, after all, a gaudy place in which to live"; Oxie, on the other hand, looks forward to the moment when he can leave Gimlet Street, when "he would turn his back on this feverish gaudy place for good."

Within a larger context, the people in *The Gaudy Place* share a problem with protagonists of

Chappell's other novels: they have been displaced by a new society which has usurped an older, more stable culture. Chappell's books unfold during the period in which the traditional mountain culture is disintegrating. According to the author, one of the reasons for the complications faced by his characters is their removal from contact with the land. To a certain extent, each character shares Andrew Harper's sense of separation from the familiar world. Each is isolated in both time and space, and the result is a reluctance to accept the limitations which define man's experience. Cultural displacement, then, becomes a metaphor for a more pervasive sense of isolation; man is unable to understand his emotions, his needs, and more importantly, he is incapable of communicating that shortcoming to others.

Since the publication of *The Gaudy Place*, Chappell devoted much of his creative energy to his four-volume poem, *Midquest*. This work grew out of the materials the author had dealt with in *It Is Time, Lord*; and part of the reason for its genesis was his feeling that many of the issues raised by that novel had been inadequately explored. *The World Between the Eyes*, Chappell's first volume of poetry, had been initially designed to bring the themes of *It Is Time, Lord* to a successful conclusion; but, though the book reveals an impressive ability to handle tone and an amazing technical dexterity, it was, according to Chappell, "not very admirable." The reason for Chappell's low valuation of *The World Between the Eyes*, however, may be merely that the book fails to give ultimate expression to the questions suggested by his first novel.

This ultimate expression is more successfully achieved in *Midquest*, which Louisiana State University Press calls a "novel in verse." It comprises four individually published volumes, each unified by variations on a single image from one of the four elements: *River* (water); *Bloodfire* (fire); *Wind Mountain* (air); and *Earthsleep* (earth). Since the impulse to write *Midquest* arose from Chappell's feeling that *It Is Time, Lord* represented a mine of inadequately explored material, many characters in the author's first book reappear in the poetry: the author's grandparents and Virgil Campbell are examples. Chappell's parents play a more direct role in *Midquest* than their fictional counterparts had been allowed in *It Is Time, Lord*. The use of real characters does not mean, however, that all the events of *Midquest* are directly autobiographical. Chappell remains at liberty to join fact and fiction in presenting both characters and events.

The major theme of *Midquest* is rebirth, an idea which Chappell borrowed from his model, Dante. But this theme has clear antecedents in *It Is Time, Lord* as well. Even the techniques used in the tetralogy arise in part from the narrative experiments in the novel, as the author himself has explained. The plan for the entire work was not solidified until halfway through the composition of *River*, the first installment. At that point, Chappell constructed an outline of *Midquest*: "I didn't know where all the pieces were going to fit or anything like that, but I knew that I was going to have the outline of a day, and the day would include his [the central character's] whole past life in one sense or another."

Each volume follows a similar structural principle: the persona awakens on the morning of his thirty-fifth birthday and considers a variety of impressions concerning his life—family, friends, background. Chappell uses a multitude of poetic forms and moods in constructing each book , but the themes remain constant, and they too are reminiscent not only of *It Is Time, Lord*, but also of the author's entire body of fiction. Chappell, who still considers himself primarily a poet, tends to think that his achievement resides in *Midquest*; but the four-volume poem is so intimately connected with the characters, structure, and themes of *It Is Time, Lord* that in some respects they comprise a single work. According to Chappell, though, even *Midquest* does not complete this unusual cycle of writing. He projects a third section: "a kind of mystical little novel about getting married in the mountains." Typically, he relegates this completion to "some later milieu or some millenium from now." Other projects will perhaps intervene; a first collection of short stories, *Moments of Light*, was published in 1980, and he is currently working on both poetry and a new novel. But his plan for a further extension of these materials indicates that Chappell continues to explore new directions for the development of his art.

—David Paul Ragan

Periodical Publications:

FICTION:

"For the Time, Being," *Sewanee Review*, 71 (Spring 1963): 251-267;

"A Property of Hope," *Saturday Evening Post*, 237 (May 1964): 62-64;

"Linnaeus Forgets," *American Review*, 26 (November 1977): 173-191;

"A Penance on Ember Mountain," *Appalachian Heritage*, 6 (Winter 1978): 58-65.

NONFICTION:

"Six Propositions about Literature and History,"

New Literary History, 1 (Spring 1970): 513-522;

"Two Modes: A Plea for Tolerance," *Appalachian Journal*, 5 (Spring 1978): 335-339;

"The Comic Structure of *The Sound and the Fury*," *Mississippi Quarterly*, 31 (Summer 1978): 381-386; originally published as "Structure comique de *Le Bruit et la fureur*," trans. Robert Loriet, *Magazine Littéraire*, no. 133 (February 1978): 30-32;

"The Image of the South in Film," *Southern Humanities Review*, 12 (Fall 1978): 303-311.

Interviews:

Craft So Hard to Learn: Conversations with Poets and Novelists about the Teaching of Writing, ed. George Garrett (New York: Morrow Paperback Editions, 1972), pp. 35-40;

James L. W. West III and August J. Nigro, eds., "William Blackburn and His Pupils: A Conversation," *Mississippi Quarterly*, 31 (Fall 1978): 605-614.

References:

Maurice-Edgar Coindreau, Preface to *Le Dieu-Poisson*, trans. Maurice-Edgar Coindreau (Paris: Christian Bourgois, 1970);

R. H. W. Dillard, "Letters from a Distant Lover: The Novels of Fred Chappell," *The Hollins Critic*, 10 (April 1973): 1-15.

ELEANOR CLARK
(6 July 1913-)

BOOKS: *The Bitter Box* (Garden City: Doubleday, 1946; London: Joseph, 1947);

Rome and a Villa (Garden City: Doubleday, 1952; London: Joseph, 1953; revised edition, New York: Pantheon, 1975);

The Song of Roland (New York: Legacy / Random House, 1960; London: Muller, 1963);

The Oysters of Locmariaquer (New York: Pantheon, 1964; London: Secker & Warburg, 1965);

Baldur's Gate (New York: Pantheon, 1970);

Dr. Heart: A Novella and Other Stories (New York: Pantheon, 1974);

Eyes, Etc.: A Memoir (New York: Pantheon, 1977);

Gloria Mundi (New York: Pantheon, 1979).

Despite winning the National Book Award in Arts and Letters in 1965 and then having one of her novels chosen as the primary Book-of-the-Month Club selection in 1970, Eleanor Clark has never enjoyed the degree of success and recognition that America has bestowed upon many far less talented writers. Her career began auspiciously with a well-received first novel and a highly praised book of nonfiction, but then after her marriage to Robert Penn Warren, her writing took second place to family life and their two children. Within the last fifteen years, however, her output has included two more novels, a novella and story collection, and two additional books of nonfiction. An original and serious artist, she has demonstrated from the start an uncompromising avoidance of the formulaic best-seller approach, producing instead a relatively small but solidly impressive body of fiction and nonfiction that continues to merit attentive reading and appreciation.

Coming to maturity during the 1930s, Clark joined a number of other American writers in experiencing an awakened social consciousness. For her, "it took the form of a certain immersion in what can be called the Trotskyite periphery," she has recalled; and the awareness gained then is evident in her fiction from her first novel to her latest, completed almost four decades later. Other constants inform her writing as well, among them her knowledge of music and architecture, her love for the outdoors, her distrust of easy consolations and life without struggle. All of her writing—fictional and nonfictional—presents a wealth of visual detail as captured by a fiercely independent and perceptive observer. And her style—which varies from the early surrealistic stories, through the almost baroque descriptions in *Rome and a Villa* (1952), to the somewhat elliptically spontaneous flow of *Eyes, Etc.* (1977)—occasionally poses a challenge but usually serves very effectively in carrying the energy of her writing.

A native New Englander—"rockbottom & 100%"—Eleanor Clark received her earliest education in a one-room school in her hometown of Roxbury, Connecticut, and in boarding schools where her mother worked. Portions of her childhood were spent in Europe, where she attended a convent in France before she returned to the United States to study at Rosemary Hall and, eventually, at Vassar College. While at Vassar, from which she received her B.A. in 1934, she collaborated at different times with classmates Elizabeth Bishop and Muriel Rukeyser to produce literary magazines.

Following graduation Clark began publishing extensively as a free-lance writer and translator, while working as an editorial member of W. W. Norton & Company from 1936 to 1939. In the years following 1937 her reputation grew steadily, with short stories appearing in the *Kenyon Review, Southern Review, Sewanee Review*, and elsewhere, along with numerous essays and book reviews in such publications as the *New Republic*, the *Nation*, and *Partisan Review*.

Immediately after World War II, during which she had worked in Washington for the U.S. Office of Strategic Services, Clark's first novel, *The Bitter Box* (1946), was published by Doubleday. Probably based upon some of her experiences from the 1930s, this work is a remarkably mature piece of writing, convincingly evocative of the social and political ferment of the Depression years during which its action takes place.

The unlikely protagonist of *The Bitter Box* is a meticulous but naive bank teller named Mr. Temple, whose precisely ordered Weltanschauung is challenged and eventually lost (along with his job), after he finds himself swept into a leftist organization referred to only as "the party." Drawn to one of the party's more charismatic leaders, Mark Brand (and perhaps even more to Brand's wife, Hilda), Mr. Temple attempts to substitute the orthodoxy of the party for that of the capitalistic system he had so unquestioningly served earlier. But his loyalty is shaken when he discovers he has been used by the organization, and his initial bewilderment over changing party lines leads eventually to disillusionment with the movement.

The economic and political rise and fall of Mr. Temple are not, however, the only focal points of *The Bitter Box*. Even though Clark never allows us to get particularly close to her main character, one can observe his sterile emotional outlook also changing as the plot progresses, aided both by his curious and comic sexual engagement with an obese party worker named Rose and by his slowly developing friendship with Francine, the young daughter of the apartment janitor. And when, at the end, he rescues this child from almost certain death in the snow, the extent of his development as a person is clearly offered as equal to or greater than

Gabriel Penn Warren

Eleanor Clark

the losses he has suffered. Adherence to dogma is replaced by an awareness and acceptance of more humane values.

The Bitter Box was well received by the critics (James Laughlin of *New Directions*, for instance, associated Clark immediately with Eudora Welty, Carson McCullers, and Jean Stafford as important new writers), and it led to her receiving a grant from the National Institute of Arts and Letters (1947) and Guggenheim Fellowships (1947 and 1949). Clark's interests at this point, however, were turning toward nonfiction, and the first impressive result of her labors was *Rome and a Villa*, a richly personal response to a city and its architecture, a history and a culture—past and present interwoven. A powerful and original work, *Rome and a Villa* has continued to hold the attention of serious readers, receiving high praise not only when first released in 1952 but also when its slightly revised and expanded version was published in early 1975.

Following her 1952 marriage to the novelist and poet Robert Penn Warren, Clark continued writing steadily, dividing her time between her career and her family. There was also a good deal of family travel to Europe, which led to her major literary product of this period: another highly acclaimed work of nonfiction, *The Oysters of Locmariaquer* (1964), winner of the 1965 National Book Award in Arts and Letters. Set in Brittany, this book relates the story of the famous oysters grown on that coast and of the people who cultivate them. In no sense a travelogue, *The Oysters of Locmariaquer* offers a personal reaction to and meditation on the genius loci as seen freshly by one who has the rare capability of making it come alive by placing it within a larger perspective.

In dramatic tension and narrative flow, *The Oysters of Locmariaquer* comes close to being a novel, and one can easily understand why Clark has remarked that "concerning impulse, motive and kind of personal involvement, I find no clear line of demarcation between my novels and nonfiction books." Genre distinctions are useful, of course, and neither *Rome and a Villa* nor *The Oysters of Locmariaquer* should be read as fiction. To regard them as mere "travel books," however, would also be a significant error. Any serious study of Clark's fiction must also give her resonant nonfiction its due. As she noted in a 1978 interview, "My Rome book and my oyster book are both, in one deep aspect, mirror images of America. . . . I think one who has any pretensions to writing literary work and not merely journalism is always writing out of his own sense of place and his own country."

Over twenty years passed between the publication of Clark's first novel and that of her second, *Baldur's Gate* (1970), generally regarded as her major novel to date. One reason it is so much more successful than *The Bitter Box* is found in its setting—the village of Jordan, Connecticut—a locale that comes alive in vital ways that the vague urban setting of her first novel never did. New England is the region Clark knows best and obviously feels most comfortable in portraying. Equally important, the action here is seen through the eyes of a far more perceptive and inviting persona than the confused Mr. Temple of *The Bitter Box*. Both factors encourage the incorporation of more subtle insights and more involved themes, resulting in an intensely complex world, persuasively created.

The basic story here belongs to Eva Buckingham Hines, whose point of view controls the action. Married and the mother of a son, Eva's outlook at the opening of the novel is conditioned by shame for the social disgrace of her once proud family (her father a failure; her alcoholic mother a suicide; her beloved brother, now also dead, a homosexual; the family wealth gone). Her sole hope for the future is for the return of her first love, Jack Pryden, who will somehow—she vaguely believes—set things right. That his return leads to no such resolution comes as little surprise in a plot summary as abbreviated as this, but within the intricacies of multiple subplots Eva's growing understanding of her past and eventual acceptance of a life with fewer illusions evolve with compelling force.

Paralleling Eva's struggle is that of the village itself, also trapped by its past, fearful of its future. Both are influenced by the charismatic Baldur Blake, a seventy-year-old sculptor who had earlier forsaken his art for alcoholic escape. Now reformed, he returns to Jordan and becomes the dominating presence in the life of the community. Although Baldur seems to possess many of the powers of his namesake (the Norse god of light, virtue, and wisdom), he denies none of the human weaknesses Eva discovers in his past and even reveals some that surprise her. Nevertheless, he inspires the community to move toward a future which, he is convinced, could be both beautiful and meaningful—even though it involves housing developments and other feared changes. And he leads Eva "to accept the curse of our humanity" while still having the courage to live creatively—which is, ultimately, the central thematic concern of the novel.

None of this is as neat and simple in *Baldur's Gate* as it may appear in summary. Baldur's dream community is never realized; his goals, in fact, are

29. The good opinion of. "I guess we had to do it, didn't we? Only ..."

"I dunno. We had no choice is all I know." And for the first time felt he was failing the boy, who was about to go beyond him, somehow in that rocket, wd. learn things Bert wd. have liked to only he hadn't known that at 18 — even if there'd been a way.

* enough to have hung around the house in Coyoacán & done some translating for the Old Man as they all called him, because he had the secret strength of a divine will.

~~[illegible]~~ Hannah Pale a good many years, & her gentle husband ~~[illegible]~~ had made their life here, year-round, some years before we came, when a taxi accident ~~[illegible]~~ his career as a violinist.* She'd been a Trotskyite of sorts in her youth & in the right mood & company talks very well about that period. Here they've been mainly sugar farmers, with a toy-making business of theirs on the side & they've written a few books together & separately. Nothing very brilliant or ambitious but the last one about their way of life ("~~[illegible]~~ must they say lifestyle?") having sold [illegible] brought them quite an influx of devotees — disciples, boarders, spongers — depending. She was ~~[illegible]~~ rather not somehow surviving a year or so in Europe or the Far East [illegible] them,

* causing him to miss 2 fingers of his left hand

Manuscript, here reduced 84%

9/10
one ! -over all the lunacies and evils chewing away at it. Like that time we stumbled upon the two forgotten children's graves in the woods up the mountain, where the village used to be, of about the same time, the 1820's; one a baby, one a girl of sixteen, wasn't it? Maybe in an ugly city courtroom that defense lawyer would have sounded more frightening and I'd have disgraced myself, and helped bring on more crimes. A tall, quick, angry young man, everything narrow about him -shoulders, hips, forehead, set of eyes - feeling very superior to his surroundings and especially to our old friend Milo Sims, the State's Attorney I think they call him now. The defense one was going for us hammer and tongs, don't ask me why but it didn't matter. He had a long chunk of dark oily hair that he'd whip back from his eyes to emphasize a point. Our next Senator Joe McCarthy... Oh yes I'm sure he'll rise from these ashes all right, I'd bet you anything. Give him five years."

He had had reason beforehand to think it was all open and shut the other way, and did set great store by it. The case was much publicized, a brilliant performance would

What mysterious strength it does give, when our past gets through to us, as I guess some mystic-oids would say it's trying to do all the time.

Gloria Mundi, *revised typescript*

misunderstood and his sculptures destroyed by vandals—youths who had once viewed him as a guru. The sordid and the painful thrive in Jordan as they do elsewhere, and the world of this novel reflects them honestly without finally yielding to despair. Perhaps this is why *Baldur's Gate* enjoyed not only a favorable critical response but also selection by the Book-of-the-Month Club. Certainly it is one of the main reasons why the novel invites and sustains subsequent readings.

The best of Clark's short fiction was brought together in her 1974 collection, *Dr. Heart: A Novella and Other Stories*. Published originally in *Partisan Review*, *Modern Occasions*, the *Southern Review*, *McCall's*, *Kenyon Review*, and the *New Yorker*, these stories date from the late 1930s to the mid-1970s. Although Clark asserts that "it is all one voice, mine—and I don't disown it," its unity is open to some question. Certainly there are some gems among the early stories—two of the best being the brilliantly concise "Responsibility" and "The Heart of the Afternoon"—but some of the apprentice stories are strained experiments, self-consciously surrealistic, and others (particularly "A Summer in Puerto Rico") are disappointingly tedious. The quality of the later stories is more consistent—highlighted by "The Fish" and "The Man for Her," an intriguing tale featuring a sadistic exterminator—but the irony is broader now and the concise edge of the earlier stories is lost.

Occupying the center of the book (and the majority of its pages) is her ambitious novella, "Dr. Heart," the portrait of Tom Bestwick, an American scholar in France trying to write a dissertation on Stendhal. Few would question Clark's knowledge of the France and Italy in which the novella is set, and she obviously knows Stendhal's works intimately. Consequently, anyone familiar with *The Red and the Black* (1830) will be delighted with the cunning ways Clark weaves her allusions and echoes of that work into a contemporary setting, as her protagonist attempts essentially to live as a Stendhalian character. Unfortunately, perhaps because Clark's male protagonists are seldom as convincing as her women, the novella too seldom comes alive as fiction. Despite some marvelous passages of writing, the dramatic tension never controls enough to convert this from an admirable idea into a believable fictional world. Thus, while the novella and the stories accompanying it illuminate some interesting facets of Clark's mind and art, they are unlikely to divert much attention from her longer works.

Probably the most original—certainly the most courageous—of Clark's books is *Eyes, Etc.: A Memoir*. An intensely personal account (but one that, like all her nonfiction, assumes more universal proportions), *Eyes* details Clark's response to the serious impairment of her vision (macular degeneration) she experienced beginning in 1976. Writing with felt-tip markers on large drawing pads, she works / writes out her reactions and reflections as she adjusts to her affliction and moves to compensate for it. Since she refuses to indulge in self-pity, the book quickly moves away from the initial stage of shock toward an engagement with issues and people. Though the narrative presence is never masked, portions of the writing come very close to fiction—especially the memorably humorous portrait of "the Tidies," a compulsively neat family so busy straightening up their summer home that they appear never to relax. But the energy propelling this writing flows toward a more open-ended resolution, and it remains a vigorously alive work of nonfiction, adding new dimensions to the genre of memoir.

"Sic transit gloria mundi.—So passes away the glory of this world." With this epigraph from Thomas a Kempis, Clark opens her most recent novel, *Gloria Mundi* (1979), and the parable she presents does indeed carry with it a sense of loss—much greater, in fact, than that found in her earlier novels. The central core of *The Bitter Box* had been an ideology, while in *Baldur's Gate* it was the charisma of one creative individual, but in *Gloria Mundi* she moves ambitiously to take the pulse of an entire New England community as its traditions and values are rapidly being overwhelmed by commercialism and the gratuitous violence of our time.

The cast of convincingly authentic characters populating the novel's Boonton, Vermont, is extensive, and by shifting the point of view Clark allows a number of differing perspectives to emerge. These shifts, sometimes disturbingly abrupt, do not ultimately fragment the novel as much as they first threaten, for the action is unified by the community's response to two dramatic incursions from the outside world.

The first of these threats to Boonton derives from the resort development plans of Jim Pace, whose aggressive ambitions give focus to the battle of values within the village, even as his bulldozers—machines in the Garden—push Boonton inevitably into a future for which it is little prepared. The other major event (the shocking murder and mutilation of two hikers) occurs offstage, the sickening act of an escaped psychopath. No one from the community is directly involved except in the discovery of the bodies, but all feel the impact and the unsettling questions it raises. The murders, together with drugs, vandalism, shootings, and the other violence new to the area, would doubtless have occurred even if the exploitive land development projects had not begun, but their combined force assumes apocalyptic overtones—particularly to couples like Lem and Hannah Palz, sensitive and cultured, and their good friends, Brit and Louise Horton. These characters serve as moral touchstones, and all of them are more aware than most of the glory that is passing away.

One of the well-integrated subplots that combine to advance the novel deals with a reticent newcomer who calls himself Johnson. Eventually he is revealed as John Philipson—a minister who had deserted his midwestern church and his wife by staging a fake death by plane crash in Canada. Philipson is recognized, however, by one of a gang of motorcyclists (a former neighbor of the minister); and not too long after, his supposed widow, Margo, comes looking for him. Unlike most of the outsiders who enter the region searching ("Practically everybody in Vermont just then [was] looking for something—Truth, identity, ripoffs, drug deals, lost dogs, new mates, . . . sociopolitical this and that."), Margo Philipson finds even more than she hopes for; she is one of the few characters who is stronger at the close of the novel than she was at the beginning.

None of Clark's fiction has yet been made into a movie. Some of the fiction hardly invites film adaptation, of course: *The Bitter Box* is lacking in exterior action, and *Baldur's Gate* is intimidating in its complex symbolism and plot intricacies. But *Gloria Mundi* appears to have far more potential than the earlier works for translation into the film medium, and perhaps Clark's novels will eventually attract the wider audience they deserve following film adaptation.

More puzzling than the proportionately small popular audience, however, is the absence of extended critical examination of Clark's writings. At a time when feminist reexaminations of the literary canon are widespread, it is somewhat surprising that Clark has not received more of this critical attention. One possible explanation for the relative silence from these critics is that her novels deal primarily with themes other than women overcoming male exploitation; she has, in fact, gone on record as having "no time for Women's Lib." More importantly, one must remember that her publication of fiction has occurred, for the most part, within the past ten years (during which time three of her four fiction books were published). Perhaps, then, more extensive critical assessment is already underway.

In any case, the fiction of Clark deserves more notice—critical and popular—and one hopes that her later novels will not be allowed to go out of print (as *The Bitter Box* now is). Both her nonfiction and her fiction reveal Eleanor Clark to be one of our most perceptive writers—and one of our most original. Her uncompromising attitude toward her art has resulted in a demanding and impressive group of books, and the fertile results of the past few years encourage hope that more of her strong and vivid prose will be forthcoming.

—Stanley W. Lindberg

Other:

New Letters in America, edited by Clark and Horace Gregory (New York: Norton, 1937);

Ramón José Sender, *Dark Wedding,* translated by Clark (Garden City: Doubleday, Doran, 1943; London: Grey Walls, 1947);

"A Man of Worth," *New England Review,* 2 (Winter 1979):248-256;

"Monday We Change Our Clothes," *New England Review,* 2 (Winter 1979):233-247.

Interviews:

R. W. B. Lewis, "Talk with Eleanor Clark," *New York Times Book Review,* 16 October 1977, pp. 11, 40-41;

"Interview with Eleanor Clark and Robert Penn Warren," *New England Review,* 1 (Autumn 1978): 49-70.

References:

Stephen Arkin, "An Enlargement of Delight: Eleanor Clark's Non-Fiction," *New England Review,* 2 (Winter 1979): 257-259;

Kenneth Pitchford, "Of Time and *The Bitter Box,*" *New England Review,* 2 (Winter 1979): 260-267;

F. D. Reeve, "A Review of Eleanor Clark's *Gloria Mundi,*" *New England Review,* 2 (Winter 1979): 268-271.

PAT CONROY

(26 October 1945-)

BOOKS: *The Boo* (Verona, Va.: McClure, 1970);

The Water is Wide (Boston: Houghton Mifflin, 1972);

The Great Santini (Boston: Houghton Mifflin, 1976; London: Collins, 1977);

Lords of Discipline (Boston: Houghton Mifflin, 1980).

Pat Conroy's writing is marked by an obsessive interest in the love/hate relationship and its ensuing tensions. Whether between Citadel cadet and "The Boo," young teacher and school superintendent, or teenage son and "Great Santini," this search for balance dominates the themes of Conroy's fiction and nonfiction.

Born in Atlanta, Georgia, Conroy was, as he writes in *The Water Is Wide* (1972), "sired by a gruff-talking Marine from Chicago and a grits-and-gravy honey from Rome, Georgia." He is the oldest son of seven children of Donald Conroy and Frances "Peggy" Peck Conroy Egan. His early years were spent as a military "brat" living short tours in "some of the more notable swamplands of the East Coast" and attending various Catholic schools. While his father was on overseas duty, the family returned to the Peck family home in Atlanta.

Conroy's was a conservative upbringing: "Mom's people hailed originally from the northeast mountains of Alabama, while Dad's greased the railroad cars in Chicago, but attitudinally they could have used the same sheet at a Klan rally." His later high school years were spent in Beaufort, South Carolina, adjacent to the Parris Island Marine base. The beauty of Beaufort's antebellum mansions, Spanish moss, and stately trees was addictive to the young Conroy and his fiction is still reflective of this response: "[it was] a town I grew to love with passion and without apology for its serenity, for its splendidly languid pace, and for its profound and infinite beauty." After graduation in 1963 from all-white Beaufort High, he journeyed some seventy miles up the King's Highway to Charleston and The Citadel, South Carolina's military college, the obvious choice for the son of a military-minded father and tradition-imbued mother. This institution engendered Conroy's earliest writing as editor of the college's literary magazine and became the subject matter for his earliest book as well as his recently completed novel *Lords of Discipline*.

Conroy's first book, *The Boo* (1970), is, as the author himself admits, "sentimental and unashamedly nostalgic." It is about "The Boo," Lieutenant Colonel Thomas Nugent Courvoisie, Assistant Commandant of Cadets at The Citadel from 1961 to 1968 and the symbol of the institution itself during this time. As Conroy noted in the preface: "The book, in essence, is the love affair of Courvoisie for the cadets and his school. The stories within this book were not written maliciously or callously; they were written to show an inside view of the long gray line, an intimate view not often afforded to the general public. The Citadel is quirky, eccentric, and unforgettable. 'The Boo' and I collaborated on this book to celebrate a school we both love—each in our different ways." The Citadel is not only "quirky, eccentric, and unforgettable." It is also an anachronism of the 1960s with a general disregard of the existence of the outside world. Thus, in this insular universe "The Boo" becomes guardian of discipline, the "Blue Book," and the Citadel way, part father, part confessor, part detective, and all soldier.

The Boo in style and format is little removed from juvenilia, the language generally bland or affected, transitions weak or nonexistent. But it does presage the later Conroy with its wry humor (occasionally misdirected), the iconoclasm balanced with a certain respect for authority, and the biographical insights into Conroy himself. The book has gone through several reprintings; its literary merits, however, are negligible.

Following graduation from The Citadel, Conroy opted for high school teaching instead of a military career, color blindness preventing his becoming a pilot like his father. He returned to Beaufort, to the high school from which he had graduated only four years before. But in that time many changes had been made. The student body was now integrated (although the faculty was still all white), and Conroy anticipated the challenge imposed by the prejudices of both races.

After the insularity of The Citadel, he was coming into a growing awareness of the world situation of the late 1960s. A trip to Europe with several of his friends after that first year of teaching gave him even greater insight and spelled an end to much of his naivete of human nature: "If man was good, then Dachau could never have happened. Simple as that." Perhaps it was not as simple as that; but as Conroy matured, his cynicism concerning mankind hardened. He "was becoming convinced that the world was a colorful, variegated grab bag full of bastards." His first real attempt to transfer this feeling to paper culminated in *The Water Is Wide*, a taut, revealing book, retelling a school year or so on a remote South Carolina coastal island while Conroy battled the ignorance of school personnel and the illiteracy of the island population in an attempt to transport young blacks into the modern era. His style is often muddled, his tone occasionally too cynical or self-righteous; but the book moves swiftly, stabbingly, to a predictable conclusion. After all of his efforts and innovations Conroy loses his teaching position because he broke the most sacred rule of all to a school administrator: "Don't rock the boat." And Conroy's boat was the only lifeline between the island isolation and the mainland contemporary society.

Although *The Water Is Wide* is basically autobiographical, the author does manipulate characterization and an occasional incident, telescoping here and there; but it is a work reveling in Conroy being himself—gregarious, committed, overreacting, but never indecisive. As the novel relates, Conroy wanted a position in the Peace Corps which was not forthcoming. Martin Luther King, Jr., had been assassinated; tensions were high. And as Conroy describes it:

> Toward the end of each school term, my draft board gets a restless desire to know my intentions for the following year. I did not wish to return to the high school. I was through with teachers more concerned with the length of mini-skirts and hair than with education. But I certainly did not wish to join the Marine Corps, romp about the marshes of Parris Island, and emerge the product of a military system I had come to loathe. So I decided to go to the superintendent and ask about Yamacraw Island.

His fictional Yamacraw Island (Daufuskie Island near Beaufort) would never be the same after contact with "Conrack." Of his forsaken black pupils, Conroy writes:

> Seven . . . could not recite the alphabet. Three children could not spell their names. Eighteen children thought Savannah, Georgia, was the largest city in the world. Savannah was the only city any of the kids could name. Eighteen children had never seen a hill—eighteen children had never heard the words *integration* and *segregation*. Four children could not add two plus two. Eighteen children did not know we were fighting a war in Southeast Asia. . . . Five children did not know their birth dates. Four children could not count to ten. The four oldest thought the Civil War was fought between the Germans and the Japs.

The odds were too great. The job he had taken "to assuage the demon of dogooderism was a bit more titanic" than he could ever have imagined. His efforts did not please those in power and his iconoclasm was such that he seemed to relish each confrontation. In retrospect he could have done more for both the children and himself by being less inflexible. But this is one of the charms of *The Water Is Wide*. It is Conroy and it is also countless other young people in the late sixties when causes and liberalism were badges to be worn and were more antiestablishment than long hair and beads.

Anatole Broyard in the *New York Times* commented perceptively about Conroy's intent: "He refuses to make a villain out of the school superintendent who fired him. Unlike many liberal do-gooders, Mr. Conroy does not see all conservatives, racists, reactionaries or rednecks as one-dimensional monsters. In his eyes, they are as much victims of their history—at least in their thinking—as the black people whose problems they haven't even begun to understand." Citing many of Conroy's artistic shortcomings, Broyard nevertheless concludes that *The Water Is Wide* "is a hell of a good story."

The motion picture industry thought so too, and in 1974 Twentieth Century-Fox released *Conrack* starring Jon Voight in the title role with screenplay by Irving Ravetch and Harriet Frank, Jr., based on Conroy's book. It received almost uniformly good reviews, although Walter Trammell, Beaufort's superintendent of education (depicted by Conroy as Dr. Henry Piedmont), called the production "a fictional farce, a typical Hollywood stereotype of the South."

But for Conroy the most important aspect of *The Water Is Wide* was cathartic. He spent a year on the island. He tried:

> I don't think I changed the quality of their lives significantly or altered the inexorable fact that they were imprisoned by the very circumstances of their birth. I felt much beauty in my year with them. It hurt very badly to leave them. For them I leave a single prayer: that the river is good to them in the crossing.

While still teaching on Daufuskie Island, Conroy married a mainlander from Beaufort who taught school there. Barbara Bolling was a Vietnam War widow with two children, Jessica and Melissa. Conroy and Barbara also have a daughter of their own, Megan. The marriage ended in divorce in 1977.

The Great Santini (1976) is Conroy's first novel, although it too is replete with autobiography. "The Great Santini" is the nickname Bull Meecham, colonel in the U.S. Marine Corps, calls himself in his most authoritative family roles. Meecham is a hard-boiled Marine aviator unable in most instances to differentiate between family and military. The Corps and flying are the premier loves of his life, with his wife and children falling in somewhere behind his macho image, his Catholic religion, and his flying and drinking buddies. Suffering most obviously in such a relationship is his oldest son Ben, a high school basketball star, generally nice kid, and typical teenager. Bull's intense desire for his son's success is almost totally misguided, creating conflict each step of the way between father and son, wife and husband, patriarch and family; but love is still predominant. Conroy has deftly turned what could have been simply an entertaining Bildungsroman of Ben into a story with more depth, because, unlike the novel's jacket blurb, it is neither wholly about nor centered upon Ben but on his father. Bull Meecham, for good or ill, is the instigator of action and the catalyst for movement, just as Colonel Donald Conroy, U.S.M.C., provided the image and impressions chosen by his son to be fictionalized. Colonel Conroy offers these comments: "Pat embellished everything. Where's the truth in all these incidents? There is a moment of truth. Where it is, I suspect only Pat and I recognize. You get mad with your dad, but you get glad with him. . . . People read the book, and fiction becomes truth to them. It's not fiction, it's fact, they think. If you asked Pat if it was true, he'd say, 'All of it.' But if you were serious, he'd give you a straight answer."

Pat Conroy

Two episodes in the book stand out above all others: the father-son basketball competition and the transfer of the flight jacket from father to son. Bull is much larger than Ben, six-feet-four to five-feet-ten, but as Ben thought, "he had a great equalizer working for him, called youth." The basketball game is rough, dirty, the epitome of Bull's win-at-all-costs attitude. The family cheers for Ben, Ben chides and kids Bull. And finally as the game winds down to a tight conclusion: "Do you know, Dad, that not one of us here has ever beaten you in a single game? Not checkers, not dominoes, not softball, nothing." And then for the decisive basket:

> At the foul line, Ben left his feet for the jump shot, eyed the basket at the top of his leap, let it go softly, the wrist snapping, the fingers pointing at the rim and the ball spinning away from him as Bull lunged forward and drove his shoulder into Ben's stomach, knocking him to the ground. Though he did

> not see the ball go in, he heard the shouts of his mother and sisters; he saw Matthew leaping up and down on the porch. He felt his father rise off him slowly, coming up beaten by a son for the first time in his life.

Bull refuses to admit defeat, challenging Ben to win by two baskets. Lillian Meecham confronts her husband with the fact of his beating. He responds by kicking "her in the buttocks with a swift vicious kick." He then begins throwing the basketball at Ben's forehead, and as Ben turns Bull bounces the ball against his son's head as Ben ascends the stairs, not in playfulness but in rage. Bull stays on the court dribbling and shooting, practicing set shots and hooks into the night.

Bull becomes the vanquished instead of the victor, a situation which he abhors but with which he also must learn to cope. Lillian knows he will not admit such, "but the real reason he's down on the court tonight is that he knows you'll hear him. You've got a strange father, Ben, but in his own way, that's him down there saying, 'I'm sorry, Ben. I was wrong.' "

On 11 October at four in the morning, Bull enters Ben's room with a present for his son's eighteenth birthday. The flight jacket "I wore when I flew in WW Two with the Cobras" is Bull's greatest gift. It is, in a sense, an admission of the passing of the order, the begrudging acknowledgment of respect for his eldest son, and a genuine show of love.

Bull does not outwardly change. He still blusters, curses, flashes toughness and resoluteness, but his family has become more to him than before. When Colonel Meecham's plane crashes and he is killed, one learns that the crash was unavoidable, but Bull's death was not: "Am commencing starboard turn to avoid populated area. Will attempt to punch out when wings are level. Wish me luck. Over." The priority was to avoid populated areas, "where people lived and slept, where families slept. Families like my family, wives like my wife, sons like my sons, daughters like my daughters." He never punched out.

Ben Meecham's hatred for his father gradually turned to understanding, then to respect and love. Flashes of hatred would return, frustrations fester; but Ben had gained an insight into his father and he had learned what it meant to be a son.

Filming for the movie version began in September 1978 on location in Beaufort, the thinly disguised Ravenel of the novel. Screenwriter-director Lewis John Carlino handled the translation from paper to film with Robert Duvall as Bull Meecham and Michael O'Keefe as Ben. Both book and movie lay open the father-son conflict, the rage, passion, growth, and love. It is a personal relationship minutely detailed in all its glory and horror. It is confessional. It is intense.

Conroy's life experiences have become for him the laboratory of his fiction, but it is anything but a sterile environment. Yet cynicism remains; an insecurity and inquisitiveness wrestle with the writer's outward ease. In *The Water Is Wide* he describes his speech as "an indefinable nonspeech, flavored subtly with a nonaccent, and decipherable to no one, black or white on the American continent." Such an impediment, obviously exaggerated for the humorous impact, is perhaps responsible for his continuing search for a more acceptable form of expression in his writing, an emphasis on effective communication. A legitimate strain of self-doubt still pervades both the fictional and real pose of the author. Don Conroy comments, "Pat's a pessimist. He never remembers the sunrise. Dealing with Pat on a day-to-day basis—you know how many clouds come over. He remembers every one." His memory and his grasp of insignificancies bring to his fiction a breadth of reality, not just a slice of life but an approximation of the whole pie.

Conroy is still maturing as an artist and craftsman; his forthcoming novel *Lords of Discipline* is anticipated as a touchstone by which to gauge his continued artistic development. Conroy has the potential and the skills to become an exceptional figure in contemporary literature. He must now harness the self-confidence necessary to accomplish it.

—Robert M. Willingham, Jr.

JOHN WILLIAM CORRINGTON

(28 October 1932-)

SELECTED BOOKS: *Where We Are* (Washington, D.C.: Charioteer Press, 1962);

The Anatomy of Love and Other Poems (Fort Lauderdale: Roman Books, 1964);

And Wait For The Night (New York: Putnam's, 1964; London: Panther Books, 1977);

Mr. Clean and Other Poems (San Francisco: Amber House, 1964);

Lines to the South and Other Poems (Baton Rouge: Louisiana State University Press, 1965);

The Upper Hand (New York: Putnam's, 1967; London: Blond, 1968);

The Lonesome Traveler and Other Stories (New York: Putnam's, 1968);

The Bombardier (New York: Putnam's, 1970);

The Actes and Monuments (Urbana: University of Illinois Press, 1978).

John William Corrington is a contemporary Southern writer of some distinction whose reputation rests largely on his achievements in poetry and short fiction. His first book of poems, *Where We Are* (1962), won the Charioteer Poetry Prize, and his short stories have received awards from the National Endowment for the Arts and have appeared in *Best American Short Stories* and *Prize Stories: The O. Henry Awards.* Corrington's three novels—*And Wait For The Night* (1964), *The Upper Hand* (1967), and *The Bombardier* (1970)—commanded generally favorable reviews when they first appeared, but they have received virtually no critical or scholarly attention since. That is unfortunate, for all three show signs of superior craftsmanship. A Roman Catholic in the deep South, Corrington shares a great deal with Flannery O'Connor and Walker Percy: like them, Corrington combines a keen historical sense with a theological perspective that gives full play to grotesque characters, paradox, dark humor, and the symbolic significance of setting. His fiction shows considerable narrative skill; it is invariably well paced and often very funny.

Born in Memphis, Tennessee, Corrington grew up in Shreveport, Louisiana—which he still claims as his spiritual home. As he writes, "The aesthetics of Shreveport when I was growing up had to do with doing one's duty, with trying to be brave, with handling situations as a man would be expected to—and, at last, to die well. Stoicism? I think so." Though he began as a music major at Shreveport's Centenary College, he was graduated with a B.A. in English in 1956. Corrington completed an M.A. in English at Rice University (1960) and his Ph.D. at the University of Sussex (1964), where he wrote a dissertation on James Joyce directed by David Daiches. After serving with the *Houston Post* as a special correspondent in Europe, Corrington spent most of his early career in academe, teaching English at Louisiana State University in Baton Rouge (1960-1966) and at Loyola, a Jesuit university in New Orleans (1966-1973)—where for a while he served as chairman of the English department. Corrington's brief tenure at LSU proved immensely influential, for there he encountered the work of Eric Voegelin—the man who was to become, Corrington admits, "my philosophical mentor." In 1972 Corrington entered law school at Tulane University and received his J.D. in 1975. He, his wife (Joyce Hooper), and their four children still live in New Orleans, where Corrington practices law and continues to write. Though his latest novel was published in 1970, Corrington produced a volume of short stories, *The Actes and Monuments,* in 1978. He and his wife served from 1978 to 1980 as headwriters for the daytime television serial, "Search for Tomorrow," and are currently headwriters for the television series, "Texas."

Most of Corrington's fiction and poetry treats the South, and his intellectual interests for the most part gravitate to Southern culture and literature. His first novel, *And Wait For The Night,* earned Corrington the reputation of traditional Southern apologist. His introduction to the two volumes of *Southern Writing in the Sixties* (edited by Corrington with Miller Williams, 1966, 1967) is a somewhat militant defense of the Southern literary and historical perspective and, combined with *The Lonesome Traveler and Other Stories* (1968), solidified the critical consensus that Corrington is an old-line Southern traditionalist. In a review of *The Lonesome Traveler,* Granville Hicks writes in the *Saturday Review* (21 December 1968) that "Corrington, perhaps more than most Southern writers, is preoccupied with the past and particularly with that supremely important event in Southern history, the War Between the States." Though Hicks grants that "Corrington [is] not merely a very good Southern writer but is a very good writer," he seems never to have recovered from his response to Corrington's first novel, a book Hicks believes attempts "to demonstrate that the Confederacy should have won the War Between the States" (*Saturday Review,* 23 May 1964). The stereotyped characters of *And Wait For the Night,* Hicks argues, result from Corrington's anger and pride over the war, and "in spite of his talents, [Corrington] is playing a game with puppets."

Admittedly Corrington's fiction—with the

notable exception of *The Bombardier*—focuses on the South and attempts to capture the spiritual quality of a region he knows well. To an impartial observer, Corrington may well seem an apologist for the Old South; his 1971 critical essay on Faulkner's *Sartoris* (1929), for example, refers to the Civil War as the "War for Southern Independence." But Corrington's real concerns are psychological and metaphysical, reflecting his considered reading of Voegelin, the Church fathers, and the Gnostic gospels. Like Walker Percy and Flannery O'Connor, Corrington presents in his most characteristic fiction a portrayal of the soul's metaphoric quest for spiritual wholeness. He thrives on paradox, irony, and self-contradiction; his fiction offers a gallery of Southern stereotypes—most of whom border on the grotesque—and implausible plots. Yet because of Corrington's superior craftsmanship, the often absurd juxtaposition of characters and events seems authentic and, at its best, yields profound insight into the nature and ambiguity of evil. The gallery of grotesques embodies the many perversions and distortions of spiritual health that modern man must confront, understand, and transcend. But for Corrington, the grotesque always offers striking and memorable testimony to the existence and viability of the ideal norm he distorts.

"Pleadings," a story in Corrington's most recent collection, *The Actes and Monuments*, documents the Louisiana author's confidence in the possibilities of history and his interest in the varied dimensions of justice—themes implicit in both *And Wait For the Night* and *The Bombardier*, and no doubt fostered by his formal study of law and interest in Voegelin. His theoretical premises receive clear statement in such essays as "Order and Consciousness/Consciousness and History: The New Program of Eric Voegelin" and "The Structure of Gnostic Consciousness," a paper delivered at Vanderbilt University in 1977. Though *The Bombardier* explores the rationale and significance of violence in contemporary American life, Corrington's primary aims in fiction are never social realism and satire. He is instead a metaphysical novelist whose narrative skill, lively humor, and subtle probing of character motivation provide focus and dramatic structure for what might otherwise seem abstract, self-conscious intellectual speculation.

Because Corrington's fiction rests firmly upon a metaphysical base, some critics have objected to what they perceive to be belabored intellectual posturing. William Koon, reviewing *The Actes and Monuments* for *Library Journal* (1 February 1979), argues that "Sometimes . . . these stories fall into heavy epistemologies that sound like Walker Percy—without tongue-in-cheek." But Lewis P. Simpson sees the title story of this volume as in many ways culminating Corrington's achievement and vision; in *The Harvard Guide to Contemporary American Writing* (1979), Simpson calls "The Actes and Monuments" an "impressive tour de force in the grotesque and absurd" that "brings into persuasive focus a southern metaphysic of 'grace as history transcendent.' "

The action of Corrington's first novel, *And Wait For The Night*, takes place in Shreveport in the summer of 1865, though there is a long flashback to the seige of Vicksburg two years earlier and shorter flashbacks of scenes from the Mexican War of 1848. The book treats the aftermath of war: the conflicting loyalties, even among Southerners, of father against son, brother against brother. Corrington admits that his is "not a historical novel" and argues that it should not be judged for its historical accuracy. Instead, *And Wait For The Night* re-creates the Southern frame of mind during the closing days of the Civil War as the novel portrays the moral and social chaos of a civilization in abrupt transition.

The two figures at the center of the novel are Amos Stevens and Edward Sentell, former Confederate officers who come to represent a dying breed: the Southern gentleman of honor. Sentell, paroled by the Union army, has vowed never again to bear arms, while Stevens returns to his Louisiana plantation only to see it overrun with Union soldiers. Stevens supports an elderly slave, Rye Crowninshield, whom he has actually freed years earlier. Their sons had gone off to war together—Mo Stevens to become a rabid Ku Klux Klan night rider, and Philippe Crowninshield to become a traitor to the South. In the end, Philippe is disowned by his father Rye—a character reminiscent of Firs in Chekhov's *The Cherry Orchard* (1904); Mo kills his father Amos for refusing to participate in the defeated Southerners' last attempt to flush out the Yankees from Shreveport.

Juxtaposed to these honorable Southerners is Colonel Jonathan Lodge, a Yankee officer who occupies the Stevens mansion and is in charge of subduing Shreveport. An educated Machiavellian leader who intensely hates the South, Lodge desires to destroy the Old South and purge it of its iniquities before raising a new world fashioned according to his own vision. His younger brother had died for the abolitionist cause, and so that his death will not have been in vain, Lodge vows to eradicate slavery and the Southern way of life that engendered it: "He could imagine whole cities given to the torch, populations

Pleadings I

Dinner was ready when the phone rang, & Joan just stared at me.

— Go ahead. Answer it. Maybe they need you in Washington.

— I don't want to get disbarred, I said. — More likely they need me at the parish prison.

I was closer than she was. It was Bertram Bijou, a deputy out in Jefferson Parish. He had a friend. With troubles. Being a lawyer, you find out that nobody has trouble, really. It is always a friend.

— On the level, Bert said. — You know Howard Bedlow?

No I didn't know Howard Bedlow, but I would pretty soon.

They came to the house after supper. As a rule, I put people off. They've got eight hours a day to find out how to incorporate, write a will, minimize their taxes or whatever. In the evening, I like to sit quiet with Joan. We read & listen to people like Haydn or Boccherini & watch the light fade. Sometimes, though I do not tell her, I imagine that we are a late Roman couple sitting in our atrium in the countryside in the south of England not far from Londinium. It is always summer, & Septimius Severus has not yet begun to destroy Britain, but it is twilight now, & there is nothing before us. We are young, but the world

"Pleadings," manuscript

handed over to the sword: it was a dream of cleansing and purgation to equal the Last Judgment, except that the god of this judgment would be named Lodge." Jonathan Lodge seems almost too evil for Corrington's thematic purpose; several reviewers were quick to point out that Corrington's characters are one-dimensional, his Southerners almost angelic, his Yankees satanic. Yet in Lodge and, to a lesser extent, Mo Stevens, Corrington exposes the deficiencies, the essential inhumanity, inherent in reformist zeal. For the uncompromising idealist, allegiance to an abstract cause (no matter how just or moral) dwarfs compassion and perverts human relationships, claiming the innocent for its victims and wreaking profound social havoc. Though Lodge is too much the melodramatic villain, his motivation and monomaniacal fury are nevertheless consistent with Stanley Elkins's study of the abolitionist mind in *Slavery: A Problem in American Institutional and Intellectual Life* (1968).

The novel ends ironically with the black traitor Philippe buying Major Sentell's plantation and hoping to restore its former glory. But this very symbol of the new, "redeemed" South becomes the scene of the novel's final bloodbath. Southern troops converge on the place to protest a black man's right to own what had once been theirs, and Northern troops—tipped off by a white Southerner—lie in wait for the Southerners to arrive. In the ensuing conflict, Amos Stevens is killed by his own son. Corrington drives his theme home with grim precision: war always blots out the essential humanity of men, results in broken family ties, and obliterates human dignity.

Corrington's second novel, *The Upper Hand*, explores the dimensions and ambiguities of evil. The novel opens with an epigraph from Newton—"in the remote regions of the fixed stars or perhaps far beyond them, there may be some body at rest"—and from Camus's *Le Mythe de Sisyphe*: "Does life's absurdity require one to escape it through hope or suicide. . . . Does the absurd dictate death?" Beginning in a state of existential angst, Christopher Nieman, a twenty-nine-year-old disenchanted Catholic priest, rejects the superstition of his church—its "alien" language—and tries to adopt, like Newton, a rationalist's perspective. But then he encounters evil in all its grotesque forms and amorphous ambiguity; it lurks in every nook and cranny of a modern urban environment that in its multi-layered depravity recalls the castle or monastery of eighteenth-century Gothic fiction. As one of the novel's gallery of grotesques asks Christopher: "Did you ever think we could all maybe be in hell?" Nothing in life is as it should be; paradox, irony, and ambiguity shatter rationalistic humanism and render one open to faith. The universe in *The Upper Hand* seems God's extended metaphorical joke; and as Christopher comes to realize, pride is the ultimate sin because it is a gnostic rejection of the minute part we all play in existence. The brief last section of the novel opens with an epigraph from Tertullian's *On the Flesh of Christ*: "The Son of God died; it is by all means to be believed, because it is absurd. And he was buried and rose again; the fact is certain because it is impossible. . . . I believe because it is absurd." For Christopher, evil throws its opposite into clearer focus.

Set in Shreveport and New Orleans during the summer of 1946, *The Upper Hand* traces the spiritual progression of its central character, whose name suggests his ambiguous relation to the net of evil that ensnares him: he is Christopher, the "Christ-bearer," and Nieman—from the German *Niemand*, or "nobody." A blinding, hammering summer rainstorm opens the novel's first section, "Catabasis" (descent), as Nieman rides a Greyhound bus from his former parish in Alexandria to Shreveport, back to mother and his origins. But, as the bus driver laments, "This wind is going to land us in hell." At a bar adjacent to the Shreveport bus station, Christopher meets Mary Ann Downey, an attractive, sensual girl from East Texas with "the impulses of a St. Bernard." Thus begins Christopher's initiation into evil: while the formerly celibate priest makes love to Mary Ann, he "feels her arms close about him like a collar of damnation."

With the novel's second and longest section—"Là Bas" (down there)—the scene shifts to New Orleans, a veritable hell replete with all manner of grotesque characters whose interaction with one another enmeshes Christopher in a tangled web of evil: dope peddling, abortion, murder, prostitution, pornographic films, extortion, and so on. The cast of what Bruce Cook in the *National Observer* (17 July 1967) calls "memorable freaks" becomes the novel's most striking feature. Corrington develops these characters through a series of short vignettes devoted to each. Sometimes narrated in first person, sometimes third, these flashbacks are compelling and artfully done; each of the characters seems psychologically plausible given his particular history. All are riddled with paradox: Mrs. Mailer, with "the face of the archetypal mother," seems the innocent peddler of flowers but in fact she is a vicious street tough whose real business is heroin distribution and abortion referral; the abortionist Dr. Aorta, a German Jew who hid his ethnic origin while he worked as an SS torturer at Dachau, is the physician

John W Corrington

who butchers; Blackman, the heroin addict, wages a vengeful war on God but begs absolution from Christopher when he dies; Billy Bob Stoker, star of porno films and the feared "Buggar Man" of Mississippi, retains a religious belief even as he murders the evil Dr. Aorta; Benny Boundoch pimps, exploits women and cranks out porno films, dreaming all the while of one day directing a film masterpiece with redeeming social value. Corrington succeeds with these characters in large part because he neither condescends nor condemns; he is never righteous about their misdeeds.

Through this inferno of grotesque characters, Christopher makes his way, always the "Christ-bearer" his name implies. Delivering bread for the Staff-o-Life bakery and living in the same French Quarter apartment that houses Dr. Aorta's abortion mill—in a room his mother chose for him—Christopher comes into contact with all the grotesques, sinking spiritually into an abyss of moral disorder: "If there is no Big Daddy," Christopher wonders, "do you go to killing automatically? . . . The answer comes as quickly as the question. Yes. Not everyone all at once. But yes. Sooner or later they go to killing. No reason not to. A million reasons, but no Reason." Following his incestuous union with his mother, Christopher touches bottom. But when he learns that Mary Ann is pregnant (possibly with his child), Christopher starts to ascend toward spiritual health. He refuses to allow her contemplated abortion, threatening Aorta with exposure should he perform it. In a milieu that places no value on human life, Christopher learns that it is precious. He ends as an agent of salvation for Mary Ann, Billy Bob, and Christian Blackman, unwittingly forced to assume the priestly responsibilities he had earlier abdicated. The last, three-page section of the novel, "Anabasis," shows Christopher walking along the river's edge, musing: "Somewhere in the deserted stretches of Christopher's memory the light recalls something. A hunger he cannot bring into focus. Those circles intertwined, merging with one another, then reaching out to permeate all the universe. . . ."

The Upper Hand is probably Corrington's best and most highly acclaimed novel. Thomas Lask, writing in the *New York Times*, calls it "a grimly comic novel, genuinely funny in many places, moving and powerful in others," and praises Corrington's "well-developed sense for the grotesque" (29 July 1967). Though he protests the 1946 setting (the novel seems more contemporary), Bruce Cook lauds Corrington's craftsmanship in what he calls "a great, sweaty, dark alley of a book" (*National Observer*, 17 July 1967). Granville Hicks finds "it hard to suppose that the religious argument will convince anyone not already committed to orthodox Christian theology" and laments the novel's "lapses into melodrama," but thinks its "vision of hell" unforgettable and Corrington's characters superbly conceived (*Saturday Review*, 24 June 1967). And Lloyd Griffin, in *Library Journal*, notes Corrington's capable handling of narrative in "a witches brew of sex, perversion, addiction, and murder [that] simmers with increasing intensity until it boils over in a gripping climax and catharsis" (15 April 1967).

Corrington's last novel, *The Bombardier*, explores the causes and ramifications of violence in American society. The novel traces the lives of six specially trained and accomplished American bombardiers during World War II. It begins with their intensive preparation in Texas under the direction of Michaelis—their leader who is a "priest in black magic"—and charts their successful war missions which culminate in the saturation bombing of Dresden, a grisly event that claimed 135,000 civilian lives. The novel then follows the six men as they return home from war, tracing their separate careers up to 1968. One or more is involved in the political campaigns of George Wallace, Eugene McCarthy, Robert Kennedy, or the riots following the assassination of Martin Luther King. All converge at the Democratic National Convention, a cataclysmic event in American history that brings the six together for the first time since Dresden.

Corrington's narrative progresses as each of the six tells his own story. Michaelis, Jacobs, Poole, Krepinski, Boyd, and Boileau represent a microcosm of American society, a diverse bunch that includes a Greek, a Jew, a Negro, a Pole, a WASP, and a Southerner. Though to a certain extent Corrington's characters are stereotypes, they are nevertheless "unflinchingly representative," James Boatwright contends, of the diverse threads that make up the fabric of American society. Corrington gives each of his major characters full development, showing particular skill in handling speech patterns. In his exploration of their diverse responses to the bombing raids, and their understanding of contemporary political and social events, Corrington offers a coherent and convincing reading of the American character.

The most objective and articulate of the six men is Boileau, a Louisiana native who after the war becomes a distinguished historian. His professional interests gravitate to the phenomenon of rebellion. Boileau is asked by an English newspaper to cover the 1968 Democratic National Convention, an epochal event that is to bring together all the revolutionary strains in contemporary American society. In the violent street confrontations between police and antiwar demonstrators, the jockeying for power within the convention hall among those who represent the poor and those who represent the traditional power structure, and the futile, staged attempt to clamp an illusion of unity upon irreconcilable factions within the Democratic party, Boileau sees the meaning of his private history as well as that of American culture come into clearer perspective.

Boileau's dispatches to his sponsoring English newspaper sum up the novel's basic theme. Violence is a very real by-product of America's attempt to fulfill some blind destiny. The United States, Boileau writes, "has destroyed all internal and peripheral opposition: Indians, Southerners, Latin Americans. She has broken the continent to her will." Her victims have been "smashed in the headlong attempt of the masterless to find some essence of freedom, an abstraction hypostatized, and settling, on a continental scale, for money. For power. . . . And in Chicago today, those who have shouted freedom are at bay. It just may be that the last of the American illusions is going to die. Here and now." There is, all six men come to realize, no real tie between Americans. Even among the six bombardiers there is nothing to bind them to one another save their common responsibility for carnage. Boileau, thinking of Boyd, realizes "that our common servitude to Michaelis' black art twenty-five years ago had made us neither kinsmen nor fellow citizens. There was blood between us, true. But it was the blood of those others we had butchered impersonally, not blood we shared." The novel ends as Boileau discovers Poole, the black ex-bombardier, lying semiconscious in the streets of Chicago, the victim of a policeman's bullet while trying to toss bombs. Poole, recognizing Boileau, thinks they are back in Germany in 1943, and he fears reprisals from the Nazis.

Reviewers discovered *The Bombardier* to be a probing, sensitive analysis of contemporary American culture. In a *New York Times* review, James Boatwright calls *The Bombardier* "ambitious in its time span, diversity of characters, dramatization of public, epochal events," and Corrington's "work as anatomist of a culture—or worse, as its pathologist—strikes" Boatwright "as right and just."

At present, Corrington's law practice, philosophical essays, and television work occupy most of his time. However, he remains an active fiction writer. He has written an unpublished novel, "The Disintegrator," and plans another novel, which he describes as "a 1950's north Louisiana version of *Don Giovanni*" entitled "The Man Who Slept with Women."

—*James D. Wilson*

Other:

Introduction to *Southern Writing in the Sixties*, edited by Corrington and Miller Williams, 2 vols. (Baton Rouge: Louisiana State University Press, 1966, 1967);

"Escape into Myth: the Long Dying of Bayard Sartoris," *Recherches Anglaises et Nord Américaines*, 4 (1971): 31-47;

"Order and Consciousness/Consciousness and History: The New Program of Eric Voegelin," in *Eric Voegelin's Search for Order in History*, ed. Stephen A. McKnight (Baton Rouge: Louisiana State University Press, 1978), pp. 155-195.

Reference:

Lewis P. Simpson, "Southern Fiction," in *The Harvard Guide to Contemporary American Writers,* ed. Daniel Hoffman (Cambridge: Belknap Press of Harvard University Press, 1979), pp. 153-190.

HARRY CREWS
(6 June 1935-)

BOOKS: *The Gospel Singer* (New York: Morrow, 1968);

Naked in Garden Hills (New York: Morrow, 1969);

This Thing Don't Lead to Heaven (New York: Morrow, 1970);

Karate Is A Thing of the Spirit (New York: Morrow, 1971; London: Secker & Warburg, 1972);

Car (New York: Morrow, 1972; London: Secker & Warburg, 1973);

The Hawk Is Dying (New York: Knopf, 1973; London: Secker & Warburg, 1974);

The Gypsy's Curse (New York: Knopf, 1974; London: Secker & Warburg, 1975);

A Feast of Snakes (New York: Atheneum, 1976; London: Secker & Warburg, 1977);

A Childhood: The Biography of A Place (New York & London: Harper & Row, 1978);

Blood and Grits (New York & London: Harper & Row, 1979).

Harry Crews is the author of ten books—eight novels (the first published in 1968), an autobiography, and a collection of magazine nonfiction pieces. He is one of the most original, prolific, uneven, and compelling novelists of the Southern post-Styron generation.

Crews's family were Georgia tenant farmers; their life, as he describes it in *A Childhood* (1978), was hard, sometimes brutal, stripped to the essentials. The restrictive realities of his early years figure prominently in his fiction. Things relentlessly go wrong, yet self-discipline and craftsmanship do not altogether fail; people suffer and die after struggling to make their lives mean something. Crews left his birthplace, Alma, Georgia, in 1953 for the U.S. Marine Corps, was discharged as a sergeant in 1956, received B.A. (1960) and M.S.Ed. (1962) degrees from the University of Florida, and has taught English since 1962, first at a junior college in Fort Lauderdale and then at the University of Florida, Gainesville. He is married and has one child.

Though he has achieved his still somewhat cultish reputation as a novelist and, to a lesser degree in recent years, as an *Esquire* columnist and *Playboy* contributor, Crews's finest book is his autobiography. In fact, of his last half-dozen volumes, four of them (three novels) are first class, and one imagines that within a short time he will be more widely recognized as a substantial talent. Already, what had been for some years the common reductive comparative practice among bemused reviewers of his work is receding; today one is less likely to read, after exclamatory plot summary, that Crews is like or is up to, or is not like or is not up to, such diverse notables as Flannery O'Connor, Terry Southern, George Garrett, or—to nail down the point—William Faulkner. Crews, at his best, writes only like Crews: he is a genuine original.

In terms of fictional techniques, Crews is a traditional storyteller; it was from his analytical study of Graham Greene's fiction that he began to learn how to fashion a story, what would work. Yet the essence of Crews's art and vision is experiential and aesthetic risk taking: excess is his mean. His fiction is fast, mean, extraordinarily violent, and often horrifyingly funny, altogether an unsettling combination.

His first novel, *The Gospel Singer* (1968), features a golden boy, with voice to match, from Enigma, Georgia (population 600), to which he returns most reluctantly, accompanied by his business manager and spiritual counselor, Didymus, and followed by a traveling Freak Fair, directed by Foot, one of whose feet is twenty-seven inches long. Prior to the Gospel Singer's arrival, his long-time sweetheart, MaryBell Carter, voluptuous virgin and doer of good works, has been murdered and—the white townspeople believe—raped by a local black man, Willalee Bookatee Hull, who anticipates (quite accurately) that he will be lynched.

The Gospel Singer is, as the dust jacket says, in public an angel and in private a satyr, on which facts the desultory plot turns. That his arrival in Enigma breaks a two-month drought is consistent with his local reputation—he is their savior; he gives meaning and purpose and excitement to claustrophobic, spiritually depleted, poverty-stricken lives. It is the belief of Didymus, who murdered his predecessor, that suffering is God's greatest gift to man; certainly very few of the characters escape it. After a day described as one long sustained shock, the Gospel Singer is finally moved to tell the truth at the widely advertised giant tent show: that he could not be what they have said he is, that he hates those who demand that he bless them, and that MaryBell Carter was the biggest whore who ever walked in Enigma. Within a few pages, in the ensuing pandemonium both Hull and the Gospel Singer are lynched.

It is a vivid, funny, and horrifying novel, but it lacks focus. The plot circles, vignettes bulge. Crews knows the prison-place and the desperate inmates, but alternates caricature (pigs in a newly carpeted living room) and portentousness (Foot, of Freak Fair). "Promising"—the reviewers' general declaration—seems accurate.

Though *Naked in Garden Hills* (1969) is not on most counts a better novel than *The Gospel Singer,* it was widely and admiringly noted—by *Harper's, Life,* and the *New York Times Book Review.* The scene is a played-out phosphate mine in mid-Florida (the biggest in the world), owned once by the mythic Jack O'Boylan and subsequently turned over to Fat Man (upwards of 600 pounds). Contending for local supremacy with Fat Man is Dolly Furgeson, a frustrated virgin, who sets up with Fat Man's last capital a lewd, blatant, and highly profitable tourist attraction, Dolly Doo and Her Dimple Review. Supporting characters, all of whom Dolly lures away from the hapless Fat Man, include Jester, a black ex-jockey, a perfect physical specimen 3′8″ tall, and his loved one, lately a performer in an obscene circus show.

As in *The Gospel Singer,* Crews works up to a horrific conclusion. Fat Man, helpless and starving without attendants, is left a prisoner in the great house, offered either a 1000-calorie-a-day diet or a cage at Dolly's establishment. Finally, bleeding, beaten by the mob of tourists, naked, and drooling, he crawls to his waiting cage and is lifted high in the light.

Though it has its moments, in particular a wonderfully funny beginning, Crews's third novel, *This Thing Don't Lead to Heaven* (1970), represents a notable step backward; adjectives such as "uninteresting," "disgusting," "repetitious," and "preposterous" set the tone of reviews. For this judgment the challenging scene and circumstances of the novel are in good part responsible: a day of suffering and dying at Axel's Senior Club, an old folks home in another of the author's godforsaken hamlets, Cumseh, Georgia. Prominent in the cast—all of them decidedly freakish—are Jefferson Davis Munroe, a midget masseur seeking the magic touch which will restore to him the three feet which life has cheated him of; Carlita, a large, voluptuous, non-English-speaking Haitian, who—as luck would have it—is looking for a dwarf to actualize her voodoo powers; Sarah Nell Brownstien, a six-foot substation mail sorter from Atlanta and would-be contributor to *True Confessions* ("I Gave Birth At My Wedding" is her best title), who is searching for Munroe in the belief, sustained by his carefully posed photographs, that he is six and a half feet tall; and Junior Bledsoe, a demon cemetery plot salesman, to whom death has been very good and who, after Munroe's desertion, looks promising to the proprietor of the establishment, Axel, a.k.a. Pearl Lee Gates, daughter of a sardonic father.

Rather as in a Marx Brothers film, the plot, a tissue of comings and goings and discoveries and reversals, defies sensible summary. At the heart of the matter, however, is pain, Munroe's massages being ordeals (he calls them cleanings), the subjects proud of their ability to "take it." An elderly would-be couple, Jeremy and Molly, are displayed in various attitudes of geriatric lust and hope—doomed, of course, to extinction. The novel is uneconomically organized. Marred by set pieces and extraneous subplots, it never comes fully into focus and ends in a gasping fall. Crews seems not to know or to sympathize with his characters, even to delight in

Charné

Harry Crews

demeaning them. All they want, to paraphrase Axel's lovesick plea to Junior Bledsoe, is what's natural; all they get is what isn't.

For all of the brutal twitching of their strings, one character, Jefferson Davis Munroe, survives into Crews's next novel, *Karate Is A Thing of the Spirit* (1971), in which Munroe's picture holds honored place in the dojo of a troupe of outlaw *karateka,* barred from competition because of their unmatched and deadly skills. Munroe was the first teacher of the troupe's leader, a middle-aged black belt by the name of Belt, once Alonzo Fiber, court-martialed for cowardice during the Korean War and now practitioner of nonviolent violence. Munroe, it is revealed, was tragic master of a system that did not work and never could since his killing side kick to the heart would strike a normal opponent two inches below the knee.

Into this mystical commune, whose members earn a worldly living as bouncers and bodyguards around Fort Lauderdale, Crews sends John Kaimon, a young drifter from Oxford, Mississippi, wearing a blue William Faulkner jersey. On the miles of open beach and in the dry swimming pool of an abandoned motel, Kaimon is initiated into the regimen of pain and its transcendence. Choosing to suffer is to achieve purity. Also in residence are a nubile blond ex-beauty queen and brown belt, Gaye Nell Odell; a reborn and friendly member named Lazarus; a deranged, one-eyed, sixtyish yellow belt; and a squad of neophyte white belts. Crowds of homosexuals and the usual crazed tourists complete the cast.

In *Karate Is A Thing of the Spirit* Crews invented a near perfect vehicle for his obsessional drama. The commitment of Kaimon is credible, even moving; his pain, humiliation, will, and rage, whether from the burning sun on his shaved head, from broken hands, or from homosexual rape, all shape and energize his quest. In an author's note, Crews writes of his respect for the ancient and honorable way of life known as karate; nothing that follows contradicts his assertion.

Under the two portraits, Munroe's and Faulkner's, Kaimon achieves journeyman karate status, a Faulknerian who has never read a word of that master but who has admired him for being, he thought, different from the mass of men. It is perhaps the Faulkner of the Nobel Prize speech who comes to mind as successfully countering Jefferson Davis Munroe's killing side kick to the heart; but it is not in such exalted terms that Kaimon endures and prevails and ultimately departs the dojo. Rather he finds that Gaye Nell Odell is pregnant with his child and discovers that he believes not in the great world but in her and in her having his baby. They are last seen in a Volkswagen bus heading north up U.S. 1.

One might argue that, as Southern Gothic parable, *Car* (1972) is pure Crews. It is a fully achieved piece of fiction, well planned and not unambitious, in which nothing is wasted. Metaphysical variations on "you are what you eat" constitute the essence of *Car,* in which Herman Mack, car-loving idealist of the junkyard-owning Mack family, undertakes to eat a red 1971 Ford Maverick (half a pound a day for ten years) in the ballroom of the Sherman Hotel in downtown Jacksonville, Florida. This is the consummation of a national love affair with the machine, which shortly evolves into a media spectacular with the networks competing, Howard Cosell and Vice President Agnew expected, with the presence of promoters, a doctor, a nurse, the family, state troopers, proud bidders at the semipublic defecation of Maverick bits, and a chorus of Mongolian idiots. The reader is caught up in the gruesome process and believes implicitly (see the *Guinness Book of World Records*); we sweat, laugh, and receive Herman Mack as mythic actor and hot property performer worth who knows how much. Pain and death, those familiar Crews presences, are everywhere on display, from the hotel ballroom to the twenty- and thirty-car pileups north of Jacksonville, which furnish the Macks their livelihood.

Herman, swallowing his first sterilized half-ounce, experiences erotic bliss, shortly dreams that he is a car and then that he is full of cars; but eventually, because he loves the Maverick and cannot bear for it to cause him such pain, he begs off. As this true believer backs away, he is followed by his brother Mister, conveniently his twin, who had been his promoter. Mister, however, does his car eating solely for the money and suffers appropriately.

Despite its dubious quasi-happy ending—Herman and Margo, a house whore from the Sherman Hotel, finding peace back at the junkyard—*Car* is a fearful and bizarre story, precisely because it is continually in contact with and grows out of a vision of life the reader knows well and instantly recognizes, and is yet, simultaneously, a closed system from which there is no escape.

With *Karate Is A Thing of the Spirit* and *Car,* Crews had two fine novels in a row; *The Hawk Is Dying* (1973) made it three. The hero of this sixth novel is a forty-three-year-old bachelor named George Gattling, who has a profitable automobile upholstering shop, a subdivision house, a sister—Precious, deserted by her husband shortly after the birth of their defective son, Fred—and a deepening sense of rage and despair. The one sustaining delight of his life is a large female chicken hawk trapped on a nearby state wildlife preserve and destined either to be "manned" (broken and trained to hunt) or to die of starvation in the hall closet, as her two predecessors have. The issue in *The Hawk Is Dying*, as might be said of *Car*, is the nature of man: what is and is not natural for a man to want and do. The issue is worked out in a drama of dominance, pain, and will through George's engagement with the hawk, an extension of himself, against the well-nigh universal contention (of other characters and some reviewers) that such things are not natural. The only character who never reproaches George for his unnatural desires and atavistic practices is his retarded nephew, Fred, who is destined for a carefully calculated, shockingly ludicrous death—he drowns in his water bed, accidentally or suicidally, the reader never knows.

The reader does know that he dies because the world is the way it is, because he is not normal, because his death deprives George of such unspoken support as his presence had provided, because George had wanted him dead, and because his death and funeral bring friends, employees, family, clergy, doctors, and attendants down on George and his hawk. The trap is closing. With his recurring fear of madness breaking through, only the hawk and her naturalness make good sense to George. They survive, both of them, and on the last page of the novel, the hawk is launched.

About *The Gypsy's Curse* (1974), the less said the better, for in it Crews passes unexpectedly into a mawkishness reminiscent of John Steinbeck. It is a tale told by Marvin Molar, a legless, deaf and dumb hand balancer, who lives in a Florida gymnasium and survives by guile and one-finger handstands. His cohorts include Al, a protofather, several punchy fighters, and a lover named Hester, who is a "normal" and whose impact on his life is a curse. *The Gypsy's Curse* reengages a thematic concern central in the canon as Molar seeks meaning in disciplining and training his upper body to perform scarcely credible feats of strength. That he ends up in jail is substantially beside the point, since for Crews's protagonists integration within any sort of social order is either impossible or abhorrent, or both. Crews maintains a semblance of detachment from his agonizing victims, yet betrays his tour de force into sickly melodrama.

In happy contrast, *A Feast of Snakes* (1976) testifies to the return of the author's powers; the dust jacket of the novel is bedecked with the admiring remarks of such luminaries as Joseph Heller and Norman Mailer, and reviewers in the main tended to follow suit. With the advent of *A Feast of Snakes* a new, valid, and long-delayed insight into Crews's work began to be registered: that beneath and sustaining the pain and violence evoked by his characters' desperate sense of human limitation is a radical sadness beyond the sentimentalism that infected *The Gypsy's Curse*.

The protagonist of *A Feast of Snakes* is Joe Lon Mackey, lifelong resident of Mystic, Georgia, not too far from Enigma and Cumseh. In Mystic is held a yearly rattlesnake roundup, an occasion of the sort of ominous, violence-prone gathering of average citizens featured in all of Crews's novels. Joe Lon is a former student leader and high school All-American football star, whose life since graduation has been a series of trials increasingly hard to bear. He is introduced as a twenty-one-year-old, illiterate wife-beater who earns a marginal living selling moonshine and renting chemical toilets to snakers. He drinks heavily, drives one-handed at suicidal speeds, experiences powerful, unfocused rages, and finally, mercifully, inevitably, goes berserk, killing four people before he is himself thrown into the snake-collecting pit. Well before his death Joe Lon realizes that there is no debating or improving his life; killing others and himself gives him what he has never had: the power to decide, a sense of being at last in control.

Beyond the background that Crews's autobiography, *A Childhood*, implicitly provides for interpretation of his fiction—and Crews could almost be a character in one of the novels—the work is fresh, beautifully crafted, and very touching. After writing about himself in the various guises of fiction, Crews has said, he wanted to do it naked, to get it down before it is gone, to discover in the process who he is and how he got that way.

Seventeen nonfiction pieces make up *Blood and Grits* (1979), an uneven collection treating subjects from L. L. Bean to Charles Bronson, from vasectomy to hawk culture. On hawks as on cars, sideshows, jockeys, and rural violence, the essays have their relevance to the author's fiction.

Crews's vision, in whatever form it is manifest, is powerful and idiosyncratic, not in service of any conventional moral message, social insight, or economic imperative. All of his novels are of necessity tragicomedies; all of them, even the least inspired, are illuminated by flashes of brilliance, and all of them, even the most successful, are marred by stylistic lapses and self-indulgent grotesqueries. Of critics' objections to Crews's work, the most common are that his novels are gratuitously violent, generally heartless, and occupied exclusively by freaks, all of this epitomized in *Southern Gothic*, which is as good a term as any. In some volumes, *This Thing Don't Lead to Heaven* and *The Gypsy's Curse*, for example, the charges seem substantiated; in Crews's best fiction, *Karate Is A Thing of the Spirit* and *The Hawk Is Dying*, for instance, they are irrelevant.

Reading Crews is not something one wants to do too much of at a single sitting; the intensity of his vision is unsettling. By writing of what the world is pleased to call abnormality, it is Crews's intent to illuminate normality, and his obsessive depth of penetration amply compensates for conventional breadth and verisimilar variety. What Crews will come to there is no telling, beyond wider recognition. All the evidence to date identifies him as a writer of short novels; he appears to have no interest in the multigenerational epic favored by some of his Southern contemporaries.

—*Allen Shepherd*

Interviews:

V. Sterling Watson, "Argument Over An Open Wound: An Interview with Harry Crews," *Prairie Schooner*, 48 (Spring 1974): 60-74;

Steve Oney, "The Making of the Writer," *New York Times Book Review*, 24 December 1978, pp. 3, 17.

References:

Frank W. Shelton, "A Way of Life and Place," *Southern Literary Journal*, 11 (Spring 1979): 97-102;

Allen Shepherd, "Matters of Life and Death: The Novels of Harry Crews," *Critique: Studies in Modern Fiction*, 20 (September 1978): 53-62.

BORDEN DEAL
(12 October 1922-)

SELECTED BOOKS: *Walk Through the Valley* (New York: Scribners, 1956);

Dunbar's Cove (New York: Scribners, 1957; London: Hutchinson, 1958);

The Insolent Breed (New York: Scribners, 1959; London: Hutchinson, 1960);

Dragon's Wine (New York: Scribners, 1960; London: Hutchinson, 1961);

A Long Way to Go (Garden City: Doubleday, 1965; London: Joseph, 1966);

The Tobacco Men (New York: Holt, Rinehart & Winston, 1965; London: Joseph, 1966);

The Least One (Garden City: Doubleday, 1967; London: Joseph, 1968);

The Other Room (Garden City: Doubleday, 1974).

Loyse Youth Deal (known as Borden Deal) was born in Pontotoc, Mississippi, and raised in Union County near New Albany. The economic struggles of his family during the Depression years made an indelible impression on him and later provided abundant material for his fiction. His father, like many other farmers, lost his land when the price of cotton dropped disastrously. Aided by Roosevelt's rehabilitation program, the family procured two mules and traveled to a communal, government-sponsored farming project in Enterprise, Mississippi. This small community of renters was depicted years later as Bugscuffle Bottoms in *The Least One* (1967). The Darden community, the site of a later farming venture, became Hell Creek Bottom in *The Other Room* (1974).

Deal left home in 1938, the year of his father's death in a truck accident. The next few years he went through a variety of occupations, including hauling sawdust for a lumber mill, working on a showboat, battling forest fires with the Civilian Conservation Corps, and following the wheat harvest with other migrant workers by freight train.

His first publication occurred in 1948 when he was in college. His short story "Exodus" won first prize in a national contest and was reprinted in *Best American Short Stories of 1949*. Deal received his B.A. from the University of Alabama in 1949 and in 1950 was a graduate student in Mexico City. He began writing full time in 1954, and by 1957 he had achieved national recognition with his first novel, *Walk Through the Valley* (1956), which received an honorable mention in the American Library Association Liberty and Justice Awards. In the same year he received a Guggenheim Fellowship for creative writing.

At present, Deal has written twenty-one novels and about one hundred short stories, along with other miscellaneous works. Although his novels are invariably set in the South, they have gained far more than regional acceptance. His work has been adapted for the screen, the stage, radio, and television. *The Insolent Breed* (1959) was the basis for the Broadway musical "A Joyful Noise." *Dunbar's Cove* (1957), along with William Bradford Huie's *Mud on the Stars*, was made into the movie *Wild River*, directed by Elia Kazan. Deal's works have been translated into more than twenty languages. The author resides in Sarasota, Florida. He has three children by his former wife, Babs Hodges, who is also the author of several novels. He is a MacDowell Colonist and a member of Authors Guild and P.E.N.

In Deal's estimation, the value of his work lies "in the progressive panorama of the 'real' South (not the 'Gothic' South so beloved by the literary critics). . . . If someone two hundred years from now wants to know about the *real* South, of people working and living, they'll have to go to my books." What Deal means by the "real South" is that his fiction is woven from the ordinary, practical lives of contemporary Southerners: the people who make music, raise horses, build dams and highways, and run for political office.

A major theme in the Deal canon—and perhaps that for which he has received the most critical attention—is man's mystical attachment to the earth itself. His first novel, *Walk Through the Valley*, distinguished him as a novelist who writes with the authority of experience of farming and the rhythms of the seasons. This tale is about a dream-seeking pilgrim named Fate Laird who leaves the sterile land of his father's Texas farm in search of a more fertile and prosperous country. Central to this novel is the romantic kinship Fate feels with the forces of nature and with the land he works. Deal's characters are typically honest and uncomplicated people who are motivated by some elemental drives of human nature: family pride, the desire for independence, and the longing for land that will yield security and those material comforts that tell a man he is progressing toward the better, more gentle life.

There is perhaps no Deal novel in which the land itself looms as a more important element than in *Dunbar's Cove*. This story revolves around two men with conflicting dreams: Matthew Dunbar, farmer and ordained guardian of his ancestral land, who vehemently fights against the massive dam-building project of the Tennessee Valley Authority, and the young and idealistic engineer Crawford Gates, who represents the federal government. Although his land is destined to be flooded, Dunbar refuses to sell to the TVA because he feels a mystical pact with the ancestral defenders of the cove—an obligation to preserve the cove as a sanctuary for any Dunbar who should ever want to return.

However, the preoccupation with land is not the only theme of the novel. Matthew Dunbar finally sees that the long and intense association of Dunbar pride with a piece of land had come to have tragic consequences for the family. The cove is destroyed, but Matthew is strangely revitalized. He moves to virgin land and builds anew, much in the constructive spirit of the engineers who build the dam that destroys his home. Deal's earth theme is thus tempered by the motif of spiritual renewal, man's perennial need for a new frontier. These early novels received critical acclaim chiefly for their clearly delineated characters and the emotional honesty with which the author describes rugged, unsophisticated people in times of crisis.

Dragon's Wine (1960) represents a deeper and perhaps darker side of Deal's creative character. This facet of his writing might best be referred to as the mythical or archetypal mode. A student of Jungian psychology, Deal has shown a fascination with the atavistic behavior of man individually and collectively. A striking characteristic of Deal's more profound books is his tendency to superimpose his plots and characters upon the primeval patterns of behavior: the classical rituals and dramas of birth, death, sexual and social initiation, and the realization of self.

Dragon's Wine is a dark and bloody tale that treats the outbreak of greed and demonic ambition in the human personality. The novel revolves around Homer and Kate Greaves, two larger-than-life characters who dominate the sawmill manor where they are tenants. Homer and Kate are sketched as characters who are massive and ferocious in their ambition and in their physical lust for each other. The tiny sawmill community finds the couple's passionate intensity food for endless gossip, but secretly the people feed upon the pair's awesome strength.

The tale is a graphic description of the consuming greed that destroys Homer, Kate, and the mill owner. Deal's story is strengthened by his introduction of an albino sow, a bizarre animal that serves throughout the novel to mirror Homer's greed. The Jungian overtones are strong. The sow and Homer die together in a gruesome duel; but the animal manages to perpetuate itself by giving birth to a tiny, white piglet that escapes, squealing, into the wilderness. Symbolically, greed survives to repeat the tragedy of Homer and Kate another time, another place.

A Long Way to Go (1965) is a treatment of the ritual of initiation. Three precocious children embark on a six-hundred-mile journey to their home after being mysteriously abandoned by their parents. The book is a sensitive account of how innocent children, suddenly severed from family dependency, adjust to the not-so-innocent world. The young trio finally arrives safely in the backyard of their home in the dead of night. They have with them the strange companions they gathered during their travels—three animals, a white mule, a goose, and a dog. Since pets are forbidden by the father, the animals stand silently in the darkness of the backyard as the children slip into the house; the animals seem to represent new extensions of each child's character, or perhaps a growing awareness in the children which the parents unconsciously fear but cannot prevent. A deceptively simple tale, *A Long Way to Go* is filled with provocative symbolism that lends itself to different levels of interpretation.

Also appearing in 1965 was *The Tobacco Men*, a fictional account of the Kentucky tobacco wars of the early 1900s and J. B. Duke's American Tobacco Company in the last decade of the nineteenth century. Deal based the novel on notes by Theodore Dreiser and Hollywood writer Hy Kraft. He obtained the notes on the condition that he be allowed complete artistic freedom in writing the book. The novel is about a shrewd robber baron named Oren Knox, patterned after J. B. Duke, and the stormy expansion of his tobacco empire. Knox is opposed by Amos Haines, an altruistic country doctor and night rider. The novel reaches its climax when Knox and his barn-burning opponent clash in a confrontation that determines the fates of both men. *The Tobacco Men* shows Deal's love of detail and his ability to weave fact and fiction. The novel's appearance marked a slight revival in attention given to Deal's work at that time. Some reviewers felt the dialogue and "cinematic techniques" would have been more suited to the screen, and the novel was noted primarily for its documentary value.

The Least One and its sequel *The Other Room* are semi-autobiographical novels about the Sword family's search for the elusive land of promise. These tales have a strong existential flavor with self-actualization as a key theme. Central to the novels is the idea that a person's values and identity are not so much superimposed by family and society as they are internally generated by certain vital experiences. In *The Least One*, Lee Sword leaves his son, simply called Boy, the task of naming himself. Deal reflects upon the biblical creation story in which Adam, through naming the living creatures and by exercising his will, shaped the world to some degree into a creation of his own making. This is essentially the responsibility left to Boy. In a sense, his struggle for self-definition is complemented by his father's economic struggle to come fully into his own as a provider, to break away from the communal life of the government farm and reestablish his independence.

The Other Room is essentially a continuation of Boy Sword's initiation. Early in the novel, Boy, now called Christian, describes his tender and humorous sexual affair with Miss Edna Bryant, his English teacher. Christian moves from this physical attraction to a more temperate and spiritual love for a girl named Vance. The critical point in Christian's initiation, however, is his struggle with the reality of death—the death of his father. Lee is killed in the prime of life with his dreams unfulfilled. The senseless nature of his death shakes Christian's faith in the entire scheme of life.

As was true with *Dragon's Wine*, this novel revolves around a central symbol, in this case the room given to Christian as a Christmas present. To Christian the room represents his move into the world of freedom and autonomy; but the room takes on an aura of horror when it is used to keep Lee's body during the long, tedious days before the funeral. The room, always referred to as "the other room," becomes the room of an unjust God and a dead father. Despite Christian's revulsion, however, he eventually becomes reconciled to the fact of human mortality and is able once again to sleep in "the other room" without a feeling of horror. Ultimately this novel is a celebration of life and death as inseparable agents in the process of spiritual maturation. Christian steps from "the other room" into "the enormous *other* room" of the adult world.

In all his work, Borden Deal is, first of all, a product of his region and past. Like many of his Southern contemporaries, his writing shows a strong sense of place and time. Undoubtedly his family's perseverance in the Depression years accounts greatly for the pervasive themes of land quest and personal ambition as well as the host of stubborn dreamers in his books. There is, however, much in Deal's work that transcends its regional flavor. A universal quality in his writing stems, in part, from his preoccupation with the timeless ritual of self-discovery. Underlying Deal's fiction is the vital conviction that modern man has an inescapable bond with his tribal past. In simple terms, Deal believes that the individual mind is composed of more than the knowledge and experience internalized during the life span of the person. Like Jung, Deal maintains that the individual mind is a recapitulation of the entire psychic history of the human race. Consequently there are, deep in the "collective unconscious" of every person, timeless symbols and images that have played profound roles in the religious, cultural, and political histories of past generations. To Deal it is the artist—owing to his sensitivity to this archetypal reservoir—who has the peculiar task of transmitting these archetypal images and symbols to his fellowman. In doing so, the writer, through his fiction, aids the human community in the process of self-discovery.

Borden Deal is a sensitive and intuitive writer. Because his novels are, as he would say, "given" to him through spontaneous eruptions of the collective unconscious, it is difficult to anticipate the future course of his fiction. Thus far, however, he has secured a wide popular readership and a reputation as a storyteller who re-creates man's most ancient conflicts within the context of the contemporary South.

—James R. Waddell

Periodical Publication:

"The Function of the Artist: Creativity and the Collective Unconscious," *Southwest Review*, 51 (Summer 1966): 239-253.

Papers:

Borden Deal's manuscript materials are deposited with Boston University.

NICHOLAS DELBANCO
(27 August 1942-)

SELECTED BOOKS: *The Martlet's Tale* (Philadelphia: Lippincott, 1966; London: Gollancz, 1966);
Grasse 3/23/66 (Philadelphia: Lippincott, 1968);
Consider Sappho Burning (New York: Morrow, 1969);
News (New York: Morrow, 1970);
In the Middle Distance (New York: Morrow, 1971);
Fathering (New York: Morrow, 1973);
Small Rain (New York: Morrow, 1975);
Possession (New York: Morrow, 1977);
Sherbrookes (New York: Morrow, 1978);
Stillness (New York: Morrow, 1980).

Nicholas Delbanco, though not yet forty years old, has produced one of the most extensive and interesting, if relatively unknown, series of novels of any writer of his generation. From a prodigy of a novelist whose early parables were dazzling in their language, Delbanco has matured into a writer of first-rate dramatic fiction. His most recent books, the chronicles of a southern Vermont upper-class family, have demonstrated his deep concern with the problems and feelings of family life, human character, history, and time, and have won him a serious and well-deserved following among his contemporaries.

Delbanco is a naturalized American, born in London in 1942. At the age of six, he immigrated to the United States with his parents, Kurt and Barbara Delbanco (of German-Jewish and Sephardic origins). He attended elementary school in Westchester County just outside New York City and graduated from the Fieldston School, a private high school in The Bronx in 1959. He went on to receive a bachelor's degree from Harvard University in 1963, graduating magna cum laude, and a master's in English and Comparative Literature from Columbia University in 1966, where the subject of his thesis was the fiction of Malcolm Lowry. In that same year (which saw the publication of his first novel, *The Martlet's Tale*) Delbanco joined the faculty of Bennington College in Vermont to teach writing workshops and literature courses. With the exception of sabbaticals and teaching terms at the Iowa Writers Workshop and the writing program at Columbia University, Delbanco has taught at Bennington ever since. For the past four years he has also served as general director of Bennington Summer Workshops writing program.

The Martlet's Tale was an auspicious and well-received first novel which, as Albert J. Guérard remarked, managed to avoid becoming "in almost every conceivable way the usual overlong and tedious first novel of subjective torment." Set in Athens and the island of Rhodes, its characters are modern Greeks who act out the drama of Sotiris, a prodigal who survives a dalliance with a seductress and returns home to prove himself worthy of his inheritance. The novel's surface is carefully sculptured, its prose as stately and decorous as its fable is passionate. If the story fades upon rereading, what remains is the keen sense of shrewdness with which a young writer masters the problem of narrative distance.

In his next two books, Delbanco seemed determined to expend all of the credit he earned with his first. *Grasse 3/23/66* (1968) turns distance into remoteness from the reader; and, with its allusive language and excessive punning, it tends to obscure any interesting psychological and emotional elements present in the Dionysian tale of love and disaffection among expatriates in France. It plays with language at the expense of the reader's concern for its action and characters.

A similar problem mars Delbanco's third novel, a complex narrative about the intricate sexual, psychological, and social relationships among six aesthetes who inhabit houses in Barbados, Martha's Vineyard, and Manhattan. Despite moments of psychological insight, *Consider Sappho Burning* (1969) seems determined to call attention to its linguistic virtuosity often at the expense of obscuring the human element. Yet in one crucial aspect, *Consider Sappho Burning* remains linked to a world beyond its tortured rhetoric. The main character, a lesbian poet named Aurore, creates a sense of reality in her otherwise chilly and perverse account of decadence on assorted islands by splicing into her journal passages from records of their colonial pasts. A similar sense of the importance of the past in the formation of a balanced view of contemporary society carried Delbanco to the American mainland for the setting of his fourth novel, *News*, published in 1970.

News is probably the most fully realized and yet most neglected political novel in recent decades. It weaves together narratives of the lives of four middle-class white American males, three of whom destroy themselves in their quests for social change. The settings in which they do business are Vermont, Mexico, and the South, and the book is much more accessible than its predecessors without sacrificing Delbanco's sense of the exotic to banality. *News* is devoted to the historical past as well as to contemporary America. Its language, while self-conscious, avoids melodrama and polemic and tends more toward clarity than obscurity while synthesizing the yea and nay of a tumultuous political period with great skill and intelligence. Some of its characters—and meanings—remain slightly blurred, but in Sam, the white organizer who heads south armed only with historical documents and a vision, Delbanco presents a man, a voice, and a mind to remember.

Few of the impurities and all of the riches of Delbanco's earlier books find their way into his fifth novel, the avowedly experimental *In the Middle Distance*, published in 1971. A novel in the form of a journal, it tells the story of a middle-aged architect-turned-writer named "Nicholas Delbanco" whose efforts to remodel a farmhouse in Upstate New York parallel his attempt to render his life into art. All of the incipient themes from the previous novels—the problems of identity and paternity, modernity versus the past, myth against reality, language versus action, and society against itself—emerge boldly in these pages. Delbanco's tendency to remain aloof from human passion and to cloud his action in a haze of allusive language yields here to a finely rendered portrait of a man's angst and happiness. While *News* is probably the most neglected political novel in recent decades, *In the Middle Distance* is probably the most neglected experimental fiction of the same period.

Joel Gardner

Nicholas Delbanco

Fathering, which appeared in 1973, has all of the aspects of a major novel, and yet among all Delbanco's books it promises the most and delivers the least. This story of a young actor named Robert Mueller who attempts to uncover certain compromising secrets about his paternity is built upon the Oedipus myth and steeped in the by now familiar Delbanco rhetoric. Though it is a book which lesser writers might have been pleased to claim as their own, something is askew in its pages. While the language does not obscure the characters, the figures themselves seem less than completely present, more like cartoons for a canvas the artist had already presented in previous books.

But the uneasiness of *Fathering* also suggests the imminent transformation in Delbanco's imagination, which had taken place by the time *Small Rain* was published two years later in 1975. Two European adults both in late middle age serve as the focus of this small and carefully constructed novel about a love affair: Anthony Hope-Harding, a frame maker and connoisseur, and Maija von Einzeedle fall in love. In depicting their passion, the novel delivers emotions which heretofore had been shrouded by Delbanco's rhetoric. At the same time, he avoids sentimentalizing these autumnal lovers and maintains for the reader an appropriate distance from their plight as well as their pleasures.

In *Small Rain*, Delbanco's ability to depict powerful and deeply felt emotions within the framework of a carefully shaped and managed story has matured, leading, in the late 1970s, to Delbanco's major work of the decade, the Vermont trilogy comprised of *Possession* (1977), *Sherbrookes* (1978), and *Stillness* (1980). The main characters of this trilogy are not only the author's most interesting and appealing, but also (and more importantly) his most carefully and successfully realized to date. Judah Sherbrooke, the patriarch of the old Vermont family in and around whose "Big House" much of the action takes place, stands out as the most attractive and mature member of the family, as much for his stubbornness and passionate self-regard as for his wisdom. Maggie, his young wife, and Hattie, his aged sister, are two of the most intelligently drawn female characters in recent fiction. Ian, the actor-playwright son, is the apotheosis of earlier Delbanco prodigals, and his return to the family mansion after the death of Judah precipitates a crisis of emotions and vision.

As John Updike has written, Delbanco "wrestles with the abundance of his gifts as a novelist the way other men wrestle with their deficiencies." This is particularly true in the Vermont trilogy. The language and the construction work in harmony with the psychological aspects of the novel as never before in Delbanco's fiction. By controlling, without muting, the rhetorical element and by balancing a propensity for allusive internal monologue with a stark, sometimes gothic sense of tableau, Delbanco achieves here his most mature and most pleasing fictions. Moreover he eschews the use of the self-conscious fabular patterns onto which he stitched earlier books and invents a family full of fascinating characters out of his own imagination and observation. "Without anyone's much noticing," John Gardner wrote about *Sherbrookes*, Delbanco "has turned into one of the country's best novelists." Yet few readers are aware of his work, an unfortunate situation when one considers that Delbanco's style partakes so much of the vitality of contemporary life and the history of the Republic.

—Alan Cheuse

Other:

"Reprise," in *On the Vineyard*, ed. Peter Simon (Garden City: Doubleday, 1980), pp. 119-123.

Periodical Publications:

"The Executor," *Iowa Review*, 9 (Fall 1978): 89-96;
"Ostinato," *Atlantic Monthly*, 244 (July 1979): 31-37;
"Traction," *Tri-Quarterly*, 46 (Fall 1979): 58-73;
"Composition," *Seattle Review*, 2 (Fall 1979): 14-19.

DON DELILLO
(November 1936-)

BOOKS: *Americana* (Boston: Houghton Mifflin, 1971);
End Zone (Boston: Houghton Mifflin, 1972);
Great Jones Street (Boston: Houghton Mifflin, 1973);
Ratner's Star (New York: Knopf, 1976);
Players (New York: Knopf, 1977);
Running Dog (New York: Knopf, 1978).

Don DeLillo writes novels that are loose-knit fabrications of the tensions, preoccupations, and manias of modern America. His books are usually shaped around a central character whose behavior is a means of defending against the stresses in his life. Only in his sixth novel, *Running Dog*, is much attention paid to plot; thin plot lines serve mostly as excuses for stringing together series of episodes. DeLillo's grasp of the contemporary myth-making process is strong, for he fastens onto his materials—football, mathematical logic, rock music, scenarios for nuclear devastation—and works them over firmly, imparting to them a satisfying glaze of bright language. His characters owe something to comic books, and his narratives cut swiftly from scene to scene, a technique perhaps picked up from films. The bizarre and extraordinarily witty dialogue of his characters often casts a surreal haze over their presence, producing much of DeLillo's unique effect.

Born in New York City, DeLillo lived as a child and adolescent in Pennsylvania and in the South Bronx. After completing his studies at Fordham University, DeLillo lived in New York and Canada. Through a grant from the Guggenheim Foundation, he is currently in Greece at work on a novel.

In DeLillo's first novel, *Americana* (1971), David Bell, twenty-eight-year-old hireling of a television network, tells his own story. Bell is caught up in a career he finds increasingly meaningless and is nagged by the failure of his marriage. He then does what so many American fictional heroes have done—he lights out on a spiritual odyssey meant to renew the flagging soul. For Bell the opportunity arises when he is assigned to do a documentary film on the Navaho Indians. He insists on making the trip west by car, for "cars are religious now and this is a religious trip."

In New York Bell recruits Jack Watson Pike, a sixty-year-old chain smoker "fascinated by animals," and an enigmatic young woman sculptor known only as Sullivan. The three of them drive to Maine's Penobscot Bay, where they stop at Bobby Brand's "ascetic garage." Brand, an old buddy of Bell's, is "a one-man dispensary of meth, acid, hashish and various amphetamines."

A week on the road in Brand's pickup-camper truck finds them in Fort Curtis, somewhere in Middle America, and at the very heart of their "mysterious and sacramental journey." They meet various people here: a skinny teenager walking across the country whom Bell renames Kyrie Eleison; several devotees of the drama from McCompex—the McDowd Communications Arts Complex; and Glenn and Bud Yost, father and son, who raise bloodworms. Although by this time Bell is supposed to be shooting a documentary in Navaho territory, he chooses instead to focus his 16mm Canon Scoopic on Fort Curtis folks reading the absurd monologues and fantastic scenarios he creates for them. When relationships sour among the four travelers, Bell hitchhikes solo and ends up in Rooster, Texas, where his "sacramental journey" culminates in a drunken orgy.

Americana has much to praise. The office scenes are amusingly loony, highlighted by the employees' speculations on the identity of the mysterious Mad Memo-Writer, whose compositions turn up signed by the likes of Zwingli, Chekhov, and Charles Olson. Long flashbacks flesh out Bell's youth and give occasion for more sketches of zany characters: fat and lonely Leonard Zajac, known as the Young Man Carbuncular; Simmons St. Jean, professor of film criticism who takes seriously the need for an appropriate persona ("He worked on his pallor"); and Beastly, a frenetic radio star apparently fueled by superspeed. The language of *Americana* is first-rate throughout, and it alone does much to justify Joyce Carol Oates's description of *Americana* as "a robust and intellectually exciting work."

DeLillo's second novel, *End Zone* (1972), is a plotless collection of scenes depicting the lives of varsity football players at Logos College in west Texas. These lives are sketched with wit and feeling, and the players are likeable human beings who generally approach both football and life with courage and as much self-understanding as most people are capable of. Squarely in the middle of *End Zone* occurs a crucial football game, which DeLillo turns into a marvelous set piece. *End Zone* has no themes to speak of—no large points to make about existence—but the characters are so engaging and the tone so friendly that its cumulative effect is bracing.

At the center of events is Gary Harkness, a talented halfback whose eccentric behavior at Syracuse and Penn State has ruined his athletic career at those schools and made Logos College his last chance to redeem himself. Much of his time off the football field at Logos is spent with Myna Corbett, a classmate in Mexican geography, who keeps her weight at 165 pounds so that she will not have to face "the responsibility of being beautiful." She wears boots studded with blue stars and gorges her mind on science fiction novels. (She is engrossed in a trilogy by the Mongolian savant of outer space, Tudev Nemkhu.) When he is not picnicking with Myna, Gary often raps about warheads with Major Staley of ROTC. Gary's fantasies about nuclear ruin are lush and epic, mordant visions of a fiery apocalypse; and in his preoccupation with nuclear catastrophe can be sensed a fear that humanity is threatened by its collective Freudian death wish.

Gary's teammates are colorful existentialists. Anatole Bloomberg, left tackle on offense, is "a voluntary exile of the philosophic type." Anatole has enuresis and a weight problem. ("I'm like a bridge. I expand in hot weather.") Because of "enormous nagging historical guilt," Anatole is "unjewing" himself in west Texas: "You go to a place where there aren't any Jews. After that you revise your way of speaking. You take out the urbanisms. The question marks. All that folk wisdom. The melodies in your speech. The inverted sentences. You use a completely different set of words and phrases. Then you transform your mind into a ruthless instrument. You teach yourself to reject certain categories of thought."

Gary, Anatole, and Myna are memorable people. One cares about them. They hang on, they keep control, and they even triumph in small ways with wit, courage, and resourcefulness. Their inspired depiction in the funny, irresistible dialogue that DeLillo excels in makes *End Zone* the "visionary novel and major triumph of the imagination" that one reviewer called it.

Bucky Wunderlick is the central figure of *Great Jones Street* (1973). Bucky is a rock-and-roll star who abruptly leaves his group in Houston and returns to New York City, where he hunkers down on Great Jones Street in a "small crooked room, cold as a penny, looking out on warehouses, trucks, and rubble." Bucky is a hot property of Transparanoia, which markets a "Superlick Mind-Contracting Media Kit" for those attracted to "The Bucky Wunderlick Story Told in news items, lyrics and disfunctional interviews." The lyrics are unique documents of the age: "VC Sweetheart," "Cold War Lover," "Protestant Work Ethic Blues," and the piece that made Bucky famous, "Pee-Pee-Maw-Maw."

Bucky's withdrawal to Great Jones Street is complicated by a visit from a tarnished flower child named Skippy, who stashes a package of dope from the Happy Valley Farm Commune with Bucky. The dope is a new synthesis, its powers yet untested, and when word of its existence gets around, Bucky's visitors increase. For instance, Opel Hampton (educated—one year—at Missouri State Women's College in Delaware, Texas) shows up as an agent for Dr. Pepper, well-known drug dealer/chemist. Dr. Pepper is earnest: "Buck, I want this product badly. This may be my last venture in the field of drugs and drug abuse."

Competition thickens the plot. An overseas eminence turns up to bid on the pharmaceuticals. He is Watney, "England's anti-king and duplicate bishop of hallucination." And Azarian, number two man in Bucky's abandoned band, appears complete with a black female bodyguard, Epiphany Powell. But while the dealers are wheeling, a boy named Hanes has taken the parcel of dope and replaced it with a package containing the Mountain Tapes, vapid but valuable tapes made by Bucky and the source of all hopes held by Bucky's manager, Globki.

The upshot of all this is that the drug is found out to be only nasty (users lose their voices), the Mountain Tapes are blown up in a Cincinnati warehouse by Dr. Pepper's evil minions, and the same minions slit Azarian's throat and give Bucky a punitive dose of the disappointing dope.

Great Jones Street has DeLillo's usual comic skill ("bursting with colorful inventions" was one critic's response), but the piling up of Doonesbury-like characters finally seems not much more than mechanical. And whereas his first two novels had characters for whom one could feel affection, those in *Great Jones Street* seldom come across as real people. Many readers will agree with the reviewer who called *Great Jones Street* "more of a sour, admirably written lecture than a novel."

Ratner's Star (1976) is a long, dense narrative packed with characters from DeLillo's special universe of baroque loonies and startling constructions, all stitched together with verbal lightning. This 438-page work has a strong impact; and the facile use of concepts and thinkers from mathematical logic is truly dazzling. It is, as one critic remarked, "a red giant of a book." But eventually the piling up of episodes becomes a lavish waste of talent, for no heightened intensity results and the episodes do not develop a plot.

Ratner's Star builds around a simple but extremely enticing gimmick. In part one ("Adventures: Field Experiment Number One") Billy Twillig, a fourteen-year-old genius and winner of the first Nobel Prize in mathematics, is summoned to the School of Mathematics of the Center for the Refinement of Ideational Structures, a think tank in Pennyfellow, Connecticut. The year is 1979. Billy's prize was for his work with the "zorg," "a kind of number" but a "useless" one. The Center is housed in a huge cycloidal structure, impossible to visualize. Billy's assignment is to decode a radio signal—fourteen pulses, gap, twenty-eight pulses, gap, fifty-seven pulses—thought to have come from a planet circling Ratner's star.

Billy's coworkers are a memorable lot, and observation of them constitutes the chief pleasure of the story. First, there is Endor, the world's greatest mathematician. He came to the center with great confidence, studied the pulse pattern for weeks with no success, and then sat in his room for seventy-two hours before going to live in a hole in the ground. Billy finds him there, smeared with dirt and eating plants and worms. Among the others, Peregrine Fitzroy-Tapps is from Crutchly-on-Podge, pronounced Croaking-on-Pidgett, which is near Muttons Cobb, spelled Maternity St. Colbert. Fitzroy-Tapps, like Rahda Hamadryad, a rat-talk scholar, is a zoologist.

Diverting pedants abound. Gerard Pence wears "old khaki shorts, bark sandals, and a string headband ornamented with eucalyptus nuts." He gives a rambling talk on myth and mysticism, introducing a white-haired aborigine who remains hidden, however, beneath a white canvas on a miniature flatcar. Finally the canvas moans, whirls, snaps inside out, and lies motionless. Hoy Hing Toy is a renowned obstetrician notorious for the Toy-Molloy incident in which he delivered a baby in a famous hospital and then ate the placenta in "five huge gulps." Molloy was the mother. "Elux Truxl" is a nom de nom—"the sound identity I have assigned to my nom." Elux, who speaks a mad, funny, Joycean pseudo-Spanish, is a big dealer out of Tegucigalpa in charge of a cartel that wants to regulate the "money curve" of the world. Elux's companion, a head shorter than Elux, is Grbk, who is "mal y bizarro" and has been "officially rebuked many times for exposing his nipples to little children. A tragic person, very sadiensis." Armand Verbene, S. J., is a practitioner of red ant metaphysics. He is "haunted by the thought that red ants don't need red ant metaphysics." One of the more striking complaints of the characters is that of a young woman named Thorkild, whom Billy finds one day in his bath. She works at "decollation control" and will not let Billy see her naked, for she has no lap.

A standout in this incredible gallery is Orang Mohole, twice winner of the Cheops Feeley Medal and the "kingpin of alternate physics." (Cheops Feeley himself is a lapsed gypsy, a state of apostasy for which "a simple announcement usually suffices," according to Cheops.) Mohole pops greenies as he discourses on the "value-dark dimension," or "mohole totality." His model of the universe is a "stellated twilligon," and he postulates "eventual collapse in a sort of *n*-bottomed hole or terminal mohole." Orang Mohole uses a vomitorium (he eats with the expectation of vomiting). He invites Billy to a party where there are "artificial fragrances packaged in aerosol cans" (e.g., "wood-burning fire," "heaped garments," "nude female body (moist)—sense of urgency arises").

At a torchlight ceremony held in the Great Hole under the cycloid, Billy meets the aged, desiccated Shazar Lazarus Ratner, who exists tenuously in a capsule called a biomembrane. He is attended by Dr. Bonwit, who owns a yacht named the *Transurethral Prostatectomy* and keeps Ratner fluffed up with silicone injections. Fifty pigeons are released at the ceremony.

As these strange characters come and go on their diverse hobbyhorses, Billy deduces that the pulses reveal a "positional notation system based on the number sixty" and that "What was being transmitted was the number fifty-two thousand one hundred and thirty-seven." But then he meets Dr. Softly, the head of the math section, who says Ratner's star is no longer of interest and reassigns Billy to work on "a logistic cosmic language based on mathematical principles." Thus ends part one.

Part two ("Logicon Project Minus-One") pursues the new problem and is narrated in a series of rapid cuts from character to character. The scientific eminences in part two are no less kin to those of Jonathan Swift. Among them is Chester Greylag Dent, a ninety-two-year-old polymath attended by Jumulu Nobo, whose Malayan forebears had settled in a small town in Louisiana called Oslo, Norway.

Softly's workers make several important discoveries that allow Softly and Billy to intuit the significance of the pulse sequence. Maurice Wu, Softly's anthropologist and guano expert, learns that "In the very distant past on this planet, there was a species of life that resembled modern man both outwardly and otherwise." Furthermore, Walter Mainwaring, authority on the "exo-ionic sylphing compounds" that occur with moholes, concludes that "In the untold past on this planet a group of humans transmitted a radio message into space." The picture is now clear: the pulses came from earth millions of years ago. What do the pulses say? Billy knows—fourteen, twenty-eight, fifty-seven is sixty-base notation for 52,137—and Billy realizes these are seconds, or twenty-eight minutes and fifty-seven seconds after two o'clock in the afternoon on an unknown day. Billy then notices that the clock on the wall gives exactly that time, and a convenient radio announcement tells of an imminent total eclipse of the sun, heretofore unexpected. Softly evidently takes in the meaning of these revelations, for he burrows into a hole already dug nearby by Endor, the crazed mathematician. *Ratner's Star* concludes with Billy's pedaling for the same refuge.

The satirical vision in *Ratner's Star* is irresistible, and the imagination that energizes it is impressive and delightful. It demands close attention, however, and most readers will probably find it a book to sample for its Swiftian fun with the enterprises of science.

A change of tone occurs in DeLillo's last two novels, *Players* (1977) and *Running Dog* (1978). Each of the previous novels had had a protagonist whose vulnerability invited sympathy and perhaps helped the reader feel that he and the author were involved together on the side of goodness and justice. The cynicism of the last two novels disallows any such illusion, for they are parables of betrayal and degeneration. The frail, confused youths of the early novels are here displaced by characters influenced by popular espionage fiction.

In *Players* the author speaks directly to his readers in the prologue and epilogue, confiding and commenting, calling attention to the fact that these are "players" whose lives we observe briefly but whose inner selves remain mysteries to us. Lyle and Pammy are the featured players. He works on Wall Street and she writes brochures for the Grief Management Council, whose "trained councilors served the community in its efforts to understand and assimilate grief." Their marriage is shaken by two events: the terrorist murder of a broker on the floor of the stock exchange and an affair Lyle initiates with Rosemary Moore, a secretary in his office building. Pammy then goes off to Maine with two homosexual male friends, but their attempts to live idyllically are blasted by the suicide of one of the men. Lyle becomes more and more involved with Rosemary, meeting through her several members of the terrorist cell responsible for the stock exchange murder, and he acts as a double agent between the cell and the FBI.

Players is a disappointing work, a letdown after a novel with so much vitality as *Ratner's Star*. The *Harper's* reviewer called *Players* "slack and shapeless," and the judgment is hard to dispute. DeLillo's language is, as always, elegant as he dramatizes the boredom of Lyle and Pammy; but this is not sufficient reward.

Running Dog, however, is another matter. The brittle tone of *Players* is applied to an elaborate plot, and the result is a genuine story featuring a cast of reptilian hired killers, porn peddlers and collectors, and petty gang-lords. Part one of *Running Dog* is entitled "Cosmic Erotics," a reference to the gallery run by an aging smut dealer named Lightborne. He has been negotiating for "The century's ultimate piece of decadence," a home movie reportedly shot in Hitler's bunker just before the Nazi collapse; but unfortunately his contact with the film is found murdered, mysteriously dressed in women's clothes. One of Lightborne's regular customers is CIA-trained Glen Selvy, who fronts as purchaser for Senator Lloyd Percival. But Selvy also reports on Percival to a shadowy agent named Lomax, who wants information about Percival because the Senator is probing PAC/ORD, a clerical intelligence organization—at least ostensibly. PAC/ORD, however, has a secret arm—Radial Matrix—so successful as a straight business firm that it has become a breakaway unit under its powerful and autonomous head, Earl Mudger. Mudger is Lomax's boss; and Christoph Ludecke, the murdered movie peddler, had also been in the employ of Mudger, who had sought to get the bunker film from him.

Moll Robbins, a journalist from *Running Dog* (a publication mentioned first in *Great Jones Street*), consorts for a while with Selvy and penetrates the Senator's secret cache of erotica. A more appealing female lead is provided by Nadine Rademacher, a Texas girl Selvy retrieves from her ignominious Times Square employment as a teller of so-called "nude stories" (i.e., erotic stories told by a girl in scanty clothing).

When Selvy flees from two Asian hit men hired by Mudger (who thinks Selvy has sought to deal independently with Ludecke's widow for the film), Nadine accompanies him, and they visit her father in Arkansas. Selvy then retreats instinctively to the Mines, the bleak Texas training ground for covert agents of violence, where he faces with only a bolo knife the death that he feels all his training has prepared him for. After Selvy's death in a brutal showdown, the surviving assassin packs Selvy's head in a bag to take back to Mudger.

Meanwhile, Lightborne has finally gotten the film and gives a private screening of it for Moll and a Texas pornography dealer, Odell Armbrister. The film turns out to be an amateurish and innocuous narrative of women and children, enlivened only by the appearance of Hitler parading as Chaplin aping Hitler. Interesting history but worthless as pornography is the consensus. The screening is concluded when a thug aptly named Augie the Mouse bursts in and carries the film off to his boss, who is Mudger. Thus *Running Dog* concludes with little concluded.

Running Dog was praised by Anthony Burgess, who said that "DeLillo has his own voice, harsh, eroded, disturbingly eloquent." That is a good appraisal of the tone of the last two novels, especially. DeLillo has shown over the course of six novels that he is inventive, witty, and extraordinarily gifted in his ear for dialogue and his feel for mood and atmosphere. For the most part, critics have dealt kindly with DeLillo, describing him as a writer with great promise. *Ratner's Star* shows signs of having been meant as a "big" novel, one that fulfilled the promise of his earlier works, but it must be considered a disappointment despite its remarkable comic characterizations and genius for contriving episodes. DeLillo has not yet had a breakthrough novel, one that would perhaps fix him on reading lists in university courses. But a writer with his intelligence and ear for language is bound to produce more fiction that shows close observation of life; this work is to be anticipated with pleasure.

—*Frank Day*

PETER DE VRIES
(27 February 1910-)

BOOKS: *But Who Wakes the Bugler?* (Boston: Houghton Mifflin, 1940);
The Handsome Heart (New York: Coward-McCann, 1943);
Angels Can't Do Better (New York: Coward-McCann, 1944);
No But I Saw the Movie (Boston: Little, Brown, 1952; London: Gollancz, 1954);
The Tunnel of Love (Boston: Little, Brown, 1954; London: Gollancz, 1955);
Comfort Me With Apples (Boston & Toronto: Little, Brown, 1956; London: Gollancz, 1956);
The Tunnel of Love: A Play, by De Vries and Joseph Fields (Boston & Toronto: Little, Brown, 1957);
The Mackerel Plaza (Boston & Toronto: Little, Brown, 1958; London: Gollancz, 1958);
The Tents of Wickedness (Boston & Toronto: Little, Brown, 1959; London: Gollancz, 1959);
Through the Fields of Clover (Boston & Toronto: Little, Brown, 1961; London: Gollancz, 1961);
The Blood of the Lamb (Boston & Toronto: Little, Brown, 1962; London: Gollancz, 1962);
Reuben, Reuben (Boston & Toronto: Little, Brown, 1964; London: Gollancz, 1964);
Let Me Count the Ways (Boston & Toronto: Little, Brown, 1965; London: Gollancz, 1965);
The Vale of Laughter (Boston & Toronto: Little, Brown, 1967; London: Gollancz, 1968);
The Cat's Pajamas & Witch's Milk (Boston & Toronto: Little, Brown, 1968; London: Gollancz, 1969);
Mrs. Wallop (Boston & Toronto: Little, Brown, 1970; London: Gollancz, 1971);
Into Your Tent I'll Creep (Boston & Toronto: Little, Brown, 1971; London: Gollancz, 1972);
Without a Stitch in Time (Boston & Toronto: Little, Brown, 1972; London: Gollancz, 1974);
Forever Panting (Boston & Toronto: Little, Brown, 1973; London: Gollancz, 1973);
The Glory of the Hummingbird (Boston & Toronto: Little, Brown, 1974; London: Gollancz, 1975);
I Hear America Swinging (Boston & Toronto: Little, Brown, 1976; London: Gollancz, 1976);
Madder Music (Boston & Toronto: Little, Brown, 1977).

Peter De Vries has been called by Kingsley Amis "the funniest serious writer to be found on either side of the Atlantic" and by W. J. Smith "the greatest punster the world has ever known." The author of a large number of popular and widely read novels, he retains a charming lack of seriousness about himself and his work, preferring to be thought of as a devoted craftsman rather than a tortured artist. He deals with sexual themes, often explicitly, but four-letter words are rare in his work, and he is never pornographic.

He was born in Chicago of immigrant parents, Joost and Henrietta Eldersveld De Vries, and was raised among other members of the strict and Calvinistic Dutch Reformed Church. He was graduated from Calvin College in Grand Rapids, Michigan, in 1931. Instead of entering the ministry as his family expected, he embarked during 1931 to 1938 on a series of jobs as a writer, a radio actor, and candy vender. For six years (1938 to 1944) he was an editor of *Poetry* magazine. In 1944, with the assistance of James Thurber, he began a long and fruitful association with the *New Yorker* magazine (he is still a part-time cartoon editor and contributor). On 16 October 1943, he married Katinka Loeser, a poetess and short-story writer of great sensitivity. Between 1945 and 1953, the couple had four children—Jan, Peter Jon, Emily, and Derek. They live in Westport, Connecticut.

Sometimes thought of by critics as too autobiographical, De Vries's novels often concern the problems of men in their early middle age who, like De Vries, have ventured into a moral wilderness of urban society after a strict upbringing. However, the fictional characters have not grown older as De Vries has, and their problems have changed to reflect more contemporary situations, while still focusing on the early years of marriage, which De Vries considers the crisis years.

In his first three novels, *But Who Wakes the Bugler?* (1940), *The Handsome Heart* (1943), and *Angels Can't Do Better* (1944), De Vries displayed hints of his dazzling wit and sure command of language, but little profundity. Not until the collection of short stories *No But I Saw the Movie* (1952) and the novels *The Tunnel of Love* (1954) and *Comfort Me With Apples* (1956) did De Vries begin his analysis of the modern moral and philosophical predicament as it is evidenced in suburbia. The characters encounter parallel artistic and ethical problems which prove too complex for their seemingly sophisticated paradigm. In *The Tunnel of Love* should Augie Poole and his unsuspecting wife adopt Augie's child by his emancipated mistress? Should he prostitute himself by selling the captions to his cartoons without the cartoons? Should Chick Swallow of *Comfort Me With Apples*, an avant-garde aesthete, continue to debase himself by writing "pepigrams" for the local newspaper? Should he hold himself responsible for the troubles of a poetess to whom he has recommended the bohemian life? *The Tents of Wickedness* (1959) continues the adventures of Chick Swallow, and contains excellent parodies of the works of Faulkner, Hemingway, Wolfe, and others.

In *The Mackerel Plaza* (1958) De Vries expanded a type of character introduced in *The Tunnel of Love*, the ultraliberated clergyman. Such clergymen find that strict nonconformity is as demanding and no more intellectual than strict conformity. Reverend Mackerel cuts his Sunday sermons short (he is "the Hemingway of the pulpit") to please his liberal parishioners, but feels compelled to heckle fundamentalist street corner divines on Saturday night. Mackerel's accidentally drowned wife becomes a kind of secular saint when a shopping center is named for her.

De Vries enriches his next four novels, *Through the Fields of Clover* (1961), *Reuben, Reuben* (1964), *Let Me Count the Ways* (1965), and *The Vale of Laughter* (1967), with both structural and thematic complexities. Instead of restricting himself to the standpoint of one character, De Vries covers the same narrative sequence from the point of view of several characters. These points of view contrast older with younger narrators, traditionalists with ultraliberals, the less educated with intellectuals. In *Through the Fields of Clover*, Ben and Alma have a less than perfect marriage, but it hangs together. Their children, who as adults do not trouble themselves with making an effort at traditional marital or parental duties, have different but no less vexing problems.

Similarly, *Reuben, Reuben* contrasts differing perspectives. For instance, a middle-aged chicken farmer named Spofford drives a Model T because he cannot afford a newer car, but the suburbanites who have invaded his rural neighborhood think he is an old car buff. Spofford is the narrator of one-third of the book, while another third is told from the point of view of an English fop named Mopworth, and another from the point of view of a poet-satyr named McGland (he much resembles Dylan Thomas). Thematically, De Vries deals with two aspects of modern mythology, the deficiencies of Freudianism as a metaphysic (Mopworth is assumed to be a homosexual because he chases girls, a sure sign, say the intellectuals, that he wants to chase boys) and the post-Romantic concept of art as a redemptive religion.

Let Me Count the Ways also is divided into three narrative sections, the first and last narrated by a piano mover named Stan Waltz and the middle one by his son Tom, a young English professor. Stan is a "bigoted atheist" while his wife is a crusading fundamentalist, and Tom reflects the confusion in his upbringing. Like many unbelievers who appear in De Vries's works, Stan's militancy indicates an uneasiness with atheism, and he flirts with orthodoxy. Tom has a hilariously strange career as an English professor and is the enemy of a group of faculty intellectuals he calls "The Three Little Prigs." At first Tom uses his divided family to his advantage, extricating himself from affairs with unreligious girls by citing his mother's fundamentalism, and from relationships with religious ones by calling on his father's atheism. Ultimately, Tom's religious confusions are resolved when he becomes "miraculously ill" at Lourdes.

The Vale of Laughter, the most underrated novel of the four, has two narrators, the gifted comic Joe Sandwich and his rival, a humorless professor of the psychology of humor, Wally Hines. Sandwich effortlessly generates paronomastic names—Justin Case, Woody Dare, Iona Ford, Willy Maker—but Sandwich cannot cope with his job as a broker in his wife's father's firm nor his familial duties, and he spends some time in a sanitarium. Hines, who narrates the second section, envies Sandwich's command of humor, a subject which evades his understanding despite his research into Hegel's and Kant's theories about it. Ironically, Sandwich is killed when, failing to realize that a racing bicycle has only hand brakes, he rides over a precipice furiously pedaling backwards.

In the midst of these novels, De Vries wrote *The Blood of the Lamb* (1962), which has puzzled many readers with its somber material, but De Vries merely allowed the seriousness of his vision to become more manifest. It is in some ways his most ambitious work, for De Vries dares to find the humor in the disastrous life of Don Wanderhope. Wanderhope's narrative begins with his remembrances of the theological discussions in his childhood home of man's innate depravity and moves through a series of misfortunes. His brother dies of pneumonia; one mistress dies of tuberculosis and another goes insane. Wanderhope tries to compensate for causing the mental problems of the mistress by marrying her; but after giving him a daughter, the wife experiments with the gamut of emotional panaceas—alcoholism, Freudianism, and religious fundamentalism—and finally commits suicide. The last half of the book chronicles the death from leukemia of Wanderhope's daughter (De Vries drew upon his own loss of his daughter Emily to leukemia). Although the book is filled with horror and theological debate, De Vries succeeds in making it funny. (A mother who catches

Wanderhope in bed with her daughter vents her anguish by calling him a "prude," knowing only that the word is pejorative in connotation and concerns sex.) Throughout the book, De Vries carefully prepares for the affirmative climactic scene in which Wanderhope throws a pie (actually a cake) in the face of a statue of Jesus, emphasizing that the comic who gets a pie in the face expects and chooses to be a scapegoat for the agonies of others.

In the novelettes *The Cat's Pajamas* and *Witch's Milk* (published together in 1968), De Vries introduces a concept he was to develop in later novels, the dangers of compulsive intellectual role playing. Hank Tattersall, who rejects both his careers as a college professor and advertising writer with melodramatic gestures, finds real enjoyment in portraying an Italian street singer on television. When the show is cancelled, he continues to play the role in "real life," strolling about selling vegetables from a cart. His wife leaves him and his finances decline, but Tattersall more and more relishes the proletarian role, adopting a mongoloid child and a drunken dog. In a splendid final scene, Tattersall freezes to death wedged half in and half out of a small door made for his dog. In *Witch's Milk* another role player is rejected when Tillie Shilepsky chooses to stay with Pete Seltzer, her unfaithful and crude but kind husband, rejecting a life with the effete aesthetician Jimmy Twichell.

In an essay in *Poetry* in 1943, De Vries praised

ONE

Given a little money, education and social standing, plus of course the necessary leisure, any man with any style at all can make a mess of his love life. And given these, plus a little of the right to self-realization that goes with modern life, a little of the old self-analysis, any woman at all can make a shambles of her marriage. Statistics show it every day. Romantic confusion, once the privelege of a few, is now within the reach of all. Even of me, a chicken farmer. I'm not going to say "mere chicken farmer," like you might expect, because in the first place I lack the humility for it, and in the second there's nothing mere about running a poultry ranch in Connecticut, as they now call them there. Nothing could be less mere, as the facts will show.

I was born here in Woodsmoke, but not this Woodsmoke. I no longer recognize the place. I'm that most displaced of all persons, your native son in a modern town. My father was the last of his line to live without being made an alien in his birthplace by turning it into a tentacle of New York. Good thing he went out with his time, as he would of had strong emotions on the subject--The Losing of the East. We were not taken captive into Babylon-- Babylon came to us-- but our harps hang on the willows just the same.

My father was a man of feeling who always wanted his family to

Reuben, Reuben, *revised typescript*

Charles Péguy for his "artless essence," and called him "an articulate peasant." In the title character of *Mrs. Wallop* (1970), he created such a peasant. Mrs. Wallop, a delightful straightforward widow, dominates the lives of a drunken novelist (obviously a parody of Thomas Wolfe) and her novelist son. Mrs. Wallop narrates most of the novel, although the middle of the book contains an autobiographical novelette by the son. Mrs. Wallop combats the modern notion that mothers are the cause of all of their children's problems, attempting to prove that sexual repression is more to be desired than sexual license. Left on his own, her son experiments with sexual anarchy and with raising a child in a home free of sex roles. To get day care for his child, he is forced to become a transvestite and is arrested as a hooker. To rescue him from the shambles he has made of his life, Mrs. Wallop goes along with her son into the world of high culture, where she underwrites a movie and exasperates the "artists" on the set.

Although perhaps the poorest of De Vries's mature work, the collection of short stories *Without a Stitch in Time* (1972) and the novels *Into Your Tent I'll Creep* (1971) and *Forever Panting* (1973) show De Vries continuing, sympathetically but surgically, to point out the shortcomings of modern life. Families and personalities disintegrate in the search for secular redemption through sex and art. Al Banghart of *Into Your Tent I'll Creep* swaps roles with his wife, she earning their living as a French teacher while he keeps the house (and keeps company with the neighborhood wives). It is the wife, a crusading advocate of women's liberation, who finds the arrangement upsetting. Ironies abound—although a simple philanderer, in order to preserve his marriage, Al must pretend to ever greater depravities, ultimately pretending to be a flasher ("no woman deserving the name," says his wife, "would walk out on a man who is sick"). Stew Smakenfelt of *Forever Panting,* fighting a losing battle with "Blodgett" (his Mr. Hyde), divorces his wife to marry his stepmother. After many complications involving the conflicting artistic careers of his wives, Stew is forced to vandalize his own house—the police see a huge modern painting hanging in his home and assume that no one would do that to a wall on purpose, and Stew must destroy the rest of the house rather than let the painter find out that the police thought his painting was the work of vandals.

The Glory of the Hummingbird (1974) is De Vries's most masterfully constructed work. After a strict and religious upbringing, Jim Tickler marries Amy Wintermoots and begins working in the morally chaotic world of advertising and television. Amy proving infertile, they bring into their home an adolescent criminal who proves incorrigible, although they make every effort to be model parents. At the same time, Jim originates a national quiz show called "The Little Red Poolroom." To boost the ratings, he becomes a contestant on the subject of the Bible. Up to that point, he had assumed that the show was legitimate, but he learns that while the show is not "fixed," the producer of the show can predict, on the basis of tests, what questions a contestant can and cannot answer. In the debate about the morality of the game, the producer invokes the philosophy of Hans Vaihinger, insisting that television, like all life, is managed illusion. Although he is never given answers, and although he goes on trying to win after he is supposed to "take a fall," Tickler cannot decide himself whether he is culpable or not. In penance, after the rigging of the show is exposed, he goes to work for a consumer testing agency. The testing agency is a kind of antiadvertising agency, dedicated to truth and honesty in marketing, but his boss, Mrs. Flamsteed, demands his sexual favors. The consumer advocates, Jim comes to realize, are "Puritans of the marketplace," but quite without moral guides in more important areas of life. Ironically, Jim's exposure as a party to quiz show fraud and as an adulterer "saves" him as a parent. The punk, it turns out, resented Jim's and Amy's perfection, and loved them only when they showed themselves as humanly flawed. Thus De Vries is able to convey in this very funny book a great deal about the Fortunate Fall and its relationship to the illusory nature of what we call reality.

De Vries's technical command is also much in evidence in *I Hear America Swinging* (1976) and *Madder Music* (1977), both of which concern the ravages of "freedom." In the first, as a marriage counselor ("an ambulance driver in the battle of the sexes"), Bill Bumpers stumbles through the nightmarish world of several modern marriages. He attends a "sexual Smorgasborg" and winds up with "somebody's foot in my mouth," tries a skinny-dipping club called the Baredevils, and helps with arcane marriages in which each spouse tries to be more liberal than the other. Along with the moral inversions of the modern sexual ethic treated in *I Hear America Swinging,* De Vries comments on modern theories of aesthetics by chronicling the adventures of a farmhand who accidentally became an art critic, the first "primitive critic," the "Grandma Moses of criticism." *Madder Music* concerns Bob Swirling who begins by playing the role of Groucho Marx but finds he cannot stop playing it. His troubles start when he mistakenly thinks he is going to die and has an affair as a last fling. By the time he finds out he is going to live, his marriage is ended, so he marries his lover. When his second marriage disintegrates, he embarks on a series of affairs, including one with a black art broker, who pretends to be his cleaning girl to hide the affair from Swirling's stepmother. As his life disintegrates, he more and more takes refuge in Groucho imitations, until he thinks he is Groucho. (This allows De Vries to air a delightful store of Groucho-esque jokes—reading rationalist philosophers on the subject of death is "putting Descartes before the hearse.") Rescued from the compulsion to play Groucho by his black mistress, he later finds marriage to her too demanding and is last seen having become W. C. Fields.

Over the years, reviewers have objected to several aspects of De Vries's work. With the exception of Mrs. Wallop, there are few well-developed female characters. Women tend to be stolid, not-too-bright foils to their more mercurial and clever husbands or lovers. De Vries's cavalier attitude toward narrative sequence gives rise to many afterthought explanations, such as "She happened to be with me," or "who had by then returned from his journey." Other critics find this nonchalance part of the character of the narrators.

From his earliest novel, in which a frying egg is said not to be sizzling but to be "squeligulating," through Joe Sandwich's strange names to the Groucho jokes, De Vries has sought to point out the inadequacy of language as a key to reality. The existence of the pun and the light aphorism drives home this inadequacy, and thus these are De Vries's favorite forms of humor. Although De Vries never fails to delight many readers, he often puzzles others by forcing them to laugh at what they think should appall them. Like the humor of Aristophanes, Swift, and Twain before him, De Vries's comedy contains much horror and terror. De Vries does not like to be called a black humorist because, as he says, they are not funny. He might also object because, unlike them, he does not really find the universe chaotic or meaningless. He does not recommend a return to the Christianity of an earlier America as a remedy for current ills, but he regrets modern man's loss of belief. He obviously knows and loves modern literature and art, but he sees its absurdities. Likewise he seems to feel for the suburbanite more sadness and pity than rancor, and tempers his criticism with genuine affection.

—*William R. Higgins*

Interviews:

Douglas M. Davis, "An Interview with Peter De Vries," *College English*, 28 (1967): 524-529;

Richard B. Sale, "A *Studies in the Novel* Interview: An Interview in New York with Peter De Vries," *Studies in the Novel*, 1 (1967): 364-369.

Bibliography:

Edwin T. Bowden, "Peter De Vries—The First Thirty Years: A Bibliography, 1934-1964," *Texas Studies in Literature and Language*, 6 (1964): 543-570.

References:

James H. Bowden, *Peter De Vries* (Boston: G. K. Hall, 1980);

Louis Hasley, "The Hamlet of Peter De Vries: To Wit or Not to Wit," *South Atlantic Quarterly*, 70 (Autumn 1971): 467-476;

Roderick Jellema, *Peter De Vries: A Critical Essay* (Grand Rapids, Mich.: Eerdmans, 1966).

J. P. DONLEAVY
(23 April 1926-)

BOOKS: *The Ginger Man* (Paris: Olympia, 1955; expurgated, London: Spearman, 1956; New York: McDowell, Obolensky, 1958; unexpurgated, London: Transworld, 1963; New York: Seymour Lawrence / Delacorte, 1965);

Fairy Tales of New York (New York: Random House, 1961; Harmondsworth, U.K.: Penguin, 1961);

The Ginger Man: A Play (New York: Random House, 1961); republished as *What They Did in Dublin with The Ginger Man* (London: MacGibbon & Kee, 1962);

A Singular Man (Boston & Toronto: Little, Brown, 1963; London: Bodley Head, 1964);

Meet My Maker The Mad Molecule (Boston & Toronto: Little, Brown, 1964; London: Bodley Head, 1965);

A Singular Man: A Play (London: Bodley Head, 1965);

The Saddest Summer of Samuel S (New York: Delacorte / Seymour Lawrence, 1966; London: Eyre & Spottiswoode, 1967);

The Beastly Beatitudes of Balthazar B (New York:

Seymour Lawrence / Delacorte, 1968; London: Eyre & Spottiswoode, 1969);

The Onion Eaters (New York: Seymour Lawrence / Delacorte, 1971; London: Eyre & Spottiswoode, 1971);

The Plays of J. P. Donleavy (New York: Delacorte / Seymour Lawrence, 1972; Harmondsworth, U.K.: Penguin, 1974);

A Fairy Tale of New York (New York: Delacorte / Seymour Lawrence, 1973; London: Eyre Methuen, 1973);

The Unexpurgated Code: A Complete Manual of Survival and Manners (New York: Delacorte / Seymour Lawrence, 1975);

The Destinies of Darcy Dancer, Gentleman (New York: Seymour Lawrence / Delacorte, 1977);

Schultz (New York: Seymour Lawrence / Delacorte, 1979).

If there is an archetypal post-World War II American writer-in-exile it may well be James Patrick Donleavy who, in 1967, renounced his American citizenship to become an adopted son of his parents' native Ireland. Though frequently explained away as a mere dodge to take advantage of Ireland's liberal tax laws for artists, Donleavy's decision to forsake his homeland may reflect a much more complex attitude toward America than simple economics would explain. "Something in one's bowels was saying no to this land," Donleavy writes as he recollects his inability to survive as an artist in the United States, "where my childhood friends were growing up, just as their parents did, to be trapped trembling and terrified in a nightmare." Much of Donleavy's reaction to America is based upon his early recognition that "obscurity and rejection" are all "America gives in abundance" to her writers, and his realization that "a lyric voice could not be heard unless heralded coast to coast by a throbbing promotional media campaign. And that that country, be it the home of my birth and where I grew up, was not about to give it to me. And if I stayed, they would, without even trying, kill me."

Donleavy has since been accorded the "throbbing promotional media campaign" prerequisite to success in contemporary American letters, but that fact has not lessened his ambivalent attitude toward the homeland he rejects as "a country corrosive of the spirit. . . . Each time you arrive anew in America," he writes, "you find how small you are and how dismally you impress against the giantness and power of this country where you are so obviously and with millions like yourself, so totally fatally expendable." In spite of his repudiation, however, Donleavy looks back on America with some longing as he recalls, "except for my first twenty years in the king of cities, New York, I have been an alien nearly everywhere for most of my life." And, though having escaped the American nightmare to Europe, which "throughout one's American upbringing somehow . . . seemed a strange and more tolerant clime," he still feels that, "as far away as you may go, or as foreign as your life can ever become, there is something American that always stays stained American in you."

These perceptions, all taken from Donleavy's most personal essay, "An Expatriate Looks at America," are important not only because they emphasize his sense of himself as an American expatriate, but also because they point toward so many themes and motifs which find expression in his works—both those with American locales and those set in Europe. All Donleavy's characters, for example, inhabit societies which seem, "without even trying," to threaten to destroy them either physically or spiritually or both. The exile is the most recurrent figure in his works, and, exile or not, all his leading characters are aliens in whatever society they inhabit. Even the idea of America as nightmare can be seen displaced into the worlds of Dublin, London, or Vienna, all equally nightmarish, but, for Donleavy, more comprehensible than the vastness of America which is too much larger than life to be comprehended adequately in literature. "Each time I go to these United States I start anew trying to figure them out," he writes. "And after two weeks I decide that like anywhere, greed, lust and envy make them work. But in America it is big greed, big lust, big envy." These vices are to a large extent the qualities that drive Donleavy's characters and the societies they inhabit, and, whatever the specific setting, they are but reflections on a more human scale of the vices which have turned Donleavy's America into a Kafkaesque nightmare.

It was not always so, according to Donleavy's recollection of his rather bucolic and sheltered childhood in the Bronx. Raised by immigrant Irish parents in a secure middle-class atmosphere, Donleavy remembers a happy youth in which America seemed filled with promise and hope, its tensions and failures too far away to be quite real. "Everywhere and everything said that America was big, strong, and beautiful," until that innocent world was shattered when "a foreign power did something evil on a Sunday morning." Donleavy, expelled from one prep school, was "narrowly graduated from another. Just in time to go to war." While training in the Naval Reserve as a radar operator on amphibious landing craft, he developed an aversion to such duty, particularly given "the suicidal attitude of the enemy." A turning point in his life came when he managed an assignment to the Naval Academy Preparatory School where, "While the Japanese war was daily coming closer to an end, . . . I first heard among these incredible naval collected intelligensia the name James Joyce. And listened to an extremely human and erudite literary English instructor talk about good writing." There too he "heard of Dublin's wide wide O'Connell Street, a big brewery, and the drinking word stout," all of which would become essential parts of his own life after the war.

With visions of Joyce's Dublin dancing in his head, and "with my piss poor high school record being instantly rejected by every university I applied to in America, and my mother's information that there was a college called Trinity, I wrote to Ireland to ask could I come. And I ran around for days looking at a letter emblazoned with an escutcheon of a lion, book, harp and castle which said yes, please do." From 1946 to 1949 Donleavy was a student at Trinity College in Dublin at least nominally reading microbiology though *Time* suggests his major activities may have been "wenching, pubcrawling, and street fighting" with his "close enemy" Brendan Behan. After leaving Trinity, Donleavy was for a time a painter, and his first serious literary efforts were introductions to exhibitions of his work in Dublin. He returned to the United States while working on his first novel during the early 1950s, but during the McCarthy era he found "there is no good life here. It is sad and bitter. Where no man has the opportunity to feel any love. This is a land of lies. The whole country is strangling with the tentacles of the Church and the various American legions of Decency. It's all vulgarity, obscenity and money. A country of sick hearts and bodies. So tragic that I just sit and sit full of pain." To a friend he recommended that the "best thing is to bring the books of Franz Kafka and read them here."

"And now with the myth of America as the place you could return to shattered," Donleavy returned to Europe and to the sense of exile and alienation that seems to haunt his life as well as his work. "My work," he has said, "has an attraction for the independent thinking loner. My readers appear to be people who are not particularly from any kind of larger society, but they are mostly of a very highly intelligent caliber." Like a mirror image, this description of his audience fits Donleavy as well, capturing the alienation which seems as much personal attribute as literary device. Even achieving the literary success he thought America would deny him has not lessened his alienation from his country, though it has enhanced the style in which he expresses his exile status. In 1968, *Time* reported "now at 42, he has six residences—three in London, the rest in the Isle of Man, Zurich, and Manhattan—and carries currency of several nations to protect his 'non-skid agility.' " Donleavy was married to Valerie Heron, with whom he had two children, Philip and Karen. He is presently married to Mary Wilson Price, and they have a daughter, Rebecca Wallis. Though he now claims a 180-acre estate in Ireland as his permanent home, Donleavy remains essentially the exile who once wrote of America, "there it goes, a runaway horse, with no one in control."

Among honors and awards received by Donleavy are the *London Evening Standard* drama award for *The Ginger Man*; Brandeis University Creative Arts award for *The Ginger Man* and *Fairy Tales of New York* (1961-1962); and a National Institute of Arts and Letters Award (1975). Donleavy completed his first novel in 1951, but was unable to find a publisher willing to accept *The Ginger Man* until 1955 when, following the advice of Brendan Behan, he submitted the work to Maurice Girodias, who agreed to publish it in Paris through his Olympia Press. Though the arrangement led to publication of *The Ginger Man*, it was also the beginning of a long dispute between Donleavy and Girodias which eventually culminated with Donleavy buying Olympia Press after it went bankrupt. Aware of the reputation of Olympia as a purveyor of pornography to the tourist trade, Donleavy submitted his novel there only because Girodias used the proceeds of his erotic potboilers to underwrite publication of such serious authors as Miller, Beckett, Nabokov, and Genet. To Donleavy's dismay, his work was included in the notorious Traveler's Companion Series, Olympia's pornographic library. Regarding this as damaging to his literary reputation, Donleavy claimed that Olympia Press was in breach of contract and arranged for publication of expurgated editions in England (Spearman, 1956) and America (McDowell, Obolensky, 1958). Girodias sued and gained a judgment against Donleavy only in France. That decision was rendered moot when Donleavy eventually purchased Olympia Press to end what he regarded as harassment over the negative ruling by the French court. After resolving the suit, Donleavy has promised to describe his conflict with Olympia in a work to be called "The History of the Ginger Man" which will celebrate "the culmination of 22 years of litigation. At the end of which I turned out to be the

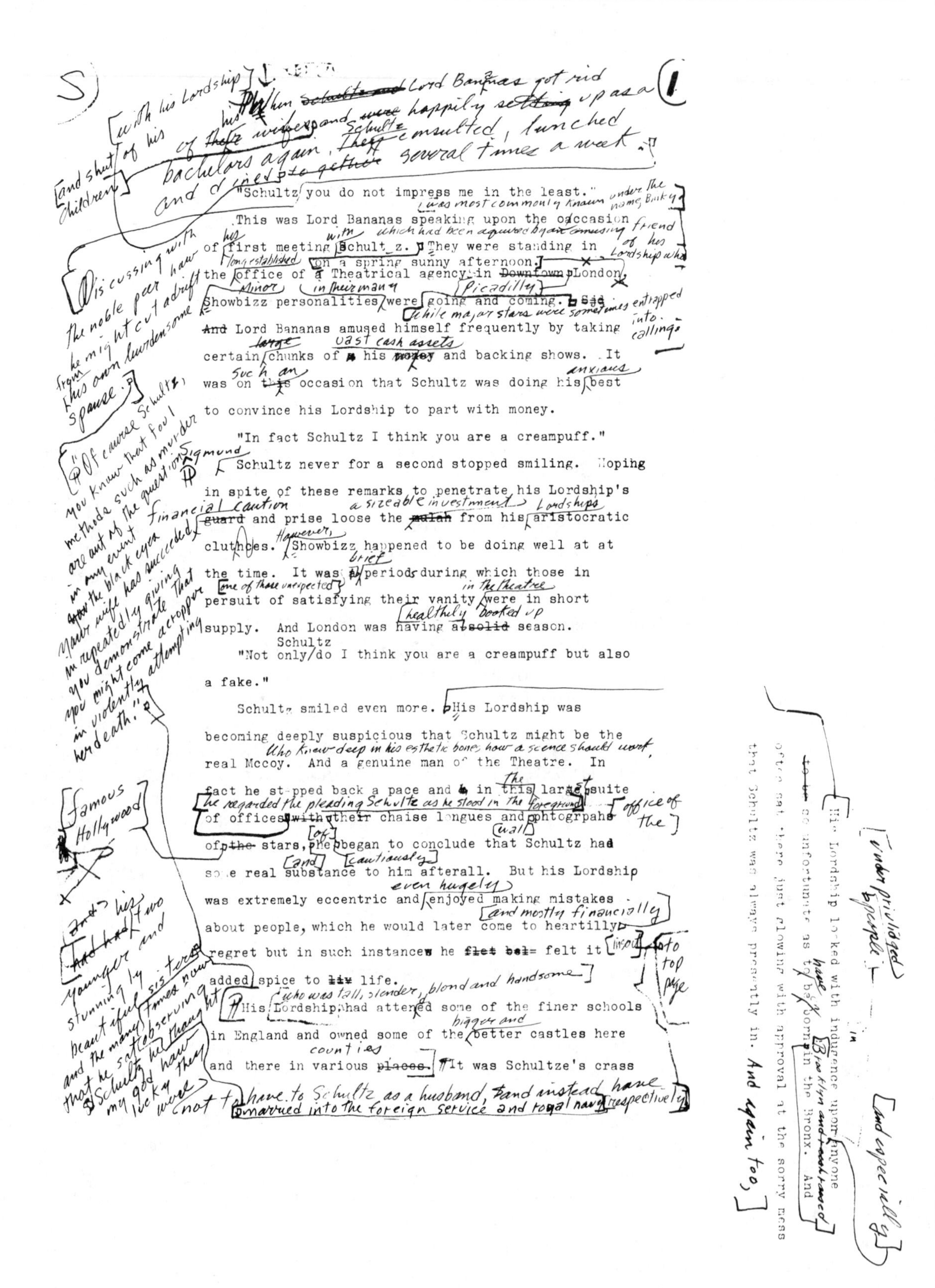

"Schultz you do not impress me in the least."

This was Lord Bananas speaking upon the occasion of first meeting Schult z. They were standing in on a spring sunny afternoon. the office of a Theatrical agency in Downtown London. Showbizz personalities were going and coming. And Lord Bananas amused himself frequently by taking certain chunks of his money and backing shows. It was on this occasion that Schultz was doing his best to convince his Lordship to part with money.

"In fact Schultz I think you are a creampuff."

Schultz never for a second stopped smiling. Hoping in spite of these remarks to penetrate his Lordship's guard and prise loose the mulah from his aristocratic clutches. Showbizz happened to be doing well at at the time. It was a period during which those in persuit of satisfying their vanity were in short supply. And London was having a solid season.

"Not only/do I think you are a creampuff but also a fake."

Schultz smiled even more. His Lordship was becoming deeply suspicious that Schultz might be the real Mccoy. And a genuine man of the Theatre. In fact he stopped back a pace and in this large suite of offices with their chaise longues and phtogrpahs of the stars, he began to conclude that Schultz had some real substance to him afterall. But his Lordship was extremely eccentric and enjoyed making mistakes about people, which he would later come to heartilly regret but in such instances he felt it added spice to life.

His Lordship had attened some of the finer schools in England and owned some of the better castles here and there in various places. It was Schultze's crass

His Lordship looked with indulgence upon anyone so unfortunate as to be born in the Bronx. And often sat there just glowing with approval at the sorry mess that Schultz was always presently in.

Schultz, *revised typescript*

owner of Olympia Press. It makes me feel that there is justice in the world, albeit self-administered. I had, I think, 14 lawyers at one time, and some of the incidents were fascinating, so I decided to sit down and write a history of it."

In spite of the potential for literary damage, publication by Olympia Press had the generally salutary effect of establishing the unexpurgated edition of *The Ginger Man* as an underground classic before complete editions became available in England (1963) and America (1965). Though it seems tame in retrospect—and especially in comparison to some of Donleavy's more recent work—the bawdy aspects of *The Ginger Man* did not suit the literary taste of the 1950s. Even the 1958 expurgated edition inspired Vivian Mercier to charge that the book, which she conceded to be an "Irish comic masterpiece," contained portions that are "obscene and/or blasphemous." Richard Sullivan felt that "disgust, indignation, and boredom . . . are the most likely responses to be anticipated among readers of . . . this nasty, rather pompous novel"; but most other critics were more positive in their responses. As Carl Bode observed, life in the novel derives its strength from sex, "and this is what the novel dwells upon. To justify that fact . . . we might keep in mind Judge Woolsey's remark in his opinion admitting *Ulysses* to our country. It should be remembered, said the judge, that the locale was Celtic and the season spring."

The bawdy tone of *The Ginger Man* helps place it in the great tradition of the comic-picaresque novel from which virtually all of Donleavy's work derives. The picaro figure at the heart of the work is Sebastian Dangerfield, a likeable rogue. An ex-Naval officer now attending Trinity College in Dublin under the GI Bill, Sebastian reads law but creates chaos. Rabelaisian in his carnal appetites, Dangerfield exemplifies in his relentless search for alcohol and women all the excesses and failures of character society normally condemns: he lies, cheats, steals, and sponges without conscience; his most positive attitude toward his wife and child is neglect when he is not downright cruel to them; he callously tramples on the feelings of the women he seduces; and, in spite of occasional generosity, he is selfishly egocentric to the point of monomania. Though in total conflict with society, Sebastian Dangerfield is too complex to be simply another social rebel rejecting society and its values. Though widely regarded by critics as an anti-hero in rebellion against the privileged world, Sebastian is seen by Donleavy himself "as a spiritual outsider who nonetheless, wants in, as a conformist and would-be member of the upper class, but who simply lacks the money."

Thus, Sebastian might aspire to become "Sebastian Bullion Dangerfield, Chairman of Quids, Inc., largest banking firm in the world," but he cannot make the compromises necessary to material success. Another character says to him, "you got to realize there's compromise wherever you go in this world," but Sebastian, even while he shows contempt for the "common people" who should be kept "back down where they belong," cannot take what he regards as his rightful place among the "professional classes" because "they want to make a mock of me and drive me out, rip my privates away and put them on a public pole with a sign, Dangerfield is dead." Like the America Donleavy describes, Sebastian Dangerfield is driven by such unsavory qualities as greed, lust, and envy, but unlike most others, he refuses to sacrifice his spirit to attain the material success he wants. For him, "life is a matter of resistance," not of the good things money might buy, or even of the values of the upper classes with which he identifies, but of the life-denying compromises which lie on the road to success. Thus, Sebastian is a rebel in spite of himself, contradicting even his own sincerest desires by alienating himself from the accommodations that might gain him the material comfort he craves. Trapped by his own uncompromising nature, Sebastian is a failed conformist rather than a romantic rebel, and there is more than a touch of pathos in the tension of his prayer, "And dear God / Give me strength / To put my shoulder / To the wheel / And push / Like the rest."

For the critical establishment as well as the young readers who lionized Donleavy, it was the unique presence of the rebellious Sebastian Dangerfield which distinguished *The Ginger Man*. Recalling retrospectively the impact of the work on his generation, Geoffrey Wolff writes that while the professors lectured on anti-heroes, "outside our reading lists we fetched up with the rogue of our dreams, the Ginger Man himself" who "made his presence felt . . . immediately and theatrically." For young American and British "beatnicks" studying in Paris at the end of the 1950s, *The Ginger Man* was required reading and smuggled copies of the Olympia Press edition established Dangerfield as a college hero well before the novel was in general circulation. While some critics debated whether Donleavy belonged with Britain's Angry Young Men, America's black humorists, or France's existentialists, others recognized with Granville Hicks that Dangerfield existed almost totally outside any system of ideas. He simply *is*, Hicks argues, and "Donleavy doesn't care in the least why Sebastian is what he is, what disorders in the world or, for that matter, what frustrations in the nursery may have shaped him. . . ." To an era characterized by J. D. Salinger's term phony, or by the prevailing image of conformist man in his gray flannel suit, Sebastian Dangerfield was a powerful antidote to our image of ourselves. "In the absence of faith," T. T. Curley said of *The Ginger Man,* "it requires courage to live without substitutes, without churlish hope or subservience to that most contemptible of tyrants, the Spirit of the Age." Sebastian Dangerfield symbolized that courage for a generation.

Along with the freshness of Sebastian Dangerfield, the most critically acclaimed aspect of *The Ginger Man* was its style. Somewhat reminiscent of Joyce's lyrical prose—though with less than his complexity of metaphor and grammar—Donleavy's style relies on rapidly moving, nearly staccato sentence fragments which capture brilliantly the chaotic and fragmented qualities of Dangerfield's world. Shifting rapidly from first-person stream of consciousness to objective third-person narration, this nervous flow of language seems almost to generate a schizophrenic tension in which Sebastian becomes simultaneously observer and observed, audience and spectacle, in a Kafkaesque world of meaningless confusion. Combined with a richness of poetic imagery that at its best rivals the finest Irish prose lyricism, Donleavy's unique and original style contributed measurably to comparisons of *The Ginger Man* to the works of Joyce, Cary, Miller, and Beckett and their comic traditions. It is particularly ironic that this style, so admired early because it seemed, as Donald Malcolm wrote, to "promise immense good things for the future," should degenerate to a mannerism which would as surely detract from Donleavy's reputation as it had initially contributed to it.

One of the most pervasive qualities that distinguished Donleavy's comic vision in *The Ginger Man,* and which would become increasingly evident in the later novels, is a melancholic tone which underlies the surface humor, frequently finding expression in the hero's preoccupation with the finality of death, the final absurdity in an absurd world. Charles G. Masinton comments that "one side of the private vision that Donleavy gives expression to in his fiction is . . . dark and melancholy, clouded over by an obsession with death and a preoccupation with sadness and loneliness. It is this aspect of his worldview that accounts for the growing somberness of his works, an almost palpable mood of dejection that after a time quite obscures the lighter, or comic, element that reflects the other side of his vision of life. . . . A spirit of vigor or confidence is lost after *The Ginger Man,* and a pervasive gloominess begins to settle over his works." Commenting on this same quality in relation to several of Donleavy's works, Thomas LeClair writes, "The novels range from variations of the humorous—slapstick, scatological, sardonic—to the sentimental in an idiosyncratic style that conveys the pressure of time on language. But such features of Donleavy's work are finally extensions of and returns to death, the test of man's mettle in landscapes made pale by death's presence."

Oddly, the critics and reviewers who regularly compare Donleavy to the comic tradition of Fielding, Sterne, Joyce, Miller, Cary, and others rarely take into account that Donleavy is a far more melancholic writer than these, who tend generally to affirm life in their works. While all these writers no doubt contributed to Donleavy's sense of style, his characteristic tone of pessimism, melancholia, alienation, and human failure is more likely to suggest Jonathan Swift's misanthropic humor than that of more optimistic comic spirits. Within the tradition of American humor (to which Donleavy is rarely compared beyond the general categorization of his novels among those of the black humorists), Mark Twain's later work, which like Donleavy's combines pessimism and humor in an elegiac, melancholic, and misanthropic voice, invites a comparison that has not yet been explored.

James Korges has suggested that Donleavy might be like Betty Smith who "often said she wished she had written her novels in reverse order, since the first one, *A Tree Grows in Brooklyn,* overshadowed everything else she wrote." The comparison is apt in that Donleavy is widely regarded as a one-book author whose claim to reputation rests entirely on his first novel. So far as most critics and reviewers are concerned, the later works have been but pale shadows of the first brilliant success, and the publication of each succeeding novel has seen a decline in critical attention. At the same time, however, Donleavy has cultivated a steady readership, reaching "best sellerdom" according to his publisher by "the cumulative route rather than by the big splash. Sales of *The Ginger Man* have not varied in twenty years, and each new work adds to sales and readership of the entire canon." Donleavy himself observes, "I've been saved from the syndrome of being a successful author. Nevertheless all my books have become bestsellers, in time. Although America is my smallest market, my largest group of fans certainly seems to be here, but I suspect that they buy my books elsewhere in the world." Out of favor with the literary and critical establishment since the appearance of his second novel, *A Singular Man* (1963), and never among the ranks of conventional best-selling authors, Donleavy has become somewhat of a cult writer. The unfortunate effect of the decline in reputation that followed *The Ginger Man* is that some of Donleavy's more substantial work has not been generally appreciated. Though none individually rivals the first masterpiece, several of these later works deserve wider attention than they have had from the American reading public and critical establishment alike. Along with *A Singular Man,* which attracted considerable but mixed notice, *The Beastly Beatitudes of Balthazar B* (1968), *A Fairy Tale of New York* (1973), and *The Destinies of Darcy Dancer, Gentleman* (1977) are Donleavy's best works, and most deserving of critical study.

A Singular Man seems to take as its point of departure a passage from *The Ginger Man* which both underscores the preoccupation with death in his first novel and points toward Donleavy's growing concern with that topic in subsequent works. Meditating on his own death, Sebastian Dangerfield would

> like to feel the end would be like closing leaves of honeysuckle, pressing out a last fragrance in the night but that only happens to holy men. Find them in the morning with a smile across the lips and bury them in plain boxes. But I want a rich tomb of Vermont marble in Woodlawn Cemetery, with automatic sprinkler and evergreens. If they get you in the medical school they hang you up by the ears. Never leave me unclaimed, I beg of you. Don't hang me up all swollen, knees pressing the red nates of others when they come in to see if I'm fat or lean and all of us stabbed to death on the Bowery. Kill you in the tenement streets and cover you in flowers and put in the juice. By God, . . . keep the juice away from me. Because I'm a mortician and too busy to die.

But, while Sebastian Dangerfield makes his life a resistance to death and rituals which would turn his existence into a life-in-death, George Smith, the title figure of *A Singular Man,* devotes his existence to the construction of a monumental mausoleum in the Renown Cemetery which "when finished will, it is rumored, be the largest of its kind anywhere and will contain every modern innovation including plumbing." For George Smith, life is more burden than adventure, and, when it seems too oppressive, he contemplates how pleasant it might be to "go to the mausoleum while still alive and live in it. Withstanding the regulations that say you must be dead." Though in love with the idea of death and building his tomb as a house of death, George, like Sebastian, implicitly recognizes that the living of life is a fit monument only for a holy man; others must provide more solid testaments to their existences. When almost shot by his secretary, George thinks, "if the bullet hit me I might be plopped into a plain pine coffin. Unclaimed. Lift on a barge. With hundreds of others. A number and body photographed on a slab. Don't want to go down that way dead. Like an amputated arm or leg. On an island in the river estuaries. With muskrats big as dogs."

Even less structured than *The Ginger Man, A Singular Man,* as Thomas LeClair suggests, "takes a protagonist very like Dangerfield into a paranoid separation from life and death symbolized by both his fixation on his mausoleum and the novel's title." Unlike Dangerfield, however, who meets the slings and arrows of outrageous fortune with courage, aggressiveness, and defiance, George Smith is more often the passive victim of forces over which he has no control than an active rebel like his predecessor. Several critics have suggested that George Smith is, in fact, the kind of figure Sebastian Dangerfield might have become had he realized his dreams of success and conformity, and that we ought to see him as representative of the plight of modern, urban man in American society. As Geoffrey Wolff in rather uncomplimentary terms summarizes this reading, "*A Singular Man* . . . shows such a wealthy man, powerful, lonely, and divorced from grubby enterprise, as Sebastian Dangerfield dreamt of becoming. Because his origins and intentions are banked in mystery, George Smith invites the suspicion that he is an allegorical figure, what the semiliterate like to call a 'modern Everyman.' " But in spite of Smith's generalized qualities—including his existence in a city only vaguely suggested as New York—and the surreal atmosphere in which he performs his comic role, this singular man is in his own way no less unique than the Ginger Man. Like Howard Hughes, who in some respects George Smith resembles, Donleavy's character is the creator of his own legend by the mystery in which he cloaks himself. Scarcely better known to the reader than to the fictional world he inhabits, Smith seems determined that only in death when he lies in his mausoleum will there be any certainty that he in fact existed.

What we do know about Smith is that he is immensely wealthy from some business enterprise which represents a rise from humble beginnings. He lives in a virtual fortress, rides about in an armored limousine, and goes to great lengths to protect his identity and affairs from the public eye. In the story, he engages in cryptic correspondence with mysteriously threatening "enemies" who are neither identified nor given motives for their harassment of George. Separated from wife and children, he engages in sexual relations with his ex-wife, his black maid, his secretary, a mysterious older friend identified as the Queen, and with Sally Tomson with whom he falls in love and then loses when she dies in an automobile accident. Haunted by a character named Bonniface—a double who might be a paranoid delusion of some aspect of himself that George Smith denies—Donleavy's protagonist lurches haphazardly through a series of misadventures which ultimately reveal the nightmare cityscape he inhabits to be little less than a jungle where violence threatens at every turn.

The world of *A Singular Man* is clearly irrational and chaotic, but it is unclear if it is meant as the paranoid response of one individual who experiences the world through his madness, or whether Donleavy means to represent modern America as an absurd horror to which the only rational response is that of the black humorist. Seen in this latter way, the novel may demonstrate Donleavy's comment that "fiction is probably a watered-down version of reality because reality is too strong for fiction. When reality has the mask of fiction it is more believable, and certainly if you can laugh at it, it's more acceptable." At any rate, the result in *A Singular Man* is a work which seems to hover somewhere between psychological fiction and absurdist fantasy, and which, as Charles G. Masinton points out, calls to mind the world of Franz Kafka.

As most reviewers of the novel recognized, Donleavy employs many of the same stylistic devices—shifting point-of-view, fragmentary sentences, flights of lyricism, and aphoristic little poems to end the chapters—that he had made familiar in *The Ginger Man*. This redundancy of style, along with a suspicion in some quarters that the obscurity of Donleavy's first two novels might mask an absence of meaning, led to serious reservations in the critical reception of *A Singular Man*. Granville Hicks, for example, had found *The Ginger Man* a "powerful and original" new novel but thought *A Singular Man* "a disappointment." Only slightly more generous in his response than Hicks, David Daiches found the work "amusing and intriguing," but complained that "it frustrates the reader at the same time as it amuses him. . . . The humor is altogether too irresponsible, so that it doesn't add up to anything in the end." Hilary Cooke conceded the second novel to be in some ways better than the first, but, like Daiches, he found fault with form and meaning in *A Singular Man*. Its style, he writes, "wearies"; "One starts to skim and then to skip."

These critical responses mark a turning point in Donleavy's career so far as public reception of his work is concerned. Hailed after his first work as a young novelist of great promise, he was after his second book a novelist already in decline. Finding *A Singular Man* flawed "to the point of unreadibility and a bit beyond," Nelson Algren thought Donleavy's failure symptomatic of a decline in modern culture itself. Further compounding the situation, Donleavy followed *A Singular Man* with perhaps his weakest work to date, the collection of stories and sketches entitled *Meet My Maker The Mad Molecule* (1964). Suggesting that Delacorte (Donleavy's publisher) was unwise to release the book, Richard Kostelanetz wrote that "to follow a bad book with a worse one can only confirm the critical judgment that Donleavy's talent is in decline." Pointing to the failure of *A Singular Man* and the weakness of Donleavy's dramatization (1959) of *The Ginger Man*, Kostelanetz is among the first to suggest that Donleavy may be "merely a one-book author." Whether or not these opinions are just, the critical reception of *A Singular Man* and *Meet My Maker The Mad Molecule* contributed strongly to the beginning of Donleavy's reputation as a cult writer, a stigma that continues to damage his reputation in established literary and academic circles.

The Saddest Summer of Samuel S (1966) (the alliteration is a mannerism popular in Donleavy's titles and character names, especially after *Meet My Maker The Mad Molecule*) departs in several respects from the examples of his first two novels, though he does continue here the characteristic stylistic devices of the earlier novels. Rather than the picaresque structure of *The Ginger Man* and *A Singular Man*, *The Saddest Summer of Samuel S* is entirely set in Vienna which provides a restraint against the antic motion that is characteristic of most of Donleavy's work. Unlike Dangerfield and Smith, both sexual athletes, Samuel S has retired from the pursuit of sex to become a celibate whose resistance to their advances frustrates the women in his life. Unlike his predecessors who resist domestic responsibility, Samuel S wants more than anything else to get married and have children. He despairs of doing so, however, because after five years in the hands of his analyst he is no nearer to breaking out of his isolation than when he started. "Five years ago he had a plan to straighten himself out and now these many thousands of dollars later he still went, clocking in twice a week to this small rotund doctor who sat askance in the shadows quietly listening and sometimes chuckling. And at long last he had an insight. That one grows older faster staying in the same place." Longing for a love he has never had and cannot find because in spite of his need he cannot give, Samuel S is the victim of a life that cannot be lived over and a destiny that cannot be changed. His summer, which should be his productive season, is barren—a meaningless life-in-death. His sadness is the outward expression of hopeless despair.

Like *The Ginger Man* and *A Singular Man, The Saddest Summer of Samuel S* is about a character preoccupied with death. But while Sebastian Dangerfield confronts life head-on in a madcap rush toward experience, and George Smith, even while obsessed with the death that awaits him, is at least a passive participant, Samuel S is almost totally withdrawn from life. Waiting to be "cured" so he can establish human contact, he recognizes that he is trapped in a life-in-death state of mind with neither belief nor passion to motivate him. "Pull in the outposts of life," he says, "the dreams, ambitions, the distant deals. So that some passing grabber, swishing his scimitar doesn't lop them off. End up just being alive, the only thing that matters at all. Feel the way carefully while there are still teeth in one's head. Beware reaching for that little flower, its stem earthed to a buried electric cable to send you flying clear across the grassy field." And finally even life no longer matters to Samuel as the novel ends with his vision of his own death—a dream untold to his doctor who has given up on him as a hopeless case. Imagining his last moments, Samuel searches for the dignity that had eluded him in life, but even in death human dignity is only a forlorn hope: "And then he was dying and you think that you don't want your friends to know you died screaming in pain but that you were brave, kept your mouth shut and said nothing at all."

Samuel's forlorn hope that he might find happiness with a wife and family relates him back to Sebastian Dangerfield and George Smith, both of whom also hoped to find meaning for their lives in the love of a woman. In *The Beastly Beatitudes of Balthazar B*, Donleavy further develops this theme, particularly exploring the tragedy of losing a loved woman, a motif he would return to again in *A Fairy Tale of New York*. In *The Ginger Man*, Sebastian recalls the funeral of his first love who "had driven her long Cadillac through the guard rails of a St. Louis bridge and her car shone like a clot of blood in the mud and murk of the Mississippi." In *A Singular Man*, Sally Tomson, who provided George Smith his only moments of happiness, was destined also to die in an automobile accident. Elizabeth Fitzdare, Balthazar B's beloved, dies a lingering death as a result of an accidental fall from her horse, and in *A Fairy Tale of New York* Cornelius Christian's wife dies a natural death on board a ship bound for New York, leaving her widowed husband "nothing but the pain of missing you." A strangely tragic motif for a writer characterized by his absurdist comedy, this theme of love and loss is central to much of Donleavy's work, and it introduces a thread of melodrama into the fabric of his novels.

Elegiac, melodramatic, and sentimental as well as bawdy and comic, *The Beastly Beatitudes of Balthazar B* does, in fact, resemble a Victorian novel in somewhat the same way as other Donleavy novels resemble the works of Fielding and Sterne. The plot traces the adventures of a young French nobleman, early orphaned, from childhood to middle age and explores along the way themes of change and loss, as the young man's innocence and hope give way to the bitter lessons of experience. As a child, Balthazar B reached from his crib in the solarium among the endlessly green plants and "touched where a chinaman fished forever in the river, to make him move. And he stayed the same. Like the cuddling kissing rocking arms I knew. Until the sweet nut flavor and milk white beauty of my mother's breasts were taken away. And I made my first frown." This early experience of loss and pain becomes a paradigm for Bathazar's life, as again and again he learns that life is change and change is loss.

This first awakening to the pain of loss is soon followed by the death of the boy's father which brings to an end the idyllic world of childhood. Soon sent away to school in England, he thinks "all wan smiles and waves. They push you away, and say goodyby.Then you are lonely and afraid with all the emptiness deeper and deeper everywhere." With that lonely note, Balthazar begins an endlessly unsuccessful search for someone who might fill "all the emptiness" of his life. At twelve, he is seduced by his beautiful governess, Bella, with whom he falls in love, but she is sent away when the affair is discovered by his mother. Later, while at the university in Dublin, he meets and loves Elizabeth Fitzdare only to have her reject him to spare his experiencing the agony of her slow death. Instead, he experiences the tragedy of that rejection as he repeatedly dreams that she "sat by moonlight on her little brother's tomb stone in a wedding dress. And I would climb the hill up from the lough and cross to her and try to take up the white splendid vision in my arms. And wake with tears." Balthazar eventually marries a loveless and frigid woman with whom he has a son, but he loses this child when the marriage comes apart, as he had earlier lost without even seeing him the son he fathered with Bella. The novel ends on a final note of loss as Balthazar crosses the channel "to bury a mother. And chase others gone goodby in my years. Calling after their names. Come back again." But these losses cannot be reclaimed as time cannot be turned back, and Balthazar ends "as all hearts are. Worried lonely. Your eyes quiet. By the waters cold. Where the sadness lurks so deep. It doth / Make you / Still."

This melodramatic plot could be the stuff of pure bathos, but the tone of the novel is regularly relieved by Donleavy's irrepressible spirit of comic absurdity and bawdy adventures, especially those involving Balthazar's friend (and double according to some critics) Beefy. Also, the writing in this novel is some of Donleavy's best, especially the convincing treatment of the adolescent's love for an older woman which is made very appealing. It is, however, the theme of change and loss which is at the heart of the novel, making it second only to *The Ginger Man* among Donleavy's works. Reviewers were virtually unanimous in their praise for the first time since Donleavy's first novel. Philip Toynbee wrote that Donleavy has "shown again that he is a splendid writer even if he has not yet managed to make himself into a great novelist." Highest praise came from Robert Scholes who called *The Beastly Beatitudes of Balthazar B* "a better book than *The Ginger Man*, richer in its moods and sympathies. Its prose honed to a fine edge of humor and tenderness that stops, as it should, just short of poetry." Commenting on the universality of Donleavy's theme, Scholes says the novel is about "separation. Not fashionable alienation, but plain old loneliness and loss," and, he concludes, "in laughing or weeping over this poor little rich boy we find ourselves denying Scott Fitzgerald's famous maxim about the very rich; for we laugh and weep not for Balthazar but for ourselves."

Donleavy, who may be, as Mark Twain was, his own worst critic, followed the success of *The Beastly Beatitudes of Balthazar B* with his least impressive novel to date, repeating in effect the error of following *A Singular Man* with *Meet My Maker The Mad Molecule*. In a review of *The Beastly Beatitudes of Balthazar B*, *Time* quoted Donleavy as guaranteeing that his next novel, *The Onion Eaters* (1971), would "be even more scandalous than *Balthazar B*." Unfortunately for Donleavy's critical reputation, most reviewers would seem not only to agree with this introduction to the new work, but also to argue that being scandalous may be the novel's only accomplishment. The surreal plot deals with Clayton Claw Cleaver Clementine, a young man who inherits both the three testicles characteristic of his male line and Charnal Castle, the Irish family manor, and who finds his domain invaded by a host of improbable guests who turn the castle into a madhouse of absurdist comic fantasy. Mad scientists, sexually overactive women, pretentious gentry, and even an invading army contribute to the general insanity which at novel's end leaves Charnal Castle in ruins and Clementine alone, broke, and uncertain of his future. In spite of some possibility that the work is meant to be a Kafkaesque allegory of modern life—Charles G. Masinton, for example, sees it as "vaguely symbolic: Charnal Castle . . . suggests a microcosm in which the insanities and obsessions of mankind destroy order, peace, and reason"—the work is unimpressive. The general critical reaction is summed up in the words of L. J. Davis who wrote that "the tone of the book is somewhere between unsuccessful comic surrealism and unsuccessful pornographic comedy; the funny parts are told all wrong and the dirty parts are nothing special. There is a lot of apparent symbolism, but none of it amounts to much." The book had its admirers, but one suspects they belong to the Donleavy cult.

Masinton suggests as a reason for the shortcoming of both *The Onion Eaters* and the novel which followed it, *A Fairy Tale of New York*, that Donleavy had "run out of ideas to begin another novel" after *The Beastly Beatitudes of Balthazar B* and was forced to refurbish old material to keep the books coming. *The Onion Eaters* was listed as a work-in-progress as early as 1964, while the material of *A Fairy Tale of New York* had already been used as a play and as a short story in *Meet My Maker The Mad Molecule*. Thus, in reworking or resurrecting earlier work, Donleavy offers up two novels inferior in style and content to those that both preceded and followed them. At any rate, neither of these works enhanced Donleavy's reputation, and they probably gave credence to the assessments of critics like Wolff, a disenchanted early admirer of Donleavy, who concluded that Donleavy is overrated by those who compare him to the great comic tradition: "he is not to be confused any longer with Sterne or Joyce or Beckett, those Irish talkers who have committed, as Donleavy has not, art."

Though not up to Donleavy's best, *A Fairy Tale of New York* has more to recommend it than its detractors willingly admit. For one thing, the focus on New York—much more graphically presented here than in *A Singular Man*—makes it the most personal of Donleavy's works since *The Ginger Man*. (Read in conjunction with his essay, "An Expatriate Looks at America," the novel's treatment of the violence, greed, and spiritual poverty of the city becomes a kind of gloss on the reasons Donleavy finds America an uninhabitable country.) Certainly in his reactions to the city, Cornelius Christian, the hero of *A Fairy Tale of New York*, is closer to his author than any other of Donleavy's characters. It is his creator's feelings as well as his own Cornelius dramatizes when, sickened by New York and despairing of ever saving the money to leave, he "finally saw a composed face on the subway train. And looked down at the lady's luggage. To get an address from where she came or where she was going. And it said Devon, England. And I nearly sobbed."

In his seventh novel, Donleavy returns to the familiar terrain of Ireland, but in this and his most recent work he seems to be casting about for a new direction after the relative failures of *The Onion Eaters* and *A Fairy Tale of New York*. Often compared to the picaresque tradition, *The Destinies of Darcy Dancer, Gentleman* resurrects that literary form almost intact to present an oddly anachronistic novel in which a contemporary story is told in a manner closely resembling Fielding's *Tom Jones*. Though he continues to use the shifting point of view, fragmentary sentences, and flights of lyricism that are the hallmarks of his style, Donleavy here combines them with the pell-mell adventures of a rogue hero who would have been quite at home in an earlier century. Darcy Dancer, though actually living in modern Europe, inhabits a world of country estates, fox hunting, family retainers, and leisured wealth in which Fielding's characters would have been quite at home. Such characters as the comic servants Crook and Sexton, Mr. Arland the tutor, the mischievous stableboy Foxy, and even Miss Von B, the seductive housekeeper who initiates the adolescent Darcy to sex, could all be stock characters from comic novels of the eighteenth-century English tradition. Likewise the plot, which follows Darcy through his adventures and misadventures and rising and falling fortune from birth, through his one day of formal education at boarding school, his term as an adolescent lord of a crumbling country manor, his disenfranchisement from the estate following which he becomes first a servant and then a confidence man briefly, until finally, in a nice parody of the self-made man, he becomes wealthy by a fortuitous wager on a horse descended from the noble stallion for which he was named. Along the way, a variety of subplots like that of Mr. Arland's tragic love affair with a lady appropriately named Clarissa, add to the antique quality of the novel. Though few critics noticed that *The Destinies of Darcy Dancer, Gentleman* was a new departure for Donleavy, the novel is quite different in some major ways from the earlier books, and, after the weakness of the previous two, represents something of a recovery of his powers.

Early on in *The Destinies of Darcy Dancer, Gentleman* Donleavy suggests a theme for this novel when Darcy, having broken his collarbone falling from bed, "was carried sobbing and trembling in my nurse's arms to her bedroom further down the hall to mend and convalesce. And learn to know that just as poison lurked in the beauteous soft tissue of yellow meadow flowers, so did pain and sorrow lie before all one's footsteps. And only / Some knowing / Loving hand / Could / Guide you / By." Though he repeatedly encounters the pain and sorrow the world offers, Darcy never finds any knowing, loving hand to guide him. Alone in a bleak and darkening world at the end of the novel, he recalls "Miss Von B said love was like catching a train, don't be late. And I was late. Late for her. Departed with all her little beauty into the life of another man." Noting from its title that this is a novel about destiny, we must recognize that Darcy was late for his only chance at love merely through the accident of birth. No knowing and loving hand shapes Darcy's end, but those accidental and coincidental events over which he has little or no control. As the novel closes, Donleavy develops an image of Darcy as the hunted, but momentarily safe, fox. Sooner or later, Donleavy seems to suggest, time will run out for Darcy and he will meet the destiny that finally awaits him.

With his most recent work, *Schultz* (1979), Donleavy continues his apparent pattern of following a relatively successful work with a weaker one. In terms of narrative style, *Schultz* is Donleavy's most conventional work as it minimizes the use of those stylistic devices he came to overuse in the earlier novels. At the same time, however, the work is generally tasteless, excessively obscene in its language, and far too reliant on slapstick bedroom scenes for comic effect. Based on the antics of a Jewish-American theatrical producer who is attempting to stage a tasteless farce in London's West End, the novel has been compared to a Buster Keaton film for its madcap comedy and slapstick situations. On his way to producing his play, Schultz is in and out of countless beds, gets blackmailed into marriage to a frigid bitch with a gross mother, spends a weekend doing all the wrong things at an English country estate, wrecks a society wedding and a diplomatic reception, and so on, but all to little purpose beyond the implicit humor in some of the scenes. Donleavy's indiscriminate satire manages along the way to insult the English, Jews, Africans, women, theatrical performers and owners, and anyone else represented in this menage of zany types. Venal, amoral, inconsiderate, cruel, and deceitful, Schultz is perhaps the ultimate survivor in Donleavy's novels, but his story makes a very poor case for survival. "Life at best is just a Jewish joke," Schultz believes, and that may be as close to meaning as Donleavy gets in this tedious novel.

It is too early to pronounce a final judgment on Donleavy's work or to place him securely in the contemporary tradition. At fifty-four years old, he already has produced an impressive array of works, including as well four plays based on the subject matter of various of the novels, several essays, and a parody etiquette book for the determined social climber called *The Unexpurgated Code* (1975). At the very least, he represents the example of a writer who goes very much his own way, eschewing both the popular success of the best-sellers and the literary acclaim of the academic establishment. At best, a case can be made for a few of his novels as primary expressions within the black humorist tradition of modern literature. Certainly he is a foremost American exponent of the Kafkaesque vision of the modern world, and his better works strongly express that sense of universal absurdity at which we can only laugh. If the sense of Donleavy's works can be summed up simply, his own comment in *The Unexpurgated Code* "upon encountering happiness" catches their essence: "Be wary at such times since most of life's blows fall then."

—*William E. Grant*

Plays:

The Ginger Man, London & Dublin, 1959; New York, 1963;

Fairy Tales of New York, Croydon, Surrey, England, 1960; London, 1961;

A Singular Man, Cambridge & London, 1964.

Periodical Publications:

"An Expatriate Looks at America," *Atlantic*, 238 (December 1976): 37-46;

"The Author and His Image," *Saturday Review*, 6 (20 January 1979): 44-46.

References:

Kenneth Alsop, *The Angry Decade: A Survey of the Cultural Revolt of the Nineteen-Fifties* (London: Owen, 1958);

Dean Cohen, "The Evolution of Donleavy's Fiction," *Critique: Studies in Modern Fiction*, 12 (1970): 95-109;

Robert A. Corrigan, "The Artist as Censor: J. P. Donleavy and *The Ginger Man*," *Midcontinent American Studies Journal*, 8 (Spring 1967): 60-72;

Grace Eckley, "Two Irish-American Novelists: J. P. Donleavy and Jimmy Breslin," *Illinois School Journal*, 55 (1975): 28-33;

Richard Gilman, *Common and Uncommon Masks: Writings on Theater—1961-1970* (New York: Random House, 1971);

Ihab Hassan, *Radical Innocence: Studies in the Contemporary American Novel* (Princeton, N.J.: Princeton University Press, 1961);

John Johnson, "Tears and Laughter: The Tragic Comic Novels of J. P. Donleavy," *Michigan Academician*, 9 (Summer 1976): 15-24;

Thomas LeClair, "A Case of Death: The Fiction of J. P. Donleavy," *Contemporary Literature*, 12 (Summer 1970): 329-344;

LeClair, "*The Onion Eaters* and the Rhetoric of Donleavy's Comedy," *Twentieth Century Literature*, 18 (July 1972): 167-174;

Charles G. Masinton, "Etiquette for Ginger Man: A Critical Assessment of Donleavy's *Unexpurgated Code*," *Midwest Quarterly*, 18 (January 1977): 210-215;

Masinton, *J. P. Donleavy: The Style of His Sadness* (Bowling Green, Ohio: Bowling Green University Popular Press, 1975);

John Rees Moore, "Hard Times and the Noble Savage: J. P. Donleavy's *A Singular Man*," in *The Sounder Few: Essays from the Hollins Critic*, ed. R. H. W. Dillard, George Garrett, and Moore (Athens: University of Georgia Press, 1971), pp. 3-17;

Moore, "J. P. Donleavy's Season of Discontent," *Critique: Studies in Modern Fiction*, 9 (1967): 95-99;

Donald E. Morse, "The Skull Beneath the Skin: J. P. Donleavy's *The Ginger Man*," *Michigan Academician*, 6 (Winter 1974): 273-280;

Norman Podhoretz, "The New Nihilism and the Novel," in his *Doings and Undoings* (New York: Farrar, Straus & Giroux, 1964), pp. 159-178;

Patrick W. Shaw, "The Satire of J. P. Donleavy's

Ginger Man," *Studies in Contemporary Satire*, 1 (1975): 9-16;

William David Sherman, "J. P. Donleavy: Anarchic Man as Dying Dionysian," *Twentieth Century Literature*, 13 (January 1968): 216-228;

Gerald Weales, "No Face and No Exit: The Fiction of James Purdy and J. P. Donleavy," in *Contemporary American Novelists*, ed. Harry T. Moore (Carbondale: Southern Illinois University Press, 1964), pp. 143-154.

WILLIAM EASTLAKE
(14 July 1917-)

BOOKS: *Go in Beauty* (New York: Harper, 1956; London: Secker & Warburg, 1957);

The Bronc People (New York: Harcourt, Brace, 1958; London: Deutsch, 1958);

Portrait of an Artist with Twenty-Six Horses (New York: Simon & Schuster, 1963; London: Joseph, 1965);

Castle Keep (New York: Simon & Schuster, 1965; London: Joseph, 1966);

The Bamboo Bed (New York: Simon & Schuster, 1969; London: Joseph, 1970);

A Child's Garden of Verses for the Revolution (New York: Grove, 1970);

Dancers in the Scalp House (New York: Viking, 1975);

The Long Naked Descent into Boston (New York: Viking, 1977).

William Derry Eastlake possesses a distinctive talent that allows him to combine luminous, lyrical description with satire in coruscating prose. The style of his early work is frequently compared to that of Hemingway, but Eastlake's scintillant art is unmistakably his own. While Eastlake has not been neglected by literary and academic circles, his work has received less critical attention than one would expect for a writer of such high literary caliber.

Eastlake was born in Brooklyn, New York, of English parents, Gordon Opie and Charlotte Derry Eastlake; he was reared in Caldwell, New Jersey. His upbringing was greatly affected by his mother's being committed to a mental institution when he was still an infant. When he attended the Bonnie Brae School in New Jersey, a boys' boarding school that incorporated farming chores into the curriculum, his early difficulties stemming from his "neurotic beginnings" increased. Eastlake recalls his "poor work at school when I bothered to show up, inability to cooperate with people, and a need to do something great that would attract attention to me." During the Depression he traveled widely throughout the United States and Mexico until he settled in Los Angeles where he worked at Stanley Rose's Bookshop, a popular gathering place for writers. There he met Martha Simpson whom he married 22 October 1943; they were divorced in 1971. He also became acquainted with such literary figures as Theodore Dreiser, Nathanael West, and Clifford Odets. The beginning of Eastlake's writing career was delayed by four years' service in the U.S. Army Infantry during World War II in which he was wounded at the Battle of the Bulge. After the war, Eastlake lived in Europe and attended the Alliance Française in Paris from 1948 to 1950. When he returned home, he deliberately established himself on an isolated New Mexico ranch located between the Navaho and Apache Reservations, not only because of the natural beauty of the area, but also because he saw the literary potential of the region and believed that the American West had been completely neglected by serious artists. From those surroundings, Eastlake created the fictional Checkerboard region used as the setting for four of his seven novels and populated it with a variety of pensive cowboys and philosophical, stoical Indians whose attitudes were largely unprecedented in American literature.

Eastlake's first novel was published when he was thirty-nine; during his relatively long apprenticeship he was aided by the comments on rejection slips sent by the editors of avant-garde publications whose judgment he valued and respected. His models were Conrad, Melville, Twain, Hemingway, and Faulkner, whom Eastlake had visited at his home in Oxford, Mississippi.

Although Eastlake is best known for his innovative southwestern novels, he has also written three war novels: *Castle Keep* (1965), based on his experiences in World War II; *The Bamboo Bed* (1969), a result of his more than a dozen reports from Vietnam which appeared in the *Nation*; and *The Long Naked Descent into Boston* (1977), a satire of the Revolutionary War.

He has published a multitude of short stories, beginning with "Ishimoto's Land" (1952), and a book of verse and essays, *A Child's Garden of Verses for the Revolution* (1970). In addition to numerous articles on war and on cowboys and Indians, including one for *Sports Illustrated* on an Indian rodeo, Eastlake has tried writing stage plays "to escape the discipline of the novel, but without success." He has served as writer in residence at Knox College, Galesburg, Illinois, 1967. He has been a lecturer at the University of New Mexico, Albuquerque, 1967-1968; the University of Southern California, Los Angeles, 1968-1969; and the University of Arizona, Tucson, 1969-1971.

His first novel, *Go in Beauty* (1956), is the story of Alexander Bowman, a writer who becomes an expatriate after he absconds with his brother George's wife, Perrette. Alexander eventually becomes a well-known author, but when he stops writing about his home, the Indian country of New Mexico, his books become less successful; he reacts by trying to create exciting experiences in real life to write about. Finally, he is killed with a machete by a crazed drunken Mexican boat captain.

Concurrent with Alexander's story is that of his brother George who remains wifeless in the Indian land that Alexander so aptly describes in his novels. Like his father and grandfather, George devotes his life to the Indians, looking out for their welfare and trying to protect them from the greed of outsiders and the insensitivity of the government.

The dramatic tension in the novel begins with Alexander's stealing his brother's wife, but that becomes, in itself, much less important than the fact that Alexander is slowly dying, as one character puts it, "not only literarily but literally too," because of his exile. Fifteen years elapse, and as time passes, both brothers become increasingly obsessed with their unnatural separation. The torture for Alexander is that he cannot go home and he cannot write successfully about anything but home. On the other hand, George has the added burden of the prophetic words that the medicine man had pronounced the day before Alexander and Perrette ran away: that something would be stolen and a drought would result until the item was returned. The fifteen-year drought ends when the Indians take Alexander's body, returned home for burial, off the train. In the mind of the medicine man, it was not the wife that was stolen, but the brother.

Eastlake effectively used the natural scenic beauty of the Southwest without allowing it to become obtrusive to the narrative. The Indian lore, beliefs, and customs are more predominant than the setting, but these are interwoven skillfully to create a believable and successful novel, effective on its myriad levels.

Eastlake's second novel, *The Bronc People* (1958), is *The Scarlet Letter* of Southwestern literature. Big Sant Bowman is branded with a flaming scar on his face when he attempts to rescue a neighboring black rancher from his burning home. The scar, however, is not a badge of courage, but one of shame and guilt for Bowman, who had been battling the Gran Negrito over water rights and inadvertently caused the fire. Two Indians calmly and objectively observe the fight and comment on the inconsistency of the whites who one moment try to kill a man and the next minute try to save him. The Indians, named My Prayer and President Taft, notice the Gran Negrito's son running from the burning cabin and capture him; they take the child to Albuquerque, where they leave him on the steps of an orphanage.

When the boy, Alistair Benjamin, finds his way back to the Checkerboard region he is adopted by Big Sant and his wife, Millicent, who have only one son, also named Sant. When Alistair, who seeks the truth of his roots throughout the novel, finally discovers that his father was killed by Big Sant, he seeks revenge by killing Big Sant's horse in a symbolic sacrifice. Ironically, it is Alistair who fulfills Big Sant's dream of attaining education and success in the outside world while Sant's own son achieves fame in the world of the bronc riders.

Time, especially as the Indians perceive it, is a prevailing theme in *The Bronc People*; it is an integral part of life and also of the land from an archaeological point of view. Traveling down an arroyo, the young boys descended through twenty million years of geological history, kicking up the dust of the strata and complaining of the twenty minutes it took them to pass the layers. Eastlake masterfully integrates themes, imagery, and plot in this novel that has become a minor classic.

Eastlake's third novel, *Portrait of an Artist with Twenty-Six Horses* (1963), is a series of episodes, some of which have been published as short stories, drawn together as the reminiscences of a man dying slowly in quicksand. Ring Bowman is a young white man who is experiencing negative feelings about going home to his father, the trader George Bowman. On the summer solstice his judgment falters, and he becomes entrapped in quicksand while his black horse, Luto, watches almost diabolically from the distant shade. The horse, a symbol of evil and fate, is finally struck by a rattlesnake and falls into the quicksand, allowing Ring to use its body as a means of escape. While Ring is slowly sinking in the death trap, in sight of the art work drawn on the Sleeping Child mesa by his best friend, Twenty-Six Horses, he reviews the major events of his life in the Checkerboard area of New Mexico.

As in Eastlake's earlier novels, the dominant theme is time, expressed in the dialogue, the Indian philosophy, and the primitive landscape. In the major incidents the theme of time merges with that of death, resurrection, and the place of art in man's existence. Eastlake builds effectively, through thematic repetition, the idea of death as both an illusion and a temporary state particularly to artists who continue to live through their works.

Although critical opinion has been generally favorable, some critics have objected to the episodic structure that Eastlake uses in *Portrait of an Artist with Twenty-Six Horses*. The most discernible connecting thread throughout the episodes is the consistent viewpoint of Ring's narrative. Toward the conclusion of the novel, Ring, whose name suggests the eternal circle of timelessness, indirectly comments upon the structure of the novel as he thinks out loud at the end of his ordeal: "Eight hours to relive one life. One life is composed of about ten separate incidents that you remember." And finally that thought, coupled with the strong thematic continuity, is what saves the novel from being simply a recapitulation of fragmented episodes.

Castle Keep represents a complete change in subject matter and setting from Eastlake's three previous novels. The story, based on Eastlake's experiences in World War II, takes place at a remote castle in France that is occupied by a small group of American soldiers; the inhabitants of the castle are an elderly Duke, his seventeen-year-old niece and wife, Thérèse. The Duke, who breeds horses as a hobby, is physically and metaphorically impotent but so desirous of an heir that he encourages Thérèse to fall in love with the leader of the Americans, Major Falconer.

Castle Keep is divided into chapters, each narrated by a major character, a device that reveals the characters' various viewpoints of events in the novel and exposes the varying degrees to which the war has affected their personalities. Gradually the castle develops as a symbol bearing a different meaning for each of the soldiers. When the battle intensifies, some of the soldiers doubt the very existence of the castle because it has come to represent a beauty and a civilization that they also doubt. Major Falconer finally convinces his men that the castle is within the heart so that each soldier decides for himself what the castle symbolizes and dies for that meaning.

Mainly through the obsessions of the Duke and Beckman, an art historian, Eastlake emphasizes the problems created by the priceless art treasures in the castle. The Duke is willing to compromise himself and to assist the Germans in destroying the Americans in order to save the art; Beckman, on the other hand, concedes that art is secondary to life and freedom. In two separate incidents, music and art draw the Germans and Americans at the castle together in a temporary peace. The answer, in the end, to the question of what happens to music and art in war is that they exist simultaneously although art must always be at the mercy of the power of war.

In 1969 *Castle Keep* was made into a major motion picture by Filmways which resulted in an increased popularity for the novel. The film, however, received mixed reviews. Eastlake was totally dissatisfied with the final movie script, saying that "they castrated the book." He had written the original screenplay, which, he said, "Columbia rejected as obscene." Despite this negative experience, which one suspects might be at the root of some of Eastlake's satiric depictions of Hollywood directors and public relations men, he believes that his other novels could be successful films. "The Hollywood crowd has improved a great deal since *Castle Keep*," he says.

The Bamboo Bed graphically presents Eastlake's historical, sociological, and philosophical views on the Vietnam war, which was still raging when the novel was published. "The Bamboo Bed" is the name of the search and rescue operation helicopter

Richard Byrd/Latent Image Gallery

William Eastlake

of cold morning sunrise; it is truly the ecstasy and somber fulfillment of the human spirit in watching the sun come down red red redding all in magnificent effulgent blaze from in back of the Sangre de Cristo mountains. The red snow-drenched mountains. The undiscovered country is the gamboling of the sheep. It is the myriad dancings of the yebechais of Blessing Way, of Healing Way. The undiscovered country is the crisp mornings and the piñon smoke and the brother sister and peoplehood of all Indians on a July day; it is all the sweetness of infant Navajo babes in cradle boards and the way a coyote looks at you when you talk at him. The undiscovered country is love and compassion and an inkling into the sufferings of others and the smack of lightning and the tintinnabulation of a small rain on the hogan roof, and the joy in the feeling for life. The undiscovered country is not the complications and dismay at life's problems but the ease and wonderment at life's mysteries. It is the only country that abides.

The red canoe continued up the blue and deep river, guided by the eagle -- the Indian's yonder star.

"Double Space," revised typescript

whose mission it is to remove the remains of A Alpha Company, which failed disastrously in an attempt to gain ground at Red Ridge Boy. The story is complicated by the issue of the missing Captain Clancy, a Custer figure. Clancy's childhood friend-turned-intelligence officer is sent to search for him and while doing so encounters a series of characters who expose their various moral interpretations of the war. These characters function as representatives of groups active in the United States during the war years: flower children, hawks, and conscientious objectors.

Eastlake's stylistic techniques in *The Bamboo Bed* are similar to those used in his earlier novels. He is successful in expressing the frustration of soldiers and civilians both in the war zone and at home through the constant obscenity in the dialogue which is itself a component of the major theme of pervading impotence.

Against the "symphony of mortars," Eastlake repeatedly juxtaposes an ominous jungle silence. This image gains significance with the rumor that Clancy and his men collect ears from the dead enemy. Interspersed throughout the novel is a religious theme that involves crucifixion, resurrection, and rebirth in the "communion of war" with an infinite variety of saviors, most explicitly the black Sargeant Pike and Clancy himself who is at least once referred to as Christ. The helicopter, which is a savior bringing alternately life and death, becomes a phoenix rising from the dead. Animal imagery dominates the novel, expressing the bestiality of man while anthropomorphizing the animals, particularly in an extended monologue by Clancy who addresses both a tiger and a cobra that are in positions to kill him at will.

In this complicated and troubling novel, Eastlake expounds his dissatisfaction not only with the Vietnam War, but also specifically with General Westmoreland, Secretary of Defense McNamara, and President Johnson, while exposing the psychological, moral, and physical problems of soldiers carrying both the burdens of war and jammed M-16 rifles.

The Bamboo Bed received a wide range of strong critical responses. The novel was dismissed by Guy Davenport in the *Hudson Review* as a "garishly colored comic book." But it was also praised by a *Harper's* reviewer as "a superb surrealistic novel" and by a *Time* critic as "a brilliantly grotesque fantasy."

Dancers in the Scalp House (1975), Eastlake's sixth novel, is comprised of a series of slapstick caricatures of whites in positions of authority. But underneath the humor is the Indians' pervading problem of the Atlas Dam which is designed to flood the Checkerboard region and will annihilate the wildlife as well as the Indians. A group of Indians resist under the leadership of Mary-Forge, an atypical teacher who appreciates the Indian culture and encourages radical action, which is all they believe the whites can comprehend. With the opening of the Atlas Dam looming in the background, the Indians still must cope with day-to-day harassment by the whites that runs the gamut from cattlemen shooting the eagles and coyotes to unscrupulous real estate agents selling Indian land as ranchettes.

Throughout these small battles the Indians manage to hold their own although the futility of it all is underscored by the impending flood from the dam. They feel both security and anxiety with the knowledge that the Indian, Tom Charlie, well educated in an American university, has prepared an atomic bomb with which to blow up the dam during its dedication ceremony. Finally, however, the Indians of Mary-Forge's unorthodox school dissuade Tom Charlie from detonating the bomb, and he subsequently commits suicide while the others pile into a canoe and drown together as they attempt to escape the rushing flood waters.

Eastlake effectively employs satire and broad humor to expose the plight of the Indian civilization that is becoming extinct as a result of the greed and shortsightedness of the United States government. In an interesting reversal of traditional roles, Eastlake endows the Indians with individuality, morals, and distinctive personality, while the whites are stereotyped, bestial characters totally devoid of respect for the environment.

The Long Naked Descent into Boston, Eastlake's latest novel, is a farcical history of the events that led up to the Revolutionary War. The setting is Boston, and the main characters are employees of the *New Boston Times* newspaper, who attempt to approach the political situation objectively. The simple plot consists of the adventures of these young journalists as they observe and record the behavior of both the British and the Patriots preparing for the battle of Breed's Hill. The vantage point of the journalists is improved by their use of the first hot-air balloon in the New World, although they are forced to burn their garments as fuel. Finally, as they descend naked into Boston, they are received as heroes who have brought together their countrymen through their defiance of the laws of gravity and the British. Eastlake is surprising and varied in his depiction of characters, historical and fictional, but overall they have little substance or depth. In fact, most of the characterization depends upon recognition of historically displaced figures or upon one-line jokes that are repeated throughout the novel. Moreover, Eastlake depends too heavily upon the inherent but evanescent humor of anachronisms in character and dialogue. A positive function of the anachronisms is to underscore the analogies of present history to past: the Revolutionary War compared to the Vietnam War and the balloon expedition to the moon mission. A noticeable structural weakness occurs late in the novel when Eastlake abruptly deviates from the fiction to include what appear to be excerpts from real historical sources such as letters or diaries of Revolutionary soldiers. The result is that instead of showing how dull history can be, Eastlake unfortunately points out how inappropriate his dialogue and characters are to their setting.

Currently Eastlake is working on "The Hanging at Prettyfields" which he describes as "a novel based on my miserable experience at a boys school in northern New Jersey." Prettyfields was introduced briefly in *The Bamboo Bed* as the school attended by Captain Clancy and his friend Mike.

Overall Eastlake's philosophical attitude toward his writing is reflected in his statement: "The task of a writer is to write well. This challenge is timeless and universal, and all other problems are pure rationalization. Writing is not a craft, it is an art. Consequently it cannot be taught. But it can be nurtured with wise counseling, which I got from a few women who were close to me. The techniques and values can be acquired at any library through the great masters who have achieved survival value. The great trap for the writer is the need for immediate applause—the dangerous influence of the latest best-seller soon to be forgot."

Eastlake is at his best, indeed he may be unsurpassed, when he writes of the Southwest: the beauty of the land and the strength, humor, and philosophy of its people. His articulate descriptions display not only the majesty of the land, but also a metaphysical significance that aesthetically unifies the land, nature, people, and time. Eastlake masterfully manipulates his plots, even in his less successful novels, to provoke interest through artistic tension. All seven of his novels have in common a thematic concern with man's relationship with his fellowman and nature, and raise the question of man's responsibility toward humanity and nature. He deals sensitively with the concept of time and the place of art and beauty, whether created by man or nature, in the overall scheme of man's existence.

—*Mary Ellen Brooks*

Periodical Publications:

"Ishimoto's Land," *Essai*, 1 (Summer 1952): 9-18;

"The Unhappy Hunting Grounds," *Hudson Review*, 9 (Summer 1956): 399-415;

"The Barfly and the Navajo," *Nation*, 189 (12 September 1959): 133;

"Three Heroes and a Clown," *Evergreen Review*, 3 (November-December 1959): 87-98;

"What Nice Hands Held," *Kenyon Review*, 22 (Spring 1960): 194-205;

"A Long Day Dying," *Virginia Quarterly*, 34 (Winter 1963): 64-80;

"The Night We Bombed Peking," *Nation*, 203 (4 July 1966): 8-11;

"Alone on an Elephant," *Nation*, 203 (22 August 1966): 155-156;

"Dragon Train to Singapore," *Nation*, 203 (26 September 1966): 283-284;

"To Die in Vietnam," *Nation*, 203 (24 October 1966): 418-419;

"The Biggest Thing Since Custer," *Atlantic Monthly*, 222 (September 1968): 92-97;

"The Message," *New Mexico Quarterly*, 37 (Winter 1968): 368-371;

"Whitey's on the Moon Now," *Nation*, 209 (15 September 1969): 238-239;

"Today is joy to their world," *Sports Illustrated*, 41 (23 September 1974): 32-34.

References:

Gerald Haslem, *William Eastlake* (Austin: Steck-Vaughn, 1970);

Delbert W. Wylder, "The Novels of William Eastlake," *New Mexico Quarterly*, 34 (Summer 1964): 188-203.

JESSE HILL FORD
(28 December 1928-)

BOOKS: *Mountains of Gilead* (Boston & Toronto: Little, Brown, 1961);

The Conversion of Buster Drumwright (Nashville: Vanderbilt University Press, 1964);

The Liberation of Lord Byron Jones (Boston & Toronto: Little, Brown, 1965; London: Bodley Head, 1966);

Fishes, Birds and Sons of Man (Boston & Toronto: Little, Brown, 1967; London: Bodley Head, 1968);

The Feast of Saint Barnabas (Boston & Toronto: Little, Brown, 1969; London: Bodley Head, 1969);

The Raider (Boston & Toronto: Little, Brown, 1975).

One of the more steadily productive of recent Southern fiction writers, Jesse Hill Ford has acquired a reputation for accomplishment in the craft of short fiction and a mixture of regard and notoriety for his best-known novel, *The Liberation of Lord Byron Jones* (1965). The fine early work, *Mountains of Gilead* (1961), and the distinct achievement of his latest novel, *The Raider* (1975), ought to ensure Ford a clearer standing than he has been accorded on the basis of the inadequate testimony offered by *The Liberation of Lord Byron Jones*. The body of Ford's work to date witnesses its author's attempt to understand what the South now is, in the light of what it once was and by continual reference to what it ought to be. His portrayal of the Southern soul comprehends an examination of what constitutes human excellence at any place and at any time.

Born in Alabama, raised in Nashville, and educated at Vanderbilt (B.A., 1951) and in Andrew Lytle's writing program at the University of Florida (M.A., 1955), Ford was a successful public relations director for the Tennessee Medical Association (1955-1956) and assistant for public relations for the American Medical Association (1956-1957). He has been awarded Guggenheim and Fulbright fellowships, studied at the University of Oslo (1961), and held a visiting professorship at the University of Rochester (1975). In addition to novel writing, he has worked briefly as a television script writer. He produced a script with Stirling Silliphant for the movie version of *The Liberation of Lord Byron Jones*. In 1971 Ford was acquitted of all charges in the rifle slaying of a black soldier whom Ford shot on the property of Ford's house in Humboldt, Tennessee, not long after the film version of *The Liberation of Lord Byron Jones* had played in Humboldt. In the trial Ford testified that resentment over his portrayal of characters who resembled locally known people gave rise to phone calls threatening his son. The *Memphis Commercial Appeal* reported Ford to have said that he shot into the man's car out of fear for his son.

Ford has produced a promising body of work, including four novels, a collection of short stories, and a play. He finds his subjects in the people and the region he knows at firsthand. All the stories are set in Tennessee at a time contemporary with Ford's own life or close enough to be known from the recollections of his parents and grandparents. Literary allusions are infrequent in his works, and the fiction succeeds without the self-conscious techniques which many current novelists impose upon their audiences. Ford appears intent upon proving the teaching of his master, Donald Davidson, who sought to impress upon a generation of young writers the wisdom of allowing their art to grow out of the communal experience of their people.

Fishes, Birds and Sons of Man, published in 1967, contains his earliest work; it collects nineteen short stories that are indicative of the range of his fiction. Three hunting tales—"The Savage Sound," the title piece, and the haunting death tale, "To the Open Water"—rank with the best recent work in this genre. "Winterkill," "The Britches Thief," "The Messenger," "How the Mountains Are," "Wild Honey," and "Act of Self-Defense" comprise a group distinguished by its subject—honor—and by a notable Anglo-Saxon reserve of understated emotion. "Look Down, Look Down," "The Rabbit," "The Bitter Bread," and, again, the title story, make up a marriage group. "The Cave," "The Cow," "A Strange Sky," and "The Trout" portray youth making the difficult transition from naivete to experience. "The Surest Thing in Show Business" and "Beyond the Sunset" revive the tall-tale tradition of old Southwest humor. Although the stories are all regional in setting, idiom, and characterization, they usually contain a moral realm which transcends narrowly localized concerns. Ford achieves universality by deploying finely tuned lyric passages that make the reader aware of a subtler intelligence standing behind the prosaic consciousness of the characters. Complementing his power for creating memorable language is Ford's grasp of moral constants. He puts his characters in situations where they must confront the perennial human problems such as divided loyalties, passions in conflict with self-respect, adult responsibilities, coming to honorable terms with women, with society, and with such natural limitations as aging and death.

In 1961 Ford followed his collection of short fiction with his first extended work, *Mountains of Gilead*. The novel continues the exploration of love entangled in dictates of honor, which had figured as one strand of the short stories, but the novel enlarges the scope of the shorter fiction by introducing a sense of history. Its central plot, which depicts a breach of faith avenged by murder, is enveloped by a chronicle of several families which portrays the characters partially as products of their familial past and partially as cut off from a tradition which might have sustained them in a better life. Gratt Shafer is Ford's contribution to twentieth-century fiction's roster of deracinated men. The young man impregnates Patsy Jo McCutcheon, his childhood sweetheart, induces the girl to have an abortion, then gives her up for a bland Memphis socialite. The jilted woman goads her father until he attempts to avenge the wrong by killing Shafer at his wedding, where, because of McCutcheon's ignorance in handling firearms, he inadvertently kills Shafer's bride.

The three central characters—Gratt, Patsy Jo, and her father, Tom McCutcheon—are all moral failures. Gratt Shafer is epitomized in Patsy Jo's comment that he is "an accident going somewhere to happen." Although he can remember a father who "had worked hard, and with all of himself," the young man lives his life randomly and lacks the sense of a purpose beyond himself, which alone would have enabled him to dedicate his will to work and a woman. The girl can see this flaw in her lover but is herself adrift and therefore cannot balance his weakness with a stabilizing strength. When she becomes aware of Gratt's indifference, she gives herself spitefully to a string of casual lovers while nursing a rage for vengeance which eventually provokes her father to his desperate attempt on Gratt's life. The father also suffers the consequences of his own vertiginous moral sense. Years before, his brief adulterous affair estranged his wife from him, whereupon, instead of acknowledging his own culpability, he blamed his wife for leaving him, neglected the upbringing of his daughter, and allowed himself to ease into a seedy senility. Nonetheless, Tom McCutcheon also possesses a memory of honorable conduct, and his struggle belatedly to square himself with the ideal he has betrayed makes him the most substantial character of the novel. Ford's best writing emerges in the lengthy retrospective upon McCutcheon family history that occupies Tom's mind as he sits waiting in the church for his chance to kill Shafer. He remembers the deathbed testament of his mother, who had charged him to "never humble yourself. Defend your honor and your name," and he thinks of the example set by his grandfather who, having shot a man to avenge his honor, never lost a night's sleep over it. McCutcheon's pathos lies in his own defection from the code of his fathers, a defection that undermines his right now to exact blood for a violation he himself has abetted. Still, a residual dignity attaches to his forlorn trust in the possibility of a world "where there was Honor, shining in a white, a brilliant light . . . Somewhere . . . And somewhere heroes."

Town and Country Studio

Jesse Hill Ford

After failing to kill Gratt Shafer, Tom McCutcheon turns his gun upon himself. His death makes him a scapegoat for his daughter and Shafer, who eventually reunite and produce a son out of their somber union. This resolution must answer the criticism that the education Ford provides for the rootless protagonist is bought at a price which exceeds the worth of the character. In defense it should be noted that the ending of the novel does not promise happiness from the marriage but only a beginning in a difficult process of moral reclamation. Shafer's willingness to undertake responsibilities is apparent in several moments of lucid self-assessment and is shown in his grief over the death of Bojack Markam, an aged family servant. He revisits the Indian mounds dear to his father, pays his respects to the deceased Bojack, and reestablishes his love for the surrounding land before announcing to his wife "I'm ready to go home."

Ford's stage play *The Conversion of Buster Drumwright* (1964) evolved from a television script written for the CBS Television Workshop. The play weds Bible-Belt fundamentalism with a fierce allegiance to kinsmen, redolent of Scandinavian saga, to produce a story of Christian piety overcoming the sanctions of blood. By posing as a preacher zealous to recover the soul of the hardened killer Drumwright, Ocie Hedgepath gains access to Drumwright's jail cell and plans to avenge his sister's murder by drowning Drumwright at his baptism. However, the scripture Ocie has read in preparing for his part works a conversion on his own soul and, as a result, at the decisive moment of immersion, he relents. As Ocie emerges from the jail triumphant yet somewhat bewildered over his turnabout, his enraged brother slays Ocie with a knife thrust. The strength of the playwright's invention overcomes the uncertain pacing at the beginning and moments of discursiveness throughout. Ford's story powerfully evokes a vivid sense of conflicting ethical codes; his characters stand unpropped; and his ability to modulate from scenes of tense gravity to moments of grotesque humor steers him safely past sententious moralizing.

The Liberation of Lord Byron Jones works a vein rather heavily exploited by recent writers, and, if some of Ford's characters consequently betray a thinness of conception which allows them to be too quickly perceived as the products of an increasingly standardized protest fiction, others give evidence of a mind which knows its subject intimately and can therefore envision their plight with freshness and unconventional specificity.

The subject invites sensationalistic treatment,

featuring, as it does, the obligatory array of mean-tempered segregationists engaged in violent oppression of long-suffering blacks who are provoked, finally, to bloody reaction. Three racial killings, several beatings, a rape, a suicide, and instances of police torture punctuate the main plot involving an adulterous alliance between a wealthy black undertaker's wife and a white policeman. The title character finds himself caught between an unfaithful wife intent upon profiting financially from his death and the town's legal authorities, who conspire or consent to his death from their fear of having the scandal of adultery and miscegenation exposed. Byron Jones's determination to secure a legal divorce sets in motion a sequence of injustices culminating in his murder at the hands of his wife's lover. With the murder as its focus, the novel develops a complicated indictment of both races' various evasions of responsibility, which set up the slaying.

Only the hard-pressed Jones succeeds in facing the moral challenge with dignity and honor. He attempts to salvage his marriage for as long as there seems hope of regaining his cynically promiscuous wife. He will forgive the adultery if she will promise to break off with her white lover, but, when she refuses his offer of reconciliation, Jones, knowing the danger he puts himself in, nevertheless insists upon the public divorce. His decision assumes its full moral weight as the natural outcome of his personal past. He has chosen to make his way in a compromising world by quietly observing the personal code of a gentleman. He thinks of death as the last of the series of ordeals which he must confront in order to liberate himself from a world that holds out assurances of security and comfort only if one is prepared to forego one's claim upon justice and honor. The fact that a brutal death is the condition for liberation substantiates the irony of the novel's title. Yet the biblical associations which Ford brings to his narration of the death scene suggest that Jones has gained a vision of moral independence superior to the awareness possessed by any of the other figures in the story.

Ford counterpoints the story of Jones's self-liberation with instances of dishonorable accommodation, moral obliquity, and ideological intransigence. He depicts a society in which the pressures for change exerted from the federal government and from homegrown liberals provoke an equally doctrinaire reaction in favor of the status quo from the townspeople who are so preoccupied with the impending threat to their way of life that they see Jones's case as part of the larger problem and lose sight of his rights as an individual.

The largest share of blame for the town's moral failure lies with Oman Hedgepath, the central character and the man placed in a position of critical moral authority. Not only does Hedgepath represent legal justice in his capacity as attorney, but he also enjoys, by virtue of his patrimony as the scion of a long-established family, a reputation for fair dealing which has earned him the trust of his white and black neighbors. Because Ford endows Hedgepath with a sense of principle, he figures as the only man from whom one might expect a firm stand on behalf of justice. He reluctantly yields to the pressure of his liberal nephew and accepts the black client, out of a feeling of regard for Jones's character. More than anyone else in the town, Hedgepath shares the ideals of honor and exacting decorum which Jones has attempted to uphold. For this reason his ultimate refusal to provide his client with the defense he deserves is more than dereliction in his duty as an officer of the court. By acting outside the law in the name of a "higher" justice, the attorney perverts the very standards which should have bound him to Jones, and in the cause of preserving the town, actually corrupts his community. By the end of the novel the most that can be said in his favor is that he acknowledges his pride: "At least I know that when I die I'm going to walk through that gate marked 'White Only,' be it fire or pearls." Although Ford does not encourage his audience to surmise an equal chance of pearls or flames, he does grant the self-corrupted Hedgepath sufficient stature to make his fall closer to tragedy than social caricature.

Critical reception of *The Liberation of Lord Byron Jones* was mixed and localized. Southern reviewers resented what they considered its tendentious and exaggerated portrayal of the region and pointed up artistic shortcomings. Northern reviewers professed themselves to have been instructed in truths about "the South" that presumably had hitherto eluded them. The novel received critical acclaim in Great Britain, Norway, Spain, France, and Japan.

The Liberation of Lord Byron Jones was followed by *The Feast of Saint Barnabas* (1969) and *The Raider* (1975). Taking its title from the Episcopal feastday celebrating the follower of Saint Paul, the earlier novel depicts a race riot in a city on Florida's west coast. Ford again employs the technique of dispersing the narration among several characters, but no single personage controls the action of *The Feast of Saint Barnabas* in the way Hedgepath pulled together the various threads of *The Liberation of Lord Byron Jones*. The story rises to moments of power, and the bizarre confusions of the riot allow Ford to exercise his particular talent for grotesque treatment of grim subjects. Yet because Ford finds no single character worthy of a sustained development, the final effect is diffuse and uneven. None of the contending centers of interest possess depth sufficient to capture more than momentarily the attention of the author.

The Raider is Ford's only historical novel and his most accomplished work to date. Set in West Tennessee and covering a span from early settlement through the Civil War, the novel evinces a firmer control of language, emotion, and pace than that of the two novels with contemporary settings. Given this distance from the present, Ford regains the talent for understatement which distinguishes his best fiction. He also creates a protagonist capable of controlling a considerable galaxy of interesting but clearly subordinate secondary figures. Elias McCutcheon, frontiersman, plantation owner, and cavalry leader, provides Ford with a hero in the vein of Odysseus. With similar intensity (yet innocent of the resentment, impiety, and ruthlessness of a Sutpen), Elias establishes a prosperous household in a plentiful but unindulgent land, defends his family against natural calamities and human marauders, reluctantly accedes to his neighbors' demand that he lead the local Confederate forces, loses his plantation house, his wife and a son in the war, and returns to live out his last years in the modest cabin he had built with his own hands. Ford's chronicle is unsentimentally elegiac. Despite a somewhat perfunctory denouement, the novel succeeds in portraying human beings whose worth is perceptible even in their moral transgressions. In Elias McCutcheon, Ford creates the rarity in modern fiction of an integral man capable of endurance without complaint and of effective action without rapacity. Elias answers Ford's quest for an image of conduct that incorporates old Germanic self-reliance, a classical sense of moral proportion, and Christian forebearance.

According to Ford, his legal debts and domestic troubles led him to Hollywood "sweat shops" and seven years of work as an anonymous rewriter of screenplays. A work in progress for G. P. Putnam's Sons is an as yet untitled novel set in Nashville during the Reconstruction. Except for *The Conversion of Buster Drumwright*, everything that Ford has written is now out of print in English, a distressing circumstance not only for the author but also for that part of the English-speaking world that could profit by sharing Ford's effort to recover his past.

—John Alvis

Screenplay:

The Liberation of Lord Byron Jones, by Ford and Stirling Silliphant, Columbia Pictures, 1969.

Periodical Publications:

"Whistlin' Dixie: The Southern Governors in Caucus," *Atlantic*, 218 (December 1966): 80-82;
"Collector," *Atlantic*, 221 (February 1968): 77-80;
"Doctor," *Atlantic*, 223 (January 1969): 86-88;
"Destruction," *Esquire*, 72 (July 1969): 96-98;
"Debt," *Atlantic*, 229 (June 1972): 68-72;
"Big Boy," *Atlantic*, 233 (January 1974): 66-70.

References:

Donald Davidson, Foreword to *The Conversion of Buster Drumwright*, pp. xv-xxiv;
Edith Schimmel Irwin, "The Revenge Motif in the Fiction of Jesse Hill Ford," Ph.D. dissertation, University of Alabama, 1974;
Madison Jones, Review of *The Liberation of Lord Byron Jones*, *Mississippi Quarterly*, 20 (Winter 1966-1967): 61-64;
Thomas H. Landess, "The Present Course of Southern Fiction: Everynegro and Other Alternatives," *Arlington Quarterly*, 1 (Winter 1967-1968): 61-69;
Jack Matthews, "What Are You Doing There? What Are You Doing Here? A View of the Jesse Hill Ford Case," *Georgia Review*, 26 (Summer 1972): 121-144;
Franklin D. Sexton, "Jesse Hill Ford: A Biographical and Critical Study," Ph.D. dissertation, University of Southern Mississippi, 1973;
Helen White, "Jesse Hill Ford: An Annotated Check List of His Published Works and of His Papers," *Mississippi Valley Conference Bulletin*, 7 (1974).

Papers:

A substantial collection of Ford's papers is in the care of the John Willard Brister Library at Memphis State University.

GAIL GODWIN

(18 June 1937-)

BOOKS: *The Perfectionists* (New York: Harper & Row, 1970; London: Cape, 1971);

Glass People (New York: Knopf, 1972);

The Odd Woman (New York: Knopf, 1974; London: Cape, 1975);

Dream Children (New York: Knopf, 1976; London: Gollancz, 1977);

Violet Clay (New York: Knopf, 1978; London: Gollancz, 1978).

Like many other women writers of the 1970s, Gail Godwin focuses sharply on the relationships of men and women who find their roles no longer clearly delineated by tradition and their freedom yet strange and not entirely comfortable. But unlike many other contemporary women writers, her themes outreach the general feminist preoccupation with What They Did To Us. She explores the complexity of relationships, the conflict and complicity of them. She is more appropriately placed with Jane Austen, George Eliot, and Edith Wharton (all of whom she admires) than with Doris Lessing or Joyce Carol Oates. She writes from the tradition of "the realistic novel which deals with people trying to understand their lives and live them fully," and she has written incisively of the relationship between the artist's life and her art, notably in her most recent novel *Violet Clay* (1978). Her development as a novelist can be viewed directly as a progression in understanding her own life and relationships and weaving them into increasingly masterful, matured novels. Anne Mickelson writes in *Reaching Out: Sensitivity and Order in Recent American Fiction by Women* (1979), "How to achieve freedom while in union with another person, and impose one's own order on life so as to find self-fulfillment, is the major theme that runs through Godwin's work. . . ."

Godwin was born in Birmingham, Alabama, and raised by her divorced mother Kathleen Godwin and her widowed grandmother. They lived near Asheville, North Carolina, and as well as teaching Romantic literature, Kathleen Godwin wrote love stories on weekends to support her family. Both these women influenced strongly Godwin's perception of woman's role: her mother was practical, energetic, ambitious, yet romantic; her grandmother was a Southern lady of traditional values. Later Godwin was to draw heavily on the figures of these two women, from her mother for the characters of Kate in *Glass People* (1972) and Kitty in *The Odd Woman* (1974), from her grandmother for Edith in *The Odd Woman*. The figures of her stepfather—her mother married Frank Cole when Godwin was eleven—and her real father, Mose Godwin, whom she first met at her high school graduation, also contributed to several of the male characters in her works: her stepfather to the stepfather Ray in *The Odd Woman* and the "villain stepfather" in "Some Side Effects of Time Travel" (a builder who destroys an old convent and rebuilds it to look like "a grasshopper about to jump"); and her real father to Uncle Ambrose in *Violet Clay*.

Godwin attended Peace Junior College in Raleigh, North Carolina, from 1955 to 1957. In 1959 she was graduated from the University of North Carolina with a B.A. in journalism and became a reporter for the *Miami Herald*. A year later she was reluctantly fired (her bureau chief wrote her, "I really feel badly that I have failed to make a good reporter out of obviously promising material"). In 1960 Godwin married *Herald* photographer Douglas Kennedy. After they divorced, she worked from 1962 to 1965 with the U.S. Travel Service at the American Embassy in London. There she met and married British psychotherapist Ian Marshall in 1965, and though the marriage ended a year later, she concludes, "this man who was impossible as my mate was the person who may well have made it possible for me to start being the writer I knew I could be." Her first novel, *The Perfectionists* (1970), was based largely on this marriage, "the figurative truths of that year, if not the literal."

From 1967 through 1971, she attended the University of Iowa and was an instructor of English there while earning her M.A. (1968) and Ph.D. (1971). In 1972-1973 she returned to teach on the faculty of the University of Iowa Writers Workshop. She has been awarded a grant from the National Endowment for the Arts (1974-1975) and a Guggenheim Fellowship (1975-1976) and has been a fellow of the Center for Advanced Studies, University of Illinois (1971-1972). She now lives in Woodstock, New York.

Godwin's first novel, *The Perfectionists*, won her early praise from writers Joyce Carol Oates ("a most intelligent and engrossing novel, and introduces a young writer of exciting talent"), John Fowles, and Kurt Vonnegut, Jr., ("a strong, darkly beautiful book"), as well as from critics. Robert Scholes called it "too good, too clever, and too finished a product to be patronized as a 'first novel.'" *The Perfectionists* examines the relationships between an American, Dane Empson, and her recent British husband John, a psychiatrist of sweeping visionary ideas, during a week's vacation on Majorca. Isolating her characters from their normal setting of London, Godwin highlights the emotional interactions between them, using flashbacks from Dane's past to reflect on present incidents and introducing minor characters as symbols and foils: John's fiercely aloof three-year-old son Robin, who accompanies them, personifies both the psychiatrist's emotional vulnerability and his intellectual remoteness; John's current patient Penelope, who also vacations with them, parallels Dane in her initial admiration for the doctor; and contrasting with Dane's cerebral and abstract relationship with John is the purely sexual, earthy marriage of Karl, a Nordic painter of nudes who sleeps with his models, and Polly, his alarmingly accommodating wife. The thematic conflict of the romantic ideal versus gut sensuality (Dane muses at one point, "She was glad that the wall hid his body. She liked his head best anyway. The rest of him gave her problems") also finds an equal and opposite conflict in Dane's drive to establish her own identity versus her need to lose herself in romantic union with her husband ("All she wished for now was to complete her self-abnegation to the will of this determined man"). These conflicts converge in the final scene, in which Dane symbolically breaches her husband's fortress of cool rationality by first spanking savagely, then kissing passionately his son Robin. But the resolution is only momentary—on the hotel balcony she watches her husband waving to her from a distant island to which he has been swimming, and she imagines his reaction to her account of the incident with his son. In her fantasied confrontation, he reasserts his intellectual superiority, and once again the "infernal balance" is established, here significantly not between her husband and herself, but between her image of her husband and her self. Just as Polly, earlier in the novel, had taken a perverse delight in photographing her husband unawares with his numerous lovers, Dane now conspires with her husband's superior image against her own self-acceptance and fulfillment. Godwin offers no solution at this point; she simply holds the mirror to modern woman: if not the self-abnegating wife and mother nor the vindictive bitch, then who?

Though *Library Journal* termed her second book, *Glass People,* "tense and witty . . . a minor literary feat," the novel seems more to have confirmed her talent than to have fulfilled the promise of her first novel. Though *Saturday Review* states, "The characters in *Glass People* are meticulously drawn and effectively realized, the facets of their personalities subtly, yet precisely laid bare," Sara Blackburn in the *New York Times Book Review* observes, "But the author, in not allowing Francesca even a glimmer of life beyond her victimhood, doesn't give us much to care about." In *Glass People,* Godwin explores a theme introduced in *The Perfectionists,* that of a resolution of woman's dilemma through complete self-abnegation; but the author, already suspicious of this alternative in her first novel, presents it here as neither fully convincing nor ironic.

Glass People is a kind of *aria da capo.* The first chapter, titled "The Bolts at Home," introduces Cameron and Francesca Bolt, the perfect couple: he the slim and elegant and formidably intelligent district attorney, she the dazzlingly beautiful wife. Unlike John Empson, the psychiatrist/husband of *The Perfectionists,* however, Cameron Bolt does not encourage his wife's personal growth and self-actualization; rather he works relentlessly toward crystallizing and preserving her beauty, adoring the image he makes of her and subverting her efforts to find herself. Francesca states, "I think there's a perfect me inside his head and I often catch him looking or listening to me and comparing me with her." Not wanting "a single sign of effort to leave its mark on that exquisite face," Cameron cleans their apartment meticulously, cooks gourmet snacks, and reduces Francesca's raison d'etre to occasional eyebrow tweezing. Stifled into acute and chronic apathy, Francesca travels east to visit her mother for diversion but finds her remarried and pregnant, living a back-to-basics life in a mountain cabin with a friendly, if somewhat doltish, health-food-store-manager-turned-farmer. Francesca's mother has found a "meaningful life" close to the earth, has been renewed as a woman (is pregnant), and keeps Francesca at a suspicious distance. On the first leg of her return flight to Los Angeles, Francesca has a two-night affair in New York City with Mike, a friendly man who encourages her struggle for independence. She stays in New York, realizes through her efforts to find a job that she is qualified to do little besides look beautiful, and finally takes a part-time position with an eccentric woman recently obsessed with anonymity and working on her magnum opus. The woman, M Evans, desperately needs someone to take charge of the business of her life, so for a while Francesca cleans house and cooks, buying soap and food for M with her own money. Francesca falls ill, however, and Cameron arrives to care for her. She explains that she wants to stay in New York, to be her own woman, and Cameron agrees, all the while planning for Francesca's homecoming. Before he leaves for Los Angeles, he takes her to Bergdorf's to buy her a

Gail Godwin

winter coat, convinces her to try on a Byzantine madonnaesque gown, and wins her back with the adoration in his eyes. She returns with him to Los Angeles, finds herself pregnant with Mike's child (Cameron is happy for her), and the novel ends as it began, with "The Bolts at Home," Francesca once more the dazzling wife and now soon-to-be mother, her life defined by her roles and insulated by her husband.

Marking a major advance in Godwin's development as a novelist, her third book, *The Odd Woman*, is twice as long as either of her previous novels, not from extension of plot but from a wealth of incidents told in flashback and in fantasy and a more thorough realization of present action. Lore Dickstein in the *New York Times Book Review* called it her "best and most ambitious book, . . . spanning several generations and a remarkable range of female characters, all successfully realized." Rather than a synoptic past, the characters in *The Odd Woman* have a history; rather than a rarified microcosm, they inhabit a world richly detailed and real. Rather than personifying the problems of modern woman in her characters, Godwin here creates an individual woman trying to live a life of integrity and order in a present world that offers no acceptable models from the past. Though notably devoid of any sympathetic male characters, the novel offers engrossing characterizations of several women, among them the heroine's mother Kitty and grandmother Edith, models of the romantic yet accommodating wife and of the Southern lady secure in tradition; her best friend Gerda, a militant feminist grown contemptuous of men; and her colleague Sonia Marks, who seems to have achieved both a successful marriage and a successful career.

Jane Clifford, the novel's consciousness and the odd woman of the title (*odd* meaning not paired), teaches Romantic poetry in a temporary position at a midwestern university and is having an affair with an art historian at a neighboring university. He is married, and she speculates what their relationship means to him and what future it can have, continually torn between the need to protect the freedom their love requires to remain romantic and mysterious and the need to establish some commitment within it. He is above reproach (his name, Gabriel Weeks, suggests an ineffectual angel, possessed of a God's-eye view, yet unable to act in the present); but Jane doubts that she can continue their affair as it is. With the death of her grandmother, Edith, she returns to her home in western North Carolina and begins an odyssey of self-examination and retrospection which leads her to seek some resolution of her relationship with Gabriel. They meet in New York City, where she realizes she can no longer accept their arrangement, and she leaves him, returning to her midwestern university town. As in *The Perfectionists*, Godwin here supplies no answer; but unlike her previous novels, *The Odd Woman* draws the reader intimately into the question.

Her collection of stories, *Dream Children*, which appeared in 1976, drew mixed reactions. The stories themselves vary widely in form and effectiveness. Though Katha Pollitt charges in *Saturday Review* that "some read like sketches for longer works and so seem to gallop across their 20 pages breathlessly, loose ends flying," she also points out that "the best have the sharp humor and sharp eye that marked her earlier work." The best indeed are gems: "False Lights" uses the epistolary form to exquisite ironic effect; "An Intermediate Stop" captures with precision and gentle humor the clash between divinely inspired vision and mundane reality; "The Woman Who Kept Her Poet," an account of the meeting, love, and marriage of a young girl of Amazonian proportions and an older poet, evokes a depth of sympathy impressive in a short story; and "Notes for a Story" scrutinizes the relationship between two women, friends since childhood—their ambitions, rivalry, struggles for identity, and continuing loyalty.

Godwin's most recent novel, *Violet Clay*, confirms her mastery of the full, free narrative technique of *The Odd Woman*—the integration of fantasy and flashback into the narrative line—while also recalling the clean, classic structure of her two earlier novels. In *Violet Clay* Godwin raises a question that is central to understanding her work as a whole: what is the relationship between the artist and her art? The answer implied in Violet Clay's achievement as a painter reflects directly Godwin's ideals as a writer. Violet Clay, when the novel begins, is an illustrator of Gothic romances for Harrow House, a publishing company in New York. She has "kept limber" for nine years by painting beautiful heroines running from dark mansions, a scene in itself symbolic of her stasis, but a series of crises forces (and allows) her to face her past and confront her future as an artist: her lover has recently left her; she is fired from Harrow House by an icy new art director bent on documenting terror rather than evoking intrigue (she will use photographs of women's faces screaming in real anguish); and her uncle Ambrose, the fatherly figure in her life and the author of one early successful novel about Violet's mother, commits suicide in a cabin in the Adirondacks. Violet travels to the mountains to Plommet Falls to settle his affairs, and through conversations with Ambrose's former wife Carol and with his landlady (a woman immersed in her own past and overshadowed by her late father), Violet attempts to gain more insight into her uncle's last effort to fulfill his promise as a writer. She decides to move into the cabin where he shot himself and there try to resolve her own similar struggle as a painter. Always aware of Ambrose's example of failure and depleted hopes, she paints with fervor and discipline for a while; and when her momentum stalls, she reenacts Ambrose's suicide with the fatal Luger, now de-pinned, invoking the thoughts he must have had. She is interrupted, though, by her neighbor, a strong, independent woman, whose ten-year-old daughter had found Ambrose dead. The woman, Sam (Samantha), resents vehemently this intrusion of the Clays' "sickness" and despair into her and her daughter's lives, but after Violet explains her purpose for moving into this cabin and for reenacting the suicide scene, the two women grow to appreciate each other and become friends. Violet's nude portrait of Sam that results from this friendship marks the beginning of her maturity as an artist. Her comment on the portrait, "what you see there is the last in a long line of frustrating attempts," echoes a statement of Picasso's she recalled at the outset of her stay in the cabin: "a good picture . . . is a sum of destructions." Either description applies to Godwin's achievement as a writer: her novels are the distillation of her life; and as her ability to weave her experience deftly into fiction has increased, so have the control, artistry, and impact of her novels.

Consistent throughout Godwin's writing is a concern with the relationship of life and art and the power of words to affect one's perception and consequently his actions. In *The Perfectionists* John Empson claims to have discovered "the basic pattern of human thought," which he describes as a snowflake with the abstract terms for human responses (joy, grief; praise, blame; love, hate) arranged in polarities around the circle. In the first paragraph of *The Odd Woman,* Jane Clifford asserts, "If you truly named something, you had that degree of control over it. Words could incite, soothe, destroy, exorcise, redeem. Putting a nebulous something into precise words often made it so—or not so. The right word or the wrong word could change a person's life, the course of the world. If you called things by their name, you had more control of your life, and she liked to be in control."

Godwin's concern with the power of words, their ability to shape feelings and experience and to give them form, parallels her concern with the patterns of relationships, the ways one tries to shape them into comprehensible forms. In all but her second novel she has progressively rejected the traditional patterns for women imposed by society—the expected modes of outward behavior—for the more organic, individual inner patterns that emerge only through self-examination and discovery. The end of *The Odd Woman,* though hardly optimistic, affirms Godwin's belief in the power of art to give shape to existence and reflects her own artistic ideal: "From the little concrete house behind came the barely audible tinkle of a soul at the piano, trying to organize the loneliness and the weather and the long night into something of abiding shape and beauty."

—*Carl Solana Weeks*

Periodical Publication:

"A Writing Woman," *Atlantic Monthly,* 244 (October 1979): 84-92.

References:

Lore Dickstein, *New York Times Book Review,* 20 October 1974, p. 4;

Susan E. Lorsche, "Gail Godwin's *The Odd Woman*: Literature and the Retreat from Life," *Critique,* 20 (Winter 1978): 21-32;

Anne Z. Mickelson, *Reaching Out: Sensitivity and Order in Recent American Fiction by Women* (Metuchen, N.J. & London: Scarecrow Press, 1979), pp. 68-86.

MARY GORDON

(8 December 1949-)

BOOK: *Final Payments* (New York: Random House, 1978; London: Hamilton, 1978).

In 1978, with the publication of her first novel *Final Payments,* Mary Gordon appeared on the literary scene, not as a promising apprentice but as an accomplished and mature writer deserving of the extraordinary amount of critical attention her work received. Prepublication remarks from such distinguished novelists as Mary McCarthy and Margaret Drabble brought the book to the immediate attention of several prominent critics, and when the book was published, the reviews indicated that the promise of the book was justified.

The author of this novel about a woman emerging from an intensely Catholic neighborhood in Queens, New York, after the death of her intensely Catholic father, comes from a background that is part Catholic, but also part Jewish and part midwestern. Her mother was a New York Catholic of Irish descent, but her father, who died when Gordon was eight, was a Jew from Ohio who converted to Catholicism in the 1930s. Nonetheless, the relationship between Gordon and her father was extremely close. Gordon's mother, in her daughter's words "full of courage, full of endurance," was struck with polio as a child and was crippled as a result. Yet, she was the one who worked and supported the family as a legal secretary. Gordon and her father stayed home together every day and Gordon remembers "the years with him with clarity and aliveness and luminosity." Her father brought his daughter up to be a lady and a scholar. "Fantastically literate," he knew seven languages; fantastically Catholic, he "wouldn't read much that was done after the Reformation."

After his death Gordon went through a furious time, angry that no one at the Holy Name of Mary School in Valley Stream, New York, where she attended grammar school, recognized her intelligence and spirit. High school at Mary Louis Academy was not much better, but in 1967 she received a scholarship to Barnard College of Columbia University. She was anxious to get out of the Catholic ghetto she felt herself stuck in, but there was opposition. Gordon reports that when she and a friend applied to Barnard, the principal of her high school refused to send their transcripts, so suspicious was she that girls who attended Columbia would lose their faith. Gordon's mother, however, approved of Barnard; and while there Gordon met the novelist Elizabeth Hardwick, a gifted teacher who later was to help her with some serious problems of narration in *Final Payments.* It is perhaps most important that Hardwick encouraged Gordon to try prose instead of poetry, a switch that was not made until Gordon attended the writing program at Syracuse University. Later Gordon would enroll as a graduate student in the English Ph.D. program at Syracuse, where she met James Brain, an Englishman whom she later married.

Gordon began *Final Payments* in 1975 while teaching freshman composition at Dutchess Community College in Poughkeepsie, New York. When several publishers rejected the completed novel, Elizabeth Hardwick recommended that Gordon try a shift of narration from third person to first person. This change and other changes took three months, and soon after Random House picked up the book. The critical and popular success of the book brought Gordon a $300,000 paperback contract with Ballantine Books. By the end of 1979, this paperback edition had sold 1.25 million copies. Gordon is currently working on a second novel.

Mary Gordon's favorite authors are Jane Austen, Charlotte Brontë, and Virginia Woolf, on whom she has completed much of a doctoral dissertation. Her interests, besides literature, are theology and musical comedy.

Final Payments is the story of Isabel Moore, a thirty-year-old woman who has spent eleven years of her life in a house in Queens, caring for her stroke-ridden father, a Catholic intellectual. The book begins with his funeral. Isabel does not cry for her father and soon sets out to find a new life. With the help of old parochial-school friends, she buys clothes, looks for a job, and begins to make a completely new sexual adjustment to the world of the late 1970s. After a humiliating affair with her best friend's husband, she finds a good man in Hugh Slade, a Protestant, a married man, and a country veterinarian. But guilt, church-related and father-related, builds throughout the book, and Isabel cracks. She forsakes all the new-found pleasures and moves upstate to a dank, sour world to give herself over to caring for a foul, stupid, malicious, unpitiable, and superficially religious old woman, Margaret Casey, the former housekeeper in her father's home. Isabel wants to love the unlovable, as her father seemed to love Margaret. Isabel accepts the spiteful treatment of this old woman but finally snaps back, gives Margaret the $20,000 remaining from the sale of the Moore house, and heads back to New York, to life, to friends.

Isabel Moore has held on to the guilt of her Catholic childhood, but she has been abandoned by, or rather has abandoned, the joy, the absolution, the "fire in the heart of God" her father knew until his death. Isabel Moore is a failed Catholic, but her failure is not a simple one. Her sense of the church and of God has fallen from the fiery vision to the smell of cheap soap and cabbage in the near medieval world of Upstate New York box factories. The great problem is that she hardly realizes that her faith has changed and thinks that in some oblique way she is doing her father's will.

Final Payments is about a perversion, first religious, but primarily secular, and it tells the story of a woman who serves such a stern Yahweh, half deity and half dad, that she denies herself until spiritual hunger becomes galloping neurosis. The habit of self-sacrifice for love becomes so great for Isabel Moore that, given the choice of a new, pleasurable life, she chooses self-sacrifice, even if no love at all accompanies it. Before the book is over, she gives up all care for her body and happiness and grows fat and fatter, and slovenly besides, until her friend Father Mulcahy reminds her not to break the fifth commandment—"Thou shalt not kill"—"It means slow death, too," he tells her. Isabel Moore's crisis is one many modern Catholics might share: the loss of everything but a feeling of guilt developed during a religious childhood.

Although much of the power of this book comes from the force with which the guilt overtakes the heroine, the guilt at the end sometimes seems excessive. Since Arthur Dimmesdale laid the lash to his body in *The Scarlet Letter,* few books have presented a more complete lust for self-punishment than *Final Payments.* In Hawthorne's novel, however, Dimmesdale's guilt is so well-defined that penance comes terribly specifically to the breast of the minister on the scaffold. The guilt in *Final Payments* is modern guilt, diffuse, sexual, social, historical, intellectual, and at the end, she literally pays for her guilt by giving Margaret money. *Final Payments* goes beyond the Catholic theme to treat the crisis of loss of belief in modern America. Things have died on us, things we loved and hated at the same time, and perhaps, like Isabel Moore, we do not weep. Nonetheless, we want them back, and *Final Payments* is the story of a woman's struggle with such a desire. It takes a long while, however, before she realizes this. At first the young woman emerges from an empty monastic house and heads straight for Bloomingdale's department store, a promised land on Lexington Avenue; then, dressed for the modern world, she finds a man. A new life seems easy at first, but it is not going to be easy.

Guilt hits and payments have to be made. After her final payment to Margaret, Isabel reenters the world, really entering it for the first time. But she has regressed so very far back to the world of a childhood she sought that old friends ask at the end, "Who did your hair? Annette Funicello?" This in 1978. Everyone laughs, but one realizes that "final" payments are just a beginning; certainly no easy end is in sight. The clue to what the life will be like, however, comes in the last line—"There was a great deal I wanted to say."

She will talk and talk some more, a rather mild and gradual venture into that world she had previously entered too quickly, disastrously, by the wrong roads. Talk, intelligence, analysis, discrimination are great catholic values throughout *Final Payments,* values which the heroine loses in her confusion of suffering with purification. With Margaret Casey she forgets the mind almost completely and only remembers the brutality of the body, the sin of the flesh and the mortification of the flesh. Heart and body sink to such a profound level of debasement in the sodden home of Margaret Casey, and Isabel only begins to come back when an offense against the mind is made. Isabel forces herself to turn an infinite number of swollen cheeks to her old housekeeper, until one day, when she is reading *Jane Eyre* to Margaret, the old woman asks her to stop—"All that stuff is old hat." "Who are you to criticize Charlotte Brontë?" Isabel asks, and rage lifts her up for the first time. The intelligence of Charlotte Brontë, like the intelligence of Jane Austen, which Gordon and Isabel Moore esteem so much, cannot be crushed as everything else can be crushed. Isabel bucks and soon will buck again when, in a moment of greater intelligence, she realizes the meaning of a rote phrase she learned in schoolgirl days—"The Poor you have always with you: but me you have not always." She realizes that Christ himself knew man needs to indulge his "extravagant affections."

Intelligence and wit are part of a final salvation in *Final Payments.* Isabel Moore is a modern woman and will not go back to the comfort of Holy Mother Church at the end. She will probably go back to a world where the pleasures of the heart and the body will play important parts; but throughout the book such pleasures are shown to be difficult, ephemeral, deep parts of life, but terribly unsure. It is an irony that the most grace in the book comes with the line about Annette Funicello—"The three of us laughed. It was a miracle to me, the solidity of that joke. Even the cutting edge of it was a miracle. And our laughter was solid. It stirred the air and hung above us like rings of bone that shivered in the cold, gradual morning." Mary Gordon is talking about the hardness of intelligence here, the intelligence of Jane Austen which sees with utter clarity and without sentimentalism, which lifts and sustains, which gets honed and gives strength. The world of the spirit and the flesh will probably be of secondary importance to Isabel Moore, secondary to a life of the mind she will share mostly with women.

But even the sense of intelligence in the book comes from Isabel's Catholic childhood and from her father. On the first page of the novel Joe Moore and the priests are described as arguing about the "precise nature of Transubstantiation" and the baptism of desire, laughing at what "non-Catholics thought that they argued about." The life of the mind, almost before the life of the heart and certainly before the life of the body or soul, was taught to Isabel in her childhood as the way to salvation. Margaret Casey would complain that Isabel does not pick up her room and "does *not* even give me the courtesy of looking up from her book even" when told to do so. Isabel's father would answer, "But Margaret, she can always get someone to pick up after her, but she can't have anyone else do her reading and thinking for her." Isabel's father always said "he was raising a Theresa of Avila, not a Thérèse of Lisieux: someone who would found orders and insult recalcitrant bishops, not someone who would submit to having dirty water thrown on her by her sisters and die a perfect death at twenty-four." When Isabel returns to the world at the end, it is from the world of Lisieux to a world where brilliant friends insult each other in an act of love. A strong and brittle intelligence for the modern world comes out of the Catholic childhood Isabel Moore leaves behind.

The critical reception of *Final Payments* was extremely positive, but Walter Sullivan felt that the passion "we are told about is never matched by either the thoughts and perceptions of the people or the thrust of the language." Perhaps this is true, for even some of Gordon's strongest admirers have admitted to feeling the immersion in guilt at the end as being overdone. The novel received perhaps most of its attention from critics who called it one of the best feminist novels in years. Although the energy of the Catholic theme is always present in the book, it is certain that some of the cleanest and most powerful moments come in scenes with women and with women alone. There is a growing feeling of escape or desire to escape from men in the novel, whether father, God, priest, lover, or cad. Yet as a "feminist" work the book falters, perhaps because the author's treatment of men does not display sufficient maturity, a sureness that is clearly there with the women she presents. Among critics who have examined Gordon's feminism, both David Lodge and Wilfrid Sheed have spoken of Gordon's difficulties in dealing with the depiction of men, young and old. It may in fact trouble some readers that one character who seems to be the author's spokeswoman speaks of the "loneliness that men never have," relegating them to a lower level of consciousness which seems to undermine them all in the book. Gordon has a much firmer hand with her women. The only man who is large, real, and fascinating is Isabel's father, and he is gone from the start. Part of his effectiveness, nonetheless, is that his absence creates something of a vacuum at the center of the book, a hollowness not unlike the hollowness after the loss of faith. Much of the book works toward filling that void.

The feminism at the very end, expressed in the sisterly reunion of Isabel Moore and her two dearest school friends, offers a bracing momentary energy, but one which can just begin to fill the great emptiness that has been building throughout the book. The power of father, God, and even lover has drawn away in *Final Payments*; and the reader feels something awfully big must be found to fill the void. The feminism at the end of the novel comes as a turn in the direction of optimism, but that optimism can hardly satisfy as a solid or developed reality.

—John Auchard

Periodical Publications:

"Now I Am Married," *Virginia Quarterly Review*, 51 (Summer 1975): 380-400;

"The Other Woman," *Redbook*, 147 (August 1976): 59-60;

"The Thorn," *Ms.*, 5 (January 1977): 66-68;

"Sisters," *Ladies Home Journal*, 94 (July 1977): 78-79;

"A Serious Person," *Redbook*, 149 (August 1977): 61-62;

"Kindness," *Mademoiselle*, 83 (October 1977): 224;

"The Writing Lesson," *Mademoiselle*, 84 (April 1978): 246;

"Delia," *Atlantic*, 241 (June 1978): 42-45;

"More Catholic than the Pope: Archbishop Lefebvre

and the Rome of the One True Church," *Harper's*, 257 (July 1978): 58-69.

References:

David Lodge, "The Arms of the Church," *Times Literary Supplement*, 1 September 1978, p. 965;

Wilfrid Sheed, "The Defector's Secrets," *New York Review of Books*, 25 (1 June 1978): 14-15;

Walter Sullivan, "Model Citizens and Marginal Cases: Heroes of the Day," *Sewanee Review*, 87 (Spring 1979): 337-344.

BEN GREER
(4 December 1948-)

BOOKS: *Slammer* (New York: Atheneum, 1975; London: Hale, 1977);
Halloween (New York: Macmillan, 1978).

With two serious, well-received, and distinctly different novels published before his thirtieth birthday, Ben Greer has already proved himself the exception to a number of cliches of our times, truisms so generally accepted that they have almost the force of guidelines if not law. At a time when serious fiction is in serious trouble and when it is probably more difficult for a beginning novelist to find a publisher than any time earlier in this century, Greer has simply written his novels and seen them published with reasonable promptness and in the sequence of his writing them. This latter fact is rarer than many critics and scholars of contemporary literature may realize. A surprising number of our newer writers have written several novels before one of them, usually the last one to be completed, was published. With some success and attention they can eventually see the earlier work published, in one form or another, but almost invariably in an order that bears little or no relation to the sequence of composition. Greer's publishing history is therefore at once unusual and old-fashioned. It is also unusual in that the two books published—*Slammer* (1975) and *Halloween* (1978)—are, at least outwardly, utterly different from each other not only in general subject matter, but in all the details of tone, style, voice, and technique. This sort of variety, introduced right at the outset of an author's career, is also unusual and old-fashioned in the contemporary literary scene. You have to go back half a century, to the generation of the American masters, the great novelists like Fitzgerald, Faulkner, Hemingway, and Dos Passos, to see writers trying out different ways and means, in published book form, in the way in which Greer has already demonstrated that his interests lie. Truly, the differences between *Slammer* and *Halloween* are as clear-cut and as startling as the differences between William Faulkner's first two novels—*Soldier's Pay* (1925) and *Mosquitoes* (1927). And, judging by the brief excerpt from a forthcoming novel, published in the October 1979 issue of *Sandlapper* magazine as "The Lie," his next work will, again, be sharply different from the first two, as different as was Faulkner's *Sartoris* (1929) from his first two novels. In a literary situation which is radically different, at least economically and socially, from that of the earlier years of this century in America, it is astonishing to see a young and beginning writer following the old ways and succeeding at it. Which is yet another unusual aspect of the career of Ben Greer—his relative success. At a time when very few first novels, indeed very few serious novels of any kind, sell more than a few thousand copies in the hardcover (and then only by dint of extensive publicity, promotion and advertising), Greer's *Slammer* (according to both his agent and publisher) sold an extraordinary number of copies in hardcover, something in excess of ten thousand copies. And at a time when very, very few first novels manage to have a second and different life in paperback edition, when, in fact, paperback publication has become severely limited, restricted to only the most popular work and only the most universally celebrated of the more serious fiction, Greer's *Slammer* was published in a mass-market paperback edition and evidently did quite well.

Greer's success with *Slammer* was achieved with a bare minimum of promotion and advertising, although the timely subject matter of that novel—life and death in a contemporary prison—together with his own experience and expertise as a former prison guard, made the book and its young author ideal subjects for the television talk show circuit and created, to the undisguised surprise of his publisher, a good deal of influential publicity for Greer and for *Slammer*. The book also received an unusually large number of favorable reviews, in and around New York and throughout the country. All this, together with other conventional pressures, might have pointed Greer toward the goal of producing more of the same—another novel on a timely and controversial subject straightforwardly developed. Instead, with *Halloween*, he invited the reader on an excursion into myth and the world of the "Southern gothic." *Halloween* was widely and respectfully

Mark Morrow

Ben Greer

reviewed all over the country, but not in and around New York. The emphasis on this last fact derives from the publishers' generally accepted rule of thumb that without prominent and favorable reviews in New York publications, a book, especially a serious novel, is almost certainly "dead," regardless of any and all attention it may have received elsewhere. And yet *Halloween*, like *Slammer* (only with even less advertising and promotion, and next to no publicity), sold in excess of ten thousand copies in hardcover. Some cynics have suggested that this success was an accident, based on the coincidence that a horror film with the same title appeared at about the same time the book did. (And, in fact, a few reviewers, who had not seen the film, seem to have assumed a relationship between the two.) But this suggestion ignores the fact that the American hardcover book public, small as it is, is not at all the same public which buys mass-market paperback "novelizations" of movies.

In short, then, Greer has broken most of the rules and proved himself an exception to others and has nevertheless succeeded, developing naturally and chronologically as an artist, with, at this stage, every evidence and indication pointing toward a significant and long-lived career as a serious novelist. On these grounds alone, not mentioning yet the genuine literary merit of his work, Greer deserves consideration among the important working American novelists.

Born in Spartanburg, South Carolina, Greer is the son of Margaret Phillips Greer and the late

Bernard Eugene Greer. (His father, a prominent television newsman in the Greenville-Spartanburg area, died mysteriously in 1968 under circumstances indicating that he may have been murdered by or for underworld figures he was investigating.) Young Greer attended Wade Hampton High School in Greenville and entered the University of South Carolina in 1967, graduating with a B.A. in 1971. While studying at South Carolina, he paid his way by working as a prison guard in the South Carolina Correctional Institution in Columbia. During his time at the university he studied writing with both James Dickey and George Garrett. Following graduation from South Carolina, Greer attended the small and highly regarded graduate program in creative writing at Hollins College in Virginia, and earned his M.A. degree in 1973. There he worked closely with the poet and novelist R. H. W. Dillard, William Jay Smith, and others. In the fall of 1973 he moved to York Harbor, Maine, where he lived with friends, worked on a fishing boat, and did some construction labor (digging foundations). It was during that winter that he completed a draft of *Slammer*, writing on a long zinc worktable in a wind-swept boathouse on the York River, sometimes writing with gloves on (Greer works first in longhand) when a smoking potbellied stove could not contend with subzero chill. While in Maine, Greer became friends with the distinguished novelist and poet, May Sarton, with fellow Southerner John Yount, and with the poet, Richard Pevear. By spring of 1974, *Slammer* had found a publisher, and Greer returned to South Carolina to finish revising the book. From 1973 to 1979, he held a number of odd jobs in South Carolina, in Savannah, and on Cape Cod while writing. In 1979 he joined the faculty of the University of South Carolina.

Greer is a devout Roman Catholic. At one time he believed his vocation to be the priesthood, and he often spends time in retreat, prayer, and meditation with the Trappist monks. He plays folk guitar, draws and paints with some skill, and is especially gifted at impersonation. Perhaps his outstanding example of the latter is a double impersonation—of James Dickey and Yevgeny Yevtushenko doing a joint poetry reading from the center of the basketball court in the South Carolina Coliseum. His acknowledged literary influences are various. He knows and greatly admires the poetry of James Dickey; he has studied the work of William Faulkner with care, especially concentrating on Faulkner's structural innovations and ways of scene-making; stylistically his impulses, which he holds tightly in check, are toward the lyricism of James Agee. Weightlifting is his sport, cooking is a passionate hobby, and fishing is a favorite outdoor pastime.

There are certainly autobiographical elements in *Slammer*, but it is interesting (and proves to be characteristic) that these are more or less equally distributed among the four principal characters in the story—Walsh, a young prison guard; Childs, a prisoner; Moultrie, a passionately committed black revolutionary; and Breen, a Catholic priest and chaplain at the prison. It is Walsh who spent some happy time on the Maine coast; but Moultrie learns to bake bread and loves it; the middle-aged Breen lifts weights; and Childs, a country boy, loved to fish when he was free. As Greer has managed to distribute (and thus to convert) aspects of himself among his chief characters, so he also manages, with maturity and a high degree of professionalism, to give each of these characters his due. With the exception of Father Breen, whose life is preserved by an accident and by a hair's breadth, all the principals come to bad or sorrowful ends as the prison erupts in a savage riot. All fail and fail others. Yet each is developed with a remarkable sympathy and understanding. Each has a past, each has a dimensional life. Ordinarily, one might honor the author for his objectivity in dealing fairly and dramatically with a variety of characters in conflict with one another. But here the depth of engagement is as much subjective as it is objective. Each of these characters is known, by thought and feeling, from the inside as well as by inference from outward and visible appearances and actions. If nothing at all were known of the author and all must be surmised from the context of this book, except for the authentic, documentary details of prison life, it would be almost impossible to guess the writer's age or color or background, let alone such complex realities as political and social affiliations and preferences. Moreover, Greer is able, whenever that proves necessary to the main line of his story, to give the same sympathetic depth to a minor character—Montana Red, a savagely depraved homosexual who lusts for Childs; Chief Freeman, who had been passed over for the job of warden; Father Michael White, the young assistant to Breen; Shebaar, the Muslim; and others. And there are mysterious characters, fished out of the depths of dreams, none more so or more memorable than Darcy, called "the Angel of Death," a black man who kills silently and efficiently (for hire) with an ice pick and is known only by "a strange dreadful odor" in the dark. All this is accomplished—a complex, panoramic plot, a large cast of characters including at least four created as major characters, a vivid re-creation of place and

Apparently Beal thought that if you kept at peace with yourself and working the positive energy levels and concentrated on good vibes all would go well. To Cody this was rather like keeping sober and using all of your strength to make sure the plane did not fall. There was no difference. But he had had only one drink though he was frightened by air pockets and lied and told Beal midway in the flight he thought he had made another step on a progression towards peace. Beal seemed flattered and very close to him because of this. Cody sensed very keenly now that he was winning Beal over.

Beal continued to explain though very carefully and not allowing too much recent information to pass who his Uncle was. Gladstone Burden was now seventy years old. He came from one of the wealthiest parts of the family which had made all of their money in the Civil war from horseshoes. His Uncle's grandfather had developed a kind of horseshoe PRESS and made them by the millions. He had then helped back a fellow named Henry Ford. Beal went through the financial part of the story quickly and not looking at Cody, thick conical white fingers going through his beard, these money cards being played tight to his chest. He loosened up some then and said that Uncle Gladstone was voted one of the ten most eligible bachelors in the U.S. by Harpers in 1927. He had explored almost the whole world by back packing and canoeing, written several books on the wilderness and archaeology. He had flown with Amelia Earhart and scaled peak 245 in the Himalayas with Lowell Thomas. He had walked part of the great March with Mao, tobogganed the Ingitok with Stalin and sucked the blood out of the arm of Jack London after having been rattler bit. In the last few years he had heavily bet on movies and now owned one of the largest companies. The company now had like almost every facet of the family business had been losing money for ten years. His newest film project had cost a great deal of money (Beal was careful not to say how much) and Beal believed it would work if he could control it, keep it from being cut up by the editors. If they could sell his Uncle they could have all of his company's assets behind them and the profits from the movie as well.

Beal told Cody to knock. They allowed Fanny to sleep. The knocker was warm in the California temperature. The heavy warm brass head of a gazelle. A small philippino came to the door. He had gray

totally reworked.

Kangaroo hyde SANDALS for Beal AS nice detail.

HO CHI MIN -- Burden met him in 1927 his SANDELS.

Cody wins Uncle over. He begins to conquer with his heart. At end Beal's Uncle says to call him "Uncle Gladdy."

Bessemer Company

On Isis went just before they go he gives Cody a manual on movies to read. Build! Build! How this excites Cody to FANTASY at the time.

-2-

Untitled manuscript

a sense of climate, weather, seasons—with amazing economy of means. *Slammer* is not much longer than the definitional minimum of sixty thousand words. And this is done without any slighting of the sensuous affective surface. All five senses, and particularly the sense of smell, which comes cumulatively to acquire symbolic weight, are fully alive from beginning to end. The lyric impulse in style is rigorously and appropriately suppressed—except where it can suddenly, and by sharp contrast with the primary texture of the story, make a point which could not otherwise be made evident. For example, early in the book, the rough and ready, often crude-spoken Father Breen imagines the child molesters who were once segregated from other prisoners in the very same space that is now his rectory. Of course, the passage has larger implications for the story, but, in abstraction, it serves to dramatize Breen's imaginative awareness of and compassion for the most hated of all the prisoners in the prison hierarchy, and to demonstrate an essential conflict of his character, the war between the tough-acting, tough-talking outward man and something else, close to a poet in sensitivity, within:

> Gray and ravening, they lay in their cells, hearts wild as rats, dreaming of dark things. One dreaming of some child he has watched at the seesaw all the long, hot day. Waiting in the dark stand of pines, weak from hunger, listening to the school bells, marking the time, listening to the last farewells as the child walks slowly toward the silent pines in wrinkled pants and shirttails. By the barefoot creek he binds the small hands. By the running water he does his dreadful work. . . .

That it is possible to imagine, as Breen does, such a human being with charity and pity and compassion, yet without an inhibiting loss of implacable morality, is one of the themes of *Slammer*, where men, already in extreme situations, are pushed to and beyond their limits.

Certainly *Halloween* also includes a sense of people in extreme situations pushed to unexpected limits. It has that much in common with *Slammer*, together with an even stricter economy. But there are sharp-edged differences from the first book. For one thing, the crisp, controlled style of *Slammer* was perfectly apt to its raw material, decorous in the eighteenth-century literary sense of the term. Here, however, the style is in conflict with the dreamlike, often surreal story, a story in which dreams and fact have equal weight and validity or are equally amorphous. *Halloween* is told as it is filtered through the perceptions of the central character who is ill and under the effects of Valium and antibiotics, as well as booze, throughout. There is a certain level of credibility for all the grotesque and exaggerated events and happenings of the long, demonic night. There is also a credible reason for the consciousness of the single central character, Blake Pasque, who has returned to his hometown (a dream version and vision of Savannah) on All Hallows Eve to save his mother from the clutches of their cruel, clever, game-playing theatrical family. Blake, in turn, is pursued by a psychopathic killer named Raphael who works best with a razor and with pictures from Gray's *Anatomy*. In an interview in *Sandlapper* magazine (February 1979), Greer described the essence of *Halloween* as follows:

> The book opens with a murderer who's psychotic and who tells the reader he plans to murder a family, and we go from there. The book takes place in twelve hours, starting from about six-thirty in the evening until about six-thirty the next morning, so it all takes place in the night. Essentially, it's about how a son rescues his mother emotionally and psychologically from the murderer and from the tyranny of their own family. At the same time, he incurs a great deal of damage himself.

Gothic then, Southern Gothic, though not treated that way in style and manner, *Halloween* was recognized as such by most of the reviewers. But most of them (often invoking the example of Poe) saw something else, something more than the chosen genre at work in the book. The review in the *Los Angeles Times* (31 December 1978) argued that the extra dimension Greer achieved in this novel was a subtle matter of mood. "What's truly fine in 'Halloween' is its lush and sinister mood," the reviewer wrote, "suggesting at times a Mardi Gras at which all the lights have been suddenly turned off. The decaying South theme is anything but new; still Greer wears the tradition well." Perhaps equally important with mood, indeed an important part in the creation of it, is *place*. The prison of *Slammer* offered a stark and fixed place which could only be relieved, for the prisoners as well as the reader, by memory and fantasy and by the passage of time measured by the changing seasons. Here, in the one-night time scheme of *Halloween*, place must be constantly developed and discovered and is even more important in the absence of the possibility of passing time. For example, here is a view of the black slums of the town as seen by Blake:

> Badly paved streets and long rows of airless, bleached-board hovels, the rusting tin of their roofs holding city heat and despair. The front yards of the houses were grassless, but by the streetlights you could see that the dirt had been carefully raked. A blue ceramic Madonna stood in one patch of earth, while before another dwelling tomato plants grew from cans painted blue and brown, yellow and white. This part of town had no oaks. No moss. No trees at all. Just sandy porches and grim steps and raked city earth with the heat of the day still there. On the corner, even though the air was still warm enough to make you sweat, a fire burned in an ashcan. Two or three old colored men sat on peach crates beside the fire, hats cocked over their eyes. When Blake said hello, they grinned and looked away.

In such descriptions as "the rusting tin of their roofs holding city heat and despair," Greer has developed his own kind of landscaping, much as Hemingway did within his own style years before. It works; it speaks to theme and subject.

Here, then, is a young and developing novelist, a serious novelist whose work, though not obscure, is not easy, a writer with two books published. These two books have each broken the contemporary rules and have succeeded beyond anyone's expectations. For his third novel, now nearly done, he has already received a very large advance from a new publisher (Delacorte). Not much is known about the new book at this writing, except that a major commercial publisher has deemed it worth a major advance investment. And the little glimpse seen in "The Lie" indicates only that it will be very different in setting, subject, and theme from the other two. It appears to be a story concerned with boats, sailing, and the lives and manners of the very rich in northeastern America today. Whatever else, it looks to be interesting, as young Greer himself, who has apparently not heard that the novel form is dead or in a rut, is unfailingly interesting in everything he writes. If he had not already achieved so much, he could be called a promising novelist. He is much more than that, but on the strength of what has been accomplished, there is great promise for the future. As the reviewer for the *Los Angeles Times* has said: "We'll be looking forward to Ben Greer books for a long time. The man can write."

—George Garrett

DAVIS GRUBB

(23 July 1919-24 July 1980)

BOOKS: *The Night of the Hunter* (New York: Harper, 1953; London: Hamilton, 1954);

A Dream of Kings (New York: Scribners, 1955);

The Watchman (New York: Scribners, 1961; London: Joseph, 1962);

The Voices of Glory (New York: Scribners, 1962; London: Joseph, 1963);

Twelve Tales of Suspense and the Supernatural (New York: Scribners, 1964); republished as *One Foot in the Grave: Twelve Tales of Suspense and the Supernatural* (London: Arrow, 1966);

A Tree Full of Stars (New York: Scribners, 1965);

Shadow of My Brother (New York: Holt, Rinehart & Winston, 1966; London: Hutchinson, 1966);

The Golden Sickle (New York: World, 1968);

Fools' Parade (New York: World, 1969; London: Hodder & Stoughton, 1971);

The Barefoot Man (New York: Simon & Schuster, 1971);

The Siege of 318: Thirteen Mystical Stories (Webster Springs, W. Va.: Back Fork Books, 1978).

Davis Alexander Grubb is a prolific writer and self-styled storyteller whose novels and tales have chronicled the people and events of the Ohio River Valley region of West Virginia, where he was born and raised. He is best known for his first published novel, *The Night of the Hunter* (1953), now considered a minor classic in modern American literature. In the works that followed, however, Grubb has continued to expand his panorama of this region. Given to the idea that "no one book should be like any of the others," he has experimented with a number of novelistic techniques and styles; and among his novels can be found examples of the historical romance, the mystery or detective story, the fantasy, the novel of social consciousness, the proletarian novel, and the tall tale. What has resulted is a large, often uneven body of work, which is nevertheless impressive in its scope, aspirations, and ultimate achievements.

Grubb was born in Moundsville, West Virginia, a small town on the Ohio River. He was the first child of Louis Delaplain and Eleanor Louise Alexander Grubb. His mother's family had lived in this section of West Virginia for over 200 years and had developed a strong heritage that Grubb would use in his writings; his great-grandmother's name Cresap, for example, would often appear in his work. Grubb himself was named for his mother's father, Captain William Davis Alexander, a steamboat pilot in the 1880s, and Grubb was raised on the lore of the river and its region. In his reminiscence of Moundsville, written for *Holiday* magazine in 1960, he explained, "In those years I remember it as a place of daily astonishment, entertainments, mysteries, myths, brags, facts and holy awe. Even the commonplaces of those times were days different as bright, colored beads, strung in endless novelty upon the cord of myth, hearthside hearsay and outrageous history. That cord, of course, was the great Ohio River. . . ."

Grubb's father was an architect who, according to Grubb, "first interested me in the use of the pencil—to draw and to write." By the age of five Grubb had decided to become a writer, and by eight he had composed and illustrated his first book for his family. His mother was a worker for the Department of Public Assistance and often brought home stories of the people and the poverty she had to deal with. If Grubb's father first interested him in the power of communication, his mother gave him many of the actual subjects he would write about. His father he remembers as a conservative, a man whose business slowly dwindled away during the Depression. His mother, however, he recalls as an iconoclast, a fighter for change and justice; and throughout the hard years of the Depression Grubb was raised in a house that "always took the side of the underdog." Grubb would return to these experiences many times, and the majority of his novels are set in the Depression era.

He was educated in the public schools of Moundsville and later of Clarksburg, West Virginia, where the family moved in 1938. In Clarksburg, he worked for a time at a local radio station, WBLK. In 1938-1939, thinking that he might be able to combine his interests in writing and drawing, he attended the Carnegie Institute of Technology in Pittsburgh, Pennsylvania, to study painting, but had to drop out because of color blindness. From this point on, he concentrated on becoming a professional writer.

In 1940, Grubb moved to New York City and worked as a page for NBC. By 1941 he had begun to write copy for radio, living on a salary of fifteen dollars a week (plus five dollars weekly from his mother), while he composed fiction in his spare time. During the next few years he worked as a radio announcer and copywriter in Florida and in Philadelphia, where he became employed by the Al Paul Lefton Advertising Agency.

Grubb sold his first story in 1944 to *Good Housekeeping* for $500, and for the next nine years he published widely in journals such as *Collier's*, *Ellery Queen's Mystery Magazine*, and *American Magazine*, usually signing his name as Dave or David Grubb. By 1950, finding the short-story market drying up, he turned to the novel. He wrote two unpublished novels, "Not in Our Stars" and "And Spring Came On Forever," before the success of *The Night of the Hunter* in 1953.

The Night of the Hunter tells the story of John and Pearl Harper, children whose father, Ben, distraught by the Depression, has robbed the bank in Cresap's Landing and killed two men in the process. Before he is captured, Ben hides the stolen money in Pearl's doll, swears the children to secrecy, and entrusts John with the responsibility for both the money and his sister. While awaiting execution, Ben has as cell mate Harry Powell, known as the Preacher, a psychopathic murderer who has been jailed for a minor crime. Powell is torn by the struggle of *Love*, which he has tattooed on the fingers of one hand, and *Hate*, which is inscribed on those of the other. After Ben is executed and the Preacher is released, he comes to Cresap's Landing, posing as the prison chaplain, and insinuates himself into the family in order to find the money. The novel then describes, in an often brilliant fashion, the encroaching evil that threatens the children and breaks up the family, an evil that John alone recognizes and fights.

The Night of the Hunter is a compelling book. Dreamlike, indeed, nightmarish at times, it often defies the strict bounds of reason and logic; it is closer to the world of tale and legend than that of reality. Grubb himself compares it to "a strange Appalachian song." The story is told largely from the viewpoint of John, and Grubb's depiction of a child asked to bear too much is skillful and convincing, although he is less successful with Pearl. Also, Grubb's tendency to rely too heavily on psychosexual explanations for his characters' actions, a problem that mars a number of his works, undercuts the mythic quality of the story. What remains with the reader is the sense of evil that Grubb conjures up, an evil embodied foremost in Harry Powell, but found in less obvious forms everywhere in the adult world of the novel.

Critical reception of the book was, in general, quite favorable. Reviewers were struck by the suspense Grubb managed to create and sustain, by the perversely fascinating figure of Powell, and by the freshness of Grubb's telling, the pure elements of "story" in the book. Some found the poetic language at times overwrought and were irritated by the less realistic sections; but, on the whole, Grubb was hailed as an original voice, a writer to be reckoned with.

For many, Grubb's second novel, *A Dream of Kings* (1955), failed to match the expectations set forth by *The Night of the Hunter*, although its reception was by no means negative. In this novel, Grubb undertook a historical romance, set near Elizabethtown, West Virginia (then Virginia), just before and during the Civil War. It is an ambitious work, recounting the love-hate affair that grows between Tom Christopher and Catherine Hornbrook, the orphan girl with whom Tom is raised. The novel describes their childhood together, as they are brought up by Tom's strict, confused, but well-meaning Aunt Sarah Christopher, and their entry into adolescence, when they slowly become aware of their sexual attractions toward each other. When they finally have sex, they do not understand what they have done. Tom, in a panic, thinks that he has killed Cathie, runs away, and eventually becomes a soldier for the Confederacy. After being wounded, he deserts, returns home to find Cathie still alive, and resumes his disturbed and ultimately tragic affair with her. Unlike the Harper children, Tom and Cathie are doomed by a world that offers no haven.

A Dream of Kings is a rich but often exasperating book. Although its story recalls such a work as *Wuthering Heights* (1847), its emotional power is diminished by lapses into melodrama, such as when Tom and Cathie single-handedly attack a flotilla of Union gunboats. When Grubb concentrates on establishing the background of the story and develops his cast of supporting characters, the novel is entertaining and, at times, even absorbing. But the central relationship between Tom and Cathie is often unbelievable. Cathie's childhood dreams of her father, who has gone south to establish a new "kingdom," become foolish, even mad, delusions when she becomes an adult, but her obsession is too outrageous to hold the reader's attention or sympathy for the length of the book. And Tom and Cathie's continuing ignorance of the basics of sex, although possible, becomes less plausible as the novel develops. Any man who had been through army life should know more than Tom does. Thus, *A Dream of Kings* is an appealing work, but one that ultimately fails on both romantic and realistic levels.

Between 1955 and 1961, Grubb worked at length on two books: *Shadow of My Brother*, which was not published until 1966, and *The Watchman* (1961). *The Watchman* is ostensibly a murder mystery, focused on the brutal killing of young Cole Blake in the town of Moundsville, West Virginia (Grubb's hometown). The prime suspect is Luther Alt, the chief lawman, the "watchman" of the town. Alt's almost fanatic possessiveness toward his daughter Jill, whom Cole was dating, leads to this suspicion. Alt's other daughter, Christi, who is as sexually free as her sister is reserved, apparently knows the truth of the crime; but it remains for Jason Hunnicutt, who is attracted to both sisters, finally to discover the murderer.

As a mystery story, *The Watchman* is not especially effective: what should be a shocking denouement comes as no surprise to the attentive reader. Also, in this novel Grubb indulges even more his tendency to manipulate plot and character in too obvious a manner. The first chapter is an extended sketch of grotesque graveyard humor, which introduces a variety of town "types" but adds little to the story's development. The ending is so bizarre as to be absurd, and there is a temptation to read the whole book as an example of very black humor. But it is clear that Grubb's main interest is less in plot than in the strength of evil it portrays. His epigraph—"For what is Hate but Love that has lost its way in the dark?"—points to his continued involvement with the complexities of love and hate, innocence and corruption, found in each of his previous works. The plot of *The Watchman* is secondary to the author's fear of and fascination with man's capacity to do wrong.

The Voices of Glory (1962) presents most clearly Grubb's concern with social injustice. His most ambitious work to that time, it describes the trial of Marcy Cresap, a nurse for the U. S. Public Health Service, who is accused by the medical establishment in Glory, West Virginia, of exceeding her professional qualifications in her attempts to supply free tuberculosis immunization to the poor of the town during the Depression. The trial itself makes up only the last chapter of the novel and is rather anticlimactic. Grubb concentrates instead on the people affected by this woman, allowing twenty-eight "voices"—of both the living and dead of the town—to tell their own stories. Grubb has acknowledged that Marcy Cresap is based in part on his own mother, and he has drawn on both family and lore in creating this story. But *The Voices of Glory* is an impressive work of the imagination as well, for Grubb creates a diverse group of characters and gives them detailed backgrounds to explain their involvement with the central figure. Critics were quick to compare the book to Sherwood Anderson's *Winesburg, Ohio* (1919) and Edgar Lee Masters's *Spoon River Anthology* (1915); the influence of these works in both content and technique is unmistakable. *The Voices of Glory* is overlong, the writing is often overblown, and the characters are sometimes too simply drawn, too easily identified as "good" or "evil." Still, Grubb does successfully establish a sense of town and community, and the book deserves more attention than it has received.

In 1964, a collection of Grubb's stories, written in the 1940s, was published under the title *Twelve Tales of Suspense and the Supernatural.* Of these, the best are "Nobody's Watching," a comic tale of revenge; "Wynken, Blynken, and Nod," a mystery with a nice twist at the end; and "Where the Woodbine Twineth," a fine, understated horror story.

This book was followed by a Christmas tale, *A Tree Full of Stars* (1965), which tells of a family whose Christmas tree takes root in their house after they give each other the gift of love on Christmas morning. Although it begins as a fantasy, the novel soon develops into a parable concerning man's need for love and understanding. Set during the Depression, the story describes the town's inability to accept a family which tries to celebrate Christmas all year. The tale ends with the family as wanderers in the dark world of the 1930s, penniless and yet still together. The tree remains and eventually becomes a symbol for the town, which learns too late what it has lost.

A Tree Full of Stars is, in effect, a variation on the story told in *The Voices of Glory*. However, there are simply too many plot lines for the small book; Grubb's symbolic devices, which should unify these threads, do not always work. The book, as a result, is an unsuccessful mixture of fantasy and reality; the charm of the central image is too quickly and irretrievably lost to the demands the parable places on it.

Shadow of My Brother, published nearly ten years after Grubb had begun work on it, is closely related in tone and style to *The Watchman.* A tale of racial hatred and murder, *Shadow of My Brother* is one of Grubb's bleakest works and also one of his most disappointing. Although located in modern-day Elizabethtown, the book has less sense of place than Grubb's other works. In it, George Purdy and his girl friend, Amy Wilson, accidentally witness the murder of a black man by three whites, one of whom is Amy's father, Loy, a leading political figure in the town. While the couple decides whether to remain quiet or to risk telling, Loy discovers that his crime is known and sets out to have George killed. Counterposed to this story, which is told in chapters entitled "Loy," is the story of Loy's background—his relationship with his sister, Nelly; their part-Negro companion, Toby; and their father, Isaiah—which is told in chapters identified by the father's name. Grubb apparently wanted these two stories, which contain parallel scenes and characters, to set up a certain resonance with each other, but such is rarely the case. Although there are powerful set pieces throughout, the writing is often uncontrolled and the characters stereotyped. Indeed, nowhere else does Grubb's tendency to strike his characters in one-dimensional poses hurt him so much as here. The critical reception generally acknowledged that while the values and beliefs expressed in the book were admirable, the novel was too melodramatic and contrived to be an effective statement.

With *The Golden Sickle* (1968), Grubb returned to the world of children and produced another good adventure, a mixture of *Treasure Island* and "The Gold-Bug." Set near Elizabethtown just after the American Revolution, it is the story of a young boy, Daniel Cresap, whose father, on his deathbed, sends him a complicated riddle by which to find a pirate treasure. Daniel is aided in his search by a blind orphan girl, Sally Cecil; a British ex-soldier, Major Henthorn; and the major's companion, a patriot named Wherry. Daniel is pursued by a vicious and malevolent dwarf known as Elisha, one of Grubb's nastiest villains; and the book contains enough mysterious characters, narrow escapes, severed heads, and grisly murders to entertain the young audience for whom it was intended.

Grubb's next book was *Fools' Parade* (1969), which critics have ranked with *The Night of the Hunter* as his most successful works. It follows the same general story line as *The Night of the Hunter* and *The Golden Sickle,* being, in effect, an extended chase in which the innocence of the main characters is challenged by those who represent unrelieved evil. Mattie Appleyard, after having served forty-seven years in Glory prison, is released with two other prisoners, Lee Cottrill, an inept robber, and Johnny Jesus, a boy who had been sent to prison unjustly. Appleyard has, during his forty-seven years, saved his small prison pay, which with interest now amounts to $25,452.32. It is 1935 when they are set free, and the local bank is unwilling to pay such money to a former convict. The banker, Homer Grindstaff, hires a local prison guard, Uncle Doc Council, and two professional gunmen, Steve Mystic and Alvin Kilfong, to kill Appleyard before he can cash his check, which can be done only in Glory. The story recounts the three ex-convicts' attempts to get Appleyard's money while they avoid the murderous trio in search of them.

What sets this tale apart are the main characters,

Mattie Appleyard and Doc Council. An old, one-eyed man, Appleyard is an expert with dynamite. Although he killed two men in his younger days (in self-defense), he is basically an innocent released into a world he has not seen in almost half a century; but he has native wit, charm, and courage to see him through. Council is clearly an embodiment of evil, but Grubb gives him enough idiosyncrasies to make him a real and threatening figure. Grubb breaks no new ground with *Fools' Parade,* but he does tell a heroic and satisfying tale.

Grubb's most recently published novel is *The Barefoot Man* (1971), again set in Glory during the Depression. It describes the fight between striking coal miners and the strikebreakers sent in to control them. Its protagonist is Jack Farjeon, a farmer who has lost his land and wanders, with his pregnant wife, into the middle of the strike. After his wife is killed in a fight between the miners and hired thugs, Farjeon swears revenge against the mine owners and sets out to kill the three men he feels are most responsible for his wife's death. While doing so, he falls in love with Jessie Dunne, the widow of a man killed at the same time as Farjeon's wife. The novel sets forth in detail the wretched life of the coal miner and the violence that was common on both sides during the coal strikes of the 1930s, although Grubb's sympathies are clearly with the miners. He creates in the character of Mother Dunne (Jessie's mother-in-law) his own version of Mother Jones, the almost legendary leader of the miners during these hard times. Despite the strength of Grubb's writing, there are distracting contrivances in the plot; and some critics, unfairly, found the book almost anachronistic in its emphasis on the coal wars. It remains another of Grubb's works that deserves reevaluation.

Grubb has published no novels since 1971, although he has continued to write. From 1973 to 1976, he lived in Louisiana, but he now lives in Clarksburg, West Virginia. He has recently finished two novels which await publication. The first, "Ancient Lights," he describes as a "comic fantasy" in the manner of G. K. Chesterton's *The Man Who Was Thursday.* The second, entitled "The Scallop Shell," is a novel of the Civil War. Grubb feels that he has never been understood by the critics because he has continued to experiment with each new work: "They seem to get very upset when you don't write the same thing. They say you have sold your talent." The fact is that many of Grubb's books do tell the same story, and all are hurt, to varying degrees, by his tendencies toward stereotypes and plot manipulation. But Grubb can be an eloquent writer, and his best works transcend the sometimes formulaic stories he imposes on them. And throughout them all can be found Grubb's basic theme, best expressed by Marcy Cresap in *The Voices of Glory*: "Where's the beginning to any life's true tale told truly?—and where's its end? *There's only the ebb and wane of things—comeback and loss—leavetaking and return—nothing lasts, yet everything endures. . . . And through the queer, imponderable riddle of that there run the threads of simple things we seem to see: life and death; love and hate; goodness and wrong. For those are woven together so alike that it's an impudence of us, in our piteous little wisdom, to call one from the other.*"

—*Edwin T. Arnold*

Periodical Publications:

FICTION:

"Checker-playing Fool," *Collier's,* 115 (23 June 1945): 26;

"The Gift," *Collier's,* 116 (11 August 1945): 20;

"A Pair of Spectacles," *Collier's,* 116 (15 September 1945): 15, 33-34;

"Beauty Treatment," *Collier's,* 116 (22 December 1945): 12, 41, 44;

"The Hero," *American Magazine,* 141 (January 1946): 36-37;

"Make Way for Uncle Freem!," *Collier's,* 117 (26 January 1946): 40, 54, 56;

"The Horsehair Trunk," *Collier's,* 117 (25 May 1946): 46, 81-82, 84;

"Banjo Twichell and the Democratic Dogs," *Collier's,* 118 (9 November 1946): 24, 56-58;

"A Child in the House," *American Magazine,* 143 (January 1947): 30-31;

"The Lollipop Tree," *Collier's,* 123 (23 April 1949): 15, 71, 74-75;

"The Rabbit Prince," *Woman's Home Companion,* 76 (June 1949): 22-23, 50, 53-54, 56;

"The Last Days of Poncho Pete," *Collier's,* 124 (15 October 1949): 24-25, 41, 44-45;

"Fifty of the Blue," *Collier's,* 124 (3 December 1949): 23;

"Count Heads in the Land," *Collier's,* 125 (27 May 1950): 32;

"The Return of Verge Likens," *Collier's,* 126 (15 July 1950): 22-23, 63;

"Buck Lindsay and the Woman Scorned," *Collier's,* 126 (11 November 1950): 22-23, 46-48;

"Gone From Glory," *Saturday Evening Post,* 235 (29 September 1962): 42, 44, 46;

"The Enchanted Room," *Good Housekeeping,* 156 (March 1963): 84-85, 181-182;

"A Tree Full of Stars," *Ladies Home Journal*, 82 (December 1965): 62-63, 118-119, 121-124.

NONFICTION:

"Valley of the Ohio," *Holiday*, 27 (July 1960): 56-57, 129-130, 132-133, 135-137.

References:

Don Crinklaw, Review of *A Tree Full of Stars*, *Commonweal*, 83 (4 February 1966): 539-540;

W. P. Fitzgerald, "The Great American Novel and *The Night of the Hunter*," *Bulletin of the West Virginia Association of College English Teachers*, 2 (1975): 18-31;

Anne Wood, comp., "New Creative Writers," *Library Journal*, 79 (15 February 1954): 373.

A. B. GUTHRIE, JR.

(13 January 1901-)

SELECTED BOOKS: *Murders at Moon Dance* (New York: Dutton, 1943);

The Big Sky (New York: Sloane, 1947; London: Boardman, 1947);

The Way West (New York: Sloane, 1949; London: Boardman, 1950);

These Thousand Hills (Boston: Houghton Mifflin, 1956; London: Hutchinson, 1957);

The Blue Hen's Chick (New York: McGraw-Hill, 1965);

Arfive (Boston: Houghton Mifflin, 1971; London: Eyre Methuen, 1972);

Wild Pitch (Boston: Houghton Mifflin, 1973).

Alfred Bertram Guthrie, Jr., is best known for his writing about the American West. His three most famous novels—sometimes referred to together as a trilogy—cover the eventful decades between 1830 and 1890, vividly depicting the lives of Americans involved in the settlement process over three generations. Guthrie's most notable achievement in these books is his demonstrated ability to assert the range, complexity, and intensity of his large subject—the colonization of the Missouri and Columbia drainage basins by real people.

Part of Guthrie's sense of the West as an actual, rather than a mythical, place may be traced to the fact that he grew up there. Born in Bedford, Indiana, during the winter of 1901, he was transplanted that spring to the village of Choteau, Montana, where his father had been hired as principal of the high school. In his autobiography, *The Blue Hen's Chick* (1965), he describes his Montana childhood as colorful, rigorous, and benign. His father's strict Methodism did not keep him from noticing that life in Choteau had an unruly side that expressed itself as drinking, gambling, and prostitution—and the fact that six of the eight children his mother bore in Montana died as infants showed him how hard the frontier could be on families. However, he learned early to love the land, with its changing moods. Perhaps most important, he developed a feel for its vast space, that quantity which informs even the titles of *The Big Sky* (1947), *The Way West* (1949), and *These Thousand Hills* (1956).

At the age of fourteen, Guthrie went to work part-time in the office of the *Choteau Acantha*, a weekly newspaper. The skills he acquired during the four years he held this job served him well during the twenty years he later spent as a journalist and editor in Kentucky. They also doubtless contributed to the insider's sense of community affairs he used subtly but effectively in his fiction. While none of his novels is "journalistic," all of them treat with confidence the details of interrelationships among people in groups—whether such groups are temporary communities of families on their way to Oregon, as in *The Way West*, or permanent towns, as in *These Thousand Hills* and *Arfive* (1971).

In 1919, eighteen-year-old Guthrie went to Seattle to attend the University of Washington but returned the following year to continue his education at the University of Montana in Missoula. In 1923, he completed his journalism degree and left again to find a job. First, he and a friend drove to Mexico, where they worked briefly harvesting rice. Then they made their way to California, where Guthrie worked on an assembly line and in a grocery store. In the fall of 1924, he gratefully came back to Montana to become a census taker for the U.S. Forest Service. However, the Forest Service job ended when the census was completed, and Guthrie soon left home for a third time, first to become a salesman for a feed company owned by relatives in Attica, New York, and then to accept his first newspaper job since his apprenticeship on the *Choteau Acantha*. Although his career on the staff of the *Lexington* (Kentucky) *Leader* spanned twenty years and saw his rise from cub reporter to executive editor, it did not diminish his strong and complicated attachment to the region where he had grown up. Indeed, it culminated in the publication of his first major novel, *The Big Sky*, which tells the story of a young Kentuckian's powerful experience of the Rocky Mountain frontier. The value the Montana foothill country of his youth had for Guthrie's imagination was not diminished by time or distance.

Guthrie joined the staff of the *Lexington Leader* in 1926, when he was twenty-five years old. Five years later he marred Harriet Larson, a childhood sweetheart from Choteau. In 1936, he began his first book – a western published as *Murders at Moon Dance* in 1943, the same year he contracted encephalitis and was forced to return to Montana for convalescence. He there began to formulate his plan for *The Big Sky*, which he soon began to write back in Lexington. In the fall of 1944, he left with his wife and two children for Cambridge, where he spent a valuable year of study and writing at Harvard as a Nieman fellow.

The Nieman fellowship program, begun in 1938, provided generous stipends for newsmen from around the country to attend classes at Harvard and take advantage of the university's cultural and intellectual opportunities. During his fellowship year Guthrie became acquainted with Bernard DeVoto, with whom he later traveled the length of the Missouri River, and profited greatly from the advice of Theodore Morrison, to whom he later dedicated *These Thousand Hills*. When he returned to Kentucky and the *Leader* in 1945, *The Big Sky*, nearly completed had been accepted for publication.

The Big Sky enjoyed instant popularity when it appeared in 1947. William Sloan Associates, the book's publishers, pressed Guthrie to write another novel, which he did in six months of intense effort. This sequel to *The Big Sky* was published in 1949 as *The Way West* and won a Pulitzer Prize in 1950. After a brief stint in Hollywood, where he wrote the film script for Jack Schaeffer's novel, *Shane*, in 1951, Guthrie moved permanently back to Montana, where he has written *These Thousand Hills*, *The Blue Hen's Chick*, *Arfive*, and *Wild Pitch* (1973), as well as a number of articles, short stories, and poems.

Although Guthrie deserves his reputation as a writer about the American West, his work has much more than regional interest, and its themes transcend regionalism. Unlike most writers about the West, Guthrie has concentrated on the domestic, familial, and political dimensions of the region's history, rather than the heroic dimension of its myth. This is a very important distinction. It means that Guthrie's heroes are all, finally, collective rather than individual, and that the huge backdrop of prairies and mountains against which they are placed serves not to magnify them into gigantic figures like James Fenimore Cooper's Natty Bumppo or Owen Wister's Virginian, but to be used by them in discovering themselves in weakness, strength, and human vulnerability. Neither do these heroes vanish into the blankness of a territory like that fashioned by Mark Twain for the permanently adolescent Huckleberry Finn. The great valleys where Guthrie's novels are set contain trails, sweethearts, homesites, and villages. The collective focus of the novels is not conquest, and it is not escape: it is settlement.

The Big Sky addresses an early phase of the settlement process, beginning in 1830 when seventeen-year-old Boone Caudill runs away from his home in Kentucky and ending in 1843 when he returns. During the twelves of his absence, Boone traverses the Missouri River from its confluence with the Mississippi at St. Louis to its headwaters in the foothills of the Rockies. His colorful adventures as fur trapper, trader, explorer, and guide are themselves arresting and engaging, but ultimately serve to state the novel's larger and deeper design – a compelling study of displacement, orphanhood, and loss.

When Boone takes leave of his mother and his brother in 1830 to escape the restrictions imposed upon him by his father, a former Indian fighter, he mistakenly believes he has killed his father by braining him with a piece of firewood. On his way to St. Louis, he encounters Jim Deakins, a restless, red-haired youth who has been hired to haul the corpse of an old man to Louisville for burial. Significantly, the old man has been a father with "chirren beyond countin" (sixteen), gotten by him with five wives four of whom are dead. Guthrie thus establishes at the outset the domestic emphasis that dominates the whole novel, deftly highlighting the urgent motive that propels Boone in his wanderings up and down the great river. The big sky that arches over the wilderness where Boon will himself become a father is neither a void nor a blank. It is a distinctly human space. All of Boone's ensuing attempts to escape from the obligations of family life only cement family ties he does not understand and therefore proves ultimately unable to accept. The freedom Boone thinks the frontier promises remains illusory. This is shown when the family group Boone sought to leave behind at the outset begins almost immediately to be reconstituted in different terms but with the same roles – a brotherly Jim Deakins hauling the corpse of a departed father to the grave. When Boon and Jim embark from St. Louis aboard a keelboat bound up the Missouri to trade with the Blackfoot Indians, the cryptic reconstitution of family is complete with the entrance of Teal Eye, a Blackfoot girl whom Jourdonnais, the leader of the expedition, has taken as a hostage, and who will later bear Boone's son. Only Teal Eye, Boone, Jim Deakins, and a frontiersman named Dick Summers survive an Indian attack.

The next part of *The Big Sky* begins after a seven-year interval, in 1837. Boone, Summers, and Deakins have meanwhile learned to live by their wits and their guns in the wilderness, journeying farther upstream to the Wind River plains at the base of the Tetons. Here they live a life Boone associates with his ideal of freedom—trapping, hunting, and meeting with other frontiersmen for yearly rendezvous at Jackson's Hole, where accommodating Indian women make love with them. However, Boone still remembers Teal Eye and wonders what sets him constantly "thinking so keen about her" as he hears "the faint honk of geese driving north to the nesting grounds." The same force that draws the geese north to nest pulls Dick Summers east to Missouri, where he marries. Supposing himself immune to this force, Boone goes north with Jim Deakins in search of better trapping. He there encounters Teal Eye at a Blackfoot village on the banks of the Teton River and marries her.

Boone lives among the Blackfoot Indians for five years, content with "his lodge, . . . his meat, . . . his woman." In 1842, after Teal Eye has become pregnant, Boone and Jim Deakins are hired to find a northern pass across the Rockies for wagon trains on their way to Oregon. Barely surviving a desperate winter in the mountains, the two friends return in the spring to find that Teal Eye has had her baby—a boy with red hair and blue eyes—born blind. Boone notices that the baby's hair and eyes resemble Jim Deakins's coloration, which is blond, rather than his own, which is dark. Goaded by grief, he suspects Deakins of being the father and kills him. His act clearly parallels his earlier rebellion against his own father in Kentucky, and—just as he ran away from the Kentucky farm, believing he had killed his father, to meet Jim Deakins transporting a dead father to the grave—he runs away from the Blackfoot village, returning to Kentucky, where he finds that his father has died, his mother has gotten old, and his brother has married and become the father of two children. When Boone asks about his nephews' blond coloration, he learns that his grandfather, who died before his birth, had red hair. The blindness of the infant he has left at the Blackfoot village thus springs into focus as emblematic of his own blindness in doubting Teal Eye and killing Jim Deakins—the mark of his own deeply flawed nature.

Boone is invited to join his brother as a partner in farming but cannot accept. After casually seducing a neighbor girl, he wanders away, again attempting escape and again meeting only more reminders of his weakness and guilt. At Dick Summers's Missouri farmstead, he finds his former friend going soft in the middle and married to a woman "yellow with fever and heavy with the young one in her." He becomes drunk, confesses to Summers that he has killed Jim Deakins, and departs, "weaving big and dark into the darkness." Boone's anguished departure from Dick Summers at the close recalls the other departures he has made since leaving home as a boy twelve years earlier. Yet his reasons for running away have been progressively removed, until only one remains. Consequently, his final departure into the darkness confirms the other departures as attempts to escape from self. Boone's repeated attempts to escape himself signal his inability to understand or control himself. Each of these attempts eventually comes back to the place where it started—a rejection of manhood. The big sky to which Boone looks for freedom therefore only binds him to the limitations men share with other creatures.

In *The Way West*, however, the departure motif is both magnified and humanized as a journey with real destination. The participants are the families that make up a wagon train bound for Oregon in 1845, two years after the close of *The Big Sky*. Dick Summers, his wife now dead, leaves his farm to guide the party from its starting point at Independence to its destination at the Willamette River, and at last returns to the Rockies, where he sojourned with Boone Caudill and Jim Deakins, explaining, "I'm bound to chase my tail, I reckon, like a pup." The others accept a more difficult maturity and are consequently transformed into "Crossers of plains. Grinders through the dust. Climbers of Mountains. Forders of rivers. Meeters of danger. Sailors at last of the big waters. Nation makers. Builders of the country." Guthrie insisted in *The Big Sky* that settlement necessarily involved displacement; in *The Way West*, he acknowledged that it also ordained transit and that the transit had a goal.

Dedicated to Guthrie's father, *The Big Sky* explored the intricacies of relationships between fathers and sons; dedicated to Harriet, his wife, *The Way West* correspondingly examines relationships between husbands and wives, centering on five such pairings. Ambitious Irvine Tadlock, from Illinois, has organized the wagon train with the secret hope of finding a place in the West where he can enter politics and thus bolster his faltering marriage. Charles Fairbanks and his wife are taking their son, Tod, to Oregon for his health. Indigent Henry McBee and his "woman" have come away from Ohio with their flock of ragged offspring, hoping to escape creditors. Amanda Mack, a beautiful but frigid Kentucky woman, is afraid to become a mother, and thus unwittingly drives her husband, Curtis, to adultery with Mercy, one of the McBee girls. Lije and Rebecca Evans (whose son, Brownie, marries Mercy McBee after she becomes pregnant with Curtis Mack's child) discover along the way the depth and strength of their reliance on each other, so that Lije's final words—which are also the final words of the novel—constitute an affirmation not only of their completed journey, but also of their successful union: "Hurrah for Oregon!"

Guthrie shows that husbands and wives can be cruel to each other, as in the case of Curtis and Amanda Mack. Yet he also shows that a strong marriage, like that of Lije and Rebecca Evans, can survive both the difficult conditions of the frontier and the more insidious perils of politics, caste, and sex that inevitably threaten to destroy the party and its families from within. The book makes a sensitive but rarely sentimental demonstration of how the powerful ties that support husbands and wives can redeem even the terrifying fractures that separate fathers from sons.

The first leg of the way west is the journey from Independence to Fort Laramie, much of it across the arid, treeless plain that lines the Platte and North Platte rivers. The second takes the party across the continental divide and into the upper Columbia basin, ending at Fort Hall on the Snake River. The final stage sees them down the Snake to Fort Boise, northwest across the Blue Mountains to the desert, and down the Columbia at last to its confluence with the Willamette at Fort Vancouver. Politics dominate the first part, in which Tadlock tries to keep his position as captain of the party but is replaced by Lije Evans before they reach Fort Laramie. At Fort Laramie, Curtis Mack seduces Mercy McBee, with whom young Brownie Evans has already fallen secretly in love. Sexual tensions, complicated by Lije Evans's reluctance to approve a connection with the generally disreputable McBees, thus plague the journey across the divide; but Mercy proves herself worthy of Brownie, Mack attempts to make up for his earlier indiscretion, and Mercy and Brownie are married at Fort Hall with the blessing of Lije and Rebecca. In *The Big Sky*, Boone's suspicion that Jim Deakins had lain with Teal Eye led to murder. In *The Way West*, the fact that Mercy carries Curtis Mack's child can be accepted and dealt with calmly by Brownie and his parents as a difficult circumstance love and reason together are capable of resolving.

The statement Guthrie makes about the settlement process in *The Way West* is intelligently humanistic in the best and largest sense. Although the terrain and climate of the frontier put serious obstacles in the way of emigration, obstacles that are even more serious originate with the emigrants themselves. Once greed, lust, jealousy, and aggression are tamed, Guthrie seems to argue, then the mountains and rivers can be crossed—not easily, but with sanity and courage. Furthermore, he convincingly demonstrates that the only effective defense couples like Lije and Rebecca Evans have against themselves is that provided for each by the other. This is the defense Boone Caudill rejects when he kills Jim Deakins instead of keeping faith with Teal Eye. It is also, of course, the defense that not only preserves the marriage of Lije and Rebecca—promising a happy married life for Brownie and Mercy as well—but also sees the emigrant train, under Lije's leadership, safely to its destination at the mouth of the Willamette. The same sky that destroys Boone threatens the emigrants at every point of their long journey. However, those husbands and wives who resolve to rely on each other survive by asserting the power of their union—not the primal urge that pulls wild geese north to nest or draws Boone to the Blackfoot village on the banks of the Teton River, but the ordinations of restraint repeated in their marriage vows, and through which they can become "nation makers . . . builders of the country."

In *These Thousand Hills*, Guthrie examines at a later stage the nation such builders are said to have shaped and finds it imperfect but beautiful. The story begins at the Evanses' Oregon farm a generation after the family's 1845 removal from the East. Rebecca has died, and Lije has become an old man. Mercy and Brownie, still true to each other, have made an orderly life for themselves. Yet their son Lat, a young man as the story opens, feels trapped. Against his father's determined opposition, Lat has therefore decided to leave home, hiring out as a cowhand on a cattle drive east to Montana, where he hopes to be a rancher. With his usual deft touch, Guthrie meaningfully joins at the outset of this book the domestic themes that informed the previous two: like Boone Caudill, Lat Evans leaves home against his father's will—even heading for the same place, albeit from the opposite direction—but Brownie and Mercy, whose life together has been founded on the wise example of Lije and Rebecca, can let Lat go with love rather than sending him away in anger. Family ties are thus preserved rather than broken, and Lat is never deprived of their humanizing influence. Indeed, the example of his parents' decency and mutual respect finally guides him to conditional success in the three perilous relationships that tempt him to ruin—those he has with his best friend, his mistress, and his wife.

On the drive to Montana, Lat takes up with Tom Ping, the charming reckless young cowboy who quickly becomes his best friend and later nips in the bud his promising career in politics. When the drive comes to an end at Fort Benton, Lat successfully rides an outlaw horse and is taken by Tom and the other hands, who have bet money on him, to the brothel where he meets Callie, a beautiful prostitute who falls in love with him and becomes his mistress. Callie later gives Lat her life savings of one thousand dollars to bet on a horse race in which he wins the stake he uses to start a ranch in the foothills near the settlement of Tansytown. Hard work and shrewd planning help Lat succeed while neighboring ranches fail, and he is soon being mentioned as a likely candidate for the U.S. Senate. Meanwhile, Tom Ping marries a prostitute despite Lat's bitter opposition, and Callie sets up a brothel in Tansytown. Lat's marriage to Joyce Sheridan, the pious daughter of a respected local businessman, completes the threatening design. Only intelligence of the kind that preserved the families of *The Way West* saves Lat from the self-betrayal that would be involved in deserting Tom Ping, repudiating Callie, and deceiving Joyce.

The bitter winter of 1886-1887 brings each of the three relationships to a crisis. Married, respectable, and beginning to think about running for the Senate, Lat yields to pressure applied by his neighbors and potential constituents, agreeing to join a vigilante band made up of ranchers who aim to end the cattle rustling hard times have fostered. As it happens, Tom Ping is one of the rustlers, but Lat contrives to manage his friend's escape from a raid in which he would otherwise be discovered and killed. When Tom soon afterward insults Lat publicly, Lat refuses to respond, seeming to behave as a coward and thus damaging his political chances. Henry McBee, Lat's maternal grandfather, then shows up, threatening to tell an unpleasant secret about Lat's birth, but at last confesses that Lat is not a bastard. Mercy's firstborn, begotten by Curtis Mack, died an infant. Soon after Joyce bears Lat's first son, a murder is committed at the brothel, and it seems certain that Callie will be charged. Lat must therefore decide whether to testify in her behalf, which would require him publicly to acknowledge his relationship with her. Courageously, he chooses to do so, but the case is solved without bringing Callie to trial. Lat nonetheless confesses the relationship to Joyce, who finds the courage to sustain him, finally entreating him to "come in! Come in out of the wind!"

The Big Sky, *The Way West*, and *These Thousand Hills* establish Guthrie as an important American writer. *Arfive* and *Wild Pitch*, his latest novels, are best seen as works in which Guthrie examines the origins of his own very considerable achievement. *Arfive* tells the story of a Montana ranching community named for the nearby R-Five Ranch and contains a number of characters and incidents that recognizably parallel elements in Guthrie's account of his Choteau boyhood. *Wild Pitch*, also set in a small Montana town, is presented as the first-person account of teenage Jason Beard's part in solving a murder case. Both works have merit, but neither comes up to the standard Guthrie set in his trilogy.

The reason may well be that *The Big Sky*, *The Way West*, and *These Thousand Hills* so thoroughly explore the broad subject Guthrie mapped out for himself. The flawed runaway of the first novel, the aspiring nation makers of the second, and the shrewd, lucky gambler of the third adequately express the range and clarity of Guthrie's vision, in which the transcontinental wilderness is calmly and intelligently insisted upon as a cluster of interrelated human problems. Since each character plays multiple roles, a larger cast would only cloud the issues. Guthrie's three great novels identify and celebrate the human values of courage, wisdom, justice, and love. It is as an American humanist that Guthrie will be remembered.

—Ben Merchant Vorpahl

Screenplays:

Shane, Paramount, 1953;
The Kentuckian, United Artists, 1955.

Periodical Publications:

"Sheep and Goats," *Atlantic Monthly*, 175 (April 1945): 113-114;
"Characters and Compassion," *Writer*, 62 (November 1949): 358-362;
"Montana," *Holiday*, 8 (September 1950): 34-51;
"Kentucky," *Holiday*, 9 (March 1951): 34-49;
"Nothing Difficult About a Cow," *Harper's*, 207 (January 1953): 73-76;
"Adventure with History," *Holiday*, 14 (July 1953): 58-63;

"Roads Running West," *Harper's*, 28 (May 1954): 68-70;

"Idaho," *Holiday*, 25 (June 1954): 34-45;

"The Rockies," *Holiday*, 18 (July 1955): 98-100ff;

"Action, Sir, Action," *Saturday Review*, 41 (12 April 1958): 56-57;

"Our Lordly Mountains," *Holiday*, 24 (July 1958): 54-55ff;

"The West is Our Great Adventure of the Spirit," *Life*, 46 (13 April 1959): 79-98;

"I Know Where I Am From," *Reporter*, 27 (22 November 1962): 50-52;

"The Great Rockies," *Holiday*, 34 (August 1963): 28-41.

Bibliography:

Richard W. Etulain, "A. B. Guthrie: A Bibliography," *Western American Literature*, 3 (Summer 1969): 133-138.

References:

Walter Van Tilburg Clark, "When Settlers Began to Take Over," *New York Times Book Review*, 18 November 1956, pp. 1, 54;

James K. Folsom, *The American Western Novel* (New Haven: College & University Press, 1966), pp. 64-76;

Thomas W. Ford, *A. B. Guthrie, Jr.* (Austin, Tex.: Steck-Vaughn, 1968);

Dayton Kohler, "A. B. Guthrie, Jr., and the West," *College English*, 12 (February 1951): 249-256.

EARL HAMNER
(10 July 1923-)

BOOKS: *Fifty Roads to Town* (New York: Random House, 1953);

Spencer's Mountain (New York: Dial, 1961);

You Can't Get There From Here (New York: Random House, 1965);

The Homecoming (New York: Random House, 1970).

Born in Schuyler, Virginia, to Earl Henry and Doris Marion Gianinni Hamner, Earl Henry Hamner, Jr., was the eldest of eight children—three girls and five boys. The historical circumstances of his birth—both time and place—account, in varying degrees, for the nature of his writings. Schuyler, situated in sparsely populated Nelson County, was a typical small Southern town, a "community" in the Eudora Welty sense. Community is at times both the means to and the ends of man's aspirations. With Charlottesville, Virginia, just thirty miles away, the spirit of Jeffersonian democracy is integral to the town. The unity of man and land which Hamner expresses in his best work may, indeed, be seen as Jeffersonian Southernness and may well be the key to the image of Hamner's fictional Spencer's Mountain which symbolizes the human freedom possible through man's interaction with the land and with his tradition.

In addition to place, a sense of family—past and present—is integral to Hamner's work. He once observed: "When I was growing up in the foothills of Virginia's Blue Ridge Mountains in the thirties . . . , I was certain that no one on earth had quite so good a life. . . . Many years later, after I had grown up, I learned that we were 'economically deprived,' that we lived in a 'depressed area' and that we suffered from a disease called 'familism.' The sociologists define 'familism' as a 'type of social organization in which the family is considered more important than either social groups or the individual.' "

Hamner's evolution as a writer is owed, in large part, to a Southern folk tradition: vernacular storytelling. Margaret Fife Tanguay observed that the grandparents who lived with the Hamners frequently amused the family with stories at night. That oral tradition remains a major ingredient in his style today and accounts, in no small way, for the strong rhetorical voice he exhibits in *The Homecoming* (1970) and in the current television series "The Waltons." Indeed, Hamner's own voice is the concluding narrative overlay of every weekly television episode.

From 1940 to 1943 Hamner studied at the University of Richmond, a small, Protestant liberal arts college. The university, its dean, its registrar, its assumption of the role of parent are easily identifiable and of considerable importance to the plot of *Spencer's Mountain* (1961). After service in World War II and a year at Northwestern University (1946), he completed the B.F.A. at the College of Music of Cincinnati in 1958.

Hamner soon discovered what Southern writers like Thomas Wolfe, Carson McCullers, and Katherine Anne Porter knew before him: to leave home better enables one to place it in proper literary perspective. After a stint (1946 to 1948) at writing for WLW Radio in Cincinnati, Ohio, Hamner took up residency in New York, where he wrote radio and television scripts for NBC from 1949 to 1960. Away

Earl Hamner

from family and familiar surroundings, Hamner found that "being Southern and going to New York, suddenly you don't have the family for solace and comfort. I think that most Southerners are such talkers and storytellers that being there and having nobody to tell the stories to, and to be lonely, you are drawn into writing."

Scriptwriting for radio gave him the kind of experience that would later help him move from fiction writing into television writing and production. His early radio writing included scripts for "Eva La Gallienne Theatre," "Biography in Sound," "NBC Theatre," and "Dimension X." Hamner's television writing in the early period of the medium included scripts for "Today," "Wide, Wide World," "Theatre Guild of the Air," and "Matinee Theatre."

On 16 October 1954 Hamner married Jane Martin of Davenport, Iowa. Jane Martin was, at the time, an editor of *Harper's Bazaar.* Hamner and his wife and their two children—Scott Martin and Caroline Spencer— now live in Los Angeles, where he is currently co-executive producer and executive story editor of "The Waltons."

Beginning in the mid-1960s Hamner won steady critical acclaim, especially for his work in radio and television. Among his numerous honors are the TV-Radio Writers Award (1967); Writers Guild Prize for "Heidi" (1969); George Foster Peabody Award (1972); Virginian of the Year Award from the Virginia Press Association (1973); and an Emmy Award for best program for "The Waltons" (1974).

Fifty Roads to Town (1953), Hamner's first novel, focuses on the unattractive aspects of Southern life. Set in the mountains, the novel portrays themes important in his later work—freedom and bondage, initiation and maturation. The tradition from which Hamner was writing at this time, unlike that of his best work, was Southern Gothic. The spirit of Erskine Caldwell's *God's Little Acre* (1933) is indeed apparent in the novel. Tanguay notes, for example, that "hill country religion, opportunism, and ignorance play a strong part in this expose." Hamner chronicles his heroine's growth into womanhood. Young Althea stands in sharp contrast to her morally loose mother, her degenerate father, and her zealous grandmother. The mountains, moreover, rather than symbolizing freedom, imply entrapment, imprisonment, and bondage while the city offers escape and the promise of freedom.

In his best work, however, Hamner generally appears the romantic conservator of traditional Southern values:

> But the value of roots, too, I think becomes more and more critical when we become such a huge technology and so many of the so-called traditional values are being questioned and discarded. . . . if people can revisit the scenes and places where the values did exist, possibly they can come to believe in them again, or . . . to adopt some kind of belief in God, or faith in the family unit, or just getting home again.

Spencer's Mountain, his second novel, exhibits those values and is a classic Bildungsroman, a warm and loving portrait of Clay-Boy Spencer's growth into manhood. As a study in maturation, the novel depends heavily upon tradition, family as community, and ritual. When the hero Clay-Boy, for example, receives as a gift from his family his first knife, the Freudian overtones of his discovery as he studies the knife foreshadow his awakening sexuality. The scene is acted out within the family: "The handle was of beautifully polished wood and when he withdrew the blade from the sheath he found it razor-sharp. Self-consciously Clay-Boy attached the sheath to his belt and returned the blade to its place."

Much like Faulkner's insight in "The Bear," Hamner's instinctive awareness of the significance

109.

58 CONTINUED:

BECKY'S VOICE
Good night, Daddy. Good night, Mama.

NARRATOR'S VOICE
(Clay-Boy as a man)
Christmas is a season when we give tokens of love. In that house we received not tokens, but love itself. I became the writer I promised my father I'd be, and my destiny led me far from Spencer's Mountain. My mother lives there still, alone now, for we lost my father in 1969. My brothers and sisters, grown now with children of their own, live not far away. We are still a close family and see each other when we can, and like Miss Emma Staples' fourth cousins, we are apt to sample the Recipe, then gather around the piano and hug each other while we sing the old songs. For no matter the time or distance, we are united in the memory of that Christmas Eve in 1933. More than thirty years and three thousand miles away, I can still hear those sweet voices:

The voices, almost like whispers on the wind, become more and more faint as the CAMERA CONTINUES TO PULL BACK from the house.

OLIVIA'S VOICE
Good night, Becky. Good night, John.

JOHN'S VOICE
Good night, Mama. Good night, Shirley.

SHIRLEY'S VOICE
Good night, John. Good night, Mark.

MARK'S VOICE
Good night, Shirley. Good night, everybody.

The voices are silent. The earth is still and the people sleep. The CAMERA RESTS for a beat on the distant house, the brilliant winter's night and the enduring mountain.

FADE OUT.

THE END

The Homecoming, *television script*

of the hunt as folk tradition and ritual is integral to Clay-Boy's trial and maturation. Clay-Boy, moreover, perceives early in the novel that in the hunt "his very manhood would be challenged and he would either maintain his position among the men of his clan or would lose something of himself." Faulknerian communion follows that recognition: "Before the food was placed on the table and all during breakfast the bottle of bourbon was passed from one man to another."

Clay-Boy attains his manhood when he kills the legendary white deer. The killing of the deer—traditional symbol of shyness and chastity—suggests his loss of boyhood innocence. His father's subsequent selling of land to educate the son at the University of Richmond proclaims not only acceptance of the son's manhood, as Tanguay has observed, but also the ritualistic changing of the old order and a yielding to the new, that is, movement from the Southern agrarian to the Southern urban experience.

Although some reviewers took issue with Harper Lee's tribute on the dust jacket to the novel, her words suggest what may be a compelling explanation for the later popularity of the novel (and the subsequent television series, "The Waltons"). Noting that "It is easy to create a villain or an eccentric," Lee concluded that "One finds pure joy in reading, for a change, a positive statement on the potentialities of man."

You Can't Get There From Here (1965) takes as its theme the search for a father—both literally and psychologically—and further emphasizes the importance of community. Joe Scott, the father of the adolescent hero, recalls in part Eugene Gant's father in *Look Homeward, Angel.* Wes's search for his absent father, which occupies only a course of hours but which takes him through the urban wilderness that is New York, acts as the basic metaphor for his initiation into manhood. Perhaps because the novel is set in New York and not in Hamner's native Virginia, it never attains the natural fusion of character and theme found in *Spencer's Mountain.*

The Homecoming is a more successful novel, in part because the setting is once again in Virginia. A significantly shorter work than *Spencer's Mountain,* the novel is set in the mountains during the Great Depression and focuses on Clay-Boy Spencer's Christmas Eve search for his father, who is long overdue in his return from his out-of-town job for the celebration of the family Christmas.

Revelation and growth through pilgrimage, as in the legend of the Magi, fuse organically with the theme of love and the importance of community and traditional Christian celebration. Traveling through the snowbound night in search of his father, the hero recognizes the sense of community and time and place that bind mankind together: "As he made his way past the Negro faces it came to him that he did not really know any Negroes. He knew those in the village, but he had never been in one of their homes and did not know what they yearned for or what their dreams were. He felt a sense of loss that an entire community existed within the larger community and he did not know one of them beyond his name and face." The cohesion of setting and narrative and the tie to Christian myth—the coming of light, knowledge, and love through sacrifice—is admirable.

No assessment of Hamner's contributions to American art would be complete without recognition of his tremendous impact on the American television audience. Of his major teleplays, four are outstanding: "Heidi" (1969), "Appalachian Autumn" (1970), "The Homecoming" (1971), and "The Waltons" (September 1972-present). An appreciation of tradition, love of family, and a Platonic faith in timeless and unchanging values permeate everything he has written for television. None of his works to date, however, has been so phenomenally successful as "The Waltons." "The Waltons" first aired on CBS television in September 1972, following the success of "The Homecoming." The cultural significance of the show has been succinctly interpreted by Philip Wander: "The Waltons symbolize Family, the ideal family undergoing one ordeal after another. [They] . . . are, of course, a particular kind of family, even though they stand for an ideal. They are a white, Anglo-Saxon, Protestant family, politically insulated and culturally provincial." Wander further points out that Walton's Mountain is Eden, and the threats to Eden are the realities of privation and hardship wrought by time. The virtue of the family is natural as opposed to religious. The author's depiction is largely Jeffersonian-agrarian in origin; the Waltons are the "natural aristoi," men and women of virtue (in the classic sense) and talent. As a consequence of his success in television, Hamner has devoted more and more of his energies to television production. At the present time, he is, however, at work on a novel, "Fenwick's Landing."

His work, in both the novel and television, continues to attest to basic Southern values—man's relationship to nature, the relationship of the individual to his community, consequences of change, and the preservation of classic values. Certainly, few

Southern writers of his generation have had so great an impact on the American mass audience.

—*George C. Longest*

Screenplays:

"Spencer's Mountain," Warner Brothers, 1963;
"Palm Springs Weekend," Warner Brothers, 1963.

Television Scripts:

"Highway," 1954;
"Heidi," 1969;
"Appalachian Autumn," 1970;
"Aesop's Fables," 1971;
"The Homecoming," 1971;
"Where the Lillies Bloom," 1972;
"Apple's Way," 1973.

Other:

"We Called It Love," *New York Times*, 5 October 1969, p. 21.

References:

Ted Allrich, "Earl Hamner: From Backwoods to Hollywood," *Writer's Yearbook*, 48 (1977): 44-48, 72;

Jack Gould, "T.V.: C.B.S. Playhouse Explores Appalachian Misery: Drama by Earl Hamner to Be Seen Tonight," *New York Times*, 7 October 1969, p. 95;

Martin Levin, "A Reader's Report," *New York Times Book Review*, 20 June 1965, pp. 31-32;

John J. O'Connor, "T.V.: 'Apple's Way' and Search for Human Values," *New York Times*, 15 February 1974, p. 67;

William Peden, "Southern Hill Folk," *Saturday Review*, 45 (10 March 1962): 26;

Antoinette Roades, "Earl Hamner, Jr.," *Commonweal*, 44 (April 1977): 23-29;

Margaret Fife Tanguay, "The Man Behind the Waltons," *Sky*, 3 (March 1974): 26-29;

Philip Wander, " 'The Waltons': How Sweet It Was," *Journal of Communications*, 28 (Autumn 1978): 148-154;

John Cook Wyllie, "A Boy Grows Up in Nelson County, Virginia," *New York Times Book Review*, 14 January 1962, p. 40.

BARRY HANNAH

(23 April 1942-)

BOOKS: *Geronimo Rex* (New York: Viking, 1972); *Nightwatchmen* (New York: Viking, 1973); *Airships* (New York: Knopf, 1978).

Since 1972 Barry Hannah has published two novels and a prize-winning collection of short stories. His third novel, *Ray*, is scheduled for publication in fall 1980. While some stories and novel segments are set in the South during the Civil War, the setting of most of his fiction is the contemporary South. Because of his prolific output, the lyricism of his prose, and his Gothic sense of humor, some have heralded Hannah as the heir apparent to the Faulkner crown. Like his Mississippi brother in letters, Hannah uses the South as microcosm. In his fiction, the South, its people, its traditions, its social ills, and its violence all become emblems of the universal human condition.

Hannah was born and grew up in Clinton, Mississippi, a town near Jackson. He received his B.A. degree from Mississippi College in Clinton and his M.A. and M.F.A. degrees from the University of Arkansas. He has taught literature and fiction writing at Clemson University and at the University of Alabama. He has also been writer in residence at Middlebury College. He has received a Bellaman Foundation Award in Fiction (1970), a Bread Loaf Fellowship (1971), and the first Arnold Gingrich Short Fiction Award for *Airships* (1978).

Hannah began *Geronimo Rex* (1972) while he was a creative-writing student at the University of Arkansas. It is an initiation novel which tells the story of Harry Monroe, the novel's protagonist and narrator, as he grows up in Dream of Pines, Louisiana, a squalid paper-mill town. The novel begins with eight-year-old Harry listening to the Dream of Pines Colored High School band, a miracle of sound and marching drama. One of its members, Harley Butte, a French-horn player who loves military music and thinks of himself as the spiritual son of John Philip Sousa, is a foil for Harry in some ways—in race, in occupation, in age—but in important sections of the novel, the fates of these two become interlocked. They become friends despite the segregated social structure of the South.

Harry's life as a high school and college student constitutes a comic quest, a search for certitude, symbolized by his longings for the bright world outside the oppressive boundaries of the provinces. Harry dreams of a passionate life at Malibu and of the sophistication of New York City, and the story of his quest is often characterized by surreal humor and violent accident. His youth is a time of frightening social upheaval in the South—of the Brown decision, the integration of the University of Alabama and the University of Mississippi, and the assassination of Medger Evers. Social unrest around Harry is matched by his internal turmoil. He decides to be a medical doctor, but he quits that for music. When he fails at music, he decides to be a poet. He falls in love frequently and hopelessly, creating Helens of Troy out of mill-town whores and bovine illiterates. He drifts away from his family and becomes tragically entangled with a rabid bigot.

Midway in the novel Harry finds a guide for his quest: the rebel Apache chief Geronimo, whose phantom appears to him at crucial moments. As Harry reports, "What I especially liked about Geronimo was that he had cheated, lied, stolen, usurped, killed, burned, raped, pillaged, razed, trapped, ripped, mashed. . . . I thought I would like to go into that line of work."

In college Harry and Bobby Dove Fleece, a sickly genius who is trying to escape the domination of his mother and stepfather, live with other of the novel's main characters in a boardinghouse run by Mother Rooney, a comical old widow who pretends not to hear the profanity her boarders direct at her. In the most important conflict in the novel, Harry and Bobby oppose their nemesis, Whitfield Peter, an insane racist who makes a profession of persecuting blacks and writing pornographic letters. Eventually, during a gun battle Bobby wounds Whitfield Peter, who is also shooting at Bobby and Harry. The novel ends with Harry's marriage to Prissy Lombardo, a mysterious woman who is sometimes disgusted with Harry's strange behavior, and the beginning of Harry's career in graduate school.

Although *Geronimo Rex* has some characteristics of the picaresque novel and owes small debts to several American initiation novels, its dialogue, narrative, and metaphors are refreshingly original, and almost all of its characters are ingenious creations. It was received by the majority of its reviewers as a brilliant first novel, and it was nominated for a National Book Award.

In Hannah's second novel, *Nightwatchmen* (1973), Harry Monroe reappears, still married to Prissy, and studying for a Ph.D. in English; but the main narrator of this arcane and outrageous murder mystery is Thorpe Trove, a wealthy eccentric who gathers a crew of graduate students in his mansion in Pass Christian, a short distance from the mythical Southern Mississippi University. Like Mother Rooney's boardinghouse in *Geronimo Rex*, Thorpe's mansion is a meeting place for the central characters of the novel. These people bring Thorpe out of his loneliness and ennui by introducing him to a life of romance and intrigue.

The university campus is beset by the "Knocker," an unknown assailant who clubs graduate students and faculty who study late in Old Main building. Harry's theory is that only "certifiable bores" are being knocked out, that the Knocker is an angel of revenge against pedantry and boredom, but the situation becomes desperate when two decapitated corpses are found in Old Main. Thorpe Trove becomes obsessed with finding the killer and he gathers tape-recorded evidence from those who might have clues. Many chapters of the novel are transcriptions of the tapes, which offer evidence from various characters about the knockings and the murders. Finally, Thorpe enlists the aid of seventy-year-old Howard Hunter, the most unconventional and engaging private detective in contemporary fiction. Together, Thorpe and Howard find, murder, and bury the killer.

Hannah's successful experiment with minor narrators speaking through the tape transcriptions allows the development of a complex texture, offering a telling counterpoint to Thorpe's sad and comic story. *Nightwatchmen* is pervaded by violence, both natural and man-made. In the midst of beheadings, rapes, and shootings, there is also death and mutilation from hurricane Camille. Hannah molds this violence around a core of humor that in its irony is reminiscent of Nabokov and Céline.

Hannah's *Airships* is composed of twenty stories, nine of which first appeared in *Esquire*. Three others first appeared in other magazines and journals, and eight are new stories. Most of these stories are told by physically wounded and handicapped narrators. The stories' subjects range from the Civil War to an American apocalypse in the future.

Several stories have been gleaned from two of Hannah's aborted novels, one about the exploits of Confederate General Jeb Stuart and the other about the lives of professional tennis players. The Jeb Stuart stories are among the most consummate in the book. "Knowing He Was Not My Kind Yet I Followed" is narrated by Confederate Corporal Deed Ainsworth, an outcast homosexual who expresses unrequited love for Stuart: "There is nobody who does not believe in Jeb Stuart. Oh, the zany purposeful eyes, the haggard gleam, the feet of his lean horse high in the air, his rotting flannel shirt under his old soiled grays, and his heroic body odor! He makes one want to be a Christian." The influence of Stuart also appears in "Midnight and I'm Not Famous Yet," a story about the Vietnam War in which captured Viet Cong General Li Dap is a student of Stuart's strategies and argues that there is a strict parallel between the Vietnam War and the American Civil War. From the unfinished novel about tennis players comes "Return to Return," the longest story in the collection, which tells of the seriocomic career of French Edward, a handsome tennis pro who is haunted by his onetime coach, Dr. Word, and is protected by his friend, Dr. Baby Levaster. This wistfully droll story of misdirected love has the narrative twists, time lapses, flashbacks, and surrealism one might expect in a John Hawkes novel.

Hannah returns to the boardinghouse setting in two stories, "Eating Wife and Friends" and the concluding story, "Mother Rooney Unscrolls the Hurt." The characters of "Eating Wife and Friends" gather at Mrs. Neap's boardinghouse during a desperate time of famine and eventually become cannibals, while "Mother Rooney Unscrolls the Hurt" is an expanded version of an episode in *Geronimo Rex*. As Mother Rooney lies injured in her house with the pin of her brooch sticking three inches into her bosom, she remembers the pain of her marriage and the pain of her silent love for her young male boarders.

The short stories of *Airships* display Hannah's development of new narrative voices and his increased exploration of surreal humor and action. Also noteworthy are his experiments with the use of time and place in such stories as "Quo Vadis, Smut," "Escape to Newark," and the neogothic thriller "Coming Close to Donna." Set in fantasylands in no determinable era and thus freed from the strictures of conventional time and place in fiction, the stories gain their strength from concentration on character, language, and incident.

Much of Hannah's fiction is experimental and belongs in the category of dark comedy. All of it composes a highly original portrait of American life, both past and present, particularly American life in the South. It is a fiction that is consistently poetic, with a language and style both dazzling and believable.

—*Charles Israel*

ELIZABETH HARDWICK
(27 July 1916-)

SELECTED BOOKS: *The Ghostly Lover* (New York: Harcourt, Brace, 1945);

The Simple Truth (New York: Harcourt, Brace, 1955; London: Weidenfeld & Nicolson, 1955);

A View of My Own: Essays in Literature and Society (New York: Farrar, Straus & Cudahy, 1962; London: Heinemann, 1964);

Seduction and Betrayal: Women and Literature (New York: Random House, 1974; London: Weidenfeld & Nicolson, 1974);

Sleepless Nights (New York: Random House, 1979; London: Weidenfeld & Nicolson, 1979).

Elizabeth Hardwick is an accomplished essayist, short-story writer, and novelist. She first was published in 1945 with her novel *The Ghostly Lover*. Since then she has written two more novels and numerous short stories. However, she is known primarily for brilliant literary and social criticism, which has graced the pages of many of the country's leading liberal journals, most notably the *Partisan Review* and the *New York Review of Books*. All of Hardwick's writing, regardless of its literary form, is distinguished for its wit, understanding, and polished prose style.

Born and raised in Lexington, Kentucky, the author was one of eleven children of Eugene and Mary Ramsey Hardwick. Her father had a plumbing and heating business in Lexington for some years and later sold oil furnaces. He also worked for the city as an inspector; and as his daughter describes it, "He did a lot of fishing, which can indeed be an 'occupation' if not a profession." She attended local schools, receiving a B.A. in 1938 and an M.A. in 1939 from the University of Kentucky.

The city and surrounding countryside, famous for the breeding of racehorses and the growing of tobacco, held little interest for her. Looking back on her childhood in Lexington, she says,

> I loved only Main Street, the ten-cent store, the

> old cigar store, where newspapers and magazines were sold, the Ben Ali, the Strand and the State movie theaters, the lobbies of the Lafayette and Phoenix Hotel, Liggett's, sandwiches on soft, white Kleenexy bread at Morford's Drug, the July dress sales at Emby's and Wolf-Wiles.

After finishing her master's degree in English literature at the University of Kentucky, she, at the age of twenty-three, left for New York City and Columbia University, where she studied from 1939 to 1941.

The sophisticated urban environment of New York City, with all its excitement and diversity, appealed to her; and there she soon began work on her first novel. *The Ghostly Lover* draws its settings from the author's experience of life in the South and in New York City. The first half of the novel is set in a small southern town that remains unnamed, where a young woman, Marian, lives with her effeminate brother and indolent grandmother. In the second part of the novel, Marian travels to New York City to study music for a year, returns home when her grandmother becomes ill, but finally decides to leave again for New York, this time for good, after her grandmother's death and her brother's marriage.

Throughout the novel, Marian is presented as a profoundly lonely young person. Her brother and grandmother are uncommunicative, each living in a strange, private world. Searching for a successful job and happy life, Marian's father and mother wander the country, making only brief visits home between their failures. Marian longs for connection and intimacy with another person but finds it impossible to break through the separateness of the characters in the novel. She is especially disappointed at the failure to establish a close relationship with her mother, whom she adores from a distance.

In New York City, Marian finds only more isolation. The other women in her dormitory worry about their studies and private lives. One of the few friends that Marian does make among her classmates is a foreign student named Gertrude, who often goes out with strange men at night and then one evening does not return. And while she is away from home, Marian begins to question her own love and loyalty for her family. She has hoped that her mother might object to the fact that a divorced, older man from the southern town was paying for her study in New York; but her mother shows no sign of disapproval.

The novel's climax occurs when Marian, after her grandmother's death, visits her parents who are now living in a run-down western town. During the visit, it finally becomes clear to Marian that she will never have a close, loving relationship with her parents; and this realization, in a strange way, sets her free to establish her own emotional stability. There are now, according to the narrator, "no ghosts in the background, none whom she must think of when she made a decision. The mother's mystery had vanished." Marian, hardened but matured, returns to New York to build her own future.

The Ghostly Lover received a mixed critical response. Most of the critics found the novel weak in plot and character development but strong in its subtle descriptions of place and person. Hardwick's prose style received much praise, and she was called by Gertrude Buckman in the *New York Times Book Review* "a new writer of great talent and promise" (29 April 1945).

Soon after her first novel was published, she was contacted by Philip Rahv, one of the editors of the *Partisan Review*, and asked to become a contributor. She accepted the offer eagerly and thus began her long and successful career as social and literary critic. Noted for her elegant prose, wide-ranging interests, and liberal sentiments, she has perfected her work in the essay form. As she is quoted in *World Authors*, "I have great affection for the form and have given to it everything and more than would be required of fiction, that is, everything I possibly could. Indeed I have always written essays as if they were examples of imaginative writing, as I believe them to be." Some of her best essays that appeared in *Partisan Review*, *Harper's*, the *New Republic*, and the *New York Review of Books* were collected in *A View of My Own: Essays in Literature and Society*, published in 1962.

In 1947, Hardwick was awarded a Guggenheim Fellowship for fiction, which she used to write several short stories. On 28 July 1949, she married the poet Robert Lowell. They had one child, a daughter named Harriet Winslow Lowell, who was born on 4 June 1957. The marriage lasted until 1972 when Lowell divorced her to marry the English writer Caroline Blackwood. In 1977, the last year of his life, Lowell returned to Hardwick. They summered together in Castine, Maine, before Lowell died of heart failure in New York on 12 September. In an interview with Richard Locke of the *New York Times*, Hardwick described Lowell as "the most extraordinary person I have ever known, like no one else—unplaceable, unaccountable."

During the early years of their marriage, the Lowells traveled extensively. They spent 1950 to 1953 in Europe. Returning to the United States they went to the Midwest where Lowell taught in brief

Thomas Victor

Elizabeth Hardwick

succession at the University of Iowa, the University of Indiana, and the University of Cincinnati. In 1954, after a short stay in New York City, the Lowells moved to Boston, where they remained for six years. In Boston, she worked on her second novel, *The Simple Truth,* which was published in 1955.

The Simple Truth is a novel about a murder trial, though not so much about the actual crime or trial proceedings as about the ideas generated by the trial in two of its spectators. Rudy Peck, a poor but clean-cut college student, is accused of strangling his girl friend, Betty Jane Henderson, the daughter of a prosperous Des Moines banker. The crime shocks the quiet university town in Iowa where it takes place, and the ensuing trial becomes the focus of attention for many of its citizens. Two who are especially fascinated by it are Joseph Parks, a twenty-eight-year-old writing student from New York, and Anita Mitchell, the middle-aged wife of a chemistry professor.

Joseph and Anita have little in common except their shared, passionate belief in Peck's innocence. Joseph sees him as the victim of class injustice: a rich father objects to his daughter's associating with a poor boy. Anita, who is interested in "psychology," cannot hold Peck responsible for the dark, violent impulses that can erupt in anyone. As the trial progresses, Joseph and Anita discuss their views with each other, think about their own pasts, but spend most of their time passing judgment on all the other people present at the trial. The lawyers, the newspaper reporters, the policemen, the jurors, the witnesses, and the other spectators do not, according to Joseph and Anita, understand the complexity of the crime. They both feel certain that the local Iowa merchants and farmers who make up the jury will find Peck guilty on the basis of superficial evidence. However, in an ironic ending, he is acquitted by the jury. Joseph and Anita are stunned by the verdict, surprised and even disappointed that their "profound uncertainty" about the understanding of the other characters was not confirmed.

The critical reception of *The Simple Truth* was similar to that given her first novel. Again the critics complained about the lack of character development: Peck and Anita are stock characters, flat and uninteresting. But the prose style and the handling of the novel's ideas are done with skill and originality. John Brooks, reviewing the novel for the *New York Times,* compared it favorably to Aldous Huxley's novels of ideas. Although Brooks considered the novel not very effective on the human level, he found that the ideas in *The Simple Truth* "march forward, join ranks, and then explode like fireworks" (13 February 1955).

In 1960 the Lowells moved from Boston to the Upper West Side of Manhattan, where Hardwick has lived ever since. In 1961 she edited and wrote an introduction to the *Selected Letters* of William James; and in 1963, with some friends, she helped begin the *New York Review of Books.* Several years earlier, in 1959, she had written an article for *Harper's* magazine in which she surveyed the state of book reviewing in the United States. She found that "Sweet, bland commendations fall everywhere upon the scene; a universal, if somewhat lobotomized, accommodation reigns." A long printers' strike in New York, which shut down the book reviews of the *New York Times* and *Herald Tribune,* gave Hardwick and her friends an opportunity to change this situation. Working with a shoestring budget, they would create a review that would examine the best books being published and do it in an interesting and critically honest manner.

The *New York Review of Books* has been a success, one of the leading and most controversial intellectual journals in the United States. Hardwick has remained a frequent contributor and advisory editor to the review since its founding. In 1969 she became the first woman to receive the George Jean Nathan Award, presented for her outstanding drama criticism. And in 1974 her essays on women in literature, written for the review, were collected and published under the title *Seduction and Betrayal: Women in Literature*.

Her third novel, *Sleepless Nights*, published in 1979, is a difficult work to classify. Much of it appears to be autobiographical, and it is structured as a series of reminiscences. In the opening paragraph, the narrator calls it "a work of transformed and even distorted memory." The narrator is a woman named Elizabeth, who from her apartment in Manhattan remembers certain people and places from her past: her mother in Kentucky, a bachelor friend in New York, a doctor in Amsterdam, a maid in Boston, a laundress in Maine, and many more. The narrator's compassion for her old acquaintances and her careful observations as she brings these memories to life give the work its power and unity.

Elizabeth's memory focuses on the unhappy, lonely lives she has seen in the past. She tells the reader she has "a prying sympathy for the tendency of lives to obey the laws of gravity and to sink downward, falling as gently and slowly as a kite, or violently breaking, smashing." Her strongest, most poignant memories are of rootless, disappointed, and lonely people who somehow manage to survive and find relief in such things as Arthur Murray dance lessons or the gadgets on their new mobile home. And memories of her mother, a woman with nine children whose "fateful fertility" dominated her life, recur throughout the work.

Sleepless Nights shows Hardwick at her best. Its prose is, according to Daphne Merkin in the *New Republic*, "sheer loveliness . . . sentences so burnished you can skate across them" (9 June 1979). And the critics have been unanimous in their praise of the novel's content: it is a moving, intensely powerful work about the way people come together, separate, and find the courage to endure the cruel fates of modern life.

The fame of her late husband, Robert Lowell, has frequently overshadowed her own productive and unique career. But with the success of *Sleepless Nights* and her continuing presence as a discerning social and literary commentator, her writing is beginning to receive critical attention. Her novels present vivid portraits of the fragility of human relationships and the loneliness of the rootless individual in modern society. The role that women play in struggling with these contemporary problems is the primary concern of all her imaginative writing.

—*Joseph J. Branin*

Other:

William James, *Selected Letters*, edited with an introduction by Hardwick (New York: Farrar, Straus & Cudahy, 1961).

Periodical Publications:

FICTION:

"Golden Stallion," *Sewanee Review*, 54 (Winter 1946): 34-65;

"Friendly Witness," *Partisan Review*, 17 (April 1950): 340-351;

"Florentine Conference," *Partisan Review*, 18 (May 1951): 304-306;

"Two Recent Travelers," *Kenyon Review*, 15 (Summer 1953): 436-454;

"Season's Romance," *New Yorker*, 32 (10 March 1956): 36-44;

"Oak and the Axe," *New Yorker*, 32 (12 May 1956): 49-50;

"Classless Society," *New Yorker*, 32 (19 January 1957): 30-38;

"Purchase," *New Yorker*, 35 (30 May 1959): 28-34;

"Faithful," *New Yorker*, 55 (19 February 1979): 36-42.

NONFICTION:

"Decline of Book Reviewing," *Harper's*, 219 (November 1959): 138-143;

"Going Home is America: Lexington, Kentucky," *Harper's*, 239 (July 1969): 78-82;

"Domestic Manners," *Daedalus*, 107 (Winter 1978): 1-11.

Interviews:

Richard Locke, "Conversation On a Book," *New York Times Book Review*, 29 April 1979, pp. 1, 61-62;

Francine Du Plessix Gray, "Elizabeth Hardwick: a Fresh Way of Looking At Literature—And At Life," *Vogue*, 169 (June 1979): 202-203, 250.

References:

Steven Gould Axelrod, *Robert Lowell: Life and Art* (Princeton: Princeton University Press, 1978);

Joan Didion, "Meditation on a Life," *New York Times Book Review*, 29 April 1979, pp. 1, 60.

JOHN HERSEY

(17 June 1914-)

SELECTED BOOKS: *Men on Bataan* (New York: Knopf, 1942);

Into the Valley (New York: Knopf, 1943; London: Hodder & Stoughton, 1943);

A Bell for Adano (New York: Knopf, 1944; London: Gollancz, 1945);

Hiroshima (New York: Knopf, 1946; Harmondsworth, U.K.: Penguin, 1946);

The Wall (New York: Knopf, 1950; London: Hamilton, 1950);

The Marmot Drive (New York: Knopf, 1953; London: Hamilton, 1953);

A Single Pebble (New York: Knopf, 1956; London: Hamilton, 1956);

The War Lover (New York: Knopf, 1959; London: Hamilton, 1959);

The Child Buyer (New York: Knopf, 1960; London: Hamilton, 1961);

Here to Stay (London: Hamilton, 1962; New York: Knopf, 1963);

White Lotus (New York: Knopf, 1965; London: Hamilton, 1965);

Too Far to Walk (New York: Knopf, 1966; London: Hamilton, 1966);

Under the Eye of the Storm (New York: Knopf, 1967; London: Hamilton, 1967);

The Algiers Motel Incident (New York: Knopf, 1968; London: Hamilton, 1968);

Letter to the Alumni (New York: Knopf, 1970);

The Conspiracy (New York: Knopf, 1972; London: Hamilton, 1972);

My Petition for More Space (New York: Knopf, 1974; London: Hamilton, 1975);

The President (New York: Knopf, 1975);

The Walnut Door (New York: Knopf, 1977; London: Macmillan, 1978);

Aspects of the Presidency (New Haven: Ticknor & Fields, 1980).

In 1950, John Hersey was considered one of the nation's most promising young writers. His first novel, *A Bell for Adano* (1944), had won a Pulitzer Prize in 1945, while his journalistic masterpiece of 1946, *Hiroshima,* with its successful depiction of individual survivors of the atomic bombing of Japan, had an enormous emotional impact on both domestic and international audiences. His second novel, *The Wall* (1950), evoked a similar kind of emotional response from its readers. A classic description of the Holocaust, it still stands as one of the few books that has been able to relate in human terms the destruction of European Jewry by the Nazis. Since that time Hersey has remained popular and prolific, publishing many works of fiction and nonfiction that deal with an enormous range of subjects and interests. However, he has been ignored by most literary scholars while others such as Leslie Fiedler have accused him of naively believing that problems such as racism have simple solutions. Hersey himself suggested recently "that there are several reasons why my work has not been written about more than it has. Leaving the issue of quality, or lack of it, aside for the moment, one fundamental reason, I would guess, is that I have always written against the grain, both of literary fashion and of establishment values." As early as 1949, he called his type of fiction "the novel of contemporary history," that is, "a specific genre: the novels which deal with contemporary events." They are, he says, part of the larger mode of the historical novel. In contrast to more avant-garde writers Hersey dedicated himself to the goal of chronicling the events and issues of his time ranging from World War II itself, the atomic bomb, and the Holocaust to the dominant social issues of the postwar decades such as racism, overpopulation, education, the generation gap, the attack on democratic institutions, and, more generally, the malaise of modern life.

Hersey's political ideology is related to his concept of his role as a writer. "I don't think of myself as a traditional American liberal," he has written. "I'm not given to compromise. And I've been too skeptical of dogma to be an attached radical—attached, I mean, to any party line. So politically I'm not exactly anywhere; I work in small ways for what I believe in." Despite his claims to nonalignment, Hersey's idealistic individualism is actually in the tradition of the old-fashioned liberalism that goes back at least two centuries in American cultural history. Hersey's continuing faith in the value of education, progress, and democracy is apparent throughout all his writings. Indeed, for him the writer ought to be an educator who brings about social change. Thus, in a speech presented at Yale University and later printed in 1952 in the *Yale University Library Gazette,* Hersey described the motives behind *The Wall* by saying that writing is "the only hope man has of rising above his unmentionably horrible existence, his foul nest of murder, war, greed, madness and cruelty. Only the poets can persuade us to move up out of the slime into a hopeful shore, there by evolution to transform ourselves into higher and more intelligent creatures." He expresses a similar belief more than twenty years later in his introduction to *The Writer's Craft* (1974), where he writes: "Art praises and nourishes life, art hates death. This is what we mean when we say we recognize power in a work of art: The life forces in us are encouraged. . . ." He goes on to say that "True art is neither revolutionary nor reactionary. This does not mean that it is neutral. No. It is rebellious in any setting."

Hersey believes that his penchant for nonconformist views may stem from his origins. Born in Tientsin, China, where he spent his childhood, he now expresses the suspicion "that there is something subtly alien in my work that has come from the fact that the regions of memory, for me, from which imaginative material has to come, are on the other side of the globe. Perhaps this is *why* my work has gone against the grain." In addition, Hersey's zealous proselytizing for faith in democracy may derive from the religious zeal of his missionary parents, Roscoe and Grace Baird Hersey. In 1924, Hersey's father contracted encephalitis, and the family returned to the United States and settled in Briarcliff Manor, New York. Hersey attended public schools there for three years. He then went on scholarship to Hotchkiss, where he supported himself by working as a waiter and by cleaning classrooms. A 1936 graduate of Yale University and an Oxford scholar, Hersey takes considerable pride in the fact that he had to work to survive as a student. While at Yale, Hersey was vice-chairman and music critic on the *Yale Daily News*, earned a letter in football, and paid his way by waiting on tables, tending telephones, working as a librarian, and by working during summers as a lifeguard, an electrician's assistant, and a tutor. His first postgraduate job in the summer of 1937 was as a secretary, driver, and factotum for the novelist Sinclair Lewis. Following his service with Lewis, he worked for several years as a journalist, including a stint from 1937 through 1944 for *Time* magazine which early on included covering events in China and Japan. During the early part of World War II, he covered the South Pacific and was cited in 1942 by the Secretary of the Navy for helping to remove wounded men from the battlefield while under fire on Guadalcanal Island. In 1943 he was a correspondent in the Mediterranean theater in the Sicilian campaign and moved on to cover Moscow in 1944. After the war, he went to work as a correspondent and editor for *Life* and the *New Yorker*. In the decades following the war, he continued active involvement in various groups concerned with educational and social issues. He also received numerous awards and honors for his work, which include the Anisfield-Wolf Award, 1950, for *The Wall*; Sidney Hillman Foundation Award, 1951, for *The Wall*; the Howland Medal, Yale University, 1952; membership in the American Academy of Arts and Letters, 1953; National Association of Independent Schools Award, 1957, for *A Single Pebble*; Sarah Josepha Hale Award, 1963; and presidency of Authors League of America, 1975. From 1965 to 1970 he was a master of Pierson College at Yale University and then was writer in residence of the American Academy in Rome from 1970 to 1971. Since then he has taught one term each year at Yale as an adjunct professor of English.

Hersey married Frances Ann Cannon in 1940, and the marriage ended in divorce in 1958. Their children are Martin, John Jr., and Baird. Married in 1958, Hersey and Barbara Day Addams Kaufman have a daughter, Brook.

In 1975 he received publicity for his coverage of former President Gerald Ford's daily activities for a week. He continues to write both nonfiction and fiction. A journalistic study of the presidency was published in 1980, and he is presently writing a "fictional biography of a missionary in China—an attempt to get at a deep impulse in the American psyche."

Since the beginning of his career, Hersey has sought to examine such deep impulses in American culture and politics. His first book, *Men on Bataan* (1942), is a journalistic account of the fall of Bataan in April 1942. Hersey's fears about the ability of democracy to function in the midst of the war is reflected in his concern over the power, prestige, and fame of General Douglas MacArthur. In a second journalistic work dealing with the war, *Into the Valley* (1943), Hersey covered a small group of Marines involved in a skirmish on Guadalcanal. The book earned him much praise and was compared to the war fiction of Stephen Crane. A brilliant piece of war reporting, the book details the life of the common soldier in war.

Hersey's fears about the internal threat to democracy represented by an ambitious and egotistic leader and his faith placed in the abilities of the common man come together in his Pulitzer Prize-winning novel, *A Bell for Adano*. When Hersey covered the Sicilian campaign in the summer of 1943, he became interested in the activities of the American governor of Licata, a Sicilian seaport. *A Bell for Adano* focuses on the character of the main figure, Major Victor Joppolo, whom the first readers of the novel saw as a heroic figure trying to bring democracy to a small Italian village. In retrospect, it is evident that there is a basic conflict in the novel between the traditional idea of democracy and the new concept of social control and political organization typified by the American military government. In dramatizing this conflict Hersey anticipated the radical attack on the liberal social programs of the 1960s. Joppolo represents a modern version of an authentic American vernacular hero in the tradition of Mark Twain's Hank Morgan in *A Connecticut Yankee* (1889). Joppolo is the common man raised to high places who believes devoutly in democracy. He tells the people of Adano that democracy means "that the men of the government are no longer the master of the people. They are the servants of the people." Like Hank Morgan he succeeds in reforming and modernizing the society over which he assumes control, emphasizing the importance of popular government, education, and honesty. His positive influence is symbolized by his providing the town with a new bell to replace the one that had been taken by the Fascists and turned into gun barrels. However, the world Joppolo creates for his innocent followers holds unforeseen dangers related to the rise of a modern corporate and technological society. The army which Joppolo represents not only brings change and reform, it also foreshadows in its use of power the modern state. This aspect of the novel is symbolized in the character of General Marvin. Hersey finds this one figure so repulsive and dangerous that he directly addresses the reader about Marvin: "But I can tell you perfectly calmly that General Marvin showed himself during the invasion to be a bad man, something worse than what our troops were trying to throw out." The major operates in conflict with Marvin and countermands one of the general's orders banning all carts from Adano, an act that would ruin the commerce and economic life of the town. He also stands in sharp contrast to some of the other American officers, such as navy lieutenant Crofts Livingston, who seem more like modern corporate personalities than military men. However, the ultimate effect of Joppolo's work is to make the American occupation easier. Although eventually removed by the general, Joppolo works like a tool of the system by serving to effect Adano's transition to a modern consumer-oriented culture. He helps to make the people responsive to and dependent upon the new economic and political order. Thus, when an Italian child is killed while trying to get close to a passing military vehicle whose occupants toss candy to the children, the incident can be seen as symbolic of the relationship of the people to the new government. Following the death, Joppolo arranges for the children to get their presents safely just as he helped to organize the town so that it could experience the benefits of modern society. However, the price of such organization to both individuality and traditional culture clearly bothers Hersey.

Hersey's next major work, *Hiroshima,* is a modern classic partly because it incorporates so well the techniques and style of the novel within a work of journalism. Thus, in this book Hersey anticipates what later critics and writers celebrated as the new mode of the nonfiction novel, a term which Hersey himself disdains. When the work first appeared as the entire 31 August 1946 issue of the *New Yorker* magazine, its impact was instantaneous and unprecedented. Charles Poore of the *New York Times* noted that "Talking to people in that week, listening to the commentators on the air, reading the editorials and the columnists, you soon realized what a profound impression the story had already made." When *Hiroshima* appeared in book form, Albert Einstein ordered 1000 copies of it, and Bernard Baruch ordered 500. Free copies were distributed by the Book-of-the-Month Club on the grounds that nothing else in print "could be of more importance at this moment to the human race." The American Broadcasting Company had the book read on their radio stations. The interest around the nation was so great that some stations felt compelled to repeat the broadcasts, and recordings of it were made available to educational institutions. Poore summed up the reaction of most readers to the book when he wrote that "*Hiroshima* penetrated the tissue of complacency we had built up. It penetrated it all the more inexorably because it told its story not in terms of graphs and charts but in terms of ordinary human beings." The dropping of the bomb is experienced through the eyes of six survivors—two doctors, a widow with two children, a German priest, a Japanese pastor, and a woman clerk—whose experiences become personal events for the reader. He does this simply by showing rather than telling what each of the six was doing when the bomb was dropped, how they reacted to it, how they behaved afterward, and how they felt throughout their ordeals. Interior emotions and attitudes are illustrated by external action. Through his combination of journalism and novelistic character development, Hersey educated his audience about the human significance of an event so terrifying as to be nearly incomprehensible.

A similar problem confronted Hersey in his next work, *The Wall,* the story of the destruction by the Nazis of five hundred thousand Jews in the Warsaw ghetto. Here again Hersey devised a way of depicting what seemed like an unimaginable horror. He created the fictitious personal diary of the character Noach

Levinson to place the story of the deterioration and destruction of Warsaw's Jews under the Nazis within a historical and cultural context. Although the diary entries cover only the period from November 1939 to May 1943, Levinson's clear memory allows him to see the connection of the present crisis to the past. Even before the advent of Nazi persecution many of the characters had deeply ambivalent feelings about their own identities, as individuals and as members of an ethnic minority. These were fed by their equally ambivalent feelings about Jewish culture and religion; but in more normal times these problems could remain submerged in the routines of everyday life. In their insecurity and defensiveness as a vulnerable minority in a crisis situation the characters in *The Wall* discover the need for systems of belief and loyalty upon which to rest individual and group identity. In an early scene in the novel Dolek Berson, who later in the novel approaches traditional heroic proportions, resists identification with the problems and crises of his own people, telling Levinson: "This has nothing to do with me," but Levinson replies, "Yes, this has to do with you, too. And with all your mishpokhe: it concerns all your family ties."

In *The Wall* as in *A Bell for Adano*, Hersey is deeply concerned about the ability of modern man to deal with the threat of totalitarianism. Modern man, he feels, may not only prove unable to resist the forces of totalitarianism, he may also invite them as a result of prolonged alienation and insecurity. In the novel, several characters reveal such alienation in their self-hatred and self-derision. Moreover, as individuals crumble before the Nazis so also do families and finally the community as a whole. At the same time, Hersey refuses to see such capitulation as the only alternative open to modern man. He steadfastly insists that human individuality and responsibility may prevail. He believes man is capable of assuming moral responsibility and authority for his own actions.

Hersey's next two novels are less successful at depicting the confrontations between individuals and the dangers of modern life. Both *The Marmot Drive* (1953) and *A Single Pebble* (1956) seem somewhat abstract and allegorical. *The Marmot Drive* is Hersey's attempt to write a modern New England novel with a contemporary Hester Prynne as a heroine. Her experiences indicate that she has no usable past or tradition upon which to base a system of values and no confidence about her ability to find such guidelines in the future. Similarly, the way in which modern life cuts one off from the traditions of the past is treated in *A Single Pebble*, which concerns the journey of a young unnamed American hydraulic engineer up the Yangtze River on a Chinese junk during the 1920s. His experiences on the river cause him to rethink his own relationship as a Western technocrat to the Orient.

Hersey was far more successful in *The War Lover* (1959) in finding an adequate means to dramatize a complex set of ideas, in this case the examination of the impulse that leads some men to love war. *The War Lover* is a novel about the psychology of death as it manifests itself in the relationship between Buzz Marrow, the war lover, and Charles Boman, his copilot. As in other works by Hersey, it is the psychological enemy within that concerns him as much as the external threat. Sections called "The Raid," which deal with the hours involved in a long mission against the Germans, are interspersed with sections called "The Tour," which describe earlier missions and incidents on the ground up to the time of "The Raid." This device allows Hersey to manipulate time artfully in order to place the present in a living historical context and to present a sophisticated psychological study of human character.

Richard De Combray

John Hersey

Boman and Marrow, as their names indicate, are two aspects of the same personality. Their dual controls over the plane, which is called by Marrow "The Body," further develops the suggestion that they are bone and marrow of the larger organism. At first both men seem quite different. Marrow is the dashing flying ace, while Boman is the defensive short man who has no desire to be a hero, thinking of himself as "not your typical cocky shorty. No would-be Napoleon he. No Little Corporal." However, as the novel progresses we see that the men are mutually dependent. Boman is too comfortable in his position of inferiority and self-denigration before Marrow. Accordingly, the counterpart to Boman's self-deprecation is Marrow's self-celebration and self-inflation. However, Marrow's seeming bravery and defiance of death really mask his enormous fear of it. At one point in the novel he castigates death as "that bastard in the sky" and says "I'd like to kill death." Boman's defensive posture provides a needed corrective.

In order to find himself, Boman must break this cycle of interdependence and does so through the help of Daphne, an English woman, who teaches him how to love by forcing him to have the courage to face his own strength and power and to deal more effectively with external threats. In contrast, Marrow, with his lack of self-knowledge, finally succumbs to his fears. In a sense Hersey is suggesting that when a democracy is at war, each participant must have the self-knowledge and the sense of purpose that can justify self-sacrifice and violence. A spokesman for this position is the character "Kid" Lynch, who says, "Well it strikes me in this century something awful has been let loose among the so-called civilized peoples, something primitive and barbaric. I don't say the Germans have a monopoly on this . . . regression. But I figure I'm here to help put down the Nazis because right at the moment they're the most dangerous representatives of this sort of throwback we're liable to. If I can do my part in keeping this worse side of mankind in hand, I'll be satisfied, whatever happens to me."

Hersey's fear that democracy is undermined if individuals live without awareness of self and higher purpose is echoed in his next novel, *The Child Buyer* (1960). The novel dramatizes the conflict between a philosophy of education that emphasizes the need to foster individual growth and fulfillment and the demands upon educators to produce more scientists, engineers, and technicians. Presented as a transcript of hearings before a state senate committee on education, welfare, and public morality, the novel focuses upon the educational community of Pequot, where the child buyer, Wissey Jones, wants to buy boy genius Barry Rudd in order to make him part of a technological learning network that will take full advantage of the boy's genius and develop it to its utmost. Jones works for a corporation that buys children like Barry under a defense contract and puts them through an enormously complicated but scientifically controlled dehumanizing process that ties off their emotions and senses and enables them to develop intelligence quotients of close to 1000. The children are then connected to computers. They spend the rest of their lives as education machines improving upon the work of the computer. When Jones is asked, near the end of the book, what end such a dehumanizing process serves, he calls it "a foolish question. He didn't even know himself. He believed it had to do with satisfying man's greatest need—to leave the earth."

In a less extreme form Jones's attitude toward education dominates the Pequot educational system. The testimony of Barry's parents, teachers, and others in the community dramatizes the inability of the educational institutions to deal with the students as individuals; instead schools tend to compartmentalize, categorize, and stereotype children. The main opponent to this inhumane philosophy is the elementary school principal, Dr. Frederika Gozar, who attacks the educational philosophy of the state department of education because it "is based on the notion that education is a science, that the process of learning is like a process of catalysis or combustion or absorption—observable, definable, manipulable; and that Barry—volatile, mysterious, smoldering Barry—is inert experimental material." She believes that "You can't package talent, you can't put it in uniform bottles and boxes with labels," and she knows that Jones's educational philosophy is part of a larger social and political philosophy that manipulates and controls the society as a whole. Dr. Gozar realizes that the child buyer's friendly manner disguises "just one slogan: We Must All Obey." Moreover, there are many who favor his approach to education and life. Dr. Gozar's emphasis on individuality and freedom runs absolutely counter to the dominant trend. She says, "The only real defense for a democracy is improvement. Crisis and triumph over crisis. It's a failure of national vision when you regard children as weapons, and talents as materials you can mine, assay, and fabricate for profit and defense." Ultimately, however, even Dr. Gozar sells out to the child buyer as does Barry, who decides to go with him so that he can reach the I.Q. level the man promises.

Written after Hersey had spent ten years as a

member of and consultant to education groups on the local, state, and national levels, *The Child Buyer* excited considerable controversy. The 10 October 1960 issue of the *New Republic* magazine published extensive commentary on the questions the book raised including articles by Margaret Halsey, B. F. Skinner, Carl F. Hansen, Robert Gorham Davis, and William Jay Smith.

Following this novel Hersey had published *Here to Stay* (1962), a series of articles dealing with the survival of people in the face of natural disasters and social upheaval. Two year later *White Lotus*, a novel that received considerable critical attention because of its unusual approach to racism, appeared. The plot of *White Lotus* (1965) involves the enslavement of whites by the Chinese. The story is narrated by a white American girl called White Lotus. In effect, Hersey encapsulates within the years of Lotus's adolescence and early youth the history of blacks in America. Each stage of black history from slavery through the civil rights movement is represented in Lotus's life. In so doing Hersey demonstrates an acute historical, sociological, and psychological insight into black history in America as well as a deep knowledge of the Orient of his own youth. He also demonstrates a brilliant insight into the nature of racism itself. Moreover, what makes the novel especially significant as a contribution to our understanding of racism is the way in which Hersey elaborates on the relationship between racism and liberalism. For the dominant yellow race of the novel the liberal creed of China means a government of laws and justice and a culture based on serious religious principles. "Hurt no living creature" is one of the key principles of Lotus's first master, the Venerable Shen. However, the liberal philosophy of the best minds of China takes an interesting twist when directed toward enslaved whites. Since slavery and racism so strongly contradict the philosophy and attitude of the liberal culture toward human life, the culture dehumanizes the slaves and regards them as either dependent children or animals. Lotus comes to learn early that she must work to sustain this fantasy of her oppressors. Even before fully understanding the meaning of her behavior, she learns from another slave "the slaves' basic law: *No matter how frightened you are before a yellow person, no matter how angry, no matter even how happy, control your face and body; show no feeling; have a face as impassive as a figure painted on a china bowl.*" The effect of this attitude on the slaves is to make schizophrenia a natural psychological condition for them: "What double meanings our life had!" Lotus says. This psychological state gives the slaves a sense of "numbness" which in turn affects their attitudes toward sexuality and violence.

The novel also includes a parallel to the American civil rights movement with leaders who strongly resemble in style and tactics Martin Luther King, Jr., and Malcolm X. A contrast between the slaves in the liberal society in this novel and the situation of the Jews at the end of *The Wall* dramatizes the stark differences between the way liberal and totalitarian states deal with resistors and minorities. By the end of the novel, White Lotus is startled to realize how continuing change and reform have caused her to expect fair treatment from the dominant culture. In addition, she also comes to realize how responsible she is for creating her own freedom: "I had come to realize that freedom could be felt at best only for moments: that even for the powerful, even for yellows, it was inconstant, elusive, fickle and quickly flown. . . . Freedom was not to be bestowed but grasped—and only for a moment at a time."

Freedom is to some extent a theme in *Too Far to Walk* (1966), Hersey's second novel about education in America. In writing this novel Hersey had in mind the growing number of students throughout the country in the mid-1960s who were finding themselves disenchanted with all they saw around them but were unable to come up with satisfactory programs of action for change. John Fist, who "had always thought of himself as a good boy," attends Sheldon College like his father before him and initially plans to follow a career and life pattern very much like his father's. However, he decides that being good comes to mean little more than accommodating himself to others' expectations and demands, and he becomes alienated. At college he dreams about "fusion" and cutting across the intellectual boundaries defined by the traditional curriculum, but he finds that graduation and traditional success will require him to conform intellectually and socially. Attracted to the drug culture, Fist falls in with a devilish character named Breed who promises, "I'll give you all that you want. You'll pay for this service by turning your id over to me." With Breed, Fist will attempt to find a new consciousness through a fusion of science and the humanities, electricity and poetry. The two sign a blood pact, and feeling an affinity for "something known as the New Morality," Fist begins a kind of Faustian adventure of experimentation with drugs. In his quest for a new freedom, John finds that he lost his sense of self. Thus, at the end he tells Breed that he cannot renew his contract "Because I can't go on living in a world that's on a knife-edge between hallucination and objective truth." He goes on to tell Breed: "I can't live with frenzy, visions, stupor, hangovers—and finally a tremor, a dragging foot as I walk. You sold me a bill of goods. You sold me illusions. I prefer the real world, crummy as it is." In spite of the fact that he has no firm answer to Breed's challenge of "Who's to say what's real? Do you know what's real?," Fist decides to turn away from a world that denies the existence of reality and affirms false "breakthroughs," realizing that "what you put me through was a series of flights into myself, away from other people." Instead of such a world Fist, like Hersey, prefers one involving "friction" with reality and human contact. "I've come to see," he says, "that there can't be any shortcut to those breakthroughs I yearn for. You can't imbibe them, or smoke them, or take them intravenously, or get them by crossing your legs and breathing deeply for twenty minutes."

In a sense Hersey's next novel, *Under the Eye of the Storm* (1967), is about the graduate who never learned Fist's lessons and so must gain Fist's experience and knowledge in other ways, in this case a sailing adventure. Dr. Tom Medlar, a liver specialist, tends to see people only in terms of this organ. Not yet thirty-five, he is already sick of himself and "earnestly sick of the organ of his choice." As Tom's last name suggests he must learn to stop meddling in others' lives and start living his own. With his wife and another couple, Tom goes out to sea and runs into a storm that frees him temporarily from the false consciousness and false sense of reality that have plagued him. Unfortunately, once the danger of the storm ends, Tom is "oppressed by a heavy sense of the discrepancies between his reading of the experiences of the storm and the versions his crew had brought away." Finally, his experiences during the storm serve only as the source for an entertaining story that Tom tells to please people.

Hersey's next two books, *The Algiers Motel Incident* (1968) and *Letter to the Alumni* (1970), were works of nonfiction on the subjects of racism and education. They were followed by *The Conspiracy* (1972) in which Hersey returned to the novelistic mode to examine the problems of freedom and political corruption in modern society through the metaphoric use of Roman history. In the process he liberally alters the original accounts of Tacitus and Suetonius to tell his version of the 64 A.D. plot to kill Emperor Nero, making it clear that his inspiration for the novel comes more from recent American history rather than from Roman history. The exchange of letters between the poet Lucan and the philosopher Seneca constitutes a discourse and debate on the subject of freedom. Thus, Seneca writes to Lucan: "Who is to blame for tyranny—the tyrant or the tyrannized? Who is to blame for your outbursts against me—you or I?" In the novel tyranny destroys itself through its insatiable hunger for more power, for as Seneca notes, "The aim of power is to keep power. The only real and lasting power, it should be clear is that of character, that which obliges others to follow because of admiration and love." Moreover, Seneca voices Hersey's view that the writer must express his concern for morality in public life to encourage life-enhancing impulses.

Since writing *The Conspiracy* Hersey has shown even more interest in the subject of writing itself. He edited *The Writer's Craft* (1974), which includes major writers' essays on their art, and he edited a collection of essays on the writer Ralph Ellison, which includes his own introductory interview with Ellison. He has also written two journalistic works dealing with the institution of the presidency. With all of these interests, however, Hersey continues to write fiction. *My Petition for More Space* (1974) presents Hersey's dystopian vision of a world in which overpopulation, a scarcity of resources, mind control, the growth of bureaucracy, and dehumanizing administration, all define the human condition. The setting for the entire novel is a mob scene in which innumerable people are crammed together in long lines, like passengers on a rush hour subway train, sometimes waiting for days to reach the government's "petition windows." In the society of the novel changing a job, marrying, going to school, moving to a new residence require a verbal petition to an anonymous authority hidden behind opaque glass. Invariably, the petitioners are turned down, and most of them, in fact, seem so demoralized and dehumanized that approval would probably terrify them. These people do not have homes but are allotted set amounts of space, and the narrator of the story wants to petition for more of it even though his space of seven feet by eleven feet makes him relatively well off.

The petition lines are so crowded that people are often unable to see the faces of those in front of or behind them. But there are conversations and some of those on the lines get vicarious pleasures from the close physical contact. The narrator, for example, has fantasies about the woman in front of him, encounters hostility from another man, and is bored by a grandmother who says she appears regularly on the lines because she enjoys meeting the people on them. When he reaches the window, his petition is denied, but he decides that he probably will return to make another petition. The process of making petitions is a kind of neurotic activity that becomes an end in itself because of its capacity for providing distraction.

With *The Walnut Door* (1977) Hersey returns once again to the subject of education. Elaine Quinlan, a Bennington graduate, and Eddie Macaboy, a former Reed College student, were both, in different ways, part of the youth culture of the late 1960s and early 1970s. Macaboy especially is obsessed with understanding his past experience in "the movement," listing his reasons for leaving college as "Disillusionment. Vietnam. Ego dilution. Deep-seated toxic reactions. 'The Movement seemed like a better education than Sociology 24.' " But Macaboy soon learned that "So many of the big talkers were cowards because they'd never learned how to be afraid." The result, he feels, was the growth of a near-mystical fascination for violence and evil. Rather than continue with either politics or formal education, Macaboy moves in a different direction. Hersey portrays him as a genius who turns his newly chosen crafts of locksmithing and carpentry into an art form, and the novel becomes a study of the nature of art.

Hersey's symbol for artistic creation is the walnut door, a masterpiece of craftsmanship, that Elaine has hired him to install because someone has broken into her apartment. Ironically, Macaboy is the perpetrator of this crime. The safety Elaine craves turns into a danger in itself as she becomes his prisoner. "The company wants you to feel safe," he says sardonically to her. Accustomed to retreating within herself, Elaine finds her victimization both frightening and fascinating. She eventually grows to trust her new jailer and admits that he "had begun to make her feel supersafe." Forced by the death of his father to return to his hometown in Connecticut and confront his past, Macaboy leaves her and her new fear is that he will not return. "For a flickering moment she wondered if Macaboy had abandoned her. Then it came to her that actually it was he, not she, who was being held captive by the walnut door." In love with him now, she feels safe and believes that an unhappy affair of a few years earlier will not be repeated. But there is a touch of irony to the novel's conclusion. Not being his prisoner creates a new sense of insecurity. Although he seems ready to move in and to establish a more permanent relationship in her apartment ("I'll have the door open," she says), the novel ends with Macaboy striving to complete his new work of art, the oak door, for another woman. He informs the new customer of his concern for "your personal safety, Mzz Creeley. Like people breaking in."

The Walnut Door integrates many of Hersey's most pervasive themes into an artistic whole illustrating his belief that a changing and dangerous world provides a continuing challenge to individual freedom. Throughout his long career Hersey has believed that as a writer he could maintain such freedom through the creative act of writing about the political and moral issues that have dominated modern times. He has tried steadily to ameliorate the contemporary human condition by challenging and enlightening public consciousness. In *The Walnut Door* Hersey once again connects his theory of art to his liberal social philosophy. His overriding concern remains human survival with freedom and dignity.

—*Sam B. Girgus*

Other:

The Writer's Craft, edited by Hersey (New York: Knopf, 1974);

Ralph Ellison: A Collection of Critical Essays, edited by Hersey (Englewood Cliffs, N.J.: Prentice Hall, 1974).

Reference:

David Sanders, *John Hersey* (New Haven: College & University Press, 1967).

EDWARD HOAGLAND
(21 December 1932-)

BOOKS: *Cat Man* (Boston: Houghton Mifflin, 1956);

The Circle Home (New York: Crowell, 1960);

The Peacock's Tail (New York: McGraw-Hill, 1965);

Notes from the Century Before: A Journal from British Columbia (New York: Random House, 1969);

The Courage of Turtles (New York: Random House, 1971);

Walking the Dead Diamond River (New York: Random House, 1973);

The Moose on the Wall: Field Notes from the Vermont Wilderness (London: Barrie & Jenkins, 1974);

Red Wolves and Black Bears (New York: Random House, 1976);

African Calliope: A Journey to the Sudan (New York: Random House, 1979);

The Edward Hoagland Reader, ed. Geoffrey Wolff (New York: Random House, 1979).

The details of Edward Hoagland's life and personality shed light on both the materials and the style of his writings. He was born in New York City, and went to Deerfield Academy and then Harvard. His first novel, *Cat Man* (1956), was accepted by Houghton Mifflin before he graduated from Harvard in 1954. He had already shown a dislike of conventional sports, preferring to tramp the woods alone. His love of solitude and silent observation of wildlife rather than social conversation may have resulted from a severe stammer that still persists. This stammer has, according to Hoagland himself, influenced how he writes: "Words are spoken at considerable cost to me, so a great value is placed on each one. That has had some effect on me as a writer. As a child, since I couldn't talk to people, I became close to animals. I became an observer, and in all my books, even the novels, witnessing things is what counts." His reluctance to speak may account for his desire to write—and be read—and for the sensitive visual, tactile, and olfactory images in his writings.

As a young man he had varied experiences that were to appear, sometimes with only minor modifications, in his essays and fiction (for he is at times a very candid, even confessional writer despite his reticent manner): he looked after a morgue while he was in the army, tramped across the country, worked as a circus hand, became fascinated with the behavior of the big cats, and had brief brushes with sadism. He thought of himself as something of an "oddball," of being "a little askew," and wondered whether he was homosexual.

Much of his time is divided between the wilderness and the urban scene. Thus, with his second wife, Marion Magid, who is managing editor of *Commentary* magazine, and his daughter, Hoagland likes to divide the year between his home, well off the beaten track and without electricity, in northern Vermont, and his apartment in New York City, that urban world he observes and writes about with both detachment and sympathy in essays and fiction. His travels to more distant areas have resulted in the widely acclaimed travel narratives, *Notes from the Century Before: A Journal from British Columbia* (1969) and *African Calliope: A Journey to the Sudan* (1979). He has been awarded several prestigious literary awards, including a Houghton Mifflin Literary Fellowship for *Cat Man* (1956), two Guggenheim fellowships (1964, 1975), an American Academy of Arts and Letters Traveling Fellowship (1964), an O. Henry Award (1971), and a

Nancy Crampton

Brandeis University Creative Arts Citation (1971-1972).

Hoagland's writing career has shown a remarkable but foreseeable movement from fiction to nonfiction. After producing three novels and a handful of short stories during the period from 1956 to 1969, he contributed, between 1968 and 1980, more than one hundred essays and book reviews, many of them not written on assignment, to such diverse outlets as the *Village Voice, Sports Illustrated*, the *New York Times* and the *New York Times Book Review*, the *Atlantic Monthly*, and the *New England Review*. Since March 1979 Hoagland's unsigned nature editorials have appeared occasionally in the *New York Times*.

Yet whether in essay, travel book, short story, or novel, Hoagland has his own distinctive voice and is often concerned with similar matters: animals, particularly those man hunts to kill or seeks to tame; the lives of ordinary people, whether in American cities or British Columbian hinterlands, whose hold on life is often threatened by poverty, alcohol, or lack of skills. His work contains an unusual blend of Thoreau's interest in nature and the urban naturalism of Dreiser. In addition, in a manner reminiscent of Hemingway, he sometimes employs

challenge and
There were two American dreams---the idea and/rhapsody of the
both cruel/ apparently/ equally seize the day and opportunity
frontier, savage and innocent, and/limitless opportunity/to/found
a fortune

Manuscript

the imagined feelings of animals (as in *Cat Man*), a staccato style, and a code (or erosion of a code) to evaluate both users of the wilderness and the city dwellers. The world of Hoagland's writing, too, is most often a man's world. His sentences are, however, recognizably his own, for they are more complex, more metaphorically detailed, more obviously a reflection of the author's ranging, discursive mind than Hemingway's though the subjects may be similar. Furthermore, the structure of his works, often built around a journey or quest, appears circuitous and dependent in the essays upon the wishes, even whims of the narrator, or in the novels upon the travels and searchings of a protagonist who has insufficient intelligence or strength of will to shape the future to his wishes. Thus death, uncertain fates, or unrealized hopes come at the end of the novels.

Although his novels have received some critical acclaim, they have not won a wide audience, perhaps because the protagonists—drifters, misfits, failures—seem to have no significance beyond their own individual, at times trivial, selves. (Of his seven books in print at present, only one is a novel—*The Circle Home*, 1960.)

The first novel, *Cat Man*, describes life in a traveling circus. Though the details are often petty and sordid the reader is led to sympathize with some of the circus hands and look down upon the outsiders, the townspeople. Much of the book portrays the activities of Fiddler, a cat man, and his relationship, always fraught with danger, with his charges. The differences between the various species of big cats are presented with the love of an admiring but not sentimental naturalist. At times man and beasts seem one; indeed, they gruesomely become one when the book ends climactically with Fiddler being torn to death by the lions:

> And one by one the goatee points on all the chins flattened until they looked no better than boxer snarling dogs, eyes buried in flame-yellow folds. Back of the wreck of the ribs they groped, tearing and hauling, wincing because of the clattering stakes on the bars. And the fire seared up and burned out his eyes. And strips of face and bone. The honey, fondling hands were gone. The elephants blared and rumbled and bawled. The elephants blared and rumbled . . .

Denny Kelly, a prizefighter and the protagonist of *The Circle Home,* is a misfit. Unable to win a crucial fight when striving to become a champion and incapable of committing his love to one woman (his wife, Patsy), he seems doomed to become a skid row derelict like his father or to be forever seeking forgiveness from his wife. At the close of the novel, he begs to be allowed to return to her:

> "No, but I won't! You don't know. Oh God, I'll promise, I'll swear I won't! I wouldn't come if I thought it was going to happen again, I promise you I wouldn't. I know what I've done and I'm going to be good to you and I want to do it for you and the kids too, for Annie. I only called so you'd know I was coming. I'm coming, my darling, I'm coming back, Patsy, I'm coming back!"
>
> He couldn't let go of the phone. He felt next door to her and not in Philadelphia. He clung to it. "I'm coming back."

The final words of the novel, Patsy's "Try this time. *Try,*" are full of pathos but give no assurance of Kelly's reform. Hoagland shows insight, however, into the plight of a married woman doomed to love a man who yearns to be faithful but lacks the will to be so.

Ben Pringle, the main character of the third novel, *The Peacock's Tail* (1965), has a more conventional background than Fiddler or Kelly, but he too is maladjusted. He is unlucky in love and, contrary to expectations, a failure in his career. Taking up residence among society's misfits in New York City, he has some success as a storyteller to hordes of young children. He turns from his former effete life to a happier, more primitive existence.

The nature of Hoagland's main characters is both a strength and a weakness of the novels. The author, filled with compassion, insight, and a detailed knowledge, can sharply etch their milieux. In *The Circle Home,* for example, Better Champions' Gym lives for the reader in all its sweaty action and shady dealings; but since many of the characters are drifters, incapable of expressing their feelings or plans subtly, with their actions governed by the basic needs for shelter, food, alcohol, and sex (with some yearning for love), the reader has to rely on Hoagland's sharp depiction of scene and event to suggest any depth to the characters.

The attractiveness and worth of Hoagland's novels do not arise from a subtle exploration of complex characters, nor, despite good use of flashbacks in *The Circle Home,* from any innovation in fictional technique. The movement of the novels, in fact, often seems to stop while the author pauses to give a quasi essay, sometimes with humor, on the nature of big cats or the use of a punching bag. Instead, we appreciate the individuality of the chapters, the varied nature of the prose (Hoagland has a good ear for dialogue), and the sympathetic re-creation of life among the misfits and the oddballs; but he is not in the muckraking tradition. The primitivism of his fiction may exclude a Jamesian exploration of a character's psychology, but it leads nevertheless to deeply moving and disturbing scenes: Hoagland skillfully depicts Kelly, the defeated and demoralized boxer, as traveling across the country and back like a wounded, crazed lion trying to identify its quarry, but finally limping back to its lair.

Throughout the fiction, as throughout the essays and travel narratives, one senses in Hoagland an educated sensitivity, a sturdy intelligence, and a tenacious individualism. The picture of a reborn Thoreau, but one more obviously exposed to and fascinated by the life of the modern city, is not so inapt after all.

—James A. Hart

WILLIAM HUMPHREY
(18 June 1924-)

SELECTED BOOKS: *The Last Husband and Other Stories* (New York: Morrow, 1953; London: Chatto & Windus, 1953);
Home from the Hill (New York: Knopf, 1958; London: Chatto & Windus, 1958);
The Ordways (New York: Knopf, 1965; London: Chatto & Windus, 1965);
A Time and A Place (New York: Knopf, 1968; London: Chatto & Windus, 1969);
The Spawning Run (New York: Knopf, 1970; London: Chatto & Windus, 1970);
Proud Flesh (New York: Knopf, 1973; London: Chatto & Windus, 1973);
Ah, Wilderness! The Frontier in American Literature (El Paso: Texas Western Press, 1977);
Farther Off From Heaven (New York: Knopf, 1977; London: Chatto & Windus, 1977);
My Moby Dick (Garden City: Doubleday, 1978; London: Chatto & Windus, 1979).

The publisher Alfred Knopf called William Humphrey's first novel, *Home from the Hill* (1958), the finest novel to come out of Texas. More than twenty years have passed since Knopf made the statement; and though a number of good Texas novels have appeared since then—two more by Humphrey himself—Knopf's judgment of the novel's place in Texas literature has not been questioned seriously. Though Humphrey's writings are almost all about his small corner of the state, and though he is definitely a regional novelist, his reputation is not confined to the Southwest, where he was born in the summer of 1924.

Humphrey spent his first thirteen years in Clarksville, Texas; and those years furnished him with the material for his three novels, almost all of his short stories, and his recent autobiographical volume—*Farther Off From Heaven* (1977). The county seat of Red River County, Clarksville is in the far northeast corner of Texas not more than ten miles from the Oklahoma line (the Red River) and not more than twenty from the southwestern corner of Arkansas. Northeast Texas is a land of rolling hills, scattered scrub oak thickets, and red dirt. In Humphrey's boyhood, Red River County was cotton country and as Southern in tone as any county in Georgia or Mississippi. It is this Southern, cotton-oriented small town and its surrounding area that Humphrey writes about, and his picture of Clarksville makes him seem much more a Southern novelist than a Southwestern one.

Humphrey moved from Clarksville in July of 1937 when his father was killed in a car crash; he did not visit it again until 1969. Clarence Humphrey, in many respects the original of Captain Wade Hunnicutt of *Home from the Hill*, was fatally injured in a one-car accident on July Fourth. Within three days of his father's death, William Humphrey and his mother left Clarksville to move to Dallas, and as he tells in *Farther Off From Heaven*, "My last night's sleep in Clarksville, with my father's body lying in the next room, would be my last ever, I vowed. No visits home for me, no reopening of wounds. It was a vow I was to keep for thirty-two years."

During the thirty-two years when Humphrey kept his vow, he attended public schools in Dallas, Southern Methodist University, and the University of Texas at Austin. In the early 1940s he moved to New York and began writing fiction. Several stories appeared in the late 1940s in *Accent* and *Sewanee Review*; in the early 1950s, he published stories in the *New Yorker, Harper's Bazaar*, and the *Quarterly Review of Literature*. These stories, along with four original pieces, were collected and published in 1953 as *The Last Husband and Other Stories*.

Home from the Hill appeared in 1958, and its success allowed Humphrey, his wife Dorothy, and their daughter to move to northern Italy, where he wrote his second novel, *The Ordways*, a part of which was published in *Saturday Evening Post*. *The Ordways* was a Literary Guild Selection, and the Knopf edition appeared early in 1965; before the year was out the book had been through six printings. The reviews of *The Ordways* were excellent, and the Texas Institute of Letters awarded it a prize of $1,000 as the best book of fiction for the year, the same award *Home from the Hill* had won in 1958.

Humphrey's second collection of short stories, *A Time and A Place*, was published in 1968 and contains ten stories, nine of which had appeared in *Esquire, Saturday Evening Post*, and the *Atlantic*; one was original in the volume. The short stories were followed in 1973 by his third novel, *Proud Flesh*, which received good reviews and had good sales, but which did not receive the acclaim of his first two novels. The only other important work which Humphrey has produced is *Farther Off From Heaven*, a memoir of his early days in Clarksville. The book received excellent reviews both in Texas and across the country.

Humphrey has lectured and taught at Washington and Lee University, University of Texas at El Paso, and Smith College, but he has pursued his writing career, for the most part, without academic connections. He has received two awards from the Texas Institute of Letters and was awarded a grant in 1963 by the National Institute of Arts and Letters, but he has supported himself solely as a professional writer for most of his adult life. He now makes his home in Hudson, New York, but he continues to write about Texas, a small part of Texas at that—the few hundred square miles surrounding Clarksville in Red River County. It is, in fact, only his first-published book, *The Last Husband and Other Stories*, that gets away from the region—and then for only four of the ten stories. These four stories are the weakest in the collection; and it is perhaps from those stories that he learned, as James Joyce did, that he must never live in his home country but never write about anything else.

The Last Husband collection is like many first books of short stories in that it shows a writer of talent who is obviously still struggling to find his voice. The book reveals, in embryonic stages, both Humphrey's weak and strong points. He writes clearly and well in most of the stories, and when he is treating Clarksville and environs, he manages to give a strong rendering of a sense of place—a thing he does superbly well. He captures the language, customs, and life-styles of the people of his native region. But in many of these stories, as in much of Humphrey's work, there are difficulties with plotting. There are also problems with focus and point of view, though in the first story, "The Hardys," the shifting focus, the plotting, and the treatment of Southern characters are very well done.

The Hardys are an old couple who must sell their home and go to live with their children. The story takes place on moving day as each one goes through the house in an unsuccessful attempt to decide what to keep and what to abandon. The reader is allowed inside the minds of both main characters. In the wife's mind he learns of her overwhelming jealousy of the first Mrs. Hardy, who is long dead. The present Mrs. Hardy has spent her life in the shadow of Mr. Hardy's first wife, she thinks, and on graveyard cleaning day has been scrupulous in tending her rival's grave and planting flowers on it. Once in Mr. Hardy's mind, one sees that he has completely forgotten the first wife, is totally devoted to Mrs. Hardy, and is unaware that any jealousy ever existed. The touch of irony gives a neat turn to the story, but the chief value of "The Hardys" lies in the excellent characterizations and the expertly handled shifting focus. The reader sees first with Mr. Hardy's eyes, then with his wife's; and Humphrey handles the shifts between the characters well and integrates them into the framework of the story.

Even the stories in this volume that are less than successful are well written, for everything Humphrey has published, successful or not, is marked by his excellence of style and his clarity. The flaws in the stories—the problems with shifts in focus and especially the failure to plot carefully—appear in later works. His depictions of characters are generally strong, though some of the characters do not come across as real and believable people—another problem with some of Humphrey's later works. But, all in all, the book of stories is a good piece of work and a worthy precursor to his first novel, which was published five years later.

Home from the Hill was an instant success. It had extremely good sales, very favorable reviews, and was made into a successful motion picture. The book has been through a number of printings in both hardback and paper; in fact, it has never been out of print. The novel is about the Hunnicutt family of a northeast Texas town like Clarksville. Specifically it is about the coming to manhood and early death of Theron, son of Hannah and Captain Wade Hunnicutt. The family is the richest in the whole county, for Wade owns cotton farms all over the area. He and Hannah have been married in name only since shortly after the conception of Theron when Hannah learned not only that Wade had not come to the marriage bed in a state of purity but also that he had, in fact, the reputation of being the leading womanizer in Red River County. She plans to influence Theron to be unlike his father in sexuality but like him in other ways. Wade is the greatest hunter and woodsman in northeast Texas, a thoroughgoing man's man who is admired by all the men and desired by the women.

The novel opens on a day in the early 1950s when Hannah's body is returned home from the insane asylum where she died. But most of the novel, told in a long flashback, takes place in the late 1930s when Theron is coming into manhood and full sexuality. He marries a girl whose child he mistakenly thinks is fathered by Wade; the father of the girl whose child Theron fathered kills Wade thinking he, not Theron, is the father; and Theron disappears and presumably dies in the Sulphur Bottoms after tracking and killing his father's murderer. Wade and Theron die on 28 May 1939, and Hannah has three stones erected for the family—all with the same date. The date marks the end of all their lives, though Hannah survives for fifteen years in the nonlife of an insane asylum.

Home from the Hill has a well-unified plot until almost the end of the book. The first three-quarters of the novel, the section which develops the estrangement of Wade and Hannah and the initiation into adulthood of Theron, is well plotted and seems to grow naturally out of the characters; but the last part of the book relies a bit too much on coincidence and obvious manipulation. A reader can believe one or two coincidental happenings, but the seven or eight at the end of the novel test the reader's credulity.

The flaws in the book's conclusion are not, however, enough to mar the novel seriously, for there are too many parts of the novel done exceedingly well to cause anyone to label it a failure. Some characterizations are first-rate, and while some characterizations never rise above caricature, the caricatures are eminently successful. The most successful of these is that of Wade Hunnicutt, Cap'n Wade, as the citizens call him. He is not the center of the novel; but he is certainly its star, and it is no accident that the movie relied for its appeal on Robert Mitchum's portrayal of Wade Hunnicutt. He is everything that Robert Mitchum represents best: he is strong, masculine, laconic, handsome in his ruggedness, and remote. For Humphrey to have attempted to probe into his character as he does into Theron's would have defeated the novel, for Captain Wade is a remote presence brooding over the lives of his family and his domain. It is Theron, however, on whom the novel focuses and on whom the theme centers. Theron is torn between the gentility of his mother and the sexual crudity of his father. He is a youth who comes to awareness of the world; and this familiar motif seems neither old nor overdone in Humphrey's hand.

The best thing about *Home from the Hill*, about all of Humphrey's best work, is the sense of time and place. The reader knows and feels that he is in the South of the 1930s. The idiom is perfect, the descriptions of Clarksville and the surrounding areas are exact, and the people *are* cotton farmers and small tradesmen. But though the book depicts the customs, folklore, and language of rural northeast Texas, at its core the novel is about people who could have lived anywhere at any time. The ability to re-create a region exactly and yet not so limit the characters to it so that they lose believability is the heart of great regional writing and is what separates it from local color. *Home from the Hill*, with the brilliance of its regional flavor, is a very good novel, and its wide readership all across the country was not gained as much by its depiction of Clarksville as by its portrayal of an authentic human experience.

The Ordways, Humphrey's second novel, is less successful than his first. The flavor of rural Texas is not diminished, nor has his style become patterned. The novel is good, but the interest is a little more in the time and the place than in the people. The novel traces four generations of Ordways from the Civil War in Tennessee to Clarksville in the 1920s. Divided into four parts, the novel's first section is devoted to Thomas and Ella Ordway who came west with their family after Thomas was wounded at Shiloh, with their possessions, including the bones of dead ancestors sealed in kegs. The last three sections are centered largely on their son Sam's search for his kidnapped child. The novel begins as a family saga and in the last three-fourths of the book turns into a comic picaresque when Sam Ordway sets out to find Little Ned, the stolen three-year-old. The story is begun by a fourth-generation Ordway who has learned almost all of what he knows at the annual graveyard cleaning days at the family plot in the town of Mabry just outside Clarksville. The narrator appears and disappears as the focus shifts from generation to generation, but at the end he returns to tell of the return of a grown-up Ned some thirty years after Sam gave up his search.

The themes of the novel are familiar to readers of Southern writers—the impact of the Civil War on Southerners and the importance which Southerners place on the family. One or the other of these themes appears in some form in most of Humphrey's writing. In *The Ordways* the Southern family theme predominates; in fact, most of the novel is a dramatization of the idea that family loyalty gives one roots which many residents of industrial areas lack. As the narrator says early in the novel, "Conscious of a long and vigorous lineage, the Southerner is assured of a long continuity to follow him. Meanwhile in his time he is priest of the tribal scripture; to forget any part of it would be sacrilege. He treasures the sayings of his kin. . . . If he forgets them, he will be forgotten. If he remembers, he will be remembered."

In *The Ordways* the family is symbolic of the South. And much of the novel is an attempt to explain the loyal and proud family and the equally proud land. But some of the point of the theme gets lost when Humphrey allows the adventures of Sam Ordway to take over the book. The parts of the book devoted to the search are comic, often extremely so, but they seem an indulgence on the author's part, a chance to tell tall tales and present comic characters and situations. This is not to say that the search section is devoid of all serious intent; it is just that the point gets overwhelmed by the multitude of adventures.

Partly based on actual events in Humphrey's mother's family, *The Ordways* is not deficient in showing the land as it was from the Civil War to the 1920s. In fact, some parts of the book are as good as anything Humphrey has written. The opening scene, the graveyard cleaning, is as good a depiction of local customs as there is in American literature. Graveyard cleanings are festivals in the rural South, occasions when members of the clan who have moved to cities can come home to honor their kin and to be reunited with the relatives who never left. These are times for retelling the legends of the family and the land, and Humphrey's use of the homecoming festival is brilliant. It not only allows him to deliver a tour de force of description, but also provides him a framework to allow his narrator to tell the story. The narration of *The Ordways* marks an advance over *Home from the Hill,* which is similar in some ways. In both novels a narrator, who begins as an individual, fades into the background to let the omniscient narrator take over. The first novel's narrator was a citizen of the town who disappeared after a few pages, but in *The Ordways* the young boy who tells the story appears and reappears as he is needed. He witnesses some things, but when things occur that he could not have seen, he fades out. Such a device is hard to manage, but Humphrey does it in a most believable way.

The characterizations are in some ways better than those in *Home from the Hill,* though there is no figure like Captain Wade Hunnicutt to dominate the novel. The plot is not up to that of the first novel, chiefly because the author gets carried away telling stories which detract from the main purpose. The sense of locale is, as always, of a very high order. *The Ordways* sold well, remained on the best-seller lists for weeks, and was bought but not filmed by a movie company. The reviews were generally good, but no one is likely to rank it above *Home from the Hill.*

In *A Time and A Place* most of the short stories seem to be incidents left over from the novels, and there is little that needs to be said of them. In this collection Humphrey remains strictly in the Red River area, though he crosses the ten miles into Oklahoma for some of the stories. But the important thing is that he has not one single story about Eastern or Northern life; apparently, he had learned after his first collection that he could do better avoiding the sort of *New Yorker* fiction he tried a few times. The title of the work is accurate, for the stories are set in the poor farm and small town areas of northeast Texas and southeast Oklahoma during the middle 1930s—the years of the Depression, the dust bowl, and the first oil strikes in that part of Oklahoma.

Once again, the sense of place in the stories is up to Humphrey's usual high standards; but the stories, while interesting enough, are not remarkable. The best of the lot, and one which will serve to give the tone and substance of the work, is "The Ballad of Jesse Neighbors," the opening story. Jesse is a "poreboy" who works hard on the land so that he can someday own a small place of his own. His father has always been a tenant farmer; and he hopes to move one rung up the ladder into the yeoman class that Naomi Childress, whom he loves, was born into. Her father, Bull, owns outright twenty-seven acres of hardscrabble and therefore looks down upon the Neighbors family. The first part of the story details Jesse's courtship of Naomi despite Bull's displeasure; the middle part tells of Bull's oil strike; and the final part focuses on Jesse's attempt to rob the Clarksville bank, his capture, trial, and execution.

The theme of the story—of the book—is the uncertainty of rural 1930s life. Before the 1930s one could count on subsistence-level farming and on having the same kind of life that had been lived in the South for a hundred years. During the 1930s Fate was more capricious. The land underwent great change, first by the severe drought and later by the oil boom that swept various parts of the Southwest. Some tenant farmers and small owners starved or left the land; others became rich overnight when oil was discovered. The first part of Jesse's story is a typical recital of dirt-farm life; the second part is a humorous sketch of a dirt-farming family rushing off to Dallas to stay at the Adolphus Hotel and shop at Neiman-Marcus as soon as the gusher comes in; the final section shows Jesse being overcome by Bonnie-and-Clyde fever and suffering the odd quirk of fate involved when he robs a bank in Texas—a capital crime—instead of one in Oklahoma where the penalties are less severe. All the stories deal with the same general theme. The stories are generally satisfactory but not up to the level of Humphrey's best work.

William Humphrey's most recent novel is *Proud Flesh.* Set in northeast Texas once again, it is a novel about the Renshaw clan, who, like the Ordways, have mostly scattered away from the home country, but who are called home to the deathbed of Edwina, the matriarch. The returnees come from as far away as Dallas, Waxahachie, and Nacogdoches. All but one. Kyle, the favorite son of Edwina, is the only one of her ten children and thirty-seven grandchildren and in-laws who does not appear. When he does not return, two of the older sons of Edwina set out to New York City where they vaguely think he might be. It never really occurs to them that he cannot be found, and they decide to take the city street by street, house by house. They, of course, are still looking as the book ends.

The theme of the book is the same one treated in *The Ordways*—the allegiance of the family members to the family above all else. The members of the Renshaw tribe are a collection of grotesques—misers, fanatics, kidnappers, and lunatics—and the book suffers because Humphrey seems to be doing a Texas version of one of Faulkner's novels about an aberrant Southern family. There is no real point to *Proud Flesh* except for the depiction of the clan. The events of the novel are a little too fantastic to be real, and the characters are not much above the level of simple caricatures. Though there is still some vestige of the Humphrey touch in giving a sense of place, even much of that is lost. The novel is set in the 1960s, and Humphrey is still writing about a Texas he knew in the 1930s. The book is a failure. The style is good, but there is little else to recommend it.

In addition to his novels, short stories, and his memoir, Humphrey produced three minor pamphlet-length works. The first, *The Spawning Run* (1970), is a small book—eighty pages of large type on 5 x 7 sheets—which had run as an article in *Esquire*. It is mostly his observations of salmon fishing and salmon fishers along various streams in Dorset and Wales. The book is interesting, even delightful in its way, but not a significant part of the Humphrey canon. A lecture on American literature which he gave at Washington and Lee University when he was Glasgow Visiting Professor—*Ah, Wilderness! The Frontier in American Literature*—was published by Texas Western Press in 1977 when Humphrey went to lecture at the University of Texas at El Paso that year. The lecture is of mild interest, but certainly not a publication that will increase his stature as either writer or critic. His most recent work is *My Moby Dick* (1978), a fishing story similar to *The Spawning Run*. The book has barely fifty pages of type. The story details Humphrey's sighting, catching, and losing a forty-two-inch trout in the Berkshire Mountains of Massachusetts.

Farther Off From Heaven is an autobiography of the first thirteen years of the author's life, the only years Humphrey lived in Clarksville. The book covers the three or four days between Clarence Humphrey's accident and his burial. But using the various events of the short period as points of reference, Humphrey weaves in the whole of his thirteen years and his parents' early lives in Clarksville. He re-creates from the point of view of a child the sights, sounds, and feelings of Clarksville as it was in the 1920s and 1930s. Readers of Humphrey's novels and stories see the raw material from which the fiction was created: his parents and grandparents are originals of a good many of his fictional characters, and the child's knowledge of the details of Clarksville and Red River County are translated into setting.

The book's purpose may at first seem somewhat obscure to the reader, for it is neither self-advertisement nor a series of answers to frequently asked questions. But close inspection will reveal the purpose the book serves for its author: it is his coming to terms with his father and with the time and place that he must have hated in 1937 but came to love in a curious way in later years. That the book is both Humphrey's portrait of the artist and sentimental journey does not deter the casual reader, for it is above all a brilliant and highly readable account of a sensitive and intelligent boy coming, slowly at first and then suddenly, into awareness of the world.

In some of Humphrey's fiction it is possible to point to one or two aspects of the works as outstanding and to complain that other parts are deficient. Such is not the case with *Farther Off From Heaven*. The book is an almost perfect example of the partial autobiography; the style is Humphrey's best so far; the characterization of his parents is unflawed; the sense of time and place has never been done better in his other works; and his complex handling of time-shifts and shifts in moods is made to seem simple and unobtrusive.

Writing with love and affection about one's parents—especially when one or both died early—is most difficult to do without bathing the whole work in a flood of sentimentality. It is so rarely done well that after one has listed Virginia Woolf's *To the Lighthouse* and James Agee's *A Death in the Family*, he is hard put to find many examples. To write such a book without benefit of the fictional distancing used by Woolf and Agee is doubly hard. But Humphrey has done it in *Farther Off From Heaven*. Both parents come across as real because Humphrey has understood their flaws and has forgiven them, and he is not afraid to present them to the reader for as close an inspection as he has given them. The quick-tempered bantam rooster of a father is depicted entire—his women, his love of hunting, his self-destructiveness, and his often misdirected love of his wife and son. The equally quick-tempered mother, who pushes her son and longs to move upward in society, is seen steadily and whole. The portrayal of the parents is the triumph of the book.

Other qualities follow hard upon the excellence

of characterization. The reader sees Clarksville, Texas, woven throughout the narrative as he saw it in the best of the fiction, but here he sees the town and people also as informing aspects of Humphrey's fiction. The descriptions in this book are not repetitions of the descriptions used in the fiction; here the descriptions are simpler, less artistic. One gets the feeling that these were written—or lived—first and were later translated into the stuff of fiction. The artistry lies in going back to the source and not giving way to the temptation to use the already published descriptions in the novels and stories.

Farther Off From Heaven may mark the end of Humphrey's Clarksville in his work. The progress of his novels seems to indicate that he has mined the vein thoroughly. The latest novel—*Proud Flesh*—is a parody of the first two, and if he is not to keep repeating the stories of the clans and the descriptions of a region, he may, as Huck Finn did, have to "light out for the territory." *Farther Off From Heaven* seems to be his last goodbye to Clarksville, for in that book he comes to terms with his beginnings and the place where he began. He says in the book that he was surprised when he returned to Clarksville, after an absence of thirty-two years, that what was once South has now become West. Maybe the place has changed utterly, or maybe the change is in the observer.

—James W. Lee

Bibliographies:

James Boatwright, "William Humphrey (1924-)," in *A Bibliographical Guide to the Study of Southern Literature*, ed. Louis D. Rubin, Jr. (Baton Rouge: Louisiana State University Press, 1969), pp. 224-225;

James W. Lee, "William Humphrey (1924-)," in *Southwestern American Literature: A Bibliography*, ed. John Q. Anderson, Edwin W. Gaston, and James W. Lee (Chicago: Swallow, 1980), p. 322.

References:

Frederick J. Hoffman, *The Art of Southern Fiction* (Carbondale: Southern Illinois University Press, 1967), pp. 103-106;

James W. Lee, *William Humphrey* (Austin: Steck-Vaughn, 1967);

Louis D. Rubin, Jr., *The Curious Death of the Novel* (Baton Rouge: Louisiana State University Press, 1967), pp. 263-265, 268, 280, 283-284.

JOHN IRVING

(2 March 1942-)

BOOKS: *Setting Free the Bears* (New York: Random House, 1969);

The Water-Method Man (New York: Random House, 1972);

The 158-Pound Marriage (New York: Random House, 1974);

The World According to Garp (New York: Dutton, 1978; London: Gollancz, 1978).

John Irving was born in Exeter, Massachusetts, the son of F. N. and Frances Winslow Irving. His father was a teacher of Russian history at Exeter Academy, the prep school which Irving attended during his adolescence. There he acquired his lifelong interests in wrestling and writing. Irving knew from an early age that he wanted to be a writer. Although he was not a distinguished student, averaging grades of B and C, he credits the vigorous apprenticeship of Exeter composition classes with teaching him how to write. In 1961 he enrolled at the University of Pittsburgh, where he began to realize that he lacked the ability of a truly first-class wrestler. As a result, he decided to devote himself full-time to writing, though he has continued to wrestle as a hobby ever since.

After leaving Pittsburgh in 1962, he enrolled at the University of New Hampshire and there met Thomas Williams (author of *The Hair of Harold Roux*, 1975 National Book Award winner), but again he grew disenchanted. He traveled to Austria, where in 1963-1964 he attended the University of Vienna. During his stay there he married Shyla Leary, a painter whom he had known for some time. Vienna is of central importance in Irving's fiction. According to one commentator, it gave him the sense of history which he had never developed in America; recent Viennese history, especially of the World War II years, is particularly significant in his first three novels. In a 1979 *Rolling Stone* interview, Irving called the Austrian capital "a real place for me. . . . It was so old and strange . . . that it forced me to pay attention to every aspect of it." But the Vienna in his books is different from the actual city: "It's not the *Vienna* Vienna—and that gave me great freedom. I didn't have to be responsible to Vienna. Vienna was a place I could *make up*." In each of his novels Vienna is tied to the past, to the imagination, to youthful ideals and fantasies. His experiences there provided the subject matter for much of his fiction, but his writing is *not* autobiographical, though it may contain some autobiographical elements. "Any writer uses what little experience he or she has and translates it," he has said. "It's the translating, though, that makes the difference." The principle of translation characterizes the relation of Irving's life to his fiction.

After his return from Vienna, he reenrolled at the University of New Hampshire and was graduated cum laude with a B.A. degree in 1965. In the following two years he worked under such novelists as Vance Bourjaily and Kurt Vonnegut, Jr., at the University of Iowa Writers Workshop, where he earned an M.F.A. degree in 1967. During those two years he also wrote his first novel, *Setting Free the Bears,* published by Random House in 1969. Critically well received, it earned him a modest sum of money and was even considered as the subject for a movie (Irving worked on an unproduced screenplay for a year). His next two novels, *The Water-Method Man* (1972) and *The 158-Pound Marriage* (1974), were less successful financially, and Irving was disappointed with Random House's failure to publicize them. His dissatisfaction led him to move to E. P. Dutton, the publisher of his fourth novel, *The World According to Garp* (1978), which in hardback and paperback together has sold more than three million copies and earned him the reputation of an accomplished writer.

Irving has held several teaching positions, most prominently as an assistant professor of English at Mount Holyoke College (1967-1972, 1975-1978) and writer in residence at the University of Iowa Writers Workshop (1972-1975). He has also received a Rockfeller Foundation grant (1971-1972) and a fellowship from the National Endowment for the Arts (1974-1975). Although the success of his fourth novel has freed him from financial pressures and left him more time for writing, he continues to teach on a part-time basis. Currently he lives in Putney, Vermont, with his wife and his two sons, Colin and Brendan. He is at work on his fifth novel, "The Hotel New Hampshire," which he characterizes as a "very simple first-person narrative about a family in the hotel business, and . . . a love story."

The concerns of Irving's novels are inherently contemporary. Yet often they bear little similarity to other recent fiction, for their author is more interested in affirming certain conventional values—art and the family, for instance—than in condemning the status quo or heralding the arrival of a new age. Still, he also regards favorably recent trends in feminism and sexual behavior. What is needed, he seems to suggest, is a fusion of the compassion and common sense of the old with the egalitarian open-mindedness of the new. Only when people treat one another with the same malice and amoral insensitivity that have characterized human relations for thousands of years do contemporary social changes wreak havoc. His last two novels—*The 158-Pound Marriage* and *The World According to Garp*—portray a society torn by such violence and insensitivity that total collapse sometimes seems imminent. Irving's calm, objective style veers away from moral sermonizing and instead allows the characters and their experiences to speak for themselves. The reader's sympathy grows from his recognition that Irving's characters are typically human, full of strengths and weaknesses, virtues and foibles, enmeshed in the common trauma of modern life.

Philosophically Irving seems a stoic pessimist. His characters have no gods to turn to but themselves; left to their own resources they more often than not make a botch of things. But sooner or later they seek to solve their problems and pull their lives into a semblance of order. In this sense Irving is a cousin to Walker Percy, whose heroes struggle out of their own spiritual dissolution to reassert their identities. Both Percy and Irving point out the amorality of modern society, but from considerably different vantage points. While Percy provides a spiritual source of personal strength for his protagonists, Irving leaves his characters to fend for themselves, forced to create their own havens of sanity. In his last three novels this haven resides somewhere within the long-term relationships between men and women, in the stability of the family. In a society of flux and relative values, such personal relationships offer one of the few sources of happiness. Their absence likewise becomes the cause of considerable grief.

Irving's fiction is occasionally marked by a whimsical, sometimes bizarre sense of fantasy, of the unlikely, firmly grounded in a hard-nosed reality. One character dreams of finding a sunken Nazi tank at the bottom of the Danube, while another is rescued from a nervous breakdown by the CIA. A young child is hidden from the Russians in the belly of a dead cow; a unicycle-riding bear appears in the water closet of an Austrian pension. Fantasy has been a frequent quality of contemporary American fiction, but Irving's novels possess only the *sense* of fantasy, which often proves to be nothing more than a character's inability to deal with reality or with his deluded attitude toward the past, toward people and events that influenced his life. In *Setting Free the Bears* Siggy Javotnik writes in his notebook: "all *anyone* has is a pre-history. Feeling that you live at an interim time is something in the nature of being born and all the things that never happen to you after birth." Much of this novel is taken up by "The Highly Selective Autobiography of Siegfried Javotnik," which chronicles the enslavement, violence, and dehumanization that eventually kill most of Siggy's family during and after World War II. Metaphorically he associates his oppressed forebears with the animals in the Heitzinger Zoo of Vienna. His fantasy of freeing the animals and thus avenging his family's fate lies at the novel's core. Bogus Trumper of *The Water-Method Man* is haunted by memories of a wild friend from his youth, while Utch in *The 158-Pound Marriage* believes her past pursues her in the nightmarish form of a Russian agent. T. S. Garp, of Irving's fourth novel, moves constantly in the shadow of his famous mother. For these characters, the past is a personal myth which often, for very different reasons, has serious consequences.

Irving also records contemporary human behavior, especially the so-called sexual revolution. His support of conventional sexual relationships is complemented by his favorable attitudes toward the feminist movement. He seems to oppose only those elements of social change which are bogged down in pointless, self-defeating extremism. His attitudes toward human relations are tolerant and expansive; he is severe only when dogma becomes dehumanizing. Hence, in *Garp* he sympathetically portrays a young girl named Ellen James, a mute whose tongue was ripped out by rapists. The Ellen James Society, however, whose members cut out their own tongues in symbolic protest of sexual oppression, is ridiculed. Emotional and physical violence are apparent throughout his writing, especially in *Garp*, where in some sense the protagonist lives out his life in their grips. Significantly, while in the first three novels it is the past which dehumanizes and inflicts suffering, in *Garp* it is the present.

Though Irving explores serious and often tragic themes, his fiction is essentially humorous. Much of his humor is black. Speech impediments, death, suicide, emotional trauma, theft, castration, mental cruelty, hospital patients, reckless driving, crippled ballerinas are all at times the objects of humor. Siggy Javotnik's quest to free the zoo animals and Bogus Trumper's fumbling life are both described comically. But Irving's humor always has a point. On one level it entertains and enlivens the narrative. On another it satirizes and exposes hypocrisy. His characters often possess comic traits and do funny things; but they are meant, for the most part, to be taken seriously. Roberta Muldoon, in *Garp*, is a transsexual tight end from the Philadelphia Eagles who at first is presented as a comic figure; however, the reader soon discovers that she is a quite admirable person whose problems, like everyone else's, are serious ones. Humor also strengthens the ever-present irony. Javotnik's comic quest to free the zoo animals causes a horrible catastrophe. That

Shyla Irving

John Irving

Bogus Trumper is regarded by so many around him as a ridiculous failure serves only to point out his pathetic condition more clearly. Irving's humor is rarely, in the long run, cruel; often it calls the reader's attention to serious issues indeed.

Irving's novels also possess a continuity which links them thematically and stylistically. Vienna in particular holds special meaning in each of the books. It is associated with youthful experiences and youthful idealism, with a past splendor that no longer survives. It is a main setting for the first novel; it lies at the heart of Bogus Trumper's sense of failure; the two couples in the third novel first meet there; and it provides Garp with the material for his first successful story. In addition, the tale of an attempt to free the animals from the Heitzinger Zoo recurs in some form in all four novels. Like Irving, two of his protagonists are wrestlers. Each book has one or more characters who are writers, and what they write helps to narrate their stories. Such repetitiveness might be evidence of a limitation in Irving's imagination or in his experience. More likely, however, he has been building each successive novel on the web of echoes, symbolic resonances, and narrative situations developed in the books he has already written. Such places as Vienna or the Heitzinger Zoo thus acquire a kind of mythical power which informs each book differently. Writing, of course, is one of Irving's major subjects—an important way of gaining self-knowledge, a refractory mirror of life.

Setting Free the Bears introduces many of the ideas, character types, and methods found throughout Irving's fiction: it depicts a character obsessed with his personal history, deluded by his own personal myths; his journal and autobiography contain much of his story; parts of the novel are set in Vienna. But in other ways it is unlike its successors: its characters are Europeans; none of the story occurs in America; the plot concerns a picaresque quest absent from the later novels. Although similar to certain other picaresque novels of the 1960s and 1970s (novels by Thomas McGuane or Tom Robbins, for example), its philosophical outlook is essentially pessimistic, grounded in realism, its irony finally leveled upon its characters and their ideals. When the story ends, one of the protagonists is dead, and the other seems to have suffered a nervous breakdown.

The narrator is Hannes Graffe, a young student who has flunked an important examination. He describes his meeting with Siggy Javotnik and their decision to purchase an old 700cc Royal Enfield motorcycle to ride to Italy. After Siggy convinces Hannes to visit the Vienna Zoo, he begins planning to free the animals from what he regards as their unnatural oppression. Later, as they ride toward Italy, they give a ride to a young woman named Gallen, whom they carry to her aunt's house. Siggy goes back to scout out the Vienna Zoo, but when he returns he wrecks the Enfield beneath a truck and is stung to death by thousands of bees. At this point Hannes inserts Siggy's zoo journal and his "Selective Autobiography." Hannes returns to Vienna with Gallen and convinces her to help him free one of the animals. Once in the zoo, he frees all the animals, who then either devour each other or are killed by the townspeople.

The heart of the novel lies in Javotnik's Zoo Watch journal and his autobiography. The apparently well-researched, historically accurate prehistories describe the suffering of Siggy's family before, during, and after World War II. They are victimized not only by the Nazis and the Russians who defeat the Nazis but also by internecine feuds in Hungary and Yugoslavia. Siggy is the only surviving member: his grandmother is killed by a Russian guard; his father is kidnapped by Serbo-Croat activists; his mother runs away; his grandfather commits suicide. Siggy apparently comes to believe that he can avenge his family's oppression by freeing the zoo animals. He is encouraged in this belief by the fact that one of the zoo's night watchmen is a former SS officer who tortures the animals. By dividing up the Zoo Watch and Pre-History narratives and then placing them side by side, Hannes shows that he has recognized the same parallels and reached the same conclusions about the zoo animals as Siggy.

Because of his belief in "pre-history," Siggy can find his identity nowhere but in the past. Hannes is so influenced by Siggy's quest that his personality begins to dissolve; he even dreams about the characters of Siggy's past as if they are his own. Both of them mythicize the past; they also mythicize the zoo animals: the oryx (an antelope with balloon-sized testicles), the terrible Asiatic black bear, and the rare spectacled bears become their personal symbols of oppression. Hannes virtually adopts Siggy's identity and determines to live out his fantasy. When fantasy becomes nightmare, however, he is left without an identity. The fate of the zoo animals uncovers the shallow delusions of Siggy's idealism. He believed in a free and harmonious world, while in fact he inhabited a world of brutality and violence where animals are confined in zoos and families are torn apart by war. At the end of the novel Hannes has to begin adjusting to this world and understanding that it cannot be changed, that he must accept it as best he can. The final appearance of the rare spectacled bears, the only survivors of the zoo holocaust, hints that he may retain a degree of his idealism, but it must be tempered with realism.

Though Irving's first novel is readable and entertaining, it also has serious flaws. Characterization is often poorly realized: of the three important characters, only Gallen seems real (she is characteristic of the women throughout Irving's fiction). Siggy seems too much of a joke at times, vacillating too freely between humor and pathos, perhaps because he is seen through his own writing and through Hannes's narrative—both tainted by shallow, unrealistic perceptions of the world. In tone the novel is unbalanced: Siggy's prehistories are so well written and intricately developed that Hannes's narrative is brittle by comparison (which perhaps Irving intended). The novel's conclusion is shrouded in unnecessary doubt about what Gallen and Hannes are going to do and why. Such flaws are understandable in a first novel, and Irving overcame them with considerable success in the ones that followed.

The title of *The Water-Method Man* refers to a treatment which the main character, Fred "Bogus" Trumper, receives for a condition in his urinary tract which makes urination and intercourse painful. Faced with the choice of a painful operation or a less agonizing water-method treatment (which requires him to drink large quantities of water and urinate frequently), he chooses the second, less effective solution. Trumper's urinary problem is a metaphor for his own life; the novel returns to it repeatedly in a seemingly obsessive, grotesque, and comical way. It is fundamental to what Trumper, and other characters, seem to consider his essential failure as a human being. Urination and sex are necessary functions of life. Trumper can have neither without serious pain, which warps his attitude toward love and life in general.

The narrative structure and point of view reflect Trumper's sense of inadequacy. The plot is divided into the two levels of Trumper's present-time affair with a woman named Tulpen and his past-time failed marriage to Olympic skier Biggie Kunft. Episodes alternate between these two levels, suggesting that Trumper's guilt over his unsuccessful marriage has a specific effect on his relationship with Tulpen, that his life has convinced him of his worthlessness as a husband, student, lover, son, and father. The past-time episodes end with his divorce from Biggie, his nervous breakdown in Europe, and his return to America where he meets Tulpen. The present-time episodes portray his fear of permanent involvement with Tulpen, a fear which leads him to desert her and return to graduate school to finish his dissertation. Eventually he is reconciled to all the people whom he has injured—his father, his ex-wife, his son, his best friend, and Tulpen.

The reasons for Trumper's guilt are reflected in numerous ways. His father disowns him for his marriage to Biggie. A friend named Ralph Packer makes a film about him entitled *Fucking Up*. Biggie blames him for her failure to become a professional skier. An intensely introspective character, he keeps a journal of his experiences on a tape recorder, writes numerous letters, and takes considerable creative liberty in his dissertation, a translation of the only "Old Low Norse" epic, "Akthelt and Gunnel." It is an obscure, clumsy saga of Nordic sex and violence so boring and uninteresting that Trumper stops translating and begins rewriting so that the tale develops similarities to his own life. The sexual rivalries between Akthelt and Gunnel come to reflect similar rivalries in Trumper's own experience—sexual competition with his friends and his fear of betrayal by them. Of course, the film *Fucking Up* is a more literal reflection of Trumper's life as seen by Ralph Packer.

Trumper's basic problem lies in the way he looks at himself. His life is a mess only because he believes it cannot be anything better. His treatment of Biggie, his disappointment of his father, his counterfeit dissertation, his desertion of the pregnant Tulpen all serve to reinforce his sense of worthlessness. He is afraid to assume responsibility because he believes he cannot adequately handle it.

Eventually, his love for Tulpen begins to give him a sense of self-esteem. His quest for self-understanding also helps him and is reflected in the novel's point of view. Although at first the novel seems to alternate between first- and third-person narration, it gradually becomes apparent that the narrator throughout is Trumper. In the final chapter, Trumper sits down and composes a sentence he has written before without knowing its significance: "Her gynecologist recommended him to me." The sentence is important because it is the opening sentence of the novel, which is really Trumper's own autobiography. In the final chapter the alternating viewpoints essentially merge as Trumper is at last able to accept his past and his mistakes, to begin living for the present and the future. By this time he has faithfully retranslated "Akthelt and Gunnel," made up with his father, reached an understanding with his ex-wife, and reconciled with Tulpen, who has borne their child. He has also undergone the painful operation necessary to cure his urinary condition. Through the personal record of Trumper's failed life and his groping attempts to understand and define himself, the novel affirms his ultimate success as a human being.

The Water-Method Man is thus about the disintegration and reintegration of a personality in modern society. It depicts sexual rivalry as a necessary but often destructive force in human relations. It also concerns the interrelation of life and art in the translated Norse epic, Packer's film, Trumper's tape recordings, his letters, and his narration of the novel. This interrelation remains an important theme in the next two novels.

Irving's shortest novel, *The 158-Pound Marriage*,

is his most tightly focused and coherently organized. Concerned with one major theme—sexual tension—it portrays two married couples who decide for various reasons to "swap" partners. The motive in such an arrangement is supposed to be wholly sexual, with a complete lack of emotional involvement. Severin Winter, a German teacher and wrestling coach, explains: "It's *just* sex, and that's all it can be in a thing like this. There's nothing very romantic about hurting anybody." Unfortunately for the couples involved, "hurting" becomes the point of it all; their four-way relationship produces far more pain than pleasure.

The opening chapters describe briefly the lives of the four main characters. The unnamed narrator is a historical novelist from Massachusetts who meets his wife, Utch, a tour guide, while on a tour of Vienna. As a child she had been adopted and raised by a Russian officer. Her name is the Russian word for cow. When her mother learned of the Russian approach at the end of World War II, she slaughtered a cow and hid her daughter in its hollowed-out belly. Severin Winter is the son of a minor Austrian painter and a beautiful model; he meets his wife, Edith, an aspiring writer, when she comes to examine some of his father's paintings. Irving is careful to describe the past lives of these characters in order to establish the circumstances leading up to the affair. Again he uses the backdrop of Vienna to connect the suffering and oppression in Europe during World War II with the turmoil and conflicts of his characters.

Utch and the narrator evidently view the relationship as a casual way of relieving boredom. For Severin and Edith, however, it is a means of saving their marriage. Severin's affair with a crippled ballerina in his wrestling loft has crushed Edith, and she vows to have her own affair to equal the score, to hurt her husband as he hurt her. Neither Utch nor the narrator is aware of these motives. Utch falls in love with Severin, while the narrator seems to fall in love with Edith. Edith pretends to love him in order to hurt Severin, while Severin pretends to love Utch only to hurt Edith. Jealousy, anguish, hostility are rampant. When Utch and the narrator learn the true reasons underlying the swap, the injuries are multiplied, then multiplied again as the vindictive narrator keeps finding ways to convince Utch that Severin never really loved her.

The novel's epigraphs come from John Hawkes's *The Blood Oranges* (1971) and Ford Madox Ford's *The Good Soldier* (1915)—fictional studies of adultery and sexual jealousy. (In his *Rolling Stone* interview, Irving said, "If I'd not read those two books, I would not have written *158-Pound Marriage*.") Ford's novel in particular poses an interesting contrast. In *The Good Soldier* an adulterous affair is conducted with the greatest secrecy; the novel is fastidious in its treatment of this subject. Nonetheless, the results are disastrous for those involved. Adultery is hardly the issue for Irving. All moral laws have collapsed. Instead of deception there is total honesty, with each couple seeking to carry on a normal marriage at the same time as the affair. But "honesty" leads to more fraudulent deception than would ever have occurred had the affairs remained secret. The emotional pain which two of the characters suffer is devastating. Utch is severely wounded. The narrator is reduced from a relatively decent, civil man to a scheming, jealous beast intent only on wounding and torturing his wife. Severin and Edith initiate the relationship as a strange kind of ritual which would save their marriage, but the two people whom they choose to exploit are virtually destroyed.

The characters of *The 158-Pound Marriage* inhabit the contemporary American world of narcissism, self-realization, and situational ethics. For Severin and Edith, whatever means they choose to resolve their marital problems are acceptable as long as they work. The novel implies that certain trends in sexual morality and human relations are verging toward social anarchy, undercutting traditional values and sources of human identity. Irving's comments in the *Rolling Stone* interview point to the discord underlying the book: "The lives of so many of my friends seemed to have been just *wiped out*. I knew people who were living in appalling situations and not moving out, and I knew people who seemed to me to move out of situations too soon—into appalling situations. It seemed a rampant kind of time. . . . everybody I *knew* was either at the thread, or reaching up for it with a scissors—or chewing on it with their teeth. The book is about lust and rationalization and restlessness: I decided I wanted to write a really dark tale of sexual intrigue; in the end nobody would know *anything* about each other." The novel reflects the social chaos which gave birth to it.

Much of the story's pathos derives from the irony which gradually eats away at the narrator's confidence and assurance. As he becomes aware that his lover has deceived him and his wife has fallen in love with another man, as he slowly realizes the cruelty he has inflicted upon his wife out of jealousy and spite, his whole world seems to crumble. He is left a pathetic ruin. In an otherwise fundamentally pessimistic novel, his recognition of the pain he has caused his wife, his resolve to follow her to Europe to begin their lives anew, is the only true note of optimism.

The World According to Garp is Irving's most vividly realized, thoroughly developed work of fiction. It lacks the occasional weaknesses of the earlier novels and improves upon their strengths. It also explores in greater depth and detail those themes which have been important throughout his fiction—the effects of "pre-history," sexual rivalry, survival in the modern world, the quest for self-knowledge. Two major strengths are its diverse range of characters and its plot, which simply encompasses the circumstances of T. S. Garp's birth, life, and death. Another strength is the omniscient narrator and his attitude toward the story, which is treated much like a historical event to be described in objective, analytical detail. Omniscient narrators are not common in contemporary novels; but Irving uses his to good effect so that his book is suffused with a gentle but firm ironic force, a warm sense of humor, and a faint but ever-present ambience of sadness and despair which is finally overwhelmed by the narrative's refusal to become mired in maudlin, tragic pessimism, and by the narrator's avoidance of literary histrionics.

T. S. Garp is the novel's main subject and character. Despite his illegitimacy and his moderately successful writing career, in some ways he is the archetypal modern man, but his life is far from typical. Irving has explained that he "created a sort of perfect childhood" for Garp. He gets into the usual kinds of trouble, worries about a career and what sport he should pursue in prep school, becomes a state wrestling champion, is introduced to sex by the daughter of the school's secretary. He travels to Vienna with his mother, where he writes his first good story and she writes her autobiography, *The Sexual Suspect*, a book which makes her a feminist hero when it is published in the United States. He returns to America to marry the woman he has always intended to marry, Helen Holm, the daughter of his wrestling coach. She becomes a professor of English; he writes and keeps house. They have two children, over whom Garp worries incessantly. His three novels enjoy a modest but secure reputation. When he and Helen have extramarital affairs, one of which leads through rather bizarre circumstances to the death of their youngest son, Garp's ideal existence comes to an end, and at times he verges on collapse. After recovering from their son's death, Garp and Helen have another child, a daughter. By this time Garp has become involved, somewhat unintentionally, in the feminist affairs of his mother. Though personally he favors the liberation of women, publicly he becomes identified as the sexist son who has exploited his mother's well-earned fame. He returns to his old prep school to coach wrestling and there is killed by an enraged feminist.

Such a summary hardly does justice to the rich intricacies of plot and character in *Garp*. Garp's mother is an amazing woman who decides to bear a child without the benefit of husband or lover. "I wanted a baby," she writes in her autobiography, "but I didn't want to have to share my body or my life to have one." Garp is fathered by a brain-damaged World War II ball turret gunner in the hospital where Jenny works as a nurse; he dies a few weeks after Garp's conception, totally witless of his progeny. *The Sexual Suspect* records Jenny's life and beliefs, her experiences in rearing a son outside of marriage. She becomes more famous than her son ever does—a fact which plagues him—and she works until her death helping women and serving various feminist causes. Helen Holm is a strong-minded woman who both loves her husband and children and is determined to pursue her own career. She encourages and sustains Garp but remains her own woman, with her own ideas; she never surrenders to him. The sexual tension between them is the source of their love as well as their rivalry; it is also one of the wellsprings of Garp's writing. Irving's portrayals of women successfully avoid most of the usual stereotypes; they are, for the most part, self-reliant human beings, individuals struggling to adjust to changing social and sexual attitudes. Those who fail to adjust are pathetic cases; those who succeed—Helen, Jenny, Ellen James, Roberta Muldoon—are among Irving's most vividly realized creations.

Unlike Irving's other protagonists, Garp seems a relatively healthy, self-assured, stable man. He grapples with his own problems—self-doubt, jealousy, a tendency toward bombast, a more dangerous tendency toward complacency—but they never overwhelm him. He is essentially normal, a typical American of the 1970s. His quest for a successful career, marriage, and family encounters considerable opposition. His society in many ways has fallen into chaos; the old sexual values have disintegrated and as yet are unreplaced. Garp himself is fatherless and illegitimate. Helen is motherless. They briefly swap partners with another married couple (in an episode reminiscent of *The 158-Pound Marriage*). Jenny Fields is surrounded with victims of sexual oppression. Examples of sexual chaos abound. But *Garp*'s feminism is combined with its opposition to those elements in society which sacrifice common sense and compassion for the sake of abstract doctrine: the Ellen James Society and the man who shoots Jenny are examples. Jenny, Ellen James, Roberta Muldoon, Helen, and Garp himself possess a strength of will and character which enables them to endure the chaos without ever overcoming it. Irving thus characterizes the novel as "life-affirming, even though everybody dies."

Violence, which has affected many lives during the past two decades, is another natural force in *The World According to Garp*. It comes in emotional as well as physical form. In one way or the other, nearly every character falls victim to it. Rape in particular becomes the encompassing symbol of violence.

Irving suggests several escapes from the social and sexual chaos. One is Helen and Garp's marriage and their children. Another is Garp's writing, which is as strongly influenced by social discord as his family. As in *Setting Free the Bears* and *The Water-Method Man*, *Garp* employs the words of its main character to reflect his basic concerns and attitudes. Both Garp's and Jenny's autobiographical writings are frequently quoted. Two of Garp's stories and a chapter from his third novel are printed intact, and each of his books is fully summarized. His writing is thus made to seem more real than the works of fictional writers in other novels; what he writes is as much a part of his story as he is.

Garp's first two novels seem fairly similar to Irving's first two books. *Procrastination* has a plot much like that of *Setting Free the Bears*, while *Second Wind of the Cuckold* resembles *The 158-Pound Marriage* (and takes its title from a phrase uttered by Severin Winter). Garp's third novel, *The World According to Bensenhaver*, bears much in common with *Garp* itself. There are a number of interesting similarities between Irving and his protagonist; both, for instance, are wrestlers, spend parts of their youth in Vienna, and are writers. It is tempting to speculate over *Garp*'s possibly autobiographical elements, but to do so would be irrelevant. Irving himself on several occasions has emphatically denied that the novel is autobiographical, and Garp is unlike his creator in many more ways than he is like him.

Garp's stories clearly demonstrate life's impact on art. They also show that Garp, while a good writer, is not a great one: he does not work hard enough or live long enough, and too many factors—his family, social conflicts, personal calamities—interfere with him. That he dies with his talent and ambition partially unfulfilled imbues the novel's conclusion with a special poignance. Though art is certainly an important part of Garp's life, it is crucial to the novel's meaning that he is only incidentally an artist, and art is only incidentally a theme. Had Garp been a fireman or a lawyer, his essential story would not be much changed. According to the *Rolling Stone* interview, Garp's first occupation was wrestling; only when Irving had written half the novel and realized that Garp needed a "voice" did he decide to make him a writer as well. Even so, as a detailed account of one writer's life and times, the book explores in depth the shifting factors which underlie the creation and substance of art.

Perhaps the book's most important theme is life's continuity. Irving has a special preoccupation with noting the deaths of practically all his characters. "Life After Garp," the final chapter, describes what happens to each of the main characters after Garp's death. Although such a summing up was characteristic of certain Victorian novelists, Irving sums up at greater length and in more detail. Garp survives in the books he wrote and the children he fathered. His daughter, Jenny, who barely remembers him, is the last chapter's prime symbol of life's continuation—she raises her own family in addition to making certain that Garp's books remain in print and continue to be read. The social and sexual pessimism of the novel is thus ultimately overshadowed by a sort of stoic optimism—human life will endure, in spite of itself, whatever the obstacles which arise to challenge it.

Despite the abundance of themes, *Garp* is primarily a novel about human character. Except for the inclusion of Garp's stories, the narrative structure is fairly conventional. The third-person narrator's evident sympathy for the characters allows the reader to admire and identify with them, to feel a real concern for what happens to them. Frequent reversals and advances in their fortunes maintain the reader's curiosity about, for instance, the outcome of Helen's affair with her graduate student Michael Milton or of Garp's feud with the Ellen Jamesians. A wide range of major and minor characters assures that no one character will predominate. Both Helen and Jenny are nearly as important as Garp, and there are in fact more women in the novel than men. An essentially melodramatic narrative structure—surely the author's intentional decision—guarantees the reader's attention and provides Irving with an appropriate metaphor for contemporary American life, which has, after all, proved melodramatic if nothing else.

Irving's prose style has consistently improved since his first novel, and in his fourth it complements the structure and the emphasis on character. Unlike the richly turgid prose of Styron, Hawkes, Pynchon, or Barth, Irving's writing is fairly simple and lucid, with little subordination and an unchallenging vocabulary. It is lively and full of contemporary slang, but classically precise. Rather than condescending to the reader or pandering for a place on the best-seller lists, Irving uses his style to focus attention on character, reinforce humor, and instill his narrative with a compelling momentum which draws the characters forward toward their final conclusions.

The rich diversity of *The World According to Garp* makes it one of the most lively, entertaining, affecting, and readable serious novels in recent years. It also establishes John Irving as a writer of considerable proportions whose true potential may yet be unrealized. Whether his future novels climb to the best-seller lists or not, his peculiar synthesis of dark humor, social upheaval, and the tragic tenor of modern life with realistic and likable characters may well exert a profound influence on the fiction of the 1980s. What Irving will ultimately achieve for himself remains to be seen; but his fiction so far—especially his fourth novel—has heralded the arrival of an indisputably significant figure on the American literary scene.

—Hugh M. Ruppersburg

Interviews:

Barbara A. Bannon, "PW Interviews: John Irving," *Publishers Weekly*, 213 (24 April 1978): 6-7;

Greg Marcus, "John Irving: The World of 'The World According to Garp'—The Rolling Stone Interview," *Rolling Stone* (13 December 1979): 68-75.

References:

L. B. Francke and M. Malone, "What Hath Garp Wrought?," *Newsweek*, 93 (26 March 1979): 98;

Lawrence O'Toole, "John Irving Adjusts: Is There Life After Garp?," *Macleans*, 92 (11 June 1979): 4-6;

Thomas Williams, "Talk With John Irving," *New York Times Book Review*, 23 April 1978, pp. 26-27.

Papers:

Irving's papers are deposited in the library at Phillips Exeter Academy, Exeter, New Hampshire.

SHIRLEY JACKSON

(14 December 1919-8 August 1965)

SELECTED BOOKS: *The Road Through the Wall* (New York: Farrar, Straus, 1948);

The Lottery Or, The Adventures of James Harris (New York: Farrar, Straus, 1949; London: Gollancz, 1950);

Hangsaman (New York: Farrar, Straus & Young, 1951; London: Gollancz, 1951);

Life Among the Savages (New York: Farrar, Straus & Young, 1953; London: Joseph, 1954);

The Bird's Nest (New York: Farrar, Straus & Young, 1954; London: Joseph, 1955);

The Witchcraft of Salem Village (New York: Random House, 1956);

Raising Demons (New York: Farrar, Straus & Cudahy, 1957; London: Joseph, 1957);

The Sundial (New York: Farrar, Straus & Cudahy, 1958; London: Joseph, 1958);

The Haunting of Hill House (New York: Viking, 1959; London: Joseph, 1960);

We Have Always Lived in the Castle (New York: Viking, 1962);

The Magic of Shirley Jackson, ed. Stanley Edgar Hyman (New York: Farrar, Straus & Giroux, 1966);

Come Along With Me, ed. Stanley Edgar Hyman (New York: Viking, 1968).

Shirley Jackson's name is most often associated in readers' minds with the haunting short story "The Lottery," which was originally published in 1948 and has since become a frequently anthologized American classic. To those familiar with the rest of Jackson's fiction, her stories and novels have earned her a reputation as a "literary sorceress," a writer with a peculiar talent for the bizarre, a creator of psychological thrillers, an adroit master of effect and suspense. In spite of her popularity, however, her work has received little critical attention. Jackson's remarkable versatility may account partly for the silence. In her lifetime she published novels, short stories, plays, children's books, television scripts, and humorous sketches of domestic life—all of which prevented her easy classification.

Above all Jackson is a storyteller; her stories aim to entertain. Yet the entertainment value of her fiction masks a pessimistic view of human nature; social criticism, overt or implicit, is central to every one of her works. Humankind is more evil than good. The mass of men is profoundly misguided, seemingly incapable of enlightenment. Lacking either the capacity to reason or the strength to act upon moral convictions, their lives are dictated by habit and convention. They often behave with callous disregard of those around them. Set against this backdrop are the victimized protagonists. They may be victims of society, of family or friends, or victims of their own fragmented and disintegrating personalities. Yet even in the novels and stories that deal almost exclusively with the private worlds of individuals, the isolation of these lonely figures is intensified by the sense that the world surrounding them is cruel—peopled with weak or malignant characters. Emotional warmth and closeness are rare in Jackson's fictional universe; there is little to sustain a healthy personality.

The origin and development of Jackson's vision of society and mankind necessarily remain speculative, since she was reluctant to discuss either her fiction or her life before the public. The daughter of Leslie Hardie Jackson and Geraldine Bugbee Jackson, she was born into a family of successful San Francisco professionals. She seemed to have wanted to be a writer from an early age. She wrote poems and kept journals throughout her childhood. These journals reveal an interest in superstition and the supernatural, and one entry (a 1933 New Year's resolution) is interesting and perhaps revealing: "seek out the good in others rather than explore for the evil."

When Jackson was fourteen, the family moved from California to New York. After one unhappy year at the University of Rochester, she dropped out of school to spend the next year (1936 to 1937) at home, pursuing a career as a writer. She set herself a quota of at least a thousand words a day and established a disciplined routine that she was to follow the rest of her life. The following year she entered Syracuse University, where she made her first acquaintance with the texts of anthropology, including James G. Frazer's *The Golden Bough* (1890), which were to influence her later work. She also published both fiction and nonfiction regularly in campus magazines. Her editorials championed the underdog and denounced prejudice on campus, particularly against blacks and Jews.

Upon graduation in 1940 she married fellow student Stanley Edgar Hyman and moved to New York City. A clerical job she held there became the subject of her first nationally published short story, "My Life With R. H. Macy." Over the next few years she continued to publish short fiction regularly, despite the birth of her first child, Laurence, in 1942. In 1945 a daughter, Joanne, was born, and in that same year she and her growing family moved to North Bennington, Vermont, where she was to remain, apart from brief absences, "comfortably far from city life" for the rest of her writing career. The Hymans had two more children: Sarah in 1948 and Barry in 1951.

The first few years in Vermont were outwardly less productive ones, but in 1948 *The Road Through the Wall,* her only novel set in suburban California, was published. Several households on the same block form the subject of the novel, and the rather spiteful interactions between individuals and between families become the basis for the plot. The characters' lives reflect a certain moral bankruptcy, which is passed from parents to children. The novel was received with moderate acclaim and demonstrated that Jackson could sustain reader interest through the novel form. On 28 June of that year the *New Yorker* printed "The Lottery." The story occasioned so much public outcry that Jackson's reputation—and notoriety—were assured from then on.

"The Lottery" is about the reenactment in contemporary society of an ancient scapegoat ritual. Its genius lies in the juxtaposition of the savage and the modern. A public stoning performed in the town square of an otherwise peaceful community communicates a powerful shock to the reader, an effect heightened by Jackson's unemotional narrative style. A modern fable, "The Lottery" reveals men and women to be timid, conformist, callous, and cruel. Although Jackson published dozens of short stories during her lifetime, she never again produced such a satire of the evil in human nature. She turned instead to studies of individuals, exploring the private worlds of lonely, often mentally ill, characters. Her short stories contain a diversity of themes and employ a variety of techniques, including what may well be her hallmark, a deliberate blurring of the lines between reality and fantasy. Some of these techniques were reproduced to even greater effect in the novels, yet the short fiction is striking in its own right.

"The Lottery" was included in *Prize Stories in 1949: The O. Henry Awards.* Appearing in *Best American Short Stories* were "The Summer People" in 1951; "One Ordinary Day With Peanuts" in 1956; and "Birthday Party" in 1965. Jackson received the Edgar Allen Poe Award for "Louisa Please" in 1961. She was honored by Syracuse University in 1965 with the Arents Pioneer Medal for Outstanding Achievement.

In her second novel, *Hangsaman* (1951), Jackson writes about a young woman who is perilously close to mental disintegration. Natalie is seventeen, highly intelligent, and under the shadow of her father's dominating personality. She enrolls in an exclusive women's college (her father's choice) and, from the first, experiences the sensation of being an outsider. Her keen mind and reserved nature seem to act as a barrier between herself and others, and the passing months only increase her sense of estrangement. Correspondence with her father becomes more strained; her journal entries reveal at least a tendency toward schizoid patterns of thinking. A brief infatuation with her literature professor is quashed when she sees his insensitive treatment of his wife. At this point she meets Tony, a young woman who appears on the campus at unexpected times and places, a seeming loner like herself. Friendship with Tony is at first satisfying and seems to promise relief from Natalie's acute loneliness and rejection by the other girls. The two friends study together, tell each other's fortunes, even sleep side by side. But is Tony real, or a creation of Natalie's disturbed mind? As in the shorter works of fiction, it is difficult to establish her existence for certain.

The novel's final scene has puzzled critics. It is nighttime, and Tony and Natalie have taken a bus to a lonely wooded area outside of town. The bus is making its last route; when it departs the girls will be stranded. Natalie is frightened and wants to return to the college, but Tony, laughing at her fears, leads her deeper into the woods. Natalie loses sight of her in the dark. She calls out. When Tony refuses to answer, the uneasiness which she has always subconsciously felt with Tony surfaces, and Natalie succumbs to pure panic. Tony reappears then, and coaxes her into an embrace. Surprised and bewildered, Natalie runs away. When she regains control of herself she finds her way back to town, and the novel ends on a hopeful note: "She was now alone, and grown-up, and powerful, and not at all afraid."

Interpretations of *Hangsaman* vary, depending upon whether the reader accepts Tony as Natalie's real or imaginary companion. On a realistic level, the book has been regarded as a study of adolescence, a perceptive tale of a young girl's initiation into adulthood. In this context, a possible implication is that Natalie has rejected a homosexual liaison with Tony, and that this is part of her growing-up process. If, on the other hand, Tony is a figment of Natalie's imagination, then the book becomes an exploration of the private world of a schizophrenic. If the reader is meant to believe that Natalie has recovered her sanity at the end of the book, critics have noted that the return to normality is too abrupt, and her full recovery seems implausible. If her recovery at this point is implausible, the optimism in the last lines becomes extremely ambiguous.

Whatever Jackson intended in *Hangsaman*, she clearly set out to fictionalize a dissociated personality in *The Bird's Nest* (1954). This book was the fruit of Jackson's extensive study of mental illness, and the multiple personality of Elizabeth-Beth-Betsy-Bess is based on an actual case history she turned up in the course of her research. The book is divided into six sections, each assuming the point of view of one of several characters, including Elizabeth's aunt and Elizabeth's attending psychiatrist, Dr. Wright.

The first section of the novel establishes the basic situation. Twenty-three-year-old Elizabeth works on the third floor of a museum which is in bad need of repair but nevertheless provides the perfect refuge for "cringing scholarly souls." Subject to severe headaches since her mother's death four years before, Elizabeth lives with her aunt and seems to do little besides eat, sleep, and work. Her life is vague and undirected. She has no friends.

Elizabeth begins to discover quasi-obscene letters in the carriage of her typewriter. Is she writing them to herself? This is the first indication to the reader that another personality is about to disturb the surface of Elizabeth's uneventful life. The second, then the third and the fourth personalities emerge. They wage a terrific struggle for dominance, distorting Elizabeth out of all recognition. She is now under the care of Dr. Wright, whose journals describing his progress with his patient form the greater part of the book. The juxtaposition of his point of view with Betsy's is extremely effective; to plunge back into the point of view of the fragmented personality after dwelling in the saner world of Dr. Wright is disturbing and frightening.

Jackson's mastery of effect is evident in *The Bird's Nest*. She shapes what would in any event be a fascinating case study into a dramatic tale of psychological suspense. The story climaxes in a dreary New York hotel room, where Betsy, the most vicious of the personalities, attacks the passive Elizabeth. In other words, one of the inner selves actually destroys the other, and Elizabeth nearly loses her life in the process. She wakes up in a hospital, is rescued by her aunt and doctor, and returns home. Eventually, she gets well. Aided by the basically kind, if erratic, attentions of her aunt, and by two and a half years' therapy with Dr. Wright, Elizabeth's recovery is convincing, unlike Natalie's in the previous novel.

In spite of the harrowing subject matter, *The Bird's Nest* sparkles with wit and humor. The book was well received critically, even hailed as "a kind of twentieth-century morality play." In this novel the problems which plagued *Hangsaman* were less

Erich Hartmann

Shirley Jackson

evident, in that there was less room for ambiguity in the interpretation of the central character. Metro-Goldwyn-Mayer purchased film rights and eventually made a movie of the book. The film was released in 1957 under the title *Lizzie*.

Jackson's fame received another boost when MGM purchased film rights to a novel published in 1959, *The Haunting of Hill House*. The movie, *The Haunting*, was released in 1963. In this book, the themes of isolation, loneliness, and emotional deterioration are explored through the character of a young unmarried woman, Eleanor. A ghostly manor is the setting, and at first the novel seems to conform to the pattern of the formula Gothic. Thirty-two-year-old Eleanor, orphaned and drab, is on the threshold of an adventure. Because of an association with a poltergeist phenomenon in her childhood which led to some small stir of publicity in her hometown, she has been invited by Professor Montague to participate in a study of a supposedly haunted house in New England, some distance from her home. She, along with two or three others, will assist the professor in his investigation into the psychic spirits which he believes inhabit Hill House.

Eleanor is the first member of the group to arrive at Hill House. From the moment that she sees it, the looming manor fills her with foreboding. An inner voice warns her that she must get away at once, but she stays nevertheless, held by a sort of fascination for the place and, even more pathetic, a need to belong to someone, or to something. Dr. Montague, a young woman named Theo, and Luke, the nephew of Hill House's owner, arrive soon after. They make themselves ready for a stay of several weeks. With frightening promptness the spirits of Hill House manifest themselves. During the second night of their stay, Eleanor is awakened by a violent pounding down the hall. She creeps into Theo's adjoining bedroom and the two of them huddle against the sudden draft of supernatural cold, listening to the hammering on the wall, then to the "small seeking sounds" at their very door. This is no human agent, nor can natural explanations account for the words HELP ELEANOR PLEASE COME HOME she finds scrawled on the wall the next day.

The spirits continue to scrawl messages and hammer on walls and to despoil clothing, singling out Eleanor as the weakest, most vulnerable member of the group. The pleas to COME HOME ELEANOR may be playing upon Eleanor's guilt for her imagined neglect of her invalid mother prior to her death three months before, or the messages may be referring to Hill House. When she first meets the other members of the group at Hill House she is happy—happier, one suspects, than she has ever been. She experiences a brief infatuation with Luke and appears to be making friends with Theo. But both attempts to bridge the lifelong isolation between herself and others are doomed to failure. Luke proves disappointingly weak; he is drawn to her primarily as a mother figure, and Theo turns out to be narcissistic and insensitive to the point of cruelty toward Eleanor. Furthermore, Luke and Theo begin to form a romantic attachment which conspicuously excludes her. Eleanor becomes more and more lonely and isolated. Her retreat into a private world of fantasy is pathetic and as chilling as any of the more flamboyant supernatural effects in the novel.

At last Dr. Montague asks Eleanor to leave. Her mental disturbance is evident but he believes she will be better when she gets away from the atmosphere at Hill House. Luke and Theo simply wish to be rid of her. Once again, as in other Jackson works, a thin veneer of sympathy and kindness hides a layer of human nature that is fundamentally uncaring. Eleanor, dazed and humiliated, is escorted to her car. Driving down the long driveway away from the house, convinced that at least the ghostly inhabitants of Hill House wish her to remain even if the human ones do not, she accelerates her car wildly and crashes into a tree. "*Why* am I doing this?" she thinks with terrifying lucidity as she dies. "Why don't they stop me?" That plea is a clue to what may well be a weakness in Jackson's fiction. There are few close, warm human ties in any of the stories or novels. The characters are nearly always seen in isolation from one another, and the predominating emotions are fear and anxiety. Nor is there a God in Jackson's fictional universe. Even in *The Sundial* (1958), a novel which comes closest to exploring metaphysical questions and the issues of belief and faith, no mature interpretations of the meaning of life are proffered by any of the characters.

In *The Sundial* the Hallorans and a few select associates are waiting for the end of the world. The spirit of Father Halloran has notified them, through the agent of eccentric Aunt Fanny, that on 31 August the world outside the walls of their estate will be consumed by storm and fire. Only those persons who take refuge in the Halloran house will survive the catastrophe. Father Halloran is the patriarchal founder of the family, and it is he who designed the estate, including the sundial from which the novel takes its name. This sundial is inscribed with the motto WHAT IS THIS WORLD?

With the aid of a few unexplained phenomena, such as the timely appearance of a brightly colored snake and the mysterious shattering of a plate glass window, the lunatic prophecy is accepted by the group as truth. Curiously apathetic, they allow themselves to be dictated to by the strong-willed Mrs. Halloran, wife of Father Halloran's son Richard, who is confined to a wheelchair. They burn all the books in the library (except a *World Almanac* and a Boy Scout handbook) and cram the empty shelves with crates of canned olives, antihistamines, and plastic overshoes. The only one who seems to have doubts about any of it is Essex, a young man who was originally hired some months before to catalogue the library. But like other young men in Jackson's fiction, he proves ultimately weak and bows to Mrs. Halloran's more powerful personality.

With everything readied for the world's end, they have nothing to do but wait. They are a nasty, irritable bunch, riddled with small sins. To pass the time they play bridge and squabble about who is to do what in the next world. That this singularly unenlightened group of people is to replenish the earth is of course the final irony. But the statement the novel makes about the hollowness or sheer idiocy of human beings is a pessimistic one. Critics were not sure whether *The Sundial* was written primarily for entertainment or intended as a serious satire. Some reviewers said that the lack of counterbalancing qualities of strength or goodness in any of the characters weakened the novel. Most agreed that it was not one of Jackson's better books.

Jackson returns to the theme of mental pathology in her last completed novel, *We Have Always Lived in the Castle* (1962). Writing in the first person, a technique she rarely employed, she develops the central character of Mary Katherine Blackwood (Merricat), a sociopathic girl who, at the age of twelve, poisoned four members of her family, including mother and father, with arsenic. The exploration of the mind of this queer and oddly pathetic character is considered by many to be Jackson's finest fictional achievement. Certainly the novel is more consistently successful than any of her previous works, sustaining a tone that can only be described as eerily poetic.

> My name is Mary Katherine Blackwood. I am eighteen years old, and I live with my sister Constance. I have often thought that with any luck at all I could have been born a werewolf, because the two middle fingers on both my hands are the same length, but I have had to be content with what I had. I dislike washing myself, and dogs, and noise. I like my sister Constance, and Richard Plantagenet, and *Amanita phalloides*, the death-cup mushroom. Everyone else in my family is dead.

The excellence of this opening passage has been justly remarked. With arresting precision the exact quality of Merricat's voice is established—disarmingly simple and childlike; clever, but crippled with queer logic. The last sentence twists like a knife. It hints at the unpredictable turns of thought which are the clue to Merricat's pathology and the source of the novel's suspense.

The setting is the Blackwood house, six years after the murders. Like the houses which are central to other Jackson novels, the Blackwood estate is at a distance from the nearest village and surrounded by a wall. Isolated and aloof, the Blackwood family has long been the object of community jealousy, which turned to outright persecution after the sensational scandal which attended the poisoning. Constance, the eldest daughter, was tried and acquitted of the deed, but the village is only too ready to believe her guilty. Merricat, Constance, and Uncle Julian now live as virtual recluses. Only Merricat goes into the village to shop. Merricat dwells in a highly imaginative world of her own making. The walk to town, for instance, becomes like a children's board game in which "there were always dangers"; and indeed, the villagers taunt her cruelly. Magic and superstition also play a role in her make-believe world. Events are omens of good luck or bad; to ward off evil she buries small objects—a doll, or blue marbles—or nails them to trees. She cares only for her cat Jonas and for Constance, whom she loves with fierce possessiveness.

Constance is loyal to Merricat too, although she seems to know that her younger sister is guilty of the murder of their parents and siblings. At any rate, they live in undisturbed domestic harmony until Charles, a young male cousin, comes to visit. Infatuated with Constance, he nearly convinces her to leave her secure retreat and venture into the real world. But Merricat, instinctively fearing change, determines to drive him away by the force of her "magic." In the process she accidentally sets the house on fire. The blaze is put out before the entire house burns, but the villagers who have come to help extinguish the blaze, in a burst of pent-up hate toward the Blackwoods, vandalize the rest of the house. While the fire rages around him, Charles seems only concerned with preserving the family safe, which is too heavy to move. When the mob leaves he goes too. The Blackwood house is in ruins.

Alone, with only two or three cups and spoons, Merricat and Constance barricade themselves in the kitchen at the back of the house. A few villagers, apparently conscience stricken, begin to leave food on the doorstep. Yet these offerings are not likely to continue indefinitely and at the end of the novel the sisters' fate is uncertain. Merricat, however, has what she has always wanted: Constance. The queer force of her personality triumphs over the potentially healthier personality of her sister. Without a moral sense, Merricat will never be tortured by guilt for the murders, nor aware of the sacrifices Constance has made for her. "We're on the moon at last," she announces to Constance in satisfaction. She has won.

During the writing of *We Have Always Lived in the Castle*, Jackson suffered from a number of health problems, including arthritis, colitis, asthma, and anxiety. Yet she worked with great care on this book and spent more time on it than on any other. Almost universally recognized as her finest novel, it was nominated for the National Book Award. It became a best-seller and was adapted for a Broadway production. The play had a short run at the Ethel Barrymore Theatre in 1966.

We Have Always Lived in the Castle was lauded especially for its imaginative treatment of Merricat, who is far removed from a textbook sociopath and made into a believable, even sympathetic, character. Though at the end of the novel the two sisters are sleeping on the floor and living behind boarded windows, their absolute dependence on one another is made to seem oddly appealing. Their narrow existence does not lack warmth, laughter, and kindness. The reader, though recoiling from a world which he logically knows to be grotesque, is brought to view the sisters with sympathy, even to share some of their happiness, which is no easy task for a writer.

But again, some readers may be left with the uneasy feeling that there are no choices for the characters. The world outside the Blackwood estate offers little to Constance and Merricat. That world is filled with the same weak or malignant characters who peopled "The Lottery." The reader has been entertained by the novel, even moved; but it is clear that Jackson's fictional world must be taken on its own terms.

In between the publication of her fiction, Jackson was writing humorous sketches of domestic life for publication in various women's magazines. These were later arranged chronologically and collected in two autobiographical works, *Life Among the Savages* (1953) and *Raising Demons* (1957). Together they form a domestic saga spanning from the time of her family's first house in Vermont until the year her youngest child enrolls in school. Ostensibly autobiographical, the anecdotal accounts of life in the Hyman household clearly have been embellished for the reader's entertainment. Lighter in tone than her fiction, they celebrate in an unsentimental way day-to-day life in a large and active family. They also reveal Jackson as a comic writer who at her best belongs in the ranks of the great American humorists.

At the age of forty-six Jackson died suddenly of heart failure. She had been active during her last years, delivering lectures at colleges and writers' conferences; three of the lectures are included in the same volume with the novel she was working on at the time of her death, *Come Along With Me* (1968). Two of these lectures, "Biography of a Story" and "Notes for a Young Writer," discuss the art of writing. Written for her daughter Sally, the latter imparts information and advice that should interest any writer or student of Jackson's fictional technique.

In Jackson's children's book, *The Witchcraft of Salem Village* (1956), she attempts to explain in necessarily simplified terms the "seeming madness" that swept seventeenth-century Salem. Men and women are susceptible to evil, Jackson seems to suggest. It surges up in society at certain times and in response to certain social conditions, then subsides again. But an elemental mystery also surrounds the presence of evil. There is no completely satisfactory cause for it, and no cure. It will spread until people "simply stop believing"; until, remorseful and repentant, they are "sick with the weariness of it all."

This children's book illuminates her fiction, touching upon many of her fundamental themes: superstition, community scapegoat rites, social prejudice, conformity, mass hysteria, violence. But development of themes is only part of Jackson's message. In "Notes for a Young Writer" she makes it very clear: the writer's only real job is to catch the reader's attention and hold it, to tell a good story. Some of her works have been aptly labeled "psychological thrillers," but others provide acute insights into the minds and hearts of her characters and have the magic power to move the reader as well as to entertain.

—Martha Ragland

Other:

"Shirley Jackson reads 'The Lottery' " (Folkways Recording).

Bibliographies:

Robert S. Phillips, "Shirley Jackson: A Checklist," *Bibliographical Society of America Papers,* 56 (January 1962): 110-113;

Phillips, "Shirley Jackson: A Chronology and a Supplementary Checklist," *Bibliographical Society of America Papers,* 60 (April 1966): 203-213.

References:

Cleanth Brooks and Robert Penn Warren, "Interpretation," in their *Understanding Fiction* (New York: Appleton-Century-Crofts, 1959), pp. 72-76;

Chester E. Eisinger, *Fiction of the Forties* (Chicago: University of Chicago Press, 1963);

Lenemaja Friedman, *Shirley Jackson* (Boston: Twayne, 1975);

Robert B. Heilman, *Modern Short Stories* (New York: Harcourt, Brace, 1950), pp. 384-385;

Stanley Edgar Hyman, *The Promised End* (New York: World, 1963), pp. 264, 349, 365;

Seymour Lainoff, "Jackson's 'The Lottery,' " *Explicator,* 12 (March 1954);

John O. Lyons, *The College Novel in America* (Carbondale: Southern Illinois University Press, 1962), pp. 62-67, 100, 158, 186;

H. E. Nebeker, " 'The Lottery': Symbolic Tour de Force," *American Literature,* 46 (March 1974): 100-107;

S. C. Woodruff, "The Real Horror Elsewhere: Shirley Jackson's Last Novel," *Southwest Review,* 52 (September 1967): 152-162.

JOHN KNOWLES

(16 September 1926-)

BOOKS: *A Separate Peace* (London: Secker & Warburg, 1959; New York: Macmillan, 1960);

Morning in Antibes (New York: Macmillan, 1962; London: Secker & Warburg, 1962);

Double Vision: American Thoughts Abroad (New York: Macmillan, 1964; London: Secker & Warburg, 1964);

Indian Summer (New York: Random House, 1966; London: Secker & Warburg, 1966);

Phineas (New York: Random House, 1968);

The Paragon (New York: Random House, 1971);

Spreading Fires (New York: Random House, 1974);

A Vein of Riches (Boston & Toronto: Little, Brown, 1978).

John Knowles, the third of four children of James Myron and Mary Beatrice Shea Knowles, was born in Fairmont, West Virginia. He has an older brother and sister who are twins, and a younger sister. Knowles left West Virginia at fifteen to attend the Phillips Exeter Academy in New Hampshire during the World War II years. After graduating in 1945 he enlisted in the U.S. Army Air Force's Aviation Cadet Program, eventually qualifying as pilot. Following his discharge after eight months, Knowles attended Yale University, served briefly after graduating in 1949 as an assistant editor for the *Yale Alumni* magazine, and then worked from 1950 to 1952 as a reporter and occasional drama critic for the *Hartford Courant.* Knowles was a free-lance writer during 1952 through 1956. After a year or so abroad, touring Italy and southern France and writing his first novel, "Descent into Proselito" (which he decided not to publish, partly on the advice of his mentor Thornton Wilder), Knowles returned to the United States in 1955. He took up residence in New York City's Hell's Kitchen section, where he shared an apartment with actor Bradford Dillman. He wrote occasional drama reviews while his first short stories (including "A Turn with the Sun" in 1953 and "Phineas" in 1956) were being published. During this period he continued to benefit from Wilder's interest in his work and began to write *A Separate Peace.*

After *Holiday* magazine published his article on Phillips Exeter Academy in late 1956, Knowles moved to Philadelphia in 1957 to assume the post of associate editor for *Holiday.* During this time *A Separate Peace* was published, first in England (1959) and then in the United States (1960). When it became clear soon after its American publication that *A Separate Peace* was to be highly successful, Knowles, then thirty-five, resigned his editorship in August 1960 to embark on a two-year tour of Europe and the Middle East, a sojourn recounted in his 1964 travelogue, *Double Vision: American Thoughts Abroad.* His second novel, *Morning in Antibes* (1962), was published while Knowles was still abroad. Established as a professional writer, Knowles returned from Europe and moved into a New York City apartment, where he lived throughout the 1960s while continuing to go abroad for short periods. During these years he served as a writer-in-residence, first at the University of North Carolina for the 1963-1964 session and then at Princeton in 1968-1969; had published his third novel, *Indian Summer* (1966), which was dedicated to Thornton Wilder, and a collection of short stories, *Phineas* (1968); and had published two essays in the *New York Times,* "Where Does a Young Writer Find His Real Friends?" in 1962 and "The Writer-in-Residence" in 1965. In 1970, the year his father died, Knowles took up permanent residence in Southampton, Long Island, where his neighbors in nearby villages have included Truman Capote, Winston Groome, Willie Morris, and Irwin Shaw. His fourth novel, *The Paragon,* appeared in 1971, followed by *Spreading Fires* in 1974 and *A Vein of Riches* in 1978. A motion picture version of *A Separate Peace* was released in 1972. Knowles is currently at work on his seventh novel, "Peace Breaks Out," designed to be a "companion piece" to *A Separate Peace.* Outside of commentaries on *A Separate Peace,* there has been very little serious critical attention paid to Knowles's work.

The settings of Knowles's novels reflect those environments he himself feels most influenced by. *A Vein of Riches,* which traces the fortunes of the Catherwood family from 1909 until 1924, is set in Middleburg, West Virginia, a coal-boom community not unlike Fairmont. The Phillips Exeter Academy takes on fictional form as the Devon school, where Gene Forrester spends most of the World War II years in *A Separate Peace*; the academy appears again (though less recognizably) as the Wetherford Country Day School attended by both Cleet Kinsolving and Neil Reardon prior to World War II in *Indian Summer.* Cleet returns to Connecticut after his military discharge in 1945 to see his brother off to Yale; in *The Paragon,* Louis Colfax comes to Yale in 1953 following an early discharge from the U.S. Marine Corps. Knowles's own strong affinity during the early 1950s and early 1960s for the French Riviera is reflected in the settings of both *Morning in Antibes* and *Spreading Fires* (which takes place at the villa Mas Tranquilitat, "overlooking Cannes").

Knowles's talent for describing local atmosphere, nurtured during his years with *Holiday,* has been frequently admired by his critics and is one of the mainstays of his appeal as a fiction writer. Knowles typically employs such local description to forward the thesis that cultures are to a significant degree products of their geographical limitations, so that individual personalities are to be understood as ultimately shaped as much by the characteristics of their native climates and terrains as by heredity. The wanderlust of many of Knowles's protagonists reflects their needs to escape the subtle determinism of such environmental shaping. This thesis plays an especially strong part in the thematic development of his two Mediterranean novels, *Morning in Antibes* and *Spreading Fires,* as well as in *Indian Summer,* in which Cleet Kinsolving's desire to "roll out his life full force" is complemented by his "fear of being trapped" into returning to Wetherford, Connecticut, his small hometown; and in *The Paragon,* the "irascible climate" of Connecticut shapes a people who become "unresting, ever on the alert to what's next, brittle from the fatigue of ever adapting to their commanding climate." A similar line of speculation about how climate and geography determine the characteristic "climates" of various national cultures runs throughout *Double Vision: American Thoughts Abroad,* a collection of impressions gathered during Knowles's transatlantic junkets to England, southern France, Greece, and the Middle East. In *Double Vision,* Knowles tests his own acquired assumptions and expectations against a variety of external milieux; this process of self-testing is a major recurring motif in his novels, and Knowles's work is perhaps best understood as his series of attempts to work out the psychological implications of his crucial observation in *Double Vision* that "the American Character is unintegrated, unresolved, a careful Protestant with a savage stirring in his insides, a germ of native American wildness thickening in his throat."

The ineluctable shaping power of environment is a constant against which Knowles's fictive protagonists must struggle; an apposite constant in Knowles's work is his thesis that every individual has within himself a metaphorical "seam of value" (a term which occurs in both *Morning in Antibes* and *The Paragon*), a "vein of riches" composed of all the urges, desires, and other innate drives which naturally resist the benevolent or malevolent totalitarianism of "the Given," be it the local shaping environment or the cultural institutions created by men as part of their collective adaptation to the environment. The major struggle for each of Knowles's protagonists is to acquire an identity which resolves "the careful Protestant" and the "savage stirring in his insides," which reconciles the personal, moiling "seam of value" within to those impersonal and rigidifying forces without. This struggle is central to the process of character development in all of Knowles's novels, and though Knowles has returned to it again and again in his six novels to date, his critics generally agree that his first novel is clearly his best demonstration of this process.

The idea for Knowles's first published novel, *A Separate Peace*, grew out of his previous short story "Phineas," which appeared in *Cosmopolitan* in May 1956 and which prefigures the first five and one half chapters of the finished novel's story line. Frequently compared critically to J. D. Salinger's *A Catcher in the Rye* (1951) and written despite Wilder's initial skepticism about the feasibility of the project, *A Separate Peace* is today one of the most widely read postwar American novels; it was in its eleventh Macmillan printing and its forty-third Bantam paperback run in September 1976, with a total of over four million copies in print. It won in 1960 the first William Faulkner Award for a notable first novel as well as the 1960 Rosenthal Award of the National Institute of Arts and Letters.

A Separate Peace represents Knowles's discovery of those psychological forces informing what he came to call in 1964 the prototypically New England "American Character." This paradigmatic self is composed of two elements: the "germ of wildness," an essentially libidinal, creative primary element bent on expressing itself upon the world, and the "cautious Protestant," a secondary element committed essentially to defending, protecting, and conserving that primary self. This secondary element corresponds roughly to Freud's concept of the superego and to Jung's notion of the animus impulse, while the primary element corresponds to Freud's id and Jung's anima. The impulses and urges of the primary self manifest themselves in the form of anarchic human needs and desires and in the emotions of love and hate; the most obvious manifestations of the secondary self in Knowles's work are the institutions—governments, academic curricula, cultural ethos—which evolve out of the impulse of the secondary self but which, once created, take on an independently self-protective character and end up stifling the very spirit they exist ontologically to protect. At their deepest level, Knowles's novels (including *A Separate Peace*) are designed to isolate and study these two complementary but conflicting elements in the American Character; hence the frequent appearance of doubles and alter ego figures in his work. The novels focus upon the limited variety of adaptive strategies his protagonists invent to reconcile the urges within themselves to the prevailing shaping forces—the characteristic "Givens" of culture and climate—Knowles sets them in.

The retrospective first-person point of view of *A Separate Peace* allows Gene Forrester to review his adolescent personality's disintegration and the subsequent process of reintegration through the detaching distance of fifteen years, a distance which enables Knowles's protagonist to analyze as well as evaluate the evolution of his identity. As a prototype of the American Character, Gene comes to Devon school controlled by the "cautious Protestant" in his character; various cultural and climatic images of conservatism at the school, including the adamantine First Academy Building, the frozen New Hampshire winterscape, and the "dull, dark green called olive drab" which he identifies as "the prevailing color of life in America" during the World War II years, all serve to reinforce this strain of his character. He is drawn to Brinker Hadley, the epitome of the "cautious Protestant." Student leader and class politician, Brinker, "the standard preparatory school article," is New England conservatism personified. At the same time, the repressed "germ of wildness" in Gene's character is attracted to Phineas, an indifferent student but a natural athlete and eccentric individualist who rules the playing fields of Devon during the summer session with a spirit of spontaneous anarchy. In contrast to the patriotic (and military) olive drab, which is the color of defensive conservatism for Gene, Phineas's emblem is an outrageously bright pink shirt.

Gene's shifts of allegiance back and forth between these two projected versions of his own potential identity constitute "a study," according to Knowles, "of how adolescent personality develops, identifying with an admired person, then repudiating that person." Gene's early attempts to identify with Phineas (by reluctantly joining the Super

Suicide Society, by accompanying Phineas on an overnight trip to the Atlantic Ocean) activate a direct inner conflict between the "cautious Protestant" and the "germ of wildness" within Gene's character, a conflict won by the cautious Protestant. When Gene causes Phineas to break a leg in a fall from the jumping tree, from which boys have been jumping into the river as a test of courage, Gene is forced to recognize the part of himself which identifies with Phineas. After Phineas has left school to recuperate from his injury, Gene secretly tries on Phineas's pink shirt and finds it fits. Gene's attempts to cultivate this awakened "germ of wildness" within himself are inhibited, however, by the presence of Brinker Hadley, who moves into the room across the hall from Gene's and immediately forces Gene to confront his disloyalty. Guided by Brinker, Gene decides to enlist in the armed forces, thus reducing the pains of coming to terms with his evolving identity by letting the military design his identity for him. Before Gene actually enlists, Phineas reappears at school, and Gene once again finds himself unable to repudiate completely either the anarchic forces within himself or his conservative defenses against those forces. Tutored by Phineas, Gene begins to train himself for the chimerical 1944 Olympics. At the same time, Brinker, having lost his direct sway over Gene's allegiances, "had begun a long, decisive sequence of withdrawals from school activity ever since the morning I deserted his enlistment plan"; having changed his uniform from "well-bred clothes" to "khaki pants supported by a garrison belt," Brinker represents Gene's own lessening but nonetheless active commitment to the prevailing olive-drab way of life. As attractive as Phineas's "choreography of peace" is to Gene, the part of himself which identifies with Phineas's emotional hedonism once again finds itself at odds with the relentless shaping forces of the outside world, which finally intrude upon Devon irresistibly in the form of a telegram from Elwin "Leper" Lepellier, a schoolmate who enlisted and has gone "psycho" in boot camp. Gene sees in Leper's condition a warning against going out into the world unprepared for dealing with hostility, a reminder that the "cautious Protestant" is a necessary element of an identity which hopes to survive in the world. Thus reminded of his dual commitment, but once again unable to reconcile the unintegrated forces within and without himself, Gene becomes a helpless observer of a climactic kangaroo court scene in which Phineas, and by extension the part of Gene identifying with Phineas, is put on trial by Brinker for refusing to cooperate with the "Givens" of a world at war, with Leper serving as chief witness for the prosecution. Phineas rejects the trial, only to stumble blindly down the marble stairs of the First Academy Building, incurring a second and ultimately fatal fracture of his leg. Gene then isolates himself, at least temporarily, from these three characters and by extension their three separate strategies for coming to terms with one's self in the world; thus removed from the shaping forces of his past, he finally succeeds in achieving an integrated "double vision" which fuses, albeit tenuously, the warring parts of his character. The "separate peace" of the title refers to this valuable but temporary act of self-integration, which produces a personality which is replication of neither of the essential forces which generated it but rather a delicate orchestration of those forces.

Where Gene Forrester seeks peace against the backdrop of World War II, Nick Bodine in *Morning in Antibes* seeks love to the rhythms of the French-Algerian crisis of the late 1950s. The use of a world crisis as a metaphor for an individual struggle is only one of several major motifs which have been transposed from *A Separate Peace* into *Morning in Antibes* and so into the cultural and climatic milieu of the French Riviera, in many ways the antithesis of the frozen New Hampshire setting of the first novel. A grown-up Gene Forrester, Nicholas Petrovich Bodine, the emotionally exhausted narrative voice of the novel, is a congeries of acquired attitudes and institution-oriented habits of thinking (his father a White Russian and his mother French, Nick himself has been raised in New England); his culturally conditioned personality holds, enveloped and stifled for most of the novel, a "seam of value" which however is in danger of "withering from disuse." The novel traces the process by which Nick's attenuated capacity for loving is reactivated and finally liberated, a process which involves the simultaneous dismantling of his acquired identity. To do so, Knowles has Nick instinctively seek out the languid summer climate of Antibes and Juan-les-Pins, as though the climate itself might help to thaw his frozen New England personality and draw out whatever urges and impulsions might be lying dormant within him.

A necessary ingredient to the process of Nick's rehabilitation is the figure of Jeannot the Algerian, who is Phineas's counterpart and who serves similarly as a role model for Nick's hidden, redeeming self. Jeannot's personality expresses directly his anarchic heart: "he didn't care about goals . . . ," and his sentiments, which he does care about, "began with himself and arched iridescently over into certain friends . . . they did not include anything so abstract as patriotism, either French or Algerian." For Nick, Jeannot stands as the archetype of a personality formed out of the single drive for authentic self-expression: "the crude battering prow of this drive, with him and with all of us, was engulfing desire, was love." Jeannot's struggle in the novel is to maintain this loving personality, unencumbered by forced commitments to the causes of others; when finally he is forced by circumstances arising out of the French-Algerian conflict to become a warrior, he predictably aligns himself with the National Liberation Front against the colonialist French establishment.

Counterbalancing the figure of Jeannot in the novel is Marc de la Croie, a much older and more intractable version of Brinker Hadley. M. Marc, still desperately committed to the Pétainist mentality he adopted in 1940 and currently a ringleader of the Ultraist conspiracy to suppress the Algerian revolt (and thus the liberation-seeking spirit of Jeannot), is as bent on drawing Nick into the witheringly civilized spirit of the de la Croie villa as Jeannot is on drawing Nick's other self out into the warming circle of his loving spirit. M. Marc represents the oppressive anima figure which Nick must overcome both within and without himself in order to redeem his capacity for love.

Poised like Nick between the forces represented by Jeannot and M. Marc is Liliane, Nick's estranged wife, whom Nick married because he was strongly attracted to "not herself but the uncontainable excitement I saw in her." Though Nick desires to possess the giving, outgoing self he sees in Liliane, their marriage "came apart" because Nick has held back from expressing the corresponding streak of giving within himself. Nick's divided self becomes at least tentatively consolidated at the end of the novel when he affirms the "hidden seam of value" he detects within himself and identifies in Liliane. Though his own capacity for love has become diminished, he exercises what is left of it first by recklessly denying M. Marc possession of Liliane and then by reconciling himself maritally with Liliane.

Morning in Antibes is a flawed novel. Though Knowles's talent for rendering atmosphere does justice to the setting, his hastily sketched characters seem underdeveloped and "perfunctory." Offered as a paragon of individualism, Jeannot seems rather a paradigm of those cultural characteristics attributable to Algerian Arabs, while Knowles's rendering of Nick fluctuates unevenly between presenting Nick as suffering from a failure of personal will and as being a helpless victim or by-product of adverse cultural conditioning. The heavy-handed use throughout the novel of the French-Algerian crisis as a metaphor for Nick's internal struggle of liberation is an unconvincing version of the more successful analogy Knowles creates in *A Separate Peace* between the progress of World War II and the progress of Gene's evolving vision of peace. General critical consensus holds *Morning in Antibes* to be an unfinished book which was, "unhappily," rushed into publication, perhaps to capitalize upon the prior success of *A Separate Peace*.

Following publication of his travelogue, *Double Vision*, in 1964, Knowles turned his concerns back to a more familiar Connecticut landscape. The dominant themes of *Indian Summer* are familiar: here again, the totalitarian forces of culture and climate tend to overwhelm the people who must coexist with them, and personal adaptations to these forces in turn give rise to the dual and usually imperfectly integrated identity sketched in *Double Vision* and explored in the first two novels. The vehicles Knowles chooses for presenting these themes, however, are new. A shift to a relatively detached third-person point of view allows Knowles to supply motivational insights into his characters which, as he acknowledges in a 1962 essay for the *New York Times*, are unfortunately missing in *Morning in Antibes*; this narrative device also creates new opportunities for both dramatic irony and for occasional corrective satire, both of which appear in *Indian Summer* and, even more inventively, in *The Paragon*. A second major shift involves Knowles's choice of protagonists; whereas in his earlier two novels the focus is on the rediscovery by the "careful Protestant" in the American Character of his more fundamental and unconservative self, in *Indian Summer* and in *The Paragon* the focus is clearly on the process through which the "savage stirring in his insides, a germ of native American wildness" attempts to insure its continuing viability.

A Phineas figure endowed with a capacity for survival, twenty-three-year-old Harold "Cleet" Kinsolving returns from the Pacific in 1946 to an America trying to demobilize its wartime identity. Cleet, like America, having adapted imperfectly to the rhythms of military priority for four years, dreams now of staying mobile and unregulated, if only to give himself time to "work the war-induced knots out of his character" in private "and without risk of hurting anybody close to him"; accordingly, he drifts from Texas to St. Joseph, Missouri, where he begins working with a small crop dusting outfit and dreams of creating a small cargo line running between Seattle and Alaska, a dream which combines his needs for the freedom he finds in flying and the creativity he would express in being able to "produce something." Coupled with Cleet's need for freedom is his lifelong "fear of being trapped": a runaway at age twelve from "the feeling of bare survival, an antiquated hollowness and brittleness" which characterizes old houses in Wetherford as well as the town in general, an escapee from a hasty marriage at seventeen, barely able to tolerate the academic rigors of Wetherford Country Day School, Cleet is by nature a "privateer," and he attributes this nature to the "Indian" strain inherited from his maternal grandmother. Like Phineas and Jeannot before him, Cleet's energy and emotions run close to the surface of his personality, so close that emblematically he cannot wear a wristwatch: excess static electricity in his body renders one inoperable.

The animus figure for Cleet is Neil Reardon, heir to High Farms and the history of exploitation it represents, the "formidable and fortress-like" Reardon estate built on coal, oil, iron ore, and most recently on real estate. Conditioned by a life of wealth coupled with an upper-class education at both Wetherford Country Day School and Yale, fresh from a shining military career, Neil has become the spokesman for old-fashioned New England intellectual and economic conservatism masked in Marxist rhetoric, lecturing the nation on the "bankrupt values and flabby laissez-faire anarchy of the pre-World War II generation in economics, politics, and sex." Like his father, Neil has become a paragon of the Wetherford spirit, the symbol of which—the 250-year-old Wetherford Elm—has begun to die back, "inevitably." Like Gene Forrester and Nick Bodine before him, Neil is dimly troubled by an inner conflict between his adopted capitalist values and a subconscious resentment against the constraints they impose upon his life's shape; predictably, Neil deals with this germ of an anarchic self first by selecting as his mate Georgia Sommers, whose "proletarian mentality" is "one of the principal reasons he married her," and second by hiring his alter ego Cleet to do odd jobs for him. Unfortunately, Neil's psychological adaptation to the Reardon way of life compels him to establish a possessive rather than a giving relationship with Georgia, the "unreplaceable part of himself."

Neil's possession of Georgia, in whom Cleet detects the same "something unguarded and aspiring, something brave and a little vulnerable, gaiety and strength" he values in himself, serves in the novel as one model of a relationship between the "cautious Protestant" (actually Neil is a Catholic) and the "savage" in the American Character. A second paradigm is represented by "The Heir," the child Georgia is carrying, who represents to both Cleet and Neil some future hybrid of the adaptive individualist in Georgia and the frozen cultural spokesman in Neil. Georgia's father, Mr. Sommers, represents to Cleet "what he himself might be someday" should he fail to try to realize his dream of owning an independent airline, a man who has "failed, missed, thrown himself away, not gotten to the priceless core of himself and used it and made something of it, not contributed it to life and so become immortal." Lynn Sommers, Georgia's sister, represents a final strategy for relating the "savage" to the "cautious Protestant": Lynn decides to leave the Reardon enclave to strike out on her own while she still can.

Cleet finally chooses to follow Lynn's example, and he flees the various traps which Wetherford and the Reardons pose for him, but not before he wreaks havoc on the Reardon empire. After discovering that Neil's father and Neil, who have become "partners... two adult millionaires" during the war years, intend to renege on their promise to finance Cleet's dreamed-of airline, the "ignorant Indian" within Cleet takes "animal revenge" on Neil by venting its sexual energies upon Georgia, "mate of Neil, enemy." Georgia in turn suffers a miscarriage that leaves her sterile, brought on by her "profound emotional shock" at the ease with which Cleet has managed to resurrect the "savage" in her. Having symbolically destroyed any hope for a reconciliation between the savage and the cautious in the American Character, Cleet's final act before leaving is an act of "love" in which he draws all Neil's awakened anger and outrage onto himself, thus protecting Georgia and at the same time providing himself as an object upon which Neil can express his otherwise self-destructive emotions.

Most critics view *Indian Summer* as being allegorically overweight, and indeed perhaps too much is made of Cleet's Indian heritage and his "magnetism." Though motivation of character is vastly more discernible in *Indian Summer* than in *Morning in Antibes*, these motivations clearly are designed to fit the demands of Knowles's thesis about the components of the American Character, and consequently it is a patently "written" novel in which symbolic implications tend to overwhelm the demands of psychological realism.

Knowles resumes in *The Paragon* the careful third-person exploration of the "germ of native American wildness in the American Character" begun in *Indian Summer*. Again the novel is set in New England, where the "commanding climate" of a 11

CHAPTER TWO

Nick Blackburn ~~Amo~~ mounted the ~~spirl~~ ~~spirl~~ spiral staircase to the small Readers' Retreat Room, about twenty feet square, ~~with~~ long shelves crowding the wallspace with ~~wa~~ volumes of every size, shape, and degree of importance, upward TOWARD ~~to~~ the ceiling and a big, foggy-looking ~~skylirh~~ skylight.

Buckley was slouched in ~~anan~~ easy chair in the ~~teer~~ corner, pouring over a massive volume. He looked up, nodded briefly, and IMMERSED ~~imersed~~ himself ~~a~~ again in his book.

The word "wayward" popped into Amo's mind as he covertly studied Buckley's head , hair, hunched shoulders, long hands. The ~~hai~~ hair was rather long for Devon, ALMOST AN AFFECTATION, as though he saw himself as ~~a~~ Maestro of ~~an~~ some symphony. IT WAS reddish brown in color. He had a straight nose, slightly sloping hazel eyes, remnants of freckles on his rather long face. His shoulders were tense, despite his slouch. Amo had earlier noticed ~~theno~~ no nicotine stains on his long hands.

"I'm glad ~~it wasn't~~ ~~no~~ you aren't some creep coming up here. I can't concentrate with creeps around," ~~sa~~ said Buckley. His voice was mellifluous, urbane, ~~and~~ almost ~~pedantic~~ pedantic; Amo felt it was an appropriate ~~accompaniemo~~ accompaniment to his somehow singular appearance, a ~~ref~~ reenforcement of it; ~~the~~ there was a languor to his voice and his ~~m~~ movements and whole demeanor which, Amo ~~sid~~ ~~suddenly~~ ~~conclud~~ ~~concluddd,eeeeeeeeee~~ ~~concluddeddddddddddddd~~ ~~concludddddddddddddddddddddddddddddddddd~~ ~~dddddddddddddddddddddddd~~ SUDDENLY concluded, was designed to mislead, the steely languor of a cat creeping up upon an unaware bird.

Revised typescript

a Connecticut autumn is clearly analogous to Yale University's architecture, depicted by Knowles as having been designed for "self-defense" and looking like "some long-established and only infrequently attacked permanent military installation." Yale University, even in 1953, is adamantly committed to preserving its fixed form at all costs, thus becoming a haven of that "Bastille psychology" associated with the institutionalized past and its human allies characteristic in Knowles's work. And Yale is not only intent on preserving that identity but promulgating it. As Clement Jonaz, an Afro-Brazilian Marxist misfit at Yale whose antiestablishmentarianism is emblematically genetic as well as political, puts it, "They're brainwashing us here with the dogmas of capitalism with a thin overlay of bourgeois government planning, plus ancestor-worship."

Throughout *Indian Summer* Cleet Kinsolving dreams of escaping the shaping totalitarianism of the New England climate and ethos; in contrast Louis Colfax, designed to become a paragon of American Character, tries to make a place for himself within this ethos without being assimilated by it. Lou represents that heir to both strains in the American Character who was miscarried in *Indian Summer*, the union of the potentially self-annihilating separation of the "cautious Protestant" and the "germ of wildness" within the individual psyche. Cleet's wildness is part of the personal past Lou brings back to Yale as the novel opens. This past is tied to the image of the "Black House" (located in the wilderness an hour from New Haven), Lou's inheritance from his mad Aunt Alice and representative of some "Colfax madness," in which Lou senses "an overpowering feeling of isolation, of holding fast to some bleak inner fact." Knowles uses the device of frequent flashback to sketch out Lou's earlier attempt to ally his ego's New England heritage with his alter ego, represented by Charlotte Mills, a British-born drama student who has come to America to escape her upper-middle-class rearing and in whom Lou identifies "some kind of anarchy" which he needs to nurse within himself, much as Nick Bodine has married Liliane for her "uncontainable excitement." Lou's early attempts to take psychological possession of his own capacity for love by displacing it onto Charlotte and dealing with it externally leads to calamity when Charlotte leaves him and the Black House in pursuit of her drama career. Like Cleet, Lou runs from the place which has become a symbol of hollow possessiveness; unlike Cleet, though, Lou runs to the Marine Corps, where he submits himself to the training designed to "break down previous personality and put in its place a human machine conditioned for combat," only to find himself discharged after eight months for the good of the corps.

Thus having already failed at three different strategies for coming to terms with his divided psyche, Lou returns to Yale to resume his college career and to take up the struggle on behalf of that American "germ of wildness" where it ends in Knowles's three preceding novels; the two prized possessions he brings with him, a carton brimming with two thousand unsent letters and a mammoth Soviet flag, symbolize his need to reconcile rather than divorce the warring impulses within himself. The measure of desperation in Lou's need to find some way of expressing his volcanolike "seam of value" within the constricting framework of a New England mentality is his reckless strategy for coming to terms with the forces that have defeated him three times already: an almost suicidally impulsive expression designed to take these forces by surprise.

Lou's first test is his new roommate, Gordon Durant, scion of the Durant Chemicals empire which has contributed heavily to the Yale endowment fund for three generations. Gordon's "code of life," a crystallized version of the wealthy New England ethos, has no place in it for the "spooky wraith" of creative but unpredictable individualism he sees in Lou. Gordon, who at one point characterizes Lou as being like certain thoroughbred horses on his family's stud farm, "a mass of nervous impulses barely held together by a desperate will, a being the French would call *fin de race*, the end of his line," ultimately concedes the value of Lou's aggressively proffered friendship after Lou manages to return to its stall the high-spirited polo pony Gordon has drunkenly ridden into their dormitory room one Saturday night. Gordon and Lou reach their separate peace the following morning, when during "the last crisis of their friendship" Gordon uncharacteristically apologizes for being so unlikable and Lou responds by vowing he loves Yale.

Lou's second and more difficult campaign involves his need to come to terms with the part of himself invested in Charlotte Mills, a need reactivated early in the novel when he finds a photograph of her with her young son (who might be Lou's) hanging on the wall of the Black House. Lou's need to somehow work the figure of Charlotte back into his own reevolving identity is the product of the terror of incompleteness which informs his recurring nightmare about not being allowed to graduate because he has neglected to take a course from each Yale department. Under the patient tutelage of Norma, Gordon's young but delphically wise Greek ex-stepmother, Lou comes to see that the sense of inner emptiness associated with the Black House is a psychological prerequisite for expressing the positive creative impulses which constitute the "seam of value" in his character. After attempting for most of the novel to repossess Charlotte and then, failing that, kidnapping her child, "the image of Charlotte in a distinctly male recasting," Lou finally gives up trying to fulfill his inner emptiness by taking from the world and reconciles himself instead to a future of giving *to* the world—a course of creative effort which may compensate for, but never eliminate, the "devastating sense of nothingness and emptiness and vulnerability" underlying all human desire. As Knowles has Lou put it, "partial people do the great things in this world . . . to make up for the inner knowledge that they were condemned all their lives to be incomplete people."

Spreading Fires, Knowles's fifth novel, is his shortest and perhaps his most unusual work to date. Dedicated to Truman Capote, the novel for the first six of its nine chapters blends themes common to Knowles's earlier works with the spare surface suspense of Capote's best terror stories (the protagonist's sister's name is Miriam, after the character in Capote's short story of the same name); the final three chapters, however, sacrifice this surface tautness in order to examine the underlying psychological terrain Knowles seems more predisposed to working with.

Knowles returns for this setting to maritime France in the languid months of July and August, and here again as in *Morning in Antibes* the benevolent climate operates to draw out whatever suppressed and pent-up urges and emotions people bring to it. The protagonist, Brendan Lucas, is a twenty-nine-year-old career diplomat, the third generation of Washington, D.C., Lucases to serve in the foreign service, who has rented the villa Mas Tranquilitat both to remove himself for a while from his professional world of "deceptions and lies and betrayals and cynicism" and to host a prenuptial party for his sister Miriam and her fiance Xavier Farel de Dornay, who was Brendan's Georgetown University schoolmate and wrestling partner. The season, the setting, and the occasion converge to trigger long-repressed adolescent emotions in all three characters: Brendan and Miriam spent their adolescent vacation years in this region, "thrown together a lot" during the years of their sexual awakenings, and this return to the area strikes Miriam as "weird . . . like having a dream about your childhood." The atmosphere within Mas Tranquilitat, itself "girded for attack on all fronts," becomes supercharged with a network of powerful and thinly displaced sexual desires (Brendan's for his sister and for Xavier, Miriam's for Xavier, Xavier's for both) which constitute some of the "spreading fires" of the title.

The counterbalancing spirit of repression is represented by the villa's resident cook, Neville, whose personality is "satisfactory on the surface" but is ravished at a deeper level by a severe degree of dissociation of the "cautious" from the "savage." Neville has committed himself the past three years to "extreme solitude and ceaseless work." Knowles likens Neville's "arid childhood—and not much of a fertile life since" to the "decadent strain" of deformed orange trees growing in the villa orchard, draped with sour inedible oranges and with the bags of arsenic Neville has hung there to ward off fertilizing insects, suggesting his bizarre total rejection of the anima within himself and in the world around him. With the occasion of the prenuptial party Neville feels himself attacked from without by the libidinal energies he has imperfectly repressed within, and his latent paranoia surfaces with terrifying force. Clearly, Neville's threatening personality gathers its energy in part from the inhibitions being shed by Brendan and his party, and Neville's increasingly overt threats against the lives of the members of the party (suggested first by his use of words, then by his method of hacking and partially decapitating chickens in the kitchen, and finally by his wielding a butcher knife) correspond in intensity to the degree to which the members of the party become more clearly controlled by their reawakened adolescent passions.

In the final three chapters, Neville comes to represent more specifically Brendan's private double, the repressive part of himself with which he has unconsciously been struggling for the past fifteen years. Brendan's earlier ambivalence about his libidinal affinity for Miriam leaves his dual identity open to the puritanical control of both his mother and Neville, who comes to replace her, and Brendan himself lives his dual psychological existence only vicariously through Xavier's love for his sister and, finally, Neville's inhibitions against love. From Knowles's point of view Brendan's inner struggle cannot be finally resolved until he undiplomatically chooses to ally himself firmly either with the "cautious" or with the "savage" in his own character. Not surprisingly, he aligns with the former near the end of the novel, when, interpreting Neville's gesture of embrace as a gesture of attack,

Brendan plunges a butcher knife into Neville's stomach. Brendan's identity thus seems designed to confirm Knowles's fundamental thesis about the hold of the past over the shape of the present: in Brendan's genealogy an inescapable part of Brendan still remains "the result of his [predominantly Anglo-Irish] ancestors and who they were and what they believed."

Critical reception of *Spreading Fires* reflects the uneven tonality of the novel's two-part structure. Proponents of Knowles's earlier work find the first part of the novel perhaps too hastily developed, while others feel the descriptive and analytic components of this novel are imperfectly synchronized.

In *A Vein of Riches* is presented a more ambivalent cultural and geographical climate. The West Virginia in this sixth novel, neither unilaterally repressive nor unilaterally evocative but rather a composite of the milieux of Knowles's earlier works, is designed to reflect in its composition both of those shaping forces at work on the American, and more generally the human, identity. Knowles emphasizes West Virginia's precarious achievement of statehood during the Civil War, a time of shifting allegiances and ambiguous political affiliations during which West Virginia took on neither Northern nor Southern identity but remained passively resistant to the forces at war on her soil. The unresolved tensions of the state's compound cultural heritage become strained by the discovery of vast reserves of coal throughout West Virginia and her consequently sudden preeminence as a "vein of riches" at the turn of the century. The novel is set during 1909-1924, a period during which the northern part of the state, controlled by exploitative coal barons who in turn are backed by "many millions of eastern dollars," finds itself pitted against the long-repressed forces of anticapitalist sentiment, vested in the southern part of the state, which finally surface in the form of the United Mine Workers uprising of the summer of 1921. The conflicting forces are in turn replicated in the social, cultural, and economic composition of Middleburg, West Virginia, a product of the coal boom founded by pioneers of the coal industry who became within a decade "the great Middleburg coal barons, rulers of the biggest, the best, and the richest coalfield in the world" but surrounded by the shantytowns of the impoverished miners.

The novel focuses upon the Catherwood family, itself bracketed by the Clifton family above it and the Hayes family below it on the social ladder of Middleburg. The personality of Knowles's protagonist, Lyle Catherwood, is, like West Virginia, determined at birth to be an arena of conflicting allegiances; Lyle is not only the son of Clarkson Catherwood, and thus heir to the sprawling Clarkson Coal Company and the future burdens of ownership, but is also the child of Minnie, a "whimsical" spirit who intuitively mistrusts her husband's self-investment in the vast but finite natural resources of King Coal and who devotes herself instead to the small farm she acquires.

As in Knowles's previous works, the protagonist's struggle is to achieve some coherent identity, a process through which the inherent dualism of his American Character becomes resolved by his responding appropriately to externalized images of those forces operating within him. Outside shaping forces, however, conspire from the novel's beginning to make this process difficult. Clarkson and Minnie have had no sexual intercourse since Lyle's birth; to exacerbate their separateness, Minnie's sympathies lie not with her husband's need to defend his coal holdings but rather with the inevitable by-product of his "greed," the squalid living conditions of the miners and their families in nearby Poundville. Lyle's identification with his father is thus offset by the values inculcated by his mother during his preadolescent years. The constant internal strife in Lyle's family prepares Lyle for the economic friction informing the charged political atmosphere of West Virginia, which surfaces as the labor-management showdowns of the early 1920s and especially in the Logan County incident of August 1921.

Lyle's first major attempt to come to terms with the warring forces within and without himself is to try to remain a neutral party to these conflicts; at eighteen he adopts the pose of a reporter for the *Middleburg Exponent*, changes his name to Lew Jenkins, and fantasizes reportorial coups to be acquired by infiltrating the ranks of the labor union army then marching from Charleston upon Logan County, where the entrenched forces of nonunion mining interests (including Lyle's father) await to repel the invasion. As though to force Lyle to reject his simplistic strategy of dissociation, Lyle's identity as the son of Clarkson Catherwood is exposed during the march and the subsequent effort to rescue Lyle from the enemy camp brings about the accidental shooting death of Clarkson's aide, Virgil Pence. Lyle's immediate reaction to the unfortunate consequences of his escapade is to deny any personal responsibility for them; this conclusion, however, proves unsatisfactory to that need for a sense of personal value and purpose which, in Knowles's vision, personal identity exists to confirm, a sense

Lyle recognizes as "the elemental animal inside his personal self" which refuses to stay "trapped inside" the incoherent pastiche of contrary impulses Lyle currently has for an identity. Attempting to redeem this elemental self, Lyle imitates the strategy his mother uses earlier to verify her "salvation" and consults with the Reverend Ramsey Fullylove Roanoke. Lyle's prayer session with Reverend Roanoke is, however, inconclusive. Lyle's evolving relationship with Doris Lee Pence, widow of the man whose death Lyle now holds himself responsible for, in whom Lyle identifies a quality of "vitality" and "a kind of breeziness which she herself seemed unconscious of," qualities which significantly go generally unrecognized and unappreciated in the Middleburg community, measures his growing awareness of the value of the corresponding germ of vitality in himself: "I have a lot of deep feelings, he thought. It's something running right through me, very deeply, a vein or seam, . . . it's what I've really got, what I've always really lived for, and I guess always will live for." As in the cases of Nick, Cleet, and Lou, the redemption of Lyle's creative possibilities depends upon his ability to free himself from his psychological bondage to the "cautious Protestant" in his nature. Lyle's discovery of this need coincides in the novel with the almost overnight collapse of West Virginia's coal industry in the first two weeks of April 1924, a collapse which forces Clarkson and Lyle to draw upon their respective hidden reserves of character. Thus disencumbered of his social status, Lyle experiences, in sympathy with that "germ of wildness" which constitutes his personal "vein of riches," "a weird sense of exhilaration, almost somehow of hope fulfilled, a wildest dream realized."

Despite its epic proportions and its fidelity in acknowledging the socioeconomic forces which may be considered to have shaped Knowles's own family background, *A Vein of Riches* is considered by most of Knowles's critics his weakest novel artistically. The problem lies not with the interpretation of West Virginia history which the novel offers or with the psychological motivation of the characters per se, but rather with the obtrusive and relentlessly methodical presentation of precise correlations between outside force and evolving identity, a technique used in all of Knowles's fictions, but used in *A Vein of Riches,* as before in *Morning in Antibes,* perhaps to excess.

Knowles's reputation, as of this writing, is based almost entirely on his achievement in *A Separate Peace.* Only occasionally has any of his subsequent works received unqualified praise in a major book review, and none has drawn the substantial critical attention usually paid to a writer of Knowles's stature. At its best, Knowles's work is generally regarded as showing admirably his "understanding of emotion and a sensitivity to the psychological struggles between love and enmity, between loyalty and freedom, between the need to accept guilt and the need to be absolved from it"; the flaws in his later work are generally attributed to a characteristic "mechanical neatness" in Knowles's handling of plot and setting as vehicles for dramatizing these psychological struggles, a handling which strikes many reviewers as being contrived. Critics both pro and con, however, generally concur in their assessment of Knowles as both a master craftsman and a serious student of that seemingly irreducible dualism he perceives at the heart of the American Character.

—Robert M. Nelson

References:

William Barrett, "The Calculated Second Shot," *Atlantic Monthly* (March 1962): 148-149;

Bernard Carragher, "There Really Was a Super Suicide Society," *New York Times,* 8 October 1972, section 2, p. 2;

Anne Duchene, "Straight from the Record," *Manchester Guardian,* 6 April 1962, p. 13;

John Gardner, "More Smog from the Dark, Satanic Mills," *Southern Review,* 5 (Winter 1969): 224-244;

Wayne J. Henkel, "Pas de Feux," *Washington Post BookWorld,* 23 June 1974, p. 2.

TOM LEA
(11 July 1907-)

SELECTED BOOKS: *Randado* (El Paso: Carl Hertzog, 1941);
A Grizzly From the Coral Sea (El Paso: Carl Hertzog, 1944);
Peleliu Landing (El Paso: Carl Hertzog, 1945);
Bullfight Manual for Spectators (El Paso: Carl Hertzog, 1949);
The Brave Bulls (Boston: Little, Brown, 1949; London: Heinemann, 1950);
The Wonderful Country (Boston: Little, Brown, 1952; London: Heinemann, 1953);
The King Ranch (Boston: Little, Brown, 1957);
The Primal Yoke (Boston: Little, Brown, 1960; London: Macmillan, 1961);
The Hands of Cantú (Boston: Little, Brown, 1964; London: Hammond, Hammond, 1966);
A Picture Gallery (Boston: Little, Brown, 1968);
In The Crucible of The Sun (Kingsville, Texas: King Ranch, Inc., 1974).

One of those rare individuals to gain recognition both as a painter and a writer, Tom Lea exhibits in both mediums a love for and knowledge of the desert Southwest; and through both mediums he has contributed significantly to our understanding of the coming of progress and change to this section. Because most of his writings are set in the Southwest, he is best known as a regionalist. But like other good regionalists, his writings transcend regional constraints, projecting universal meanings.

Born in El Paso, Texas, at a time when El Paso was a crossroads for Mexican revolutionaries, ranchers, and prospectors, Lea spent his early years getting to know the mountains, deserts, and people of the Southwest. Throughout his career, the harsh reality and the awesome grandeur of the region have blended to form a backdrop for his characters—whether in his paintings or in his novels. His familiarity with the region enables him to develop detailed descriptive material which conveys much more than plot and dramatic action.

After graduating from high school in El Paso, Lea followed his interest in art and went, at age seventeen, to study at the Art Institute of Chicago. During Lea's eight years in Chicago, John Norton, a noted muralist, helped him develop a sense of historical panorama, which is evident in his art and his literature. After a brief study tour of Europe, he returned to receive commissions for murals in several public buildings, including the Benjamin Franklin Postal Station in Washington, D.C. Most of his murals depict vast landscapes and the struggles of explorers and settlers against the land and the elements. And always, the murals show his awareness of the role of history in shaping modern American character. During his career, Lea has drawn illustrations for his own books, as well as for many other authors. He worked especially closely with J. Frank Dobie, illustrating Dobie's *Apache Gold and Yaqui Silver* (1939), *The Longhorns* (1941), and others. Early on, Dobie and Lea formed a friendship that endured for decades as both sought to portray the development of the historical Southwest.

As an artist and correspondent for *Life* magazine, Lea spent World War II describing beach landings, fighter convoys, the sinking of aircraft carriers, and the everyday activities of America's fighting men and women. His realistic sketches and writings helped many Americans realize for the first time the violence and grim harshness of the war. He took part in military actions in the Pacific Islands, China, and the North Atlantic. After returning home, he published two fictionalized accounts of his war experiences, accompanied by illustrations of battle scenes (*A Grizzly From the Coral Sea* in 1944; *Peleliu Landing* in 1945). The war experiences had a profound impact on him, developing his concern for realism and for sharp depiction of accurate details. "I learned sharp gaunt prose from the sharp gaunt events of Peleliu," he commented.

After the war, Lea returned to his Southwest material, producing his first full-scale novel, *The Brave Bulls,* in 1949. This novel was widely acclaimed as a manual to the art of bullfighting and has gone through some thirty printings. Because of its popularity, it was serialized by the *Atlantic Monthly* and several newspapers, was published in ten foreign countries, and was made into a movie which starred Mel Ferrer as Luis Bello, the central character of the novel. The novel presents meticulously detailed information about the raising of bulls for the ring, the training of the bullfighter, the ritualistic movements of the bullfighter, and the business operations necessary for staging a large bullfight. The kaleidoscopic details serve as an important staging device for the study of Luis Bello.

Bello is a classic example of the poor, uneducated youngster who makes it to the top, enjoying the lucrative benefits of the hero worship accorded top bullfighters. The novel centers on the psychological trauma he experiences while enjoying, on the one hand, fame and fortune, and struggling, on the other, with constant fears of injury, disgrace, and death at the horns of the bull. Lea's hero has no death wish; instead, he wants only to meet each challenge, to survive the dangerous encounter with the bull, and to enjoy the material rewards he earns.

Lea successfully creates a blend of romanticism and realism—elements found in most of his novels. Bello revels in a world of make-believe where he is adored by beautiful women and honored by all; at the same time, the cold reality of the sharp horns and agonizing injury and death are always near. Lea's stark black and white illustrations in *The Brave Bulls* suggest the contrasts in this romantic-realistic world.

James K. Folson calls Lea's next novel, *The Wonderful Country* (1952), "one of the very best of recent Westerns." It has also been one of the most popular, selling over a million copies. The 1958 movie version starred Robert Mitchum. In developing the theme of this novel, Lea has Texas Ranger James B. Gillett comment, "Oh, how I wish I had the power to describe the wonderful country as I saw it then." Lea wants to describe not only the geography of "the wonderful country," the desert Southwest, but also the exuberant, full lives many Americans lived there in the post-Civil War era—a romantic, idealistic period in American history. Set along the Rio Grande, the novel depicts the struggles of Martin Brady, an American who grew up in Mexico, as he attempts to find his true identity and to determine his national allegiance and future. Brady, a hired gunman for the unscrupulous Castro brothers, lives a double life: known as Martin Brady in the United States, he is Martín Bredi in Mexico. He moves freely back and forth across the border, experiencing the pleasures and hardships of both worlds. Eventually he must decide whether to remain in Mexico, which represents his carefree and irresponsible youth, or to move to Texas, which, though often "plain and unromantic," represents reality and maturity.

Though many of the thematic elements in *The Wonderful Country* appear in a number of other Western novels, Lea handles them with sensitivity and freshness. For instance, Brady must make the traditional choice between his horse (and all that it symbolizes) and a woman. Brady's magnificent black stallion, Lágrimas, stands for everything in Mexico that he dreams about and treasures in the romantic past. Louisa Rucker, the woman whom Brady loves in Texas, stands for reality, responsibility, and the future. Once Brady chooses Louisa and Texas, he loses his home in Mexico, his job, and ultimately Lágrimas.

Lea often addresses, as he does here, the impact of progress and the coming of civilization to the frontier. To help explain this impact, he thoroughly and accurately describes the historical, geographical, and cultural background of the area. He embroiders a tapestry of sensual description and experience, incorporating scenes involving Texas Rangers, soldiers and their wives, Texas settlers, Mexican bandits and villagers, and Indians. And, as always, the stark beauty and harshness of the desert help put these scenes in perspective. Progress comes to the El Paso area with the completion of the railroad and the eradication of the Apache. The cavalry and the Texas Rangers are no longer necessary. Texas is, at last, a civilized place, no longer like the romantic and colorful Mexico of Brady's youth. Similarly, Lea says, America has now matured and faces a plain reality, void of romantic delusions. Lea's illustrations for *The Wonderful Country* are much more detailed and softer than those for *The Brave Bulls*, perhaps because of the greater need for descriptive elements. Always the visual correlation of Lea's illustrations with his story creates a sensory experience which could not be achieved by text alone.

Although the massive two-volume *The King Ranch* (1957) is essentially a history of that enterprise, Lea dramatizes and embellishes the historical framework so that it becomes an intriguing study in Texas history, folklore, and business achievement. Commissioned by the King Ranch, this project, like Lea's other works, reflects his copious research and familiarity with his topic. The novel won the Summerfield Roberts Award and the 1957 Book Design Award (Dallas Museum of Fine Arts) for its artistic merit as well as for its content and development. In cooperation with Carl Hertzog, his friend and a graphic specialist, Lea produced two volumes that are larger than the ordinary (as is the King Ranch), attractively printed, and masterfully illustrated. The volumes capture the grandeur of the land from which the Kings and the Klebergs carved a cattle empire. Because of its topical nature, Lea does not develop theme and plot as well as he does in other books; rather he focuses on a historical figure struggling to conquer the land and the elements against such seemingly overwhelming odds as political maneuvers, marauding Indians, and Mexican revolutionaries.

Departing from works that combine realism and romanticism, he set *The Primal Yoke* (1960) in the bleak Wyoming high country, rather than in the Southwest. *The Primal Yoke* is a study in naturalism. Drawing from his war experiences once more, Lea presents Haven Spurling, a wounded American marine who returns to the Wyoming mountains to recover physically and spiritually from the war. Spurling's life is tied intricately to the high mountains, and a primal force binds him closely to Nature and its peaceful, healing qualities. Intruding into this pastoral setting is Robert Royston, a millionaire industrialist who has alienated himself from Nature. Royston's daughter has designs on Spurling, whose destiny, along with Royston's, appears to be totally controlled by the Fates. Spurling's weakness causes him to violate his pact with Nature by falling in love with Royston's daughter, who, because of her father's exploitation of material resources and disregard for people, represents a destructive, outside force, alien to Nature. While critical reception of this novel has not been especially kind, Lea's usual skill is evident in its finely turned descriptive details and the terse style that reinforces the starkness of the primal images.

In *The Hands of Cantú* (1964) Lea returned to the Southwest and to the romantic-realistic quality of his earlier works. His central character, Don Vito Cantú is a Spanish nobleman of the sixteenth century, charged with raising fine horses for use by Spanish expeditions as they settle New Spain. Like *The Brave Bulls* in its documentary effect, *The Hands of Cantú* provides detailed information on the raising of fine horses—information obviously familiar to Lea. But the focus is on the character of Cantú, always larger than life, always heroic, always gentle, and always valiant and noble. The other major character is Toribio Ibarra, a young man sent to study horsemanship (and life) at the hands of Cantú. Serving as the narrator who reveals Cantú's excellent qualities, Ibarra progresses from a naive youngster to a confident sophisticate under Cantú's tutelage. Critical reception of the novel has been mixed, but most critics have rightfully praised it as a study of one of the earliest pioneering and civilizing elements in the Southwest.

Although Lea has published no major works since *The Hands of Cantú*, he continues to gain recognition as more readers discover his works. He and his wife Sarah live in El Paso, where Lea continues to work in his studio, producing paintings and drawings now much in demand by collectors of Western art. He suggests that he has "a novel on the shelf, about one-quarter done, promising well, developing slowly. Tentative title: *Maclovio, A Story of Mexico.*"

Because of his significant output of paintings, illustrations, and literary works, Tom Lea may well be remembered for his contribution to our knowledge of the American Southwest. He has helped Americans to appreciate the contributions of early settlers of the region, and to recognize, like Martin Brady in *The Wonderful Country*, that the freedom and energy of America's youth has vanished. By reading Lea's works, we are able to remember fondly America's romantic past and her civilizing pioneers and to understand why and how this nation and her people have become what they are today.

—*L. W. Denton*

References:

Evan Haywood Antone, "Tom Lea: A Study of His Life and Work," Ph.D. dissertation, University of California, Los Angeles, 1971;

El Paso Public Library, *A Bibliography of Writings and Illustrations by Tom Lea* (El Paso: El Paso Public Library Association, 1971);

Carl Hertzog, "Two Artists in Two Mediums," *Southwest Review*, 32 (Winter 1947): 53;

John O. West, *Tom Lea: Artist in Two Mediums*, Southwest Writers Series, no. 5 (Austin: Steck-Vaughn, 1967).

Papers:

Major collections of Lea's writings and illustrations are located at the El Paso Public Library in El Paso, Texas, and the Tom Lea Rooms at the Humanities Research Center, University of Texas at Austin.

HARPER LEE

(28 April 1926-)

BOOK: *To Kill a Mockingbird* (Philadelphia: Lippincott, 1960; London: Heinemann, 1960).

Harper Lee's reputation as an author rests on her only novel, *To Kill a Mockingbird* (1960). An enormous popular success, the book was selected for distribution by the Literary Guild and the Book-of-the-Month Club and was published in a shortened version as a *Reader's Digest* condensed book. It was also made into an Academy Award-winning film in 1962. Moreover, the novel was critically acclaimed, winning among other awards the Pulitzer Prize for fiction (1961), the Brotherhood Award of the National Conference of Christians and Jews (1961), and the *Bestsellers* magazine's Paperback of the Year Award (1962).

Although Lee stresses that *To Kill a Mockingbird* is not autobiographical, she allows that a writer "should write about what he knows and write truthfully." The time period and setting of the novel obviously originate in the author's experience as the youngest of three children born to lawyer Amasa Coleman Lee (related to Robert E. Lee) and Frances Finch Lee. The family lived in the sleepy little town of Monroeville, Alabama. After graduating from Monroeville's public schools, Lee spent a year (1944-1945) at Huntingdon College in Montgomery, Alabama, and then attended the University of Alabama for four years (1945-1949), including a year as an exchange student at Oxford University. She left the University of Alabama in 1950, six months short of a law degree, to pursue a writing career in New York City.

Harper Lee became interested in writing at the age of seven. While she was a student at the University of Alabama, her satires, editorial columns, and reviews appeared in campus publications.

Living in New York in the early 1950s and supporting herself by working as an airline reservations clerk, she approached a literary agent with the manuscripts of two essays and three short stories. The agent encouraged her to expand one of the stories into a novel which later became *To Kill a Mockingbird.*

With the financial help of friends, she gave up her job and moved into a cold-water flat where she devoted herself to her writing. Although her father became ill and she was forced to divide her time between New York and Monroeville, she continued to work on her novel. She submitted a manuscript to Lippincott in 1957. While editors criticized the book's structure, suggesting it seemed to be a series of short stories strung together, they recognized the novel's promise and encouraged Lee to rewrite it. With the help of her editor, Tay Hohoff, Lee reworked the material, and *To Kill a Mockingbird* was finally published in July 1960.

To Kill a Mockingbird is narrated by Jean Louise "Scout" Finch, a six-year-old girl who lives with her ten-year-old brother Jem and her lawyer father Atticus in the small Alabama town of Maycomb during the 1930s. During the three years covered by the novel, Scout and Jem gain an increased understanding of the adult world. A key incident in their maturing is the legal defense by their father of Tom Robinson, a black man falsely accused of raping a white girl named Mayella Ewell, daughter of the nefarious Bob Ewell. In the months preceding the trial, Scout and Jem suffer the taunts of classmates and neighbors who object to Atticus's "lawing for niggers." As the trial nears, the situation intensifies, and a threatened lynching of Robinson is narrowly averted by the innocent intervention of Jem and Scout. In a climactic scene, the jury finds Robinson guilty even though Atticus has clearly proven him innocent. Maycomb's racial prejudice is so engrained that Atticus cannot influence the verdict of people reared to believe "that *all* Negroes lie, that *all* Negroes are basically immoral beings, that *all* Negro men are not to be trusted around . . . [white] women."

Another major interest in the novel is the unraveling of the mystery surrounding the neighborhood recluse Arthur "Boo" Radley, who has remained secluded in the Radley house since he was arrested many years before for some teenage pranks and then released in his father's custody. Initially a victim of his father's uncompromising religion and family pride, Boo gradually becomes a victim of community prejudice, feared by adults and children alike. When Jem and Scout befriend Dill, a little boy who is spending summers in Maycomb with his aunt, the three devote themselves to Dill's idea of making Boo come out. At first the children imagine that the recluse dines on raw squirrels and roams the neighborhood by night. But finally they learn that Boo is truly a friend who has done a number of kind deeds for them. He hides gifts for the children in a hollow tree. He secretly mends Jem's torn pants, which were badly snagged on the Radleys' fence and abandoned there by the boy during an attempt to spy on Boo. Boo leaves them on the fence for Jem to retrieve. One cold winter night, while Scout stands shivering near the Radleys' steps as she watches a neighbor's house burn, Boo, unseen, covers her with a blanket. Finally, it is Boo who rescues Scout and Jem from the murderous attack of drunken, vengeful Bob Ewell.

To Kill a Mockingbird contains a number of complex and opposing themes in a deceptively simple narrative—ignorance-knowledge, cowardice-heroism, guilt-innocence, and prejudice (persecution)-tolerance. The ignorance-knowledge theme is developed through characterization and action. Lee believes that children are born with an instinct for truth and justice. Their education, which is the result of observing the behavior of the adults around them, can nurture or destroy their intrinsic goodness. Fortunately, the Finch children have Atticus to provide the true education which the Maycomb school fails to provide. The structuring of the action around the Boo Radley mystery and Robinson's trial is well suited to the gradual revelation of truth and further develops the ignorance-knowledge theme.

The character most central to the development of the cowardice-heroism theme is Atticus Finch; in counterpoint to Atticus's courage is the bullying cowardice of Bob Ewell. In part one of the novel, the children begin to think of their father as a hero when they see him shoot a rabid dog and learn for the first time that he was once "the deadest shot in Maycomb County." Atticus reforms the children's definition of courage when he has Jem read to Mrs. Dubose, a former drug addict, after school. The day after she dies, he tells Jem about her victory over morphine: "I wanted you to see what real courage is, instead of getting the idea that courage is a man with a gun in his hand. It's when you're licked before you begin but you begin anyway and you see it through no matter what." In part two of the novel, Atticus fulfills this definition of courage in defending Tom Robinson.

The themes of guilt-innocence and prejudice (persecution)-tolerance are closely related in the novel. The characters who are innocent—Tom Robinson and Boo Radley—are judged guilty by a prejudiced society. Tom is killed trying to escape from prison but the novel expresses hope that prejudice will be overcome. Jem sheds tears at the end of the trial and vows to combat racial injustice. However, the climax of the trial is melodramatic, and the narrative flounders when characters mouth pious speeches against prejudice.

Lee's use of symbol is masterful. The mockingbird closely associated with Boo Radley and Tom Robinson represents joy and innocence. Both Atticus and Miss Maudie, an optimistic neighbor, tell the children that it is a sin to kill a mockingbird. Lee's use of the symbolic mockingbird has been compared to Whitman's in "Out of the Cradle Endlessly Rocking." When Maycomb has a light snowfall for the first time in years, Jem builds a snowman underlaid with mud to give it sufficient substance. The snowman melts when Miss Maudie's house burns. Thus, in a day the snowman's color goes from black to white and from white to black, proving how superficial skin color is.

When *To Kill a Mockingbird* appeared in 1960, its critical reception was mixed. R. W. Henderson called it "a compassionate, deeply moving novel, and a most persuasive plea for racial justice"; others praised Lee's "insight into Southern mores" and her "wit, grace, and skill." Negative comments were made about the novel's sermonizing and its melodramatic climax. Some critics found fault with the point of view. In *Atlantic* Phoebe Adams found the story "frankly and completely impossible, being told in the first person by a six-year-old girl, with the prose style of a well-educated adult." Granville Hicks noted in *Saturday Review* that "Miss Lee's problem has been to tell the story she wants to tell and yet to stay within the consciousness of a child, and she hasn't consistently solved it."

Scholars writing articles about the novel in the 1970s praise its technical excellence and recognize its place in literary tradition. R. A. Dave notes that in creating the small world of Maycomb, Lee has made "an epic canvas against which is enacted a movingly human drama of the jostling worlds—of children and adults, of innocence and experience, of kindness and cruelty, of love and hatred, of humor and pathos, and above all of appearance and reality—all taking the reader to the root of human behavior."

Fred Erisman in "The Romantic Regionalism of Harper Lee" notes Lee's awareness of traditional Southern romanticism and its pervasive influence on the South, but suggests that she sees the beginning of a new type of romanticism, "the more reasonable, pragmatic, and native romanticism of a Ralph Waldo Emerson."

With the novel's dramatic success, articles and interviews about Lee appeared in leading periodicals. The author of a 1961 *Newsweek* interview suggests that Lee "strongly calls to mind the impish tomboy who narrates her novel. There is a faint touch of gray in her Italian boy haircut and a heavy touch of Alabama in her accent."

In interviews Lee's quick wit served to protect her privacy. She describes herself as a Whig ("I believe in Catholic emancipation and repeal of the Corn Laws") and quotes as her favorite fan letter one which accuses her of playing down the serious problem of the rape of white women ("Why is it that you young Jewish authors seek to whitewash the situation?"); she fabricated a clever response signed "Harper Levy."

She did, however, speak seriously in interviews about her reading tastes and her work habits. She numbered among her favorite authors Charles Lamb, Robert Louis Stevenson ("the old gentlemen"), Jane Austin ("writing, cameo-like, in that little corner of the world of hers and making it universal"), and Thomas Love Peacock, as well as various religious memorialists of the nineteenth century. Describing herself as a "journeyman writer," she noted that "writing is the hardest thing in the world, . . . but writing is the only thing that has made me completely happy." In 1961 she was in Monroeville working on her second novel, which was also to have a Southern setting. She said that she began working about noon, after sleeping late, and worked until early evening. Because her method involved extensive revision, she completed only a page or two each day.

The reading public and the critics have been eagerly awaiting more of Lee's writing. In the early 1960s, several short pieces about personal experiences and an article discussing different types of love, "Love—In Other Words," appeared in popular magazines; none of her work has been published since. In 1980, nearly twenty years later, Lee continues to write. Although she travels extensively, Monroeville, where her sister Alice Lee practices law, remains home. Whether or not Harper Lee adds to her body of published work, her contribution to American literature is an important one. *To Kill a Mockingbird,* a regional novel with a universal message, combines popular appeal with literary excellence, assuring Harper Lee's place in American letters.

—Dorothy Jewell Altman

Periodical Publications:

"Love—In Other Words," *Vogue,* 137 (15 April 1961): 64-65;

"Christmas to Me," *McCalls,* 89 (December 1961): 63.

References:

R. A. Dave, "*To Kill a Mockingbird*: Harper Lee's Tragic Vision," *Indian Studies in American Literature,* ed. M. K. Naik, S. K. Desai, S. Mokashi (Dharwar, India: Karnatak University, 1974), pp. 311-323;

Joseph Deitch, "Harper Lee: Novelist of the South," *Christian Science Monitor,* 3 October 1961, p. 6;

Fred Erisman, "The Romantic Regionalism of Harper Lee," *Alabama Review,* 26 (April 1973): 123-136;

"Mocking Bird Call," *Newsweek,* 57 (9 January 1961): 83.

ANDREW LYTLE
(26 December 1902-)

BOOKS: *Bedford Forrest and His Critter Company* (New York: Minton, Balch, 1931; London: Eyre & Spottiswoode, 1938);

The Long Night (Indianapolis & New York: Bobbs-Merrill, 1936; London: Eyre & Spottiswoode, 1937);

At the Moon's Inn (Indianapolis & New York: Bobbs-Merrill, 1941; London: Eyre & Spottiswoode, 1943);

A Name for Evil (Indianapolis & New York: Bobbs-Merrill, 1947);

The Velvet Horn (New York: McDowell, Obolensky, 1957);

A Novel, A Novella and Four Stories (New York: McDowell, Obolensky, 1958);

The Hero With the Private Parts (Baton Rouge: Louisiana State University Press, 1966);

A Wake For the Living: A Family Chronicle (New York: Crown, 1975).

After his participation in the Agrarian symposium *I'll Take My Stand* in 1930, Andrew Lytle set himself to the task of learning the craft of fiction. Working slowly and carefully, he produced by 1958 four novels, a novella, and a small collection of short stories. This achievement, culminating in the excellent novel, *The Velvet Horn,* demonstrates almost ideally the growth of an artist toward mastery, but it has not received the attention that it deserves. One reason for this neglect may be that Lytle stopped writing novels after the publication of *The Velvet Horn* (1957). Another perhaps is the bias of critics who disapprove of the conservative social and religious views that Lytle has expressed in critical essays and in various public utterances. This tendency to associate his fiction with his personal conservatism is unfortunate since Lytle has refrained conscientiously from using fiction as a pulpit. "Polemics is one thing," he has said, "and fiction another; when a novel obviously makes an appeal other than its proper aesthetic one, you may be sure that it is written with the left hand."

There is nothing left-handed about Lytle's four novels. Each of them adheres more or less closely to the aesthetic principles developed and articulated by such novelists as Flaubert, Henry James, and Ford Madox Ford. Lytle has acknowledged his debt to these masters in various critical essays, but he expresses the sum of his learning most succinctly in his foreword to *A Novel, A Novella and Four Stories* (1958): "Fiction is an action which tells the only story which makes of the form and the subject a single whole."

Like many Southern writers, Lytle has been strongly attracted to the past. The antebellum South suffered its deathblow in the Civil War; but Lytle says that he "witnessed its ghostly presence" as a boy in Murfreesboro, Tennessee, "and yet the people which this presence inhabited were substantial enough." Many of these people were his own family, and by family Lytle means "all the complex interrelationships of blood and kin, the large 'connections' which extended to the county lines and by sympathy overlapped the states." So it was the community, regarded as family, that made the past accessible to him. As M. E. Bradford puts it in an essay on Lytle's *A Wake for the Living* (1975), "History is most visible *and* available in [the] lineaments" of his own people, the people of his community. The past and the community that remembered it, then, were the two great experiences that Murfreesboro provided him.

As Lytle relates in *A Wake for the Living*, the town was founded by his ancestors, both Lytles and Nelsons. Andrew was born there, the only son of Robert and Lillie Belle Nelson Lytle. His father was a lumberman and sometime farmer who moved back and forth during Andrew's childhood between Murfreesboro and Guntersville, Alabama, as his business interests directed him, causing one local wag to say, "Bob Lytle moves every Tuesday." Though his family joined him at Guntersville from time to time, Murfreesboro remained home for Andrew and his younger sister Polly. There, surrounded by a large family, the children grew up

Robert T. Coleman III

hearing the rich body of tales and anecdotes which embodied the values of the community as it documented the family's history in Tennessee. They learned, for example, not from a history teacher but from a neighbor, that General Bragg was confident of victory on the eve of the Battle of Murfreesboro. (As a child, the neighbor had been in the room with Bragg and watched him as he dressed his beard.) The outcome of the battle was of more than academic interest to the boy Andrew, for its loss brought about Union occupation of the town, and during this period a Union soldier fired into a group of children and hit Lytle's grandmother Nelson in the throat. The velvet choker that she wore to conceal the scar signified to her grandson something about invaders and something about poor generalship.

At sixteen Lytle went to Sewanee Military Academy at nearby Sewanee, Tennessee. When he graduated four years later, he sailed for France and after a year went on to England with the intention of enrolling at Exeter College, Oxford; but word that his grandfather Nelson was dying called him home to Murfreesboro. Back in Tennessee, Lytle continued his education at Vanderbilt University, where he met the men who influenced the direction his life would take. The year was 1921. Robert Penn Warren was a member of the same class; and he and Lytle became friends, taking courses under Donald Davidson and John Crowe Ransom. Through these associations Lytle was drawn to the Fugitives, a group of young men who, under Ransom's direction, were seeking to develop a new voice in Southern poetry. But, though he attended their meetings for a while and learned a lot from them about writing, he never became a member of their group.

Lytle spent the summer after his graduation running a sawmill near Huntsville, Alabama, and then moved in with his father at Cornsilk, a farm near Guntersville that his father had recently acquired. Lytle soon developed a deep love for Cornsilk, but after a year he decided to study drama under George Pierce Baker at Yale.

His two years at New Haven were productive ones, but by the spring of 1928 his thoughts were turning to Tennessee, to his own people and their history. Ransom had written him in the winter of 1927 that Allen Tate and his wife Caroline Gordon were in New York, where Tate was working on a biography of Stonewall Jackson. Lytle had not known Tate at Vanderbilt, but he went to New York to meet him. He and the Tates quickly became good friends and before the summer was over they set out together in the Tates' old Ford to visit the Civil War battlefields of Pennsylvania, Maryland, and Virginia.

Supporting himself by acting in a small theatre company on Long Island and on Broadway, Lytle spent most of that summer and winter reading Civil War history at the New York Public Library. He soon found that historians had tended to neglect the Tennessee theatre of war so he decided to write a biography of Bedford Forrest in order partly "to correct the impression that it all took place in Virginia and . . . to show that the plain man fought the war."

Lytle completed the Forrest biography in Murfreesboro in the late fall of 1930. At the same time he renewed his associations with Ransom and Davidson. Under their influence, his sympathy for rural life was transformed into a coherent agrarian philosophy; and when they conceived of a symposium that would undertake a defense of the agrarian South against growing industrialization, they invited Lytle to participate. His essay for *I'll Take My Stand*, "The Hind Tit," is a vigorous defense of the life of a yeoman farmer and an examination of the forces that threatened it.

With the publication of *Bedford Forrest and His Critter Company* in 1931, Lytle moved in with his father at Cornsilk, intending to farm and write at the same time. He soon began work on his first novel, *The Long Night* (1936), stripping to his shorts and taking his typewriter to a hill behind the house. But in the spring of 1936 Tate, who was teaching at Southwestern College in Memphis, asked Lytle to fill a temporary vacancy in the history department. So began Lytle's academic career. Although he was there for only a semester, living with the Tates, he completed *The Long Night* and met a student of Tate's named Edna Barker. She and Lytle were married in June of 1938.

Since Cornsilk was to be inundated by the Tennessee Valley Authority, the couple set up housekeeping in Monteagle, Tennessee, in a log cabin that had belonged to Lytle's mother. When Lytle began teaching history at the University of the South, he and Edna moved to Sewanee, and he began looking for a farm to buy. He soon found a place in Robertson County near Nashville; this was what he calls in *A Wake for the Living* a "throwed-away farm," an abandoned run-down place that required a major effort of restoration before it could be occupied and worked. Lytle relates the account of their labors in *A Wake for the Living*, and he explains his reasons for wanting the farm: "There was enough evidence that a rapidly changing society had not quite reached this area, but I didn't realize, what soon became clear, that we did not have a true community. My friends actually belonged to

Nashville, and this part of Robertson County was for them a kind of private suburb." It seems from this statement that the Lytles were seeking to realize an ideal of agrarian living in a true rural community. But the wartime economy made it difficult for them to get the materials they needed to complete the restoration, so they remained at Sewanee and worked on the farm when they could. The Lytles' first child Pamela was born in 1941, and his second novel, *At the Moon's Inn,* was published in the same year; in 1943 he took over the editorial duties at the *Sewanee Review,* and before the war had ended the Lytles were able to move to Robertson County. Established at the farm, Lytle finished work on *A Name for Evil* (1947), the story of a couple whose efforts to restore an ancestral plantation are defeated by the husband's encounter with his forebear's ghost.

Again Lytle found the responsibilities of managing a farm too burdensome to allow much time for writing, so in the spring of 1947 he gave up his dream of making his living as a farmer-novelist and returned to the academy, teaching first for two spring terms at the University of Iowa Writers Workshop and then at the University of Florida. By the time the Lytles moved to Gainesville, they had another daughter, Katherine, and Lytle had begun work on the novel that would take him nine years to complete. Published in 1957, *The Velvet Horn* established his reputation as a serious novelist, but it was to be the last novel that he would write. By 1960 Edna was suffering from cancer. When Lytle was offered the editorship of the *Sewanee Review,* he moved his family, now including their third daughter Langdon, back to Monteagle, to the cabin where they had begun their life together. There in 1961 Edna Lytle died.

Lytle spent the last fifteen years of his academic career as an editor and teacher. In 1966 he published a collection of critical essays, *The Hero With the Private Parts,* and in 1975 his memoir, *A Wake for the Living.* Beginning with the sentence, "Now that I have come to live in the sense of eternity, I can tell my girls who they are," it gives aesthetic shape to the raw material of family history and by so doing explores the meaning of being not merely a Lytle but an American in the twentieth century. Lytle retired from Sewanee in 1973, and except for a year of teaching at the University of Kentucky (1977), he has lived quietly at the cabin at Monteagle.

In several of his critical essays Lytle provides the reader with tools that help in understanding his own novels. Perhaps the most useful of these is the distinction he makes between the action proper of a story and what he calls its enveloping action. In the foreword to *A Novel, A Novella and Four Stories,* he says that the conflict is the action proper and defines the enveloping action as "that universal quality, some constant, forever true aspect of experience." The enveloping action, then, is an archetypal truth about humankind in relation to God and nature that manifests itself in the particular action of the conflict. Thomas H. Landess provides a lucid explanation of the relationship between the two in his "Unity of Action in *The Velvet Horn.*" The enveloping action of that novel, according to Landess, is the myth of Eden—the fall of man and his subsequent regeneration by suffering. In fact, the story of the Garden—its loss and men's abortive efforts to recover it—lies back of all of Lytle's novels. In each it takes the form generally of a protagonist's rejecting the family or the community in pursuit of knowledge or wealth or power. The irony of the action lies in the protagonist's failure to recognize that the freedom of Eden is already lost and that consequently the family, as the basic unit of a civilized society under God, is a microcosm of the Godsweal and therefore a means of grace. His rejection of order leads him inevitably into the dark forest, which he is inclined to mistake, at the risk of great loss, for the Garden itself. Such is the paradigm that operates to some extent in each of Lytle's novels, but Lytle's sense of the richness of the particular is so strong that the bones of the paradigm never show.

Lytle's first novel, *The Long Night,* is not as successful as his later work; but it shows the struggle of an artist to learn his craft, and it reveals his considerable power as a storyteller. Lytle got the story from another of the Agrarians, the historian Frank Lawrence Owsley, who stopped over at Cornsilk one evening and suggested to Lytle that he write a novel about a kinsman of Owsley's who had assassinated a number of his father's murderers and then disappeared after the Civil War. Lytle was intrigued by the possibilities. He named his protagonist Pleasant McIvor and, true to his source, begins the novel with Pleasant's summoning a nephew to his remote mountain farm to relate to him a matter of family history. The nephew, who has grown up believing that his uncle was dead, responds to the summons, and the long night of telling begins.

The action commences with the brutal murder of Pleasant's father as the family is passing through Alabama on its way to Texas. Though only a boy of sixteen, Pleasant vows to avenge his father by murdering all of the forty men who were present at his death. At this point in the narrative, Lytle shifts the point of view from Pleasant's first person to third-person omniscient and, according to some critics, weakens the novel. But it may be that Lytle was seeking a greater aesthetic distance as a way of emphasizing the dehumanizing effect that Pleasant's commitment has upon him. Pleasant begins this process of dehumanization by refusing to accept his older brother William's command that the McIvor men not take the law into their own hands. As an attorney and the titular head of the family, William represents the order of the community, and it is this order that Pleasant violates when he overrides his brother's proper authority. Acting from a keen sense of family honor, he ironically undermines the integrity of the family. Moreover, by killing the members of the mob that murdered his father, he strikes at the community, which, despite its weaknesses, has about it a measure of order and stability.

So Pleasant becomes an exile, living in the dark forest, or as Lytle would have it, the long night: "To be at ease in the dark. To know what the long night meant. That was the meaning of vengeance." The reader, however, comes to understand the true meaning of the long night before Pleasant does. Living in caves, wandering the forest half-naked, terrorizing the community and shunning contact even with his own family, Pleasant submits to a darkness that he does not comprehend. Lytle shows the full extent of the darkness when Pleasant knifes young Damon Harrison as he walks in the woods with his girl. The long night then is the inevitable consequence of this fallen man's rejection of the family and the community as a means of grace.

Pleasant is saved from utter damnation ironically by the Civil War. Enlisting in the Confederate army only as a means of expediting his purpose, Pleasant discovers friendship during the Battle of Shiloh (the account of which is one of the best that fiction offers), and by the influence of this friend, Roswell Ellis, he comes slowly to understand that the cause of the Confederacy is greater than his private vendetta. This realization comes finally when he passes up an opportunity to kill one of the men he has been seeking. But the night to which he has submitted has been too long. When he returns from his abortive mission, he learns that his absence has led indirectly to the death of his friend Roswell. Believing that he can never return to the community of men who suffer and love, he turns his face to the mountains, redeemed from darkness but never to be restored.

Lytle's second novel, *At the Moon's Inn*, is the story of Hernando de Soto's expedition through Spanish Florida. As Robert G. Benson says, "Lytle takes a dark view of the early European ventures in the New World; and his second novel . . . is an exemplum dramatizing the failure of that Satanic self-assertion which characterized such ventures." The main characters of the novel are de Soto and a soldier named Tovar, who begins as the Adelantado's chief lieutenant but is demoted by the time they reach Florida for having made pregnant a young ward of de Soto's. It is from his point of view that we see the explorer; and because Tovar is out of favor, we see him at some distance. This is as Lytle intends it: the figure of de Soto larger than life but two-dimensional, ruthlessly hacking his way through jungle and Indian town alike in his mad search for gold. The meaning of the novel then lies in the perceptions and responses of Tovar.

At the Moon's Inn opens with a feast at de Soto's house, where Tovar is relating to a young friend the circumstances that led to his following the Adelantado. From his account the reader learns that Tovar had joined the Pizarro expedition to Peru to escape hanging for having killed a man in a fight over a woman. As Benson says, "his flight to escape hanging is a paradigm of the whole New World venture, an attempt both intellectual and emotional to escape or deny the effects of the Fall." Now he is about to follow de Soto to Florida. But when he speaks in favor of the expedition, an old and respected marshall of Seville pronounces judgment on the venture and all who participate in it: "your Columbus made such a hole in Christendom I fear me it can never be plugged."

De Soto encounters difficulties from the moment he lands in Florida; but in his determination to find gold, he brooks no obstacle to his will. As his men grow discouraged, he becomes more ruthless, throwing an Indian woman to the dogs and burning an Indian man at the stake. When the army arrives at the town of Cutifichiqui, the men are more dead than alive, but de Soto is encouraged by the wealth of pearls these Indians possess. Feigning friendship to the gracious Lady of Cutifichiqui, de Soto gains her trust; but when his army has recovered, he despoils the town that saved them and enslaves some of its people.

As witness to this ruthlessness, Tovar is uncertain of his response. His devotion to de Soto has continued despite his reduction in rank, but he earnestly hopes that his lord will be satisfied with the pearls and conclude his blind plunge into the wilderness. Tovar's desire to remain at Cutifichiqui in harmony with its people, however, is motivated not by compassion for the Indians but by his delight in the unrestricted promiscuity of the Indian

Wake
msp 1
Doris
1-15-75

Now that I have come to live in the sense of eternity, I can tell my girls who they are. They are the rare and precious objects of my delight. But this is not enough. Two of them already prefer to be the delight of another. In either case this is a personal matter, and their being concerns more than that. The sense of eternity gives a perspective on things and events which makes for a refreshing clarity. I don't care how many rabbits jump over my grave, they don't make me shiver. But I always speak courteously to them when we meet. In mythology the rabbit is the great African hero, as the monkey is in China. From my father's childhood to mine the stories of Bre'r Rabbit and Bre'r Fox were widespread. Bre'r Fox's appetite and his huff and his puff seemed always threatening to the small and helpless, but always Bre'r Rabbit's cunning thwarted him. Their adventures instilled into a child's mind the lost resemblances between man and beast. It was a rich world for a child's education, but this is not the whole of it. I rather think that a country society, which ours was and is no more, by its habits and customs discovers the identity between the natural and the supernatural, that mystery which becomes ceremony to people who make their living by the land and the sea.

If you don't know who you are or where you come from, you will find yourself at a disadvantage. The ordered slums of suburbia are made for the confusion of the spirit. Those who live in units called homes or estates—both words do violence to the language—don't know who they are. For the profound stress between the union that is flesh and the spirit, they have been forced to exchange the appetites. Each business promotion uproots the family. Children become wayfarers. Few are given any vision of the Divine. They perforce become secular men, half men, who inhabit what is left of Christendom.

The woman is neither worldly nor spiritual. She is the vessel of life. Hence substance is a familiar mystery to her, its loss damaging. She may sell herself and never be bought. She may do and be many things. One thing she will not do: accept an abstraction as having anything to do with the business of living. Whatever life is, she knows it manifests itself in and through substance. During the Revolution in western North Carolina, when a party of Tories was plundering the Daniel Jackson house near Fairforest Creek, Miss Nancy Johnson kicked one down the stairs. I don't believe Mr. Jefferson's Declaration of Independence was in her mind when she lifted her foot. We hear much of the war of Independence from England, little of the rapine and murder between Whig and Tory. These people were of the same race and common experience. It is a part of our history and must be understood, else we fail in a crucial knowledge about what has made us and, perchance, lost us.

If we dismiss the past as dead and not as a country of the living which our eyes are unable to see, as we cannot see a foreign country but know it is there, then we are likely to become servile. Living as we will be in a lesser sense of ourselves, lacking that fuller knowledge which only the living past can give, it will be so easy to submit to pressure and receive what is already ours as a boon from authority.

The Incas understood this. They had an invariable rule of conquest: to bring back to Cuzco the gods and young chieftains as hostages. The conquered gods became courtiers of the Sun and the young caciques learned Quechua. Atahualpa, the Inca who lost to Pizarro, was carried to his doom in an elaborate palanquin with the Lord of Chinca at his feet. To lose your language and your god surrenders all that you are,

A Wake for the Living, *galley proof*

maidens. He has found his paradise and is content to remain there, for Tovar, as Lytle has said, is a man of the senses. The wilderness for him is a garden of earthly delight. When de Soto prepares to push on to the west, Tovar shows his displeasure by marrying an Indian girl according to the customs of the tribe and living with her people as one of them. He thus repudiates the pregnant Spanish wife he left in Cuba, and by so doing, rejects civilized order in favor of sleeping at the moon's inn, a Spanish phrase that means sleeping out-of-doors but in this novel implies dwelling apart from an ordered community under God.

If Tovar is a man of the senses, de Soto is a man of the will. In his overreaching pride de Soto comes finally to defy the priest who has charged him in the name of God to leave Florida. Tovar has just suffered in battle a humiliating blow to his sense of manhood by the courageous example of a dying Indian, so it is in a chastened mood that he reflects upon de Soto's defiance and explains it: "He had set his private will outside the guidance and discipline of the Church.... He, a layman, had undertaken to interpret God's mind. This is what his decision meant.... From here it was only one step further to supplant God's will by man's and call it divine.... Where would this bring him? Where would it lead them all?" The answer to both questions is the dark west, the moon's inn, or death in the coils of the world, for Tovar turns his back upon the altar and faces the wilderness in assent to his commander's blasphemy.

After de Soto dies on the banks of the Mississippi, Tovar encounters his ghost. Mistaking it for the living man, he tries to encourage de Soto: "All may yet go well. The will remains." But the ghost replies, "Did I lead the chivalry of Spain to the sacred groves, the blessed land of Jerusalem? No, I am the alchemical captain, the adventurer in gold. Gold the wanderer." And Tovar, who has bound himself to his master's will, is left, a corrupt body wandering lost in the darkening west.

Charles C. Clark calls Lytle's third novel, *A Name for Evil*, the author's "depiction of the effects of a perverted view of tradition." Modeled to some extent after James's "The Turn of the Screw," it is the story of Henry Brent, a writer who, like Lytle himself, buys a "throwed-away farm" and undertakes its restoration in the expectation of establishing for himself and his wife Ellen an ordered agrarian life. But unlike the author, Henry means actually to re-create the past. In his commitment to this task he begins to see the ghost of a collateral ancestor who had established the Grove, and it is this encounter that stands at the center of the novel's action. The enveloping action is that of fallen man's effort to reenter the Garden.

The problem the reader faces is the same as that presented by "The Turn of the Screw"—that of determining the actual nature of the characters' experiences. Henry Brent tells his own story, and he believes that he sees the apparition of Major Brent, but not wanting to alarm his frail wife he chooses not to tell her. In time Henry becomes convinced that the Major is attempting to defeat his plans to restore the Grove by claiming, or destroying, Ellen. When Ellen becomes pregnant, Henry decides to move to town for her to have the baby, but a snowstorm delays their departure. Strolling one foggy day in the snow-covered garden where the Major's wives are buried, Henry and Ellen become separated. When he finds her again, he sees her retreating from him in the fog toward the figure of Major Brent, who stands at the mouth of a well. Lured by the Major or frightened by her deranged husband, Ellen falls to her death and Henry fails in his effort to restore the lost Garden.

Clark makes a plausible case for Major Brent's being a projection of Henry's tormented mind. Because the Major had destroyed his own progeny by banishing his sons and keeping his daughter a spinster, Henry regards him as a man almost demonically opposed to the perpetuation of tradition, and he becomes the name that Henry gives to the evil that would thwart him. Thomas Carter, on the other hand, suggests that the reality of the ghost is multilayered and ambiguous, perhaps a "lingering spirit of malicious evil," perhaps a demon, either spiritually or psychologically real, that possesses Henry. And he says that the novel is "infinitely richer for its ambiguity." Whatever the nature of the ghost, Carter is correct when he observes that Henry "meant literally to restore the past, and when that happens, the result is always a Major Brent."

Lytle's most recent novel, *The Velvet Horn*, is by general agreement his most impressive achievement. Rich in texture, complex in structure, and ambiguous in meaning, it is more demanding than his other novels, but it rewards the serious reader more fully. Once again Lytle turns to the Old South for his material, setting the novel in the Cumberland hill country of middle Tennessee in the late nineteenth century, but his treatment of this society is both more profound and more extensive than it had been before. At the same time, Lytle's craft is so accomplished that he effects without any sign of contrivance an organic wholeness of the particular conflict and the archetypal action that envelops it. Lytle himself discusses this process in an essay entitled "The Working Novelist and the Mythmaking Process," one of the most helpful and revealing commentaries in American literature by a novelist on his own work.

The enveloping action in *The Velvet Horn* is basically the same as that of his other novels; in the words of Thomas Landess it is "nothing less than the fall of man from a state of innocence, his suffering as a consequence, and his redemption, partially through grace, which leads finally to reintegration into the order of things." But in this novel the archetype is required to unify a much greater diversity of material than it does in the earlier novels. Lytle accomplishes this difficult technical feat, according to Landess, by giving the archetype definition as the myth of Eden and setting that myth in the consciousness of the character Jack Cropleigh. In other words, Jack's awareness and understanding of the Eden myth provide him with a means of interpreting for himself and for his nephew Lucius Cree the actions in which they are involved. As Lytle says of Jack, he represents all of the characters for he is "the spiritual hermaphrodite" who "alone could suffer the entire myth."

The two stories of *The Velvet Horn* are those of young Lucius, which occurs in the novel's present, and his mother Julia, which belongs to the past. As Julia's brother and Lucius's uncle, Jack knows both stories, and functions for the reader as what Lytle calls "the hovering bard" who alone among the characters has enough information to make sense of the various fragments. Jack is also a mule breeder, a "water witch," and a garrulous drunk with an education in classical literature. When the novel begins, he and Lucius are going up to the Peaks of Laurel in a time of severe drought to "witch a well," or find water, for a cousin whose cattle range the mountain. There they meet the shiftless Rutter family, and Lucius is seduced by the daughter Ada Belle. The next morning word comes to the Peaks that Lucius's father, the lumberman Joe Cree, has been killed by a falling tree. Knowing that his father was too good a lumberman to make such a mistake, Lucius is forced to consider the possibility of suicide as the cause of his father's death. So begin at the same time his loss of innocence and his initiation into manhood.

In the second section, "The Water Witch," Lucius and Jack on their way down the mountain drive through a forest that reminds Jack of his early years and his sister's relations to her brothers. From Jack's reverie the reader learns that he and his brothers and sister were orphaned before they were grown. The oldest son Beverly renounced his responsibility as head of the family and took to the woods to live the primitive life of a hunter. His younger brother Duncan followed him and was followed in turn by little Julia, who went everywhere that Duncan went. Dickie went to medical school, and Jack stayed at home. When Julia was in her teens, she went to a secret place in the forest with a young man named Pete LeGrand, and there her brothers discovered them the following morning. Duncan, whose love for Julia was private and intense, eviscerated LeGrand on the spot, but Dickie sewed him up and saved his life. And Jack decided that Julia should marry their cousin Joe Cree. At this point in Jack's reverie, Lucius interrupts him to confess his sin on the mountain and to blame himself for his father's death. Jack perceives the connection between his nephew's sexual guilt and the knowledge that caused Joe Cree to take his life, but he only says, "The snarl of fatality. Who can pick its thread?"

In the brief third section Pete LeGrand, now rich and powerful, rides to the funeral remembering his love for Julia and considering the possibility of marriage. And in the climactic fourth section, "The Wake," Jack struggles to pick the thread from the snarl of fatality. The understanding that he gains by this effort brings together the disparate strands of the characters' lives, but it produces in a drunken vision the terrible truth that has brought this crisis about.

As the wake begins, Lucius wanders about in confusion as he tries to understand the cause of his father's death, and Jack, helpless amid the bustle of kinfolk and neighbors, begins to drink. The arrival of Pete LeGrand, however, calls Jack into action, for LeGrand proposes to help the widow by offering her financial security. In a series of conversations that occur among various characters during the course of the night, the garrulous Jack, who often appears merely foolish to his family and neighbors, attempts to explain for himself and for any with ears to hear the meaning of the death they attend. The means that he uses is the myth of Eden. In the process he prepares Lucius for his inevitable discovery of the truth of his paternity. This typical example of Jack's talk is addressed to Lucius:

> Your Uncle Beverly said—I won't tread the mill of this world. I'll live with the beasts. I'll begin at the beginning and know the pure image of divinity imprisoned in the darkness of nature. Your Uncle Duncan, not saying it, for he could only feel that total innocence of love before carnal knowledge. When they were young, he and your mother had no love but for

> each other, and for one to think was for the other to act. It was the pure fire that does not burn. But the garden they wandered was never there. The world was though. It destroyed my brothers, your uncles.

When Julia consents to LeGrand's offer of assistance, Jack gets drunk and, wandering about in a thunderstorm, stumbles into Joe Cree's open grave. There, in his stupor, he envisions Duncan and Julia embraced and by some means understands that such a union had taken place. Having believed up to this point that his responsibility is to assist Lucius through the trauma of learning that he is LeGrand's son, Jack crawls out of the grave next morning sobered, silent, and utterly changed.

The action of the last section, "The Night Sea Journey," occurs several months after the death of Joe Cree and involves Lucius's assumption of his responsibilities as a man. He is told, as Joe Cree had been, that he is the son of Pete LeGrand, though the reader learns from Julia that the event of Jack's vision is true. In the aftermath of knowledge, Lucius discovers that Ada Belle Rutter, whom he has continued to see, is pregnant with his child and marries her. Planning to go west, he stops at Jack's house, and there in a climactic scene he meets his mother and Ada Belle's mother and her retarded brother Othel. In a moment of misunderstanding, Othel fires at Lucius; but Jack, assuming full responsibility in his role as savior, steps in front of his nephew and receives the bullet. The full significance of Jack's role emerges in the poetry of his final words:

> See the words run out of my side!
> Why was I not put to sleep to dream this?
> Bleeding breath, oh, breathy blood
> What a grave gravity is in your fall.
> It will leave a stain worth all the books.
> Look at it sometimes, girl, when you sweep
> And remember Jack Cropleigh
> Who learned life by heart.
> Learning is a surfeit.
> Let it spill.
>
> Christ! This cannibal world.

The nature of Jack's death clearly is Christ-like. He had taken upon himself the burden of his family's guilt, the tendency among them all to wander in a garden that was never there, and in the end, he is the one who pays with his life for their transgressions. Moreover, his sacrificial death is redemptive, for it brings the family back together. Pete LeGrand, now married to Julia, says to Lucius, "Jack's death will bring us all together. Your mother mentioned it might be well for your cousin to teach Ada Belle her letters. I think that's a good sign, don't you?" And Lucius, in an act symbolic of redemption, determines to build a house for his wife and child from the lumber of the oak that killed Joe Cree.

Like his fellow Agrarians Allen Tate and Robert Penn Warren, Andrew Lytle is a writer of impressive versatility; and any assessment of his work must take into account his literary criticism, his biography of Bedford Forrest, and *A Wake for the Living*. But in spite of the merits of these works, Lytle's fiction is his greatest achievement. His narrative power and his keen sense of the manners, mores, and idiom that constitute the texture of the world he describes are as strong as those of any writer of his time. These talents alone, however, are not sufficient to establish him among the first rank of twentieth-century novelists. And Lytle's early works, despite particular merits, lack the range and depth of truly great fiction. *The Velvet Horn*, however, as Caroline Gordon has said, "is a landmark in American fiction." All that the earlier novels promise is fulfilled in the maturity of its craft and the depth of its vision. The fact that that vision is profoundly Christian does not contradict Lytle's belief that fiction must make no appeal other than its proper aesthetic one, for in *The Velvet Horn* he has found the means by which to give shape aesthetically to his Christian world view. As the crowning achievement of his long commitment to the discipline of writing fiction, it secures for its author a place of honor among the writers of the Southern Renaissance.

—James Kilgo

Other:

"The Hind Tit," in *I'll Take My Stand: The South and The Agrarian Tradition by Twelve Southerners* (New York: Harper, 1930), pp. 201-245;

"The Forest of the South," *Critique*, 1 (Winter 1956): 3-9;

"A Hero and the Doctrinaires of Defeat," *Georgia Review*, 10 (Winter 1956): 453-467;

Introduction to *Bedford Forrest* (New York: McDowell, Obolensky, 1958), pp. xi-xvii;

"A Reading of Joyce's 'The Dead,' " *Sewanee Review*, 77 (Spring 1969): 193-216;

"The State of Letters in a Time of Disorder," *Sewanee Review*, 79 (Autumn 1971): 477-497.

Bibliographies:

Ashley Brown, "Andrew Nelson Lytle," in *A Bibliographical Guide to the Study of Southern Literature,* ed. Louis D. Rubin, Jr. (Baton Rouge: Louisiana State University Press, 1969), p. 243;

Noel Polk, "Andrew Nelson Lytle: A Bibliography of His Writings," *Mississippi Quarterly,* 23 (Fall 1970): 435-491.

References:

Robert G. Benson, "Yankees of the Race: The Decline and Fall of Hernando de Soto," in *The Form Discovered,* ed. M. E. Bradford (Jackson: University and College Press of Mississippi, 1973), pp. 84-96;

Bradford, "The Fiction of Andrew Lytle," *Mississippi Quarterly,* 23 (Fall 1970): 347-348;

Bradford, "Toward a Dark Shape: Lytle's 'Alchemy' and the Conquest of the New World," in *The Form Discovered,* pp. 57-63;

Charles C. Clark, "*A Name for Evil*: A Search for Order," in *The Form Discovered,* pp. 24-34;

George Core, "A Mirror for Fiction: The Criticism of Andrew Lytle," *Georgia Review,* 22 (Summer 1968): 208-211;

Brewster Ghiselin, "Andrew Lytle's Selva Oscura," in *The Form Discovered,* pp. 73-78;

Thomas H. Landess, "Unity of Action in *The Velvet Horn,*" in *The Form Discovered,* pp. 3-15;

Allen Tate, Foreword to *The Hero With the Private Parts* (Baton Rouge: Louisiana State University Press, 1966); reprinted as "The Local Universality of Andrew Lytle," in *The Form Discovered,* pp. 79-83;

Clinton W. Trowbridge, "The Word Made Flesh: Andrew Lytle's *The Velvet Horn,*" *Critique,* 10 (Winter 1967-1968): 53-68;

Robert Penn Warren, "Andrew Lytle's *The Long Night*: A Rediscovery," *Southern Review,* new series, 7 (Winter 1971): 130-139;

H. L. Weatherby, "The Quality of Richness: Observations on Andrew Lytle's *The Long Night,*" in *The Form Discovered,* pp. 35-41;

Frederick Yeh-Wei Yu, "Andrew Lytle's *A Name for Evil* as a Redaction of 'The Turn of the Screw,' " *Michigan Quarterly Review,* 11 (Summer 1972): 186-190.

DAVID MADDEN

(25 July 1933-)

BOOKS: *The Beautiful Greed* (New York: Random House, 1961);

Wright Morris (New York: Twayne, 1964);

Cassandra Singing (New York: Crown, 1969);

The Poetic Image in 6 Genres (Carbondale: Southern Illinois University Press, 1969);

The Shadow Knows (Baton Rouge: Louisiana State University Press, 1970);

James M. Cain (New York: Twayne, 1970);

Brothers in Confidence (New York: Avon, 1972);

Bijou (New York: Crown, 1974);

Harlequin's Stick, Charlie's Cane (Bowling Green, Ohio: Popular Press, 1975);

The Day the Flowers Came (Chicago: Dramatic Publishing, 1975);

The Suicide's Wife (New York: Bobbs-Merrill, 1978);

Pleasure-Dome (New York: Bobbs-Merrill, 1979);

A Primer of the Novel (Metuchen, N.J.: Scarecrow Press, 1980);

Writer's Revisions (Metuchen, N.J.: Scarecrow Press, forthcoming 1980);

On the Big Wind (New York: Holt, Rinehart & Winston, forthcoming 1980).

David Madden is a writer who seems unafraid to tackle any project or subject. He has worked in almost every genre—short story, novel, poetry, drama, criticism, film, autobiography—and, until recently, kept as many as four projects going at once. In such eclecticism there can be, of course, great danger, but Madden has been amazingly successful as he has explored as many ways as possible to express the writer's imagination. He greatly admires Joyce Carol Oates's work and his writing bears a striking similarity to hers. His work might be described as he described hers: "produced upon the sweeping flood of an apparently inexhaustible creative energy." Repeatedly asked how he manages to balance the criticism and the fiction, he consistently replies that he has had little trouble doing so. "I think the reason I'm able to [see a critical book as a creative act] is because very early when I was a kid I took the attitude that *anything* I would do in life would be done in a creative manner; that any situation in life should be fraught with all kinds of possibilities for creative responses, and I have to be alert to them and when I sense them, then I respond with as much creativity as possible." Furthermore, "everything I write comes out of a creative energy flow and that exploration of all media and genres . . .

is part of that energy flow, reaching out, trying to affect audiences and readers in different ways." Thus, in the same year his work has been published in men's magazines such as *Adam* and *Playboy* as well as in the *Southern Review* and the *Minnesota Review*. For him, the artist must explore, must test himself in new ways continually to remain true to his imagination. Like Faulkner, he often reworks certain material, seeing it first perhaps in isolation, then in juxtaposition with other work, and finally integrated into one or more wholes.

Jerry David Madden was born in Knoxville, Tennessee, the son of James Helvy and Emile Merritt Madden. He has stated that "my infatuation with my hometown is similar to Thomas Wolfe's with Asheville and like Wolfe I look homeward but live elsewhere." Greatly influenced by his grandmother and her story telling, he began early to tell his own stories; at age eleven he wrote down the first one and during his education in the Knoxville public schools was nearly expelled on many occasions for writing stories in class. As a youth in Knoxville, he worked at many odd jobs, his favorite being as an usher at the Bijou Theater, which his "mother had used as a babysitter while she worked during the depression and the war." By the time he was fourteen he had the same literary agent as Raymond Chandler and MacKinlay Kantor. Also, from the time he was fourteen until he was a college student, he wrote, directed, and acted in about twenty-five radio plays. When he was sixteen, his first play won a state contest and was presented at the University of Tennessee. When he was seventeen, he visited New York where he saw *A Streetcar Named Desire, Death of A Salesman,* and *The Member of the Wedding,* all of which further convinced him that he wanted to be a playwright.

In 1951, after graduation from Knox High School, he entered the University of Tennessee, but his education was interrupted off and on as he traveled over the country, working briefly in Washington, New York, Boston, and California. As Madden remembers, "After my freshman year . . . I set out to encounter Life in New York, made the Greenwich Village scene in the pre-beatnik days when Maxwell Bodenheim in a trench coat was still peddling his poems. I worked as a mail clerk atop the Empire State Building, hopped the counters of numerous White Tower hamburger stands on the night shift, and finally signed as a messman on a [U.S. Merchant Marine] ship out of Edgewater, N.Y., thus satisfying a long-fermenting urge to take to the sea." From this experience would come his first novel *The Beautiful Greed* (1961). After service in the merchant marine, he joined the army as a private in 1953. Although he refused to sign the loyalty oath in basic training and was briefly detained at Fort Jackson, South Carolina, he was finally shipped out to Alaska and remained in the army until 1955.

In 1956, he enrolled as a student at Iowa State Teachers College where he continued to work on both the play and novel forms of *Cassandra Singing* (1969), begun while he was in the merchant marine. In the same year, he returned to Knoxville where he entered the University of Tennessee as a senior, and on 6 September 1956 he married Roberta Margaret Young, whom he had met in the college radio station in Iowa. They have one son, Blake Dana. After graduating from the University of Tennessee in 1957 with a B.S. in education, he took creative writing courses with Walter Van Tilburg Clark at San Francisco State College. During the year in San Francisco before he received his M.A. in creative writing in 1958, he wrote further on *Cassandra Singing* and, in addition, wrote five short stories, five hundred pages of literary criticism, two one-act plays, several poems, and another novel—his M.A. thesis which would be published by Random House as *The Beautiful Greed* in 1961.

In 1958-1959 Madden taught at Appalachian State Teachers College in Boone, North Carolina. During that year, which he calls "one of the greatest years of my life," he taught five classes and directed three full-length plays and four one acts. On the basis of his work on a dramatic version of *Cassandra Singing,* Madden was then given a John Golden play-writing fellowship by John Gassner at the Yale Drama School, where he studied during 1959-1960. (He later said that although he has written many plays he is not a good playwright and he no longer feels drawn to the theatre.) Also in 1959, he was awarded the Pearl Setzer Deal Award for his religious drama, *From Rome to Damascus*.

Between 1960 and 1968, Madden was on the faculties of a number of institutions, including Centre College in Danville, Kentucky (1960-1962), the University of Louisville in Louisville, Kentucky (1962-1964), Kenyon College in Gambier, Ohio (1964-1966)—where he was assistant editor of the *Kenyon Review*—Ohio University in Athens (1966, 1968), and the University of North Carolina at Chapel Hill (1967). Since 1968, he has been writer in residence and has taught at Louisiana State University in Baton Rouge. In the early 1960s he also taught in summer writing workshops at Morehead State University in Morehead, Kentucky, and at Alice

Lloyd College in Pippa Passes, Kentucky, and in the summer of 1979 he taught at Bread Loaf Writers' Conference, which he had attended in 1972 on a William Raney Fellowship. During the spring of 1980, he was a distinguished visiting professor of English at the University of Delaware, an honor accorded him on the basis of his criticism, not his fiction.

Certainly a major part of the impetus behind Madden's work is the view of the artist as storyteller trying to capture a different audience with every telling or trying to create anew with the same audience the bond of trust and deceit between the teller and the listener/reader. As Madden describes it, "The relationship between the storyteller and the listener is like that between the con man and his mark, who charge each other through phantom circuits of the imagination; the storyteller uses many of the same techniques for capturing attention, holding it, and projecting the reader into a totally different world from the one he is living in." There is always thus an element of risk, of being exposed; however, there is also the possibility of success when the artist creates a world more real than the one in which his "mark" lives his daily life. Madden has been such a storyteller since the age of three when he, impelled by his grandmother, began to tell stories to his brothers and friends. His grandmother herself used unconsciously all the literary techniques that the grandson would later develop to envelop her audience in what Madden calls the "pleasure-dome." Listening to her, watching movies, and participating in radio drama all helped to create the foundation upon which Madden quite early began to tell, then to write his own stories.

As a Southerner, Madden is far from unique in having been influenced by the oral tradition. Indeed, he sees himself as very consciously a Southern writer, mainly in terms of "using elements of the oral tradition in a literary context" as he does in *Cassandra Singing*, *Bijou* (1974), and *Pleasure-Dome* (1979). However, he sees the Southern experience as representative of the universal experience and acknowledges being influenced not only by Wolfe and Faulkner, but also by Hemingway, Fitzgerald, Conrad, Camus, Joyce, Cain, Agee, Nathanael West, and especially Wright Morris, about whom he has written a book-length study. Moreover, some of his most successful work, such as "No Trace," "The Day the Flowers Came," and *The Suicide's Wife* (1978), seems to have nothing at all to do with the South. Yet, even in these non-Southern stories, the central character often faces the characteristic dilemma of Southern fiction: isolation—being cut off from the past, from place, family, and community. Madden's autobiographical protagonists, like Lucius Hutchfield in *Bijou*, regardless of how they struggle to break away from the forces which shape them, always draw a certain strength and security from their sense of identity. Madden seems to suggest that when man is successful in severing his ties with tradition or has no tradition in which he can discover a place, he is cut off from vital sources which make the individual life part of a continuum rather than a separate fragment.

In order to create successful fiction, Madden has had to balance two sides of himself that he sees embodied by Thomas Wolfe and James Joyce. While writing *Bijou*, he poured forth twenty-two hundred pages in about six weeks and then spent six years trying to create the most satisfying artistic unity out of the material. From the tension between the two processes of pouring forth and shaping comes his best work. To find the subject, whether from his own life or from other sources, is not as important as discovering the technique. He believes "that technique is more important, *finally*, in the revision process at least, than inspiration or than these other romantic concepts about the writing process. . . . You can't recharge the uniqueness of the original experience—it's a contradiction in terms to recharge something that's unique. It either is unique or it isn't. But through technique it can be recharged." Fitzgerald expressed Madden's ideal when he said that "the test of a first-rate intelligence is the ability to hold two opposed ideas in the mind at the same time, and still retain the ability to function." The tension between a life of action and a life of the imagination, between raw material and polished product, between the Renaissance Man in the twentieth century and the single-minded novelist has dominated much of Madden's career so far. As he has written, "I believe life is meaningless—and yet I put all my energy into making it meaningful. Lack of control as opposed to artistic design—those have been the opposites whose tensions have generated my life."

That tension is evident even in Madden's first published novel, *The Beautiful Greed*. Based upon Madden's own experiences in the merchant marine, the novel is obviously apprentice work in which the young writer is exploring ways to transform his own raw experience into objective art. Alvin Henderlight, the central character, is a young man from Tennessee, near Knoxville and Cades Cove, who spent twelve years in an orphanage for indigent children and has now shipped out in the merchant marine for the first time, having left college after being asked what he would tell his own students when they asked why man had been put on earth. In response, Alvin left the tedious, meaningless classes behind and, like Conrad's seamen, went to sea driven by "a beautiful greed of adventures that are their own and only reward!" On the ship, he is forced to share a room with Franco, the ship outcast whom all the other men depend upon to hate, their willing sacrificial lamb. Alternately attracted to and repelled by Franco, Alvin finds himself more and more associated with the snarling, defiant man. Alvin, who reads Melville and Conrad in his spare time, recognizes his separation from the other members of the crew and begins to realize that he too is a type of outsider doomed to suffer and to discover. "He did not want to be like them, he knew he never would be, but he did not like to feel cut off either, that he could not connect with them if he wanted to." When Franco leaves the ship to go home, he will not allow Alvin to come with him. Alvin has not completed the experience, has not yet found the necessary control in life. To back out of experience is to back out of life, and the failure to find control is the failure to find one's self. Thus Alvin stays with the ship, presumably to complete the trip and to remain true to his original commitment whatever the immediate or long-range consequences might be. As Franco tells him, "perhaps you know that if you walk away from this living part of your existence—all these possibilities you created—you will die that much." Like Franco, he will never become like the other men, accepted and created by them, but, unlike Franco, he will never burn out, uncreated by himself.

Carefully written, *The Beautiful Greed* is still not very good fiction. In an essay on first novels by others, Madden himself points to the obvious weaknesses which also mark his first novel: "little natural or acquired talent for style, technique, or even storytelling." Madden agrees with the critics who chided him for having an idea to relate without a real story to tell. The lack of successful technique only adds to an essentially lifeless book with unrealized characters. We finally do not care very much about Alvin and his process of discovery. However, Granville Hicks praised Madden's "firm, vigorous prose" and saw in him "the makings of a novelist."

Madden's second novel has never appeared in book form. Madden wrote it in eleven days in 1959 or 1960 because, "I wondered if I could write a novel in 11 days as Georges Simenon claims to do regularly; I did." Published serially in *Adam* from April to November 1967, *Hair of the Dog* appeared shortly before Madden's edited collection of essays, *Tough Guy Writers of the Thirties.* It clearly shows the influence of Madden's fascination with the "tough guy" writers, especially with James Cain about whom he has written a critical book, and with the popular culture explosion, which Madden helped to spearhead with his essays on the subject, in general. *Hair of the Dog* concerns a private detective, Frank Swaggerty, a giant of a man in Knoxville, Tennessee, and his efforts to help Arabel Corum Sutterfield find her daughter Avis who had been taken away two years earlier by Arabel's husband, the Reverend Lucius Sutterfield. During the novel, one of Arabel's brothers is killed by Lucius's vicious German shepherd; Frank and Arabel discover that Lucius has blinded himself after having committed what he thinks was incest with Avis; Arabel reveals that Avis is really Frank's daughter conceived in a one night encounter in Galveston; and Frank finally corners Avis who with her Gypsy lover Rago has been conducting bogus revival meetings in south Georgia. After Frank kills Rago, he ends up on the chain gang telling his story to his cellmate Rooks, which provides the frame for the novel.

As Madden accurately says of *Hair of the Dog,* "it has a certain sweetness and innocence, I think, though it's decadent, bizarre, gothic, grotesque, etc." It also has some very fine, effective crowd scenes. However, it is what Madden, using Graham Greene's distinction, calls an "entertainment" as opposed to a serious novel. Such entertainment, though, is clearly an important facet of all of Madden's work. He believes firmly in the insights, the truths, which can be gained from the study of and the writing of "popular" fiction. The audience reached by these writers, after all, is far larger, far broader than any audience that a "serious" writer has been able to reach. That wider contact places its own demands upon the writer, demands which, if successfully met, can have greater, more far reaching effect than the majority of serious works. Even though Madden sees that period of stories in the men's magazines *Adam* and *Knight* as a phase which has passed for him, he still sees its merit and importance not only to his career, but also to any developing writer as he shifts "from one perspective to another on the same material, over several genres."

For over fifteen years Madden worked on various versions of *Cassandra Singing,* one of the least autobiographical works he has written and his third published novel. First suggested by a story told to him in the merchant marine, Madden has traced its long inception in an essay " 'cassandra singing'—on and off key" collected in *The Poetic Image in 6*

Genres (1969); before its publication in novel form, *Cassandra Singing* had gone through seventeen or more versions as drama or fiction. Ten chapters had appeared in various journals, and the one-act play version had been published in *New Campus Writing No. 2* (1957) and the two-act play version had appeared in *First Stage* (Spring 1963). Madden has subsequently written three unfilmed movie script versions of it for Warner Brothers and a radio play in which he returns to his original conception of the story with the focus on Cassie. Madden has said that "every playwright or novelist has that one work on which he really gets hung up, and *Cassandra* was mine." Even if ultimately the novel is not entirely successful, it does reveal Madden's developing style and technique, and, unlike *The Beautiful Greed*, it has a powerful story to tell. The novel and Madden's commentary on it offer a penetrating analysis of how an artist struggles to create good fiction; clearly, Madden's primary education as a novelist was the writing of this novel.

Published in 1969, *Cassandra Singing* focuses upon a brother and a sister, Lone and Cassie McDaniel. A boy with much promise, with the potential to break out of his squalid background, Lone, throughout the course of the novel, nearly destroys every chance he has by becoming too involved in the reckless world of Boyd Weaver, an ex-marine who has returned home, and Boyd's girlfriend, Gypsy Travis. Suspended from school, Lone spends most of his time riding his motorcycle with Boyd and then telling his adventures to his invalid sister, Cassie, who has never fully recovered from a serious childhood illness. Thus she stays in bed and lives through Lone's experiences, her imagination, and her songs. However, when an accident prevents Lone from bringing home stories of their adventures, she tries to enter life fully, also through joining Boyd and Gypsy in their exploits. Boyd, in a way, seduces and betrays both Lone and Cassie through a strange mixture of hatred and love.

Madden himself has stated the theme of *Cassandra*: "To live fully, one must balance the forces of action and imagination. Lone's life is an exaggeration of action, Cassie's an exaggeration of imagination. . . . A subordinate theme is the inability of people to distinguish between love and hate, to see that in a dynamic interplay each makes the other possible. When the operation of these forces is revealed to Lone as a consequence of his own actions, he makes an existential response to life." Both Lone and Cassie at the end of the novel can look squarely at each other and, consequently, at life itself. For the first time, they both truly have a self with which they can enter the world. Madden has written better novels, but *Cassandra Singing* is indeed an exciting, disturbing piece of fiction. Some of the novel's elements, the unconsummated incestuous relationship between Cassie and Lone, the consummated relationship between Boyd and Charlotte, Lone and Cassie's mother, do not completely coalesce, but they have been worked through to fulfill the promise which Granville Hicks had expected.

Brothers in Confidence (1972), Madden's fourth novel, is an expanded version of the novella "Traven," which appeared in the *Southern Review* in 1968. In 1969, Tony Bill, the producer of the film *The Sting*, contacted him about doing "Traven" as a film, and after Bill failed to get financial backing for the project, he recommended the novella to Peter Mayer at Avon, who asked Madden to expand it for publication in Avon's series of original novels published first in paperback. Madden obliged by adding sections about the childhood of the central character and his brothers. Although the series published novels by many fine authors and Mayer hoped that it would be successful not only financially but also critically, critics chose to ignore these novels. *Brothers in Confidence* is still largely unknown to the reading public even though the fact that it gets the best response at Madden's dramatic readings suggests its merit. It is closely linked to two other novels by Madden. He had made notes in 1969 for *Bijou*, a much longer novel about the same characters; and later he decided to incorporate *Brothers in Confidence* into his 1979 novel, *Pleasure-Dome*, the sequel to *Bijou*.

Brothers in Confidence is indeed Madden's most entertaining novel. Hollis Weaver, a young graduate student finishing his thesis on Henry James and already hired to teach at Transylvania College, receives a desperate call from his younger brother Cody who has been arrested for passing bad checks and is to be sent to the Tennessee chain gang. Hollis's efforts to save his brother are futile until their older brother, Traven, arrives. The ultimate con man, who is indirectly responsible for Cody's present situation and who has spent his life conning strangers, friends, and family alike, Traven poses as the smooth lawyer, Mr. French, and he not only talks his brother's way out of jail but also gets the judge to accept one of his own bad checks so that they can have some cash to leave town. The narrator, Hollis, who has tried to save his brother through his great gift of story telling, is much like Madden himself. Hollis too has been in the merchant marine (duped by Traven into believing that real adventure lay at sea even though Traven has only worn the merchant marine uniform so that he might hitchhike more easily across the country). And, like Madden, Hollis is awaiting the publication of his first novel about his experiences at sea and by the end of *Brothers in Confidence* has already begun a teaching career. Certainly for Hollis, as for Madden, life has been a combination of the two worlds, of imagination and action, represented by Cassie and Lone in *Cassandra Singing*. More importantly, out of the life has come

Peggy Bach

the art—not merely autobiography but embellished reality. After all, it is Hollis's story which lasts beyond Cody's actual rescue, Hollis's world which Madden explores in detail in *Bijou*.

Published in 1974, *Bijou*, a Book-of-the-Month Club alternate selection, was critically acclaimed by many as an important novel by a major talent. Growing initially out of the autobiographical material about his youth which had been used in "Traven" and *Brothers in Confidence*, *Bijou* began, according to Madden, with a great longing, "a kind of terrible nostalgia for the Bijou, for the place itself rather than the events which occurred there." He spent 1969 in Venice on a Rockefeller grant (for which he had been nominated by Robert Penn Warren) because it seemed to him that Venice was the best parallel for the "exotic, weird, strange place" he thought of the Bijou as being. Later, he continued to revise the novel from its initial overwhelming twenty-two hundred pages to its current five-hundred-page length and would still like to cut another two hundred pages from it. His criticism of it, as with all his criticism of his own work, is accurate; the novel is too dispersed, too episodic: "The length is a consequence of getting outside the Bijou, and I think that the book might have been more of an aesthetic achievement if I had maintained more of a unity [of place]."

Yet, despite this flaw, *Bijou* does draw together many of the aesthetic, personal, and technical concerns which Madden had been developing through his fiction and discussing in much of his nonfiction. An important example of this is his concept of the charged image, "an image that in its prepared context in a story or novel is so fully packed with implications about all the other elements in the story that whenever you encounter that image it recalls for you all those other elements that have been set up in the story. It's as if it sends a charge of electricity into all the other elements." The charged image in *Bijou* is Lucius Hutchfield, the thirteen-year-old central character, standing in the theatre where he ushers, watching images on the screen while he creates his own images in his mind. Thus *Bijou* is about the creative process at work—the ways in which even a very young artist absorbs and radiates. *Bijou* traces Lucius's development—emotionally, physically, and artistically—at school, at home, and mainly at the Bijou with his family, the other ushers, and his friends during one year of his life, 1946. Moreover, it centers upon that "terrible nostalgia" to which Madden frequently refers. Just as Lucius makes a pilgrimage to Thomas Wolfe's home in Asheville at the end of the novel, Madden takes himself and his reader on a pilgrimage into the past, not at all for sentimental reasons but to capture those moments, perhaps the moment, of an entire year frozen in time. This type of nostalgia allows for revelation not only of what the past might have been, but also of what people were at that moment. Rather than reveling in what has passed, we can then examine in all their complex facets the elements which made individuals and which, continuing into the present, make life and art a timeless reality transcending the past and the artist himself. By the end of the novel, standing in a bedroom in Wolfe's house, out of which that novelist once emerged with the power to create a pleasure-dome for himself and his reader, Lucius is also on the verge of transforming the Bijou with all its tinsel into a world of his own making for himself and for those who listen to him and, in the future, read his work.

Prefigured in tone and writing style only by some earlier short stories, *The Suicide's Wife*, says Madden, "differs in every way from my earlier novels . . . and even from my plans for future novels. . . . I became Ann [the central character] more than I have ever become one of my characters, even though I was imagining what it was like to be a woman, to be that particular kind of woman in that very specific situation. Paradoxically, *The Suicide's Wife*, then, is in one sense more my autobiography than *Bijou* is. It is the expression of the eighteen days when I was Ann Harrington, who, beyond a difference in sex, is totally different from the person I usually am." Conceived in 1967 but written in eighteen days, a chapter a day, during February 1977, Madden's sixth novel is indeed so unlike his previous work that the reader might be inclined to check the title page periodically to verify the author's name. Some critics have favorably compared *The Suicide's Wife* to Fitzgerald at his best while others have praised it mildly and expressed the hope that Madden would return to the world of his earlier fiction. Short and concise, with every word carefully chosen, the novel does beautifully present the story of Ann Harrington, who must find a life for herself and her three children after her husband's suicide.

The novel begins and ends with a death. At the beginning, Wayne Harrington has returned to his family home in upstate New York to die, leaving his wife alone in the empty house to find her way back to West Virginia where he teaches. At the conclusion, Ann has accomplished a type of rebirth after having symbolically killed the person she had been. Step by step, she sheds the identity which she had created as Wayne's wife and painfully creates a new self able to cope with the world she had previously been unaware of. She discovers that she had been living with a man who finally knew himself no better than she did, if indeed there was anything to know. Thus she can conclude: "Because the most boring man on the face of the earth died, I can begin to live. He could not act when he was alive, he could not create, but out of his death, she had been creating whatever she would become. And that she knew most clearly—that she was becoming." Against the political and social upheavals of 1968 which the media report throughout the novel, Ann goes through her own violent upheaval and emerges more fully aware of what she has been through than most of the "real" people who are participating in those background events will know of themselves. *The Suicide's Wife* is a perfect, albeit small novel.

Pleasure-Dome, the sequel to *Bijou*, was to have been entitled "A Demon In My View." Bought by Bobbs-Merrill at the same time as *The Suicide's Wife*, it began as a complex project to combine six works, some previously published, some unwritten, but ended up composed of two parts: *Brothers in Confidence* and "Nothing Dies But Something Mourns," which had originally appeared in the *Carleton Miscellany* in 1968. Madden changed his original plan because he wanted *Pleasure-Dome* to be a shorter, more intense work than *Bijou*. The end result is a novel divided neatly into the two parts, which are unified by the presence of Lucius Hutchfield as the central character. The first sixteen chapters are a not greatly altered version of the Avon paperback. Hollis is now Lucius, and many of the events of *Bijou* not in *Brothers in Confidence* are recounted by Lucius in his attempts to free Bucky (who was called Cody in the Avon version). If the reader has read *Bijou*, he knows more about Lucius and his family than *Pleasure-Dome* relates; however, Madden also fills in more detail about Lucius's life between the time spans covered in the two novels—his trip to New York and his stint in the merchant marine, for example. Thus the sequel does not depend upon the reader's knowledge of *Bijou* even though it is immeasurably richer if one has read the earlier novel.

The last sixteen chapters take the reader beyond Lucius's past and Madden's autobiographical materials into the world of Madden's imagination. Again, the novel reflects the tension between imagination and action which is a part of all of Madden's work. In this case, however, the two sides are juxtaposed, depending upon one another to spark the transition which will unify the novel. It is as if Lone and Cassie are brought together again, side by side, forcing the reader to recognize the whole which they as characters recognized in one another at the end of *Cassandra Singing*. In addition, the first part of *Pleasure-Dome* illustrates the con artist at work both in Earl's role as Mr. French and in Lucius's role as storyteller; the second part then takes the reader into a young man's awakening, not to his identity as the storyteller, for Lucius knows his identity, but to his responsibility and obligation as the artist.

As the storyteller, Lucius travels to Sweetwater near Boone, North Carolina, to discover if Jesse James, one of his childhood idols, had indeed stayed there at the Blue Goose Hotel and fallen in love with

Zara Jane Ransom, now an elderly recluse living in the doomed hotel. Finally, Lucius convinces the old lady to tell him of her past with Jesse when he deceives her into believing that the money he will pay, which she needs for taxes, is indeed real. Lucius, though, has no money and writes his own bad checks, not to free his brother from jail as Earl had done, but to satisfy his curiosity and greed for adventure, real or vicarious. Because of events and Zara Jane Ransom's death in the burning hotel, he never hears the ending to her story about Jesse. He must create his own variation and live with the guilt of how he has used Zara Jane and other characters in the small town. Thus at the end of *Pleasure-Dome*, Lucius has moved beyond nostalgia for its own sake and beyond his curiosity into a realization that the artist must be more than the successful teller of stories. He must make of the pleasure-dome not a nightmare, but a dream of possibilities and beauty. The storyteller who only exploits others and himself to gather material is finally the man who has conned himself. Only when he transcends the factual and learns to cherish what has been and can be created—not to inform, but to enlighten—can the storyteller become the artist, mingling despair and guilt with joy and forgiveness.

On the Big Wind (1980) is subtitled *Being Seven Comic Episodes In the Fitful Rise of Big Bob Travis From Disc Jockey In a Small Eastern Kentucky Mountain Town To Network Television News Reporter* and focuses upon, as Madden says, "the impact of the electronic media on the Appalachian storytelling dynamic." Even though most of the episodes had been published earlier as short stories in such diverse journals as *Adam* and the *Kenyon Review*, there is an amazing consistency of tone and quality throughout. Madden juxtaposes seven distinct stages in Big Bob's life, the earliest being in 1968 and the latest in 1979. Each time Big Bob moves from one job to another, against the background of news events, moving from being a disc jockey with a late night show to being a television commentator on the verge of becoming a big success, he changes his name, thus a part of his identity: Big Bob Travis, Daryl Don Donovan, David Epstein, and finally Robert Travis. As Big Bob's name changes, so does the nature of his stories, the ones he tells and the ones he hears. As the media, the jobs, and the names change, so does the relationship between Bob and his listeners and, more importantly, between Madden and his reader. The third-person narrator is replaced more and more by Big Bob's voice alone or his conversations with various listeners—over the telephone and in person—only to return to third person in the final episode when Robert Travis returns home. Madden brings together his recurring interest in the complexity of the story-telling dynamic with the technical expertise he has learned from writing both fiction and drama. Thus we begin to listen to Big Bob, to the immediacy of the story, as he weaves a dome over himself and us. Whether he is trying to induce drivers on the Interstate to come to a mobile home sale or acting as an oral Miss Lonelyhearts or overshadowing a political propaganda film with the story of the Singer ("The Singer," published in the *Kenyon Review* in 1966, is the heart of the novel), Madden is exploring the complex, changing relationships between storyteller, material, and listener in his most experimental work in novel form. He has done this before but never more successfully. When Robert Travis, unable to change himself as easily as he has changed names, arrives home, kept from covering the fall of Sky Lab by his mother's impending death, he has returned to the world which created him and in turn the world which he reports and imagines. The material out of which legends grow seems forever altered by the camera and the immediacy of the television commentator. Yet Madden's forthcoming novel, *On the Big Wind*, is a reaffirmation that facts alone do not create truth; only when the individual transcends the facts and creates, in a very real sense, his own legends, his own stories, does he have a chance for freedom.

Madden is now at work on a historical novel, "Knoxville, Tennessee." In it, he says that he is exploring "the schizophrenia of the East Tennessee character, focussing on my home town Knoxville, seen best during the Civil War, and in the persons of Parson Brownlow (pro-North, but pro-slavery), preacher and journalist, and James Ramsey, doctor and banker and historian, archetypal Southern farmer gentleman. In their conflicting characters, personalities, and backgrounds, I see two aspects of my own (as Nick and Gatsby are two aspects of Fitzgerald). This will not be a conventional historical novel; I want to do new things with that genre; and I want to push the omniscient point of view further than it has ever, to my knowledge, been pushed. It was abandoned by modern writers before it could be developed further in modern consciousness." Furthermore, he adds, "I have a feeling, a feeling only, that I want to explore possibilities of the imagination further . . . to stimulate those possibilities I plan to read the great imaginative works—RABELAIS, etc., fantastical leaps of the imagination. That seems to me a great adventure to look forward to." David Madden is indeed one of the most ambitious contemporary novelists in America. American fiction will be only richer for his exploration and the fulfillment of that ambition.

—Thomas E. Dasher

Plays:

Call Herman In to Supper, Knoxville, Tenn., 1949;
They Shall Endure, Knoxville, Tenn., 1953;
Cassandra Singing, Knoxville, Tenn., 1955;
From Rome to Damascus, Chapel Hill, N.C., 1959;
Casina, New Haven, Conn., 1960;
Fugitive Masks, Abingdon, Va., 1966;
The Day the Flowers Came, Baton Rouge, La., 1975.

Other:

Cassandra Singing, in *New Campus Writing No. 2,* ed. Nolan Miller (New York: Putnam's, 1957), pp. 214-237;

Proletarian Writers of the Thirties, edited by Madden (Carbondale: Southern Illinois University Press, 1968);

Tough Guy Writers of the Thirties, edited by Madden (Carbondale: Southern Illinois University Press, 1968);

American Dreams, American Nightmares, edited by Madden (Carbondale: Southern Illinois University Press, 1970);

"The Suicide's Wife," in *New American Review 10* (New York: New American Library, 1970), p. 69;

Rediscoveries, edited by Madden (New York: Crown, 1971);

The Popular Culture Explosion, edited by Madden and Ray B. Browne (Dubuque, Iowa: Brown, 1972);

Nathanael West: The Cheaters and the Cheated, edited by Madden (Deland, Fla.: Everett/Edwards, 1973);

Remembering James Agee, edited by Madden (Baton Rouge: Louisiana State University Press, 1974);

"Leda and the Paratrooper," in *New Southern Poets,* ed. Guy Owen and Mary C. Williams (Chapel Hill: University of North Carolina Press, 1975), p. 49;

Creative Choices, edited by Madden (Glenview, Ill.: Scott, Foresman, 1975);

Studies in the Short Story, edited by Madden and Virgil Scott (New York: Holt, Rinehart & Winston, 1975);

Contemporary Literary Scene, edited by Madden and Frank Magill (Englewood Cliffs, N.J.: Salem Press, 1975).

Periodical Publications:

FICTION:

"Hurry Up Please It's Time," *Botteghe Oscure,* 24 (Autumn 1959): 185-193;

"The Shadow Knows," *Deep Summer: Kentucky Writing,* 4 (1963): 93-108;

"The Singer," *Kenyon Review,* 28 (January 1966): 79-107;

"Big Bob's Night Owl Show," *Adam* (August 1966): 6;

"Lone Riding," *Southwest Review,* 51 (Summer 1966): 221-236;

"In My Father's House," *First Stage,* 5 (Summer 1966): 119-131;

Hair of the Dog, Adam (April 1967-November 1967);

"Big Bob and the Hellhounds," *Adam Bedside Reader* (June 1967): 22;

"The Master's Thesis," *Fantasy and Science Fiction* (July 1967): 87-99;

"Children of a Cold Sun," *North American Review,* new series, 4 (July 1967): 24-28;

"Traven," *Southern Review,* new series, 4 (April 1968): 346-391;

"Love Makes Nothing Happen," *Southwest Review,* 53 (Summer 1968): 266-275;

"The Day the Flowers Came," *Playboy,* 15 (September 1968): 137, 142, 254-256;

"Nothing Dies But Something Mourns," *Carleton Miscellany,* 9 (Fall 1968): 24-88;

"A Voice in the Garden," *English Record,* 20 (October 1969): 25-37;

"On Target," *December,* 11, no. 1-2 (1969): 29-37;

"No Trace," *Southern Review,* new series, 6 (January 1970): 1-24;

"Home Comfort," *Jeopardy* (March 1970): 65-69;

"Frank Brown's Brother," *South Dakota Review,* 8 (Spring-Summer 1970): 96-109;

"A Secondary Character," *Cimarron Review,* 20 (July 1972): 5-19;

"A Part in Pirandello," *North American Review,* 257 (Summer 1972): 48-55;

"The Cartridge Belt," *Massachusetts Review,* 13 (Autumn 1972): 681-701;

"Looking at the Dead," *Minnesota Review,* 3 (Fall 1972): 29-33;

"Lindbergh's Rival," *Quartet,* 6 (Spring-Summer 1973): 59-64;

"Here He Comes! There He Goes!," *Contempora,* 2 (Summer 1973): 2-5;

"Wanted: Ghost Writer," *Epoch,* 23 (Fall 1973): 44-59;

"The World's One Breathing," *Appalachian Heritage,* 1 (Winter 1973): 12-24;

"Second Look," *Fiction International* (Fall 1975);

"In the Bag," *Southern Review*, new series, 13 (April 1977): 361-369;
"Putting an Act Together," *Southern Review*, new series, 16 (January 1980): 228-233.
POETRY:
"Lindbergh's Rival," *Southern Poetry Review*, 2 (Spring 1971): 14;
"Venice Is Sinking," *Tennessee Poetry Journal*, 4 (Spring 1971): 65-66.
NONFICTION:
"Letter to a Young Critic," correspondence between Madden and Wright Morris, *Massachusetts Review*, 6 (Autumn-Winter 1964-1965): 93-100;
"Ambiguity in Albert Camus' *The Fall*," *Modern Fiction Studies*, 12 (Winter 1966-1967): 461-472;
"The Agnostic Priesthood," *Discourse*, 11 (Spring 1968): 171-182;
"College on Wheels: A Special Response to General Needs," *Discourse*, 12 (Autumn 1969): 452-461;
"The Charged Image in Katherine Anne Porter's 'Flowering Judas,' " *Studies in Short Fiction*, 7 (Spring 1970): 277-289;
"James M. Cain's *The Postman Always Rings Twice* and Albert Camus's *L'Etranger*," *Papers on Language and Literature*, 6 (Fall 1970): 407-419;
"The Compulsion to Tell a Story," *Journal of Popular Culture*, 5 (Fall 1971): 269-279;
"Notes for an Erotic Memoir of the Forties," *Film Journal*, 2 (September 1972): 2-19;
"The Necessity for an Aesthetics of Popular Culture," *Journal of Popular Culture*, 7 (Summer 1973): 1-13;
"Fallacies and Leaps of Imagination," *New Writers*, 1, no. 2 (1974): 111-115;
"The Performing Voice in the Singer," *Dramatics* (Fall 1978);
"Behind the Locked Door," *Register* (Quota issue 1978): 30, 38, 42-44.

Interviews:

"A Conversation with David Madden," *Critique*, 15 (1973): 5-14;
"An Interview with David Madden," *Penny Dreadful*, 3, no. 3 (1974), n.pag.;
"The Story-teller as Benevolent Con Man," *Appalachian Heritage*, 2 (Summer 1974): 70-77;
"An Interview with David Madden," *Southern Review*, new series, 11 (1975): 167-180.

Papers:

A collection of Madden's manuscripts is in the Special Collections of the University of Tennessee Library, Knoxville.

FREDERICK MANFRED

(6 January 1912-)

SELECTED BOOKS: *The Golden Bowl*, as Feike Feikema (Saint Paul: Webb, 1944; London: Dobson, 1947);
Boy Almighty, as Feike Feikema (Saint Paul: Itasca Press, 1945; London: Dobson, 1950);
This Is the Year, as Feike Feikema (Garden City: Doubleday, 1947);
The Chokecherry Tree, as Feike Feikema (Garden City: Doubleday, 1948; London: Dobson, 1949; revised edition, Denver: Swallow, 1961);
The Primitive, as Feike Feikema (Garden City: Doubleday, 1949);
The Brother, as Feike Feikema (Garden City: Doubleday, 1950);
The Giant, as Feike Feikema (Garden City: Doubleday, 1951);
Lord Grizzly (New York: McGraw-Hill, 1954);
Morning Red (Denver: Swallow, 1956);
Riders of Judgment (New York: Random House, 1957);
Conquering Horse (New York: McDowell, Obolensky, 1959);
Arrow of Love (Denver: Swallow, 1961);
Wanderlust (Denver: Swallow, 1962)—revised edition of *The Primitive*, *The Brother*, and *The Giant*;
Scarlet Plume (New York: Trident Press, 1964);
The Man Who Looked Like the Prince of Wales (New York: Trident Press, 1965); republished as *The Secret Place* (New York: Pocket Books, 1967);
King of Spades (New York: Trident Press, 1966);
Winter Count: Poems 1934-1965 (Minneapolis: James D. Thueson, 1966);
Eden Prairie (New York: Trident Press, 1968);
Apples of Paradise and Other Stories (New York: Trident Press, 1968);
Conversations with Frederick Manfred, moderated by John R. Milton (Salt Lake City: University of Utah Press, 1974);
The Manly-Hearted Woman (New York: Crown, 1975);
Milk of Wolves (Boston: Avenue Victor Hugo, 1976);
Green Earth (New York: Crown, 1977);
The Wind Blows Free (Sioux Falls, S.D.: Center for Western Studies, 1979);
Sons of Adam (New York: Crown, 1980).

Frederick Manfred has had two careers as a writer: the first as a writer primarily identified with the Midwest, but in the autobiographical tradition of Thomas Wolfe; the second as a writer identified with the American West, particularly the West of the nineteenth century. In the second career he has achieved his greatest reputation. The two careers are not totally distinct entities, of course; but their reality is emphasized not only by the fact that Manfred is among the minority of writers who have published under two names, but also because he changed his legal name after his career was well launched. A writer would take such a step only after careful deliberation, for the common reader would assume that there were two writers, not one. Old names die slowly: James D. Hart's *Oxford Companion to American Literature*, 4th edition (1965), gives the main entry to Manfred under his first authorial name, Feike Feikema.

Manfred, the first of six sons, was born Frederick Feikema on a farm near Doon, Iowa. The northwest corner of Iowa had a sizable contingency of settlers from the Netherlands, and the area still has a marked Dutch character. While Manfred identifies his roots as Frisian, his neighbors did not usually make such subtle distinctions. Manfred attended the Dutch Christian Reformed Church. While he attended country public schools until he was nine and in the fifth grade, in the spring of 1921 his family moved by design closer to the Doon Christian School, and Manfred was enrolled there. Thereafter he attended parochial schools: it was entirely in keeping with familial and community expectations that Manfred later enrolled at Calvin College in Grand Rapids, Michigan, for his college work.

Manfred's orthodoxy was always somewhat suspect at Calvin, but he nevertheless profited a great deal from his years there (1930-1934). However, he abandoned his mother's dream that he might be a minister, and although he earned a teacher's certificate, he was not taken with the idea of teaching. He was most attracted to his English major, and in his second year at Calvin he published his first poem, "Birth of Neumonon," in the *Calvin College Chimes*. During the rest of his college career he used the *Chimes* and *Prism*, the college yearbook, to share his creative efforts, poems and stories, with his classmates. In his reading at Calvin, Manfred was especially attracted to Chaucer and Whitman. Tall (6′9″), physical, coordinated, Manfred also found athletic outlets at Calvin; he was a great asset to the basketball team.

After his college graduation, he was at loose ends; the severe economic depression of the nation contributed to his mood of uncertainty. In August of 1934 he inaugurated a period of wandering with a trip to the West and Yellowstone National Park. He returned to Grand Rapids to work at menial labor, moved to New Jersey where he worked for U.S. Rubber in Passaic; then he went back to Doon. In 1936 he was again in New Jersey, where he began writing a newspaper column, "The World Around Us," for the *Prospector*, a weekly. But Manfred never stayed away for long from the upper midlands. He was back in Iowa in June, and in September he moved to Sioux Falls, South Dakota. In April 1937, he had his first job that looked permanent when he became a sportswriter on the *Minneapolis Journal*. That year he also commenced writing his first novel, a novel that reflected many of his wanderings. The *Journal* fired him in January of 1939.

All ambition was brought into question, however, in 1940 when the athletic Manfred was stricken by tuberculosis and had to enter Glen Lake Sanatorium, where he was to be for almost two years. He had an abundance of time to reflect on the future course of his life. He decided there that Maryanna Shorba, another tuberculosis patient, should share that life with him. He married her in Minneapolis shortly after he left the sanatorium. In Minneapolis he worked for a brief time for *Modern Medicine*. Attracted to liberal politics, in 1943 he became the assistant campaign manager for Hubert Humphrey's unsuccessful bid for mayor of Minneapolis. In June he ceased political activity, determined to devote the rest of his life to serious writing, to finish the novel he had begun six years earlier.

After many rewritings, *The Golden Bowl* was published in 1944. It portrays a farming family in South Dakota struggling to recover from the catastrophe of the Dust Bowl. The Thors are not tempted to seek any golden land further west; they are committed to faith in the promise of the golden bowl at hand; their faith is enough to transform Maury Grant, an embittered wanderer (who shares some experiences with young Manfred). The strength of the novel is attested by its reprintings, first by the University of South Dakota Press on the occasion of the novel's twenty-fifth anniversary, and in 1976 by the University of New Mexico Press as part of its Zia series, reprints designed to keep in print important novels of the West.

The year 1944 was a good one for Manfred. Not only was *The Golden Bowl* published, but he also received a University of Minnesota Writing Fellowship (renewed in 1945). A daughter, Freya, was also born that year. In the next year Manfred got a grant-in-aid from the American Academy of Arts and Letters. In April he moved to Bloomington, Minnesota, where he would live for fifteen years. Publication of his second novel, *Boy Almighty*, also came in 1945.

Boy Almighty is much more overtly autobiographical than *The Golden Bowl.* The hero is named Eric Frey, close to Frederick, but since the novel was penned under the name Feike Feikema, the autobiographical echo would not be too obvious to the novel's first readers. The novel narrates Eric's battle with tuberculosis in a sanatorium. Since his disease leads Eric to question all existence, the novel becomes too discursive, the structure too loose. Nevertheless, with *The Golden Bowl* and *Boy Almighty* Manfred had made an impressive beginning.

Probably the most important reader of Manfred's first book was Sinclair Lewis, a fellow Minnesotan. Impressed with *The Golden Bowl,* Lewis invited Manfred to visit him for a weekend in his Duluth home. Manfred accepted and passed the time with Lewis genially enough. Lewis promised to use his influence to get Manfred published by a bigger company. Manfred's first two novels had been published by a small St. Paul firm, and he realized what a publishing house like Doubleday could do for his career. Lewis read the manuscript of the novel on which Manfred was then working and recognized its merit. Because of Lewis, when *This Is The Year* was published in 1947, Doubleday was the publisher. Manfred repaid the debt by giving the commemoration address for Lewis after his death in 1951.

This Is The Year gave Manfred his first national recognition; it was reviewed widely and quite favorably. The novel was Manfred's first mining of the material offered him by his own family and that corner of Iowa with its distinct ethnic flavoring. Pier Frixen, based in part on Manfred's father, is an intriguing character, the most colorful Manfred had yet created. The novel was also longer than the previous ones—Manfred allowed himself a large canvas and achieved on it a convincing portrayal of farm life. Set in the 1920s and early 1930s, the novel was in part an indictment of attitudes toward the land that had led to the disaster of the Dust Bowl.

Manfred allowed himself an even larger canvas for another project—a trilogy of novels, novels that were Wolfean in conception, as his title for the trilogy, "World's Wanderer," suggests. Manfred coined the word *rume* for novels like his trilogy. In a postscript to its final novel, he explained: "After deep rumination, after long inner musing, a man cries out, RU-es, 'rhues' forth among men that thus and so he has felt about living. 'I was here,' he cries, 'and I had this happen to me, and this I did, and these things I saw and discovered, and this is what I think it all means. . . .' " The three volumes of the trilogy are *The Primitive, The Brother,* and *The Giant*; they appeared one year apart, 1949 through 1951. It would be a mistake to say that Manfred's hero Thurs Wraldson was uninteresting, but it became evident, most of all to Manfred, that the books had been written too hastily. As the successive volumes appeared, critical response in the more influential publications was increasingly disheartening. Feike Feikema's career was at a crisis. Doubleday dropped him, and finding a new publisher was no easy task. Manfred needed a new start.

It was then that he decided to do away with the name *Feike Feikema.* The name was often mispronounced and was annoying to Manfred on that score. He kept the Frederick with which he had been christened and put with it an acceptable translation of Feikema. And he took a surprising new turn for the subject of his next novel—a venture into the American West of the nineteenth century and a rendition of the legend of Hugh Glass, a mountain man who had been mangled wrestling a grizzly and left by his comrades to die, some two hundred miles from refuge. Hugh survived alone on sheer grit and a desire for revenge: he slowly crawled back to Fort Kiowa and there recuperated before setting out to get his revenge on the two comrades who had abandoned him. The Glass story was splendid material for Manfred, who had been badly mauled by the critics. Manfred's rendering of Hugh as *Lord Grizzly* (1954) is one of his best novels and still his most popular title.

But the strength of *Lord Grizzly* was not enough to entice Manfred's new publisher, McGraw-Hill, to publish *Morning Red,* a long, bizarre novel of two counterparting stories. Nor could Manfred interest other publishers in the work. Convinced of its merit, Manfred sought out Alan Swallow, who he had heard was especially interested in writers of the West. Swallow's Denver firm was small, but Swallow was not in business only to make a profit. He seems to have liked to gamble on the long shot: he read Manfred's manuscript and decided that it should be published as it was. In 1956 Swallow published Manfred's "romance," a tale of crime, political intrigue, and neuroses in the Twin Cities, which has yet to gain a large following.

But whatever the weaknesses of *Morning Red,* Manfred's association with Swallow was fortunate for his career. Swallow counted Manfred one of the maverick writers of the West who had not been given his due, and he promoted Manfred's work in various ways (Swallow wielded power as a critic) as well as by publishing his books. In addition to *Morning Red,* Swallow published three other Manfred titles. In 1961 he published a slightly revised version of *The*

-1

were high. Pa had left them again, busy with his own thoughts, never shared with anyone. . . .

It was sometime after the initial shock, when Alan went to bed one night, that a clear mental picture of the other twin popped into his head. Alan was on the edge of sleep when he saw him. The other twin was an inch taller than Alan. Hair a little darker red. Wider shoulders. Skin not quite so light-complected. Eyes a deeper and steadier blue. And on his lips, ~~a most wonderful superior smile. The other twin was so good he could afford~~ a confident smile. It wasn't a big smile, just an impish one. Alan could just ~~imagine~~ see the other twin breaking in a bronc, or connecting for a homerun, ~~to lifting a heaving basket of corn,~~ with always that little ~~superior~~ smile on his full lips. Where most athletes grimaced at the moment of their supreme effort, even making a horrible face, his twin brother had that superior smile of the champ.

It was also about the same time that Alan decided since he himself had the name of Alan legally, he'd think of the other twin as John. Otherwise Alan felt he'd go nuts. ~~crazy trying to keep from being pushed over into another envelope of skin with the tag of John on it.~~ Alan pretty much liked who he was, liked being called Alan, so the imaginary twin had to be John.

After that, in his mind's eye, Alan often saw ~~his~~

Sons of Adam, *revised typescript*

Chokecherry Tree. The Chokecherry Tree, originally published in 1948, was a comic counterpart of the more ambitious trilogy; its protagonist is something of an antihero. Elof Lofblom returns to his small community in Siouxland, Chokecherry Corner, a college dropout. He never quite completes anything, but he is a winning character who creates his own sense of affirmation. In the larger frame of Manfred's work, *The Chokecherry Tree* marked Manfred's commitment to his Siouxland (the valley of the Big Sioux River) as the favored arena for his fiction. Influenced by the novels of Hardy and Balzac, Manfred also began thinking of his Siouxland as a counterpart to Faulkner's Yoknapatawpha County (he dedicated *Morning Red* to Faulkner). Siouxland was also the setting for another book Swallow published for Manfred in 1961, *Arrow of Love,* a gathering of three nouvelles. The first nouvelle is a story of the Sioux Indians in the nineteenth century, and the later two show affinities with *The Chokecherry Tree* in their renditions of ordinary country folks. The last novel Swallow published for Manfred was *Wanderlust* (1962), a revision of the Thurs trilogy. Its publication was a gratifying event for Manfred: he had felt obligated to revise his "rume," and he at last had it under one cover so that readers could judge it as a single work.

While Swallow did "maverick" publishing for Manfred, elsewhere Manfred was having published (with Swallow's blessing) other works that had greater potential for monetary success. The most important of these built on the success of *Lord Grizzly* and expanded Manfred's reputation as a writer of the Western past. Collectively the series, set in the nineteenth-century West, became known as the Buckskin Man Tales. *Riders of Judgment* (1957) is based on the Johnson County Cattle Wars of Wyoming in 1892. The hero, Cain Hammett, is patterned on the historical Nate Champion, who lost his life in those wars. Manfred's Cain partakes of the mythic, as his name suggests. Like Hugh Glass, Cain is involved in violent actions, but he is concerned that any violence he perpetrates be for a right reason. Cain's problems are compounded because he is living at a time when a body of religious beliefs is not universally shared by his society. *Conquering Horse* (1959) takes the reader into a society where religious belief is a bond of the community, and the novel's orthodox Indian hero can find his way by following orthodox requirements in his search for his identity. Manfred's portrayal of the Sioux in the early nineteenth century before the white man had undermined their culture is one of his most impressive achievements. His *Scarlet Plume* (1964) is named for an Indian who lives later in the century and loses his life during the Sioux uprising in Minnesota in 1864, well aware that his society is doomed. Many readers have found Manfred's portrayal of the barbarities of that uprising excessive—though, as Manfred knew, the barbarities (on both sides) could be easily documented by history. An important part of Manfred's story has to do with the love affair between Scarlet Plume (his name is phallic in addition to being appropriate to a tale of bloody excess) and Judith Raveling, a white woman who finds her intellectual husband inadequate as a companion and lover. The novel is at times fiercely Lawrencian in its celebration of the more vital Indian sexual life. Judith's conversion is as complete as Constance Chatterley's in Lawrence's novel. But Judith is not as convincing a heroine as is Constance Chatterley. *Scarlet Plume* is the only Buckskin novel to concentrate on the female consciousness, and Manfred—who had focused all of his novels prior to *Scarlet Plume* on the male viewpoint—did not wholly succeed with Judith: she is both too intellectual and too banal. Furthermore, since Scarlet Plume is also something of a Christ figure, Manfred's novel gets a little heavy. It is of lesser stature than the first three Buckskin Man Tales.

More problematical than *Scarlet Plume* is *King of Spades* (1966), which stretches credibility in its extravagant plot. Manfred claims that he was interested in the concept of bonding when he wrote the novel: what is it that brings one to a soul mate? His suggestion tips his hand, for idea more than character carries the novel. Many readers have described the story as the Oedipus myth brought to the American West, where it does not fit very well. While still a young boy, the novel's protagonist, Earl Ransom, runs away because he thinks he has killed his father to protect his mother. Years later at a brothel he falls in love with the madam, who he later discovers is his mother. Manfred tried to make the situation plausible by having had Kitty marry Ransom's father when she was very young. But women on the frontier did not mature sexually earlier than they do now; even if one accepted that they did, Manfred's novel has a large number of coincidences; the father is not dead, as supposed, but arrives as Ransom is about to be hanged for the murder of his mother. *King of Spades* may be of most interest for its role in the Buckskin series, for it touches on motifs of the other novels and, like the rest of the series, is concerned with the American past and implications of the past for the present.

In 1975 Crown published Manfred's *The Manly-Hearted Woman,* a short novel that is most conveniently considered with the Buckskin Man Tales, particularly with *Conquering Horse,* for it also reveals Manfred's affection for and understanding of the Sioux of a bygone day. *The Manly-Hearted Woman* is, like *Conquering Horse,* a novel of faith, a celebration of community and growing. The modern reader reads it with two minds, probably. With his modern mind, he is likely to be amused at Flat Warclub's progress from tribal unfortunate to hero—particularly since the progress shows Flat Warclub in a string of sexual conquests. With the other side of his mind, the reader should envision the religious strength of the Sioux, their sense of belonging to each other and to the spirits. Sexual fulfillment symbolizes spiritual fulfillment. Flat Warclub's progress is paralleled by that of Manly-Heart, a woman who is struggling to find her sexual identity and for a time lives as a man with a wife, Prettyhead (pretty as she is, Prettyhead is also a tribal unfortunate since she has some white blood and so has not been sought by other suitors). As Flat Warclub finds his manhood, he transforms the lives of Manly-Heart and Prettyhead: they find their womanhood. As *The Chokecherry Tree* with its nonheroic protagonist seems to play against the more serious *World's Wanderer* trilogy, *The Manly-Hearted Woman* plays similarly against the more heroic adventures of No Name on his way to becoming Conquering Horse.

Had Alan Swallow not died in 1966, Manfred's *Milk of Wolves* (1976) would have, in all probability, been published sooner than it was, for its publication was delayed until Manfred located another maverick publisher—Avenue Victor Hugo. *Milk of Wolves* is as extravagant at times as *Morning Red* and as deserving of the subtitle of the earlier work: *A Romance.* The book recounts the career of Juhl Melander, a stonecutter. Juhl is a "natural" artist—largely self-taught, the more surprisingly since his medium is stone. He objects to the word *sculptor* as too high-toned, "like someone calling himself an author instead of a writer." *Milk of Wolves* suffers as apologia, which is what it is too much of the time. Manfred makes his case through Juhl for his own studied plainness, for his view of the artist as male, as prober—whom Manfred sees at his best when most instinctive. While Juhl has sex with many women, he finds his greatest personal fulfillment when he retreats from the city, from civilization, and takes an Indian wife in the far north of Minnesota. Many readers will find Juhl's adventures there marvelously strange, and Juhl's adventures as "hermit in the woods" comprise the second half of the novel. While Juhl thinks of himself as natural, *Milk of Wolves* too frequently seems designed to illustrate theory.

Manfred was infinitely more successful in *Green Earth* (1977), perhaps his most concretely autobiographical novel. But *Green Earth* does not immediately focus on Free Aldredson, the Manfredian hero: it studies him by looking at the marriage of Free's parents. A long and leisurely novel, *Green Earth* creates many convincing pictures of rural life in a particular time and place. Often it is effective genre painting, and it is an impressive backdrop for all of Manfred's twentieth-century Siouxland novels and stories. In *Green Earth* characters found in such works as *The Man Who Looked Like the Prince of Wales* (1965) and *Eden Prairie* (1968) are given a cultural foundation. It is a good starting place for studying Manfred's Siouxland novels.

Now in his late sixties, Manfred retains a youthful enthusiasm and affirmation toward life (as the title *Green Earth* suggests). He is physically active, maintains a garden, loves to take long walks. He claims to feel about twenty-seven or twenty-eight—maybe twenty-nine on bad days. In October of 1978 he divorced his wife and now lives alone—still in rural Siouxland, near Luverne, Minnesota, where he has lived since 1960. But he is a sociable man. He enjoys his children and follows their interests actively (besides Freya, there is a daughter Marya, born in 1949, and a son Frederick, born in 1954). He writes as regularly as did the Victorian professionals and gives every indication of continuing to do so. In 1979 the Center for Western Studies published *The Wind Blows Free,* a reminiscence of his trip west just after his college graduation, a celebration of the urge that made him a writer. *Sons of Adam,* his twenty-fifth book, is scheduled for publication in late 1980.

While some readers would agree with Wallace Stegner that Manfred's regionalism is sometimes "a shade too provincial," many have found Manfred's depiction of his region to be bracing and refreshing. A work like *Green Earth* preserves a part of the past with commendable precision. Realism is not the virtue in some of Manfred's other works, especially the Buckskin Man Tales and the romances. Nor is style; indeed, Manfred's style (with its unusual word coinages and sometimes flat dialogue) has tended to put barriers between his story and the reader. But Manfred's depiction of parts of the West will be read for some time to come. And his imaginative participation in the life of the American Indian is one of his greatest achievements.

—Joseph M. Flora

Other:

"Writing in the West," cassette tape (Deland, Fla.: Everett/Edwards, 1974).

Periodical Publications:

"The Evolution of a Name," *Names*, 2 (June 1954): 106-108;

"Sinclair Lewis' Funeral and In Memoriam Address," *South Dakota Review*, 7 (Winter 1969-1970): 54-78;

"Sleeping Dogs," *Fiction*, no. 8 (1974): 17-31;

"Lily Susan," *New Letters*, 41 (March 1975): 21-32;

"Hubert Horatio Humphrey: A Memoir," *Minnesota History*, 46 (Fall 1978): 87-102.

Interviews:

"An Interview with Frederick Manfred," *Studies in the Novel*, 5 (Fall 1973): 358-382;

"Milton, Manfred, and McGrath: A Conversation on Literature and Place," *Dacotah Territory*, no. 8/9 (Fall-Winter 1974-1975): 19-26.

Bibliography:

George Kellogg, *Frederick Manfred: A Bibliography* (Denver: Swallow, 1965).

References:

Anthony Arthur, "Manfred, Neihardt, and Hugh Glass: Variations on an American Epic," in *Where the West Begins*, ed. Arthur R. Huseboe and William Geyer (Sioux Falls, S.D.: Center for Western Studies, 1978), pp. 99-109;

James C. Austin, "Legend, Myth and Symbol in Frederick Manfred's *Lord Grizzly*," *Critique*, 6 (Winter 1963-1964): 122-130;

Donald Bebeau, "A Search for Voice, A Sense of Place in *The Golden Bowl*," *South Dakota Review*, 7 (Winter 1969-1970): 79-86;

Joseph M. Flora, *Frederick Manfred* (Boise: Boise State University, 1974);

Flora, "Siouxland Panorama: Frederick Manfred's *Green Earth*," *Midwestern Miscellany VII* (1979): 56-63;

Flora, "The Works of Frederick Manfred," cassette tape (Deland, Fla.: Everett/Edwards, 1975);

Madison Jones, Review of the Buckskin Man Tales, *New York Times Book Review*, 16 February 1975, p. 6;

John R. Milton, "Frederick Feikema Manfred," *Western Review*, 22 (Spring 1968): 181-196;

Milton, "Lord Grizzly: Rhythm, Form and Meaning in the Western Novel," *Western American Literature*, 1 (Spring 1966): 6-14;

Milton, "Voice from Siouxland: Frederick Feikema Manfred," *College English*, 19 (December 1957): 104-111;

Peter Oppewall, "Manfred and Calvin College," in *Where the West Begins*, pp. 86-98;

Russell Roth, "The Inception of a Saga: Frederick Manfred's 'Buckskin Man,' " *South Dakota Review*, 7 (Winter 1969-1970): 87-100;

Alan Swallow, "The Mavericks," *Critique*, 2 (Winter 1959): 88-92;

Max Westbrook, "*Riders of Judgment*: An Exercise in Ontological Criticism," *Western American Literature*, 12 (May 1977): 41-51;

Robert C. Wright, *Frederick Manfred* (New York: Twayne, 1979);

Delbert E. Wylder, "Frederick Manfred: The Quest of the Independent Writer," *Books at Iowa*, 31 (November 1979): 16-31;

Wylder, "Manfred's Indian Novel," *South Dakota Review*, 7 (Winter 1969-1970): 100-110.

Papers:

The University of Minnesota has a large collection of Manfred's literary manuscripts and correspondence.

D. KEITH MANO

(12 February 1942-)

BOOKS: *Bishop's Progress* (Boston: Houghton Mifflin, 1968);
Horn (Boston: Houghton Mifflin, 1969);
War Is Heaven! (Garden City: Doubleday, 1970);
The Death and Life of Harry Goth (New York: Knopf, 1971);
The Proselytizer (New York: Knopf, 1972);
The Bridge (Garden City: Doubleday, 1973).

D. Keith Mano graduated summa cum laude from Columbia University in 1963. He spent the next year as a Kellett Fellow in English at Clare College, Cambridge, and toured as an actor with the Marlowe Society of England. He came back to America in 1964 as a Woodrow Wilson Fellow at Columbia. He has appeared in several off-Broadway productions and toured with the National Shakespeare Company. Mano married Jo Margaret McArthur on 3 August 1964, and they had two children before their divorce in 1979. Mano left the Episcopal church for the Eastern Orthodox in 1979. He lives in New York City and is active in running the family X-Pando Corporation, which manufactures cement and other building products.

Mano's six novels emphasize religious and ethical themes and focus on contemporary issues seen from the point of view of a conservative Episcopalian. The novels are rich with comic action and written in an energetic style that occasionally caves in on itself from too much straining for effect. His narrative procedures are straightforward and conventional. His central characters always leap vividly to life, but L. J. Davis has commented fairly on Mano's "deplorable tendency to turn minor characters into unbelievable caricatures." Most readers will find Mano's fondness for scatology a flaw; he often focuses on the body functions and physical tics of his characters, presenting them in poses and acts that are repulsive and unconvincing.

Mano's first novel, *Bishop's Progress* (1968), won the MLA award for the best novel on a religious theme. It recounts the twelve days in August that Whitney Belknap, fortyish Bishop of Queens, spends in a New York City hospital being tested and prepared for a serious heart operation. The bishop is a "controversial leader of the radical movement in the Episcopalian Church" and the author of *A God for Our Time*. The bishop's medical crisis leads to two inner struggles for him: a need to cope with the pride that rises up in him as he endures the impositions on his privacy attendant upon being bedded in a room with three other patients, and his gradual shedding of his old liberal beliefs in favor of a stricter Christianity based on law. These two themes intersect ironically: as the bishop's fashionable humanism is dissipated by the human suffering in the hospital room, his religious love and understanding are toughened and matured by the same insistent human presences.

Much of the bishop's change of spirit comes about through his clash of temperaments with Dr. Snow, the wonder-working heart surgeon who plays the role of the satanic adversary. Dr. Snow is the modern humanist, the advocate of progress, a scientist-warlock who tests Bishop Belknap's faith. When the bishop enters the hospital, he wants a private room but cannot get one; and later, when he is offered one, he turns it down and chooses to maintain his human associations with patients and families whose existence he had previously, in effect, rejected. Later, the bishop learns that Dr. Snow had meant the offer of a private room as a test.

The allegorical function of Dr. Snow is intensified by the ambiguities revealed about his life and also by the problematic nature of his two assistants, Dr. Crecy and Nurse Black. One patient claims that Dr. Snow has lied about his background and that his real name is Snofski; to add to the obscurities, the menacing assistants' names cannot be found in the hospital's records of its employees. As forces of the Devil, they are defeated by Bishop Belknap in the finale, when he leaves the hospital without surgery. His salvation seems completed by his repudiation of his old liberal convictions: as he departs, he gives Dr. Snow a copy of *A God for Our Time* inscribed "To Dr. Terrence Snow. Without his inspirations this book could not have been written."

The three other patients in the bishop's room contribute to his new religious insights. When Jimmy Lopopulo, six years old, is put in with him to await a dangerous heart operation, the bishop is at first appalled by the exuberance of Jimmy's Italian Catholic family, especially when he is drawn into the family conflict over the courtship of Jimmy's sister by Sidney Kaplan, a Jew. The second patient in the room is elderly Mr. Farbstein, brought in to recuperate from serious heart surgery. He is so ill he can only goggle at the events going on around him. A foul-mouthed alcoholic, Artie Carson, occupies the third bed. When Artie learns that he has terminal cancer, he asks the bishop for help and is assigned the Book of Matthew to read.

It is in this setting of both psychic and physical suffering that Bishop Belknap learns the real meaning of his vocation. He will not let Artie read *A*

God for Our Time, rejecting his former beliefs with the observation that "Often—most often, let's face it—love is no more than a form of—well, externalized narcissism." In explaining the mysteries of suffering to Artie, the bishop can only quote Romans 7—"for without the law sin was dead"—and emphasize to Artie that the law is given by God.

One final character is important in the bishop's revision of his faith: Sarah Samson, the naive, unlettered black attendant who forces her attentions, well-meaning but clumsy, on the bishop. Her husband is a preacher, and she insists the bishop wear a lucky rabbit's foot. Bishop Belknap is at first appalled by her ignorance, but eventually understands that Sarah is one of the main instruments in the cure of his spiritual pride. The bishop faces up to the questions raised by his responses to Sarah and his fellow patients, and his honesty justifies R. V. Cassill's description of *Bishop's Progress* as "a prolonged meditation on the riddle of faith in our epoch."

Mano's second novel, *Horn*, published in 1969 but set in the 1970s, also features a clergyman. Calvin Beecher Pratt has spent all of his life in his quiet hometown, Greensprings, New York, where he teaches at the Episcopal seminary. But events conspire to change his life drastically. Pratt is disturbed to overhear a student's remark about "fat Pratt the Pharisee," topped off by the student's observation that "At least Satan got out and met people." So Pratt succumbs to his times and decides to get out and meet people, concluding "It was God's hand" that led him to Harlem's George Horn Smith and a vacancy at St. Bartholomew's Church, just around the corner from Smith's headquarters.

Pratt's first six months at St. Bartholomew's are disappointing. Not a soul attends his services, and he is bullied by his sexton, a Negro who has dropped the

J. S. Peck

D. K. Mano

name Rufus Clagger in favor of Nicholas Breakspeare. It turns out that Nicholas Breakspeare was the name of Adrian IV, the only English pope, and that the name—as well as the orange tabard with puffed sleeves, the green tights, and the orange bootlets worn by Nicholas—is part of the trappings of the Horn Power movement that dominates American Negro life.

Horn Power gets its strength from the extraordinary personality of the former middleweight boxing champion George Horn Smith, universally known as Horn for the eleven-inch growth, *cornu cutaneum,* projecting from his forehead. Horn is Caribbean-born and thought to be illiterate; but Pratt learns finally that Horn is not only literate but also quite well educated, with a library taken over from a Dr. Oddie, who had exploited Horn in his Coney Island freak show. Horn's aged and senile mother lives with him; and one night when she makes an eccentric visit to Pratt, the priest gets to meet the powerful Horn. As a result of his kindness to the mother and the rapport between the two men, Pratt finds that the insolent Breakspeare ("Nobody likes a talkin' white man") suddenly takes his sexton's duties seriously. Moreover, Pratt's church mysteriously fills up with worshipers.

But Pratt's congregation is won at the expense of John Meeker, rector of St. Catherine's Church only twenty blocks north, and the switch causes Meeker to hate Pratt. Meeker is a guilt-haunted white liberal, a scarred veteran of civil rights marches who affects a tough idiom and boasts that his congregation does not want the Bible, only love: "They are magnificent. Raw and strong." For Pratt, this approach is all wrong. At the seminary where he taught, Pratt had rejected the arguments of those who followed Bonhoeffer and Bishops Robinson and Belknap (the latter from Mano's *Bishop's Progress*), describing them as "phenomenologists; that is, they judged things by what they meant to men, not by the traditional norms of the real or the unreal." This difference in temperaments and in ideologies leads to Meeker's savage beating of Pratt in the aftermath of a Horn Power rally Pratt has inadvisedly attended.

In the climactic scenes of *Horn,* Aylbrous Purston, a contender for the movement's leadership, blows up Horn's headquarters. Horn makes his way to the rectory, and it is then that he reveals to Pratt his secret library under the church buildings. Horn leaves that night when he thinks it is safe, but Pratt learns the next day that both Horn and Breakspeare have been murdered in Morningside Park.

S. F. Caldwell said of *Horn* that it was "a fine young writer's tale about two men who might reasonably expect to find the worst in the other but instead find the best." Mano presents the big dramatic scenes skillfully, and the dialogues between Pratt and Horn are excellent vehicles for the philosophical burdens of the novel. In their last moments together, Horn tells Pratt that for the Horn Power followers human life is everything, "But human life, it isn't everything to you." Pratt answers him calmly: "No. Not everything." The treatment of Meeker, however, is less convincing and weakens the narrative. It is possible to sympathize with Mano's conservative convictions without seeing the white liberal as always such a grotesque victim of insecurities and delusions.

War Is Heaven! (1970) is Mano's apologia for America's military role in Vietnam. It is set in Camaguay, a fictitious Central American "republic" ruled by the dictator General Amayo who, with American support, is fighting Camaguayan guerril-

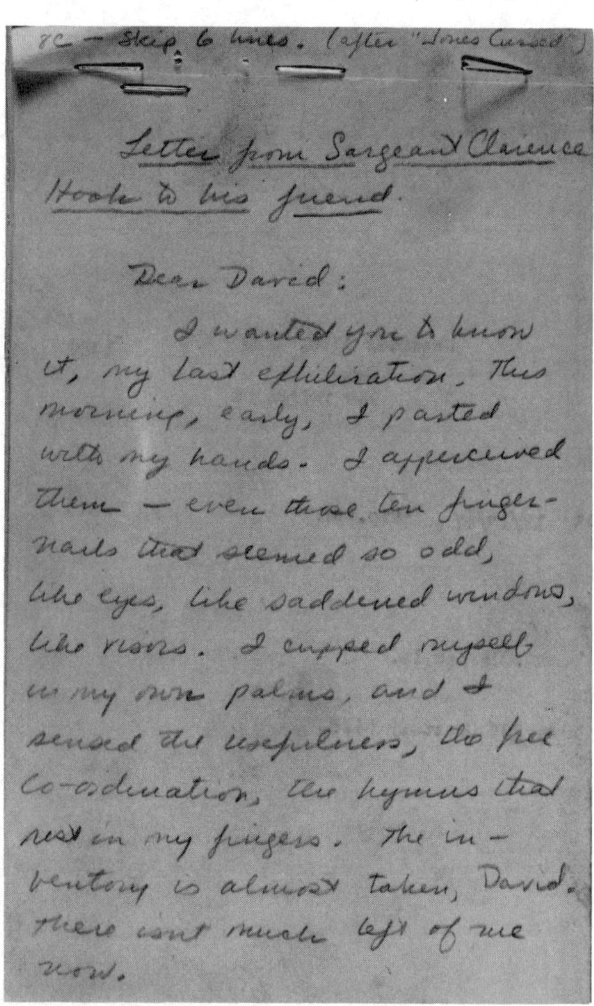
8C — Skip 6 lines. (after "Jones Cursed")

Letter from Sargeant Clarence Hook to his friend.

Dear David:

I wanted you to know it, my last exhilaration. This morning, early, I parted with my hands. I appreciated them — even those ten finger-nails that seemed so odd, like eyes, like saddened windows, like visors. I cupped myself in my own palms, and I sensed the usefulness, the free co-ordination, the hymns that rest in my fingers. The inventory is almost taken, David. There isn't much left of me now.

War Is Heaven!, *manuscript*

las in league with forces from neighboring Valencia, which has just had a communist revolution.

Like Mano's two previous novels, *War Is Heaven!* resolves into a dialogue between two characters representing opposing poles of conviction and faith. The knight of faith is Sgt. Clarence Hook, the de facto leader of a small group of U.S. Irregular Command troops who, with a contingent of undisciplined Camaguayans, are on a march through the jungle to deliver supplies. Hook's position is revealed early in a letter to a friend in the States: the war, he says, is sanctioned by "The same that sanctioned Joshua and St. Joan. The same that sanctions martyrdom." Moreover, he confides that "I am terrified now of righteous pride. Yet, at this moment, I feel totally an instrument. And I want desperately, if I can, to make myself a still better instrument of His will."

Hook's philosophical antagonist is Corpsman Andrew Jones, an intelligent young Negro just graduated from college, who feels that his expectations for life have been cruelly undercut by the war just at the moment he was poised to realize them. His bitterness contrasts sharply with Hook's faith. Hook is an expert killer, who prays over his victims, infuriating Jones, who interprets Hook's actions as hypocritical. Jones indulges in self-serving rhetoric about Americans killing innocent foreigners while blacks endure rats and other miseries of ghetto poverty, and Hook's answer to one of Jones's tirades puts the issue in clear focus:

> "Well. Let me try to explain." Hook spoke carefully, as though with an enforced patience. "I cherish two things only in life. My religion and my liberty. I am those things. In every one of its forms communism has suppressed Christianity and, with it, all human freedom. Suppressed with a ruthless and programmatic brutality. To my own way of thinking there can exist no more mortal enemy. It means to destroy me. I mean to resist it—at whatever personal cost. Is that clear enough?"
>
> "Too simple," said Jones. "Redneck simple."

In answer to Jones's taunts about "Thou shalt not kill," Hook asserts:

> But there comes a time when the sanctity of one's life, the strict purity becomes self-regarding and sinful. Paul says, "Respect the spirit of the law, not the letter." I've thought about this. If merely to keep my conscience clear, to comfort myself in a display of my own moral perfectness, I permit others to suffer and be killed—then I have killed as surely as I killed in that hut. And I believe in damnation, Jones. In heaven and hell. In eternal punishment and in eternal joy. It may well be that I have damned myself by these acts. I have to accept that. But better to lay down one's soul for another than to sit isolated, preparing for my own sterile and loveless salvation. That is what I believe.

Hook finally dies after the mission has proved a failure. Attended by a gloating Jones, he dies a painful, protracted death from wounds. Hook's death scene is long and exhausting, brilliantly written, and, with the dialogues between Hook and Jones, it forms a provocative discourse on war. The outstanding weakness of *War Is Heaven!* is the failure of the march through the jungle to generate any real suspense, leaving the debate and the characterizations in the plot void. Without being unfair to Hook's position, one could also criticize with justice the characterization of Jones. The antiwar position is represented too crudely by the bitter corpsman, for a lot of people opposed the war in Vietnam for principles as selfless as those cherished by the heroic Sergeant Hook.

Although all of Mano's novels have strong comic elements, none of them approaches the black farce of *The Death and Life of Harry Goth* (1971). Harry is one of five brothers—Philip Pray Goth, Eustace 'Til Goth, Harry The Goth, William Lord Goth, and Frankie Comes Goth—who got their middle names from a phrase much cherished by their mother: "Pray 'Til The Lord Comes Again." (John Again Goth was miscarried.) The family has a manufacturing firm—Cleano Corp., specializing in the Johnny Do toilet brush—run by William Howard Taft (Daddy) Goth, five foot three, tanned, and hard of belly.

The brothers are a diverse lot. Crew-cut Bill is vice-president and general manager of Cleano Corp., and he is a bully. Frankie has spent seven of his thirty-four years in prison and reformatory; he has a mindless daughter called Sin-sin, whose boyfriend, Adolph Fishbein, is a power in Students for a Democratic Society. Eustace 'Til Goth is a mindless giant, 6′4″, 230 pounds, controlled only by ninety-year-old Grandma Goth, who keeps thwacking Eustace in the testicles with a rod of correction. Although Grandma Goth has no real appetite, she eats voraciously "to agitate her tired system." Eustace also has a daughter, seventeen-year-old Mary

Magdalene Goth, his by a young Christian charity worker he had raped. Mary Magdalene, although introverted, is a good student. She has read *Wuthering Heights* seven times. Philip Goth resides in a monastery and signs his cards Fra Chrysostom.

Harry The Goth is married to voluptuous Lee-lee, but Harry is suffering from a wasting disease that renders him ineffectual as a husband. After a frustrating day trying to sell Johnny Do's, the hapless Harry goes to his ancient physician, Dr. Thanatobos who, after the proper humiliations of Harry's tired body, tells him he is dying of leukemia. Harry goes home despondent, only to find Lee-lee mysteriously dead in the bathtub. Lee-lee's funeral is a big event held at De Luigi's Fabulous Funeral Palace, formerly De Luigi's Famous Casa Espana, and it is presided over by a morbid Mafia lackey, Johnny (the Big Embalmer) Costello. The Funeral Palace is a front where the Mafia's hits are butchered and disposed of piece by piece in the corpses of the disemboweled dead. The high point of the funeral for Harry is his meeting an in-law, George Freezy Slocum, who, as he says, is "in" cryogenics, freezing the dear departed until their happy awakenings in a far-off age of medical miracles.

Harry's misadventures continue, including an episode in which he loses his glasses into the grinding mechanical innards of a peep show. Invigorated by a blood transfusion, Harry takes an office girl to an upstate motel; but this affair only leads to new frustrations and Harry ends up sneaking in to visit Fra Chrysostom, his brother, in the monastery. He is then treated to a conventional lecture on Christian contempt for the world, a theme he is by now sorely in need of.

Upon his return to the city, Harry takes a medicine derived from pansy seeds, and it promptly bloats his stomach and causes all of his hair to fall out. Penniless and seemingly moribund, Harry retreats to his house, blacks out the windows, and goes out only to get food at Gulbenkian's Exotic Food Emporium, a grocery chosen solely because it takes his American Express card. Thus Harry survives, meagerly, on a diet of such foods as shredded tongues of wildebeests and flies in orange mucilage, while Myrtle Goth, his pet turtle, makes do with "praying mantises impregnated with molasses and holding, in their claws, rare European berries."

Events happen fast. Grandma Goth dies (more business for the Big Embalmer); Frankie and Harry break into the Cleano Corp. and trash the place but are unfortunately nabbed by Daddy, who has bear-trapped the office; Harry takes over Grandma's job as Eustace's attendant, and he so terrifies Eustace by donning Grandma's gown and nightcap and picking up her stick that the poor imbecile flees down the street in panic, taking refuge in a subway tunnel where he is immediately killed by a train. (Another assignment for the Big Embalmer.) Eventually Harry learns that Dr. Thanatobos is dead of leukemia, having projected his own disease onto Harry, who is suffering only from pernicious anemia. *The Death and Life of Harry Goth* is talented black humor, deft and wicked, reminiscent of Evelyn Waugh, and generally well liked by critics (Arthur Curley called it "a comic delight"; Tom McHale thought it was "a marvelous book").

In *The Proselytizer* (1972) Mano returns to his most convincingly portrayed milieu, an Episcopalian congregation, and mixes comic and serious elements in an imaginative way. The Church of the Resurrection in the town of New Faith was made from blueprints drawn up for an intended primate house in the municipal zoo. The flock is in the pastoral care of Reverend Father Lambert McKee, B.A. Dartmouth, M.A. Oxford. A wealthy man, Father McKee is married to the former Chloe McKee, who is much younger and much less pious, affects bralessness, and inserts scatological epithets into dull patches in Father McKee's sermons.

Among the parishioners are Kris Lane and his mother, Thelma, the latter confined in a rigid back brace and suffering from the baseless conviction that Father McKee yearns secretly for her. Kris is wealthy, muscular, and squat of body. He is crucifer at the Church of the Resurrection, a romantic figure in his black eye patch and one black glove, made necessary, he explains, by his having been struck by a bolt of lightning that went in his eye and out his hand. The choir is made up of Esther Lee and Gretchen Kurtz, altos; Jenny Fish and Ellen Kelly, sopranos; and Flower Lee, Chinese bass. Kris, who has great charm, having graduated from Tom Teller's TV commercial school, has seduced each of these young choristers, their seductions all having been followed in but a few days by their baptisms.

Kris is well prepared for his proselytizing efforts. He has a retreat atop Lane's Bluff, a 940-acre lot overlooking New Faith, where he has erected a huge cross next to six tall, dancing fountains lighted by spotlights that accommodate the whole color spectrum in "one-to-one correspondence" with the tones of a Bach toccata erupting from dozens of loudspeakers. Each seduction is recorded on movie film and stored in a film library of numerous such exploits, each properly dated. For each convert a file card is kept, recording such data as date of baptism,

I.Q., hang-ups, suggested foreplay, and religious rating. Kris's downfall comes when, sick with frustration over Chloe McKee, he enters her bedroom one night, attempts first to rape her and then to strangle her, is apprehended, and driven away.

Much of the story of Kris Lane and his proselytizing seems not much more than an extended bad joke in not always good taste, funny as many of the incidents are. But the novel is redeemed to a great extent by the family across the street from Kris, David and Edna Smith with their four young children (and a fifth on the way). They live in financial want, on a day-to-day basis, David being an easygoing man of no special talents or noticeable ambition but a good father and loving husband. Edna is a big woman, much overweight, whose intelligence and good spirit keep the family on an even keel. They help along a novel one reviewer called "A miss for Mano this time."

The Bridge (1973) has some moments of very fine suspense. It opens with a prologue set in the Adirondacks in the twenty-seventh century. Odd things are going on. A man named Oscar is taking his three wives in a Model T (everyone else is driving one, too) to a religious ceremony called the Feast of Eater that is being held in a large crater. The characters wear clothes of animal skins. Scientific knowledge is two hundred years ahead of technology, and everyone uses the word *Priest* as an oath in place of the word *Christ*. Furthermore, one of Oscar's wives teaches speech therapy to "young Appalachia savages," whose "evolved speech was of groans and clacking yips, set behind the mouth."

The religious rite is conducted by a priest known as a "dom," who wears a black, rubberized suit with a black hood and a left sleeve that is scarlet below the biceps. The left arm is amputated at the elbow. He invites the faithful to "Come and feed at my arm. I have given my flesh for you." The response is, "I accept this gift of grace and I am full of thanks." The congregation, who have come in two thousand Model T's, are there to shoot mortars at the crater—each mortar shoots five hundred rounds a day, or fifteen hundred between Good Monday and Eater. The targets are humans. The prologue concludes with the ritual words:

> I perform this act in the name of Priest and in the name of man, who is, who shall always be, the only master of God's great creation. I kill that I may know life. Go in love without rancor—bring the grace of Priest to those who eat and those who are eaten.

Oscar recites these words as he fires the mortar. In the epilogue, it is the third day, the mortars are quiet, and Oscar and his wives are at a huge communion rail eating chunks of human flesh and drinking human blood.

The body of the novel, in which these proceedings are illuminated, is titled "The True Book of Priest," and it is set in New York City and the Hudson River area in the year 2035, known as the Ecological Age. "The True Book" tells the story of Dominick Priest, a rebel in a society that had overwhelmed itself in a fury of adulation for all life. In the Ecological Age everyone wore a special suit to protect himself from the swarming insect life, and plant life grew unrestrained everywhere. Human sewage had been outlawed by the Ecological Decree, resulting in a distasteful and unnourishing E-diet that left only a "negligible, odorless trace."

The main narrative concerns Dominick Priest's efforts to evade the decree of 7 July 2035 ordering everyone to commit suicide to stop "heinous crimes of murder and pollution committed by our race throughout history." Dominick, who has been incarcerated in a run-down Yankee Stadium, wants to cross the Hudson and return to his wife in their hometown upriver. His journey is harrowing. He has to cross the river by slithering across a bridge cable high in the air, and then he must avoid the police charged with enforcing the suicide decree. His walking trip upriver affords a view of life in the Ecological Age and evokes some of Mano's most effective satiric barbs. When Priest meets a stranger, the man comes up to him and puts his hand over Priest's genitals. This is a "sensitivity greeting" which had "evolved from encounter-group Psychology in the 1980's." Priest falls in with an aged Christian priest named Xavier Paul, who has circumvented many of the restrictions on diet and behavior for years. Priest learns about Christianity from him, is baptized, and is preparing for his first Communion when Paul is trampled by a fleeing deer herd. Priest makes his way alone to his home, finds his wife dead, and kills Ogilvy, the cruel officer in charge of the death scene. He then eats the flesh of Ogilvy's left arm, watched by a lesbian community who will become the ten Eves of Priest in the new society built around the ritual cannibalism they have just witnessed. Thus the events in the prologue and epilogue are explained.

Although *The Bridge* shows considerable narrative skill and develops a satisfying suspense story, the premise is hardly convincing. Indeed, the tone of the work is perhaps close to hysterical, and the "profound spiritual resonance" spoken of by one critic is largely bogus.

Although he wrote six novels between 1968 and 1973, Mano had no more novels published in the 1970s. His seventh novel, entitled "Take Five," he expects to finish "late in 1980." He says of it: "It's a very large work—probably 700 pages—and it will be a recapitulation and a synthesis of the themes of my first six books." While at work on "Take Five," he has written a great deal of magazine material. His expose of Colorado won the *Playboy* Best Non-Fiction Award for 1977, and he was at one time book editor of *Esquire.* He has been a regular contributor to the *National Review,* writing columns which he calls "the most consistent gauge of my thinking." His hatred for much of the life of his time seems to have peaked in *The Bridge.* It will be interesting to see what direction his career as a novelist takes in the 1980s.

—Frank Day

Periodical Publications:

"Reflections of a Christian Pornographer," *Christianity and Literature,* 28 (Spring 1979): 5-11;
"Rocky Mountain Nirvana," *Playboy,* 24 (March 1977): 80-82, 86, 178-180, 182-183.

JACK MATTHEWS
(22 July 1925-)

SELECTED BOOKS: *Bitter Knowledge: Short Stories* (New York: Scribners, 1964);
An Almanac for Twilight (Chapel Hill: University of North Carolina Press, 1966);
Hanger Stout, Awake! (New York: Harcourt, Brace & World, 1967);
Beyond the Bridge (New York: Harcourt, Brace & World, 1970);
The Tale of Asa Bean (New York: Harcourt Brace Jovanovich, 1971);
The Charisma Campaigns (New York: Harcourt Brace Jovanovich, 1972);
Pictures of the Journey Back (New York: Harcourt Brace Jovanovich, 1973);
Collecting Rare Books for Pleasure and Profit (New York: Putnam's, 1977);
Tales of the Ohio Land: Short Stories (Columbus: Ohio Historical Society, 1978).

Jack Matthews was born in Columbus, Ohio, educated at Ohio State University (where he received a B.A. in English and Classical Greek in 1949 and an M.A. in English in 1954), and has taught at Ohio University since 1964. His work benefits from its firm rootedness in place even if his national reputation seems to suffer from it. In the *Los Angeles Times* (27 February 1972) Herbert Gold pointed out that although Matthews had had six books published at that time, his readership remained small (though ardent), and "he seems to speak from a region of silence and exile."

His first book-length fiction publication, *Bitter Knowledge* (1964), was a collection of thirteen stories that illustrate Matthews's penchant for taking a simple situation and demonstrating the existence of the marvelous in what might have seemed cliche. Although the stories are strong, their themes are somewhat repetitious. They are best seen as practice in finding the right detail or the proper minor character to develop his plots—skills which he sharpens in the later novels and exhibits in his recent collection of short stories.

It was with *Hanger Stout, Awake!* (1967) that Matthews claimed a place in contemporary letters. Clyde Stout, better known by his nickname "Hanger," gives new meaning to the phrase, "hang in there!" His one real talent, aside from auto mechanics, is free-hanging: he can hang from a tree limb or door jamb longer than anyone else in the country. As Hanger narrates his own story, he unknowingly reveals his incredible naivete, and when he meets the gambler-con man Mr. Comisky, the novel becomes a classic tale of innocence confronted with evil. Even when Mr. Comisky sets up a major competition with the four-minute hanging man from Detroit, Hanger Stout is essentially unchanged by the supposed temptations of the "big time" because he is genuinely and simply concerned about the business of living and loving. Although after rigorous training he wins his match, instead of getting the promised prize money, Hanger is laughed at by the entire town. From all appearances, Hanger now stands as a lonely scapegoat, but both Hanger and the reader know that he has proved himself. And the reader senses further that Hanger will survive even the army, into which he is being drafted as the novel closes.

Matthews's second published novel, *Beyond the Bridge* (1970) uses an actual event of recent history as point of departure. Neil, who narrates by means of a diary, was on the Silver Bridge over the Ohio River between Ohio and West Virginia during rush hour on 15 December 1967, when the bridge collapsed. Narrowly escaping death, he realizes that the event offers him an opportunity to shed his middle-class responsibilities. So he impulsively begins a new life "beyond the bridge," confident that the insurance money from his presumed death will adequately provide for the family he is abandoning.

Although a short book of only 164 pages, *Beyond the Bridge* is strong and complete. Neil's old life impinges upon the new one, but he genuinely and strenuously tries to avoid his old mistakes. Having escaped physical death, Neil tries to avoid the psychological death that had been creeping toward him, and he sorrows for those around him in the West Virginia town where he has settled who, in failing to see "its wasted beauty," experience another form of death, surely. The two months of entries from Neil's diary record observations and ruminations by a man who wants to sort things out for himself, who would like to avoid what he fears is impending "craziness," and who wants to think about questions which all men, in some form or other, ask themselves. One of his final entries, "We take on new imprisonments when we despair of understanding the old," distills the major theme of the book.

The Tale of Asa Bean (1971) also concentrates on a somewhat eccentric character, but unlike the first two protagonists, this one is obviously extraordinary. Asa Bean has a genius level IQ, and he calls himself an Aphorist, Ironist, and Existential Hero. He works in the A&P warehouse loading crates, lives with his stupid sister Earlene and her Marxist real-estate salesman husband, Roy Scobie. Asa often exhibits his vocabulary of polysyllabic words inappropriately; so it is only just that Durango, with whom Asa works in the warehouse, calls him Soy Bean and seldom allows his own vocabulary to include words of more (or less) than four letters. The result is what a reviewer in the *New York Times Book Review* called "most delicious triteness"; and, he observed, "Banality rendered with full affection is one of Matthews' most appealing talents."

Central to the book is Asa's intention to vandalize a painting by Rubens at the local art museum. Seeing the acronymic basis of his name as "*A*narchist, *S*hawnee, *A*ssassin," Asa plans the act because, given the burden of his enormous intellect, the totally free and gratuitous act of the existential hero is the only act he cannot understand. He is saved from committing his crime and suffering the consequences, but not until the reader has been treated to funny, sad, and provocative moments. There is a problem of overindulgence in the book in spite of its brevity; and occasionally the asides, although many of them are at the very heart of the book's purpose, become cloying and too much like academic humor. As in earlier works, the book's strength lies in Matthews's presentation of lovable characters and small surprises and insights which work cumulatively rather than by leading toward a single overwhelming conclusion.

The Charisma Campaigns (1972) is considered by many to be Matthews's best work so far. It is the story of a middle-aged but still boyish car dealer named Rex McCoy, an all-American con man who speaks in slogans, banalities, and cliches cast in the form of headlines: "Honesty Found Best Policy," for example. Narrated in the form of an American tall tale, the novel tells the story of the investigation of Rex (the Real McCoy) by a psychologist named Professor Homer Winslow, who wants to study charisma. When McCoy learns, from the results of the professor's study, that he sells more cars than any other dealer in the state because he has charisma, he is thrilled. But he refuses to move on to "the big time," recognizing that he is a big man within his sphere of influence and taking pleasure in his one success. He even has the satisfaction of knowing that the big city psychiatrist who has come to study him has a compulsion to frequent *his* used-car lot.

The Charisma Campaigns was widely and well reviewed when it appeared, and many reviewers praised Matthews's revival of the realistic novel about small-town life. Martin Levin, writing in the

Max Schaible

135

And so it goes, on and on., trying to convert me into Adlai Stevenson or Eugene McCarthy or somebody similar damned body.

Yes, we're all caught up in the charisma game, flashing out these goddam signals from inside our heads, trying to knock every body dead and trying not to get infected by the poisonous of their charisma.

Clowns and fools, that's what we all are. But the game is fun, if you see it right, and understand that it is a goddam game, and understand that any body who doesn't think we're all crazy is crazy.

The other day I bought a fine cane. I can walk real well with it, now, and I feel like a million dollars.

I go down the street my string tie and my cane, and people look up when they see me and smile. They don't hold the Pattie Nieder thing against me, I'm happy to say.

This is a great little town, and I love it.

I can imagine them saying, there's old Rex, the son of a bitch. He's a real character, that jasper is, but he could talk the president of the United States into buying Russian Imperial Bonds.

That's the kind of son of a bitch I am, and I don't mind admitting it.

THE END

One day Bucky came up to me while I was typing this account, and he said, "Rex, just whatcha doing, typing all the time?"

"I'm writing my memoirs," I told him.

"You're what?" he asked.

"Writing my memoirs."

"What's at?" he said.

"An account of my life," I said.

He looked a second, and then nodded slowly and switched the toothpick from one side to the other.

When he left the office, I printed a sign with my felt-tipped marker, that said, "WHERE THERE'S LIFE THERE'S HOPE, AND SOMETIMES EVEN WHERE THERE ISN'T."

A-6

The Charisma Campaigns, *revised typescript*

New York Times Book Review, admired Matthews's "inclination to be upbeat about the offbeat," and his presentation of "a parade of failures, crazies, ingrates and fools," whom he "marvels at" instead of condemning.

Matthews's most recent novel is *Pictures of the Journey Back* (1973). A modern picaresque novel, the story takes place during a trip from Wichita, Kansas, to Colorado with several detours along the way. Because he considers it the "right thing to do," J. Dan Swope, an alcoholic ex-rodeo cowboy, forces Laurel Burch, a confused and alienated young hippy, to visit her dying mother. Riding with them is Laurel's lover, Jeffrey Martin, an aspiring film-maker who takes pictures of the journey. The clash of values represented by the generations in the novel and the clash between the positions of the observer and of the participants are explored throughout, as the point of view shifts among the members of the group in order to present a powerful drama of emotion and intellect.

As they travel through the vast openness of the Kansas plains, Laurel feels lost and without hope; but, as Elmer Suderman points out, Jeffrey "sees all the uncluttered land not as a threat but a challenge to be clarified and articulated" through the use of his camera. Just as Jeffrey hopes to give shape and clarity to the previously "unfocused" landscape, Matthews the novelist tries to give a similar shape and clarity to the moral landscape of all his characters. One way he provides clarity is by naming; for example, the pickup is named Betty Bump, and as Suderman notes, Jeffrey is pleased to learn this fact because the name "gives it a character, and he and Laurel and J. Dan can speak of it in mutually intelligent terms."

The act of naming is most often associated with the poet rather than the novelist, and although Matthews has published only one book of poems, *An Almanac for Twilight* (1966), his technique as a fiction writer is often poetic. The search for the telling emblem, apparent in all his work, implies a concern with presenting the most concise, and thus the most intense, version of a story. Another poetic characteristic of Matthews's fiction is his concern with language. Matthews seems to use linguistic experimentation to keep a freshness in his work and to avoid the dangers of the formulaic approach to fiction; as he himself said: "The gift of experimentation manifests itself in stories, poems, and plays as inventiveness, richness and subtlety of metaphor and thematic resonance."

The merging of his poetic concerns with his fictional craft occurs most consistently in Matthews's short stories, over two hundred of which have been published. Appearing in all the leading quarterlies and little magazines (and regularly in the prize anthologies), these stories establish Matthews as one of the contemporary masters of the genre. Perhaps the richest illustration of this is his latest book, *Tales of the Ohio Land* (1978), which skillfully blends history and myth with the art of storytelling. The cumulative power of these ten stories surpasses that of many novels, capturing a convincing sense of the past and of place that is rare today.

Jack Matthews's development as a novelist can be traced by observing each novel's increasing complexity. Yet from *Hanger Stout, Awake!*, which concentrates on a single character who tells his own story, to *Pictures of the Journey Back*, which involves three major characters and multiple points of view, Matthews continues to probe the possibilities of human interaction. In his words, "every story can be viewed as, in varying degrees, an occasion and ceremony of passionate learning." Thus he has not developed a patented formula for his work but has allowed his voice to be molded by the demands of his chosen subjects. Matthews is a "literary" writer, as critics continually note, one whose works gain by rereading and thoughtful examination. Perhaps that is the reason his readership, though faithful, remains smaller than his champions believe he deserves.

—*Bin Ramke*

Other:

The Writer's Signature, edited by Matthews and Elaine Hemley (New York: Scott, Foresman, 1972);

Archetypal Themes in the Modern Story, edited by Matthews (New York: St. Martin's Press, 1973);

George Belden, *Belden, The White Chief*, introduction by Matthews (Athens: Ohio University Press, 1974).

Periodical Publications:

FICTION:

"The Knife," *Yale Review*, 58 (Winter 1968): 249-262;

"Another Story," *Sewanee Review*, 77 (Summer 1969): 426-439;

"A Genealogy of Trees and Flesh," *Iowa Review*, 2 (Spring 1971): 49-52;

"On the Shore of Chad Creek," *Virginia Quarterly Review*, 47 (Spring 1971): 235-245;

"The Amnesia Ballet," *Mundus Artium*, 4 (Summer 1971): 74-85;

"The Colonel's Birthday Party," *Ohio Review*, 13 (Spring 1972): 71-81;
"The Kitten," *Kansas Quarterly*, 4 (Summer 1972): 98-104;
"First the Legs and Last the Heart," *Carleton Miscellany*, 13 (Fall/Winter 1972-1973): 4-16;
"The Terrible Mrs. Bird," *Western Humanities Review*, 27 (Summer 1973): 241-253;
"Invaders of the Field," *Yale Review*, 63 (Autumn 1973): 69-79;
"The Burial," *Georgia Review*, 28 (Winter 1974): 658-673.

NONFICTION:
"Browning and Neoplatonism," *Victorian Newsletter*, 28 (Fall 1965): 9-12;
"Writing a First Novel," *Writer* (February 1968): 20-21;
"The Writer as Semanticist," *RE: Arts and Letters*, 1 (Spring 1968): 44-51;
"The Descent," and comments on "The Descent," *English Record*, 19 (February 1969): 26;
"Poetry as the Act of Language," *Ohio University Review*, 1 (Fall 1970): 5-15;
"Print and the Oral Generation," *Michigan Quarterly Review*, 10 (Fall 1971): 236-244;
"What Are You Doing There? What Are You Doing Here? A View of the Jesse Hill Ford Case," *Georgia Review*, 26 (Summer 1972): 121-144.

References:

Stanley W. Lindberg, "One Alternative to Black Humor: The Satire of Jack Matthews," *Studies in Contemporary Satire*, 1 (Spring 1974): 17-26;
Elmer Suderman, "Jack Matthews and the Shape of Human Feelings," *Critique*, 21 (1979): 38-48.

PETER MATTHIESSEN
(22 May 1927-)

BOOKS: *Race Rock* (New York: Harper, 1954; London: Heinemann, 1955);
Partisans (New York: Viking, 1955; London: Secker & Warburg, 1956);
Wildlife in America (New York: Viking, 1959; London: Deutsch, 1960);
Raditzer (New York: Viking, 1961; London: Heinemann, 1962);
The Cloud Forest: A Chronicle of the South American Wilderness (New York: Viking, 1961; London: Deutsch, 1962);
Under the Mountain Wall: A Chronicle of Two Seasons in the Stone Age (New York: Viking, 1962; London: Heinemann, 1963);
At Play in the Fields of the Lord (New York: Random House, 1965; London: Heinemann, 1966);
The Shorebirds of North America, ed. Gardner D. Stout (New York: Viking, 1967);
Oomingmak: The Expedition to the Musk Ox Island in the Bering Sea (New York & London: Hastings House, 1967);
Sal Si Puedes: Cesar Chavez and the New American Revolution (New York: Random House, 1969);
Blue Meridian: The Search for the Great White Shark (New York: Random House, 1971);
Everglades: Selections from the Writings of Peter Matthiessen, ed. Paul Brooks (New York: Sierra Club / Ballantine, 1971);
Seal Pool (Garden City: Doubleday, 1972); republished as *The Great Auk Escape* (London: Angus & Robertson, 1974);
The Tree Where Man Was Born, with Eliot Porter's *The African Experience* (New York: Dutton, 1972; London: Collins, 1972);
Far Tortuga (New York: Random House, 1975);
The Snow Leopard (New York: Random House, 1978).

Peter Matthiessen's increasingly substantial reputation as a novelist rests firmly on two remarkable books. Although he wrote three promising early novels, his two best-known works of fiction are surely *At Play in the Fields of the Lord* (1965), a rich surrealistic panorama of civilization and savagery, innocence and depravity among the primitive Indians of the Amazon, and *Far Tortuga* (1975), a graphically and stylistically experimental work about an ill-fated Caribbean turtle-fishing boat and its doomed crew.

Remarkable as Matthiessen's fiction is, many critics feel that his greatest achievement is as a naturalist and nature writer. Out of twenty-five years of traveling in remote areas he has produced meticulously observed, often poetically written books and articles on a range of topics—American wildlife, shore birds, the wilds of South America, a war tribe of New Guinea, life on an arctic island, and the fastnesses of East Africa. His travel writings are all characterized by an attempt to present natural and human subjects that are strange, remote, and alien and to do so with fidelity to detail but with a fluid, sometimes rich style that brings out the beauty in rough, often crude, subjects. There is also in much of Matthiessen's work an almost chilling objectivity, which sometimes couples with a natural pessimism, to lend some of his writing a gloomy cast.

Born in New York City of a well-to-do family, educated at Hotchkiss and Yale (B.A. 1950), married in 1950 to Patsy Southgate, the strikingly beautiful daughter of a socialite and diplomat, Matthiessen was in the early 1950s the center of an attractive crowd of expatriates in Paris that included William Styron, George Plimpton, James Baldwin, Terry Southern, and Irwin Shaw—a glittering group of intellectuals that became "The *Paris Review* Crowd." In the 1950s the Matthiessens' apartment was, as Gay Talese says, "as much a meeting place for young American literati as was Gertrude Stein's apartment in the Twenties." Matthiessen, along with Harold L. Humes, was the cofounder of the *Paris Review*, and its first fiction editor.

In Paris Matthiessen wrote his first novel, *Race Rock* (1954). It is a relatively conventional psychological novel about upper-middle-class Americans struggling to cope with the burdens of their own personal histories and traditions as well as with their uncontrollable and often malevolent psyches. The main character, George McConville, is the offspring of a rich, old, decaying family on the New England coast. Aimless and confused, he is unable to escape his past or accept the responsibility of a mature future, specifically responsibility for the pregnancy of his mistress, Eve Murry. Like George, Eve is the embodiment of American traditions and values without direction. George's friend, Sam Rubicam, Eve's ex-husband, is sensitive, effete, artistic, weak, and directionless. All three are emotionally overpowered by Cady Shipmen, their brutal childhood companion, who is socially less acceptable than George, Sam, and Eve, but possesses an elemental savagery and life force that fascinates as well as threatens them. Cady's barely latent violence is echoed by Eve's intense suppressed sexuality, directed toward her father.

Race Rock moves fluidly backward and forward in time, shifting between a disturbed reunion of the major characters in the present and their memories of the conflicts and emotions that molded them in childhood. The emotional confusions of George, Sam, and Eve produce a rising tension that finally leads to a violent explosion of hatred. In a series of confrontations, masks are stripped off, hatreds bared; and George and Sam come to some kind of terms with their own immaturity. Ironically, the only character to die as a result of the conflict among George, Sam, and Cady is an Indian friend who has mistakenly tied his fate to that of the white men.

Although *Race Rock* does not anticipate the experimental techniques or exotic subject matter of Matthiessen's later fiction, the novel shows the author's early concern with fundamental emotions and with the tension between primitive vitality and the veneer of civilization. Matthiessen's association with the *Paris Review* assured wide attention for his novel, and most critics found *Race Rock* a strong work but technically somewhat awkward and lacking in focus. Both the novel's theme and its problems with characterization are represented by a scrap of dialogue between George and Eve—George: "It's hard to know what to do in these mixed-up times." Eve: "What right have you to be mixed-up?"

Matthiessen followed *Race Rock* with *Partisans* (1955), a short novel which obviously derived from his dabblings with the political avant-garde of Paris. Reflecting liberal disillusion with Communism, the book describes an American newspaperman's search for an old Communist, Jacobi, who is betrayed and hunted by his own people. Heavily ideological, the novel is filled with set-piece declarations of political and personal philosophy. The grim humorlessness that makes Matthiessen's characterization in *Partisans* a trifle tedious works more effectively in terms of the setting and atmosphere—the squalid and threatening underside of Paris. The book is heavy with both paranoia and legitimate menace, as the protagonist, Barney Sand, finds himself searching through a sordid world of poverty and betrayal. Despite his idealism, or perhaps because of it, he cannot find a pure cause to adopt. Ultimately, he feels betrayed by his own philosophical heritage as well (his father was an American diplomat). Critics again wrote of Matthiessen as a developing talent, and they praised the moral seriousness of *Partisans* but criticized its tendentiousness. As William Goyen wrote in the *New York Times*, "The characters seem only mouthpieces. . . . They do, however, impress one with this young author's serious attempt to find answers to ancient and serious questions. . . ."

In the late 1950s Matthiessen was divorced and began the series of travels that were to mark the next quarter century of his life. He also wrote his third novel, *Raditzer* (1961), a short book thematically reminiscent of Conrad's *The Nigger of the Narcissus* (1897; Matthiessen acknowledges Conrad and Dostoevski as the two major influences on his writing). The narrator of *Raditzer*, Charles Stark, is a predictable young white Anglo-Saxon Protestant liberal in the navy during World War II. Fellow sailor Raditzer attaches himself to Stark with a perverse friendship that is alternately fawning and abusive. A ratlike survivor of slums and gutters, Raditzer is a loathsome Jonah, despised by everyone; and he brings out the worst in every character in the novel, except Stark who accepts a kind of responsibility as Raditzer's keeper and protector. Raditzer's corrupt behavior finally provokes the ship's crew to want to murder him, and Stark's courage is tested when he remains the man's defender.

In making Raditzer both loathsome and believable Matthiessen showed great skill in characterization: "After two decades of hand-to-mouth survival his malnutrition had spread like a cancer to his mind." A skillful ear for dialect and an immediacy in sketching scenes of violence and depravity saved *Raditzer*'s moral weightiness from being wearisome, and the novel proved Matthiessen's ability to project his imagination into worlds far removed from that of the intellectual upper-middle class.

With *At Play in the Fields of the Lord* Matthiessen, until then a promising young novelist, became, as Jim Harrison wrote in the *Nation*, "our most eccentric major writer." With strong Conradian overtones but no specific Conradian analogue, Matthiessen tells the story of the corruption and virtual destruction of a totally primitive and innocent tribe of Amazonian Indians, the Niaruna, by the forces of "civilization," represented by a small group of myopic missionaries who come to do good but do very badly, a corrupt local military dictator, and an odd pair of soldiers of fortune washed up like jetsam on the banks of the jungle river.

Matthiessen later called *At Play in the Fields of the Lord* "ornate, full of 'fine writing,' " but "essentially an old-fashioned novel." Even so, the book shows a virtuosity and richness that few traditional novels exhibit. There is immense stylistic facility in shifting from surreal dream and drug sequences to scrupulous realistic descriptions of tropical nature. Characterization is deep and various; even the sinisterly pious and meddlesome chief of the missionaries, Les Huben, with his ridiculous religious huckstering ("We surely thank the Lord for His new outboard motor. . . . Yours for a greater harvest of souls") is a believable character rather than a caricature.

The novel's tension between vulnerable innocence and corrupt civilization is the leitmotiv of all Matthiessen's major work as a naturalist—a concern for fragile traditional cultures and natural ecologies in the onslaught of civilized destruction. In *At Play in the Fields of the Lord* Matthiessen brilliantly embodies this theme in the novel's style, endowing the writing with an almost vegetable lushness that lends description of characters and setting the semblance of organic life. He creates a subtle balance between the healthy, gardenlike fecundity of the jungle with its naked, primitive Indians and the rot of the drunken, bestial fleshiness that characterizes the world of the mercenaries and the corrupt locals. Most skillfully drawn is the sickeningly sweet, artificial life of the missionaries, whose coy and simpering rhetoric and self-conscious energy contrast with the Indians' natural spirits.

The most remarkable character in *At Play in the Fields of the Lord* is its hero, Lewis Meriwether Moon, the soldier of fortune who makes the transition from partner in the mercenary team of "Wolfie & Moon: Small Wars and Demolition" to self-proclaimed savior of the Indians. Through drugs, visionary experience, personal sensitivity, and strength of character, Moon, a Cheyenne Indian himself, launches an inward quest that leaves him, on the last page of the novel, finding, or refinding, a primal identity: "Laid naked to the sun and sky, he felt himself open like a flower. Soon he slept. At dark he built an enormous fire, in celebration of the only man beneath the eye of Heaven."

In the ten years after the publication of *At Play in the Fields of the Lord* Matthiessen published some important nonfiction—notably his fine account of his travels in East Africa entitled *The Tree Where Man Was Born* (1972)—but no novels. *Far Tortuga*, his most recent novel, proved to be as radical a departure as *At Play in the Fields of the Lord*; but where the early book was ornate, *Far Tortuga* is bare and stripped, completely lean prose. The deep penetration of character and psychology that characterized *At Play in the Fields of the Lord* yields to an almost disturbing objectivity in *Far Tortuga*, an absolute, realistic reproduction of surface phenomena—dialogue, noises, colors, shapes. From the startling opening image of the sun beginning the day ("The sun, coming hard around the world: the island rises from the sea, sinks, rises, holds.") to the image frozen in a blank expanse of empty paper at the foot of the last page ("a figure alongshore, and white birds towarding"), the novel is full of sound, light, and image but completely lacking the authorial explanation of meaning that was criticized in earlier novels.

The only characters in *Far Tortuga* are the mulatto crew of a run-down turtle-fishing boat plying the modern Caribbean in the declining days of both turtle and turtle fisherman. With these men one finds another of those threatened and vanishing traditional cultures that are the main subject of all Matthiessen's mature fiction and nonfiction. The crew of the boat, the *Lillias Eden*, exhibits a variety of personalities. Dominant is the captain, Raib Avers, whose reckless, authoritarian search for turtles and his determination to prove himself as good as the traditional standards of excellence in his trade, "de coptains of dat time," endangers all their lives; one can hardly avoid thinking of Ahab in *Moby-Dick*. Juxtaposed to Avers is the life-loving Speedy whose cheerful existential humanity defies the aura of doom hanging over the ship's last trip. "If the book has a hero, it's him," says Matthiessen, and like Ishmael, he is the last survivor of the wreck of the *Lillias Eden*.

The radical format of *Far Tortuga* makes the novel a structural tour de force and assured a range of critical reaction, from Terrence des Pres's "an outright masterpiece," to Bruce Allen's judgment that the novel is "an adventurous failure . . . lacking a harmonious whole." Matthiessen strips his prose of connectives, transitions, and most modifiers, leaving a collection of images, sounds, and fragments of dialect. These are spread like macaronic poetry between punctuating expanses of white space and pictographic symbols—a smudge for the death of a character, a long horizontal line for the horizon. Visually, the book recalls Ezra Pound's *Cantos* or Charles Olson's *Maximus* poems. And perhaps this is the best way to approach *Far Tortuga*—as a tone poem through which flows a tide of language, image, and detail forming the rich lives of the characters. Matthiessen calls himself "a closet poet" and says that writing *Far Tortuga* was an attempt to create a novel akin to a musical score, and sometimes "like writing haiku." The result is a book that approaches pure poetry as closely as anything in modern American fiction.

Although Matthiessen says he wishes to be remembered particularly for his novels and is currently outlining a new one, he is perhaps better known as a nature writer and naturalist, and the themes and concerns of his fiction pervade his nonfiction as well. His extensive wanderings around America and the world have produced a number of distinguished accounts, both personal and objective, which give him claim, as Peter Farb says, to being "beyond dispute, the finest nature writer working today."

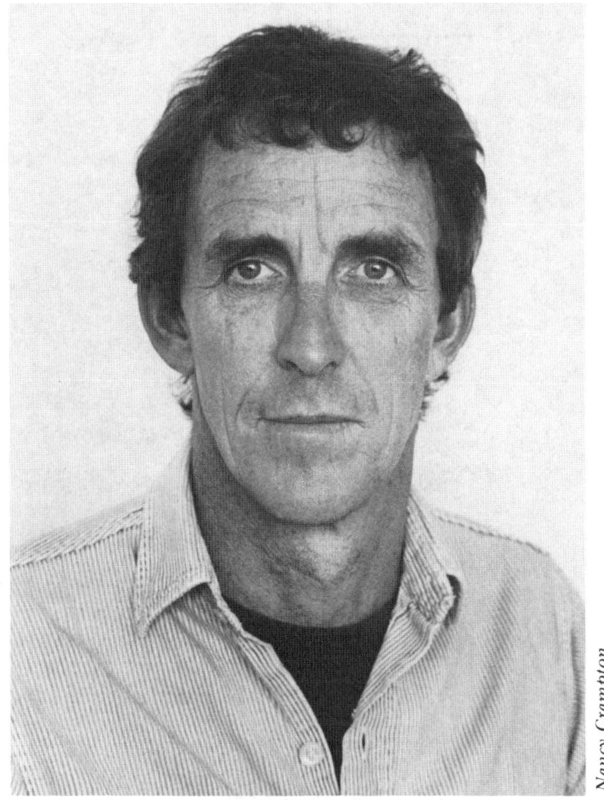
Nancy Crampton

Peter Matthiessen

Nearly all Matthiessen's nature and travel writing has demonstrated both the author's cameralike eye and his determination to provide an inflexible objectivity and honesty. Although Matthiessen calls himself a romantic, he completely resists romanticizing nature, chronicling his subjects with loving care but doing nothing to pretty them up. The depravity of the Indians of Tierra del Fuego, the ugly killing of a zebra foal by a dog pack, and the sordid grimness of a Nepalese village are impassively presented just as effectively as the beauties of the African steppe or the rain forest. Matthiessen, who is a lean, craggily handsome fifty-three, says lightly, "Most people think of me as a nature writer—eighty-five years old with a butterfly net." But anyone who has really read his nature writing knows that Matthiessen's attitude toward the natural world is hardly that of a fatuous admirer in his dotage. He brings to his work a skeptical, wary professionalism, the uncompromising eye of a scientist, and an almost cynical and often bitter knowledge of the vulnerability of nature.

X-1 text starts — p. 3

~~Setting Copy~~

1

At four miles above sea level, Martin Quarrier, on silver wings, was pierced by celestial light: ~~he marvelled at the force of the Almighty~~. The snow peaks of the Andes burst from clouds which hid the earth, sparkling in the sun like gates of Paradise, ~~Heaven,~~ and the blue dome of the mountain sky was as pure as ~~the Lord's~~ pain. Where the clouds parted, dark lakes ~~tarns~~ reflected wild demonic gleams, but the red roofs of the villages on the lone road traversing the sierra were signals of ~~signalled~~ sane harmonies, good will to men.

Shyly he expressed his joy to his wife Hazel, but Hazel only turned away again and peered out of the window, one hand fisted at ~~to~~ her mouth and the other flat upon her collarbone, in a way she had when she was apprehensive ~~most absorbed.~~ He stole a look at her. As always, he was moved, but she was not an easy person to reach out to; he drew back when she caught him watching. "You shouldn't have filled Billy's ~~his~~ head with all that business," she accused him, her hand dropping out of habit to tug down the hem of her skirt. She was a very large woman with coarse black hair tied up in back, baring her ears; the rude bun, which had collapsed during the journey, reminded her husband of a loose rat's nest he had once found in the barn. Her pale face looked lye-scrubbed, and a sour though not humorless expression camouflaged natural ~~native~~ handsomeness, as if

Revised typescript

Of Matthiessen's nonfiction, two works stand out as of particular quality. His account of his travels in East Africa, *The Tree Where Man Was Born*, is, as Paul Zweig says, "a masterpiece of understated prose and exacting description." The book, published with handsome photographs by Eliot Porter, offers an enormous amount of anthropological, zoological, and geological information, always woven into a compelling portrait of a land, its people, and wildlife. In *The Tree Where Man Was Born*, as in much of Matthiessen's best writing, there are long passages in which the intensity of the texture of the writing thickens, and the reader senses, as with good oil paintings, levels of composition and depths at which elements of that composition function. Matthiessen's canvas is suffused with a variety of light, and the images parade with an almost musical orchestration, so that as with Monet's series of paintings of haystacks, one sees Matthiessen's Africa in myriad ways. Only occasionally, and at crucial moments, does Matthiessen's sensitive consciousness penetrate to interpret, and then powerfully, as in his description of a dying lioness: "I felt sick, as if all the waste, and loss of life, the harm one brings to oneself and others, had been drawn to a point in this lonely passage between light and darkness."

Matthiessen's personal sensibility is more in evidence in his latest book, *The Snow Leopard* (1978), winner of a National Book Award in 1979. Written out of his increasing interest in and commitment to Zen, *The Snow Leopard* recounts the difficult trip Matthiessen made with naturalist George Schaller to the remotest parts of Nepal. Like Moon's inward journey in *At Play in the Fields of the Lord*, Matthiessen's trip was a search for himself and an exercise in self-awareness. Matthiessen's second wife, Deborah Love Matthiessen, whom he had married in 1963, died of cancer in 1972. In the next year, when he and Schaller walked across the Himalayas, Matthiessen's thoughts were very much on his wife, and he made of the trip a deliberate attempt to confront the primal mysteries of life and death. The arduous trek through much beauty, but also much squalor, hardship, and loneliness, is the journal of an introspective man whose consciousness is hypersensitive to the meaning of the natural world and its importance for man. In the bittersweet awareness that informs *The Snow Leopard*, one senses continually the presence of Matthiessen as a man who believes, as he has said, that "There's something mysterious and strange and violent in the world—something random in the air that shamans know how to get in touch with."

In fiction and in nonfiction, Peter Matthiessen is one of the shamans of literature. He puts his audience in touch with worlds and forces which transcend common experience. His works abound with *wildness*, in the sense that Thoreau used that word, and he constantly forces the reader to an apprehension of the natural world and to an unavoidable sharing of Matthiessen's conviction that that world matters. *At Play in the Fields of the Lord* and *Far Tortuga*, his two finest and most important novels, share with his best nonfiction the presentation of "other" worlds—human existences strange, alien, and unfamiliar to "civilized" Western man. These existences—the world of the Niaruna, the instinctive and often superstitious world of the turtle fishers—exhibit an elemental violence, an intensity of emotion, a depth of interconnection with the natural world, simplistic but traditional standards of quality, and a depth and sincerity of human conviction and commitment that the "civilized" Western world lacks. Always, this alternate human experience is presented with a careful, even ruthless, objectivity and fidelity to reality.

It is simplistic, but relatively accurate, to divide Matthiessen's career as a novelist into two parts. The first three novels—*Race Rock*, *Partisans*, and *Raditzer*—are relatively conventional Bildungsromans. Young men come to terms with their confused world, exorcise some of their psychological demons, and emerge from the rites of passage sadder but wiser.

With *At Play in the Fields of the Lord* and *Far Tortuga*, however, Matthiessen has produced two novels which lay legitimate claim to very serious consideration. Both project the reader into intense fictional states in which human feeling is intensified and man exhibits an identification with the natural world in which he lives. The identification gives meaning to life and denies the sterility that marks more sophisticated twentieth-century experience. Self-knowledge and self-respect characterize the worlds of the Niaruna and the turtle fishermen. But both worlds hang on the brink of extinction, and in the tragic consciousness of impending doom and loss lies the greatness of Matthiessen's sensibility.

—John L. Cobbs

Periodical Publications:

"Sadie," *Atlantic Monthly*, 187 (January 1951): 55-58;

"The Fifth Day," *Atlantic Monthly*, 188 (September 1951): 60-63;

"Martin's Beach," *Botteghe Oscure*, 10 (1952): 310-318;

"The Tower of the Four Winds," *Cornhill*, 166 (Summer 1952): 143-149;

"A Replacement," *Paris Review*, 1 (February 1953): 46-56;

"Late in the Season," *New World Writing* (May 1953): 320-328;

"Lina," *Cornhill*, 169 (Fall 1956): 53-58;

"Traveling Man," *Harper's*, 214 (February 1957): 57-65;

"The Wolves of Aguila," *Harper's Bazaar*, 27 (August 1958): 76-150;

"Annals of Crime," *New Yorker*, 34 (1 November 1958): 119-145;

"Midnight Turning Gray," *Saturday Evening Post*, 236 (28 September 1963): 56-67;

"A Reporter at Large: Sand and Wind and Waves," *New Yorker*, 41 (3 April 1965): 116-144;

"The Last Great Strand: Corkscrew Swamp Sanctuary," *Audubon*, 69 (March 1967): 64-71;

"The River-Eater," *Audubon*, 72 (March 1970): 52;

"Kipahulu: From Cinders to the Sea," *Audubon*, 72 (May 1970): 10-23;

"Lignumvitae—the Last Key," *Audubon*, 74 (January 1972): 20-31;

"In the Dragon Islands," *Audubon*, 75 (September 1973): 4-49;

"The Craft of Fiction in *Far Tortuga*," *Paris Review*, 15 (Winter 1974): 39-82;

"Happy Days," *Audubon*, 77 (November 1975): 64-95;

"A Track on the Beach," *Audubon*, 79 (March 1977): 68-106;

"Horse Latitudes," *Antaeus*, 29 (Spring 1978): 7-14;

"A Whale in Spring," *Westigan Review of Poetry*, 3 (1978): 38-39;

"Stop the GO Road," *Audubon*, 81 (January 1979): 48-65;

"My Turn: The Price of Tellico," *Newsweek*, 94 (17 December 1979): 21;

"How to Kill a Valley," *New York Review of Books*, 27 (7 February 1980): 31-36.

References:

Henry Allen, "Quest for the Snow Leopard's Secret," *Washington Post*, 13 December 1978, D: 1, 13, 15;

D Nicholas, *Peter Matthiessen: A Bibliography: 1951-1979* (Canoga Park, Cal.: Orirana Press, 1979).

CORMAC MCCARTHY

(20 July 1933-)

BOOKS: *The Orchard Keeper* (New York: Random House, 1965; London: Deutsch, 1966);

Outer Dark (New York: Random House, 1968; London: Deutsch, 1970);

Child of God (New York: Random House, 1974; London: Chatto & Windus, 1975);

Suttree (New York: Random House, 1979).

Cormac McCarthy has been considered a strong new talent in American fiction since his first novel, *The Orchard Keeper* (1965), was awarded the 1965 William Faulkner Foundation Award for the best first novel by an American. With the exception of *Outer Dark* (1968), all of McCarthy's novels are set in his native eastern Tennessee, either in the mountain communities of the Smokies or in Knoxville. Reviewers have often placed him in the Southern Gothic tradition of William Faulkner, Carson McCullers, and Flannery O'Connor, as his novels have in common with theirs a rustic and sometimes dark humor, intense characters, and violent plots; McCarthy shares as well their development of universal themes within a highly particularized fictional world, their seriousness of vision, and their vigorous exploitation of the English language.

Born in Providence, Rhode Island, McCarthy moved with his parents to Knoxville, Tennessee, at the age of four. His parents, Charles Joseph and Gladys McGrail McCarthy, were Roman Catholic, and their son attended Catholic High School in Knoxville. He entered the University of Tennessee as a liberal arts major in 1951-1952 and then left school to serve for four years in the U.S. Air Force. In 1957 he returned to the university, where he was encouraged by his professors to develop his writing ability. Through the English department he was chosen to receive the Ingram-Merrill Award for creative writing in 1960. While in school he began work on his first novel, and later in 1960 he left the university without having earned a degree, for the purpose of pursuing a writing career. He told an interviewer, "I don't know why I started writing. . . . I don't know why anybody does it. Maybe they're bored, or failures at something else. Look at Spiro Agnew. He's now a novelist." The facetious tone of this comment notwithstanding, it seems true that McCarthy had not long planned to be a novelist, but rather had embraced his career gradually as his talent became evident to him and to his teachers during his college years.

Though his fiction is deeply anchored in his home state of Tennessee, McCarthy has not been a sedentary writer. *The Orchard Keeper* was composed in Sevier County, Tennessee, in Asheville, North Carolina, and in Chicago. When the novel was published on 5 May 1965, McCarthy had already been awarded a fellowship for a year of travel abroad by the American Academy of Arts and Letters. He embarked for Europe in the early summer of 1965 with a rough draft of his second novel in hand. On shipboard he met a singer, Anne deLisle, of Hamble, England, whom he subsequently married. With additional support from a Rockefeller Foundation grant (1966-1968) he traveled in Europe two years longer, spending long periods in London, Paris, and on the island of Ibiza in the Balearics, revising *Outer Dark* "three or four times" during that time. The novel was finished before he and his wife returned to the United States in 1967 and settled on a small farm in Rockford, Tennessee. In 1969 McCarthy received a Guggenheim Fellowship for creative fiction writing.

After the publication of his third novel, *Child of God*, in 1974, McCarthy wrote "The Gardener's Son" for the "Visions" series of original television dramas on public television. He collaborated on the project with film director Richard Pearce, who was interested in making a film based on a historical event and who asked McCarthy to write the television play about a murder committed in 1876 in the textile village of Graniteville, South Carolina. His story of Rob McEvoy, the crippled son of a laboring family who murders the scion of the Gregg family, owners of the mill, is, like his novels, dark and complex. Of McEvoy McCarthy said, "The kid was a natural rebel, probably just a troublemaker in real life. But in our film he has a certain nobility. He stands up and says, 'No, this is intolerable and I want to do something about it.' " McCarthy was involved in the making of the film as well, accompanying Pearce on a search for actors throughout South Carolina. The film was first shown in January of 1977.

February of 1979 saw the publication of *Suttree*, a work McCarthy began after he had completed *The Orchard Keeper* and which he worked on throughout the late 1960s and 1970s, interrupting its composition to write the two shorter novels preceding it. Currently he is working on a fifth novel.

The Orchard Keeper is technically ambitious for a first novel. The story centers on young John Wesley Rattner and his coming into manhood in the isolation of the East Tennessee mountains. But the novel is composed of three main narrative strands, of which the last to be introduced is John Wesley's. The other two center on his two mentors, the men who teach him most by precept and by example. The first is Marion Sylder, the young bootlegger who kills John Wesley's father in self-defense and hides the body in an abandoned insecticide pit in an old peach orchard. This occurs in 1934, when John Wesley is six. The second is the "orchard keeper," old Arthur Ownby, who discovers the corpse and keeps watch over it for seven years until he feels its soul is at rest. Neither knows the other, nor the identity of the dead man, and neither meets John Wesley until 1940. For the most part, the novel is developed chronologically, from 1934 to 1941, with a prologue and final episode set in 1948, but it is built of discrete episodes focusing on the various characters, with little exposition to clarify the relation in time among them. Italicized passages present flashbacks to earlier events, most of these representing the present memories of a main character.

Through these characters the novel explores the relationship between the individual integrity and independence achievable in the remote natural world of the mountains and the societal obligations and strictures imposed by the community of men. The latter are most often represented by inflexible legal codes, such as the taxation of liquor, and by impersonal technological features, such as the cold and ugly tank erected atop the mountain, which so offends Ownby that he shoots an *x* on its surface to protest its encroachment on his natural environment. (The *x* as the Greek letter *chi* also represents the old man's rejection of this new mechanistic god that would replace the old human one.) Such structures of civilization make outlaws of both Sylder and Ownby, though each is possessed of more generosity, fair-mindedness, and discipline than the petty thug, Jefferson Gifford, the local constable, or his incompetent accomplice, Legwater, the humane officer who requires seven shots to kill a stray dog he has wounded with the first. Near the end of the novel, both of John Wesley's surrogate fathers are incarcerated by the machinery of the new order. Sylder is jailed and beaten by Gifford; Ownby is locked up for an indefinite term in the mental hospital.

John Wesley's grief for his friends leads him to reject the new order of the modern world. There is nothing sentimental about the boy. He has lived in the natural world of fecundity and decay, helping himself to its resources when he could use them, teaching himself to be a hunter and trapper. His gesture of repudiation of the world of bureaucracy

Dan Moore

Cormac McCarthy

and technology is accomplished in the context of his sportsman's experience. He had found an ailing sparrowhawk that he first tried to nurse back to health; but when it died, he took it to the county courthouse to collect the bounty on it. Months later, after the arrests of Sylder and Ownby, John Wesley returns to the courthouse to buy the bird back, in a rejection of the purposes of the world of courts and laws. But he is further horrified to learn that the bird has been burned, "somehow figuring still that they must be kept, must have some value or use commensurate with a dollar other than the fact of their demise." Accepting death as part of the natural order of things does not imply an acceptance of waste. The fate of the sparrowhawk reinforces the lesson of Sylder and Ownby: "And thow people in jail and beat up on em. . . . And old men in the crazy house." In a final gesture of repudiation John Wesley thrusts the money onto the counter and leaves, to return to the region briefly seven years later when the change has accomplished itself completely: "No avatar, no scion, no vestige of that people remains. On the lips of the strange race that now dwells there their names are myth, legend, dust."

The corpse decaying over seven years in the old peach orchard finally functions as an analogue for the race of John Wesley's fathers. The seven years expired, Ownby tells authorities of its presence and it is burned to ash, then sifted by the humane officer, Legwater, who hopes to find the platinum plate reputed to have been in its skull. His disappointment in finding nothing of value in the ashes leads him to kill Ownby's aged hound in a final demonstration of modern man's devotion to waste. When he returns to Red Branch at twenty-one, John Wesley is an anachronism, a ghost of an earlier age. But he has inherited from Ownby the role of orchard keeper, the guardian of old ways and values, and this is no tragic fate.

The plot of *The Orchard Keeper* is basically simple, but its episodic and periodic development makes for more complexity in form. McCarthy employs a mythic technique so infused with naturalistic detail that the possibilities for mythic interpretation are scarcely apparent until very near the end, when the design in the fabric suddenly comes into clear focus. *Outer Dark* is similar in structure to McCarthy's first novel, but much more sparse and clean lined, and its allegorical nature is made apparent with its very opening—a prologue that introduces three mysterious figures who roam the landscape:

> *THEY CRESTED OUT on the bluff in the late afternoon sun with their shadows long on the sawgrass and burnt sedge, moving single file and slowly high above the river and with something of its own implacability . . . and then dropping under the crest of the hill into a fold of blue shadow with light touching them about the head in spurious sanctity until they had gone on for such a time as saw the sun down altogether and they moved in shadow altogether which suited them very well.*

The movements of these emissaries of darkness are reported in several brief italicized passages until near the end of the novel, when their path twice crosses that of Culla Holme, the main character, and they have a profound effect on his fate.

In *The Orchard Keeper* the main characters were placed in a region so remote as to be, at least initially, beyond the reach of civil law. The characters of *Outer Dark*, Culla Holme and his sister Rinthy, live in the mountains in an unspecified locale, four miles from the nearest store and outside of any human community—in such isolation that they seem beyond the reach of any custom, common law, or moral law regulating the relations of human beings. They are guilty of incest, and their story opens as Rinthy goes into labor and delivers their son. Culla, however, is not unaware of the violation he has committed, and, driven by shame and guilt, he leaves the infant to perish in the woods and tells Rinthy it died at birth. But the baby is found by an old grotesque tinker, himself an outcast of human society; and Rinthy, intuiting this with some kind of maternal instinct, sets off to find the tinker and her child. Culla in turn wanders in search of Rinthy—or so he tells those who ask.

The title of the novel comes from Matthew 8:9-12, as William Schafer has pointed out, and is an allusion to Christ's prediction that the faithless will be cast out to wander in outer darkness. The very different fates of Culla and Rinthy, who share equally in their original sin, are parables of the fates of the faithful and the lost. Rinthy's faith is so much an integral part of her as to be almost a biological process. The mere thought of her baby, or any suggestion that she is close to finding it, causes her milk to flow, and in her months of searching her milk never dries up. She is treated with kindness by the strangers she meets, even when they sense her sin. It is as though her steadiness of purpose and her willingness to take responsibility for her child exempt her from harsh moral judgment. She is a natural creature like the doe she is often compared to.

But Culla's wandering is harsh and full of threat. He is followed in his travels by the dark figures who appear in the prologue and who dispense death and violence wherever they go. Culla is greeted with suspicion and false justice by the people he meets, often being accused of the crimes committed by the three "foot soldiers of the apocalypse," as one reviewer has called them. The distrust of the people he meets seems to arise from their instinctive recognition of his state of sin.

Culla's sin is not merely the commission of incest, however. Rather, the state of his soul—his lack of faith and of grace—seems to be both his sin and his punishment. Culla claims to be searching, but in fact he makes no inquiry, follows no lead that might bring him to Rinthy and his child. In his soul-sickness he avoids human ties, just as he has discarded his own son. The world he wanders in is described in terms of a spiritual wasteland, a limbo, in which all beings partake of the satanic. Some, like the three dark marauders, are consistently presented in demonic terms; but Culla himself becomes identified with them as a denizen of the outer dark, even though they are not precisely his companions and though when he meets them face to face, they inflict on him a stern retribution.

The lack of differentiation among the satanic and their victims is most clearly exemplified in a remarkable scene in which Culla encounters a group of drovers with an immense herd of hogs. The devilish nature of all hogs—those with cloven hoofs and those without—is established in Culla's conversation with one of the drovers, a genial man who is later carried over the river bluff to his death when the demon hogs stampede. The drovers howl in satanic despair at this disaster, yet are shown to contribute to it "as if they were no true swineherds but disciples of darkness got among these charges to herd them to their doom." Subsequently they blame Culla for the event, and at the instigation of a diabolic parson who arrives "fending flies," they drive him to follow the hogs over the bluff to save himself from hanging. Culla is ostensibly a victim, but by jumping he identifies himself with the demon hogs. He himself is a disciple of darkness and thus a victim of darkness. His pain is the pain of Milton's outcast Prince of Darkness.

Though he travels the same terrain as Rinthy, though his history is nearly identical to hers, he is brought to a different end because of his spiritual blindness. He tells one of his acquaintances that his father taught him that a man makes his own luck. The contrast between Culla's and Rinthy's fates is meant to reinforce the notion that Culla's world of darkness is of his own choosing, his own making. Rinthy, too, suffers, as any living creature must. She finds the tinker, but he refuses to give her the child. In his own bitterness he judges that she is not fit to have it. She never understands what has happened to her, nor why. But her searching is itself a kind of salvation, and finally she sleeps, whereas Culla continues to wander.

The novel is so centered on guilt and retribution that it is largely structured around scenes of judgment. Culla is brought to answer for several crimes and is invariably found guilty by his human and satanic inquisitors, both real and dreamed. Rinthy is found guilty only once, by the grotesque tinker. The ultimate scene of judgment, however, is brought about by the three dark emissaries in a repulsive version of divine retribution. Culla finds them in the tinker's camp where they have hanged the tinker (apparently in retribution for his denial of Rinthy's right to her son) and where they are in custody of the child. In emblem of his divided nature and of the opposed natures of his parents, the boy is scarred over one half of his body and blind in one eye.

With every word and action infused with threat, the leader of the three challenges Culla to own the child, much as Solomon used the threat of death to determine the mother of the disputed infant. Culla's shame prevents his acknowledgment of his human tie to the boy, and the bearded "prophet" cuts the child's throat and delivers him up to the cannibalistic enjoyment of one of his fellows. The judgment is ruthless but fair. Yet it provides no resolution to Culla's trouble. The final scene finds him several years later, still wandering. He watches a blind man progressing toward a swamp, with no insight to the relevance of such an image: "He wondered where the blind man was going and did he know how the road ended. Someone should tell a blind man before setting him out that way."

Lester Ballard, the central character of *Child of God*, is also an outcast and an outlaw, one alienated from human society and from anything else that might nurture the human soul within him. He is a child of God, "much like yourself perhaps," the narrator tells us. Yet what Ballard endures and what he does is outside the experience of most of us. The novel chronicles the process of Ballard's alienation and consequent abandonment of any of the standards that govern human behavior. Its opening scene introduces the dominant theme of dispossession, as Ballard's small farm is auctioned out from under him for nonpayment of taxes. When he protests, brandishing a rifle, he is hit from behind with the blunt side of an ax.

In one of several scenes in which Ballard's neighbors in Sevier County, Tennessee, recall events of his childhood and youth by way of explaining what he has become, one among them concludes that Ballard was never quite right after being hit with the ax. But these brief scenes of idle community dialogue—the source of a region's legends—stand in opposition to the novel's third-person narrative of the twenty-seventh year of Ballard's life. Ballard's neighbors mean to account for his behavior, but their explanations are only partial ones. In recalling his mother's abandoning him and his father, and his father's subsequent suicide, Lester's matter-of-fact report of this event in the nearby store, or his bullying behavior toward other children, the members of his community provide important background information, but they draw conclusions that do not fit the larger pattern as it is shown to the reader.

The pattern is that of dispossession. Ballard at twenty-seven is a man with almost nothing—no family, no home, no profession, no acceptance within the community. He is divested of all but his basic human needs and his ability to shoot a rifle with deadly accuracy. A neighbor allows him to live in an abandoned house on his property, and Ballard does the best he can to fill his needs within the limitations he is given, even as his range of choices becomes more and more constricted.

Ballard's predicament is dramatized primarily in terms of his human need for sexual activity. Considered peculiar, Ballard finds it nearly impossible to approach the women he knows. They rebuff him not because they are chaste, nor because he is crude and they are not, but because he is in some way marked as a pariah. As his parents and the law have dispossessed him of portions of his birthright, so do the women he approaches deny him the function of a normal male. This process of denial reaches a culmination when Ballard discovers by the roadside a sleeping whore who has been abandoned wearing only a thin nightgown. He wakes her to ask if she is cold, only to be attacked, vilified, accused of rape, and temporarily jailed.

Given his status as social outcast, Ballard does what he can to satisfy his need. In an inexorable progression of events that bear a horrifyingly logical relationship to each other, Ballard relieves his sexual frustration first by spying on a couple parked at a turnaround on the mountain road and masturbating on their car fender; then by taking home the body of a young woman who has died there of carbon monoxide poisoning so that he can possess her sexually; and finally—after his borrowed house and the woman's corpse burn—by killing people in order to possess them. He becomes a necrophile not by choice but by necessity; Ballard has an instinctive understanding of the young idiot child of the first of his murdered victims, who chews off the legs of a bird because "He wanted it to where it couldn't run off. . . ."

When the house burns Ballard retreats to a cave in the mountain, living more and more like an animal, yet still a child of God with his all-too-human perversions. Denied the society of the living, Ballard peoples his cave with a society of the dead. Suspect and pursued, he struggles to preserve his life and belongings, only dimly aware that he has become alien even from himself, dressing in women's clothing and wondering at night what stuff he is made of.

But unlike Culla Holme of *Outer Dark*, who is doomed to perpetual "blindness," Ballard does have brief glimmerings of what has happened to him, and this apparently brings an end to his life as an outlaw. The process of dispossession does not end, but Ballard seems finally to accept it. Spring brings a

Not thre weeks before this he was run out of Fort Smith Arkansas for having congress with a goat. Yes, Lady, that is what I said. Goat.

Why damn my eyes if I wont shoot the son of a bitch, said another man, and drew a pistol from his boot and leveled it and fired.

The teamster next to the kid produced a knife from his clothing and ~~xxxxx~~ unseamed the tent ~~with it~~ and stepped outside. The kid followed. They ran ~~low and ducked~~ across the mud toward the hotel ~~in the next lot~~. By now gunfire was general within the tent and people were running out like rats. As they rounded the corner the structure swayed and settled to the ground like a tattered huge and ~~sutured~~ medusa trailing guywires, stained with smoke and grease and birdlime.

~~When the entered the bar the judge was standing at the corner~~

The judge was already standing at the corner of the bar when they entered. He raised a glass but not to them. They went on to the rear and the kid bought whiskeys for himself and the teamster. The teamster drained his and looked at the kid. Or he seemed to. One eye was slightly walled and you couldnt be sure of his gaze. The kid looked toward the front where the judge stood. The bar, waist high to most men, came just to his fingertips and he stood with his hands placed flatwise on the wood, slightly leaning, as if about to give an address. Other men were coming in now, some bleeding. A few gathered about the judge. In the melee the preacher had escaped and a posse was being drawn up to pursue him.

Judge, said one of the men, how did you come to have the goods on that no account?

Goods? said the judge.

Revised typescript

consciousness of soul-sickness, and Ballard dreams of his death—the final dispossession. In an act that can be construed as one of self-destruction, Ballard tries to kill the man who had bought his home at auction, but this victim shoots back and Ballard loses his arm. A mob takes him from the hospital and forces him to lead them to the corpses of his victims, but he eludes them in the caverns. After three days of wandering underground he emerges, and after a startling vision of a little boy's face in the rear window of a church bus—a face he feels is his own—he returns to the hospital where he says he belongs.

Though the story of Lester Ballard seems a case study in depravity, and though the progression of events from cause to effect seems inevitable and logical, the emphasis of this novel is not on the psychological motivation of a psychopathic character. In fact, the narrative is designed to insist upon both the mystery of Ballard's fate and the fact that he is not inherently different from his neighbors. He dies in a state mental hospital and his corpse is turned over to the students of the state medical university, who perform upon it acts perhaps no less ghoulish than Ballard had performed on his victims. Ballard and his victims both become subjects of human inquiry. Ballard, like the students, has acted in pursuit of a kind of knowledge. The suggestions of Sevier County residents that Ballard was born different, that he was always beyond the pale, and that his family had bad blood ignore his essential humanity and thus emphasize the inadequacy of man's explanations for the violence and aberrations committed by other men. Neither does the chronicle of Ballard's progress in depravity really explain, though it allows us to see human needs and motivations at work.

The horror of this novel is that its author insists that Ballard is one of us—an example of what can go wrong with a child of God. In a set piece that serves as a kind of parable of Ballard's and of everyman's life, Ballard takes an ax to a blacksmith for sharpening, whereupon the smith delivers a discourse on the proper dressing of an ax. Lecturing as he works, he eulogizes attention to detail and careful provision of the proper conditions for fine strong steel that will hold a sharp edge. The tool must be fashioned for its function from start to finish: "Do the least part of it wrong," the smith concludes, "and ye'd just as well to do it all wrong." The implication is that it is the Craftsman who is to blame for the flawed creation that Ballard is. Through inattention or indifference—or perhaps by design—such children of God are permitted to come into existence. Earlier, and more pointedly, the smith says, "Some people will poke around at somethin else and leave the tool they're heatin to perdition but the proper thing is to fetch her out the minute she shows the color of grace." Lester Ballard, like Culla Holme, is without grace. Dispossessed of his earthly parents, he seems dispossessed of God the Father as well. He is an outcast child, unable to establish ties with the human family or to find guidance from outside of himself. As such, he—like Culla Holme—is an emblem of twentieth-century man with his loss of faith and of the sustaining traditions of Christian belief, with his human instincts perverted, and with his love of death rather than life.

Suttree again focuses on a single character who is a misfit and who suffers from a kind of soul-sickness. This is a big novel, a tremendously ambitious one that employs some of the themes and techniques of the two that precede it but with a much richer texture and on a much larger canvas. In *Suttree* McCarthy moves from the mountain settings of his earlier novels into the city of Knoxville, but his main character has a wider range of mobility and experience, and there are scenes in the Smokies, Asheville, Gatlinburg, on the French Broad River, and in other less localized places in East Tennessee, as well as in various parts of Knoxville. Most of the action is centered in the McAnally Flats section of Knoxville—a seamy district where the substrata of the black and white residents of the city exist, a half mile from the river where Cornelius (Buddy) Suttree lives in an old houseboat. Where community life was sketched in broad strokes in the earlier novels, in *Suttree* the community of drunks, derelicts, and dregs among whom Suttree lives is drawn in detail. Dozens of its denizens are introduced, and of these a good number emerge as fully conceived characters.

Suttree is a young man of a prominent Knoxville family, who—like McCarthy himself—attended Catholic schools and then the University of Tennessee. While there Suttree met a girl from a small mountain town, married her, gave her a son, and then abandoned her to retreat to Knoxville. There he makes a meager living as a fisherman in the filthy Tennessee River and drinks with the inhabitants of McAnally Flats.

The novel relates the events of Suttree's life from October of 1950, when he is in the workhouse, until the spring of 1955, when he leaves the city. Opening in the summer of 1951, its structure is predominantly chronological except for the major dislocation in time in which the novel's second most important character, Gene Harrogate, is introduced, and his life is brought into confluence with Suttree's while both are in the workhouse. Throughout, McCarthy employs a flexible third-person narration that often takes on the diction and perspective of its subject to merge almost without seam into a first-person point of view. The narration fluctuates smoothly between objective, central, and first-person perspectives, providing some of the intimate acquaintance with the main character that interior monologue might, without ever seeming to report anything but the experience of the character. Inner obsessions are projected into the external world, and inner experience such as dreaming is not differentiated from external, sensory experience. The technique is marvelously suited to emphasizing what McCarthy had used the contrasting experiences of Culla and Rinthy Holme in *Outer Dark* to demonstrate: that the world one inhabits is of one's own making, that the outer world one experiences is as much a projection of one's state of mind and soul as is the inner world of dream.

Suttree's world is often portrayed as a wasteland, the city in its state of ruin functioning as an emblem for Western civilization. Suttree is a refugee from life, especially from family life and from the life of work and achievement advocated by his father. Half in pursuit of death, half in morbid fear of it, Suttree in fact feels that he is twinned with death, since his twin brother died in infancy. He suffers, the narrator tells us, a "subtle obsession with uniqueness," and part of his rejection of his family is his compulsive denial of the genetic repetition among family members—the very repetition that makes life possible.

Dreading both death and life, Suttree has withdrawn, but neither life nor death will leave him alone. His decayed habitation is teeming with animal and vegetable life reclaiming the ruins of the city. His impoverished friends, all of whom have fewer intellectual and physical resources than he does, continually touch his humanity, drawing him into familial relations, involving him in their lives and their pain. And because he cannot divorce himself from life, Suttree is constantly confronted with death. In grim succession, his son dies, then a young girl with whom he shares a mock-pastoral love affair in one of the episodes set outside of Knoxville, then a series of his friends from McAnally Flats. His sensibilities, both physical and emotional, are constantly harrowed. His head is battered by a drunk wielding an electric floor buffer, by a boat thief slinging rocks, and by frequent exposure to alcohol of inferior quality; he witnesses other men's pain, is coerced into helping a friend submerge the corpse of his father who had died six months before, and descends into the sewers under the city to find Harrogate, who has nearly killed himself by dynamiting a sewage restraining wall, thinking it led to a bank vault.

Intelligent, often admirable, even sane by the standards of this novel, Suttree is yet another wanderer in outer darkness, a victim of life and circumstance. The metaphoric implications of existence in the wasteland of McAnally Flats are most explicitly stated in reference to Harrogate's wandering in the underground tunnels: "He began to suspect some dimensional displacement in these descents to the underworld, some disparity unaccountable between the above and the below." The nadir of Suttree's career occurs when he becomes involved with a whore who carries on some unspecified but very lucrative dealings in successive towns in neighboring states. Suttree moves in with her, holding for her the money she sends and gradually allowing her to support him. But he is unable to respond to the humanity in her or to understand why, finally, she falls into a drunken rage, kicking to pieces the car she has provided him, and tearing up the money that is the basis of their relationship.

Unlike Culla Holme, however, Suttree is at last redeemed. A near fatal encounter with typhoid fever provides a final challenge to his life and his sanity. In a series of hallucinations and dreams Suttree faces his own death, stands self-accused of squandering his life, witnesses a rebirth of Western civilization, and wakes affirming life as process and his own uniqueness as well. Returning to his houseboat, he finds a corpse in his bed, a corpse identified with himself; but he is able to face it calmly and then to leave the waste of McAnally Flats. The brief final section of the novel suggests the changed quality of his experience in quick strokes: a blond waterboy offers him a drink and a passing car stops to offer him a ride, though he has asked for neither. The novel ends with Suttree's recognition of the agents of darkness that had dominated him:

> Somewhere in the gray wood by the river is the huntsman and in the brooming corn and in the castellated press of cities. His work lies all wheres and his hounds tire not. I have seen them in a dream, slaverous and wild and their eyes crazed with ravening for souls in this world. Fly them.

McCarthy's work has generally been well received by reviewers, and he has earned the esteem of several of his contemporaries among American novelists; but his work is not widely known, and except for *The Orchard Keeper* his novels have not had more than one printing in the United States. He has been the subject of only one scholarly article, and his out-of-print books are not yet available through dealers in first editions. But with the addition of *Suttree* to his list of accomplishments, McCarthy ought to become more widely recognized. His first three novels compare favorably with the initial efforts in the genre by William Faulkner, and in *Suttree* he has reached a new level of ambition and achievement. Here his themes are dramatized in a world so fully realized, by characters so realistic in their grotesqueness, that some reviewers have missed McCarthy's serious intentions beneath the rich texture of detail lavished on often repulsive subjects. Suttree is by far the most complex and most interesting of McCarthy's protagonists—the end product of a progression toward deeper inquiry into the minds and motivations of his alienated characters in novels from *Outer Dark* through *Suttree*. In its use of all the resources of the English language, from the vernacular and slang to latinate oddities and Anglo-Saxon archaisms, *Suttree* builds on the practice of the earlier novels and develops a more consistent narrative voice. Since the publication of *The Orchard Keeper*, reviewers have rejoiced at McCarthy's ear for the dialects of his characters, but have caviled at his penchant for unusual diction in the narrative sections of his work. This feature of his style is not gratuitous, however; it is integral to his portrayal of his fictional world, and McCarthy is not likely to abandon it for the convenience of his readers.

McCarthy is in no way a commercial writer. He is a novelist by profession, and he has not supplemented his income by turning his hand to more lucrative kinds of work such as Hollywood screenwriting. Two excerpts from *The Orchard Keeper* and one from *Suttree* have been printed in periodicals, but McCarthy has written no short fiction for the popular magazine market. Perhaps as a result of this, his novels have had from the beginning a polish and discipline remarkable in a young writer. His most perceptive reviewers have consistently predicted more of the same solid work from McCarthy, and he has fulfilled these predictions. He deserves, now, serious attention from students of literature.

—Dianne L. Cox

Periodical Publications:

"Bounty," *Yale Review*, 54 (March 1965): 77-85;
"The Dark Waters," *Sewanee Review*, 73 (1965): 210-216;
"Burial," *Antaeus*, 32 (Winter 1979): 87-100.

Reference:

William J. Schafer, "Cormac McCarthy: The Hard Wages of Original Sin," *Appalachian Journal*, 4 (Winter 1977): 105-119.

JAMES A. MICHENER
(3 February 1907?-)

BOOKS: *The Unit in the Social Studies*, by Michener and Harold M. Long (Cambridge: Graduate School of Education, Harvard University, 1940);
Tales of the South Pacific (New York: Macmillan, 1947; London: Collins, 1951);
The Fires of Spring (New York: Random House, 1949; London: Transworld, 1960);
Return to Paradise (New York: Random House, 1951; London: Secker & Warburg, 1951);
The Voice of Asia (New York: Random House, 1951); republished as *Voices of Asia* (London: Secker & Warburg, 1952);
The Bridges at Toko-Ri (New York: Random House, 1953; London: Secker & Warburg, 1953);
Sayonara (New York: Random House, 1954; London: Secker & Warburg, 1954);
The Floating World (New York: Random House, 1954; London: Secker & Warburg, 1954);
The Bridge at Andau (New York: Random House, 1957; London: Secker & Warburg, 1957);
Rascals in Paradise, by Michener and A. Grove Day (New York: Random House, 1957; London: Secker & Warburg, 1957);
Selected Writings, foreword by Michener (New York: Modern Library, 1957);
Japanese Prints: From the Early Masters to the Modern (Tokyo & Rutland, Vt.: Charles E. Tuttle, 1959);
Hawaii (New York: Random House, 1959; London: Secker & Warburg, 1960);
Report of the County Chairman (New York: Random House, 1961);
The Modern Japanese Print (Rutland, Vt.: Charles E. Tuttle, 1962);
Caravans (New York: Random House, 1963; London: Secker & Warburg, 1963);
The Source (New York: Random House, 1965; London: Secker & Warburg, 1965);
Iberia: Spanish Travels and Reflections (New York: Random House, 1968; London: Secker & Warburg, 1968);
Presidential Lottery: The Reckless Gamble in Our Electoral System (New York: Random House, 1969; London: Secker & Warburg, 1969);
The Quality of Life (Philadelphia: Girard Bank, 1970; London: Secker & Warburg, 1971);
The Drifters (New York: Random House, 1971; London: Secker & Warburg, 1971);
Kent State: What Happened and Why (New York: Random House, 1971; London: Secker & Warburg, 1971);
A Michener Miscellany, 1950-1970, ed. Ben Hibbs (New York: Random House, 1973; London: Corgi, 1975);

Centennial (New York: Random House, 1974; London: Secker & Warburg, 1974);

About "Centennial": Some Notes on the Novel (New York: Random House, 1974);

Sports in America (New York: Random House, 1976); republished as *Michener on Sport* (London: Secker & Warburg, 1976);

Chesapeake (New York: Random House, 1978; London: Secker & Warburg, 1978).

James Michener has published nearly a dozen volumes of fiction, but such is his versatility that he has published more than an equal number of volumes of nonfiction, and more than one hundred articles in periodicals. He does, however, think of himself primarily as a novelist, and his narratives—often of unusual length and detail—have been widely popular both in America and in many other countries of the world. He is a master reporter of his generation, and his wide and frequent travels have given him material for colorful evocation of the lives of many characters in international settings in periods going back to earlier millennia. Most of his novels have been best-sellers and all his works, even studies of Japanese prints, are currently available. As a literary craftsman Michener has labored to entertain. Many of his books, however, also appeal to the thoughtful reader and are laden with details that reveal Michener's academic training and bestow information as well as enlightenment.

Although many standard reference works state that Michener was born in New York City on 3 February 1907, son of Edwin and Mabel Haddock Michener, they are in error. Mabel Michener picked up the young child from the streets of Doylestown, Pennsylvania, and reared him as her foster child. In 1931, when the young man received a scholarship to study abroad, he obtained a passport only after Mabel Michener and a notary prepared a statement giving him citizenship status. The fact that Michener has never known when or where he was born, or his family background, has impelled him to invent his roots and enabled him to put himself in the place of characters of exotic heritages.

James Albert Michener grew up in the Bucks County countryside in Pennsylvania and attended Doylestown Grammar School. At the age of fourteen he hitchhiked for some months through forty-five American states. On his return home he delivered newspapers, wrote a sports column for the local paper, and was saved from delinquency by his prowess in sports, especially basketball. A sports scholarship took him to Swarthmore College, and his second novel evokes feelings of an undergraduate of the time in this Quaker institution. During one summer vacation Michener traveled with a Chautauqua tent show and became imbued with a love of the drama, reflected in his fiction, which has often been adapted for the stage and screen.

Michener graduated (*summa cum laude*) in 1929 with a degree in English and history as well as a Phi Beta Kappa key. He began teaching at the nearby Hill School. A traveling scholarship enabled him to make his first trip abroad and he enrolled at St. Andrew's University in Scotland, but he also studied art in London and Siena, Italy, worked on a Mediterranean cargo vessel, and collected folk tales in the Hebrides islands. Returning to the United States during the Depression years, he taught from 1933 to 1936 at George School near Doylestown and in 1937 earned a master's degree at the Colorado State College of Education in Greeley, where he was an associate professor from 1936 through 1939. He served his writing apprenticeship as the author of some fifteen scholarly articles on the teaching of social studies, published between 1936 and 1942. During 1940-1941 he was a visiting professor at Harvard University, and in 1941 he accepted a post on the editorial staff of the Macmillan Company in New York. Despite his Quaker upbringing, he volunteered for service in the U.S. Navy in 1942, and his first assignment as a lieutenant (junior grade) was a wartime post as "a supersecretary for aviation maintenance" in the South Pacific—a region with which his name is still associated. From 1944 through 1946 Michener served as a Naval historian in the South Pacific.

Michener was able to visit some fifty islands during World War II, and as the war wound down, he retreated to a jungle shack and began writing the stories that were to appear as his first novel, *Tales of the South Pacific* (1947), which won a Pulitzer Prize in 1948.

Although *Tales of the South Pacific* is sometimes considered a collection of short stories and several chapters have been separately published in anthologies, Michener has always thought of it as a novel because of its strong theme and largely unified setting; several characters recur throughout the book, and the chapters are united through the characters' participation in a single cause—the giant anti-Japanese operation called "Alligator." The beauties and terrors of the South Seas form the background for the actions of members of almost every section of the American armed forces in the Pacific war—army, navy, air force, doctors and nurses, Construction Battalion workers, and radio operators. Likewise, the heroic actions of America's allies are given their due attention. Even the island residents are featured (including the Frenchman

Emile De Becque, lover of Nurse Nellie Forbush from Little Rock, and Bloody Mary, the Tonkinese laborer who can out-deal even the wily Luther Billis). The idyllic love of the American soldier Joe Cable for Liat, a young, slim virgin of Bali-ha'i, is the first but not the last affair in which Michener foreshadows in his fiction his own real-life interracial marriage to his third wife, Mari Yoriko Sabusawa, an American of Japanese ancestry whom he married in 1955. The preparations depicted in earlier chapters culminate in "The Landing at Kuralei," a full-dress battle piece that seems to dramatize the novel's main theme: "If you were not the man at the end of it, the ultimate man with his sweating hands upon the blockhouse, you didn't know what war was. . . . By the grace of God you would never know." However, in the epilogue, "A Cemetery at Hoga Point," the author also stresses what might be his lifelong concern: the universal human brotherhood "that we seem able to attain only in cemeteries." *Tales of the South Pacific* is one of the best novels about Americans in the Pacific theatre in World War II.

Michener had been discharged in 1946 from the navy as a lieutenant commander and had returned to Macmillan as a textbook editor when in 1949 *Tales of the South Pacific* was made into a successful musical by Richard Rodgers and Oscar Hammerstein II. When *South Pacific* ran for a total of 1,925 performances on Broadway, a share of royalties from the play (which became in 1958 a popular Hollywood film) enabled Michener to devote himself entirely to his career of professional author.

Michener's second book was the semi-autobiographical *The Fires of Spring* (1949), a Bildungsroman about David Harper, an orphan who spends time in the county poorhouse and early faces violence. David enacts many a scene from Michener's youth. He works as a cashier in a summer amusement park, goes to a college not far different from Swarthmore, travels on the Chautauqua circuit, and struggles in Greenwich Village to learn the craft of writing. However, after this book Michener was able to attain distance and concerned himself with the lives of people far from his Bucks County home.

With *The Fires of Spring* came an important change in the life of the author. When *The Fires of Spring* was rejected by Macmillan, Michener traveled by bus up Fifth Avenue and submitted the manuscript to Random House. Thereafter almost all his books were published by Random House, and Bennett Cerf and Albert Erskine became his meticulous publisher and editor.

The Pacific still beckoned, and an assignment from *Holiday* magazine to revisit his wartime haunts sent Michener to write feature articles about the Pacific, its atolls, and places like Fiji, Guadalcanal, and Rabaul. He decided to write, for every nonfiction essay, a short story with the same setting. Published in 1951, *Return to Paradise* sandwiched travel sketches with exotic tales. Some of his finest short stories appear in this volume, and several of them, such as "Mr. Morgan" and "Until They Sail," have been made into films.

Other assignments allowed Michener to range through Asia, continent of his early dreams. Interviews with fifty-three persons or groups form his first fully nonfiction volume, *The Voice of Asia* (1951). *The Floating World* (1954), a scholarly study of the art of the Japanese print, was the first of four volumes that reveal Michener's serious concern with art, especially that of the Orient. Two novels derive from the author's involvement with Americans in Asia in wartime, and both were made into memorable Hollywood films.

The first of these, *The Bridges at Toko-Ri* (1953), required Michener to spend eight days on an aircraft carrier, to study the operation of jet-fighter planes in the Korean War. The story is divided into three sections: "Sea," "Land," and "Sky." It opens with a dramatic rescue by helicopter of the leading character, Harry Brubaker—a twenty-nine-year-old veteran of World War II and a successful Denver lawyer with a wife and two small daughters. Brubaker's suicidal mission to destroy the critical bridges illustrates the theme that all through history the warriors of freedom have had to fight the wrong war in the wrong place, and civilization depends upon such "voluntary men." By contrast, *Sayonara* (1954) is an interracial love story that reveals Michener's love for Japan. Major Lloyd ("Ace") Gruber, who has just shot down his sixth and seventh MIGs in Korea, is sent to rest in Tokyo, where his affair with Hana-ogi, an actress, educates him about the differences between being engaged to a cool, spoiled American blonde and having a devoted Oriental mistress.

Another novel with an Asian setting, *Caravans* (1963), derives from Michener's visit to Afghanistan in 1955, but the book is set in 1946 and was not published until 1963. It presents Mark Miller, a former navy officer attached to the American embassy in Kabul, who on a mission joins a nomad camel caravan along with Ellen Jaspar, a beautiful and intelligent graduate of Bryn Mawr College. The exotic band of characters, including a former Nazi torturer of Jews and an Afghani tribal chief, fails to people a realistic landscape based on Michener's extensive travel notes. As one reviewer commented: "Michener tells you, it sometimes seems, absolutely everything he has learned about Afghanistan. . . . As a result, it is much like reading a bound set of the *National Geographic,* without the pictures."

The novelist returned again to the Pacific scene when in 1954 he invited A. Grove Day, a professor at the University of Hawaii, to collaborate with him on *Rascals in Paradise* (1957), a collection of ten biographical studies of colorful figures from Pacific

Antoinette W. Roades

James A. Michener

history. Working with Day in Honolulu in 1956 to complete the collaboration, Michener prepared himself to write the first of his family sagas.

Published in 1959, the year when the Territory of Hawaii was granted American statehood, the novel *Hawaii* opens with pages of nonfiction, describing the birth of the islands as a result of aeons of submarine volcanic action. Then follows a section on eighth-century life on the island of Bora Bora, a voyage of exploration in an ocean-going canoe, and the settlement of the Hawaiian island chain by early families (their invented ancestries occupy no fewer than eight pages in an appendix). Succeeding sections tell of the coming of Congregational missionaries from New England, the arrival of field laborers from China and Japan, and the mingling of many racial and ethnic strains to form a polyglot modern population that Michener calls the "Golden Men." It is not required that the inhabitants' bloodstreams mingle, but "only that their ideas clash on equal footing and remain free to cross-fertilize and bear new fruit." This million-word novel was made into two lengthy films, and the characters crowd the screen. This is not a historical novel in the usual sense, for not one actual name or event is given; rather, it is a pageant of the coming of settlers from many regions; and the main theme might well be: Paradise is not a goal to attain, but a stage to which people of many colors and creeds may bring their traditional cultures to mingle with those of the others and create what may truly be an Eden at the crossroads of a hitherto empty ocean.

An avid student of politics, Michener was turning toward involvement in the national political scene. His active campaigning for John F. Kennedy is described in *Report of the County Chairman* (1961); and in 1962 Michener himself campaigned vigorously but unsuccessfully as a candidate for the House of Representatives from the Pennsylvania Eighth District. A later study by Michener of the democratic process resulted in *Presidential Lottery* (1969), a plea for reform in the method of choosing an American president.

Michener returned to fiction, however, in 1963, living in the state of Israel and gathering material for a mammoth volume, *The Source* (1965), another best-seller. The frame for this rich book is the description of the archaeological excavation of Makor Tell, a mound on which one settlement after another has been built through the ages. Artifacts found in the various layers introduce chapters dealing with events in the Holy Land during the period in which the articles were made. The periods range from 10,000 B.C.E. (before the common era) to the Israeli War of Independence. Prominent families of several nationalities are followed through the ages; the setting is limited to the invented tell of Makor, the surrounding countryside, and the shores of the Sea of Galilee. *The Source* is one of the longest of Michener's books, and the best in the opinion of many readers. Although it may lack a clear general theme, its leading topic is certainly the various facets of religion.

When Michener published *The Drifters* in 1971—the same year he produced a big reportorial volume, *Kent State,* dealing with the riots and shootings at that midwest university—he surprised readers who expected another *Hawaii* or *The Source.* In focusing on a group of disenchanted, contemporary young people—a bearded American draft evader, a beautiful Norwegian, an irredeemable

British vixen who rejects her diplomat family, a handsome black revolutionary from the Philadelphia ghetto, a bright young veteran of the Israeli six-day war, and a rebellious blonde ballad singer from New England—the narrator, as an observant, older friend, seems to record rather than to judge. The rootless youths forgather at Torremolinos in southern Spain, and their drifting takes them to the feast of the running of the bulls at Pamplona and eventually to East Africa and drug-drenched Morocco, in the course of which the novel offers historical and geographical information about the regions through which they travel. The novel was even more popular in Europe than in the United States.

As a professor in Greeley, Colorado, in the 1930s, Michener was inspired through his friendship with an erudite newspaper editor to prepare to write a voluminous novel based on the history of that state. The result, many years later, was *Centennial* (1974), which dramatizes the lore of Colorado from the creation of the earth up to 1974. The narrator is Dr. Lewis Vernor, who is preparing a report on the history of the village of Centennial in the northeastern section of the state. Before human beings appear in the saga, however, there are no fewer than eighty pages of solid nonfiction covering geology, archaeology, and ecology. Seventy named characters—not including dinosaurs and the lowly eohippus—appear, including Indians, fur traders, trappers, cattle drivers, miners, ranchers, dry farmers, real-estate salesmen, and assorted townspeople. Again national and ethnic interminglings in a limited region are recorded through many years, and little is omitted from the panorama of the developing American West. It appears in the end that the lineage of the "golden man" of Centennial, Paul Garrett, can list thirty ancestors, all of whom have previously held center stage in the novel; Garrett's forebears include a Pennsylvania Dutchman, an Arapaho Indian grandmother, and English, Welsh, Irish, French, and German emigrants from Europe. Garrett's wife is Mexican, and his friends are the grandson of a black cowboy, a farmer from Czarist Russia, and a clan of Japanese field workers. As in earlier novels, progress is the result of ethnic intermingling, and in Michener's simple Quaker creed, all men and women are brothers and sisters.

The pattern is repeated once more in another saga, *Chesapeake* (1978). Here the setting is the great bay of Maryland and its shores; the characters go back to the American Indians, and the story incorporates much fictionalized American history. Five families and their descendants take the spotlight, and the principal locales—Devon Island, Peace Cliff, the Turlock marshes, and the town of Patamoke—are not to be found on any map. Sections in *Chesapeake* labeled "Voyages" supply preludes to the various chapters, which like those in *The Source* are narratives of regional events in successive periods. While no single theme emerges, here even more than in *Centennial* Michener is preoccupied with damage done to the land by human misuse; the ecological lesson is complete when the last fragments of Devon Island disappear through erosion into the brown waters of the bay.

James A. Michener has probably traveled more of the world than any other novelist and in spite of two cardiac attacks has led an energetic life. He has studied at a dozen universities, and has been awarded more than a score of honorary degrees, as well as the Navy Gold Cross and the Medal of Freedom.

As a scholarly novelist, Michener has won wide popularity without stooping to cheap melodrama. He may best be remembered for his family sagas in which men and women of many heritages intermingle in far-off places.

—A. Grove Day

Other:

The Future of the Social Studies: Proposals for an Experimental Social-Studies Curriculum, edited by Michener (Cambridge: National Council for the Social Studies, 1939);

The Hokusai Sketchbooks: Selections from the Manga, edited by Michener (Rutland, Vt.: Charles E. Tuttle, 1958);

Firstfruits: A Harvest of Twenty-five Years of Israeli Writing, edited by Michener (New York: Fawcett, 1974).

Reference:

A. Grove Day, *James A. Michener* (Boston: G. K. Hall, 1977).

Papers:

Collections of Michener's books and manuscripts are to be found at Swarthmore College and the University of Hawaii Libraries. The Library of Congress has a large collection of his papers.

MARION MONTGOMERY

(16 April 1925-)

BOOKS: *Dry Lightning* (Lincoln: University of Nebraska Press, 1960);

The Wandering of Desire (New York: Harper, 1962);

Darrell (Garden City: Doubleday, 1964);

Stones from the Rubble (Memphis: Argus, 1965);

Ye Olde Bluebird (Atlanta: New College Press, 1967);

The Gull and Other Georgia Scenes (Athens: University of Georgia Press, 1969);

T. S. Eliot: An Essay on the American Magus (Athens: University of Georgia Press, 1969);

Ezra Pound: A Critical Essay (Grand Rapids: Eerdmans, 1970);

The Reflective Journey toward Order: Essays on Dante, Wordsworth, Eliot, and Others (Athens: University of Georgia Press, 1973);

Fugitive (New York: Harper & Row, 1974);

Eliot's Reflective Journey to The Garden (Troy, N.Y.: Whitson, 1979).

Marion Hoyt Montgomery, Jr., is a Southern novelist, poet, and critic whose work reveals an understanding of himself as an inheritor and preserver of traditional values, particularly (though not exclusively) as they are embodied in his own region's past and present.

Montgomery was born in Thomaston, Georgia, and has lived most of his life in his native state, except for a tour of duty in the U.S. Army during 1943 to 1946 and two years (1956 to 1958) as a student in the writing program at the University of Iowa. He studied at the University of Georgia from 1947 to 1953, where he received his B.A. and M.A. degrees. Montgomery served as assistant director of the University of Georgia Press (1951 to 1953) and as business manager of the *Georgia Review* (1951 to 1953). He taught during 1953-1954 at the Darlington School for Boys in Rome, Georgia. In 1954 Montgomery became an instructor in English at the University of Georgia and, with the exception of his years in Iowa, has continued to teach there. He married Dorothy Carlisle in 1951, and they have five children: Priscilla, Deana, Marion III, Heli, and Ellyn. The Montgomerys live in the rural town of Crawford, Georgia, in an old home which they have restored.

Montgomery's first published volume, *Dry Lightning*, appeared in 1960. Though this early collection of poetry is uneven in quality, Montgomery successfully presents the nature and virtues of his region as they image traditional values such as familial piety, a love of one's own land, and a belief in God.

Montgomery's first novel, *The Wandering of Desire* (1962), is a complex work in which the diversity of characters and action further suggests the author's wide knowledge of his region and its lore. Set in the wire-grass country of Georgia, it is essentially the story of separate attempts by two men to conquer the land, ventures that ultimately end in failure. The first attempt is made by Wash Mullis, a self-made, yeoman dynast in the mold of Faulkner's Thomas Sutpen; and the second is by Doc Blalock, a veterinarian and "progressive" who hopes to enlighten his neighbors with a kind of scientific revelation concerning agriculture. Possession of The Hill is for the two men the ultimate goal in life. But in their pride and greed they fail.

Mullis, a late-nineteenth-century frontiersman, clears the swamp, converts the land into cotton fields, and then farms it for a while at great profit. He is a man of enormous appetites for money and sex; and the story of his rise and fall as a land baron provides the novel with its most important narrative thread. Blalock, a more temperate man than Mullis, represents the civilized and scientific impulses of the early twentieth century; he is soft-spoken and reasonable, yet possesses ambition that drives him to be no less self-serving than Mullis.

Mullis's venture in the raising and marketing of cotton parallels the early agricultural history of Montgomery's region and of the South at large. Like other Southerners of the late nineteenth and early twentieth centuries, his fortunes rise and fall with the accidents of nature and the unpredictability of human conduct. The boll weevil, the burning down of his cotton gin, and the theft of his crop by underlings and his son all conspire to undermine his financial resources so that finally, in 1930, he is forced to surrender his land to the bank. At this point Doc Blalock manages to buy The Hill, though he, too, is financially strapped. His efforts at establishing cattle as a profitable enterprise are met by a series of misfortunes similar to those which have plagued Mullis. Blalock's cattle die; his prize Brahma bull kills Mullis's son and has to be destroyed; his own son is castrated by another of Mullis's sons; and finally his daughter-in-law sells her half of the farm back to Mullis, though by this time the land is covered with pine seedlings. As the novel ends both Mullis and Blalock, aged and powerless, await death as the wilderness reclaims The Hill.

In many ways *The Wandering of Desire* is Montgomery's most innovative novel. For one thing, the central events of the narrative are rendered in bits and pieces, out of sequence and juxtaposed with one another in thematic patterns. Such jumbling of time sequences, however, is directly related to the meaning of the novel, which is summarized in the allusive title and in epigraphs derived from Ecclesiastes. It matters not whether Wash Mullis preceded Doc Blalock in his attempt to master The Hill, or vice versa. Their efforts meet with the same end, having little to do with the sequence of historical events, suggesting that all is vanity. Montgomery's many anecdotes and digressions—some of which are narrative in nature, others of which are more discursive—have puzzled some readers. But while such materials do not relate directly to the actions of the main characters as dramatic links or analogues, they are often relevant to the history and peculiarities of the Georgia wire-grass country in which the story takes place. Although some commentators complain about this rambling, other critics suggest that this propensity is consistent with the character of the rural bardic voice that the author is attempting to imitate. Southern novelists Flannery O'Connor, Erskine Caldwell, and

Walker Percy praised *The Wandering of Desire* for its rendition of life in general as well as its fidelity to the unique character of the region.

Darrell (1964) is simpler in its plot structure than *The Wandering of Desire*. The action is uncomplicated and is rendered sequentially. Indeed the novel is Montgomery's only conventional fictional narrative. Darrell, a young man of rural background, persuades his aging grandmother to leave their small town and move to the city. The old woman will not live in Atlanta, as Darrell wishes, but agrees to go as far as the suburbs, where they plant a plastic pink flamingo in the yard and begin to establish a new life. This lawn decoration represents a cheap mass culture which the grandmother instinctively distrusts but which Darrell, in his simpleminded ignorance, admires. For him Atlanta is the embodiment of the best things in life and therefore a place toward which his heart yearns. While living in the suburban shadow of the great city he becomes attached to Sandra Lee, a dying child whose plight has been picked up and exploited by the local media as a human interest story. The girl herself understands more about the world than Darrell does. Indeed she is hard and selfish, an exploiter as well as one of the exploited. One of her fondest dreams has been to go to the zoo; and when she is near death, Darrell, in the midst of a carnival staged by the publicity-minded media, grabs her, sets her on his motorcycle, and zooms off toward the Atlanta zoo to fulfill both their hearts' desires. On the way, either out of haste or because Darrell is seized by an epileptic fit, the motorcycle strikes a bridge abutment and Darrell and Sandra Lee are killed. Beneath this straightforward plot—which is no more than a situation out of which grows the final tragic consequence—the reader finds a statement of Montgomery's view of urban life. Suburbia is rendered as a kind of banal hell in which people are manipulated by forces beyond their control. Even Darrell, who is essentially pure at heart, is fatally attracted by the false image of the city as a place where wonders abound and dreams come true. In the final analysis, then, his death is an example of what happens when simple country people are exposed to the evils of modern urbanization.

In *Darrell* the tightly textured narrative skims too easily through sequential events, and as a result, several critics have maintained that the hero and his small friend are stereotypes rather than well-developed and credible fictional characters. Yet others argue that in their simplicity Darrell and Sandra Lee are epic figures whose actions speak for

2000

Stream

Guitar

CHAPTER ONE

On Monday, a man came out to the house and took down the sign that said FOR SALE, A. C. BRADLEY, REALTOR and put up one that said SOLD, A. C. BRADLEY, REALTOR. He had a hammer, and he drove the sign, on a pointed stick, down sharply and then before he got back in the car he looked at it to see whether it could be seen alright. from the street.

On Wednesday afternoon, after all the stores ~~were closed~~ had been closed for three or four hours, a big truck with ERNIE TRIGGS, WHOLESALE GROCER on the door turned into Mimosa Lane and went on across ~~over~~ the bridge over the little stream ~~branch~~ and past the house before its brakes squealled. Then it started backing up, with its motor whinning in the hot afternoon. Mrs. Thurston's two little boys came out of their backyard when they heard it, and started down the street toward the truck.

The truck stopped when it got ~~in front of~~ to the house with the SOLD sign in front of it, and a man got out from the driver's side. He hurried up the driveway, leaning uphill a little, and went on to the picture window and cupped his hands around his eyes to look in. Then he came back down the driveway and cranked up the truck and pulled it into the opposite curb so he could back it up the driveway. A Negro man popped out of the ~~bak~~ back and began giving directions.

"Cut it this a way," he hollered. Then, "Cut it the other way."

But the man driving didn't pay any attention. He sawed the wheel back and forth till he got the truck angled toward the little front stoop with the iron grill around it.

"That's all right," the Negro man called. But the ~~truck had~~ driver had already ~~stopped~~ cut off the motor. ~~The man driving got out~~ He got out of the cab and went over to the mimosa tree where there were two or three rocks lying against the trunk and brought one back and scotched it under the back wheel.

"All right," he said. ~~"Lets get this thing unloaded so you can take it on back. I told him I wouldn't~~

Darrell, *first draft*

themselves and who suggest a premodern purity.

Stones from the Rubble (1965), Montgomery's second volume of verse, gives the reader a clear indication of the direction in which his poetic talents have moved since *Dry Lightning*. In this later collection the subject matter of the poems is even more obviously regional and familial than that of the first volume, becoming a kind of verse affirmation of the principles that at this point begin to assert themselves in his literary criticism and occasional polemical essays. In *Stones from the Rubble* he has all but forsaken traditional prosody and the diction and syntax of modern poetry. Instead his most traditional sentiments are rendered in free verse, resulting in a loose and idiomatic poetic line. There is no "major poem" in this collection, but the cumulative effect of the volume is impressive; the reader is struck with a sense of authority that is often missing in Montgomery's earlier works.

Ye Olde Bluebird (1967) is a novella that is to some degree polemical in method and intent. Within the prose narrative is presented a play entitled *Ye Olde Bluebird*. The drama, produced in a northern university community, is reviewed for the university newspaper by Mike, a Southern graduate student. He realizes that the play is a sentimental piece of propaganda that portrays the abuses of Southern whites against Southern blacks. Mike must decide if he should tell the truth about the play, which is badly flawed aesthetically despite its social message, or lie and thereby compromise his critical values. His friend, Paul Levinson, believes that the social message of the play is paramount and either fails to see the aesthetic weaknesses or is willing to overlook them. A heated argument over Mike's decision erupts between the two men. Here Montgomery debates critics who have too readily praised poor literature, letting Mike win a victory (which some might say was too easily accorded). Though the protracted argument may appear to be merely a device to feature and justify Montgomery's polemics, the action in the epilogue qualifies some of what has been said in the discussion and ends the novel on a note of compromise with Mike and Paul as friends.

Fugitive, Montgomery's most recent novel (1974), is also his most overtly Agrarian. The novel's hero, Walt Mason, a former student of Donald Davidson at Vanderbilt, has a highly successful career in Nashville writing country music lyrics. However, he comes to the rural Tennessee town of Weaverton in order to live the life of rural simplicity that he has come to believe in intellectually. But in this new and at times perplexing environment he learns what compromises he will have to accept in order to make his intellectual ideal a reality. Weaverton, as Montgomery depicts it, is no idyllic community free from commercialism and technological dependency. In fact, television is an important influence there, and at times the air is alive with the corrupted country music that Walt has hoped to leave behind. Walt encounters local figures such as Mort Thompson, a sinister and primitive moonshiner who moves out of the shadows as stealthily and mindlessly as a wild animal to gun down the town's mayor. However, Walt does find in Weaverton some people who come close to living a life of rural self-sufficiency. The most admirable is Hugh Akers, a country yeoman who becomes Walt's guide during his initiation into the mysteries of the Southern rural community. Akers is both active and contemplative, performing a variety of roles in Weaverton and also ready to pass along his wisdom to Walt in the form of sayings, tales, and direct advice. The sparse action of the novel grows out of Walt's attempts to restore an old historic building and to marry Phyllis, a plain but attractive widow. The difficult but rewarding efforts at restoration have obvious thematic implications for Walt's desire to reestablish a collapsing order; and his union with Phyllis suggests a limited victory: the Agrarian ideal can be courted and won in the world as we know it, provided some compromise is made. As the novel closes, Walt is married to Phyllis and accepted as a father by her daughter; but Nashville has come to Weaverton in the form of a country music festival, and the encroachment of modernity continues.

Fugitive, like *The Wandering of Desire*, poses some difficulties for the critic or reader who expects a conventional plot composed of sequential events. In addition to numerous digressions and anecdotes, this novel offers long passages of philosophical discourse, the immediate relevance of which may not be apparent. Like Montgomery's criticism, it demands of the reader that he assent to the authority of the author's own logic with something like a willing suspension of disbelief. While a few commentators have been willing to submit to this discipline, others have complained that the discursive passages are tedious or irrelevant.

Montgomery's growing preoccupation with the problems of modernity, particularly as they are revealed in the works of twentieth-century literary masters, has been indicated in *T. S. Eliot: An Essay on the American Magus* (1969) and subsequent critical volumes. Montgomery exemplifies in his criticism some of the same tendencies found in his fiction: a rejection of conventional logic, and a sense of the poet/critic randomly examining the literary work.

At the age of fifty-five Marion Montgomery has established himself as an important voice in the literature of his region. Whether or not he will be heard outside the South is a matter for speculation. As yet he has been the subject of no significant critical studies, and commentary on his individual works can be found only in extended reviews and a few standard reference books. His growing body of criticism commends him to the attention of serious literary scholars. At present he is preparing for publication a critical study of Western literary tradition which will exceed two thousand pages and touch on virtually every significant poet and fiction writer from Homer to the present. It is concerned with "the prophetic poet and the popular spirit of the age."

Both his fiction and his poetry suggest a movement from the purely mimetic to the discursive. Montgomery is more and more concerned with ideas and their consequences, and his later novels and poetry are the works of a philosopher as well as a bard. He clearly believes that the direction of his own work is necessary: one must "fight fire with fire" rather than capitulate to the spirit of the age.

—Thomas Landess

BERRY MORGAN

(20 May 1919-)

BOOKS: *Pursuit* (Boston: Houghton Mifflin, 1966; London: Heinemann, 1967);

The Mystic Adventures of Roxie Stoner (Boston: Houghton Mifflin, 1974).

Berry Morgan was born into an old, landed Roman Catholic family who settled in Port Gibson, Mississippi, in 1798. Doubtless, during her childhood while she was cared for by black house servants, she formed the foundation of the acute and accurate perception of the relationships among blacks and whites that comprise the content of her art. She attended Loyola University in New Orleans (1947) and Tulane University (1948-1949), married an oil geologist, and continued to live in Port Gibson on Albena Plantation. In 1966 she was awarded the Houghton Mifflin Literary Fellowship for a trilogy to be called "Certain Shadows," and in that same year *Pursuit*, the first novel of the trilogy, was published. In the fall of 1972 and after a divorce, she accepted an appointment as writer-in-residence at Northeast Louisiana University in Monroe, Louisiana, from which she commuted on weekends to Albena Plantation. Her next book, *The Mystic Adventures of Roxie Stoner*, appeared in 1974. Later in 1974 she and the younger two of her four children moved to a pre-Revolutionary stone house on a family farm near Washington, D.C., where she currently resides.

The fabric of Berry Morgan's work is the fabric of her own life: King's Town is very like Port Gibson; the house on Ingleside Plantation resembles the house on Albena Plantation; Ned Ingles's reference in *Pursuit* to his family's having been in the county since 1789 parallels her ancestors' entry into the county in 1798; and the Ingles family is Roman Catholic, as Berry Morgan is.

While the landscape of Berry Morgan's work has led certain critics to categorize it as Southern Gothic, *Pursuit* and *The Mystic Adventures of Roxie Stoner* have little in common with novels of that genre. Phoebe Adams, for example, writes in *Atlantic Monthly* that *The Mystic Adventures* is a "delicate, ironic put-on, for the author's actual purpose is to describe a general, vicious decline in morality and manners." And Walker Percy specifically denies that *Pursuit* is "romantic" or "Gothic" or "eccentric," adding that "what the novelist is up to is not the transcription of Southern manners and oddities at all but nothing less than the deepest movements of the human spirit as it picks its way through the vast disorder of modern life."

Imperious and bizarre behavior in the Ingles family is the norm, and the rules that apply generally to human relationships never penetrate the feudal kingdom of Ingleside Plantation. *Pursuit* chronicles Ned Ingles's developing obsession with his illegitimate son, Laurence, whose death from Hodgkin's disease catapults Ned from acute alcoholism into certifiable lunacy. At forty-seven, he returns from New Orleans to Ingleside where Laurence—a dull, unattractive youth of seventeen, who, after the death of his grandmother, has had only the blacks on the place for companions—is daily and unprofitably attending a nearby Roman Catholic school and nightly sleeping with the half-black, half-Chinese cook. While fingernail shaping, tooth brushing, and hair grooming are immediately and uncompromisingly imposed upon Laurence by Ned, sex with the cook attracts no more of his attention than would the matter-of-fact use of any other convenience.

Social contact between the Roman Catholic Ingles family and the predominantly Protestant citizens of King's Town has withered away during Ned's years in New Orleans, and little is known about Laurence in town beyond the general assumption that he is "dull" because his parents were first cousins. Therefore, Ned takes on a formidable task when he realizes that Laurence will leave Ingleside if some ties to the area are not established.

Consequently, Ned seeks out his childhood friend, Anna Meredith Welles, a widow who lives in genteel poverty with her lovely daughter Annabella. After Ned outlines his problem to Anna, she offers to tutor Laurence daily after school in her home, referring offhandedly to the help that Annabella can contribute. Although Laurence submits passively to the tutoring, very little is accomplished scholastically, for, as Anna tells Ned, Laurence does not remember from one afternoon until the test the next day.

There are unanticipated developments of other sorts, however. Laurence ignores Annabella and drifts into an affair with her mother. When Anna accidentally reveals the affair to Ned, attempting to justify her actions by commenting that she "honestly did think . . . it would drive all that God business out of his head," Ned hastily restructures his plan. He bedazzles Annabella, marries her, and moves both ladies out to Ingleside—congratulating himself on how cleverly he is saving Laurence for Ingleside.

Ned refuses to acknowledge Laurence's illness at first, shifting the burden to Anna but cooperating when she decides Laurence must be taken to New Orleans for a period of treatment. Ned's terror increases with Laurence's progressive deterioration, and he tries first one thing and then another to keep Laurence alert and alive, demonstrating his surface religiosity by turning to regular prayer. The familiar routine, "the feel of the smooth beads slipping through his fingers," reassures him in the same way that viewing Grandfather Dana's portrait in its accustomed place reassures him, but he admits to Anna that he does not even believe in God. His prayer is motivated by the godlessly pragmatic concern of capturing Laurence's attention by appearing to be undergoing a crisis of faith.

Laurence's interest, however, centers on Ned and Annabella's new son, Dana, and he spends hours admiring the baby—whereupon Ned craftily plants the story that Dana is the son of Annabella and Laurence in order to assure that Laurence will inherit Ingleside Plantation, and he encourages Annabella to leave Dana behind and go to New Orleans to "study." In what seems to be an attempt to ritualize the giving of his own son to Laurence, Ned commissions a gravestone that shows Dana to be Laurence's son.

Laurence advances toward death, Ned advances toward alcoholism and insanity, and Anna advances toward exhaustion. Surely among the finest sections of the book is the description of Laurence's death. The double focus on one type of torment and suffering in Laurence and another type in Ned makes the scene both clinically accurate and emotionally volatile. Ned's long pursuit of Laurence's attention and companionship ends after Laurence is buried in the Ingles's cemetery on the hill behind the house and Ned goes with pillows, blanket, and whiskey to live beside, to talk comfortably to, a Laurence who no longer flees from him.

Roxie Stoner, a black woman whose mystic adventures comprise Morgan's second book, *The Mystic Adventures of Roxie Stoner* (1974), lives near the Ingles family and helps out on the plantation from time to time, serving as Dana's nurse. The novel consists of sequential episodes in Roxie's life, depicting Roxie in encounters with various people, black and white, including both Laurence and Dana. At the end of the book, after a stay in the "nerve hospital," Roxie is reunited with Dana who promises now to teach her how to hear the voice of God.

Despite their differences in race and social class, the protagonists in the two novels entertain similar assumptions. Each flourishes in only one small locale and "feels real" only there; each sees his life as a link in a long, long chain of his own ancestors stretching far into the past; each makes his decisions on the narrow basis of his inherited family code (Ned's an autocratic code of land barons and Roxie's a pastiche of selected moralizings); and, finally, each believes that he is exempt from local authority. (Ned's invincibility derives from his money and family background and Roxie's protection comes from God.)

Furthermore, Ned and Roxie share certain situations and experiences: each is alone without a true mate; each has been confined for a time in a mental institution; each escapes; and each finally—and almost miraculously—gets home after a long and frightening journey.

Among the stories published by Morgan in the *New Yorker* since *The Mystic Adventures of Roxie Stoner*, three stories in particular relate further episodes in the life of Dana Ingles. "The Desertion" shows Dana at fourteen years of age abandoned by Anna and left alone to nurse the dying drunkard

Ned. "The Headrag" concerns Dana and a daughter living in an old house in the woods, while "Point of Rocks" reveals Dana at thirty-nine, with a five-year-old daughter, and living near Washington, D.C. These suggest that "Fornika Creek," Morgan's novel-in-progress, will examine the moral and spiritual issues of the first two novels as they pertain to the third generation of the Ingles family. Morgan describes the projected novel as a "look at the darker, or diabolic side of human nature—the hardest to speak of."

—Martha Adams

Periodical Publications:

"The Headrag," *New Yorker*, 53 (8 August 1977): 20-23;

"The Christmas Bush," *New Yorker*, 53 (17 October 1977): 43-45;

"Arthuree," *New Yorker*, 54 (27 March 1978): 36-38;

"The Desertion," *New Yorker*, 54 (10 July 1978): 28-31;

"Point of Rocks," *New Yorker*, 55 (22 January 1979): 37-40;

"Mr. Winston," *New Yorker*, 55 (9 April 1979): 36-37.

TONI MORRISON
(18 February 1931-)

BOOKS: *The Bluest Eye* (New York: Holt, Rinehart & Winston, 1970);

Sula (New York: Knopf, 1973; London: Allen Lane, 1974);

Song of Solomon (New York: Knopf, 1977; London: Chatto & Windus, 1978).

One of the most prominent contemporary analysts of the black experience, Toni Morrison has, within a decade, established herself as a significant American novelist. As a senior editor at Random House, a visiting lecturer at Bard College, and the divorced mother of two sons, Morrison must juggle schedules in order to find time for her writing. Yet, she observes, "Writing is the only thing I do that is for me. . . . I was over 30 when I began to write seriously and intelligently and I hope, honestly." With this commitment to serious writing, she has produced three extraordinary novels since 1970 and is nearing completion of her fourth one, "Tar Baby." Each of her novels has been critically acclaimed. However, the acclaim is not unqualified, probably resulting from the difficulty in understanding the sometimes bizarre content of the books rather than from deficiencies of style, structure, or vision.

Toni Morrison, nee Chloe Anthony Wofford, was born in 1931 to George and Ramah Willis Wofford in Lorain, Ohio, a small northern Ohio town which is the setting for her first novel. Her father, a blue-collar worker, held three jobs simultaneously for seventeen years. In an article recalling her parents' and grandparents' attitudes, Morrison reports that both her grandmother and grandfather believed that white people were "in some way fundamentally, genetically corrupt." Her grandmother, however, felt that white people were capable of improvement, while her grandfather always distrusted them. Thus, she says, she grew up "in a basically racist household, with more than a child's share of contempt for white people."

After her high school graduation (with honors), she left Lorain for Howard University in Washington, D.C., where she was active in the campus theatre group. Upon receiving her B.A. degree in 1953 she went on to graduate school at Cornell University, writing a thesis on the theme of suicide in the works of Faulkner and Woolf, receiving her master's degree in English in 1955. There followed a two-year stint in Houston, where she taught undergraduate English classes at Texas Southern University. In 1957 she returned to Howard to join the faculty, a position she held until 1964. While in Washington, she met and married Harold Morrison, a Jamaican architect, and gave birth to two sons, Harold Ford and Slade.

It was during these years in Washington that she began to write, as she told Mel Watkins in the *New York Times Book Review*:

> I never wanted to be a writer, but I was always an avid reader of fiction. I really began writing myself when I drifted into a writer's group while teaching at Howard University in 1962. There were about 10 of us who got together once a month, and the only rule was that you couldn't come unless you brought something to read. The others were mostly poets, but Claude Brown was part of it for a time. Anyway, I brought all that old junk I'd written in high school. Then one day I didn't have anything to bring, so I wrote a little story about a black girl who wanted blue eyes. It was written hurriedly and probably not very well, but I read it and some liked it.

In 1964 Morrison and her husband were separated. She left her job at Howard and moved with her children to Syracuse, New York, where she took a job with a subsidiary of Random House. She also continued to work on her short story and eventually turned it into a novel. *The Bluest Eye* was published by Holt, Rinehart, and Winston in 1970. Random House transferred her to their Manhattan office in 1968 when she became a senior editor, and since 1976 she has taught classes in Black literature and techniques of fiction at Yale and Bard College, although writing is now her principal interest.

When interviewer Robert B. Stepto asked her if she felt a conflict in her three professional activities, she conceded that full-time teaching might be inimical to her writing since the critical stance required by teaching would tend to inhibit her creative efforts. She felt that possibly she might become too self-conscious about writing. However, she said that editing is not in the least incompatible with writing since the process is so different.

Each of her three novels has strikingly original structure and elements of plot, with thematic consistency among the three reinforced by the similarity of the milieu of each and the recurrence of motifs. The novels deal with members of a black community in a small northern town, with, significantly, little reference to the white community. Rather than depicting the conflict between races, as Ellison does in *Invisible Man* (1952), for instance, Morrison treats the difficulties among members of various economic levels within the black community. Violence, grotesque characters, and bizarre actions all figure prominently in her works, as do allusions to folklore and the Bible. In all three novels Morrison's characters' names are inspired. Surnames such as Breedlove, Peace, and Dead are rich with symbolic meaning; first names such as Soaphead, the twins Chicken and Pie, and Milkman provide comic irony. The many biblical names, such as Shadrack, Pilate, First Corinthians, and Hagar, are both comic and allusive. Morrison uses place names with particular acuity, such as the Bottom community that is actually on a hill, and Not Doctor Street, so called because the town tried without success to change Doctor Street to Main Street. This sensitivity to names is related to Morrison's fine ear for dialogue, another important feature of her work.

Each novel may be considered experimental. Morrison has said she finds the novel "the most demanding and most challenging" genre. She notes that the novel form is important because "People crave narration. . . . That's the way human beings organize their human knowledge—fairy tales, myths. All narration." In her first two novels Morrison tried to be "extremely suggestive" and "to say a lot in a line," but in *Song of Solomon* (published in 1977 and more than twice the length of the earlier two books) she "made a serious attempt to write it all out."

The Bluest Eye opens with a passage which resembles a reading primer: "Here is the house. It is green and white. It has a red door. It is very pretty"—and so on, through a description of Dick and Jane, Mother and Father, and the cat and dog. The passage is repeated immediately twice, once with no punctuation and once with neither punctuation nor spaces between the letters. The passage then becomes the organizing principle of the book, with various parts of it used as chapter headings throughout. On the page following the simplistic renditions, the reader is provided with a sort of poetic plot summary, set in italics, revealing that in the summer of 1941 Pecola bore her father's child, that no marigolds grew that summer, that Claudia, the narrator, lost her innocence, that Pecola lives although her father and child are dead. This passage concludes with "There is really nothing more to say—except *why*. But since *why* is difficult to handle, one must take refuge in *how*."

The book tells how those tragic events happened, principally through the point of view of nine-year-old Claudia. Claudia with her ten-year-old sister, Frieda, befriends Pecola, the little girl who believes herself to be ugly and so prays every night for blue eyes like Shirley Temple's. Interspersed within the first-person narrative are stories told from a third-person point of view about Pecola's parents, Cholly and Pauline Breedlove, and experiences Pecola has away from her friends. After Pecola is raped by Cholly, she visits a charlatan, Soaphead Church, and asks for blue eyes. That encounter drives her over the brink of madness, and the book concludes with a dialogue in which Pecola asks an imaginary friend if her eyes are the bluest of all.

The publication of the book in 1970 brought numerous favorable reviews, including John Leonard's elaborate praise in the *New York Times Book Review*: "a prose so precise, so faithful to speech and so charged with pain and wonder that the novel becomes poetry." In another critical assessment, Chikwenye Okonjo Ogunyemi notes the theme of disorder reflected in the structure and diction of the novel.

Morrison's second novel, *Sula* (1973), is not so radical in form as *The Bluest Eye*. It proceeds chronologically and episodically, with each chapter having as a title a single year: the first is 1919 and the last is 1965. The book explores life in the black community called the Bottom in Medallion, Ohio, and focuses on the vicissitudes of the friendship between Nel Wright and Sula Mae Peace, two friends from childhood who have markedly different personalities and backgrounds. Nel, an only child, is "surrounded by the high silence of her mother's incredibly orderly house," while Sula, also an only child, is "wedged into a household of throbbing disorder constantly awry." Part one relates experiences they share during their school years; the most significant and traumatic one is their being the inadvertent cause of the drowning of a small boy, Chicken Little. When the body is eventually recovered and a funeral service is held, Sula cries uncontrollably and Nel stays preternaturally calm. After their high school graduation Nel has a June wedding and Sula leaves town to go to college, staying away for ten years.

Part two begins with Sula's return in 1937. Though the community disapproves, Sula puts her grandmother in a nursing home. Sula proceeds to sleep with most of the husbands in the neighborhood, though usually for only one night, thereby insulting as well as betraying the wives. She even spends one casual afternoon with Nel's husband, Jude. Three years after she has come home, Sula dies. Although the cause of death is undetermined, it may have been an overdose of the pills she has Nel get for her. Although Nel believes that Sula was the cause of the dissolution of her marriage, she nevertheless mourns Sula's death.

Important to the novel but tangential to the main plot is the figure of Shadrack, who is prominent in the first and last chapters and appears intermittently throughout the story. Shadrack, shell-shocked in World War I, is an eccentric figure who lives on the outskirts of Medallion and has established an annual "National Suicide Day." Because he may have been a witness to Chicken Little's drowning, Shadrack is a dreadful reminder of the event to the two girls. His failure to recognize Nel when he passes her in the final scene recalls Sula powerfully to her, and she then realizes that it is Sula, not her husband, for whom she has grieved for the past twenty-five years.

> "All that time, all that time, I thought I was missing Jude." And the loss pressed down on her chest and came up into her throat. "We was girls together," she cried as though explaining something. "O Lord, Sula," she cried, "girl, girl, girlgirlgirl."

The presentation of scenes widely spaced in time maintains a continuity and causality in the novel. A casual, matter-of-fact tone is used to describe scenes of horrifying violence. The thirteen-year-old Sula, for example, watches her mother burn to death when her clothes catch fire. She makes no move to help, Sula's grandmother Eva believes, "not because she was paralyzed, but because she was interested." The characters in the novel seem to do the wrong things for the right reasons. Eva, for example, is so distressed when her son, Plum, becomes a dope addict that she sets fire to him, killing him. The book is so heavily symbolic that it may be considered mythic, with the two central characters representing variously order and disorder; rationality and emotion; conventionality and the lack of it; good and evil. Numerous other symbolic elements are present: dreams and unusual natural phenomena, such as a plague of robins when Sula returns to Medallion, mark important events in the story; Sula's birthmark, variously interpreted, becomes a motif; the violent deaths by fire and water emphasize the juxtaposition of opposites. *Sula* was nominated for the National Book Award in 1975 and was selected as a Book-of-the-Month Club alternate. Its serious recognition by critics is indicated by a closer analysis of both its strengths and weaknesses than *The Bluest Eye* received. Sara Blackburn in the *New York Times* objected to *Sula*'s lack of warmth, but other critics praised the novel.

Song of Solomon (1977) is clearly Morrison's

most elaborate, complex, and mature novel thus far. Its working title, "Milkman Dead," refers to the protagonist (this time, significantly, a man), whose search for his identity and roots is the central focus of the novel. Milkman, so called because his mother is seen nursing him when he is four years old, is the son of Macon Dead, a prosperous black businessman, and Ruth Foster Dead, the only daughter of the only black doctor in town. Macon Dead is emotionally estranged from his wife and from his idiosyncratic sister, Pilate, who lives across town with her illegitimate daughter and granddaughter. Macon's ironic advice to his son is "Own things. And let the things you own own other things. Then you'll own yourself and other people too." At the instigation of his father, Milkman and his friend Guitar steal from Pilate's house a bag that reputedly contains gold nuggets, but in it, instead, are bones. Milkman goes south to trace the missing gold and is followed by Guitar, who thinks Milkman will try to keep the gold for himself. The novel ends ambiguously with Milkman leaping from a cliff to fight Guitar.

Milkman, who has sought information about his past and ancestors from his father, mother, and aunt, uncovers on his southern odyssey the secrets of his family's history. Milkman's most important clue to his background comes from the "song of Solomon," the folk song he overhears children singing as they play a game in a little Virginia town. He knew of an earlier version of the song that used the name "Sugarman" instead of "Solomon." In the first chapter of the novel, when a crowd gathered to watch a man "fly" off the top of a building, Milkman's mother heard a woman sing a song about "Sugarman." The song had so badly startled Ruth, who was pregnant, that she began to have premature labor pains. The significance of the first chapter does not become clear until Milkman learns at the end of the novel that it was believed his grandfather could fly. He realizes that the story told by the children singing Solomon's song is a version of his own family history. In the song, history and magic merge, creating a fantastic tale of folklore. Susan L. Blake has pointed out that the song is a variant of a well-known Gullah folktale. That Morrison's grandfather, a slave born a few years before the Civil War, is named John Solomon Willis, suggests that she uses in some way her own family history or folklore, although to imply that the novel is autobiographical would be a gross distortion. The thrust of the second section of the book is far too mythic to be construed as a factual account.

Song of Solomon has been, appropriately, the best received of the three novels. It was a main selection for the Book-of-the-Month Club (the first novel by a black writer to be chosen since Wright's *Native Son* in 1940) and a paperback best-seller. In 1979, 570,000 copies of *Song of Solomon* were in print. It received the National Book Critics Circle Award for 1977 and critical attention in popular and scholarly journals. Maureen Howard, for instance, called it "a fine novel exuberantly constructed and stylistically full of the author's own delight in words." Less satisfied critics voiced complaints about subplots, choice of protagonist, and possible sensationalism.

These three novels indicate Morrison's developing talent and increasing ability to deal with materials in a complex and subtle manner. Although the novels are distinctively different from each other, Morrison comments on the similarity of themes:

> Beauty, love . . . actually, I think, all the time that I write, I am writing about love or its absence. . . .
>
> I thought in *The Bluest Eye* that I was writing about beauty, miracles, and self-images, about the way in which people can hurt each other about whether or not one is beautiful.
>
> In *Sula* I thought I was writing about good and evil and the purposes to which they are frequently put, the way in which the community can use them.
>
> In this last book, *The Song of Solomon*, about dominion. . . . And I thought I was writing about the way in which men do things or see things and relate to one another.
>
> But I think that I still write about the same thing, which is how people relate to one another and miss it or hang on to it. . . .
>
> About love and how to survive—not to make a living—but how to survive whole in a world where we are all of us, in some measure, victims of something.

Despite Morrison's creation of idiosyncratic characters and bizarre circumstances in her novels, the message she provides in her compelling theme has universal appeal.

—Nancy Carol Joyner

Periodical Publications:

"What the Black Woman Thinks About Women's Lib," *New York Times Magazine*, 22 August 1971, pp. 14-15, 63-64, 66;

"Rediscovering Black History," *New York Times*

Magazine, 11 August 1974, pp. 14, 16, 18, 20, 22, 24;

"A Slow Walk of Trees (as Grandmother Would Say), Hopeless (as Grandfather Would Say)," *New York Times Magazine*, 4 July 1976, pp. 104, 150, 152, 156, 160, 162, 164.

Interviews:

Dorothy Gilliam, " 'The Black Book' How It Was," *Washington Post*, 6 March 1974, p. B1;

Robert B. Stepto, "Intimate Things in Place!! A Conversation with Toni Morrison," *Massachusetts Review*, 18 (1977): 473-489;

Mel Watkins, "Talk With Toni Morrison," *New York Times Book Review*, 11 September 1977, pp. 48, 50;

Jane Bakerman, "The Seams Can't Show: An Interview with Toni Morrison," *Black American Literature Forum*, 12 (1978): 56-60;

Colette Dowling, "The Song of Toni Morrison," *New York Times Magazine*, 20 May 1979, pp. 40, 42, 48, 52, 54, 56, 58.

References:

Susan L. Blake, "Folklore and Community in *Song of Solomon*," unpublished paper, Modern Language Association Convention, San Francisco, 30 December 1979;

Phyllis R. Klotman, "Dick-and-Jane and the Shirley Temple Sensibility in *The Bluest Eye*," *Black American Literature Forum*, 13 (1979): 123-125;

Barbara Lounsberry and Grace Ann Hovet, "Principles of Perception in Toni Morrison's *Sula*," *Black American Literature Forum*, 13 (1979): 126-129;

Chikwenye Okonjo Ogunyemi, "Order and Disorder in Toni Morrison's *The Bluest Eye*," *Critique: Studies in Modern Fiction*, 19 (1977): 112-120;

Ogunyemi, "*Sula*: 'A Nigger Joke,' " *Black American Literature Forum*, 13 (1979): 130-133.

HOWARD NEMEROV
(1 March 1920-)

SELECTED BOOKS: *The Image and the Law* (New York: Holt, 1947);

The Melodramatists (New York: Random House, 1949);

Guide to the Ruins (New York: Random House, 1950);

Federigo, or the Power of Love (Boston & Toronto: Little, Brown, 1954; London: Gollancz, 1955);

The Salt Garden (Boston & Toronto: Little, Brown, 1955);

The Homecoming Game (New York: Simon & Schuster, 1957; London: Gollancz, 1957);

Mirrors and Windows (Chicago: University of Chicago Press, 1958);

A Commodity of Dreams and Other Stories (New York: Simon & Schuster, 1959; London: Secker & Warburg, 1960);

New and Selected Poems (Chicago: University of Chicago Press, 1960);

Endor: Drama in One Act (New York & Nashville: Abingdon Press, 1961);

The Next Room of the Dream: Poems and Two Plays (Chicago: University of Chicago Press, 1962);

Poetry and Fiction: Essays (New Brunswick, N.J.: Rutgers University Press, 1963);

Journal of the Fictive Life (New Brunswick, N.J.: Rutgers University Press, 1965);

The Blue Swallows (Chicago & London: University of Chicago Press, 1967);

The Winter Lightning: Selected Poetry (London: Rapp & Whiting, 1968);

Stories, Fables & Other Diversions (Boston: Godine, 1971);

Reflexions on Poetry & Poetics (New Brunswick, N.J.: Rutgers University Press, 1972);

Gnomes & Occasions (Chicago & London: University of Chicago Press, 1973);

The Western Approaches: Poems, 1973-1975 (Chicago: University of Chicago Press, 1975);

The Collected Poems of Howard Nemerov (Chicago: University of Chicago Press, 1977);

Figures of Thought: Speculations on the Meaning of Poetry and Other Essays (Boston: Godine, 1978).

Howard Nemerov's literary career has been a singularly wide-ranging and productive one. A teacher by profession (currently the Edward Mallinckrodt Distinguished University Professor of English at Washington University in Saint Louis), Nemerov is also a poet, a novelist, a short-story writer, and a literary critic. He was born in New York City in 1920 and educated at Harvard (A.B., 1941). After serving as a pilot during World War II, he returned to New York and completed his first book, a volume of poems entitled *The Image and the Law*, which was published in 1947. Over the years, he has taught at Hamilton College, Bennington College, Brandeis University, the University of Minnesota, and Hollins College. Although the critical response to his writing has been curiously mixed, with the

Thomas Victor

same books generating both extremely favorable and extremely unfavorable opinions, overall he has enjoyed considerable success and received many honors and awards, such as *Poetry* magazine's Oscar Blumenthal Prize (1958) and the Roethke Memorial Prize for Poetry (1968). In 1963-1964, he was Consultant in Poetry to the Library of Congress.

Despite his apparent versatility, Nemerov is primarily a poet. The sheer industry, as well as the talent, which has gone into the making of his *Collected Poems* (1977) cannot fail to be impressive. By comparison, his output of novels seems relatively slight. There have been only three to date, and the last of the three, *The Homecoming Game*, appeared as long ago as 1957. All of the novels are out of print, and, since there is virtually no commentary on them other than the original reviews, they are perhaps in danger of being totally ignored. Each of them, however, reveals the same witty, ironic intelligence that has attracted Nemerov's readers to his poetry. Most of the criticism they received when they were new was centered around the complaint that they are not realistic enough, that the characters in them are unbelievable, the plots fantastic. Now, however, it seems clear that they were not intended to be realistic at all in the usual sense. They are essentially comedies about the dialogue that goes on in everyday life between imagination and reality. They focus primarily on the complications that arise when ordinary human beings try to behave as though life were a novel and as though they themselves were characters in it. Nemerov sees this as a tendency that is deeply rooted in human nature but ultimately based on illusion.

His first novel, *The Melodramatists* (1949), gets its title from the fact that almost all of the characters go around speaking and posturing like characters in a stage play or a novel of manners. They are often unable to grasp what is happening to them because they are so preoccupied with playing a part. The effect is ludicrous, and the reader may suspect that Nemerov is indulging in pure satire. However, there are moments in the novel when at least some of these characters are treated sympathetically, and we catch a glimpse of real anxieties and real fears underneath the facade. Gradually, it becomes evident that they are more or less compelled to behave as they do, because it is impossible for them to conceive of themselves except in terms of some sort of scenario.

The action in *The Melodramatists* revolves around the family of Mr. and Mrs. Nicholas Boyne, a pair of proper Bostonians who are keenly aware of the requirements of their social position and who always respond to any situation by saying and doing what they believe is expected of them. The falseness they project does not go unnoticed, however, by their daughters Susan and Claire, both of whom are intelligent enough to seek alternatives to the life led by their parents. Susan chooses to explore the possibilities of immorality and allows herself to be seduced by a man who is considerably older than she, a psychoanalyst named Edmond Einman. Claire goes in the opposite direction toward religion, specifically the Roman Catholic church. Placing herself under the guidance of Father Meretruce, she hopes to attain the discipline and intensity of faith. Both experiments fail, and the girls become disillusioned. Susan despairs when she finds that her life of sexual abandonment is boring instead of exciting and momentous. Claire, on the other hand, becomes increasingly skeptical and cautious when she discovers that the Church does not care about her spiritual progress or even about theology but demands simply that she be obedient and cooperative in practical matters. Ultimately, the two diametrically opposed experiments, which are intended to achieve authentic selfhood or self-expression, end in personal calamity (for Susan) and chaos for the Boyne household.

The plot of *The Melodramatists* is rather zany and, at times, even macabre. Mr. Boyne, for example, goes mad one day quite unexpectedly and decides to spend the rest of his life in the bathtub. Susan is blackmailed by Hogan the butler, who later beds down with her and finally kills her in an absurd accident. Claire, for her part, allows Father Meretruce to billet a group of refugee nuns in the family mansion (after the elder Boynes retire to a rest home) and eventually permits him to turn the place into a halfway house for whores. The final catastrophe comes when the latter take over the house and stage an elaborate *nuit d'amour* while Susan and Claire and their associates are held at gunpoint upstairs. Throughout all this, the characters tend to vacillate between involvement and detachment, between strong emotion and apathy. Frequently they commit themselves to a course of action and are amazed by their own behavior. By thus exhibiting a lack of coherence or stability, they illustrate one of the novel's main lessons, which is that life is "capable of infinite, improbable expansions."

In his next novel, *Federigo, or The Power of Love* (1954), Nemerov continues to explore the consequences of the overactive imagination. The protagonist is a perfectly average married man named Julian Ghent who, at thirty-six, has become slightly bored with his wife Sylvia and, consequently, has begun to fantasize about the possibilities of an affair. Partly for the sheer adventure of it and partly to justify himself in the event that an opportunity should arise, he sends himself fictitious letters (signed Federigo) warning of a possible indiscretion on Sylvia's part. When he deliberately leaves these letters where she can read them, he creates the conditions whereby his fantasies can be turned into reality. Just as he becomes committed to the idea of having an adulterous affair, so he unwittingly encourages her to do the same with a young man she has been flirting with behind his back.

Like Susan in *The Melodramatists,* Julian is excited by the possibilities that seem to lie before him and also goaded by a sense of his own nothingness, a feeling that he is just drifting toward oblivion and must make some kind of significant gesture. For the most part, his behavior is amiably foolish, and he deserves the gentle chiding he receives from Federigo, who begins to appear in the novel as though he were real, as Julian's double in fact, ready to advise. Federigo's precise status is allowed to remain obscure to Julian, though to the reader he seems to be quite clearly a figment of Julian's imagination. Ironically, it is Federigo who tries to persuade Julian to eschew his fantasies and be more realistic. The effect, however, is to make him struggle harder to realize those fantasies. He and Sylvia both become determined to take lovers who are clearly inappropriate and not even really desired except for the purpose of making an impression. In the superbly improbable denouement, they are tricked into spending the night together in the belief that they are actually in the arms of their lovers. Their shock and relief at finding that their act of adultery has been mental or imaginative rather than real brings them back to normal and cures them of the foolishness that almost wrecked their marriage.

Federigo, like *The Melodramatists,* is largely a satire on the vanity of characters who entertain a romantic conception of their place in the scheme of things, and it shows what absurdities may result when this conception is acted on. In his third novel, *The Homecoming Game,* Nemerov shows how an ordinarily shrewd man might become the victim of such a conception. The novel tells the story of Charles Osman, a history professor at a small college who fails the star football player on an exam and makes him ineligible to play in the big game of the season. Charles is essentially a reflective man who has withdrawn from active participation in life in order to muse and speculate on the past. From the ivory tower of his aloofness and detachment, he is drawn into the fray of the present by the enormous pressures that are brought to bear upon him from different quarters. Nemerov makes it clear that the events surrounding the homecoming game are themselves a kind of game in which Charles is required to maintain his principles of honesty and fair play and, at the same time, meet and counter the complicated moves of his various antagonists, who include disgruntled students, the college president, distinguished alumni, and the football player's girlfriend Lily, to mention only a few. The situation is constantly changing and developing with Charles becoming more and more conscious of his pivotal role in determining the outcome. Thus, he tries to foil the plans of mobsters who, as it turns out, have bribed most of the players to throw the game. He also decides to marry Lily and change the basic direction of his own life. He discovers by the end of the novel that his sense of being at the center of things was an illusion. The mobsters' plan works, he loses the girl, tensions at the college evaporate, and he learns that his own part in events has been inconsequential.

Throughout the novel, Nemerov reminds us that Charles has always been fascinated by football games. They suggest to him the brilliance and brevity of life's spectacle in which he happens to be merely a spectator rather than an important player. However, the successful fixing of the football game seems to indicate that there are no important players or, at least, that they are always behind the scenes. Since the average man cannot choose but be a spectator, it is the part of wisdom to accept this condition with resignation.

Since *The Homecoming Game,* Nemerov has not published another novel. In the early 1960s, he seems to have experienced a mental block while trying to write a novel, and he recorded his efforts to analyze this block in *Journal of the Fictive Life* (1965). In many ways, the *Journal* affords the best introduction to the novels that precede it, because it contains, in addition to a large measure of Freudian self-analysis, a sort of commentary on the problems which the modern novelist must face. Among these problems, Nemerov implies, is the fact that, since we now know how infinitely complex a human being is, it is impossible to regard any character in a work of fiction as realistic. Or, rather, it is impossible to think of men and women as having fixed or definable "characters." In the course of the *Journal* Nemerov tries to identify his own character, his own fundamental motives and anxieties, but he reaches the rather negative conclusion that psychoanalysis is "mostly a plausible fraud" which can only "dissolve in dialectic the idea of character as a category." At the bottom of all analyses and interpretations, there is, according to Nemerov, "no self, only an echoing emptiness." This is precisely the intuition that Nemerov's characters in his novels are trying desperately to avoid. In adopting various melodramatic postures, they are trying to give themselves the unity and stability which properly belong only to the invented characters of literature.

By the same token, Nemerov makes the concept of narrative seem equally inappropriate to real life by suggesting that it is derived from the mind's need for order rather than from events themselves. Therefore, a novel about real life which has a carefully constructed, wholly plausible plot is highly unrealistic. In Nemerov's novels, the impression is created that almost anything can happen, because the characters themselves are trying to impose on events their own sense of what ought to be happening and these "plots" are often in conflict.

Nemerov has perhaps come to feel that the novelist himself, with his own incorrigible tendency to fantasize melodramatic scenes and situations, presents a spectacle as ridiculous as that of his own characters. In recent poems such as "Novelists" and "Reflexions of a Novelist," he observes that it is, of course, the novelist who is preeminently the man with the overactive imagination, the egomaniac, the voyeur. By choosing not to write another novel, Nemerov may be following out the implications of his own earlier fiction.

—Carl Rapp

References:

Julia A. Bartholomay, *The Shield of Perseus: The Vision and Imagination of Howard Nemerov* (Gainesville: University of Florida Press, 1972);

Bowie Duncan, ed., *The Critical Reception of Howard Nemerov: A Selection of Essays and a Bibliography* (Metuchen, N.J.: Scarecrow Press, 1971);

Ross Labrie, *Howard Nemerov* (Boston: Twayne, 1980);

Peter Meinke, *Howard Nemerov* (Minneapolis: University of Minnesota Press, 1968);

William Mills, *The Stillness in Moving Things: The World of Howard Nemerov* (Memphis: Memphis State University Press, 1975).

JOSEPHINE PINCKNEY

(25 January 1895-4 October 1957)

BOOKS: *Sea-Drinking Cities; Poems* (New York & London: Harper, 1927);

Call Back Yesterday: The First Twenty-Five Years of Ashley Hall (Charleston, S.C.: Quin Press, 1934);

Hilton Head (New York & Toronto: Farrar & Rinehart, 1941);

Three o'Clock Dinner (New York: Viking, 1945; London: Hodder & Stoughton, 1946);

Great Mischief (New York: Viking, 1948; London: Chapman & Hall, 1949);

My Son and Foe (New York: Viking, 1952; London: Chapman & Hall, 1952);

Splendid in Ashes (New York: Viking, 1958; London: Chapman & Hall, 1958).

Josephine Pinckney began her career as a poet and did not publish her first novel until her forty-sixth year. The early discipline of writing verse aided in making her five novels triumphs of meticulous craftsmanship and polish. One point that reviewers stressed time and again is the artistry of her "chiseled" style, which Pinckney explained as coming from slow and painstaking composition and a "lot of time with the pumice stone." Her novels are the conceptions of a mature mind. By her first novel, her themes had been clearly thought out, thus at least partly explaining why critics frequently praised her keen intelligence and firm grasp of reality.

Pinckney was not a sensational writer. Although violence and sex are part of the world she created, she never exploited them. Neither was she a sentimental novelist. Her hallmarks, after an effective style, are an almost eighteenth-century restraint, an urbane wit, and a carefully controlled emotional distance from her subject matter which allows seeing life's acute ironies and paradoxes. The fact that she had thought long and seriously about the human condition provided insights which, in the final analysis, are the novels' most valuable contributions. It is little wonder that Harrison Smith, writing in 1952 in the *Saturday Review*, described her as "one of the ablest women writers of the South."

Today, if she is remembered at all, it is for a single novel, *Three o'Clock Dinner* (1945). This work sold over 700,000 copies in America alone during the first four months after publication, was translated into Spanish, Portuguese, Dutch, Danish, Norwegian, Swedish, Romanian, Finnish, French, Italian, and German, and was bought by MGM for $125,000, thus representing one of the ten highest prices paid for motion-picture rights to its day. While it is a very fine novel, it is not her best and, unfortunately, has overshadowed the other works of a long and distinguished career.

Josephine Lyons Scott Pinckney was born in 1895—the only child of Thomas and Camilla Scott Pinckney of Charleston, South Carolina—into high social position and a strong sense of tradition and place. Her father was one of the last of the rice planters, and she was plantation-bred on the Santee River. Her Charleston ancestry included Thomas Pinckney, diplomat; Charles and Charles Cotesworth Pinckney, who played important roles in founding the new nation and in writing its Constitution; and Eliza Lucas Pinckney, rice planter and colonial author whose work has recently been singled out for "literary excellence" of a high degree. Thus, Pinckney's coming to writing as a career may have been more a matter of fate than free will. Understandably, the conflict between these two forces was to become one of her major themes.

Pinckney reported that as a child she "had always liked to write" and kept her copybook in use at school. In 1909, she was the first student to enroll at Ashley Hall, a private girls' school in Charleston, where she was active in dramatics and literature and where with a few friends she started the student literary magazine *Cerberus*. Because there were not enough contributors, the editors had to draw lots for filling the magazine: she got poetry and jokes, and when the magazine came out, Herbert Ravenel Sass praised her poetry in the local paper. So she continued to write verse. She graduated from Ashley Hall in 1912 and took courses in English at the College of Charleston, Columbia University, and Radcliffe. Returning to Charleston, she was instrumental in founding the Poetry Society of South Carolina in 1920, an organization in the vanguard of the Southern literary renaissance, and as Donald Davidson has written, the "model for similar organizations in nearly every other southern state." Throughout the society's first decade, she was much involved in its work and a regular contributor of poetry to its yearbook.

Her first publications in a periodical of nationwide circulation came in July 1921 in *Poetry*. From then until 1935, she published verse in such magazines as *North American Review*, *Bookman*, *Saturday Review*, *New Republic*, *Yale Review*, and *Virginia Quarterly Review*. Her first book and only collection of poems was published by Harper in 1927, a volume entitled *Sea-Drinking Cities*. These forty-two poems attempt to capture the charm of the Carolina Low Country by making use of its folklore, songs, and superstitions. In keeping with these local interests, Pinckney became a trustee of the Charleston Museum, a member of the Carolina Art Association and the Historic Charleston Foundation, and a founder of the Society for the Preservation of Spirituals, songs which she collected, transcribed, and performed. Until her death, she maintained a family plantation, El Dorado, on the Santee River, with the ruins of its great-house rising above a wilderness garden. She lived, however, in Charleston at 36 Chalmers Street in a home she restored around 1940. From the third-floor study of this structure, with its view of St. Michael's famous spire and the central city, she was to write all her novels.

By 1935, she had turned from poetry to fiction. She told a reporter ten years later: "I can't write poetry now—I don't know why." When in 1952 the same subject was broached, she commented that she was unhappy about not writing verse any more, but this time went further to give the reason: "one can't go on and on writing pastoral poetry." She had moved away from mere local color and entered the greater world of character. Her fiction had become a more successful vehicle for her ironic view of human motives and actions.

There was still some emphasis on local color in her first novel, *Hilton Head*, which she began in the 1930s and published in 1941; but this interest was not a primary one. The novel is fleshed out on a frame of historical research which sent her to London and Seville. Yet, as reviewers were quick to realize, it is "something more than the historical novel" and, in the words of one, cannot be mentioned with "such spurious historical travesties as *Anthony Adverse*, *Scaramouche*, or *Forever Amber*." The novel received high critical praise in *Atlantic*, *New York Times*, *New Yorker*, *Books*, and *Saturday Review*. It was an overwhelming success with the critics.

Several strengths save it from the mediocrity of many historical narratives. It is a solid psychological novel that convincingly portrays the main character's inner struggles, aspirations, and weaknesses. Its style, while not possessing the brilliance of the later works, shows frequent touches of poetry. (This trait does at times result in overwriting and a too conscious striving for dramatic effect, faults which Pinckney eliminated in her later novels.) One recognizes the effective wit and studied irony which were to become her hallmarks, although they are not handled quite as masterfully as in her later works. The serious intent of the novel is never in doubt. Its themes are universal and bespeak careful thought. One also notices the author's tolerance of cultures and peoples unlike her own, or, as she would say, superficially different, but essentially the same in the important ways. "We all have the same skeletons," she wrote. "It is merely the flesh that takes on the color of the surroundings." Early in the novel she notes that when looked at objectively, the curious foxtails worn by the Indians are not far different from the tails on the Englishman's coat. She is thus more interested in similarities among mankind than in the surface differences emphasized by the local colorist.

Set in 1663, *Hilton Head* portrays the life of Henry Woodward (first English settler of Carolina)—his travels to Barbados; his stay among the Indians of Santa Elena; his captivity in Saint Augustine; his settling in what is to become Charles Town; his years as surgeon, naturalist, deputy to Lord Ashley Cooper, Indian trader, and planter; and finally his exploration of the Appalachians in old age. As Pinckney writes of him in her preface, he "is one of the many enterprising spirits who, scarcely known to Americans, flavored the early history of their country with his brisk activities and stamped the American genius with its toughness and resiliency." That resiliency is a major theme of the novel: the necessity of being adaptable in the teeth of fate, a theme developed throughout her canon. In old age, Henry tells a new immigrant that "You will shortly find, sir, that here on the edge of the world necessity is the tailor and makeshift the fashion." Henry has learned early that "Every life had its direction bent by cross winds, and what could a man do in the clutch of the elements but find his legs as best he could, take a new bearing, and pursue what opportunities fate presented. He refused to lament the lives he had once intended to live." And Henry survives, while Meg, his first wife, who never can cease longing for the fashionable life she left in London, will not accept her position in the new land. In trying to escape, she is destroyed in a storm at sea. Henry concludes, " 'Well, Meg had refused to bend before the wind, her definite personality had set itself against circumstances and had gone down before them.' He admired that arrogance, but he admired it remotely, without envy, being otherwise himself."

Mary, his second wife, is very different from Meg. She is compared to King David: "at a time of calamity she weeps and lies all night upon the earth, but when she's lost the throw, she ceases to beseech God . . . she washes and changes her apparel and goes about the business of living." And Mary endures to raise strong children. Both she and Henry have learned that it is the "low tree which withstands the wind." After Henry's death, the people of the village, whose survival he has insured through his treaty with the Creeks, report that "one of the sights of the countryside is Mrs. Woodward walking barefooted with her skirts looped up through the mud of her rice fields keeping her sowers at their work."

Both Henry and Mary accept fate with resiliency, make the best of situations, draw strength from the new continent, and survive. They are practical, but also passionate in their love of the land. In old age, Henry views the familiar flat landscape, pausing "in the gate with the catch at the throat he always felt when he looked out over his fields. . . . The sharp salt smell of the big fish nets drying on the palisade; the sweet wood smoke rising like a coronet of plumes from the half-circle of servants' huts spoke to Henry's keenest sense, the sense that most directly stirred remembrance and emotion. For no reason in particular he felt his heart bursting with passion and pain." In good eighteenth-century fashion, both have an abiding faith that life must continue despite crises and cataclysms, that order will eventually assert itself through the routine daily performance of the basic human activities, and that after the inevitable tragedies of life, one must indeed get on with "the business of living." What a man becomes, therefore, is a direct result of a combination of character and fate.

Pinckney began her second novel, *Three o'Clock Dinner,* in the fall of 1941; by mid-November 1944 it had been accepted by Viking Press. At the suggestion of her editor, Pascal Covici, she made corrections in the typescript, but rejected any attempts to "ham" the story and make it conform to a formula. After traveling to New York in March with the finished manuscript, she returned to Charleston where she made further corrections, including a new last page, and she finally mailed the polished typescript to Viking in April 1945. The month of May found her at her favorite pastime—gardening—and meticulously scouring over minute details in the galley proofs. Her conscientious attention to the smallest points suggests her professionalism. As late as June 1945, she still had not settled on a title. Along with *Three o'Clock Dinner,* she was offering as alternates: "The Feast of Unreason," "The Damask Table Cloth," "The Olive Plants" (from "Thy children are like olive plants about thy table"), "The House of Cards" (for as she explained, "The building up of a family is a Manufacture very little above the building of a House of Cards"), and "The Laughing Animals: A Comedy of Manners" (from the quotation by William Hazlitt stating that man is the only animal that laughs and weeps). Although Pinckney favored the last, Viking finally settled on *Three o'Clock Dinner.* The novel's first printing of 10,000 copies was completed in July; but the book's official publication did not come until 21 September 1945. By 9 October, Viking could report that the novel was selling "with atomic speed. . . . No novel we have published in many seasons . . . has sold faster." It was a Literary Guild selection, a fact which assured a prepublication run of 600,000 copies for members; and Viking had sold another 100,000 copies of its own by Christmas 1945. In the face of all this sudden success and MGM's record purchase price, the author reported herself in a daze and not able to believe any of it.

Three o'Clock Dinner was to be her most popular book, selling more than her other four novels combined. It was likewise a great critical success. Reviewers praised its irony, fine wit, vigor, and readableness. Several singled out its style for delicacy, crispness, craftsmanship, and a classic sense of rightness. Generally, the reception marked no falling off from the high praise which greeted *Hilton Head.* After *My Son and Foe* (1952), it is probably her best work.

The novel is set in Charleston on the eve of England's entry into World War II. Book 1 is the account of a day in Judith Redcliff's life. It begins as she wakes and starts gardening, dealing "confidently with plants as she herself did not with human kind." Through inference and understatement, Pinckney implies Judith's failure to see her own worth. Her melancholy, introspective nature has a strong tendency toward fatalism. Following her is "the reproach that dogs a childless woman." Her husband, dead now for two years, still dominates her as he does this first book and, to some extent, the entire novel. Her "backward voice of remembrance" robs her of a present existence; and she finds escape from intense unhappiness only in fantasy, "the indigestible food the starved heart gnaws on." The first book ends in darkness, with the single place set at the table hurting her "with its mute statement."

Set against Judith is the main female character of Book 2, Lorena Hessenwinkle. Full of life, confident, voluptuous, extroverted, but coarse and tactless, Lorena is the center of attention of Tat

Redcliff, Judith's brother-in-law. Book 3 focuses on Wick Redcliff, Judith's father-in-law, a Broad Street businessman. Book 4 centers on Lucian Redcliff, Wick's brother, who squarely faces the truth about his family members. He rightly sees that Lorena is marrying Tat because she had loved his brother, Fen, whom Judith married. Both Lorena's jealousy of Judith and the argument Tat has with his father are quirks of fate which lead to their "choice" to marry. The author devotes much attention to the unspoken truth behind the silences, the meanings behind the gestures and nuances of manners. Books 5 and 6 have a shifting focus on various characters, including Wick, Lucian, Mr. Hessenwinkle, and Lucian's mother. Book 7, the novel's last chapter, returns to a focus on Judith and her final meeting with Lorena.

The novel's plot revolves around Tat and Lorena's marriage and involves the conflict between traditional patrician values and contemporary middle-class ones. Yet Judith is the character who matters most. Tat and Lorena's marriage is finally unimportant because it is annulled; its main import is that Judith learns about her dead husband and Lorena's illegitimate son and, as a result, is able to adopt him. The heir comes home to the Redcliff family; and no one could raise him better in the family tradition than Judith and Lucian, who Pinckney strongly implies will marry Judith. Judith has grown since the novel's beginning. She has learned to accept the truth about her husband, to adapt herself to this truth, and, like the survivors in *Hilton Head,* to carry on with the business of living. She has broken from her barren shell of fantasy and is able to begin living in the present once again. Her triumph marks the triumph of the family, or at least a tentative one for another generation. The themes of family solidarity and of the necessity to adapt to change are strong threads which run throughout the novel.

Three o'Clock Dinner is primarily a novel about family and the complicated meshings of familial interaction. Even though the plot may focus on the conflict between two families, the novel is more concerned with the tremendously complex attitudes family members have toward one another within the family unit. And although Pinckney's plot is entertaining, she might have run the risk of creating a tempest in a teapot were it not for an emphasis on the greater issues of universal value and the unmistakable humanity of the people who act out the drama. For Pinckney's portrayal of character in *Three o'Clock Dinner* is complex. One feels both pity and dislike for Lorena, who is attractive and repulsive at the same time. One admires Judith's loyalty to her dead husband and simultaneously realizes the selfishness in it. Her cool self-possession is also both a strength and a weakness. Fen Redcliff's magnetic character is reflected in the memories of the living, but the reader learns that he was also an adulterer and a domineering egotist. Wick, his father, is a warm and gentle man, but reveals his vain and foolish sides when he makes his too warmly felt toast of adulation to Lorena at the wedding party. His obvious physical attraction to her makes him depart from the impeccable manners he has shown on all occasions heretofore. In Lucian, the reader sees both kindness and a sadistic enjoyment of the sufferings of others. The characters, therefore, are all a dappled mixture of noble and ignoble impulses; and Pinckney is able to stimulate strongly ambivalent feelings in the reader from almost every action of each character. As a result, the novel runs the gamut of tones from satirical to sympathetic, comic to tragic, whimsical to poignant—with one tone following directly on the heels of its opposite or with all the tones interwoven at one and the same time in a complex mixture. As one critic has written, "a love of paradox and ironic juxtapositions is perhaps the distinguishing trait of her fiction."

In the social war waged in the novel, Pinckney does not propagandize; in fact, she never really chooses sides, for both her most sympathetic character (Judith) and her least (Tat) are of the same class. In writing to her editor, she stated matter-of-factly that in the end the Hessenwinkles come off rather better than the Redcliffs. Pinckney was too much the knowledgeable student of mankind to betray her talent for presenting character honestly by distributing virtue exclusively to one class and vice to another. Her chief aim was to provide insight into life and character; and life as it is created in this novel is simply too complex to allow such easy simplification.

She was attempting to begin her third novel, *Great Mischief* (1948), by July 1945, but was finding it difficult owing to the publicity from *Three o'Clock Dinner.* By May 1946, she reported that she was working hard on it, but getting nowhere. She was expecting to finish the first draft in late July 1946 and by 8 November was cleaning up the manuscript. On 30 December she was still revising. By 7 July, she had simplified her title, "Great Mischief; or The Blue-Eyed Hag," to *Great Mischief* and had rejected an alternate title, "A Corner of the Moon." She sent the last section of the completed typescript to Viking in mid-July 1947. Marshall Best, Viking editor, noted that her revisions took an entirely different course than he had expected: instead of moving the novel toward ironic fantasy, she had actually thrown it more toward realism. Because one or two sticky places had slowed her up, she did not complete reading proofs until 17 November.

By January 1948, *Great Mischief* had been chosen as the April selection of the Book-of-the-Month Club. Author's copies were being sent by 8 March; its official publication came 22 March 1948 and was marked by a Viking Press party at the Dock Street Theatre in Charleston. The book was another critical success; reviewers praised its style, psychological realism, rich humor, professionalism, and its treatment of the serious theme "of man's abiding preoccupation with the problem of evil." The novel was another best-seller and was published abroad. December 1964 saw a Popular Library Reprint edition, thus attesting to a continuing interest in the novel.

Set in 1886 in Charleston, *Great Mischief*'s main character is Timothy Partridge, a meek, shy druggist, thirty-six years of age, whose routine, carefully ordered life is dominated by his sister, with whom he lives. Partridge has had little experience in life and has not thought clearly about life's possibilities. As he says of himself, "he was becoming an old man without having been a young one." The title comes from one of his ancient almanacs, which prophesies that 1886 is a year "in which great mischief is to be wrought." The mischief is the Charleston earthquake of 1886; but great mischief is also wrought in Timothy's personal life, when as a result of dabbling in witchcraft, he meets evil face to face.

He is working late at the pharmacy when a beautiful woman comes calling for solanum, or nightshade. She begins to haunt Timothy's mind. His sister Penelope, the other woman in his life, is long-suffering and charitable. She gets pleasure from self-sacrifice and is "always morally right." Yet she is not perfect, for it is Timothy who pays the bills while she gets the credit. Penelope enjoys the image of the noble woman; and all her charities keep Timothy tied to home and to her. Her primary "sacrifice" is keeping Mr. Dombie in their house; he is an aging soldier wounded in the "holy war." Timothy mischievously begins to cross her in small ways, for he has had too much of her charity—especially her "sacrifices" for Mr. Dombie. His mischievous (or is it better called *evil?*) turn of mind finally leads him to view her realistically: she is no paragon, but a mixture of noble ideals and selfish motives. He realizes that she keeps Dombie in their house so that she can enjoy seeing him every day as a symbol of her role as mankind's savior. Again, as in the two earlier novels, and in the two yet to come, Pinckney demonstrates that in most actions, both good and bad motives are closely intertwined. This truth is an integral and unchanging part of her view of mankind.

Timothy, in a fit of contentiousness, throws the Bible his sister had given him into the fireplace and leaves the house. When he returns, the building has burned and his sister and Dombie have died in the flames. As part 1 ends, he sees the woman who came into his shop for solanum watching him. In part 2, she becomes a regular visitor. Timothy calls her Sinkinda the witch, and she teaches him that good and evil are closely aligned. Through his love of Sinkinda, his first consummated love affair, he decides to go over to the side of Satan. What had started as "mischief" has resulted in murder and is fast leading to damnation.

In part 3, Timothy follows Sinkinda on what he thinks is a night ride. (He actually takes solanum, jumps off his roof, falls, gets knocked out, and hallucinates what follows.) Pinckney uses local Negro folklore, the Faust legend, and other folk motifs to describe Timothy's visit to hell and his interview with Satan. All strands are nicely and ingeniously adapted to local, everyday life, and with a sprightly, sophisticated humor. On first meeting Satan, Timothy sees that he looks very much like a Charlestonian. Satan's act of putting an embroidered fire screen (like so many seen in the colonial homes of Charleston) in front of the fire of hell is a nice local touch and, at the same time, is highly symbolic: the scene is pretty, but the reality behind it is anything but, thus again emphasizing the theme that what seems to be may only be the opposite in reality. Timothy shows the deep-seated propriety of his upbringing when he describes Satan's robes of pink, red, and magenta as "a somewhat garish selection for his Western tastes." He comments further that everyone in Satan's procession looked "overdressed." Instead of participating in the "Radio City Music hall atmosphere," he goes to hell's library to read, burns the book of Evil, catches the library on fire, and probably burns down the house of hell. In part 3 comes the great earthquake, which Timothy believes to be Judgment Day. It is indeed the end for him because he jumps into the fissure caused by the quake, an act that was "no harder than jumping off the roof." Timothy leaves the reader with his final conclusion: "You have to re-examine Good and Evil constantly; they change their appearances, like Satan at the reception." The novel suggests further that it may be even safer to make no exploration of Good and Evil at all.

Great Mischief, for all its humor, imagination, and ingeniousness, is not as good a novel as *Three o'Clock Dinner.* Although Pinckney took her usual pains in rewriting and polishing, it shows more hasty initial composition than her previous work (one year, rather than three). Its strongest sections are the excellent part 1 and the account of Timothy's visit to hell.

Pinckney was aware that *Great Mischief* was composed in record time for her. *My Son and Foe* would again be slow, painstaking work requiring over two years of initial writing and a year of rewriting. She began shuffling notes on this fourth novel in April 1948. By July she was still struggling with outlining. February 1949 saw the novel getting along in spite of vernal interruptions because, as she said, spring is not a very good working time, it being "contrary to nature to hang over a typewriter at this lovely season." After much mental anguish, she decided to interrupt her work for a two-month visit to Greece. Although she became so disillusioned with the work in November that she contemplated scrapping it and starting over, by 13 March 1950 she could report her worst troubles with the manuscript behind her and that she was again working in her slow fashion. In July she reported being in the last stretch, but was certain that as usual, there was much rewriting to do. November 1950 found her "plugging away on revision and, as usual, finding it very slow and draggy." In May 1951, she was recovering from an operation and putting in hard work. She sent the first half of the typescript to Viking 18 May 1951 after purging the story of padding and moving one scene forward. The second half was mailed 3 June 1951 with the message that the typescript needed cutting and sharpening still and that she was anxious to get at it. On 7 July 1951, she wanted to give the novel what she called a major rewrite job. The current title "Susannah's Fancy" did not please her because it had the "social comedy touch which I am now trying earnestly to scratch out." The corrected typescript was sent to Viking 30 July 1951 after she had done nothing else but correct it for days, "day and night." Before leaving for a trip to London, she wrote Viking on 13 August to change her title to "Passing Strangers." This was not done. "By unanimous final vote of 9 editors" at Viking, the title became *My Son and Foe* on 15 August. From London on 21 August, she complied with the change because while she did not feel *My Son and Foe* an ideal title, she agreed that it did give a necessary seriousness to the tone of the book and was challenging. The title is taken from the passage quoted in the novel: "In opposition sits grim death, my son and foe," a quotation from book 2 of Milton's *Paradise Lost.*

Pinckney corrected galleys in London during September 1951, requiring 650 lines to be reset, thus again showing meticulous attention to her craft down to its last stage. The novel was published 11 January 1952. By 6 February, Viking could report a sales of "just under 10,000" which was "moving along, though not in best-seller fashion." Viking was having to dispose of overstock at twelve cents a copy in December 1953. Of her four Viking novels, it sold the fewest copies. Pinckney would no doubt appreciate the irony in the fact that her poorest seller is now receiving praise as her most distinguished literary work. The novel elicited mixed reviews, but the consensus was generally favorable, yet not as favorable as those of her previous novels.

My Son and Foe is her only work not set in Charleston. This departure came as a result of her perturbation with critics who expected "quaintness" and spoke of her works as "Charleston novels," thus implying that they were local color. As early as 1945, she was combating this notion. "It disturbs me a little to hear people speak of *Three o'Clock Dinner* as a 'Charleston novel, ' " she said. "I wrote it as a story about some people who, because of their natures, their loves, envies and resentments, followed a predictable course. . . . Primarily they are human beings; superficially they take color from the place they live in. Hence it is my theory that the background of a story should stay where it belongs—in the background." She commented further that she hoped her books had a different emphasis from Robert Molloy's *Pride's Way* (1945), a novel of Charleston local color, because unlike it, they stressed character, story, and philosophical implication rather than setting.

My Son and Foe is an excellent example of a novel with these emphases. The Caribbean island of St. Finbar, where it is set, is fictional. Its remoteness and timelessness are particularly suited to the novel's portrayal of the old elemental conflicts. Like *Three o'Clock Dinner,* the novel centers on the conflicts within a family. This one is highly unstable and unorthodox. Elsi[nore] Baxter has one son James before she leaves her husband and marries a Greek, Basil Metellus, with whom she has another son Rikki. The four are now living in a run-down country estate on the island. Rikki is spontaneous, instinctual, physical, natural, and emotional; James is cold, intellectual, aloof, and has a penchant for machines. The two sons are always subtly but relentlessly at odds and constantly vying for their mother's attention. As one critic noted, the novel "recreates in modern terms the old tragic patterns of brother against brother, parent against child, and man against the dark workings of fate."

Into this potentially explosive situation, Pinckney introduces Kirk McAfee, an engineer touring the world for pleasure, who "drops from the skies" in an airplane. He becomes the central intelligence of the novel, and the reader gains some objective insight into the family's affairs through his detachment. He is an aloof, clinically objective man of intellect, a spectator whose omniscience makes him a perfect narrator, but whose cool distance makes him a failure as a human being. The imagery which surrounds him suggests that he is a deity. Arriving unannounced in an airplane, he is a literal, but ironic, deus ex machina. With "God-like reticence," he dabbles in the family's affairs, "playing God," as he implies; and through his meddling, instead of preventing a crisis, he creates one which results in Rikki's death by drowning, possibly at the hands of James. Although his intervention in the story precipitates the tragedy, his self-centered emotional blindness prevents him from realizing his guilt. He merely resumes his rootless wanderings, his "circlings," by going on to some other island with his camera loaded with fresh film.

Again Pinckney's characters abound in paradoxes. The reader's responses to them are constantly changing. He sympathizes with Rikki, then dislikes him before finally appreciating his personality most of all. The reader dislikes James at first, then sympathizes with his plight before seeing that he is selfish and unfeeling. It is the same with Elsi. She is a fascinating woman and a life-force, but she is also unstable and potentially destructive to all around her. Kirk McAfee is the most complex character, but the final view of him is decidedly negative. He destroys carelessly and without conscience or even the realization he has done so. It is almost as if he has collaborated with James to destroy Rikki, for James is veritably McAfee's philosophical son: cold, mechanical, and aloof. When Rikki dies, intellectuality triumphs over instinct, and the reader feels a sense of loss.

The novel is therefore a tragedy. As in *Great Mischief*, Pinckney intertwined various myths to highlight her themes. This time she relied heavily on Greek drama, and appropriately so, for the novel deals with her concept of fate. Commenting in an interview, she said that the novel's "thematic question" is "of good and evil, and if and when a crash comes, is it you or I or fate that is to blame? Sometimes the fates grab our little sin and run away with it and bring it back outsize. You start something, and then things get rolling, and you have the conclusion that character is fate. A dreadful thing to think of." The fates and furies are thus largely projections of ourselves and our passions.

Unlike most Americans of her day, Pinckney had learned to see tragedy as a pervasive fact of life. In her view, tragedy does not totally overwhelm man or engulf him entirely, yet is ever present, yoked with the comic. (The portrayal of this paradox is responsible for imparting to her comic scenes what one critic called a "lime-tart edge.") After Rikki's death, the characters, in typical Pinckney fashion, must adapt and make the best of their lives, or be destroyed. Life goes on with its ironies, paradoxes, and absurdities.

My Son and Foe is the darkest of her novels. Its weighty theme of fate versus free will tends to make it less lively reading than *Three o'Clock Dinner*. It does not have the earlier novel's sparkling wit, and the characters are somewhat too histrionic to be pleasing. Yet these are minor faults next to the book's strengths. The complexities of the novel cannot be exhausted by several readings; it is a significant literary achievement.

Pinckney had made a good start on writing her last novel, *Splendid in Ashes* (1958), by late August 1952. She found the going difficult: two years later she reported herself stuck. "Writing books is just too hard," she said. "What I've gone and done is written two books, and it's going to be hell to disentangle them. . . . And I'm *furious* with myself for falling into that trap." Approaching the age of sixty, she was even more the careful craftsman. By January 1955 she had "reconciled" the book's two halves and reported it to be moving along toward a Christmas 1955 completion. But she took off time to visit Peru with Mrs. DuBose Heyward and to make other tours. A partial typescript of the novel was not sent to Viking until late March 1957; and the entire typescript did not reach them until September. On 7 September, Marshall Best suggested two major changes. Pinckney came to New York to discuss these; while there she became ill, entered the hospital, and died on 4 October 1957. She was buried in Charleston's Magnolia Cemetery on 7 October.

About the suggested changes, Best reported to her nephew that one problem had been practically solved before her death and the other had been discussed but not settled. He proposed to publish the novel with his revisions limited to these two places, where he felt he knew her wishes. As he explained, she was so conscious of every sentence she wrote that any cut required much patching, which is hard for anyone else to do. After completing the work, he reported that his principal change was at the end, where he cut a number of pages to speed the conclusion. The novel was published on 14 April 1958 and received favorable reviews. Viking reported the sales as "considerably better" than *My Son and Foe*, but less than her other two Viking novels.

The book's title comes from a passage in Sir Thomas Browne's *Urne-Buriall* (1658): "Man is a noble animal, splendid in ashes, and pompous in the grave." It prepares the reader for the tragicomic attitude toward man's grandiose posturings, which the novel depicts primarily through the character of Augustus Grimshawe. The novel begins in Charleston with the news of Grimshawe's death; and through town gossip and flashbacks, the reader learns partial truths about this native son who made and then lost his great fortune in New York.

Focusing on the interactions between members of the Grimshawe family and within the larger family of the community, the novel is filled with a sense of life's poignancy and tragic nature. It reflects on "what compromises life brings even to the high-minded," and on the necessity of not asking "too much of fate; [for] we aren't meant to have much." "Love certainly gets a rough treatment in this world," the novel says. "Even its vital ingredient, memory, [is] wiped out by new associations." But even so, man is still a "splendid," if vainglorious creature. The folly of his vanity and grandiose undertakings does not deter him from continuing his strutting, even in death. Fate may frustrate his individual schemes, but his kind survives. At the novel's end, Grimshawe is dead; yet his silk hat, given to his servant Annibal, "goes marching on," albeit in comic fashion, on Annibal's head, a symbol that life continues.

Grimshawe is a tragic hero, with the tragic flaws of egocentrism and materialism. His community is flawed in the same manner, and he thereby epitomizes and embodies it. This kinship is probably the reason the townspeople, while blind to the traits in themselves that they dislike so much in him, are so fascinated with Augustus and his doings without ever knowing why. He is not only one of them, but also the composite of them, a modern everyman.

The novel marked no diminution of its creator's intellectual acuteness. Her ironic sense had, if anything, sharpened. There is the same tone of gentle worldly wit, of sparkling grace and gaiety which marked *Three o'Clock Dinner*. And her faith in man's resiliency in combating a hostile fate did not fail her. *Splendid in Ashes* is probably not as good a novel as *Three o'Clock Dinner* and *My Son and Foe*, but is a solid achievement and a fitting epitaph to a distinguished career, which is, unfortunately, too little explored today. Pinckney's works never became hackneyed or formulaic. She cannot be stereotyped as a local colorist or novelist of manners; instead, she used the methods of both in rising above them. She is a genuinely gifted author whose achievement is substantial and noteworthy.

—*James E. Kibler, Jr.*

Other:

"Bulwarks Against Change," in *Culture in the South*, ed. W. T. Couch (Chapel Hill: University of North Carolina Press, 1934), pp. 40-51.

Periodical Publications:

"Charleston's Poetry Society," *Sewanee Review*, 38 (January 1930): 50-56;

"Southern Writers in Congress," *Saturday Review*, 8 (7 November 1931): 266;

"They Shall Return as Strangers," *Virginia Quarterly Review*, 10 (October 1934): 540-557;

"Marchant of London and the Treacherous Don," *Virginia Quarterly Review*, 12 (April 1936): 207-219;

"Palmetto State," *London Transatlantic* (1945);

"The Story Behind the Story," *WINGS: Literary Guild Review* (October 1945): 4-12.

Interviews:

"Up from the South," *New York Times*, 30 September 1945, section VII, p. 37;

"Miss Pinckney Tries to Put in 4 or 5 Hours of Writing a Day," *Charleston* (S.C.) *News and Courier*, 1 November 1945, p. 10;

John K. Hutchens, "On an Author," *New York Herald Tribune Book Review*, 20 January 1952, p. 2.

References:

Hamilton Basso, "Crop Without Cream," *New Yorker*, 21 (29 September 1945): 79;

Carroll Coates, "Myth and Magic Embroider Josephine Pinckney's Work," *Columbia* (S.C.) *State*, 14 August 1966, p. A17;

Florence Thompson Howe, "The Charleston Home of Josephine Pinckney," *Antiques*, 49 (May 1946): 307-309;

Herbert P. Shippey, "Josephine Pinckney," in *South Carolina Women Writers*, ed. James B.

Meriwether (Spartanburg, S.C.: Reprint Company, 1979), pp. 83-100;

Katharine Drayton Mayrant Simons, " 'If Any Man Can Play the Pipes': A Sketch of the Poetry Society of South Carolina," *South Carolina Magazine*, 14 (September 1951): 9, 21-22;

Harrison Smith, "Tropic Island and Odd People," *Saturday Review*, 35 (19 January 1952): 17;

Samuel Gaillard Stoney, "Josephine Pinckney," Book-of-the-Month Club Promotion Flier for *Great Mischief* (1948), p. 4.

Papers:

Pinckney's correspondence with Viking Press from 1944 to 1957 is deposited at the South Caroliniana Library, University of South Carolina.

SYLVIA PLATH

(27 October 1932-11 February 1963)

SELECTED BOOKS: *The Colossus* (London, Melbourne & Toronto: Heinemann, 1960; New York: Knopf, 1962);

The Bell Jar, as Victoria Lucas (London, Melbourne & Toronto: Heinemann, 1963); as Sylvia Plath (New York, Evanston, San Francisco & London: Harper & Row, 1971);

Ariel (London: Faber & Faber, 1965; New York: Harper & Row, 1966);

Crossing the Water (London: Faber & Faber, 1971; New York, Evanston, San Francisco & London: Harper & Row, 1971);

Winter Trees (London: Faber & Faber, 1971; New York, Evanston, San Francisco & London: Harper & Row, 1972).

Although most of her creative energies were directed toward poetry, Sylvia Plath produced one novel, *The Bell Jar* (1963), a striking work which has contributed to her reputation as a significant figure in contemporary American literature. A thinly veiled autobiographical account of the inner conflicts, mental breakdown, and ultimate recovery of a college girl in the 1950s, the novel is one of the earliest to express rebellion against the conventional roles of women, a forerunner of such works as Erica Jong's *Fear of Flying* (1973) and Marilyn French's *The Women's Room* (1977). Yet it is more than a feminist document, for it presents the enduring human concerns of the search for identity, the pain of disillusionment, and the refusal to accept defeat. As a novel of growing up, of initiation into adulthood, it is very solidly in the tradition of the Bildungsroman. Technically, *The Bell Jar* is skillfully written and contains many of the haunting images and symbols that dominate Plath's poetry.

Because her literary work is based so closely on her own experiences, knowledge of her life is highly important to an understanding of it. Plath was born in Boston, Massachusetts, to Aurelia Schober and Otto Emil Plath. Both were of German descent, her mother being a first-generation American and her father having come to the United States from Poland as a young man. Otto Plath, a professor of entomology specializing in the study of bees, died in 1940 after a long illness (diabetes mellitus); his death was a central negative factor in Plath's life, for the pain and anguish of this loss never left her.

In 1942 Mrs. Plath took a job in Boston; and the family, including Sylvia's younger brother Warren and her maternal grandparents, moved away from the coast, a place that Plath was always to associate with the innocence and happiness of youth. They settled in Wellesley, where Plath earned prizes for scholastic achievements, and her first short story was published in *Seventeen* just after her graduation from high school. Even this early, most of the issues, attitudes, and desires which were to dominate her entire life, especially her all-important yearning for a perfection she felt she would never attain, were established, as evidenced by the following excerpts from a diary entry of 13 November 1949 (in *Letters Home*, 1975):

> Somehow I have to keep and hold the rapture of being seventeen. Every day is so precious I feel infinitely sad at the thought of all this time melting farther and farther away from me as I grow older. *Now, now* is the perfect time of my life. . . .
>
> I still do not know myself. Perhaps I never will. . . .
>
> I am afraid of getting older. I am afraid of getting married. Spare me from cooking three meals a day—spare me from the relentless cage of routine and rote. I want to be free—free to know people and their backgrounds—free to move to different parts of the world. . . .
>
> Never, never, never will I reach the perfection I long for with all my soul—my paintings, my poems, my stories. . . .
>
> There will come a time when I must face myself at last. Even now I dread the big choices

which loom up in my life. . . . What do I want? I do not know.

Oh, I love *now*, with all my fears and forebodings. . . .

The very concerns sounded here are the dominant themes of *The Bell Jar*, which is based on the next period of her life—her college years, her suicide attempt, and her recovery.

Having received several scholarships, Plath entered Smith College in September 1950. She excelled academically, was elected to various student offices, and received awards and prizes for her short stories and poems. In the summer of 1953, she spent a month in New York as one of twenty guest editors for *Mademoiselle*'s college issue. Upon her return home, depressed by her failure to be admitted to a creative writing course at Harvard, by some of her experiences in New York, and by her personal sense of imperfection and lack of direction, she attempted suicide, crawling beneath the house and taking an overdose of sleeping pills. Found barely alive three days later, she then began the difficult road to recovery in a mental hospital.

She returned to Smith in January 1954 and graduated *summa cum laude* in June 1955. Not only had she received additional awards and written an honors thesis in English, but she had also won a coveted Fulbright fellowship for study at Cambridge University. There she fell in love with the young English poet Ted Hughes, who seemed to her a kind of ideal man, something she had never expected to find. Her wonder and joy were ecstatically expressed in letters to her mother: "I shall tell you now about something most miraculous and thundering and terrifying. . . . It is this man, this poet, this Ted Hughes. I have never known anything like it." They were married on 16 June 1956, and Plath's letters reveal her happiness in having found what seemed a perfect relationship: "I love Teddy more and more each day and just can't imagine how I ever lived without him. Our lives fit together perfectly."

After a year in England, they came to America, spending the academic year 1957-1958 in Northampton, Massachusetts, where Plath taught freshman English at Smith, and the following year in Boston, where she wrote poems and attended Robert Lowell's poetry course at Boston University. In December 1959 they returned to England and settled in London; soon afterwards Plath's first volume of poems, *The Colossus* (1960), was accepted for publication, and in April a daughter, Frieda, was born. During the next year, Hughes's career advanced steadily while Plath's seemed to her at a standstill. She was able to write little not only because of her responsibilities as wife and mother but also because of her poor health; she had recurring sinusitis as well as a miscarriage and an appendectomy.

Rollie McKenna

Sylvia Plath

However, in the spring of 1961 she began working on *The Bell Jar*, confiding to a friend that she had "been wanting to do this for ten years but had a terrible block about Writing A Novel. Then suddenly . . . the dykes broke. . . ." She had become interested in novel writing because, as she said in an interview with Peter Orr, "you can get in toothbrushes and all the paraphernalia that one finds in daily life, and I find this more difficult in poetry." In May she applied for a Saxton fellowship in order to obtain money for a study and babysitters so that she could complete the novel. The Hugheses moved to a lovely thatch-roofed house with an apple orchard and fields of daffodils in Devon on 1 September, and in November Plath was notified that she had received the Saxton fellowship. In her letter of acceptance, she noted: "I certainly do plan to go ahead with the novel and the award comes at a particularly helpful time to free me to do so." Although concentrating on *The Bell Jar* for most of the next year, she also wrote numerous poems. In February 1962 a son, Nicholas, was born.

The summer of 1962 was a very painful time in

which the Hugheses' marriage broke up. Hughes, who was in love with someone else, moved to London, leaving a bitter and devastated Plath with the two children in Devon; she wrote to her mother in August that she wanted a legal separation because "I simply cannot go on living the degraded and agonized life I have been living, which has stopped my writing and just about ruined my sleep and my health. . . ." Battling her despair and disillusionment, she kept busy with beekeeping, took up horseback riding, and wrote intense and often violent poems at top speed; in an October letter, she said that she "managed a poem a day before breakfast." She also completed *The Bell Jar*, which was accepted for publication by Heinemann, and began work on a second novel; to her brother Warren she confided, "[I] have had my first novel accepted (this is a secret; it is a pot-boiler and no one must read it!) and am ready to finish a second the minute I get a live-in nanny. . . ."

In December she left the isolation of Devon and moved to London, occupying a flat in a house where Yeats once lived. *The Bell Jar* was published in January under the pseudonym of Victoria Lucas and received relatively good reviews. Although her health was poor, her responsibilities for the children demanding, and her emotional state depressed, she continued to write and to struggle for a stable and meaningful life. Yet she seemed unable to throw off the effects of the past months, as she indicated in her last letter to her mother: "I have been feeling a bit grim—the upheaval over, I am seeing the finality of it all, and being catapulted from the cowlike happiness of maternity into loneliness and grim problems is no fun." On 11 February 1963 she turned on the gas in her kitchen and ended her life.

Often labeled "confessional," Plath's literary work is highly personal and intense, centering largely on her own negative and anguished emotions and states of mind—depression, despair, frustration, failure, and obsession with death. Not only does she use her own emotions and experiences as subject matter, but she also uses her own family and friends as characters—her father, mother, boyfriends, college classmates, neighbors in Wellesley. Her major concerns are the search for one's true identity and fulfillment of that self, the role of women, and the meaning of death. Her style is, for the most part, as personal as her content, particularly her striking images and symbols.

The plot of *The Bell Jar* is neatly divided into three parts, covering a period of approximately eight months. In part one (chapters 1-9) the novel's narrator and major character, nineteen-year-old Esther Greenwood, describes her experiences during a one-month residence in New York City as a guest editor for the college issue of a fashion magazine. In addition, she remembers key episodes from her recent past in college. All the incidents reveal her slow but certain emotional and mental disintegration, as she fails to find an identity which satisfies her and as she becomes more and more disillusioned with the world in which she lives. The opening episode recounts her isolation and naivete as she and her friend Doreen are picked up by a flashy disc jockey named Lenny. Another key scene takes place at the magazine office when Esther bursts into tears when asked what she wants to be. Several incidents, both past and present, show her unsatisfactory relationships with men: her date with Constantin, who disappoints her by making no attempt at seduction; her encounter with the brutal, woman-hating Marco, who beats her up; and various experiences with her college boyfriend Buddy Willard, who wants a conventional and ordinary marriage. On her last night in New York, she throws all her clothes off the roof of her hotel in a bizarre, symbolic "ceremony" which clearly reveals her disillusionment and disorientation.

Part two (chapters 10-13) concentrates on her psychological deterioration upon her return home and ends with her suicide attempt. Arriving home dressed in a friend's clothes and with bloodstains still on her face from being beaten by Marco, she feels terrified at being trapped there until the fall: "[The] white, shining, identical clap-board houses with their interstices of well-groomed green proceeded past, one bar after another in a large but escape-proof cage." In the following weeks she is unable to accomplish anything, cannot sleep, and refuses to wash her hair or change her clothes. Further depressed by visits to Dr. Gordon, an unsympathetic psychiatrist who gives her devastating shock treatments, she becomes obsessed by death and experiments with various methods of suicide. After an anguished visit to her father's grave, she crawls beneath the house and takes sleeping pills until she loses consciousness.

In the third section (chapters 14-20) she describes her painful return to normalcy after surviving her suicide attempt. First placed in the psychiatric ward of a city hospital, she resists all efforts to help her, being uncooperative and even destructive. However, when she is moved to a private mental hospital, she makes great progress under the care of a sympathetic woman psychiatrist, Dr. Nolan. When allowed to leave the hospital for short excursions into Boston, she obtains a diaphragm and has her first sexual encounter, an unpleasant experience with disastrous consequences. Surviving that disillusionment as well as the subsequent suicide of her friend Joan, she awaits her imminent release from the asylum and prepares to return to life—"patched, retreaded and approved for the road." Yet her future is unsure, and the ominous threat of another breakdown later in her life haunts her: "How did I know that someday—at college, in Europe, somewhere, anywhere—the bell jar, with its stifling distortions, wouldn't descend again?"

The two major themes of the novel, the search for identity and rebellion against conventional female roles and attitudes, are closely linked. The multitalented Esther is unable to decide who she wants to be: "I saw my life branching out before me like [a] green fig tree. . . . From the tip of every branch, like a fat purple fig, a wonderful future beckoned and winked. One fig was a husband and a happy home and children, and another fig was a famous poet and another fig was a brilliant professor, and another fig was Ee Gee, the amazing editor, . . . and beyond and above these figs were many more figs I couldn't quite make out." While the identity she seems most drawn to is that of the poet, the one she rejects most strongly is that of the traditional wife and mother. She sees marriage as a prison of dull domestic duties, a wife as a subservient inferior to her husband, and a mother as a drudge with dirty, demanding children. What she does want as a woman is the freedom to have an interesting life: "I wanted change and excitement and to shoot off in all directions myself, like the colored arrows from a Fourth of July rocket."

The cast of characters is quite large as numerous people touch Esther's life. She herself is the major figure, a brilliant student who has a talent for creative writing. Her inner directness and wry sense of humor make her a likable character, as do her determination to be independent and her rejection of stereotyped molds of all kinds. Both her greatest asset and her greatest liability is her compulsion to excel, which drives her to demand of herself an unattainable perfection. Thus she is constantly plagued with feelings of failure and frustration. Further, she lacks self-confidence in the social and sexual areas, and she affects an urbane sophistication as often as possible. She is touching, funny, annoying, surprising, but always a very human and very sympathetic character.

Most of the numerous female characters who revolve around her represent different identities that she might assume. In New York, Doreen with her devil-may-care attitude symbolizes social and sexual sophistication. Betsy, an all-American girl from Kansas, placidly accepts the stereotypes for women. Jay Cee, the magazine editor and Esther's boss, is an intelligent and successful businesswoman whom Esther admires and often emulates, imagining herself as "Ee Gee, the amazing editor." Yet Jay Cee is flawed by a lack of femininity, implied by her use of neutral initials rather than a female first name, her "plug-ugly looks," and her "strict office suit." Esther is drawn to but ultimately rejects each of these characters.

Three female figures, all of whom appall Esther, dominate the scene at home. Representing conventionality both in career and in standards, Esther's mother urges her to take shorthand in order to become a secretary, and to guard her virginity in order to marry a fine, clean-cut boy like Buddy Willard. Buddy's mother is a typical housewife in a conventional marriage, appearing to Esther as a drudge and an inferior. Dodo Conway, who has six small children and is very pregnant with the seventh, is to Esther a grotesque figure of woman as mother.

In the third part Joan Gilling, another mental patient who is a lesbian and who ultimately hangs herself, represents choices Esther might have made, clearly being an alter ego. Finally, the one female character who is not flawed, who is an understanding and open-minded human being and has achieved an integration of her womanhood and her career, is Dr. Nolan, Esther's psychiatrist at the private hospital. Although it is not explicitly stated, this woman who is largely responsible for Esther's salvation seems the model that Esther will use to find her own true identity as a woman.

The male characters are presented even more negatively than the female ones. The most important is Buddy Willard, who from Esther's point of view is flawed in two ways. First, he is a hypocrite, having slept with a waitress but pretending to be chaste. Second, he wants a conventional marriage with Esther as a conventional wife. The other male characters pass in and out of her experience in a nightmarish parade of cruelty, stupidity, and coldness: Lenny, the brash, sexually aggressive boyfriend of Doreen; Marco, the violent woman-hater; Dr. Gordon, the remote and unsympathetic psychiatrist; Irwin, the indifferent, unattractive math professor to whom Esther loses her virginity. All the men are portrayed almost exclusively in terms of their relationships with women, relationships in which they are at worst brutal and at best thoughtless or uncaring. While they are presented in this highly negative light, it is clear that Esther demands an ideal of perfection from men as much as from herself.

Obviously, no man can measure up, as is evident from Esther's comment, "I would catch sight of some flawless man off in the distance, but as soon as he moved closer I immediately saw he wouldn't do at all."

The style of *The Bell Jar* is conversational and informal, at first glance belying its craftsmanship and careful attention to detail. The simple sentence structure, ordinary diction, and slang terms of the 1950s are appropriate to the narrator, and the numerous concrete details bring to life in a very tangible way the places, people, and experiences that make up Esther's story. Certain aspects of the style are skillfully differentiated in each of the three parts, subtly reflecting the changes in the narrator's mental and emotional condition. While in the first part the sentences and paragraphs are of medium length and are logically developed, in the second part, as Esther's condition deteriorates, they become short and choppy, with paragraphs often containing only one sentence. The thoughts are fragmented and do not flow smoothly and logically, but jump abruptly from subject to subject. As Esther moves toward recovery in part three, the style shifts back toward longer sentences and paragraphs that are logically connected.

There is a subtle difference too in the use of humor in each section. In the New York period there are many humorous episodes, most of which are based on the juxtaposition of Esther's naivete with her affected sophistication; a prime example is her attempt to cover her inexperience in ordering mixed drinks by asking for a plain vodka, explaining casually that "I always have it plain." Her inner directness and honesty as well as her unusual way of seeing things—as when Buddy's genitals remind her disappointingly of "turkey neck and turkey gizzards"—provide other instances of humor. However, in part two there is a reduction in the amount of humor as well as a shift in kind to the grim humor of black comedy; for example, with the silk cord of her mother's bathrobe "dangling from my neck like a yellow cat's tail," Esther wanders through her house but never finds a place from which to hang herself. The last part is practically humorless; even those episodes, such as the "seduction" by Irwin, which contain incongruity and earlier would have evoked some touch of the comic, are treated in an entirely serious manner. Plath means to suggest perhaps that the breakdown has destroyed Esther's sense of humor or that the effort to recover requires a plodding, humorless concentration.

Finally, the novel is full of brilliant and effective symbols, some of which recur consistently to form major groups or patterns, while others appear only once but with striking force. One of the most significant of the dominant symbols is the bell jar, a personal and highly original symbol, which represents the condition of mental breakdown. Esther imagines her illness as a gigantic bell jar that descends upon her, imprisoning her, suffocating her, isolating her from others, and distorting her view of the world. The colors of black and white appear on nearly every page, the former conveying despair and gloom and the latter emptiness and deadness. In a striking use of both colors, Esther describes her future as "stretching ahead like a series of bright, white boxes, and separating one box from another was sleep, like a black shade." Prison images symbolize her feeling of being trapped in various ways: her body is a "stupid cage," her mother's car is like a "prison van," and her face reflected in the mirror of her compact "seemed to be peering from the grating of a prison cell after a prolonged beating." Last, her obsession with death is conveyed by numerous images, comparisons, allusions, and actual deaths, which fill the novel from the opening page with its reference to the execution of the Rosenbergs and its simile describing the cadaver's head that haunts Esther's memory to the final chapter with its account of Joan's suicide and funeral.

Although *The Bell Jar* is Plath's only novel, it is a significant one that joins such works as Salinger's *The Catcher in the Rye* and Joyce's *A Portrait of the Artist as a Young Man* in presenting the painful experiences of adolescence—and also begins a new tradition of novels exploring the experience of women. While its value lies to a great extent in these contributions, in its portrayal of the 1950s, and in its intense study of mental breakdown, its reputation ultimately will rest on its concern with the universal human problem of self-discovery.

—Nancy Duvall Hargrove

Letters:

Letters Home, ed. Aurelia Schober Plath (New York: Harper & Row, 1975).

Bibliographies:

Eric Homberger, *A Chronological Checklist of the Periodical Publications of Sylvia Plath* (Exeter, England: Raddan, 1970);

Cameron Northouse and Thomas P. Walsh, *Sylvia Plath and Anne Sexton: A Reference Guide* (Boston: G. K. Hall, 1974);

Gary Land and Maria Stevens, *Sylvia Plath* (Metuchen, N.J.: Scarecrow Press, 1978).

References:

Eileen Aird, *Sylvia Plath: Her Life and Work* (New York: Harper & Row, 1973);

A. Alvarez, *The Savage God* (New York: Random House, 1971), pp. 3-42;

Caroline King Barnard, *Sylvia Plath* (Boston: Twayne, 1978);

Edward Butscher, *Sylvia Plath: Method and Madness* (New York: Seabury Press, 1975);

Charles Newman, ed., *The Art of Sylvia Plath* (Bloomington: Indiana University Press, 1970);

Nancy Hunter Steiner, *A Closer Look at Ariel: A Memory of Sylvia Plath* (New York: Popular Library, 1973).

CHARLES PORTIS
(28 December 1933-)

BOOKS: *Norwood* (New York: Simon & Schuster, 1966; London: Cape, 1967);

True Grit (New York: Simon & Schuster, 1968; London: Cape, 1969);

The Dog of the South (New York: Knopf, 1979).

Charles Portis's reputation rests primarily on his second novel, *True Grit* (1968), which skillfully blends a dry wit much in the mainstream of American regional humor, plot conventions and stock characters from a Western adventure story, and the serious fictional themes of self-reliance and coming of age. Unfortunately, the real quality of the novel is overshadowed by the fact that its film adaptation provided one of John Wayne's best-known roles, Rooster Cogburn, and his only Academy Award. Like Portis's other two novels, *True Grit* is firmly rooted in his home state of Arkansas and its singular blend of Southern and Southwestern culture. His fiction explores the clash between the temperaments and values of the old and new South and between traditional Southern traits such as independence and gentility and the untamed, willful quality of the Southwest. In this respect, Portis is a unique, entertaining, potentially important regional writer.

Portis's upbringing steeped him in his region's culture, with its small-town life, oddball characters, rural conservatism, and love for hunting, country music, and tall tales, all of which find their way into his fiction. He was born in El Dorado, Arkansas, and attended public schools in Hamburg, in the southernmost part of the state. This area combined vestiges of the Mississippi Delta plantation culture, the backwoods of the Southern pine forests, and the boom economy of the oil industry. After graduating from high school in 1951, he served during the Korean War in the Marine Corps; upon his discharge in 1955, he studied journalism at the University of Arkansas where he received a B.A. in 1958. His first reporting jobs after graduation kept him in the mid-South: the *Northwest Arkansas Times*, the *Memphis* (Tenn.) *Commercial Appeal*, and the *Arkansas Gazette*.

In 1960, Portis became a reporter and feature writer for the *New York Herald Tribune*, where, in a city room staffed by Easterners and urbanites, he developed something of a reputation for his droll Southern wit. He moved successfully in this new environment, but his experiences in New York have entered his fiction only in minor ways. Of greater importance was his contact at the *Tribune* with some of the deacons—Jimmy Breslin and Dick Schaap—and the high priest—Tom Wolfe—of the "new journalism." Portis was never a practitioner of this approach to nonfiction; however, his first national publication, a 1966 article on Nashville-style country music in the *Saturday Evening Post*, shows the same love for scenic presentation, ear for dialogue, and emphasis on striking, almost novelistic detail usually associated with Wolfe, Gay Talese, Norman Mailer, and others like them. His fictional prose style, too, shows a journalist's instinct for taut phrasing and concrete description.

Portis's success in New York led to an attractive assignment as London correspondent for the *Tribune*, but the urge to write fiction proved irresistible. Tom Wolfe relates that "Portis quit cold one day; just like that, without a warning. He returned to the United States and moved into a fishing shack in Arkansas. In six months he wrote a beautiful little novel called *Norwood*. Then he wrote *True Grit*, which was a best seller." Both novels were serialized in the *Saturday Evening Post*: *Norwood* appeared in a considerably revised text under the title "Traveling Light," and *True Grit* in a severely condensed version that eliminated much fine dialogue and the best comic subplot. Others were responsible for the film scripts of the two novels, as well as the film script for *Rooster Cogburn* (1975), a sequel to *True Grit*. The success of the two novels and their screen and paperback rights gave Portis a measure of financial independence, and aside from an occasional magazine article, he published nothing else for over a decade. A new novel, *The Dog of the South*, appeared in 1979.

Norwood (1966) is a straightforward, unpretentious novel about Norwood Pratt, like Portis a Marine Corps veteran and aficionado of country music. The novel begins in the late 1950s in Ralph, Texas, due west on U.S. 82 from Portis's hometown; but its action takes place mostly on the highways with a young American whose wanderings prove both quixotic and serendipitous. Though Norwood shares with the flower children of the 1960s a restlessness and good-natured faith that things will work out, his is a more traditional subculture. He pumps gas and repairs cars at a discount gas station; his ambition is to sing on the "Louisiana Hayride"; and he picks up his bride-to-be on a Trailways bus. Norwood is both a Candide in his unflappable optimism and a Quixote in his resolve to re-create the world according to his perceptions. His specific quest is simple: a fellow Marine owes him seventy dollars, and he goes forth seeking repayment, first to New York, then to Old Carthage, Arkansas, via North Carolina. Along the way, he encounters the underside of modern society in an endless stream of grotesques and collects Rita Lee, a jilted girl who wants only "to live in a trailer and play records all night"; Edmund B. Ratner, a philosophical midget once billed as "the world's smallest perfect man"; a "wonder hen" he rescues from a penny arcade; and, incidentally, his money, which he promptly lends out again to Ratner.

Portis fleshes out this rather thin story line through his skill in sketching memorable caricatures and his keen ear for the rhythms and nuances of conversation, whether that of Norwood, the ne'er-do-well drugstore philosopher his sister marries, or a harried Greenwich Village writer trying to stop a gang of street urchins from burning mattresses to toast marshmallows. The book has some of the typical flaws of a first novel, also. Its humor becomes forced, especially when Portis reaches too far afield for a satiric target, and certain sequences are poorly integrated into the plot. The entire episode in New York, for example, is too sketchy to provide an effective counterpoint to the scenes of rural and small-town life; and it contains only one incident whose comic possibilities are fully realized: Norwood's encounter with the automat and the derelicts who frequent it.

Norwood is a well-conceived character type—the amiable hick—whose voice and actions ring true, but he does not seem, finally, to matter. His generosity and energy are undermined by his apparently limitless credulity. Moreover, Norwood's encounters with deceit, passivity, and some relatively mild forms of evil seem not to teach him, or the reader, anything. The novel is funny, occasionally very funny; but because it lacks both a focused target and a consistently articulated value system, it is not comic or satiric in the traditional sense.

Portis's second novel, *True Grit*, must stand as his best work, at least at present. It was a commercial and critical success even though it is, as one reviewer notes, a "strange sort of best seller" because it combines so many fictional types and conventions. The plot is that of a popular Western adventure. In the late 1870s, Frank Ross, a farmer from Yell County, Arkansas, is shot down in the streets of Fort Smith by Tom Chaney, one of his hands. Chaney joins an outlaw band in the Oklahoma Indian Territory; and after a train robbery, an ambush, a protracted chase, and a kidnapping, he is eventually run to earth by a deputy marshal and a Texas Ranger. The variations on these stock characters and plot devices give the novel its unique flavor. The most important departure is the central role of Ross's fourteen-year-old daughter Mattie, who sets the pursuit in motion by offering the lawmen a bounty to avenge her father; she then accompanies them on the chase and, after a series of near disasters, helps them kill Chaney. Mattie, who tells her story after a lapse of nearly fifty years, is a splendidly original character. She has become a spinster who, by her own admission, loves only her church and her bank; she is a shrewd, scripture-quoting, self-righteous woman with "brains and a frank tongue." She displays all of these traits, particularly the last two, as clearly at fourteen as at sixty-five. Her fastidious tongue—she eschews contractions and places even the mildest colloquialism in quotation marks—exhibits that peculiar mixture of candor and understatement available only to the completely self-assured. She drives all adversaries before her. In the novel's best comic sequence, she outdeals a hapless horse trader named Stonehill who sold her father four cow ponies just before his death. Mattie maneuvers Stonehill into buying back his stock and paying for her father's horse (which Chaney stole); she then purchases one of the ponies for herself (at a lower price) and, to complete her triumph, moves into the stable office for the night because, as she is quick to point out, it makes no sense to pay "a full rate for only a few hours sleep" at a boardinghouse.

Another significant twist is the character of Deputy Marshal Rooster Cogburn, whom Mattie hires because he is the most ruthless man available. His credentials are anything but heroic; fat, slovenly, fortyish, and missing an eye, Cogburn is much enamored of the bottle and not particular about his modus operandi: he has killed twenty-three men in four years and kills four more in the course of the novel. Nevertheless, Mattie's narration presents him in a positive light, because in her Old Testament "eye for eye" value system Cogburn is an instrument of righteousness and justice. Events also vindicate his character. At the story's climactic point, when Mattie and Cogburn share the task of killing Chaney, she falls into a pit and is bitten by a rattlesnake. At this moment, Cogburn metamorphoses into a hero: he pulls the girl out and carries her to a doctor in a mad dash that involves riding her horse to death, carrying her on his back, and commandeering a wagon at gunpoint. Even single-minded ruthlessness, the novel suggests, has merit if properly directed.

Coupled with the novel's parody of Western fiction is a strong realistic strain, the net effect of which is to demythologize the frontier. Portis's knowledge of Arkansas history and geography enables him to capture the spirit of time and place through carefully wrought details: at a triple hanging in Fort Smith, the prisoners' last words combine authentic notes of swagger, remorse, and religious fervor; the various hideouts, outposts, and settlements are rendered with depressing wealth of grubby detail; and a meeting with now aged outlaws Frank James and Cole Younger in a Pullman car "drinking Coca-Colas and fanning themselves" dramatizes the decline of the dime-novel West.

As with *Norwood*, the real strength of the novel is its dialogue. The characters speak tight-lipped, deadpan frontier idiom, as though nothing can surprise them. Although their actions are at times suitable for a comic book, their speech never degenerates into cliches. Mattie's voice is especially successful. Her verbal sparring is entertaining because it seems so incongruous coming from one so young; yet given the malevolent world she moves in, it is also satisfying in a moral sense. When Chaney's gang captures her, for example, she calmly reasons with them, explaining who she is and the justice of her cause. Absurd and futile though this gesture might be, the reader shares her indignation and her belief that rationality and justice are in short supply in her world.

True Grit, despite its comic tone, deals seriously with significant themes. It can be read as a Bildungsroman that tests Mattie's fortitude and strength of character. The "grit" of the title, which she ascribes to Cogburn, is also her own. Although the central action takes but a few days, the retrospective point of view underlines the importance of the girl's maturation. She faces down death and achieves redress of a serious wrong; in so doing, she prepares herself for life on her own terms, as unencumbered by society's conventions regarding her sex as she is by her age. Her humor, then, is a function of her clear-eyed vision of the world and a saving grace amid its genuine evil. That evil is ever present in a starkly realistic appraisal of the difficult life on the frontier. Even Chaney, who comes closest to being a stock villain, recognizes that he is to some extent both an agent and a victim of a harsh, lawless society in which "everything is against [him]." Some of the novel's best moments occur when young outlaws, such as Moon, a horse thief killed by his partner to silence him, confront death as the ultimate penalty for their wrongdoing.

Reviewers generally praised *True Grit* but were hard-pressed to categorize it. Some, taken in by the matter-of-fact tone and wealth of realistic detail, failed to detect its essentially comic nature, seeing instead a fictional memoir or historical novel. Others struggled to characterize its humor, calling it parodic, absurd, satiric, or even camp. Most agreed, however, that the character of Mattie Ross is a significant achievement in the tradition of Huck Finn and that the book contributes meaningfully to American humor. The catchall description "classic," variously defined, appeared in such diverse publications as *Life*, *Saturday Review*, and *Nation*. On the whole, however, the reviews are a disappointment. Reviewers are content to stop with the comparison to *The Adventures of Huckleberry Finn*, which *True Grit* resembles only superficially, and make no attempt to make sense of the novel's divergent strands. Metaphors to describe its special appeal abound—"a board fence . . . tight, plain, and direct, not a nail out of place," "pure, beautiful corn"—but the reviews always stop short of real analysis of Portis's achievement.

In *The Dog of the South*, published eleven years later, Portis speaks in a new, much more freewheeling comic voice. The novel is marked by an inspired zaniness; one reviewer describes the reading of it as "like being held down and tickled."

Also a first-person narrative, the novel concerns Ray Midge, an Arkansan who, like Portis's other protagonists, clings devoutly to his idiosyncrasies. His story also involves a quest, although its motivation is unclear. His wife Norma and her former husband, a would-be radical named Guy Dupree, have run off in Midge's new Ford; and he traces them to Texas, through Mexico, and eventually to a plantation in Belize. All the while, he insists that the car is his only objective, that he is "already cuckolded" but "wouldn't appear so foolish" if he were able to recover it. When he discovers that Dupree has ruined the car and sold it for junk, however, he decides that it was not important anyway. He is equally capricious about Norma, whom he literally stumbles upon and brings home, only to let her run off again at the end of the novel, this time for good.

The chase to Belize occupies about one-third of the novel and contains its best writing, largely because it gives Portis an opportunity to create the sorts of characters he does best: misfits, dropouts, and near lunatics on the fringe of society. The best of these, perhaps Portis's best comic character, is Dr. Reo Symes, a quack physician who travels with Midge. He is a born schemer, the sort of person who answers (and occasionally places) advertisements for get-rich-quick schemes in the back pages of magazines. He is also chronically insecure, a manic conversationalist, and a master of the non sequitur, a man for whom life is a series of inexplicable mysteries and unexplained rituals. His two great obsessions are John Selmer Dix, a hack writer who composed self-help books while riding a bus endlessly between Dallas and Los Angeles, and Jean's Island, a mosquito-infested sandbar his mother owns in the Mississippi Delta, for which he proposes ludicrous development possibilities.

Wherever Midge goes, he meets with bizarre behavior and situations: a blazing mop in the kitchen interrupts his lunch; he nearly comes to blows with an obstreperous artist who fashions overpriced rabbits for the tourist trade; Dupree's dog wears plastic bags on his paws; and Symes's mother runs a nondenominational mission in Belize that does little more than show ancient movies to local children. In a world where anything is possible and nothing certain, it is not surprising that most of the characters develop eccentricities to cope with the unexpected, the inexplicable, and, most of all, their own failure. The novel's apparent aimlessness underlines a key theme: in the complex modern world, life has become a frustrating, often futile search for the security conventionally supplied by money, love, and knowledge. Character after character swallows the American dream whole and finds it unpalatable, either through an Algeresque pursuit of prosperity or a simplistic utopian scheme. Moments of insight are rare and unenlightening: Norma, who at the outset wanted only "to dye her hair" and "change her name to Staci or Pam," finally opts for that most conventional of panaceas, love; Midge shares with Candide and Norwood Pratt the desire for "a good job of work to do."

The novel's principal weakness is its plot. Once Midge reaches Belize and Symes fades into the background, the comic pace slows. An absurd assault upon Dupree's jungle hideaway, several brushes with tropical con artists, a foiled love affair, and an extraneous hurricane that serves only to shake up the grab bag of characters provide action but do not advance the plot meaningfully. Finding Norma, whom he did not really want and does not keep long, seems almost an afterthought, and the novel ends with the initial situation essentially unchanged.

In his three novels, Portis has shown a sure grasp of the principles of comic characterization and a growing mastery of his personal comic style. He is not so much a writer of vision as of observation. With journalistic economy, he selects appropriate actions and descriptive details and constructs sustained, idiomatic voices for his characters, all of whom exhibit a basically good-natured, if slightly askew, view of the world. He creates downtrodden, inept, seriously flawed characters, however, without condescension or meanness. He is the whitest of white humorists at a time when such optimism has grown unfashionable. *The Dog of the South* shows his recognition that American society—at least outside of Arkansas—is undergoing profound changes, but his comic vision deals with that society only obliquely. Ray Midge articulates Portis's most consistent theme: "A lot of people leave Arkansas and most of them come back sooner or later. They can't quite achieve escape velocity." Portis seeks to capture the essence of the experience his historical and contemporary Arkansas travelers carry with them into the world, and he does so brilliantly. To characterize him as a regionalist is in no way to demean his writing, for his fictional world never dwells upon the merely local for its own sake, never becomes unintelligible to the outsider. If his novels show considerable similarity in plot and situation, it is to Portis's credit that he has managed to render that oldest of fictional conventions—the quest—consistently interesting. One does not approach his novels seeking profound insight into human nature, but many readers have apparently found his voice both funny and familiar and, ultimately, comforting.

—Michael E. Connaughton

Periodical Publications:

"The New Sound from Nashville," *Saturday Evening Post*, 239 (12 February 1966): 30-38;

"Traveling Light," *Saturday Evening Post*, 239 (18 June 1966): 54-77; 239 (2 July 1966): 48-75;

"True Grit," *Saturday Evening Post*, 241 (18 May 1968): 68-85; 241 (1 June 1968): 46-61; 241 (15 June 1968): 44-57;

"Your Action Line," *New Yorker*, 53 (12 December 1977): 42-43.

References:

R. Baird Shuman, "Portis' *True Grit*: Adventure or *Entwicklungsroman*?," *English Journal*, 59 (March 1970): 367-370;

Tom Wolfe, *The New Journalism* (New York: Harper, 1973), p. 9.

MARIO PUZO

(15 October 1920-)

BOOKS: *The Dark Arena* (New York: Random House, 1955; London: Heinemann, 1971);

The Fortunate Pilgrim (New York: Atheneum, 1965; London: Heinemann, 1971);

The Runaway Summer of Davie Shaw (New York: Platt & Munk, 1966; London: World's Work, 1976);

The Godfather (New York: Putnam's, 1969; London: Heinemann, 1969);

The Godfather Papers & Other Confessions (New York: Putnam's, 1972);

Inside Las Vegas (New York: Grosset & Dunlap, 1977);

Fools Die (New York: Putnam's, 1978; London: Heinemann, 1978).

Mario Puzo is primarily a novelist, a storyteller of uncommon gifts whose American literary ancestors are the Naturalistic writers who focus on the American "cityscape," on the lower orders of the middle class, the streets, the resourcefulness, the upward or downward mobility of emigrants or persons but one generation removed from Europe. Puzo explores the underbelly of social institutions and has a sure sense of urban social process; his vision, however, is more persuasive when he handles smaller, interlocking segments of society: a family group, a mother's role in a Lower East Side tenement neighborhood, the tensions engendered by ethnic, religious, and economic considerations. Thus his vision of society is highly personal and he seldom addresses a single, major, conceptual issue in the sustained way, for example, that Dreiser explores the nature of distributive justice in *An American Tragedy* (1925). In addressing the theme of either petty or organized crime, Puzo's artistic judgments are often made by implication and by the use of irony. A continual reliance on irony, however, is not always productive: readers overlook the points, or—in the end—irony may represent no position at all.

Along with his strong commitment to narrative structures, Puzo displays an uncommon talent for the creation and the exploration of character, of human nature. Typically, these characters-in-action also suggest many tenets of the Naturalistic creed. For example, protagonists with power, with an "edge," exploit the weak; persons are victims of circumstance, of forces they do not accurately understand. Subtle or lethal revenge is a powerful motive; endurance and cunning are traits highly respected. On the other hand, fidelity and loyalty, especially within a family, are marks of maturity if not always wisdom. In many ways Puzo's city is a contemporary, tempered vision of the so-called Darwinian jungle. A general exception to this observation is Puzo's depiction of inner-family circles and of older, maternal women.

Because all American cities are embodiments to some extent of finance capitalism and because Puzo's typical characters are of the streets or not far removed therefrom, the importance of money in the novels and the nonfiction is a major concern. Money saved through frugality or gotten quickly by a well-managed crime is presumed an acceptable end in life; when a protagonist or a family—at last—becomes prosperous, however, the struggle continues. The necessity then becomes to acquire what money buys: prestige, love, "respect." Tragic situations, understandably, involve money; the magnificent gesture is the cash-nexus gesture. The importance of money in Puzo's work strikes a significant, typically American note.

From *The Dark Arena* (1955) to *The Godfather* (1969), Mario Puzo's novels, nonfiction, and literary and cultural commentary all present a consistent view of society and human nature. The scene is American and extends from after the turn of the century to the present day: Hell's Kitchen, Las Vegas, Hollywood. There is a consistency of tone, an admirable vitality. The major and minor protagonists against these cityscapes are managed with strong, novelistic authority. At age sixty-one, doubtless, the novelist is at the height of his powers: a recognized literary artist, himself with money at last, and with it the earned respect of fellow craftsmen of the literary community.

Mario Puzo comes to his materials by direct, perhaps enforced, association. The son of a trackman-laborer for the New York Central Railway, one of seven children, Puzo grew up on Tenth Avenue, between Thirtieth and Thirty-first streets, then a part of Hell's Kitchen. Beneath their tenement were the railway yards; there cattle were unloaded at all hours for the city slaughterhouse. Over the years the six males of the family worked for the railway, as brakemen, trackmen, or messenger boys. Crime was an accepted way of making extra money and Puzo says, "I had every desire to go wrong but never had a chance. The Italian family structure was too formidable." In addition, a nearby Hudson Guild Settlement House was a strong influence; among other things, that charitable institution sponsored summer weeks in the country for its boys. In Puzo's case, he lived for two weeks during each of several summers with a Baptist family at their house in New Hampshire. To the young Puzo these outings were "magical." Thus, the influence of a maternally dominated family, settlement house programs, and the early discovery of public libraries were major formative elements in the novelist's character and his concept of what it may signify to be a literary artist. These and other facts of the author's early life are detailed in "Choosing a Dream: Italians In Hell's Kitchen" (1971). This significant, revealing essay (reprinted in *The Godfather Papers*, 1972) confirms Puzo's concept of the near-heroic stature of the immigrant Italians, their dedication to survival through hard work, their frugality, their disassociation from their European, Italian past. Moreover, Puzo strikes a strong, affirmative note of appreciation for an America which allowed illiterate peasants to achieve "economic dignity and freedom." If there are reservations about the "Fascistic . . . racially prejudiced" aspects of this country, Puzo also expresses his most consistent view when he writes, "what a miracle it once was!" He cites especially the ways in which America encouraged those brave immigrants who "Bent on survival, . . . narrowed their minds to the thinnest line of existence."

If the typical life of the 1920s and 1930s has disappeared from the neighborhoods he knew intimately, Puzo's role as a literary artist has been to reconstruct those experiences, to explore the nuances, the manners, the values. This process takes place in the imagination of the working novelist; to his credit, however, his work—as against his merely "personal" memories—is remarkably free of what he calls "retrospective falsification"(e.g., remembering only pleasant or affirmative details). Today Puzo sees life with an appropriate Hell's Kitchen cynicism; but this does not preclude the virtues of fidelity, personal honor, and a variety of emotional responses to his materials. When the novelist, the artist, treats the "facts" of past and contemporary existence, he speaks in his most authentic voice. At the same time, Puzo is not to be categorized as merely a Naturalistic author. The recurrence of the dream, the possibility of miracle, the magical, are all distinctly a part of his world view; significantly, in the latest novel, *Fools Die* (1978), an artist-hero is named Merlin, with direct reference to the King Arthur legends.

In any event, Puzo's biographical facts—his attendance at the New School for Social Research (on the GI Bill), his early career of odd jobs and administrative employment in Europe—do not fully explain his motivations as a literary artist. He, himself, suggests the complex nature of such an inquiry in the essay "Choosing a Dream": "Thinking back, I wonder why I became a writer. Was it the poverty or the books I read? Who traumatized me, my mother or the Brothers Karamazov? Being Italian? Or the girl sitting with me on the bridge as the engine steam deliciously made us vanish? Did it make any difference that I grew up Italian rather than Irish or black?" In the end, there is only the work. Puzo's novelistic career begins with *The Dark Arena*.

The first of four novels (written in twenty-three years), *The Dark Arena* is not typical, for the action takes place almost entirely in Occupied Germany, in and near Bremen. The structure dramatizes two major themes: the stirrings of a new German nation as it rises from the rubble; and the attempt at spiritual growth, of the ability to love, on the part of the main protagonist, Walter Mosca. The second theme—the inability to love—is the most demanding and also has suggestive, political implications.

At the beginning of the novel Mosca returns to New York after having served in World War II; there he refuses to marry a girl who has waited for him, dramatizing his central, emotional trait: an inability to love. He returns to Germany, to civilian employment at an air base. The novel's title has a double implication, for the "dark arena" is the rubble of Germany and also the rubble of Walter Mosca's emotional condition.

Eventually Mosca meets and begins to live with Hella, a German. Because of rules against fraternization with Germans, Mosca cannot at once marry Hella; nevertheless, they have a child, and Mosca is apparently happy in a purely domestic way. Later when they might marry and thus allow Hella to qualify for medical attention at the air base, Walter delays; then Hella urgently requires penicillin for an infected tooth. Because he has no "papers," Walter is refused penicillin by an American GI dentist and a black-market supplier, Yergen, sells Walter penicillin which he knows, or suspects, to be useless. Mosca's delay, the bureaucratic rules, and black-market conditions combine to cause Hella's tragic death.

The revengeful aspect of Mosca's character becomes dominant. With the cooperation of Eddie Cassin, another American, Mosca entices Yergen to a meeting and shoots him. By this action Mosca becomes an outlaw, a kind of a stateless person on the ruined continent of Europe "he can never leave." Mosca is last seen waiting, without destination, for a streetcar. His isolation, his desolation, is complete.

Walter Mosca's inability to love is central to the novel. By extension, this theme suggests a general criticism of American occupational policy: in general the policy was to fill only the physical needs for the survival of those conquered; therefore the emotional life of anyone still alive is sacrificed. If this first novel is flawed, there remains an austere vision of the occupation years, a time now largely forgotten, possibly because of a failure of American policy.

Five years later, Puzo published his most artistically successful novel to date, *The Fortunate Pilgrim* (1965). The pilgrim of the title is a peasant woman who comes from Italy to America as a new bride. The story focuses on Lucia Santa's rise from a Hell's Kitchen tenement to her version of the American dream, a cottage of her own, with a garden, in Long Island. Her domestic life, determination, cunning, wisdom, bravery—her strong-willed adherence to "standards," and her ability to avoid *figlio disgraziato* (disrespect)—constitute the main action of this strongly felt novel.

A contrapuntal movement in the novel concerns the nature of big-city crime: the recruitment and training of its workers, the methods and tone of management, the rewards and the punishments. A vivid example of this theme is Larry Angeluzzi's discovering the advantage of quitting his fifteen-dollar-a-week job on the railroad to work for a Mr. di Lucca who is "definitely Italian but dressed American." The older, fatherly man controls a bakery "union": Larry—through proper connections by way of family and local reputation—becomes an "enforcer," a collection agent. The occupation is described as being "like an insurance man"; the Italian-American justification for crime as a necessity, a profession, is subtly rendered. In addition, such passages are memorable because the focus of crime remains at the domestic, neighborhood level.

The rise of the "pilgrim" and the parallel consideration of criminal activity resonate to produce a hovering, effective irony; the emotional pitch is finely controlled even in overstatement. A *New York Times* reviewer suggested the book is "Harsh, abrasive, brilliant!" and so it is; in addition, however, the inclusion of the "dream," of the "magic" of life itself, of the tempered pleasure in ordinary events add an unusual dimension to a novel which has been called, "One of the two or three best novels on American city life ever written."

At forty-five years of age, with six children, in debt $20,000 to relatives (and bookmakers), with his first two novels "critical" but not financial successes, Puzo set himself a two-valued task: to establish himself as a best-seller author, and to earn the big money which was becoming a convention of publishing, largely through the sale of hardcover novels to aggressive paperback publishers. Although his former publisher (Atheneum) declined the proposal for the next novel, his present publisher (Putnam's) advanced Puzo $5,000 for *The Godfather*.

Puzo attained both his goals. The paperback rights to *The Godfather* sold for a (then) record price of $410,000 of which the author received fifty percent. In the first year after its publication as a paperback (1970-1971), the novel sold an estimated six million copies. With movie sales and other income, Puzo earned over $1 million. The novel became the number one best-seller in the United States for sixty-seven weeks (in New York) and, in translation, number one in France, Germany, and other countries. Financially secure at last, Puzo gave up his assistant editorship of a male-oriented magazine where, among other chores, he sometimes wrote the wildly imaginative, sex-oriented center section stories.

The Godfather is a study of character, exploring and extending the crime sequences of the first two novels. The central protagonist, Don Corleone, suggests Mr. di Lucca of *The Fortunate Pilgrim*. Corleone is the powerful, rebel-founder of a crime empire; yet his concerns often remain domestic, almost fatherly, as he kills off the opposition and/or those persons in his own "family" who merely make mistakes of judgment. If the larger implications of organized crime are not explored, there is a pervasive irony, a comment on the contradictions within America during the war in Vietnam.

Beyond question Don Corleone is Puzo's most fully realized character—Lucia Santa excepted. As a character, Corleone's appeal is in three areas: his style; his ability to organize and to control; and his rational, if humorless, trait of mind which causes his decisions to appear just, or at least fair, to all concerned. These traits give Don Corleone a larger-than-life, a legendary, stature. The action, the episodes of the novel are cumulative in effect; although Puzo suggests, "I wrote below my gifts in that book," it is possible that a more controlled structure would have undercut the mythic nature of Don Corleone.

In another context Puzo says, "The novelist's job [is] not to be a moralist but to make you care about the people in the book." Squared against this authorial intention, *The Godfather* is more of an artistic success than many reviewers implied. Puzo went to Hollywood and (with Francis Ford Coppola) wrote the film script for Paramount (1972). The film received three Academy Awards, for best picture, actor, and screenplay. *The Godfather, Part II,* also adapted for the screen by Puzo and Coppola, won six Academy Awards, for best picture, supporting actor, director, screenplay, art direction/set decoration, and music/scoring.

Fools Die is set in Las Vegas in the 1950s and 1960s, with ancillary action in Tokyo, Hollywood, and New York City. The main protagonist is John Merlyn, a slightly dishonest writer of fiction (he has been investigated by a grand jury for his acceptance of a bribe while a civil servant) who considers himself a modern version of the Arthurian magician. Merlyn's associates—for want of a better term—are a literary scamp (who suggests Norman Mailer); a producer-director (suggestive of Coppola); an actor (of Marlon Brando's type); a brother; and many other more or less realized protagonists. Character is central to the book and one direct comparison will suffice: Don Corleone is a fully sustained, detailed, rounded character; by contrast, Merlyn is alleged to be a novelist but there is no suggestion of how he has practiced his career. The appellation "novelist" is superimposed; the character, Merlyn, does not earn that role through his actions. As to female characters, Puzo's expectations for Janelle are not realized. Janelle is an actress with a checkered past, and she is Merlyn's sometimes girlfriend. She is also said to be a "feminist"; but, as one reviewer points out, this seems to be a "word for bisexual." This important female character is central to many episodes in this novel but remains unresolved and without—in the end—authenticity.

The strength of *Fools Die* is in the opening chapters. These episodes render the action, the "house edge," and the social context of Las Vegas. Throughout the novel there are strong biographical echoes that verify the novel's serious intention. Curiously, the extended structure of the novel seems inappropriate for the authentic, felt experiences and states of mind; on grounds of unity-of-effect, characterization, and significance, the novel has not been judged an artistic success. Nevertheless, the author received about $2.5 million for the paperback and other rights; in 1978-1979 the paperback sales were placed at 2.75 million copies.

Inside Las Vegas (1977) is an illustrated nonfiction book that effectively describes, summarizes, and, in general, defends the gambling capital of the United States. The book offers an interesting comparison and contrast with the fictional version of the same general materials in the early chapters of *Fools Die.* The photographs, by John Launois and others, are of high quality; the text, by Puzo and others, is able reportage and gives a balanced, sympathetic view of a difficult, complex situation.

Meanwhile, Puzo is said to be working on a novel about a Sicilian character, a sort of Robin Hood figure. As yet, the book is untitled. Regardless of future work in the genre of the novel, Puzo is now established as an authentic American literary voice. He has matured as an artist, especially in the area of novelistic techniques. To date, his career is an interesting comment on the life of the literary artist in America in the last half of this century. His early works were appreciated by sensitive readers, fellow writers, and a few critics; but those early books, apparently, did not claim the dedication of either his publishers or the general reading public. Whereupon, by intention, Puzo wrote two more novels: one a best-seller (*The Godfather*); one notorious for its indifferent accomplishment (*Fools Die*). Especially in the last novel, the author relies on journeyman skills to the exclusion of unifying theme, of coherent vision. Thus it is ironic that Puzo's new audience, if not his critics, should reward him most for work which is below what his gifts as an author might give in an age less commercial in spirit, less philistine in expectation. Possibly this gifted artist's current situation suggests a theme of our greatest imaginative literature: the appearance of life against the reality.

—*James B. Hall*

Screenplays:

The Godfather, by Puzo and Francis Ford Coppola, Paramount, 1972;

The Godfather, Part II, by Puzo and Coppola, Paramount, 1974;

Earthquake, Universal, 1974.

Periodical Publication:

"Last Christmas," *American Vanguard 1950,* 3 (1950): 176-182.

References:

James B. Hall, "On Mario Puzo's *The Dark Arena,*" in *Rediscoveries,* ed. David Madden (New York: Crown, 1971), pp. 121-133;

Interview, *Publisher's Weekly,* 213 (12 June 1978): 10-12.

Papers:

Boston University has a collection of Puzo's papers.

JUDITH ROSSNER
(31 March 1935-)

SELECTED BOOKS: *To the Precipice* (New York: Morrow, 1966; London: Barker, 1967);

Nine Months in the Life of an Old Maid (New York: Dial, 1969; London: Weidenfeld & Nicolson, 1977);

Any Minute I Can Split (New York: McGraw-Hill, 1972; London: Weidenfeld & Nicolson, 1977);

Looking for Mr. Goodbar (New York: Simon & Schuster, 1975; London: Cape, 1975);

Attachments (New York: Simon & Schuster, 1977; London: Cape, 1977).

Judith Rossner attained a national reputation with *Looking for Mr. Goodbar* (1975), a best-seller which presents a dramatic portrayal of the sexual dilemma of modern Americans. The movie based on the book further advanced Rossner's reputation and increased the sales of her other novels, some of which have been republished with the billing "by the acclaimed author of *Looking for Mr. Goodbar.*" *Looking for Mr. Goodbar* is not only the most popular of Rossner's novels but also the best, treating her dominant theme—the conflict between selfishness and altruism—most convincingly. Her other novels, while they show promise, are often weakened by morally ambiguous or inconsistent characters and by formulaic plots that do not satisfactorily fulfill reader expectation.

Judith Perelman Rossner was born and grew up in New York City, the setting of most of her novels. She attended New York City public schools, including the City College of New York, but dropped out at the age of nineteen and married Robert Rossner. They have two children, Jean, born in 1960, and Daniel, born in 1965. Her first novel, *To the Precipice,* appeared in 1966. The work contains a number of elements which have proved characteristic of Rossner's fiction. The plot employs a recognizable formula—in this case, that of the Cinderella love story. The poor, brave, hardworking, and beautiful Jewish heroine, Ruth, having been rejected by her irrational father while she is working as a tutor for the rich Stamm family, finally marries Walter Stamm, the divorced father of the child she is teaching. But other details vary the formula: to marry Stamm, Ruth gives up the novel's romantic hero, her childhood sweetheart David, a poor but handsome Jewish law student. Thus, at first *To the Precipice* reads like a well-written popular romance in which Ruth and David are faced with such barriers between them as their poverty and his hostile mother. Soon, however, the novel is dominated by the conflict between selfishness and altruism that was to become dominant in Rossner's work. More and more Ruth is torn between her desire for wealth and her capacity for "true love" and self-sacrifice. Ruth's mother represents the extreme of self-sacrifice: she wears the same clothes for years and is constantly scrubbing, mending, penny-pinching. It is against such a background that Ruth declares, "I wanted to be rich—with an overwhelming, painful devotion. With a disregard for any of the small things [I] might have to give up for it. With the conviction that once [I] had it, nothing could ever make [me] really unhappy again." David represents the alternative to these values and, Rossner suggests, Ruth's better and real self. Yet to marry David, Ruth would have to give up her dreams of wealth, for he is not only poor, but also disapproves of her materialism.

The weakness that emerges in *To the Precipice* is Ruth's morally ambiguous character. Given the melodramatic plot of the novel, the reader wants to see Ruth either as the good heroine who finally gets her man or the bad woman whose punishment is losing him. Instead, although Ruth loses David, she is never bad; she is merely a passive victim, paralyzed by her conflicting desires ("I could no more have arbitrarily broken with David than I could have suddenly stopped wanting to be rich"). And this impasse is finally broken not by Ruth's making a choice, but by a lovers' misunderstanding. David, in his hurt pride, pushes her into marrying Stamm, and she decides that David never meant to marry her. Several years and two children later, Ruth again meets David and realizes that he is the man she loves; but when he asks her to leave her husband and marry him, she "can't." Again, however, there is no clear moral choice: Rossner does not show whether Ruth's inability to leave is based on selfishness (love of material security) or self-sacrifice (not wanting to lose her children) or simply the inability to act. As a result, Ruth evokes neither sympathy nor condemnation.

Three years later in *Nine Months in the Life of an Old Maid* (1969), Rossner employed a popular Gothic situation—that of an insane woman living in an isolated mansion. This novel, however, rises above the conventional treatment of the situation by presenting an effective portrait of a totally selfish person—Beth, the narrator, an "old maid" of thirty. Outwardly sweet and quiet but with an undefined mental disorder, Beth has from childhood been kept isolated in Yiytzo (Russian for "egg"), an old mansion outside of New York City, with her normal sister Mimi, now married. At first, because Beth has the strange kind of insight often attributed to the disturbed, she seems to be the novel's moral center—and a sympathetic victim of her incredibly selfish parents, Lily and Josh. (They had simply abandoned their daughters to the care of a housekeeper at Yiytzo while they lived wild lives in Hollywood.) As the novel progresses, however, it becomes clear that Beth is totally self-absorbed, possessing no real feelings for others except as objects to serve her. She admits that she is the "center of the household" because she is "the person the others try to please"—and further, she takes this position as her right: "[Mimi] kept me alive by maintaining a certain set of circumstances, [so] she owes it to me to maintain those same circumstances." A chilling touch is Beth's complete lack of conscience; she regards her own nature as a given, describing herself in terms of natural but premoral forms of life—particularly flowers.

During the course of the novel several events occur to disturb Beth's position in the center of the "egg." Her father sells some of Yiytzo's land. She loses the love of her half-brother, Vincent, who comes to see her as "the most incredibly self-centered human being" he has known. Max, the man on the next estate, asks her to marry him. But most importantly, Mimi becomes pregnant, and Beth is terrified and angry at the prospect of no longer being the sole object of her sister's attention and service. The night the baby is born, Beth, in an Ophelia-like mad scene, runs to Max in her nightgown. She never returns to Yiytzo, but marries him, taking up her residence in his home, a new egg with a new protector-servant. Thus, in spite of the changes around her, Beth has arranged to remain as parasitical as ever, "a transplant [whose] form and color [will not] be altered by its new position." By the end of the novel Beth, unlike Ruth of *To the Precipice*, is clearly an unsympathetic character—one, indeed, who evokes a chill of horror.

Rossner followed *Nine Months in the Life of an Old Maid* with *Any Minute I Can Split* (1972), a work shaped by the 1960s: the chief setting is a commune, and there are detailed descriptions of sexual intercourse and a generous sprinkling of four-letter words. Thematically, the novel suggests that traditional marriage, when based on unselfish love, is preferable to communal living; but the message is weakened by some authorial ambivalence and by the inconsistent characterization of the heroine's husband.

The heroine, Margaret, is a warm, Earth Mother figure—grossly overweight during her pregnancy. In her last month, ignored by her self-absorbed, philandering husband, Roger (he "should've just rented an orgone box"), Margaret leaves home on a motorcycle, picks up a nineteen-year-old hippie, David, and goes with him to a commune where she gives birth to twins. Margaret and David stay at the commune and become lovers. Rossner both celebrates and criticizes commune life: she lingers lovingly over descriptions of bread making and canning, but presents the two commune leaders as basically unstable, disturbed individuals. DeWitt, the father figure, has been a fraudulent psychotherapist and real estate agent, and there is the suggestion that when he becomes bored with his new role as guru he will move on again. Hannah, the mother figure, lives in a trailer, ready to pull out at any moment, refusing to become emotionally or sexually involved with anyone. Most of the other commune members are portrayed as lost young people who use Hannah and DeWitt as parent substitutes. David, like Beth of *Nine Months in the Life of an Old Maid*, seems meant to possess the insight of the outcast, but his frequent descriptions of almost everyone—from the commune rebels to the traditionalists—as full of "bullshit" are without direction.

Three months after Margaret's twins are born, when Margaret has lost weight and become attractive again, Roger comes to the commune and claims her. He proves to be a totally inconsistent character, however. At first he attempts to form a simultaneous relationship with Hannah and tells Margaret, "I married you to fill MY needs, not yours"; but later he decides to become monogamous and states, "Margaret's feelings are important to me because she's my wife." When Margaret is given a large sum of money by Roger's parents, she and Roger plan to invest it in the commune, but they will return to a conventional form of marriage, living in a separate house and returning often to Margaret's family home on Cape Cod—a symbol to Margaret of stability and tradition. This happy ending, evidently meant to reaffirm traditional morality by rewarding the loving Margaret, is, however, seriously undercut by the inconsistency in the portrayal of Roger.

In 1973, the year following *Any Minute I Can Split,* Rossner and her husband were divorced. Working at secretarial jobs, with two children to support and her three favorably reviewed novels not selling, Rossner produced her best and most original work, *Looking for Mr. Goodbar*—written, ironically, to make money. Based on an actual murder of a New York Catholic schoolteacher, *Looking for Mr. Goodbar* not only became a runaway best-seller but was also judged by critics as a work of "considerable literary merit." Here indeed Rossner does not show her earlier weaknesses. The protagonist's character is clearly drawn throughout: Theresa Dunn is a split personality—part of her amorally self-serving (she is a nymphomaniac cruising singles bars by night) and part of her loving and altruistic (she is a teacher of little children by day). And here the ending of the novel—Theresa's murder—is completely convincing, the inevitable outcome of her double life.

In the beginning, Theresa's split personality is foreshadowed by the difference between her two sisters. The extreme of self-sacrifice is represented by Brigid, who is married and has a baby nearly every year. The extreme of selfishness is represented by Katherine, whose various marriages and liaisons are free and swinging: she has two abortions, neither time knowing the identity of the child's father. Theresa herself, though displaying a sense of duty and compassion in her teaching, has an overdeveloped and finally perverted sex drive. She comes to crave violent sex much as a drug addict craves his fix. The reader is left to speculate about the reason for this craving. Does Theresa's first lover (and seducer), her college English teacher Martin Engel, who simply abandons her when she graduates, make her feel that physical love does not accompany spiritual? Or is it lack of parental warmth, or the detrimental results of sexuality seen in her two sisters, or an irrational sense that her slight curvature of the spine, which had so handicapped her as a child, would make her unable to bear children herself? Whatever the causes, Theresa's intense sexual desire results in her split personality: she "didn't really feel that she *had* a life, one life, that is, belonging to a person, Theresa Dunn. There was a Miss Dunn who taught . . . and someone named Terry who whored around in bars. . . . The only thing those two people had in common was the body they inhabited."

Of the men whom Theresa encounters, two in particular mirror the conflicting halves of her personality. Tony Lapanto appeals to her sexuality. A macho hoodlum who works in a parking garage and drugs race horses, Tony visits Terry on a semiregular basis for sadomasochistic sex orgies. One side of Theresa finds him exciting: "Something there was that couldn't really be interested in a man who liked powerful, intelligent women. Something there was that wanted a man from Marlboro Country . . . with a dick so long that you rode it as though it were a horse." James Morrissey appeals to what Theresa considers her "real" and better self; he is a young lawyer, "every Irish mother's favorite son. Pink, smooth-faced, well-behaved. Hairless. Neat as a pin." Clearly there is a question regarding James's masculinity: he even had a homosexual affair once. Yet he really cares for Theresa, and "except for her sexuality," she comes to feel that "she was more herself, the real Theresa . . . with James than she'd ever been before with anyone."

Theresa can give up neither of her conflicting selves, but the result is not the paralysis of Ruth in *To the Precipice*; it is an active, dramatic pursuit of self-destruction. Surely death is what Terry, in her driven wandering through the bars of New York City, at night, alone, is subconsciously seeking. On New Year's Eve, at the height of her personal crisis, with James demanding that she choose between him and her night life, Theresa takes a man home with her, and then, after they have sex, refuses to let him spend the night: "It's one thing to fuck someone you don't know and another thing to look at him over coffee in the morning." Outraged, the man—who has doubts about his own sexuality—brutally murders her. In Theresa's fate there is an unmistakable moral: that the 1960s dream of complete sexual freedom and fulfillment—however much Rossner sympathizes with it—is ultimately an impossible, self-destructive one, while traditional morality—however limiting—at least allows one to survive, even to be a credit to family and society. *Looking for Mr. Goodbar* thus dramatizes the dilemma of many Americans of the time, who were beginning to be disillusioned by the wild sexual experimentation and rejection of past values, but were continuing to hold fast to the narcissistic ideal of sexual fulfillment. The paperback rights were sold for $300,000, the movie rights for $225,000—a clear testimony to the extent the novel spoke to the

American public. Critics lauded it too, with Carol Eisen Rinzler placing Theresa "beside Henry James' Isabel Archer . . . as another victim of the American Dream."

The public was understandably eager for the next Rossner novel, *Attachments*, published in 1977. But it was a disappointment. Rossner's theme is the individual's need for both human relationships and space for individuality, and she employs the marriage of two women to Siamese twins as her vehicle. Yet, in spite of this kinky situation, *Attachments* remains basically a 1970s "woman's novel," the story of the buxom, sexual Nadine Tumulty, her bedhopping search for a husband "to coddle [her] into passivity," and her disillusionment with marriage as the key to happiness. The use of the Siamese twins only weakens the novel: when Nadine's not very original feminist insights (such as "We never really thought about . . . whether we [and our husbands] had anything in common") are put in the context of the bizarre marriage, the effect is often ludicrous. Further, as narrator, Nadine is often needlessly intrusive (witness her comment in a 1950s scene: "I wanted a bowl of Crunchy Granola but it hadn't been invented yet") or too lengthily philosophical. And the detailed descriptions of Nadine's acrobatics to achieve intercourse with the twins are—unlike the sex scenes in *Looking for Mr. Goodbar*—gratuitous.

Still, the novel might have worked had the characters been convincing—but they lack unity of conception. Nadine has some Earth Mother qualities but seems more akin to Beth and the lascivious side of Theresa than to Margaret. Her friend Dianne, who joins Nadine in the affair with both twins, making it into a foursome (and each woman later marries a twin), is at the beginning warm and caring; but by the end of the novel she is a selfish bitch. The twins, Amos and Eddie, have no more individuality than paper dolls, and their undeveloped personalities change to fit the varying needs of the plot. Amos, for example, is by turns a novelty sex object; a warm, loving father and husband; and a lazy, alcoholic male chauvinist. At one time, after the twins are surgically separated, Rossner hints at the idea that Amos and Eddie have exchanged personalities. She also sporadically suggests that the two wives have become, like the twins, one complete person: Nadine feels that she and Dianne are attached "in the head"—and certainly the two women do function with the closeness of a husband-wife team, Dianne working as a lawyer and Nadine as the housewife. But in the end, when Dianne seems to have become as much a male chauvinist as the husbands at times have been, Nadine walks out, feeling that her friendship with Dianne "long ago got lost in our marriage" and that she had never loved the twins at all. What Nadine learns is that being too close to anyone—male or female—involves the danger of losing one's selfhood; but the message is blurred by the intrusive narration and the inconsistent and unsympathetic characters.

Rossner was married in 1979 to Mordeccai Persky, and her latest novel, *Emmaline*, is scheduled to appear in 1980. Her published works show Rossner to be a promising writer, but one whose work varies in quality and whose dramatic conceptions are often flawed. Only *Looking for Mr. Goodbar* is a truly superior novel; it will have a place in American literary history because of its convincing, finely drawn portrait of the sexual and moral confusion of its time.

—Patricia Jewell McAlexander

References:

Martha Duffy, Review of *Looking for Mr. Goodbar, Time* (7 July 1975): 60;

Carol Eisen Rinzler, Review of *Looking for Mr. Goodbar, New York Times Book Review*, 8 June 1975, pp. 24-26.

BUDD SCHULBERG

(27 March 1914-)

BOOKS: *What Makes Sammy Run?* (New York: Random House, 1941; London: Jarrolds, 1941);

The Harder They Fall (New York: Random House, 1947; London: Bodley Head, 1948);

The Disenchanted (New York: Random House, 1950; London: Bodley Head, 1951);

Some Faces in the Crowd (New York: Random House, 1953; London: Bodley Head, 1954);

Waterfront (New York: Random House, 1955; London: Bodley Head, 1956);

A Face in the Crowd: A Play for the Screen (New York: Random House, 1957);

Across the Everglades: A Play for the Screen (New York: Random House, 1958);

The Disenchanted: A Drama in Three Acts, by Schulberg and Harvey Breit (New York: Random House, 1959);

What Makes Sammy Run?: A New Musical, by Schulberg and Stuart Schulberg (New York: Random House, 1964);

Sanctuary V (New York & Cleveland: New American Library / World, 1969; London: Allen, 1971);

Loser and Still Champion: Muhammad Ali (Garden City: Doubleday, 1972; London: New English Library, 1972);

The Four Seasons of Success (Garden City: Doubleday, 1972; London: Robson, 1974);

Swan Watch, by Schulberg and Geraldine Brooks (New York: Delacorte, 1975);

Everything That Moves (Garden City: Doubleday, 1980);

On the Waterfront (Carbondale & Edwardsville: Southern Illinois University Press, forthcoming 1981).

Budd Schulberg predicted in 1950 that he would be remembered primarily as "the writer who reversed the usual process: started in Hollywood and worked East." It was an accurate forecast in that Schulberg's name most often surfaces in connection with the city where he was raised, where he has returned frequently to work, and about which he has written on many occasions. Yet while the author often refers to himself as a "Hollywoodologist" and to the Los Angeles basin as his version of Steinbeck's "Salinas Valley," he is much more than a student of the film industry or a regional novelist. In the course of a professional career which began in 1938, Schulberg has produced a varied body of work—stories, plays, essays, reportage, and screenplays—covering a broad range of subjects from prizefighting, labor racketeering, and political revolution to the price of literary success in America and the life cycle of a family of swans. During this career Schulberg has consistently eschewed the autobiographical, confessional mode which characterizes much of contemporary literature. Nor has he much concerned himself with stylistic or formal invention. The reader discovers little personal revelation or stylistic experimentation in Schulberg's work. Instead he encounters the sensibility of an author turned outward rather than inward, diagnosing the social ills that plague contemporary life and the moral dilemmas such ills pose for the individual.

Budd Wilson Schulberg was born in New York City on 27 March 1914. His father, Benjamin P. Schulberg, had quit his stenographer's position on the *New York Evening Mail* four years earlier to take a job in the fledgling motion picture industry then located in Manhattan. After World War I, the Schulbergs joined the exodus of movie families to Los Angeles; by 1925 the elder Schulberg, as general manager of the Paramount Famous-Lasky studio, was one of the industry's most powerful figures. Thus Budd Schulberg witnessed the workings of the movie colony from an early age and a privileged position.

Schulberg's parents sent him east to Deerfield Academy when he was sixteen. The following year he enrolled at Dartmouth College, where he majored in sociology and edited the daily newspaper. In his senior year he entered and won an intercollegiate short-story contest—his first literary award—and graduated cum laude in 1936. Schulberg left Hanover committed both to a career in writing and to the Marxist analysis of society which had excited many young intellectuals of his generation.

Returning to Hollywood, where he worked first as a reader and then as a junior contract writer for producer David O. Selznick, an old family friend, Schulberg spent the next three years in Los Angeles as a moderately successful screenwriter. He also began placing short stories—many about Hollywood—with *Collier's*, *Liberty*, and the *Saturday Evening Post*. He left Hollywood in late 1939, moving to Vermont where he spent a year forging his knowledge of the movie industry into his first novel, *What Makes Sammy Run?* (1941), a satiric treatment

Geraldine Brooks

Budd Schulberg

of Hollywood and the American success ethic. In this book Al Manheim, a frustrated playwright-turned-theatre critic, narrates the story of Sammy Glick's meteoric rise from newspaper office boy to movie studio mogul. Manheim first encounters Glick as a hyperactive sixteen-year-old copyboy who literally runs the columnist's reviews to the editor's desk. "The world," Manheim at once realizes, "was a race to Sammy."

Obsessed with charting the advance of his "little ferret" of a copyboy, Manheim watches incredulously as Glick scrambles his way out of the city room and to the top of the motion picture industry, stealing other people's ideas and scripts, betraying friends and double-crossing business partners, buying favorable publicity and reviews, and selling out the fledgling Screen Writers Guild along the way. Manheim's search for the reasons behind Glick's unalloyed ambition leads him to the slums of Manhattan's Lower East Side, the scene of Glick's childhood, where the grinding poverty and brutality he discovers force him to conclude that Glick is the product of this harsh environment: "I thought of Sammy Glick rocking in his cradle of hate, malnutrition, prejudice, amorality, the anarchy of the poor; I thought of him as a mangy little puppy in a dog-eat-dog world. I was modulating my hate for Sammy Glick from the personal to the societal."

In *What Makes Sammy Run?* Schulberg focuses on a theme he would return to often—the invidiousness of the American success ethic. Manheim finally sees Glick's career as "a blueprint of a way of life that was paying dividends in America in the first half of the twentieth century." As fashioned by Schulberg, Glick is a bold parody of Horatio Alger's heroes: he succeeds over more worthy men not through pluck and luck but through shameless deceit and self-promotion. Hollywood, in the scheme of the novel, represents the moral bankruptcy of capitalism run amuck in America. Glick has not been "born into the world any more selfish, ruthless and cruel than anybody else, even though he had become all three, but . . . in the midst of a war that was selfish, ruthless and cruel Sammy was proving himself the fittest, the fiercest and the fastest."

Schulberg's first novel proved a considerable commercial success. Although some reviewers balked at its large dose of coarse language and others objected to Schulberg's radical critique of American society, most reviewers found it an eminently readable and sharp-witted first novel. Critics praised Schulberg for creating in Glick a vivid—and perhaps definitive—portrait of the American heel. Sammy Glick made such an impression with the reading public that his name quickly entered the vernacular as a term for the shameless and amoral opportunist.

Schulberg scarcely had the chance to build on this initial literary success before World War II intervened. He entered the navy in 1943, serving with the Office of Strategic Service and gathering evidence for the war crimes trials in Nuremberg. Leaving the navy in 1946, Schulberg immediately coupled his lifelong love of prizefighting with his concern for social justice in writing a second novel, *The Harder They Fall* (1947). Loosely based on the career of Italian heavyweight Primo Carnera, the novel chronicles the cruel exploitation of a hulking, placid Argentine peasant-turned-boxer, El Toro Molina, at the hands of racketeer promoters and managers first in his native country and then in New York. After suffering a vicious beating in a fight arranged by Nick Latka, his American manager, Molina ends up in the hospital with a smashed jaw and exactly $49.07 to show for his entire painful and humiliating career. His managers, on the other hand, have made fortunes.

Schulberg's Princeton-educated narrator, Eddie Lewis, like Al Manheim, aspires to write plays. Yet as the story unfolds he resigns himself to serving as Latka's publicity flack, portraying the passive and awkward Molina as a skilled and brutal boxer. "The lies I told were just ordinary American business lies like everybody else's," Lewis rationalizes, but he is nonetheless wracked by guilt over his complicity in El Toro's exploitation. Wanting to help Molina after this simple peasant has been discarded by Latka, and finding himself absolutely powerless to do so, Lewis becomes filled with self-loathing for the compromised life he has led.

The Harder They Fall is a scathing indictment of the greed which had turned a "fine sport into a dirty business." It is also a more generalized attack on the "disease of the American heart" which allowed the nation's Eddie Lewises to believe falsely that they could "deal in filth without becoming the thing they touch." Some reviewers again found Schulberg's narrative coarse and profane, a frequent response to Schulberg's work throughout his career. Yet ex-heavyweight champion Gene Tunney praised Schulberg's knowledge of the fight business and his sympathy for its manipulated and defeated victims. Most critics agreed with Tunney and said that, whatever its stylistic shortcomings, *The Harder They Fall* diagnosed accurately and powerfully the abuses of professional boxing in the United States.

In his next novel, *The Disenchanted* (1950), Schulberg again drew upon his Hollywood experience, in this case his friendships with many of the eastern playwrights and novelists under contract to the movie studios. Among them was F. Scott Fitzgerald, with whom Schulberg briefly worked in 1939 on the screenplay for *Winter Carnival*, set at Dartmouth. *The Disenchanted* focuses on three main characters: Manley Halliday, a middle-aged, debt-ridden, alcoholic screenwriter who had once been America's most celebrated novelist; Shep Stearns, an idealistic but ambitious junior contract writer much like Schulberg himself; and Victor Milgrim, a well-heeled producer with intellectual pretensions who teams Halliday and Stearns on the script of a sophomoric movie musical. In a fictional analogue to a weekend spent on location at the Dartmouth Winter Carnival, Milgrim insists that the two writers accompany him to the frigid campus of a New England college for location shooting. Their harrowing cross-country plane and train trips leave Halliday ill, exhausted, and drinking heavily. The trip prompts Halliday to recall, in a series of long flashbacks, his halcyon days during the 1920s; but, in the present, Milgrim subjects him to a number of humiliating encounters with the college's faculty and students, and then summarily fires him for drunkenness. Halliday staggers back to New York only to die shortly thereafter in a hospital bed following surgery.

The Disenchanted is Schulberg's most complex and ambitious book, based in part on his experiences with Fitzgerald, but, more generally, a frontal assault on the machinations of the movie industry and a sad account of what happens to American writers who betray their talent for money and public success. Schulberg employs the Halliday and Stearns characters deftly to contrast the attitudes of two generations of writers toward American society and literary success. Halliday, who represents all the alienated artists of the 1920s, believes that the artist must withdraw from society because the money and fame which attend to literary success in America can sap the will to create. "Nothing in America," Halliday instructs Stearns, "fails like success." Stearns, like Schulberg himself, one of the generation of socially conscious writers of the 1930s, believes that American artists must engage their society; he believes it is their duty to enlighten the masses and help lead them from their economic and political bondage.

Nowhere is the contrast between Halliday's and Stearns's attitudes more striking than in their respective opinions of the art of the motion picture. Although both writers see Hollywood as an example of all that is wrong with the American system of rewards, Stearns devoutly believes that the movies are a "great new folk art," an important social agent to be conquered rather than ignored or ridiculed, while Halliday feels that the movies are an "orphan child born of artificial insemination on a box-office counter," which merely reinforce the American obsession with the outward signs of success.

Critical responses to *The Disenchanted* have focused mainly on the character of Manley Halliday. Most critics agree with Alfred Kazin that Schulberg planned Halliday to be "a gifted writer who surrenders to despair and even embraces it as a special fate," but some critics, Kazin among them, quarrel with Schulberg's execution; they find Schulberg's frequent forays into Halliday's consciousness unconvincing. Finding little evidence in the book of Halliday's supposedly great talent, such critics conclude that his downfall evokes not tragedy but merely pathos. Those critics who do, however, find a measure of greatness in Halliday invariably admire the book as a whole. Bruce Cook, for one, writing after the novel's republication in 1975, called *The Disenchanted* a "fine, honest, solid novel, one that is deeply respectful of its hero and treats the writer's vocation with a dignity and seriousness that is very rare in novels today."

Schulberg's only collection of short fiction, *Some Faces in the Crowd*, was published in 1953. Many of the stories, some of which were written as far back as the late 1930s, are satiric glimpses of Hollywood or unsentimental treatments of boxing, two familiar Schulberg subjects. Others concern army life during World War II; a few are uncharacteristically poignant tales of childhood innocence and confusion. "Your Arkansas Traveller," perhaps the best of the collection, tells of Lonesome Rhodes, an alcoholic singing cowboy who catapults to national celebrity purely on the basis of large doses of commercial ballyhoo. "Typical Gesture," about the military career of a famous actor, and "Meal Ticket," in which a has-been boxer lives vicariously through his younger brother's accomplishments, are other superior stories in the collection. Schulberg's brand of literary realism infuses most of the stories: frauds and cheats scramble to succeed, most of the realities of life are bleak, and the prognosis for the future is dreary.

In 1953 Schulberg also began work on a screenplay, in association with director Elia Kazan, about union corruption on the docks and in the warehouses of the New York harbor. *On the Waterfront* was both a popular success and a favorite of the critics, and won for Schulberg five major screenwriting awards, including the Academy

Award in 1954. The next year he reversed the usual process of adaptation by publishing a novel, *Waterfront,* based on his screenplay. *Waterfront* details Father Peter Barry's courageous but ultimately futile attempt to wrest control of the docks from the thugs and gangsters who dominated the union locals and restore it to the workers themselves. Barry enlists the aid of a reluctant Terry Malloy, a slow-witted boxer-turned-longshoreman whose brother serves as a lieutenant for a powerful union boss. Schulberg's screenplay focused on the character of Malloy, played by Marlon Brando; in the novel he expanded his focus to include other characters, as well as much social and historical background to the union power struggles.

Waterfront raises ethical questions about the nature of social commitment as Father Barry tries to convince himself and then Malloy to face up to their social responsibilities. Although intensely compassionate toward the oppressed dock workers, Schulberg, by the mid-1950s, was pessimistic about the possibility of meaningful social change. In *Waterfront* Schulberg seems resigned to the fact that man cannot be rid of corruption, but can only recognize and oppose it where it exists. "Progress," Father Barry ruefully reflects after Malloy has been killed for opposing the racketeers, "is not measured in hundred yard dashes but in painfully crawling forward centimeters."

Fourteen years passed during which Schulberg wrote for both stage and screen, before he published another novel. *Sanctuary V* (1969) is at once a cautiously sympathetic examination of a Latin American revolution and an unflinching exposé of the abuses and horrors of diplomatic sanctuary. It chronicles the purging of Justo Moreno Suarez, a learned and idealistic socialist who at the beginning of the novel serves his country's revolutionary government as its provisional president. Suarez passionately believes in the possibility of both individual freedom and "a social order based on empathy, compassion and mutual sharing" until he is betrayed by Angel Bello, a charismatic guerilla leader-turned-dictator. Once Suarez outlives his usefulness to Bello, he is forced to seek sanctuary in the embassy of another Latin American country or face imprisonment and possible execution on trumped-up espionage charges.

Suarez discovers that diplomatic asylum, rather than the refuge he imagined, is in fact a further "bureaucratic management of political persecution," where greedy diplomats "trade in human misery" by ill feeding and ill housing refugees and then forcing them to pay exorbitant bribes to gain their release. Separated from his wife and daughter and forced to fend for himself in the anarchic jungle of sanctuary life, Suarez's faith in man's free will is shattered; he discovers that any man, no matter how strong, may be "bent by circumstances like a crudely hammered nail."

Critics did not greet *Sanctuary V* with the same enthusiasm they had for previous Schulberg novels. Schulberg tried to expose the humiliations and perversities of sanctuary life with frankness and power, they suggest, but the cumulative effect of such descriptions more often numbs than shocks. While Suarez is one of Schulberg's most interesting, complex, and believable characters, Schulberg was unable to breathe life into the cast of minor characters who share the asylum barracks; a homosexual poet, the brutal former chief of the secret police and his murderous bodyguard, and the leader of a peasant revolt against Bello's regime, among others, are rarely more than stereotypes.

Sanctuary V is most impressive as an uncompromising indictment of political oppression, particularly as it affects the situation and thinking of Moreno Suarez. As the novel ends he and the reader are left with little but the depressing thought that often the most well meaning pacifist idealists, by their inability to act, contribute to the making of dictators like Angel Bello.

During the 1970s, Schulberg produced three substantial works of nonfiction, each quite different: *Loser and Still Champion: Muhammad Ali* (1972), an appreciation of the boxer's career; *The Four Seasons of Success* (1972), memoirs of his friendships with six American writers; and, with photographs by his wife, Geraldine Brooks, *Swan Watch* (1975), an affectionate and well-observed account of the life cycle of a family of swans. Of the three *The Four Seasons of Success* is the most thoughtful and accomplished, containing sharply etched portraits of F. Scott Fitzgerald, William Saroyan, Sinclair Lewis, Nathanael West, Thomas Heggen, and John Steinbeck. Schulberg displays a sure instinct for focusing on the telling moment or incident as he explores how the authors coped—or failed to cope—with success, or failure, or both. In these six essays and a long introduction, Schulberg ponders—as he did in *The Disenchanted*—the chimera of literary success in America and the strains suffered by authors in a culture where the "business of success" often gets confused with "the art of writing."

In his most recent novel, *Everything That Moves* (1980), Schulberg combines two familiar themes, labor racketeering and the moral costs of American success, but neither is treated with the insight or conviction of his earlier work. Labeled a "documentary novel" by its author, *Everything That Moves* is rather freely based on the career of ex-Teamster president Jimmy Hoffa. The novel traces the rise and fall of Jerry Hopper from his beginnings as a truck driver for a small petroleum company, through his climb to the top of the International Brotherhood of Haulers and Truckers, his conflicts with his organized crime associates on the one side and government investigators on the other, and his eventual death at the hands of mobsters once he has become more a liability than an asset to them.

When Hopper, as a young man, exhorts his fellow truckers to destroy the paternalistic company union which exploits them and to replace it with an independent local, and when he successfully leads a strike, he is in many ways an admirable character. Through the course of the novel, however, Hopper's cold-blooded expediency and lust for power lead him to abandon the principles of trade unionism in his quest to control "everything that moves" on land, sea, and air. Hopper becomes, in short, a classic illustration of Lord Acton's aphorism (which Schulberg employs as a postscript) that "power tends to corrupt and absolute power corrupts absolutely." Union abuses had become more sophisticated in the twenty-five years since *Waterfront*, Schulberg implies, yet the rank-and-file workingman still suffered at the hands of leaders who, like Hopper, believe in the dictum: "down with altruism, up with selfishism."

The basic flaw with *Everything That Moves* is not thematic but stylistic. Schulberg's use of present tense, third-person narration and the division of the novel into fifty-six very short chapters lend it the quality of a screenplay. But neither device is well suited to Schulberg's ultimate purpose of exploring the intricate collusions among organized crime, labor unions, and big business. Ultimately the novel borders on the superficial.

Although Budd Schulberg has enjoyed considerable popular success during his long career (and has several best-sellers to his credit), his work is neither much admired by the critical establishment nor often taught in the classroom. His novels are often attacked on several fronts, for one-dimensional characterization, for mechanical or melodramatic plotting, and for embodying a political viewpoint which is little more than a much-diluted Marxism and which disrupts the unity and flow of his narratives. Chester Eisinger, in *Fiction of the Forties*, perhaps best sums up this criticism when he terms Schulberg a "chronicler of the entertainment world who is himself not much more than an entertainer."

Yet there have been dissenting voices in the literary community. Some critics, while finding fault with Schulberg's style, admire his choice of difficult subject matter and his journalistic concern for the truth. They place Schulberg in the tradition of American realistic writers—beginning with Theodore Dreiser and Frank Norris—who, despite the lack of stylistic nicety, demand that the reader witness the raw reality of lives meanly led. Schulberg is at his best, however—as in *What Makes Sammy Run?*, *The Disenchanted*, and *The Four Seasons of Success*—when he explores that territory he knows so well, his "Salinas Valley," Hollywood; and he is presently working on a memoir of his childhood in the movie colony.

—Richard Fine

Plays:

The Disenchanted, by Schulberg and Harvey Breit, New York, Coronet Theatre, 3 December 1958;

What Makes Sammy Run?, libretto by Schulberg and Stuart Schulberg, New York, Fifty-fourth Street Theatre, 27 February 1964.

Screenplays:

Winter Carnival, by Schulberg, Maurice Rapf, and Lester Cole, United Artists, 1939;

On the Waterfront, Columbia, 1954;

A Face in the Crowd, Warner Brothers, 1957;

Wind Across the Everglades, Warner Brothers, 1958.

Other:

From the Ashes: Voices of Watts, edited with an introduction by Schulberg (New York: New American Library, 1967).

References:

Bennett Cerf, "Trade Winds," *Saturday Review*, 33 (14 October 1950): 4;

Bruce Cook, "Shock of Recognition," *Washington Post BookWorld*, 2 March 1975, p. 4;

Chester Eisinger, *Fiction of the Forties* (Chicago: University of Chicago Press, 1967), pp. 102-106;

Jonas Spatz, *Hollywood in Fiction* (The Hague: Mouton Press, 1969), pp. 67-72, 78-80, 89-94;

Walter Wells, *Tycoons and Locusts* (Carbondale & Edwardsville: Southern Illinois University Press, 1973), pp. 86-102.

MARY LEE SETTLE
(29 July 1918-)

BOOKS: *The Love Eaters* (London: Heinemann, 1954; New York: Harper, 1954);
The Kiss of Kin (New York: Harper, 1955; London: Heinemann, 1955);
O Beulah Land (New York: Viking, 1956; London: Heinemann, 1956);
Know Nothing (New York: Viking, 1960; London: Heinemann, 1961);
Fight Night on a Sweet Saturday (New York: Viking, 1964; London: Heinemann, 1965);
All the Brave Promises (New York: Delacorte / Seymour Lawrence, 1966; London: Heinemann, 1966);
The Clam Shell (New York: Delacorte / Seymour Lawrence, 1971; London: Bodley Head, 1972);
Prisons (New York: Putnam's, 1973); republished as *The Long Road to Paradise* (London: Constable, 1974);
Blood Tie (Boston: Houghton Mifflin, 1977);
The Scapegoat (New York: Random House, 1980).

When Mary Lee Settle was named the winner of the National Book Award for fiction in 1978, some of the newspaper and television critics were somewhat less than gracious about reporting the news. The writer was described as an "unknown." And there were complaints (in the *New York Times*, the *Boston Globe*, on television's "Today" show, and elsewhere) that the judging of the award for that year had been perhaps utterly irresponsible, at best completely whimsical. Some of the same sentiments had surfaced as early as the announcement of the five nominated books, weeks before the award itself was made. But none of the reporter-reviewers and journalist-critics in the prominent eastern publications seems to have been prepared for the eventuality that Settle's *Blood Tie* (1977) might, in fact, be the book chosen by the panel of judges. It soon enough developed, as both press coverage and controversy continued for a time, that many of these critics had not yet read *Blood Tie*, and so they found themselves in the awkward and embarrassing position of not being able to bear witness to the novel's virtues or its flaws, if any. Not familiar with this book, they were forced to fall back upon the notion that the author, herself, was unfamiliar if not unknown, a notion which can tell us a good deal both about the state of the art of serious writing in America and the condition of serious criticism in this final quarter of our century. *Blood Tie* is, as it happens, Settle's ninth book and her eighth novel. At that very moment, the time of the award (and very unusual, indeed, for all but a very few highly regarded or extremely commercially successful American writers) all of her work had been published by distinguished publishers in Great Britain as well as in America. As early as 1965, there had been a paperback publication by Ballantine Books of the volumes of her "Beulah Land Trilogy"—*O Beulah Land* (1956), *Know Nothing* (1960), and *Fight Night on a Sweet Saturday* (1964). This particular publication was graced with a special foreword to the trilogy written by the critic Granville Hicks. Hicks described and praised her body of work, especially calling attention to "the excitements and insights" of each separate novel and celebrating the "grandeur of Miss Settle's design" and the success of the work as a whole. Hicks ended by expressing his gratitude to fellow critic Malcolm Cowley "for calling Miss Settle's work to my attention." There is at least a hint of something there, a suggestion of some problem or difficulty dogging Settle's reputation, if not her career. For ten years earlier than that, following the publication first of *The Love Eaters* (1954) and then, the following year, of *The Kiss of Kin* (1955), the reviews, especially in England but also in America, had been uniformly laudatory. When Rosamund Lehmann reviewed *The Love Eaters* in the *New Statesman*, giving it what amounted to a rave review ("She has written this year's sharpest novel"), it must have seemed, by any known standards, that Settle's career as novelist had been well, indeed most auspiciously, launched. And yet, a decade and five books later, she had to be "discovered" by Granville Hicks, thanks to the interest and the persuasive powers of Malcolm Cowley. With such prominent and unquestionably powerful men of letters now on record as favoring her work, the simple question of recognition would appear to have been solved for Settle. Not so. Twelve years and four major books after Hicks's discovery, she found herself dealing with a new generation of critics, yet again classified as an "unknown," waiting to be read and rediscovered by somebody or other.

In all fairness to Settle, and in candid celebration of her courage and her style, it needs to be said, first of all, that she has never complained about neglect or bad luck. It must be said that for twenty-five years she has borne the turns and the counterturns of Fortune's wheel with a tough and elegant equanimity. In a letter she complains strongly about one thing only—the process and business side of contemporary commercial publishing: "I think that there is one thing beyond all others that is unpleasant to the point of evil about producing a book," she writes. "Not the hard work. Not the lack of reward—but the actual process of publishing itself. It ought to be a decent time. Instead it is obscene. A whole industry depends on us and treats us like shit. I call the whole process, from finishing a book, to getting it out beyond the industry and the parochial critics to the public a fire field." In contrast, no sense of bitterness or even common regret can be inferred from her acceptance speech for the National Book Award. Accepting that honor, she begins by doing honor to others: "to me the honor is in the experience itself—that of being chosen as one of five writers I respect so highly by judges who over and over again through their careers have opted, not for regions or schools or sexes, not for coteries or theories. They have sought an unnamed but recognized quality inherent in good work. I hope that quality is honored in the choice of all five of us."

The selection of *Blood Tie* for the National Book Award can hardly be called "a happy ending" to a long, conscientious, dedicated, productive, and often arduous career; for Settle is now writing at a peak of artistic ability and energy, and her work continues to grow and to develop without any slackening of power or interest. But, clearly, that reward and the consequent recognition mark what must surely (and finally) be a turning point in at least the public aspect of her life's work. C.A. Taormina quotes a number of well-known writers and critics of various ages who have now come forward to praise her and her work. The elder statesman of the group, Malcolm Cowley, remains her thoughtful and perceptive supporter:

> She has largeness, freedom, power, and she has produced a courageous body of work. I was most impressed by her West Virginia trilogy, beginning with that extraordinary prologue to *O Beulah Land* . . . that historical vision was Tolstoyan in its breadth. Settle is also good at treating characters in depth, subjectively in what she calls a post-Proustian manner, though she sometimes has trouble harmonizing the Tolstoyan and the Proustian aspects of her talent. That she may do in her next novel, and at last the public will learn to admire.

In the same piece, the younger editor, critic, and literary entrepreneur, Theodore Solotaroff, calls *Blood Tie* "a gem" that "can only have been written by a novelist whose craft had been through the fire several times before" and "a vital book, in both senses of the term: alive and necessary." Restless with her own accomplishments, aiming always for something more, something at once deeper and more deeply true, Settle sees herself as only just now approaching, artistically, the place she has been seeking for so long. Replying to a question from Taormina, looking for a way to explain "a kind of pulse, a blood pulse" that she senses at the final depth of the vision of a writer she admires and honors like Proust, she is able to relate this candidly and matter-of-factly to herself: "Somehow all three, Proust and Conrad and George Elliot [*sic*], they all get to the same point, the point at which we have to write or it's not worth writing. It's too damn hard work to tell lies. I once said to a friend of mine, 'I want to get to the clarity of vision that Pavese had and *not* commit suicide.' And the first time I felt that I had it was in *Prisons*. I had tried before, there are passages here and there that have this quality of a pulse, but *Prisons* has it, and I think there are places in *Blood Tie* which have it. I don't see that there's anything else worth doing."

Settle was born in Charleston, West Virginia, in the last year of World War I, which, she says, "so permeated the atmosphere of my birth that I can remember—as pictures—something of it." (She, herself, was to serve in England in World War II and to write about it in *All the Brave Promises*, (1966); but her latest novel, *The Scapegoat* (1980), has a whole section set in France during World War I.) "My father had a coal mine on Straight Creek in Harlan County, Kentucky," she writes. "When I was a year old we went there to live. When my mother put me out in the sun in what was called a Kiddy Koop, the mountaineers came to see the wild baby in the cage." She lived in Pineville, Ball County, and then in Orlando, Florida, where her father, a civil engineer by training, went to work during the Florida Boom. Her father both designed and laid out the substructure of Venice, Florida. Settle studied ballet and read everything she could find about the knights of the Round Table. "When I was ten we came back to West Virginia for one year to my grandmother's house. I went to school in Montgomery on the school bus, and on winter mornings I saw the miners going to work in the dark with their carbide headlamps lit and at night I saw them coming home in the dark." The following year the family moved to Charleston, West Virginia, and that was home for her until she was eighteen and, in the deepest sense, it remains the central home base for her fiction. Settle is not, by any strict definition, an *autobiographical* novelist. In many ways she stands

Thomas Victor

Mary Lee Settle

at an anonymous distance from her work. And yet it is clear that, like the novelists she most admires, she has used and made use of much of what has happened to her and around her. Thus, and perhaps ironically, the facts of her life have an importance which is even stronger than they might have had if she had written traditional autobiographical fiction. In the latter the facts would be there in the fiction, at most only lightly disguised, mildly changed. In her stories, varied as they are in geography and in historical time, the facts of the artist's life are transformed, dealt out and shared among various characters. There are any number of subtle and complex relationships among all her books, a network of things and events which serves to link them all together, much like chapters or units of one larger design. One of the links is the use of direct experience (and observation), itself invariably transformed into something new and different.

When she was eighteen, Settle was sent to Sweet Briar College in Virginia. Something interrupted her formal education—or saved her from it—if we are to judge by and from her picture of a college much like Sweet Briar in *The Clam Shell* (1971). In a letter to George Garrett she says: "Because my parents were trying to keep me 'interested'—my mother got me to the Barter Theatre in Abingdon, Bob Porterfield's theatre, as an apprentice. It was the end of my sophomore year at Sweet Briar. I was nineteen. There a scout from Selznick found me to test for *Gone With The Wind*. I did not go back to Sweet Briar. Went the rounds to agents to get a job as an actress in New York that winter of 38-39 and earned my living modeling. First for Powers and then for Harry Conover."

In 1939 she married an Englishman, Rodney Weathersbee, and they went to Canada where, with the coming of the war, he joined the Canadian army. Her son, Christopher, was born in Canada. She returned to the United States from Toronto in 1941. "It was so strange," she writes. "I had, in effect, been in a 'war-time' country for two years. This country was still belligerently at peace." Leaving her son with her parents in West Virgina, she joined the Women's Auxiliary of the RAF in 1942, and found herself "Stationed in Wiltshire, Herefordshire, and Gloucestershire—Signals. ACW 2. 2146391. Transferred to Office of War Information, London, September 1943. By doing so I escaped being invalided out of the WAAF with 'signals shock' due to enemy jamming. Returned to the U.S. Jan. 1945."

She began work as assistant editor of *Harper's Bazaar* but did not keep that job for long: "I quit when I realized on reading the introduction to *Wuthering Heights* that Emily Brontë was dead after writing it at 28 and I was 24 and had better get on with it. I swore then not to take another daily job. So I took Christopher and went back to England where everybody else was tired, too, was divorced."

In 1946 she married Douglas Newton and made a precarious living as a free-lance journalist. For a year she wrote as Mrs. Charles Palmer, etiquette expert for *Woman's Day*. Of this experience she writes, "I got twenty quid a go which kept three of us for a month." In 1949, for $100 a month plus payment for any published article, she went to work for Fleur Cowles as English correspondent for the brilliant, extravagant, and short-lived *Flair* magazine. All of this time she had been writing on her own, having not much luck. "I had written six plays by 1953," she reports. "The last one I turned into a novel called *The Kiss of Kin* which nobody would publish. Then I wrote *The Love Eaters* as the result of a bet with James Broughton. I said tragedy required recognition by the audience; he said it was inherent. So I said that if the Phedra were in a modern setting she would be treated as comic, pathetic, menopausal, but not tragically—this is the story of *The Love Eaters* but *no* critic caught it." By 1954 she had already begun to work on the "Beulah Land Trilogy," starting in the British Museum where, she says, "I found a gold-mine of material." The first novel of that trilogy, *O Beulah Land,* was published in 1956, and that same year, divorced a second time, she returned to West Virginia. In 1957-1958 she was awarded a Guggenheim Fellowship. (A second Guggenheim Fellowship was awarded to her for 1959-1960.) During this period appeared the other two novels of the "Beulah Land Trilogy," *Know Nothing* and *Fight Night on a Sweet Saturday*. She worked a time for *American Heritage,* "rewriting bad manuscripts"; and in 1965, following work on a play, *Juana la Loca,* with the American Place Theatre in New York City, she began teaching at Bard College. Since some time in 1963 she had been writing her memoir of service in the WAAF in Britain during World War II—*All The Brave Promises.* She finished this work in September of 1965, and it was published a year later. "In 1968," she writes, "I said that if Nixon was elected president, I was going back to Europe. He was and I did. I lived in London and Oxford." In 1971 she began working on *Prisons* (1973), doing research at the Bodleian Library and the British Museum. She had written *The Clam Shell,* which was published in late 1971, but by that time she was far away and deeply involved in the creation of *Prisons,* later writing in a letter:

> In February 1972 I went first to the island of Kos—started writing *Prisons*—left Kos and went to Bodrum Turkey in April—went on writing *Prisons*. . . . I finished the first draft of *Prisons* in 1972, August, and came back to teach at Bard. In 1973, I finished the rewrite of *Prisons* and returned to Turkey, with no plans to write about it—but *Blood Tie* kept demanding to be written—so, in 1974 I finally started it. The Cypriot War caught me in Turkey and I came back to this country. It took six months to find a place to live and work here. I had little money. Careful budgeting for money to work had been upset by having to get out of Turkey.
>
> I finally landed at the Colonnade Club at the University of Virginia in March 1975, where I finished the first draft of *Blood Tie* in August. Taught at Bard in the fall, Iowa in the spring of '76. Finished the rewrite of *Blood Tie* December '76 published August 1977.

The style and content of Settle's observations reveal a serious struggle to survive and to get the work done. The dedication to the concepts and the completion of both *Prisons* and *Blood Tie* carried great risk, gambling not on awards or rewards, but gambling on artistic survival. No question that the commitment to the work was complete. And in her own view *Prisons* seems to represent a great leap forward, a kind of "breakthrough" from a steadily built canon of excellent fiction to . . . something more. It should also be evident that the books, the making of them, became her life; that the facts of her life have now become the facts of doing and making her work. The rest is almost irrelevant. Almost, though not quite. She adds one more autobiographical fact, in a weighted single sentence: "I married William Littleton Tazewell September 1978, thank God." If the general history of Settle's reception as an artist, her long wait for appropriate attention and recognition in spite of some excellent reviews and some significant support, has been all too sadly familiar a story of the twentieth-century novelist in most countries and cultures; if her experience with publishers, who after all stand between the writer and an audience, if any, has been often unfortunate; and it has—Viking refused to publish the "Beulah Land Trilogy" *as a trilogy* (it took the paperback publisher to do that), and she says that Viking so cut *Fight Night on a Sweet Saturday* as to create difficulties in other, related works, such as *The Scapegoat* (she is now rewriting *Fight Night on a Sweet Saturday* "to connect with" *The Scapegoat* for publication in 1980); and Seymour Lawrence / Delacorte did such an inexcusably poor job of bringing out and promoting *All the Brave Promises,* a book of potentially very wide interest, thus a possible best-seller, that it seems an almost classic example of American publishing malpractice; if all of these things are true, as they are, then the story—even the "happy ending" of a major award for *Blood Tie* and all the large and small differences such a distinction can confer—is still, unfortunately, typical. But there are a number of particular ways in which Settle's example of growth and development as an artist, over a quarter of this century, is not at all usual.

Her beginning, with *The Love Eaters* swiftly followed by *The Kiss of Kin,* is surprising, even now. Hindsight does not clarify in any conventional sense. These two novels, both contemporary and set in West Virginia, are exceptionally professional. They are controlled, well-wrought, and smoothly executed. Only an underlying seriousness, a high gloss of irony, and a bright shine of intelligence

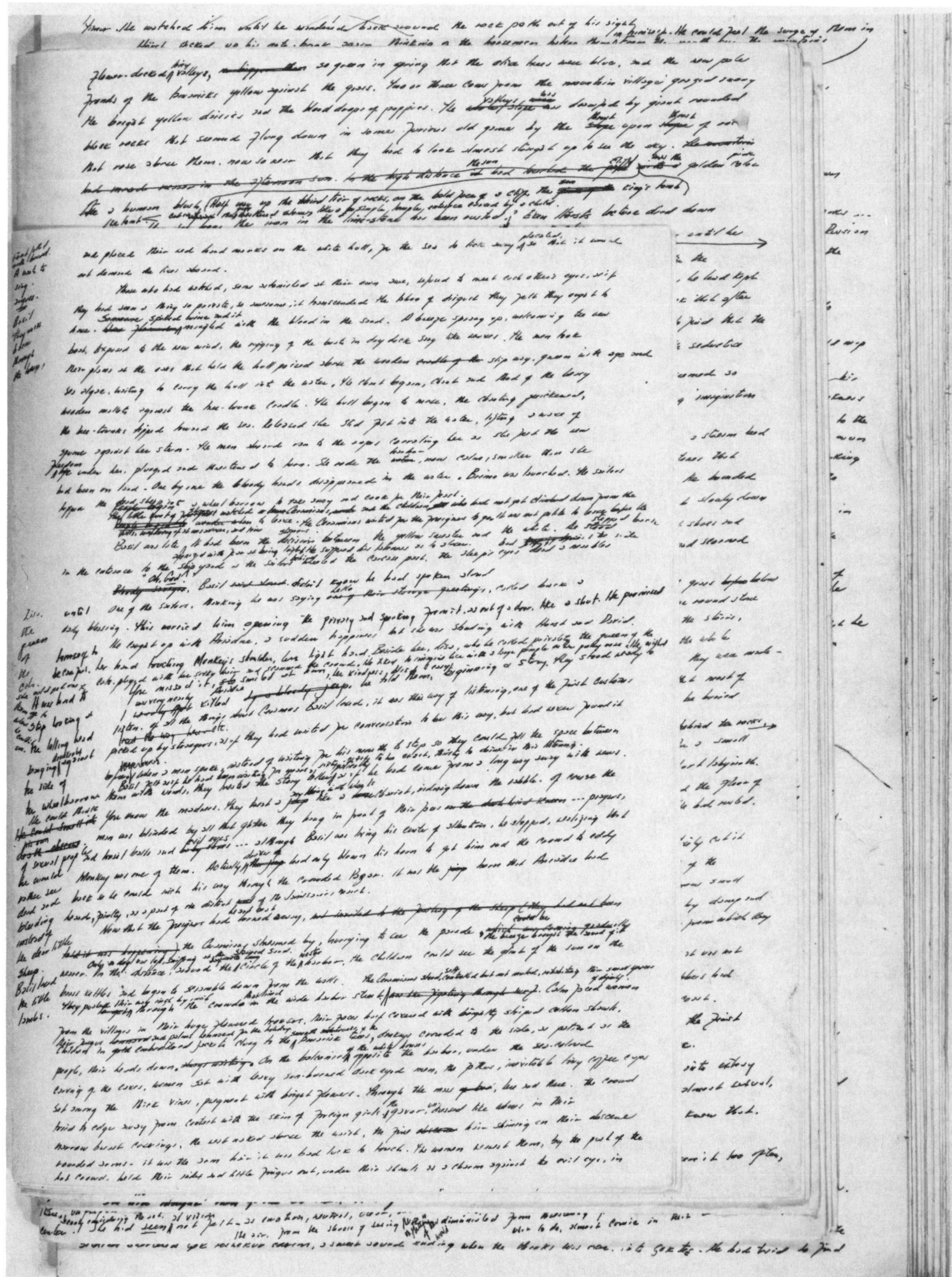

Blood Tie, *first draft*

keeps them from being "slick." They are good, solid novels, yet so *finished* in form that they give no hint of any future directions for development. *The Love Eaters,* based as Settle indicates on the Phedra story, is set in the town of Canona in West Virginia and centers around the production of a play, *Bedtime for Miranda,* by the Canona Thespians, under the direction of Tiresias-like, hired professional director, Hamilton Sacks, a cripple with a sharp tongue and a subtle understanding. The novel ends in disaster, if not tragedy, with the death by fire of the story's beautiful and amoral young man, Selby, and the destruction of the theatre.

The Kiss of Kin, written first and adapted from her own play script, is also set in West Virginia. It takes place in one day, mostly in one place, and involves the gathering of several generations and branches of one family for the funeral and the reading of the will of the family matriarch, Anna Mary Passmore. It is multiple in viewpoint (as is *The Love Eaters*), basically advancing dramatically, scene by scene, in large part depending on dialogue and presented action to make its points and revelations. It is rich with large and small ironies, as most of the characters receive more justice than mercy from the author as well as from the book's most vital and memorable character, the deceased Anna Mary Passmore, who appears at the denouement in the form and words of her eccentric last will and testament.

Neither book reads like a "first novel." They are considerably advanced in mastery of the craft; and, interestingly, they have not really dated much in the more than twenty years which have passed. Of course, she had been writing all her life. Her first published item, she says, came in her ninth year. And in England she had written six unproduced play scripts and four unproduced film scripts, so she was hardly an amateur. Both books are brightly clever, and neither, in and of itself, seems to offer any indication of the way that Settle would choose to follow. Nor do they show plainly—and this is more extraordinary—how, in fact, they were what they have come to be—first statements, an introduction to a body of work which is related, in all of its separate parts, in one larger design, in one grand myth or story. That is, these books are part of the living, growing, unraveling story she has been writing ever since. For instance, Canona is important to each and every one of her books except *Prisons,* set in the seventeenth century in England. Yet descendants of principal characters in *Prisons* do end up in West Virginia and Canona in other novels. Her most recent novel, *The Scapegoat,* concerning a coal strike in West Virginia in the summer of 1912, also involves Canona; and many of the Laceys, Catletts, and McKarkles appear in all the books. And all are ingeniously interrelated: families, blood ties, link all these people together, often without their full awareness of the linkage or its implications. It is chiefly place and kinship which link together the books of the "Beulah Land Trilogy," the stories which may be seen and taken as at the very center of Mary Lee Settle's whole saga and, as well, as exemplary of the aims and terms of it. The books are chronologically sequential. The first story begins shortly after the Fort Duquesne massacre of 1755, in the valley of the Ohio, in what becomes and now is West Virginia, flashes back to London in 1754 and moves steadily forward, through the French and Indian Wars, to the summer of 1774, just before the struggle of the American Revolution was about to begin. The principal characters, among a large cast developed through omniscient narration, are Hannah Bridewell, born in a London prison, Jeremiah Catlett, a fugitive from Virginia colony who marries her, and Jonathan Lacey, a Virginia gentleman and soldier. His daughter marries the son of Jeremiah and Hannah. "And thus Hannah, the London harlot," Granville Hicks writes, "becomes ancestress of some of the aristocratic families of the years to come." This first novel of the trilogy, *O Beulah Land,* is an accounting of the harsh struggle to survive against great odds, in the face of great perils. In the end Jeremiah and Hannah are killed in a final Indian attack, but not before founding a family in a settlement which endures. Endures to reappear in *Know Nothing,* which deals with the years 1837 through 1861, the period leading inevitably toward the tragedy of the Civil War. Primarily a story of Catletts and Laceys, *Know Nothing* is built around the narration of a central protagonist, Jonathan Catlett, following his growth and development from childhood to manhood. He ends as a captain in the newly formed Confederate army, fighting against his own brother, Lewis, who as an abolitionist sides with the North. Hicks notes that the passing of three generations since the frontier times depicted in *O Beulah Land* has made a considerable difference: "Life has become more refined, and an aristocracy of sorts has developed. There are Negro slaves, often descended from the same ancestors as their masters. The sons of the aristocracy are sent east to college, and the wives frequent fashionable summer resorts—where they boast of their forefathers." *Fight Night on a Sweet Saturday,* the final volume, is contemporary. Here kinship is crucial, kinship with all the others, from the earlier stories; and it is the discovery of kinship between victims which proves to be the turning point of this story and the resolution of the "Beulah Land Trilogy." Hannah McKarkle, herself named after the eighteenth-century protagonist of *O Beulah Land* (though she knows nothing of the first Hannah and her story), has come home to West Virginia from New York, acting on a phone call and a premonition of disaster for her brother Johnny. Johnny is killed in a Saturday night brawl, and, as Granville Hicks describes it, "Hannah discovers that the man who hit Johnny was a resentful poor white, an unemployed coal miner, Jake Catlett—a cousin, of course. The Negro policeman with whom Hannah talks turns out to be a childhood playmate of hers and Johnny's, whom they know as Toey but whose given name is John Peregrine Lacey—another cousin." In essence that is what happens in all of Settle's fiction, wherever and whenever each story is laid. Discoveries are made. Relationships, kinships of people, *and of events,* are established. Thus each new book slightly changes all the others. So it becomes important that these earlier books are polished enough to hold their own after many years; for they are not expendable as first books often are. Part of the whole story, they must hold up. If they are, at least superficially, slight and brittle, they *acquire* depth and shadows through the inexorable unfolding of the large design. No question that Settle has grown and changed, "improved" then, as a writer, book after book. But it is much more than a matter of technique. Technically the first two books were entirely satisfactory. She has, of course, tried out a variety of narrative techniques—first person, single voice, in *Prisons* and *The Clam Shell* (as well as in her own story in *All The Brave Promises*); third person, single center of consciousness in *Know Nothing* and *Fight Night on a Sweet Saturday*; omniscient and multiple visions (again) in *O Beulah Land* and *Blood Tie*; and literally everything at once, including a distinctly different first-person "written" and first-person "spoken" narration in sections of *The Scapegoat*. But at no point has technique been more (or less) than a means to an end. She is a writer who does not choose to call attention to her own virtuosity. Technique is used to disguise itself. Her aim has been clarity of focus and then the depths which are possible when technique seems to be transparent. Writing through history served as her strictest schooling. She had to find and to invent, at one and the same time, an appropriate *language* for her stories set in the historical past. Thus this was a problem particularly for *O Beulah Land* (set in the 1770s, at the tag end of the Indian Wars and just before the American Revolution), *Know Nothing* (concerned with events from July of 1837 to June of 1861), and *Prisons* (set in the springtime of 1649). In her interview with C. A. Taormina she describes *O Beulah Land* as being written "in that kind of Roman down-to-earth eighteenth century prose," and she says that *Know Nothing* "is very romantic in texture, it's a Sir Walter Scott, it's pre-Civil War." But she says that *Prisons* "was written in seventeenth century prose, which was like learning a new language." The result of this training, aside from the considerable achievement manifest in each of the novels, has been a greater ease and flexibility of style, a mastery that allows for ever greater freedom of imagination. For example, she had always been able to handle the point of view of the "foreigner," the "outsider." Hamilton Sacks in *The Love Eaters* was such, and Julik Rosen, the New Yorker, Jew, and violinist, thrust among his mistress's Southern kin, was another, credible and well realized. But, after overcoming the risks and challenges of *Prisons,* giving tragic life and language to nineteen-year-old Johnny Church, using a "true" if unknown character and an actual historical incident as the occasion for the story, she was able in *Blood Tie* to create entirely believable Turkish characters, of both sexes and of a variety of ages and dispositions, who are equal in importance and dimension to the American characters in the book. It is one of those rare books in which that which is foreign becomes familiar and ceases to be simply strange. Multiple in narration, *Blood Tie* was clearly a virtuoso work. If it was her fate to be, at last, discovered, it is apt that *Blood Tie* caught the critics' eyes.

Yet *The Scapegoat* is stronger, more daring, and an even more impressive example of graceful virtuosity. Held together by the suspense generated by the 1912 coal strike, by an enormous potential for violence and tragedy, it is a large novel without sprawl or prolixity. Its cast of characters is more extensive and various than anything Settle has attempted before, ranging from mine owners to native mountaineers and coal miners, from an English geologist and a Scots engineer to Italian immigrant families newly come to West Virginia to dig out the coal. There are "ladies" and mountain women and there is even a wonderful rendering of an amazing historical figure—Mother Jones, in person and every inch in character. People of all ages are treated (thus developed) equally and sympathetically without the protective shields of authorial cleverness or irony (except, when appropriate, in style or the working out of private dooms and destinies). Again the major events of this book are, unknown to anyone involved, set at a time just beyond the edges of imagination. For all of this way of life, the glory as well as the sadness and squalor of it, will be lost in the coming fire storm of World War I.

Even the worst of the violence, which remains more potential than realized, will fade and shrink into puny insignificance when measured against the incredible violence certain to come. There is one brief (and essential) section of the story, pushed into a future beyond the immediate action, which credibly sets the young Englishman, Mr. Roundtree, and Lily Lacey, one of the three daughters of Beverly Lacey who owns the struck Seven Stars Coal Mine, in France at the time of the 1915 Battle of the Somme. Lily, working as a nurse in a small chateau-hospital learns some of the bitter things Settle was to learn serving in the next war. She also learns sympathy and with it the capacity to place the action of the story of *The Scapegoat* in the larger perspective:

> Then the letters came, the pathos of their innocence and their blackmail, and the letters hurt her more even than what she saw every day and she could not understand then and resented it. She told herself that she let it happen to hide from herself the daily facts. 'I can't get help,' her mother wrote, meaning that she couldn't find a maid for the new house. She tried to sympathize and found that her mother's words did make her cry, like the tommy who stood in the road sobbing for his dead dog when behind him there was a pile, head high, remains of his regiment, bits of tunic, legs still in puttees, stumps that had been men, gathered with rakes and shovels, piled against the stumps of trees.

And that is it. No need to go beyond that image to present the horror of the war or to make the connection between the lives and events of a few years earlier in West Virginia and the bloody fields of France. Settle has now arrived at an artistic peak of lyrical economy and of narrative authority. The patterns she has been working with are now coming together in new, complex arrangements. In *The Scapegoat,* for instance, most of the central characters are sensitive to the coming of something terrible in the future. They sense it. They can imagine it. But imagination cannot bear it and converts it to something else. Here, in one brief paragraph—a flash as it were—we are given (once and once only) the depths of Mrs. Lacey's prescience and her inward and spiritual truth. She has gone up to the high cupola of her house to take an afternoon nap. Falling toward sleep, she has a brief vision and enters into it:

> Out beyond the protecting trees she heard the hosts of Midian prowling and prowling, even though nothing moved. She threw herself on her side into full heavy sleep. It was not a green sleep. She began to climb, and went on climbing high grey walls. If a light crack of sound like a branch breaking came through the window it only made her pause in her climbing and then go on up the bare walls of forbidden cities, where a song Shy Ann Shy Ann hop on your pony became a plea, always a plea, Ann, oh God Ann my love take down your hair for me.

By now, each new book by Settle changes and alters each and all of the others as it moves toward the completion of her design, which, intricate as it is in details, is—like the language and the world of *The Scapegoat*—ever more beautifully simple and refined as it emerges. It would be impossible to guess where she may go next. Her story is not yet done, any more than the story of this nation and its people, which is what she has been telling, is yet done either. Her story will continue. Meantime, however, it is clearly time for serious students and critics of the contemporary American novel, even as they wait for her next work, to turn back and follow where she has already traveled. In the twenty-five years of her career as novelist, Settle has created a major body of work, most unusual, if not unique, in its unity and depth. It waits to be properly studied and appreciated.

—George Garrett

Other:

"Paragraph Eleven," in *The Girl in the Black Raincoat: Variations on a Theme,* ed. George Garrett (New York: Duell, Sloan & Pearce, 1966), pp. 103-108.

Periodical Publications:

"Senator Burney's American Dream," *Paris Review,* 2 (Fall/Winter 1954-1955): 114-129;

"The Old Wives' Tale," *Harper's,* 211 (September 1955): 73-78; reprinted in *Prize Stories 1957: The O. Henry Awards,* ed. Paul Engle (Garden City: Doubleday, 1957): pp. 241-261;

"Excerpt From Novel-in-Progress," *Blue Ridge Review,* 1 (1978): 26-31.

References:

George Garrett, "An Invitation to the Dance: A Few Words on the Art of Mary Lee Settle," *Blue Ridge Review*, 1 (1978): 18-24;

Garrett, "Mary Lee Settle's *Beulah Land Trilogy*," in *Rediscoveries*, ed. David Madden (New York: Crown, 1971), pp. 171-178;

Granville Hicks, Foreword to *O Beulah Land* (New York: Ballantine, 1965), pp. xiii-xvii;

G. Dale Neal, "Filling an Empty Room—The Art of Mary Lee Settle," Wake Forest University *Student*, Spring 1980, pp. 18-22;

C. A. Taormina, "On Time With Mary Lee Settle," *Blue Ridge Review*, 1 (1978): 8-17.

IRWIN SHAW

(27 February 1913-)

BOOKS: *Bury the Dead* (New York: Random House, 1936);

The Gentle People (New York: Random House, 1939);

Sailor Off the Bremen (New York: Random House, 1939; London: Cape, 1940);

Welcome to the City (New York: Random House, 1942);

Sons and Soldiers (New York: Random House, 1944);

Act of Faith (New York: Random House, 1946);

The Assassin (New York: Random House, 1946);

The Survivors, by Shaw and Peter Viertel (New York: Dramatists Play Service, 1948);

The Young Lions (New York: Random House, 1948; London: Cape, 1949);

Mixed Company (New York: Random House, 1950; London: Cape, 1952);

Report on Israel, by Shaw and Robert Capa (New York: Simon & Schuster, 1950);

The Troubled Air (New York: Random House, 1951; London: Cape, 1951);

Lucy Crown (New York: Random House, 1956; London: Cape, 1956);

Tip on a Dead Jockey (New York: Random House, 1957; London: Cape, 1957);

Two Weeks in Another Town (New York: Random House, 1960; London: Cape, 1960);

Selected Short Stories (New York: Modern Library, 1961);

Children From Their Games (New York: French, 1962);

In the French Style (New York: MacFadden, 1963);

In the Company of Dolphins (New York: Random House, 1964);

Love on a Dark Street (New York: Delacorte, 1965; London: Cape, 1965);

Voices of a Summer Day (New York: Delacorte/Dial, 1965; London: Weidenfeld & Nicolson, 1965);

Short Stories (New York: Random House, 1966);

Retreat (London: New English Library, 1970);

Rich Man, Poor Man (New York: Delacorte, 1970; London: Weidenfeld & Nicolson, 1970);

Whispers in Bedlam (London: Weidenfeld & Nicolson, 1972);

Evening in Byzantium (New York: Delacorte, 1973; London: Weidenfeld & Nicolson, 1973);

God Was Here But He Left Early (New York: Arbor House, 1973; London: Pan, 1977);

Nightwork (New York: Delacorte, 1975; London: Weidenfeld & Nicolson, 1975);

Beggarman, Thief (New York: Delacorte, 1977; London: Weidenfeld & Nicolson, 1977);

Paris! Paris!, by Shaw and Ronald Searle (New York & London: Harcourt Brace Jovanovich, 1977; London: Weidenfeld & Nicolson, 1977);

Short Stories, Five Decades (New York: Delacorte, 1978; London: Cape, 1978);

The Top of the Hill (New York: Delacorte, 1979).

Irwin Shaw was born in New York City, the son of William Shaw, a salesman of hat trimmings, and Rose Tompkins Shaw. When he was very young the family moved to the Sheepshead Bay section of Brooklyn, where he attended local schools and developed a lifelong love for sports. Some of his best short stories, including "The Eighty-Yard Run" and "March, March on Down the Field," both about football, were drawn from his athletic experience.

At the age of fifteen he graduated from James Madison High School and entered Brooklyn College. During his freshman year he failed calculus and Latin and was expelled from college. He worked at odd jobs for a year and then returned to obtain his B.A. degree. He continued his interest in sports by playing football for four years, contributed pieces to the school newspaper, and wrote plays that were staged by the school dramatic group. In a short autobiographical sketch, he recalled how he supported himself during his remaining years in college: "To make money when I got back into school I tutored children, worked in the school library, typed manuscripts, wrote theses in English

Usually during those hours he was content just to sit reading or still, sipping at a whiskey,/staring into the fire that took the bite off the autumn nights, as the house cooled down with the fire in the furnace banked for the hours of sleep. But tonight he got out the copy books in which he had started his journal, glanced at a few pages, then began to write.

The evening after the game in which Romero made his first appearance in a game for Dunberry, he wrote, we all went to dinner at the inn at which Hazen and Conroy were staying, with Romero, neatly dressed and wearing a tie, sitting next to Caroline at the table. They seemed interested in each other and Hazen, while regarding them intently at certain moments, left them to their own conversation. The next morning, before he left for New York, with Leslie and Caroline, he told me he was favorably impressed with Romero's manners and asked me to sound out Caroline about what she thought of the boy. I had no chance to talk to her before they left, but told Leslie to speak to Caroline and find out what she could.

We still hadn't gotten our furniture from New York and Leslie and I had to sleep in the same bed, but after what had happened in Tours after we had made love, we rather self-consciously slept stiffly as far away as possible. We said nothing about it, although one day, we both knew we would have

"Bread Upon The Waters," work-in-progress

for students in New York University." Years later Brooklyn College awarded him an honorary doctorate.

After graduating in 1934, Shaw began his career as a writer by writing serials for radio. Two shows, *Dick Tracy* and *The Gumps*, both based on comic strips, were successful. During this time he also wrote his first major play, *Bury the Dead*, which had an immediate impact when it opened at the Ethel Barrymore Theatre in 1936. Overnight, Shaw was acclaimed as a promising young playwright.

The plot of *Bury the Dead* is simple. In "the second year of the war that is to begin tomorrow night," six dead soldiers refuse to be buried, arguing that society has never given them an opportunity to fulfill their lives. Despite appeals from members of their families and commands from their superior officers, the soldiers do not budge in their convictions. At the end of the play the soldiers and the gravediggers walk off the stage, dramatizing their hatred of war. Leslie Fiedler, writing in *Commentary*, said of the production: "I can remember with embarrassing clarity screaming in ecstasy as the soldiers walked portentously across the stage at the end of *Bury the Dead*; it seemed a play written for me and for my friends, *our* play." Shaw wrote many plays after this, including the moderately successful *The Gentle People* (1939), but none compared in popularity with *Bury the Dead*.

In the next few years Shaw wrote dozens of short stories for the *New Yorker*, *Collier's*, and *Esquire*, twenty of which were brought together in his first collection of short stories entitled *Sailor Off the Bremen* (1939). Until then he had been viewed primarily as a playwright, but this new collection confirmed his talent as a short-story writer as well. Some of his most famous stories appeared here, including the title story, "The Girls in Their Summer Dresses," "The Boss," and "The Second Mortgage." Critics agreed that Shaw was at his best with stories dealing with characters and scenes from large cities, particularly New York.

A few stories reveal his strong social consciousness. In "Sailor Off the Bremen," Ernest, an American artist and an idealistic Communist, has lost an eye and had his face disfigured by a Nazi tough. Ernest's younger brother, a football hero, seeks revenge for what has happened to Ernest. Shaw's description of the bloody fight between Ernest's brother and the Nazi becomes a graphic dramatization on a small scale of the clash between the forces of Teutonic fascism and communism.

Most of these early stories, however, are simple tales with no higher message. Gould Cassal, writing in the *Saturday Review*, noted: "Shaw is chiefly interested in the henpecked Jewish tailor, the young wife who cannot control her jealousy, the bartender who values his professional integrity above money, the world-weary taxi drivers, and others who are part of New York City's seven million. You may read your own lessons into them. Sympathy, honesty, and lack of pretension in 'Sailor Off the Bremen' give this young playwright an auspicious debut as a short-story writer."

Shaw's new career was interrupted by World War II. He enlisted in the armed forces in 1942 and rose from private to warrant officer in the United States Army Signal Corps. He served in Africa, France, England, and Germany. When the war was over in 1945, he began working on his first and most famous novel, *The Young Lions* (1948). While working on this novel he served as drama critic for the *New Republic* in 1947-1948 and he taught creative writing at New York University in 1948-1949.

Months before the publication of *The Young Lions*, critics were writing advance reviews, predicting it would be the best novel to come out of the war. The action covers the period from New Year's Eve 1938 until Hitler's war machine was crushed in 1945. It deals with the lives of three soldiers, two Americans and one German. They are Michael Whitacre, a stage manager who has grown disillusioned with the theatre in Hollywood and New York; Noah Ackerman, a young introverted Jew who at the beginning of the war has found happiness in a recent marriage; and Christian Diestl, an Austrian ski instructor who has joined the Nazi party. The drama of their lives, their joys and sorrows, acts of cowardice, examples of bravery, are all played out against the backdrop of World War II. Finally in 1945, as the war draws to a close, the three men confront each other outside a concentration camp in Germany. There Michael finds meaning beyond all the bloodshed which has consumed his life for the last four years. He realizes if struggle and sacrifice will bring about the survival of a few men of decency, then all their hardships have been worth the cost.

In *The Young Lions* Shaw reveals again and again his eye for detail, especially in his descriptions of army life in the barracks and in war scenes such as Rommel's retreat, which one critic compared with Hemingway's sketch in *A Farewell to Arms* of the Italians' flight at Caporreto in World War I. Lee Rogow, writing in the *Saturday Review of Literature*, said: "Shaw has turned out a fine, full, intelligent book, packed with wonderful talk and crackling writing. We have waited a long time for this novel of Irwin Shaw's. In *The Young Lions* he reveals in even greater stature the delicious wit, the dramatic sense of scene-making, and the fullhearted comparison of his short stories."

The idea for Shaw's second novel, *The Troubled Air* (1951), occurred when he learned that a radio producer had been advised to fire several people from his show because of their alleged leftist persuasions. In the novel the central character, Clement Archer, who runs the news program "University Town," is in a similar predicament. Five members of his panel have been labeled Communists by a right wing newspaper and Archer must determine the truth of these accusations.

The Troubled Air focused on Archer as the well-intentioned seeker for truth. There are perceptive insights into the workings of the Communist mind and the tactics employed by right-of-center business groups. But Lionel Trilling found the book wanting as a novel: "whatever political satisfaction *The Troubled Air* may give, it gives but little pleasure as a work of fiction. What it tells us of the ordeal of its hero, Clement Archer, is adequate for a political morality but not for a novel."

Shortly after the publication of *The Troubled Air* Shaw decided to make his home in Europe, dividing his time between his apartment in Paris and his chalet in Klosters, Switzerland, a ski resort. His stay outside of the United States has lasted so long that one critic has suggested he no longer can write about America because he has lost touch with all the changes that have taken place in the last thirty years. In a recent interview in the *Paris Review*, Shaw answered that criticism: "The charge that I've become less American is ridiculous because I went back and forth all the time. I think I gained a whole lot of insight by living in Europe, and my books reflect it: *Lucy Crown*, for example, *Two Weeks in Another Town*, *Evening in Byzantium*, *Rich Man, Poor Man*, *Nightwork*, *Beggerman, Thief* would never have been written if it hadn't been for that European experience."

Nancy Crampton

The first novel that Shaw wrote as an expatriate was *Lucy Crown* (1956). At the beginning of the narrative he sets forth a premise, which provides the underlying psychology of the book: "When we look back into the past, we recognize a moment in time which was decisive, at which the pattern of our lives changed, a moment at which we moved irrevocably off in a new direction." In *Lucy Crown*, this turning point occurred for Tony Crown when he witnessed his mother seducing his friend. As a result, Tony is sent to boarding school, and it is almost twenty years before a reconciliation takes place between mother and son.

Most of the critics found *Lucy Crown* too slick and contrived. More than once it was compared with daytime soap operas. But Charles Rolo, writing in the *New York Times Book Review*, thought otherwise: "Mr. Shaw's adventure into fresh territory, it is pleasant to report, has produced a continuously absorbing book—sharply drawn, highly charged and painfully moving."

During the 1960s Shaw wrote two novels, *Two Weeks in Another Town* (1960) and *Voices of a Summer Day* (1965). Generally, neither book was well received by the critics. Shaw's novels were frequently compared unfavorably with his superb short stories of the 1930s and 1940s. He was called a facile novelist during this time, a writer who made no effort to create three-dimensional characters, while at his peak as a short-story writer, some of his work could be compared with the best of Hemingway and Fitzgerald.

But with the publication of *Rich Man, Poor Man* (1970), the critics were more enthusiastic. This novel is large, even longer than *The Young Lions*, and covers the three decades from 1940 to 1970. The setting moves from Hollywood to New York to Paris. The central characters are the three children of Axel Jordache, a baker who resides near the Hudson River. He has two sons, Rudolph and Thomas, and a daughter, Gretchen. Rudolph is the hard-working, good, intellectual member of the family while his brother is belligerent, aggressive, and at times cruel. Gretchen is a cross between the two.

In the end, ironically, it is Thomas who achieves success and love in his life. Gretchen compromises her life through a series of cheap love affairs, and Rudolph is left unhappy by a wife who does not love him. W. G. Rogers, writing in the *New York Times*, said: "A wealth of know-how has gone into the fictional creation; even today, few of our younger technicians can beat Irwin Shaw's expertise. . . . Shaw whisks us off from a standing start to a velocity well beyond familiar limits. His pace doesn't slacken for chapter after chapter. Incidents lead to incidents—and they are uncommonly appealing."

During the 1970s Shaw wrote four novels—*Evening in Byzantium* (1973), *Nightwork* (1975),

Beggarman, Thief (1977, a sequel to his *Rich Man, Poor Man*), *The Top of the Hill* (1979)—and several short stories. Of these four novels the best is *Evening in Byzantium.* It tells the story of a once-successful producer of plays and movies, Jesse Craig, who in the past few years has become unproductive. He travels to the Riviera at the time of the Cannes Film Festival in 1970, where he mixes with celebrities from all over the world. He arrives with more than his share of problems. He is separated from his wife, and the IRS is auditing his finances. While at the film festival, he meets a young journalist named Gail McKinnon and, with her help, explores his past. All of the novel takes place in the mind of Craig, and the reader soon finds himself concerned about the protagonist. Essentially *Evening in Byzantium* is the search for lost identity in the most unlikely setting of the lights and glitter of a film festival. Reviewer James R. Frakes noted: "There's something very reassuring about watching a really professional writer at work again, especially a veteran like Irwin Shaw, who knows his way around in many worlds—literature, publishing, movies, theater, international society, velvet roped restaurants and Third Avenue saloons—and who can handle the details of a business deal, an ulcer operation and a bedroom scene with equal aplomb and economical non-exploitation."

Since Shaw began writing over forty years ago, he has turned out a large number of novels, plays, movie scenarios, and short stories. The future seems to indicate no letup in his production since he is under contract for three more novels with his new publisher, Arbor House. In a 1979 interview Shaw was asked by Esther Blaustein about his plans for the future: "I aspire to write as many books as possible—and to do as well as possible." Although some critics have dismissed his writing as shallow and slick, it is clear that others have recognized the merit of his work. Lionel Trilling voiced this positive feeling about his early work thirty years ago when Shaw was beginning as a novelist: "I am inclined to believe that nothing Mr. Shaw might write could be totally lacking in interest of one kind or another. For one thing, he always *does* observe and always *does* feel and even when he is facile in observation and sentiment, he is not insincere."

—*Walter W. Ross III*

Plays:

Bury the Dead, New York, Ethel Barrymore Theatre, April 1936;

Siege, New York, Longacre Theatre, December 1937;

The Gentle People, New York, Belasco Theatre, January 1939;

Quiet City, New York, Belasco Theatre, March 1939;

Retreat to Pleasure, New York, Belasco Theatre, 1940;

Sons and Soldiers, New York, Morosco Theatre, May 1943;

The Assassin, New York, National Theatre, October 1945;

The Survivors, by Shaw and Peter Viertel, New York, Playhouse Theatre, January 1948;

Children From Their Games, New York, Morosco Theatre, April 1963;

A Choice of Wars, Glasgow, Scotland, Glasgow Citizens Theatre, 1967.

Screenplays:

The Big Game, RKO, 1936;

Commandos Strike at Dawn, Columbia, 1942;

The Hard Way, by Shaw and Daniel Fuchs, Warner Brothers, 1942;

Talk of the Town, by Shaw and Sidney Buchman, RKO, 1942;

Take One False Step, by Shaw and Chester Erskine, Universal, 1949;

I Want You, RKO, 1951;

Act of Love, United Artists, 1953;

Fire Down Below, Columbia, 1957;

Desire Under the Elms, Paramount, 1958;

This Angry Age, by Shaw and Rene Clement, Columbia, 1958;

The Big Gamble, Fox, 1961;

In the French Style, Columbia, 1963;

Survival, United Film, 1968.

Interviews:

"The Art of Fiction, IV," *Paris Review,* 1 (1953): 27-49;

"The Art of Fiction, IV," *Paris Review,* 21 (Spring 1979): 248-262.

References:

John W. Aldridge, *After the Last Generation* (New York: McGraw-Hill, 1951);

Chester E. Eisinger, *Fiction of the Forties* (Chicago: University of Chicago Press, 1963);

Bergen Evans, "Irwin Shaw," *English Journal,* 40 (November 1951): 485-491;

Leslie Fiedler, "Irwin Shaw: Adultery, The Last Politics," *Commentary,* 22 (July 1956): 71-74;

Roy Newquist, *Counterpoint* (New York: Rand McNally, 1964);

William Startt, "Irwin Shaw: An Extended Talent," *Midwest Quarterly*, 2 (1961): 325-337.

Papers:

Collections of Shaw's papers can be found at Boston University, at Pierpont Morgan Library, and at Brooklyn College.

WILFRID SHEED

(27 December 1930-)

BOOKS: *Joseph* (New York: Sheed & Ward, 1958);

A Middle-Class Education (Boston: Houghton Mifflin, 1960; London: Cassell, 1961);

The Hack (New York: Macmillan, 1963; London: Cassell, 1963);

Square's Progress (New York: Farrar, Straus & Giroux, 1965; London: Cassell, 1965);

Office Politics (New York: Farrar, Straus & Giroux, 1966; London: Cassell, 1967);

The Blacking Factory & Pennsylvania Gothic (New York: Farrar, Straus & Giroux, 1968; London: Weidenfeld & Nicolson, 1969);

Max Jamison (New York: Farrar, Straus & Giroux, 1970); republished as *The Critic* (London: Weidenfeld & Nicolson, 1970);

The Morning After (New York: Farrar, Straus & Giroux, 1971);

People Will Always Be Kind (New York: Farrar, Straus & Giroux, 1973; London: Weidenfeld & Nicolson, 1973);

Vanishing Species of America (New York: Sheed & Ward, 1974);

Three Mobs: Labor, Church and Mafia (New York: Sheed & Ward, 1974);

Muhammad Ali: A Portrait in Words and Photographs (New York: Alskog/Crowell, 1975; London: Weidenfeld & Nicolson, 1975);

Transatlantic Blues (New York: Robbins/Dutton, 1978);

The Good Words and Other Words (New York: Dutton, 1978; London: Sidgwick & Jackson, 1979).

Born in London, Wilfrid Sheed is the son of Maisie Ward and Francis Joseph Sheed, both of whom were writers and publishers. Although his father's family were not writers, his mother's side could boast of four generations where "some kind of writing has been going on. . . ." Four years before Sheed was born his parents established the publishing house of Sheed and Ward, which became one of the most respected religious publishers in the world. In 1933 a branch of this firm was opened in New York, and Sheed and Ward became the center of the Catholic intellectual movement in America.

When World War II began, Sheed, then nine, moved with his family from London to Torresdale, Pennsylvania, a place he remembers as almost an abandoned village where there was no one to play with. "I became perhaps the outstanding solitary baseball player of my generation, whaling fungoes down the long, narrow garden and plodding after them, chattering to myself and whaling them back again." At the age of fourteen he contracted poliomyelitis. About this time his schooling in the United States ended and he entered the well-known British Benedictine preparatory school Downside, in some ways similar to Sopworth in his novella *The Blacking Factory* (1968). During these years at Downside, he recalled, "I formed a taste for English prose and began consciously talking it to myself—a curious transatlantic brew of my own which I am still working on." After graduation he enrolled at Lincoln College at Oxford, where in 1954 he earned a B.A. degree in history. He began writing a novel in 1954 while residing with his father's relatives in Australia and finished it after returning to New York.

His first published novel, *A Middle-Class Education* (1960), grew out of Sheed's experience as an undergraduate at Oxford. In a 1979 *Publishers Weekly* interview he commented on his use of autobiography in his fiction and in particular in his earliest novel: "I shift the chronology around. I use settings I know. I wait until things have distilled, fermented. The boyhood episodes in my novels are less and less based on anything that really happened. The most autobiographical novel I have ever written, not surprisingly, was my first, 'A Middle-Class Education,' about going to Oxford."

The novel is a satire on academic life in England and the United States. John Chote first attends Oxford, where he avoids classes and homework, devoting most of his time to drinking beer and telling dirty jokes. All this does not keep him from winning a scholarship for graduate work at an American university. In New York his studies suffer further when he falls in love with a glamour girl and they have a brief affair. Finally, disillusioned with education, Chote returns to England where he vows to live an upright life.

The critics praised the book for its dialogue and comical scenes, but they found the novel weak in structure and unnecessarily drawn out. Charles Rolo in the *Atlantic Monthly* said: "The trouble is that 425 pages is an awfully long stretch on which to sustain undergraduate comedy; pruned of a hundred pages the novel might well have been an unqualified success."

The Hack (1963), Sheed's second novel, is a description of the gradual emotional deterioration of Bert Flax who lives with his wife, five children, and mother-in-law in a cluttered apartment in New Jersey. For a living he writes trite little inspirational poems and stories for second-rate Catholic magazines and occasionally speaks out on the dangers of Communism. Flax is a kind and thoughtful man who tries to live according to the religious homilies that he prescribes for others. It soon becomes clear, however, that his faith is not as strong as he believed. At church his mind begins to wander and confession no longer soothes his troubled soul. Soon his writing begins to dry up. The climax comes at Christmas when, unable to write his annual inspirational poem, he has a total nervous breakdown and is put under the care of a doctor.

The Hack is a realistic portrayal of the kind of writer Sheed most abhors. Reviewer Francis Connolly said: "At bottom, *The Hack* is neither tragic nor comic, but a sophisticated, exemplary tale that discriminates skillfully between dedicated service and dessicated servility. Like other good books of the same kind, it clears one's mind of cant."

With the publication of *Square's Progress* (1965) Sheed became recognized by some critics as an important American writer. The novel concerns the search for identity of a married couple living in Bloodbury, New Jersey. Fred Cope, a young insurance salesman, is happy with his life in suburbia. However, his wife, Alison, worries that she will become ordinary if she stays in the community very long. She reads Proust and Sartre, looking for any sign of self-deception or hypocrisy in her husband. Fred cannot withstand this close scrutiny. The two begin to quarrel and eventually part, each going a separate way to find out what went wrong in their marriage. Ironically, Fred ends up living much the way his wife would have wanted him to live. He moves to Greenwich Village, changes his style of dress, and starts smoking pot. Alison returns to her childhood home and adopts a life-style similar to what her husband's had been. The novel is marked by Sheed's wry humor and skill in evoking a sense of time and place.

Though he is best known for his fiction, over the

Jacqueline McCord

Wilfrid Sheed

years Sheed has also acquired a reputation as a journalist. In a recent autobiographical piece, he explained why he had decided to divide his time between the two kinds of writing: "Circumstances have obliged me to do a good deal of reviewing (the last refuge of the light essayist): books, plays, etc. I find this work painful, but it serves a couple of selfish purposes. It enables me to work out various aesthetic ideas, while unloading my little burden of didacticism in a safe place; and it gives me a certain thin-lipped benignity towards my own critics, when they turn the cannon round and aim it in my direction."

Sheed's journalistic output has been steady. He was movie reviewer for the Catholic magazine *Jubilee* between 1959-1961 and associate editor of the magazine from 1959-1966. In 1964 he became the drama critic and book review editor for *Commonweal*, a post he held until 1967. In that year he was offered the position of film critic at *Esquire*, where he remained until 1969. He has also contributed numerous articles to other magazines including the *Saturday Evening Post*, *Sports Illustrated*, and *Life*. Since 1971 he has written regularly for the *New York Times Book Review* and in 1972 he became a judge for Book-of-the-Month Club.

Throughout this period Sheed did not neglect his fiction writing. In *Office Politics* (1966), which was nominated for a National Book Award, he analyzes the sordid struggle for power that ensues on a magazine staff after the editor-in-chief becomes ill. In *The Blacking Factory*, a short novel, and *Pennsylvania Gothic* (1968), a long short story, published in one volume, Sheed returns to a study of youth in America and England, already a familiar theme in his writing. In *Max Jamison* (1970), nominated for a National Book Award in 1971 and published as *The Critic* in England, Sheed treats a subject in which he had considerable familiarity. The novel is a study of a Broadway theatre critic whose life is consumed by his job.

In the 1970s many of Sheed's critical reviews and essays were collected in book form while he continued to write on a wide range of subjects. In 1973 he published a sociological study entitled *Three Mobs: Labor, Church and Mafia.* Two years later he wrote a biography of *Muhammad Ali* supplemented with photographs. *Transatlantic Blues,* his second novel within the decade and his ninth novel in less than twenty years, received considerable critical attention, including a front-page review in the *New York Times Book Review.* Although many critics agreed that with *Transatlantic Blues* Sheed had written enough about the effect of England and America on his characters, Sheed's ear for dialogue, command of tone, and gift for comedy all indicate a promising future for this transatlantic novelist.

—Walter W. Ross III

Other:

Gilbert Keith Chesterton, *Essays and Poems,* edited by Sheed (Harmondsworth, U.K.: Penguin Books, 1958);

James Thurber, *Men, Women and Dogs,* introduction by Sheed (New York: Dodd, Mead, 1975).

Periodical Publications:

"My Passport Was at Shortstop," *Sports Illustrated,* 29 (11 November 1968): 28-35;

"Close-Up: Novelist of Suburbia," *Life,* 66 (18 April 1969): 39-46;

"Thurber Carnival," *Horizon,* 13 (Autumn 1971): 16-17;

"Twin Urges of James Baldwin," *Commonweal,* 104 (24 June 1977): 404-407.

Interviews:

"Wilfrid Sheed," *Publishers Weekly,* 213 (6 February 1978): 10;

"Talk with Sheed," *New York Times Book Review,* 21 January 1979, pp. 9, 20-21.

References:

Francis Connolly, Review of *The Hack, America,* 109 (9 November 1963): 608-609;

"Sheed's Specters of the Past," *Time,* 92 (20 September 1968): 108-109.

ISAAC BASHEVIS SINGER
(21 November 1904-)

*SELECTED BOOKS: *The Family Moskat,* trans. A. H. Gross (New York: Knopf, 1950; London: Secker & Warburg, 1966);

Satan in Goray, trans. Jacob Sloan (New York: Noonday, 1955; London: Owen, 1958);

Gimpel the Fool and Other Stories, trans. Saul Bellow and others (New York: Noonday, 1957; London: Owen, 1958);

The Magician of Lublin, trans. Elaine Gottlieb and Joseph Singer (New York: Noonday, 1960; London: Secker & Warburg, 1961);

The Spinoza of Market Street, trans. Martha Glicklich, Cecil Hemley, and others (New York: Farrar, Straus & Cudahy, 1961; London: Secker & Warburg, 1962);

The Slave, trans. Isaac Bashevis Singer and Hemley (New York: Farrar, Straus & Cudahy, 1962; London: Secker & Warburg, 1963);

Short Friday and Other Stories, trans. Joseph Singer and others (New York: Farrar, Straus & Giroux, 1964; London: Secker & Warburg, 1967);

In My Father's Court, trans. Channah Kleinerman-Goldstein, Gottlieb, and Joseph Singer (New York: Farrar, Straus & Giroux, 1966);

Zlateh the Goat and Other Stories, trans. Elizabeth Shub and Isaac Bashevis Singer (New York: Harper & Row, 1966; London: Secker & Warburg, 1967);

Selected Short Stories of Isaac Bashevis Singer, ed. Irving Howe (New York: Modern Library, 1966);

Mazel and Shlimazel, Or the Milk of a Lioness, trans. Shub and Isaac Bashevis Singer (New York: Farrar, Straus & Giroux / Ariel, 1967);

The Manor, trans. Joseph Singer and Gottlieb (New York: Farrar, Straus & Giroux, 1967; London: Secker & Warburg, 1968);

The Fearsome Inn, trans. Shub and Isaac Bashevis Singer (New York: Scribners, 1967; London: Collins, 1970);

When Shlemiel Went to Warsaw and Other Stories, trans. Isaac Bashevis Singer and Shub (New York: Farrar, Straus & Giroux / Ariel, 1968);

*This list includes only books published in English.

The Seance and Other Stories, trans. Roger H. Klein, Hemley, and others (New York: Farrar, Straus & Giroux, 1968);

A Day of Pleasure: Stories of a Boy Growing Up in Warsaw, trans. Kleinerman-Goldstein and others (New York: Farrar, Straus & Giroux, 1969);

The Estate, trans. Joseph Singer, Gottlieb, and Shub (New York: Farrar, Straus & Giroux, 1969; London: Cape, 1970);

Elijah the Slave, trans. Isaac Bashevis Singer and Shub (New York: Farrar, Straus & Giroux, 1970);

Joseph and Koza, Or the Sacrifice to the Vistula, trans. Isaac Bashevis Singer and Shub (New York: Farrar, Straus & Giroux, 1970);

A Friend of Kafka and Other Stories, trans. Isaac Bashevis Singer, Shub, and others (New York: Farrar, Straus & Giroux, 1970; London: Cape, 1972);

An Isaac Bashevis Singer Reader (New York: Farrar, Straus & Giroux, 1971);

Alone In the Wild Forest, trans. Isaac Bashevis Singer and Shub (New York: Ariel / Farrar, Straus & Giroux, 1971);

The Topsy-Turvy Emperor of China, trans. Isaac Bashevis Singer and Shub (New York, Evanston, San Francisco & London: Harper & Row, 1971);

Enemies, A Love Story, trans. Aliza Shevrin and Shub (New York: Farrar, Straus & Giroux, 1972; London: Cape, 1972);

The Wicked City, trans. Isaac Bashevis Singer and Shub (New York: Farrar, Straus & Giroux, 1972);

A Crown of Feathers and Other Stories, trans. Isaac Bashevis Singer, Laurie Colwin, and others (New York: Farrar, Straus & Giroux, 1973; London: Cape, 1974);

The Hasidim (New York: Crown, 1973);

The Fools of Chelm and Their History, trans. Isaac Bashevis Singer and Shub (New York: Farrar, Straus & Giroux, 1973);

Why Noah Chose the Dove, trans. Shub (New York: Farrar, Straus & Giroux, 1974);

Passions and Others Stories, trans. Isaac Bashevis Singer and others (New York: Farrar, Straus & Giroux, 1975; London: Cape, 1976);

A Tale of Three Wishes (New York: Farrar, Straus & Giroux, 1976);

A Little Boy in Search of God, Or Mysticism in a Personal Light (Garden City: Doubleday, 1976);

Naftali the Storyteller and His Horse, Sus, and Other Stories, trans. Joseph Singer, Isaac Bashevis Singer, and others (New York: Farrar, Straus & Giroux, 1976);

Yentl, by Singer and Leah Napolin (New York, Hollywood, London & Toronto: French, 1977);

A Young Man in Search of Love, trans. Joseph Singer (Garden City: Doubleday, 1978);

Shosha, trans. Joseph Singer and Isaac Bashevis Singer (New York: Farrar, Straus & Giroux, 1978);

Old Love, trans. Joseph Singer, Isaac Bashevis Singer and others (New York: Farrar, Straus & Giroux, 1979);

Nobel Lecture (New York: Farrar, Straus & Giroux, 1979).

One of the most distinguished and honored of modern writers and certainly deserving of the Nobel Prize for literature awarded him in 1978, Isaac Bashevis Singer is an anomaly as an American and a novelist. Shaped by a culture which was not only Old World but derived from perhaps its most remarkable sector, Singer thinks and writes in a dying language, Yiddish, about a community which has vanished—that of East European Jewry, and specifically that of the Hasidim in Poland.

Yiddish is the thousand-year-old form of German developed by Jews, using the Hebrew alphabet and incorporating ancient Hebrew and Aramaic words. Its vocabulary expanded by adapting words from European languages with which Jews had contact, including Russian, Provençal, and English. During the Middle Ages it became the language for daily speech among Jews, especially in Eastern Europe. This was their vernacular; in it practical affairs were discussed and transacted at home and elsewhere. But Hebrew, the sacred language and therefore the language of special authority, continued to be used as it had been for thousands of years, not only for liturgical and ritual purposes but also for religious learning and written discourse, because it was the language of scripture and related texts. Until the nineteenth century, therefore, Yiddish as a written language was reserved for commercial purposes and as the medium for popular education, including religious instruction for those (particularly women) who lacked sufficient Hebrew for advanced study of religious texts and their rabbinic commentaries. But by the middle of the nineteenth century, as the cohesiveness of distinctively Jewish culture began to disintegrate, Yiddish came to be used for so-called enlightened purposes, including literary writing of a secular sort. Isaac Bashevis Singer in the twentieth century has established himself as one of the four or five masters of literary Yiddish, and one of the greatest writers of Yiddish narrative.

His writing preserves and extends the linguistic resources of Yiddish as perhaps no other writing has done. Not only is Singer's command magisterial, but he has reintroduced archaic aspects of the language, adapting them to the sophisticated needs of a modern writer to give Yiddish a vitality and versatility deriving not only from his scholarly command of traditional Hebrew and Aramaic texts but also from his genius for storytelling, equalled by few modern writers, Yiddish or otherwise.

It therefore is misleading to think of him simply as a naturalized American who has lived and worked at his writing on the Upper West Side of Manhattan since the mid-1930s, as misleading as to think of him in terms of writers of whatever origin who celebrate the values of the old country, or who in other ways seek for sentimental reasons to reestablish ties with fellow immigrants in America, or who are concerned with the complex and tragicomical processes of Americanization. And it surely would be mistaken to group him with those well-known Jewish-American and American-Jewish writers of fiction who have contributed so much to American literature during the past thirty years, especially writers such as Saul Bellow, Norman Mailer, Bernard Malamud, J. D. Salinger, Philip Roth, Herbert Gold, Herman Wouk, and Chaim Potok. The genius of Singer indeed is distinctive if not unique.

But what primarily distinguishes him from contemporary American writers of fiction is not simply a matter of language, perhaps that least of all. Almost everything he has written is either available in English translations supervised by him or has been announced for such publication; some of the English versions are of a genuine brilliance approximating that of the original Yiddish texts. Therefore it is the culture his language reflects and expresses which defines the uniqueness of Singer and establishes the scope and focus of his writing. Polish Jewry during the past three hundred fifty years, the traditions of Hasidism, and his own personal experiences provide the matrix which forms his consciousness as a man and artist, and which informs his novels, short stories, and autobiographical writing.

Born Icek-Hersz Zynger in Poland in 1904, in the *shtetl* of Leoncin not far from Warsaw, he was the third of the four children of Rabbi Pinchos-Mendel Zynger (formerly of Tomaszov) and Bathsheba Zylberman of Bilgoray. Both parents, members of pious rabbinical families, had themselves been raised in relatively obscure Jewish villages similar to Leoncin. With ramshackle wooden-frame buildings, muddy streets, and noisy market districts, little seemed outwardly remarkable about these communities. Hundreds of them were scattered throughout the rural areas of Poland, Lithuania, and Russia. But whatever their sizes, conditions, and precise locations (and these varied greatly), the Jewish religion dominated such *shtetls* and always differentiated them from comparable villages of nearby peasants. In the *shtetl* every aspect of life—public and private, communal and personal, commercial and domestic—was prescribed by traditions, laws, institutions, and public officials, all sanctioned specifically by religion.

Communities so oriented, in which ritual controlled not only household routines but conduct in the communal bathhouse and the slaughterhouse as well, in the synagogue and the *heder* (elementary school), in commerce and intimate personal relationships, in the study house and the prayer house, must necessarily hold scholarly knowledge in special esteem given the vast and intricate literature dealing with such matters. Even among ignorant townspeople, learning and the discipline of study were deemed precious, as highly regarded as worship itself and scarcely distinguishable from it. But however much Pinchos-Mendel and Bathsheba shared by virtue of their *shtetl* upbringing and their dedication to leading pious lives, Singer's parents came from religious backgrounds that not only were different but also were in basic conflict: he was a Hasid, she a *mitnagid*, an orthodox Jew who opposed Hasidism. Those distinctions would provide their son with an endowment whose tensions would always resonate, sustaining him for more than seventy years and continuously enlivening his work.

Hasidism was a pietistic movement which developed among East European Jews in the eighteenth century. Drawing upon the *Kabbalah* (the best known of the cabalistic writings is the *Zohar*, the "Book of Splendor"), it evolved a mystical version of Jewish orthodoxy which many Jews found irresistible. Hasidic Judaism, then and now, is an emotional religion which provides ecstatic encounters with the Divine Spirit. Joyful feelings were construed as an indication of sanctity; spontaneous prayers in Yiddish were encouraged to supplement the traditional Hebrew liturgy; and enthusiastic singing and dancing contributed to transcendence and spiritual communion. In such ways despair could be overcome while celebrating the ever-present God. It was a religion for the oppressed masses, for simple people who suffered from the hostility of the non-Jewish world which surrounded them. Through Hasidism they could experience the awesome power of God and replace heartache with joy. It was also a reaction against the

Jill Krementz

Isaac Bashevis Singer

relatively cold and rather detached formalistic traditional orthodoxy perpetuated by erudite rabbis and talmudists (scholarly authorities on Jewish law) who in effect constituted the Jewish intellectual elite.

By the middle of the nineteenth century, Hasidism was the most active force in the Jewish world. By then, however, it was also fragmented because of the emergence of dozens of charismatic Hasidic rabbis, each with his own personal following; some of the older communities even had an inherited dynastic leadership. Such rabbis often were considered *tsadikim* by their followers. A *tsadik* was a righteous man whose saintliness enabled him to possess supernatural powers sufficient to work miracles. By force of his personality alone, a *tsadik* could bring his followers close to his own exalted ethical and spiritual condition. Singer's father, Pinchos-Mendel, was a Hasid who yearned to become a wonder-working rabbi himself, studying, praying, and practicing a discipline of piety which made severe demands upon him and upon his family. He was also writing commentaries on rabbinical commentaries, calling his manuscript "The Righteousness of Rashi." By temperament he was an austere yet gentle and loving man.

Singer's mother, Bathsheba, possessed a different but still traditional outlook on Jewish life. Her father was a keen-witted rabbi, a pious talmudic scholar of some distinction, an intellectual with a curiosity about mathematics. Bathsheba was a remarkable woman. Tall, red-haired, with piercing cold-gray eyes set in a strong-featured face, she was a skeptical rationalist of a kind which *mitnagdim* delighted in. Moreover, she was a self-taught Hebraist, which gave her access to the sacred knowledge customarily reserved for men. (She had married Pinchos-Mendel because he was the most learned of her suitors.) She was also practical in ways that contrasted boldly with the unworldliness and naivete of her husband, who sought to avoid not only everything secular but also anything he considered spiritually dangerous. For example, he never learned to speak or write Polish or Russian, refusing to study the latter language although it was required for the civil examination which would have granted him official status as a clergyman and made him eligible for more prestigious rabbinic appointments. By contrast, although a modest and dignified matron, Singer's mother forced herself to sell yeast to the coarse women of the village in order to supplement the meager earnings of the Leoncin rabbi. Unlike her husband she was intellectually sophisticated and knew how to release her frustrations through ironies of understatement. Both, however, were apparently gifted storytellers. But while he told his children about miracle-working rabbis, angels, wandering souls, and demons, all of whom confirmed the existence and goodness of God, she told them about their relatives in Bilgoray, describing them in detail and relating the chief events in their lives so that the children might have a feeling for family history. For him, as a religious fundamentalist, history would not culminate in a Bilgoray reunion but in the literal coming of the Messiah, at which time the Jews would be restored to the Holy Land. They were in agreement, however, that police, soldiers, and the laws and customs of non-Jews were threats to the moral order of the universe.

In 1907, after having been a dedicated but unremarkable and impoverished rabbi in Leoncin for ten years, Pinchos-Mendel was appointed director of the Yeshiva in Radzymin, the religious school founded by Rabbi Yekele, the wonder-working spiritual leader of that *shtetl.* He would also serve as secretary to the *tsadik.* Accordingly, the family moved to Radzymin. But a year later, because they could barely survive on a small salary intermittently paid, they moved again, this time to Krochmalna Street in the huge ghetto of Warsaw. This was functionally a *shtetl,* located not in the countryside but within a city of some eight hundred thousand people, about a third of whom were Jews. Until World War II, Warsaw was one of the world's great centers of Jewish culture.

It would become for Isaac Bashevis Singer the preeminent city, providing him with the sophisticated urban imagination which suffuses his writing. This is nominally confirmed by Singer himself. One of the two names under which his writings have regularly been published in New York's *Jewish Daily Forward*—for many years the world's foremost Yiddish periodical—is Isaac Warshofsky, a name meaning Isaac of Warsaw. The other name, equally revealing, is the one he used first when he began to publish in Warsaw in 1927, Isaac Bashevis. This identified him as his mother's son, Isaac son of Bathsheba. Bashevis is the familiar form of that biblical name which, he has admitted, is sacred to him but also suggestive of sin. (King David had ordered Uriah the Hittite into the most dangerous part of the battle where he was killed, and then took Uriah's wife Bathsheba for himself.) Only when he began to publish in English for American readers did his name, Isaac Bashevis Singer, reveal the double heritage he received from his parents.

Thus it was in 1908 that Pinchos-Mendel settled himself, his wife, and four children in a dingy three-room apartment illuminated by smoky kerosene lamps, in a rundown fortresslike stone building with foul-smelling stairways, dimly lighted hallways, outdoor toilets, and a maze of bustling and dirty courtyards. Here in the cramped apartment, Pinchos-Mendel established himself as the unofficial rabbi of Krochmalna Street. Red-haired Isaac with luminous blue eyes was now almost four years old, but he had already begun his elementary studies at the Radzymin *heder.* His education continued in Warsaw at a rapid pace; it was not restricted to local classrooms, however.

In the shabby apartment, Singer's father established his *Beth Din,* the traditional rabbinical court (literally a place of judgment and discrimination) which was sought out by people in the neighborhood in need of authoritative opinions and advice. He received small fees for his services with which he was determined to support his family. Rabbi Zynger answered questions about ritual observances, settled domestic quarrels, adjudicated disputes over money and commercial transactions, solved problems of love and marriage, counseled the emotionally disturbed, argued fine points of Talmudic law, and listened patiently to whomever required the purgation of talk. It was a communal institution essential for the preservation of Jewish orthodoxy. As he administered it, the *Beth Din* was permeated with Hasidic customs, unworldly values, and puritanical habits of mind, and sustained by an all-pervading sense that traditional Jewishness was everywhere being threatened, even in his own household.

In both formal memoirs and casual reminiscences about the *shtetl* and Warsaw he knew in his early years, Isaac Bashevis Singer characteristically represents himself as the famous writer wishes to be remembered: Itchele (his family nickname), secretly listening to trivial and portentous matters being discussed in his father's *Beth Din*; the child-Hasid scribbling away at an early age and reading forbidden books both sacred and profane; risking heretical thoughts while asking the perennial questions about the meaning of existence; already seeing how the surrounding non-Jewish world threatened the integrity of the marginal Jewish community; experiencing inexplicable mood swings, from ecstasy at the thought of the imminent arrival of the Messiah to despair for the generations of those who had suffered and would continue to suffer; observing from a discreet distance the mysteriously complex world of adult emotions; walking along familiar but still dangerous streets; accompanying his father to the Radzymin study house which was located in one of the Krochmalna Street courtyards; envisioning the world as a gigantic slaughterhouse or an enormous hell; eavesdropping on the conversations of learned rabbis and foolish ones; being fascinated by the incomprehensible games of sexuality and love; relieving the drabness of slum dwelling with the lovely mystery of the Sabbath and the drama of Jewish holidays and holy days; learning about the domestic tensions that torment individuals and destroy families; worrying about the undeserved sufferings of the innocent and the virtuous; reading the religious texts which would prepare him for the advanced studies which might qualify him someday to be a rabbi like his father, his grandfathers, and his other forebears; dreaming incredible and indescribable dreams, more real than everyday realities; being terrified by imps, demons, and witches lurking everywhere in the shadows; already knowing that Jewish thieves, prostitutes, ruffians, and assassins lived and worked alongside pious paupers on Krochmalna Street; and adoring a worldly brother, Israel Joshua, eleven years older than himself, an impious, idealistic rebel, politically active, who was struggling to become an artist and a writer.

As such experiences were unsettling his consciousness, he was determined to define himself in terms of parents and a brother, each temperamentally and intellectually different. In its multiple aspects, Krochmalna Street represented to his imagination the infinite world which was demonic and divine, full of cruelties yet lovely nevertheless whenever butterflies fluttered into view or trees blossomed. But he knew that neither flowers nor plants were kept in the apartment because his parents considered it a pagan custom.

Singer's recollections of his precocious years in Warsaw are not only eventful but also full of books, some removed secretly from his father's library, some given by his intellectually adventurous older brother, some borrowed from libraries in Warsaw, some bought. All were read when he should still have been in the Radzymin study house located in the courtyard, studying the scholarly commentaries and explications of Jewish law recorded in Hebrew and Aramaic. Contrary to the pious wishes of both parents, he read books in Yiddish explaining the *Kabbalah,* modern science and cosmology, the economics of Malthus and Marx, and Darwinian evolution; Yiddish newspapers and penny dreadfuls; Yiddish translations not only of Poe and Conan Doyle, but also of Shakespeare, Gorky, Andreyev, Tolstoy, and Dostoevsky. (He thought that Raskolnikov—in the Yiddish version of *Crime and Punishment* he claimed to have read at the age of ten—explained the baffling ways of student-intellectuals like his own brother.)

What young Isaac perceived as the rebellious behavior of Israel Joshua was neither perverse nor gratuitous, nor was it that rite of passage by which the child repudiates parental values for the sake of his own adult status. The truth was that Israel Joshua, raised a Hasid, had actually become a *maskil* (a so-called enlightened one). He was ideologically a modern Jew who was educating himself in mainstream Western culture. He was convinced that such acculturation was not a repudiation of Jewishness nor a loss of Jewish identity; rather it was a liberation from the needlessly restrictive ways of the *shtetl* and the ghetto. Accordingly he read widely and belonged to various political and social organizations in Warsaw, and he had forsaken the external indications of the Hasidic spirit within: the untrimmed full beard, the long curled sidelocks, the ankle-length black gaberdine tied with black silk cord, the short prayer-shawl undergarment with silk tassles often visible, the large black velvet hat with fur trim worn outdoors, and the *yarmulka* (black skullcap) always worn indoors.

Maskilim like Israel Joshua were the beneficiaries of *Haskalah,* the eighteenth-century movement for modernizing Judaism, without, it was believed, sacrificing the traditional values essential to Jewishness. An intellectual and religious revolutionary struggle for fuller participation by Jews in non-Jewish society, the *Haskalah* was opposed to Jewish dogmatism and what were considered medieval superstitions.

In part as a consequence of this movement, serious fiction in Yiddish by *maskilim* began to appear in the middle of the nineteenth century, ranging widely in subject and purpose but always with substantial Jewish content. Secular writing of genuine literary merit had already been done by Mendele Mocher Sforim, Sholom Aleichem, I. L. Peretz, Sholem Asch, and David Bergelson—all writers now being read surreptitiously by young Isaac. In the years following World War I, the *maskilim* would stimulate a renaissance in Yiddish culture in Warsaw, with Israel Joshua Singer involved as coeditor of *Literarishe Bletter* ("Literary Pages"). This had special significance for Yiddish

X

A PAIR

By ISAAC BASHEVIS SINGER

Among those who ran away from Hitler and managed to reach America was the poet Getzele Tertziver, a tiny, dark-complexioned man with a small head, shoulder-length hair, and on his chin a wisp of a beard. He had a crooked nose, a mouth with small, widely-spaced teeth as black as lead, and large black wandering eyes--the right one looked up, the left one down. The humorists in the Warsaw Yiddish Press often printed jokes about Getzele Tertziver, his wild appearance and his poems which no one understood, not even the critics who believed in modernism. Getzele Tertziver had published one book, a mixture of poems, aphorisms and miniatures, titled "The World History of My Future."

Getzele Tertziver, as did his grandfather the Tertziver Rabbi Alterel, reversed everything. He slept in the daytime and was awake at night. Only one typesetter in Warsaw could decipher Getzele's handwriting. Years after pelerines for men went out of fashion, Getzele's apparel was a pelerine hanging to his ankles, a flowing tie, and a black, wide-brimmed hat. He smoked a long pipe. Even though the Tertziver Chassidim considered him a ~~non-believer~~ heretic who shamed his pious ancestors in Paradise, they surreptitiously sustained him. Old Chassidim who remembered Rabbi Alterel when he was young swore that Getzele resembled him like two drops of water--the same face, the same way of walking, the same mannerisms. True, Rabbi Alterel ascended to the highest spheres while Getzele had fallen into the abyss of apostasy. Still, they would not allow his grandson to starve.

How strange that wild-eyed Getzele, who could not make himself understood either in his writing or in his speech, using a gibberish of Yiddish, Hebrew, Aramaic, which he spewed forth quickly and in a chassidic sing-song, had married three times, and each time with a beauty. When the writers in the Yiddish Writers Club in Warsaw tired of discussing literature and reviling one another, it was enough to mention the name Getzele Tertziver to revive the conversation. Everyone asked the same question: "What had those rich girls seen in him?"

- 1 -

"A Pair," revised typescript

literature in Warsaw because modern perspectives could be brought to bear on Jewish culture past and present. If Israel Joshua could engage in philosophical debate in his mother's kitchen, citing his intellectual hero Darwin while she quoted rabbinic authorities, he was not necessarily an impudent son or a criminal non-Jew but an "enlightened one," as young Isaac eventually came to understand.

When famine and epidemics devastated Warsaw in 1917, thirteen-year-old Isaac (with his mother) fled the city. They settled in Bilgoray, living with her relatives. There he remained for four years, encountering life in the authentic *shtetl* for the first time since his infancy in Leoncin and Radzymin. Bilgoray was little changed by the modern world because of its inconspicuous location near the Austrian border. Here, as never before, he encountered the "old Jewishness" with an intensity and purity which imprinted itself on his consciousness in much the same way as the contrasting complexities and secular worldliness of life in Warsaw were fixed. Both would always remain with him, available to be remembered, experienced, and imagined whenever and however he wished. In Bilgoray he felt he had contacted the richness of his own cultural past as it actually had been, giving him the sensation that "Time . . . flowed backward." Ever after he believed he could actually experience Jewish cultural history because in Bilgoray he had "lived it." Here history, autobiography, and fiction were now beginning to merge in his mind, internalized in much the same way as the values of his father, mother, and brother had been absorbed.

But the longer he remained in Bilgoray, the greater his sense that the distinctions between that *shtetl* and Warsaw were being obscured. Even in Bilgoray the traditional world was not permanent. A Zionist society had been organized; there were members of the Socialist Bund; Bolsheviks enlisted orthodox youth; Zionism and orthodoxy united in the *Mizrachi* movement; young "pioneers" prepared to settle in Palestine; a Yiddish theatre company came from Warsaw to perform; and a small lending library was established, with secular books in Hebrew as well as in Yiddish. Where once only a tattered Russian dictionary could be found to satisfy the young Singer's hunger for worldly books, now he was able to read (in Yiddish) Strindberg, Turgenev, and Chekhov, among other European authors. Here too he found Stupnicki's book about Spinoza, forcing him to contemplate the terrifying yet potentially beautiful consequences of equating existence with deity: simply by *being*, everything was God. And from the Bilgoray watchmaker, a *maskil* with a passion for scientific and philosophical talk, he learned about Einstein and Max Planck. The *Haskalah* had finally reached Bilgoray.

But Singer's most important discovery was a copy of Hillel Zeitlin's *The Problem of Good and Evil* (1898), in which the *Kabbalah* and Hasidic writings were reconciled with Spinoza, Schopenhauer, and Nietzsche: Zeitlin's "silent God" mediated between the metaphysical despair of Schopenhauer and the joyful Messianism of the Hasidic movement. If separated from God by an impassable gulf, still man is not powerless; the master of his own existence, his first human act is to struggle up from the depths of despair. What will redeem him from his isolation is compassion, the only force which can bring him closer to other men and to God. A mystic with an extraordinary capacity for intellectual synthesis, Zeitlin learned from the *Kabbalah* that modern Jewishness needed to be rooted in religion if it were to survive, a view virtually identical to that of the mature Singer who considered Zeitlin one of the "giants." His book helped Singer reconcile the changes occurring in Bilgoray with the Bilgoray he remembered from the stories his mother had told about her native *shtetl*.

In addition to deepening his commitments to Yiddish literature and Jewish culture generally during his Bilgoray period, Singer became involved as never before with Hebrew as a modern secular language. He taught conversational Hebrew to the children of *maskilim*, thereby shocking the *mitnagid* townspeople; he read the Hebrew poetry written by the *maskilim*—Bialik, Czerniochowsky, and Schneyur; he experimented with writing his own poems and stories; and adolescent sexual fantasies intruded upon other weighty matters occupying his attention in Bilgoray, causing him unforgettable anxieties.

In 1921 he returned to Warsaw, enrolling in the Tachkemoni Rabbinical Seminary at his father's insistence. Penniless, lonely, without a settled place to live, often near starvation, and lacking interest in his studies, he later said that this period was the worst of his life. What preserved him, apparently, was reading a novel by Knut Hamsun, the Norwegian writer who had received the Nobel Prize the year before. Paradoxically, it was *Hunger* (1890) which nourished and enlarged Singer. Hamsun's great novel dealt with that condition of extreme deprivation in terms of a young writer (like Raskolnikov, Singer noted) whose intellectual energies, having been crushed by poverty, virtually border on madness. The hallucinogenic hunger of Hamsun's nameless hero is psychic as much as physiological. Although estranged from Christiania (Oslo) society and desperate, he nevertheless is deeply if invisibly rooted in the life and culture of Norway. But he releases himself from his despair by shipping out on a freighter (a virtual suicide, thought Singer). Isaac of Warsaw by contrast, after a year of misery, quit the seminary and returned to his visible roots in Bilgoray for the restoration of his psychic and physical health.

But unable to support himself by giving Hebrew lessons and still unwell, he joined his family in the nearby *shtetl* where his father now was rabbi and his younger brother Moishe was studying for the rabbinate. Here, in Dzikow ("half-bog, half-village") Singer discovered in 1922—as had Martin Buber a generation earlier in Germany—the work of an extraordinary storyteller quite different from Hamsun: Rabbi Nachman of Bratzlav (1772-1810), whose status as a *tsadik* was confirmed by his being the dynastic descendant of the founder of Hasidism, the *Baal Shem Tov* (the Master of the Good Name), who was his great-grandfather.

The contributions of the *Bratzlaver* to the development of the Nobel laureate-to-be are remarkable: partly because the tales of Nachman helped bring Singer through his own despair (or so he claimed fifty years later), partly because he was still exasperated by Spinoza's conception of God as infinite intellect but without feelings, and partly because they helped him find his vocation. Therefore, several months later in 1923, when Israel Joshua offered his brother a modest position on the staff of the *Literarishe Bletter*, Singer was ready to accept. His purpose in returning once again to Warsaw would be unmistakable—to become a writer, a writer of fiction in Yiddish, like his brother who the previous year had published an important book of short stories.

For the Hasidim, storytelling by the *tsadik* had religious value, constituting a religious experience for his followers. Because religious doctrine, dogma, and theory were believed to be fully incarnated in the narrative, Hasidic storytelling (and retelling by disciples) acquired the same central importance that academic study of Jewish law had in the rabbinic tradition strictly preserved by the *mitnagdim*. But unlike the Yiddish tales associated with other Hasidic masters, those attributed to Nachman are symbolic narratives of a strange sort: they tell of princes and shepherds instead of saints and miracles, of sages and messengers who are not recognizably Jewish, of kings and counselors whose origins are not in the Jewish world at all, and of distant lands which are infinitely removed from the *shtetl* and the ghetto.

The *Bratzlaver*'s tales ultimately are transcendent affirmations: adventures end in happiness and harmony. What is mysterious is not evil, and what is dangerous is really fortuitous. A Messianic spirit therefore pervades his stories. Nachman believed that the Messianic personality was that of a suffering victim, able to serve as the perfect helper of all the other suffering victims constituting mankind. Moreover, mystic that he was, Nachman also believed that there was something of the Messiah in everyone, and that therefore each had an obligation for the redemption of every other, the wicked along with the saintly, the former actually having a greater claim on salvation than the latter.

Singer considered Nachman a "true saint" whose stories protested powerfully against life's cruelties. But he could still fault the *Bratzlaver* for taking comfort from a God whose benevolence was completely incomprehensible. By way of corrective, yet directly under the influence of the *tsadik*, Singer would eventually write stories of his own in Warsaw after developing what he called his own "ethic of protest."

Basic to Jewishness, according to Singer, is the obligation to protest against injustices whatever their source, whether in nature or in God himself. Therefore even though nature sanctions prodigality, conflict, and death, the Jew must oppose nature, subdue it, and insist upon restraint, peace, and life—the values incarnated in the Ten Commandments. But for protesting against what is natural, nature despises the Jew and takes revenge upon him. In addition to the strength needed to bear suffering brought on by natural antagonism, being a Jew requires the courage to protest even against God on behalf of what is right. Singer rationalizes this heroic sacrilege by citing a passage in the Talmud to the effect that the cause of justice is more compelling for a Jew than a voice from heaven to the contrary. The demands of such an uncompromising "ethic of protest" elevate Messianism to a level beyond even the vision of Rabbi Nachman of Bratzlav, but the relentlessly compassionate Singer was not yet competent to embody it in narratives of his own.

When he was called to Warsaw in 1923, it was to become lowly proofreader for the journal edited by his brother. When he arrived in the city he had few acquaintances and little money, led a hermitlike existence, lived in cheap rented rooms in the ghetto, wore seedy clothes, spoke broken Polish, and had the manners of a bashful young Yeshiva student. Secretly he nourished a passionate if ill-defined yearning for life in general, but specifically for women. Ascetic by necessity as much as principle, he struggled against urges to indulge in every possible pleasure. He was only nineteen years old. Amid the excitements of Warsaw from which he was excluded, as his feelings of anomie intensified by recent years spent in the *shtetls,* Singer often contemplated suicide. He thought self-destruction was warranted as the ultimate protest against the cruelties of the world: it "hurled back" to God the "gift" of life he granted. Such moods alternated with Messianic fantasies, but these were embittered by the human cruelties which made mankind seem not worth saving.

Fascinated by what was forbidden, Singer's imagination put him in touch with whatever was harmful. It was a perverse imagination (darkly "medieval" some called it) which was fed by the tedium of reading proof for *Literarishe Bletter.* What protected him against his sense of worthlessness were the Warsaw libraries which satisfied his hunger for philosophy, psychology, natural science, and the occult. He also read Strindberg's plays, William James's *The Will To Believe* (1897), and novels by Romain Rolland and Thomas Mann. He even read such Polish writers as Mickiewicz and Slowacki, Wyspianski and Przybyszewski.

Gradually overcoming shyness complicated by morbidity, he was drawn after a while to the Yiddish Writers' Club. Filled with the aromas of herring, garlic, and cheap tobacco, the club was where the buffet, the chess, the buzz of conversation, and the possibility of borrowing money brought together professional writers, struggling young aspirants, and the usual hangers-on. Here one could sip tea alone and read the current newspapers and journals, or sit near or with genuine intellectuals and fraudulent ones, jesters and pedants, flatterers and gossips, the disreputable and the dilettantes, and the brilliant and not-so-brilliant talkers. They were attracted here from everywhere in Eastern Europe. Never having published anything, if Isaac was recognized at all at the Writers' Club he was referred to as "Singer's brother"; Israel Joshua, who had already earned an international reputation for his stories and essays, was experimenting with plays and soon would publish his first novel.

But within a year of coming to Warsaw, at the Writers' Club Isaac met young Aaron Zeitlin, the son of Hillel Zeitlin. (Several years earlier, in Bilgoray during another crisis in Singer's life, Hillel Zeitlin's book had sensitized him to the continuing values of *shtetl* culture.) Singer already knew that, like his father, Aaron Zeitlin derived enormous personal power from Hasidism, enabling him to withstand the radical, atheistic, unlearned, secularistic forces in the Jewish world. A brilliant novelist, poet, and essayist, he was thoroughly trained in traditional Jewish law, knowledgeable about Yiddish folklore, a serious student of *Kabbalah,* and widely read in the major European writers including the moderns. Like his father too, he rejected most contemporary Yiddish writing, with its sentimental cliches or its bombast about social justice, political action, and Jewish nationalism. And like his father—and therefore like Singer himself—he not only believed in God but also in demons, evil spirits, ghosts, and phantoms, all within the context of Jewish traditions.

In 1922 Aaron Zeitlin had already published two books filled with mystical insights, Messianic visions, feelings of ecstasy and pain, apocalyptic and grotesque images, prose and verse rhythms associated with the melodies and vocal intonations used in the study of the Talmud, and metaphors derived from the scrupulous dialectics of the Talmudists. Nevertheless—and this was the miracle—he was recognizably a modern writer rooted in Yiddish language and the distinctive culture inseparable from it. Although only six years older than Singer, Aaron Zeitlin became not only his most intimate friend but also his *tsadik.* Singer acknowledged him to be "one of the greatest [religious poets] in world literature."

With the encouragement and example of Zeitlin (who in 1926 became literary editor of one of the leading Yiddish newspapers in Warsaw), Singer persisted in his literary ambitions, despite the embarrassment of having to support himself as a proofreader. He was eager to become a journalist. But when his brother arranged for him to serve as a "literary observer" for a Yiddish newspaper and report on a series of sensational treason trials, Singer quickly abandoned the assignment because he said he found the proceedings boring. Writing out of his own memory and imagination apparently was becoming more exciting for him, and more appropriate.

His first published story, "Oyf der Elter" ("In Old Age"), appeared in 1927 in *Literarishe Bletter* under the pseudonym Tse. In the same journal later that year appeared "Vayber" ("Women") under the name Isaac Bashevis. Such stories angered editors even when they agreed to publish them. As did most readers, they insisted that the duty of Yiddish writers was to stress the virtues of Jews, what was lofty and sacred in their culture, and thereby defend Jews instead of defame them. His first story, for example, was considered too pessimistic; it ignored current social problems and immediate political issues, and seemed so negative toward Jews that it was almost anti-Semitic. (Naive readers have been raising similar objections to his writing for the past fifty years.) It was a story about Jewish thieves and whores, and therefore combined violence with sexuality. Nevertheless, as signified by the sacred matronymic, the literary life of Isaac Bashevis was now underway if already controversial. Such stories, and the bitter denunciations they elicited from the Yiddishists, were indications at the outset of his career that Singer had already established the general characteristics of his writing. The "ethic of protest" was also a literary strategy.

Most Yiddish writers in Warsaw, he believed, had cut themselves off from their authentic roots by ignoring or deriding the culture of the ghetto and *shtetl* for the sake of narrowly defined worldliness such as communism, socialism, labor unionism, Zionism, assimilationism, anarchism, territorialism, or other doctrinaire positions of dubious value. By contrast, he was determined to find ways to draw upon the energies of ghetto culture and *shtetl* culture suitable for an enlightened Yiddish writer like himself, even if it meant dreaming and writing about spirits, demons, cabalists, and dybbukim, or writing about the seamier aspects of Jewish life without editorializing or apologizing.

While he continued to work on his stories and occasionally publish them in the Yiddish periodicals, literary translation became the means by which he supported himself as a professional writer during the next five years. He was often employed by the newspaper *Radio* to translate and adapt popular German suspense novels for publication in installments. He was required to transpose original locales into Polish ones familiar to readers and convert the chief characters into Jewish equivalents. This was poorly paid potboiling work, and Singer could not afford to decline it. But translation need not be simply hack work. Between 1927 and 1932 he also turned seven major novels into Yiddish books: Knut Hamsun's *Die Vogler* (1927), *Victoria* (1898), and *Pan* (1894); Stefan Zweig's *Romain Rolland* (1920); Erich Maria Remarque's *All Quiet on the Western Front* (1929) and *The Road Back* (1931); and Thomas Mann's *The Magic Mountain* (1924).

No longer was he simply proofreader for the writing of others; no longer was he known only as "Singer's brother." However, as translator and struggling writer, he still was leading a marginal existence, in rundown boardinghouses or rented rooms, usually in debt, while obstinately avoiding in his writing the contemporary problems and issues which were exploited by better established and "more promising" young writers. He was not interested in writing about the struggles of the Jewish masses in a capitalist society, nor could he rest in the dogmas of others. (He was once arrested because his mistress was a communist and he spent a terrifying day in prison in the company of thieves and political radicals.)

He remained faithful to the principles he shared with Aaron Zeitlin, and wrote stories that could be called imaginatively free, modern, and inverted analogues of the brilliantly idiosyncratic tales of Rabbi Nachman of Bratzlav. He had resolved, he said, "to become a narrator of human passion rather than of a placid life-style." With Zeitlin he shared an interest in the false Messiahs, Sabbatai Zvi and his disciple Jacob Frank, and discussed the possibilities of Messianism as a literary subject and a literary form.

Although he continued to think about Spinoza's *Ethics* in this connection, his doubts about an unfeeling God persisted, but Spinoza's assertion that "everything could become a passion" was important for fiction writing. His own passionate adventures and misadventures with women—frequent subjects in his recent autobiographical writings for American readers—confirmed this and acquired special significance for him. (During this period he lived with "Runya" and in 1929 their son Israel Zamir was born.) Religious feeling and sexuality were compatible because sexual urges, Singer was convinced, were connected with spiritual rather than physical powers. Both love and sex were, he thought, "functions of the soul."

What otherwise might seem a romantic commonplace was actually a principle of *Kabbalah* well known to Singer. According to the mystical lore, even God has sexual urges. The many universes he created (of which ours is by far the worst), for example, were the products of his "divine copulation" with the *Shekhinah*, the feminine element of God's glory, also known as the "Divine Presence." (With more wit than tact, Singer said the *Shekhinah* was "God's wife.") Not only was sex attributed to God, but all the parts of his creation were either male or female, each lusting for the other so strongly that they could never be satisfied. On a more practical level, but as an extension of the mystical nevertheless, Singer considered it futile to write about love while excluding sex. This is a modern literary idea, but Singer extracted it from the *Kabbalah* as well as confirming it by his own sexual experiences. Like the students of *Kabbalah*, Singer sought the hidden world concealed by the external one; the literal details of his fiction accordingly could cover a hidden world, not unlike the spiritual dimensions of sexual passion. "The sexual organs," Singer once said, "expressed more of the human soul than all the other body parts, even the eyes."

In 1933 Israel Joshua Singer—now well known for his novel *Yoshe Kalb*—sailed for New York at the urging of Abraham Cahan, the editor of the *Jewish Daily Forward*. That year Aaron Zeitlin founded *Globus* in Warsaw and Isaac Bashevis accepted the position of associate editor. In that literary magazine a number of his stories subsequently were published. Also in 1933 he began writing *Satan in Goray*, his first novel. *Globus* printed it in installments in 1934, and in that year Singer began *Messiah the Sinner*, another novel. In 1935 *Satan in Goray* was published as a book by the Yiddish section of the Warsaw P. E.N. Club. (The American translation appeared in 1955.)

Satan in Goray could not have been written had Singer not responded to the tales of Rabbi Nachman of Bratzlav, and had he not been befriended by Aaron Zeitlin. But it is the old Jewish past that he came to know in Bilgoray, remembering it as if it were an intimate experience of his own in a timeless world, that makes it the book many consider his masterpiece. Set in the middle years of the seventeenth century in an actual *shtetl* located not far from Bilgoray but seemingly at the end of the world, the novel's form is experimental, deliberately proto-novelistic. It is a long tale told through an aggressively historical imagination derived from what appears to be an archaic tradition of oral storytelling. This form is brilliantly suited to the time, the culture, and the specific circumstances of the novel.

Colored by folk memories of the events, actual historical facts are juxtaposed by Singer: cossacks devastated the *shtetl* in 1648 and butchered its inhabitants; and independently in the same year, an Oriental Jew, Sabbatai Zvi, proclaimed himself the Messiah. Out of this conjunction of discrete events emerges the disembodied narrative voice which tells of the gradual restoration of the *shtetl* following the disaster and the extraordinary effect on the town of the prospect of the Messiah's arrival.

The narrative focus is upon Rechele, a neurasthenic woman whose hallucinations are construed by Sabbateans as prophetic. Her visions, of course, are satanic rather than Messianic, sexually induced rather than divinely inspired; but nevertheless they manage to integrate the sacred with the profane. The integrity of the community is eventually shattered by the failure of the Messiah to arrive and by the devastating information that Sabbatai Zvi has converted to Islam. But through memories of the traditional culture which formerly existed, hope for the future continues to be affirmed, however indistinctly.

The power of this extraordinary novel derives not only from the plot but also from the details which bring to life the strange customs, the superstitions, the demonic spirit, the cabalistic lore, the savagery of the physical and psychic violence, the sexual excesses, the wildly apocalyptic visions, and the pious ecstasies which are not precluded by the disappointments of the credulous millenarians. Nothing is explained; everything is evoked. What emerges from the failure of orthodox tradition, reasonableness, and fundamental decency to prevent communal hysteria and degradation, is not hopelessness or helplessness; instead it is the expectation that through suffering mankind will be redeemed, and it will redeem itself. This redemption is even now being overseen by God, but it is a God both invisible and silent. If the Messianic hope is itself life-sustaining, the prospect of immediate Messianic fulfillment is demoralizing indeed.

Piously orthodox sentiments continually are subverted by the narrative; and yet there is an irony at work which ultimately asserts the value of even the most grotesque beliefs. What Singer affirms is the power of the traditional orthodox Jewish culture to prevent the total destruction of man by man. Out of the false Messianic hope there is a Messianic reality, much more modest in scope and therefore much more effective as a life-sustaining force. In this alchemical novel Singer has managed to convert cultural anthropology into art and to transmute morbid psychology into a measure of joy which possesses profound significance for the future.

Before *Satan in Goray* appeared as a book in Warsaw, Singer had already arrived in America and was living in Brooklyn. He had been invited by his brother to join him there in 1935, just as eight years before he had been called by him to Warsaw. The understanding was that he would be able to work in New York as a free-lance writer for the *Jewish Daily Forward*. "Runya," meanwhile, had taken Israel Zamir to Russia, but she was soon expelled; eventually she settled in Palestine with her son, never again seeing her former lover.

By leaving Warsaw in 1935—never to return to Poland—Singer in effect fixed permanently in his consciousness all of the elements of his literary art. There was nothing more of importance to experience or to learn for purposes of remembering and imagining in ways that make great stories and novels. All was now in readiness. As he believed Knut Hamsun had done before him, only "searching introspection" was required. His consciousness was complete by 1935, needing only the occasion and space for release. In this sense all of Singer's work, whether in novels or short stories, is fictional autobiography, spun out of an imagination functionally identical with memory. Customary distinctions between fact and dream are therefore meaningless. "All my books are about me," said Singer. "They are myself" in the sense that fictional events "are not always what did happen but always what might have happened."

What he required from America was the opportunity to write, nothing more. That his assessment was correct accounts for the anomalous position he now occupies as an American writer. In a profound sense, all that is distinctive and valuable about Singer, all that so justly merits his having been honored as a Nobel laureate in 1978, is irrelevant to his acquired citizenship and to his forty-five-year residence in America. As a writer, functionally considered, he never left Warsaw.

Singer's initial experiences in New York were disorienting and distressful. He continued to live with the grim poverty familiar to him from Warsaw, moving from rented room to boardinghouse and back; but he was now also deeply depressed about the future of Yiddish language and culture in America. Although he wrote occasional reviews and journalistic essays for the *Jewish Daily Forward,* writing became so difficult for him that even his grammar seemed to be affected. He could scarcely write a Yiddish sentence he could take pride in. He even considered leaving America. But Aaron Zeitlin wrote to him in 1935 advising him to remain in New York and resume work on *Messiah the Sinner*.

This novel about the false Messiah, Jacob Frank, the eighteenth-century disciple of Sabbatai Zvi, was finished by 1937. Although published serially in the *Jewish Daily Forward* and in newspapers in Warsaw and Paris, Singer considered it a "complete failure." He admitted that he knew too little about the Sephardic (Spanish-Jewish) culture in which Frank developed, and therefore he would never permit the novel to be reprinted. It was evident to Singer that he could not yet resume writing at the brilliant levels he had reached in *Satan in Goray* just before leaving Warsaw.

His circumstances changed. In 1940 he married Alma Wasserman. Two years later they moved to the Upper West Side of Manhattan, and he became a regular staff member on the *Forward*. In 1943 he began writing short stories again, and in the following year his brother died. Singer's feelings toward his brother had always been ambivalent. Although acknowledging him as "my father, my teacher," "a spiritual father and master as well," Singer felt so overshadowed by Israel Joshua Singer that his own creativity in America was inhibited until his brother's death in 1944. And even then, only after thrice exorcising the spirit of Israel Joshua by writing three generational novels in the manner characteristic of his brother's two monumental triumphs, was Singer free to discharge his own distinctive genius through novels of a quite different sort. Only then was he able to resume writing with the authority of *Satan in Goray*.

Singer began writing *The Family Moskat* (1950) a year after his brother's death. It was evident that the book was commemorative because it derived its structure from *The Brothers Ashkenazi* (1936) and *The Family Carnovsky* (1943), his brother's massive social novels, family chronicles in the realistic style of classic nineteenth-century European fiction. More than any other Yiddish writer, it was Israel Joshua Singer who established the sprawling family novel as the literary form for the modern history of European Jewry. Accordingly, the three family chronicles of Isaac Bashevis Singer are generational novels of large scope. But in them, ever the subversive capable of the "ethic of protest," he asserts his own fundamental values. He celebrates lives characterized by the psychological and ethical disciplines provided by Jewish religion and culture. While doing so, however, Singer seems to exempt himself from relevant controls; he indulges himself by depicting a world perhaps too large and perhaps too full of suffering victims, somewhat reminiscent of the expansive conventions of old-fashioned melodrama and modern soap opera. And yet, as Robert Alter has observed, even in these three novels there are moments of "hallucinated dramatic power" of the concentrated sort found in *Satan in Goray* and in the best of his short stories, as well as in the "demon-ridden world" of his later, more circumscribed, and more sharply focused novels. And so at the same time as Singer acknowledged the tradition of the Jewish historical novel developed by his brother, he subverted it with his own distinctive marks.

The first of these impressive works of covert fraternal hostility, *The Family Moskat,* was published serially between 1945 and 1948 in the *Forward,* despite editorial disagreements with Abraham Cahan. As installments appeared, they were also broadcast weekly on WEVD, the ethnic radio station in New York, thereby exposing the Singer brothers to the widest possible audience. (The success of the series was so great that Singer continued the practice for subsequent novels over a five-year period, writing all the scripts himself.) In 1950 the novel was published in two volumes in

Yiddish, and in one volume in English translation in the same year.

The Family Moskat is about the disintegration and ultimate destruction of Warsaw's Jewish community in the twentieth century, the breakdown of family and society completed by the eastward march of Hitler's armies. But it is as storyteller rather than historian that Singer relates the details of everyday life, the individual hopes and drives, anxieties and defeats of members of the large Jewish community. These people are enclosed by the historical forces within the Jewish world and outside, which Singer had himself experienced, which cannot be moderated even when recognized and understood. The Jewish community had changed so rapidly in Poland between the two World Wars that the family—formerly the focus for Jewish cohesiveness—was fractured by conflicting views of life: modern values clashed with traditional ones, intensifying the generational conflicts which had always strained family unity.

In the novel, these dynamics are set in motion by the patriarch of the family, Mushulam Moskat, whose strength derives from the traditional values no longer available to subsequent generations of the family. Singer describes Jewish life in Warsaw with relentless realism, especially in the depiction of sexuality. Much to the discomfort of readers accustomed to virtuous figures being treated in sentimental fashion, neither the rabbis nor the sages of the community are spared the urgings of the flesh. But the genuinely shocking aspects of Singer's novel are found elsewhere. The decline of the family is equated with the disintegration of Western society generally. Out of the conflict of cultures emerges an anarchic imagination which understands the meaning of chaos: "Death is the Messiah. That's the real truth." The book ends with these words which echo from Singer's own previous work, not his brother's. They of course literally affirm the coming of the Nazi Holocaust. Before World War II more than three million Jews lived in Poland; when Singer wrote his novel there were fewer than ten thousand.

Still writing under the influence of his brother's earlier successes, Singer in 1952 began another long family novel, *The Manor*, a two thousand-page Yiddish manuscript (much longer than *The Family Moskat*) published chapter by chapter in the *Forward* between 1953 and 1955. When translated into English and amplified somewhat, it appeared as two volumes: *The Manor* (1967) and *The Estate* (1969). This monumental but still crowded work was conceived as a huge prelude to *The Family Moskat*, portraying the period immediately preceding, from the Insurrection of 1863 in which the Poles rose against their Russian rulers until the end of the nineteenth century. Despite the apparent structure, these are not so much historical novels as imaginative works of cultural anthropology.

The Manor, with its epic range of character and incident, takes its coherence from the pious businessman Calman Jacoby, whose commitment to traditional ways preserves him (despite his wealth) well into his old age, while other members of the family are estranged from him and from the values which might also protect them from the destructive energies being unleashed in the modern world. *The Estate* continues the process of disintegration and deterioration, exempting only a saintly ascetic rabbi, whose otherworldly visions sustain him in death, and Calman Jacoby himself, whose more conventional orthodoxy sanctifies him as he dies. Despite such drama and melodrama, there is an overriding concern with the past which can best be described as "passionately objective." It is an unsentimental view of cultural change, presented with an informed power which endows even death with vitality. The pressures of entropy are intensifying as the twentieth century draws near, yet choices still remain for the individual, not least for the intelligence behind the fictions. From the last of these grand monuments erected to honor his brother, Singer emerges purged and poised.

Whatever the ambivalent personal motivations shaping them, the three family sagas established Singer as a master of his brother's techniques. Melodramatic and heavily plotted, these are works of the sort which Henry James could respect only as "loose and baggy monsters." As such they constitute a departure from Singer's more idiosyncratic stories and more muscular later novels, which derive from imaginative sensibilities which had earlier yielded *Satan in Goray* and to which he could return now that he was no longer writing in the shadow of his brother.

Between 1945 and 1955, Singer also began to emerge out of relative obscurity as Americans in increasing numbers began to discover him. About fifty thousand Yiddish readers closely followed the installments of *The Family Moskat* in the *Forward* from 1945 until 1948, and with its publication as a book in 1950 he gained additional readers. Finally in 1950, substantial numbers of readers knowing only English read *The Family Moskat*, the first of Singer's novels to be published in English. A new and perhaps more discriminating English-reading audience was found for Singer in 1953 when *Partisan Review* published Saul Bellow's brilliant translation of "Gimpel the Fool," one of the greatest Yiddish short stories.

Gimpel's folly is saintly. Prepared to think the best of people morally inferior to himself, he believes whatever he is told, however absurd and often repeated. Gimpel is thus victimized by all in the *shtetl* who know of his unlimited capacity for belief: he is deceived by a whorish wife, diddled by prankish children, tricked by mischievous townspeople, cuckolded by treacherous apprentices, and even tempted successfully by the crafty Satan. But Gimpel's sanctity is inviolable. It is preserved by his believing that the habit of disbelief leads eventually to disbelief in God, and this he refuses to risk.

A child-man and therefore a saint despite his human frailties, he believes whatever is improbable and impossible. Appropriately, therefore, he becomes a storyteller himself, telling tales about "things that could never have happened—about devils, magicians, windmills, and the like." Artlessness and credulity transform Gimpel into an artist like Singer himself. At the conclusion of the story which he is telling about his own life, he makes his ultimate confession of faith: "No doubt the world is entirely an imaginary world, but it is only once removed from the true world." This formulation may also be a fiction, but it is one to which Gimpel is totally committed since it permits him to come to terms imaginatively with the suffering in the world. Only in the Paradise of God which awaits him at death will whatever exists be nonfictional and nondeceptively real.

An even larger English-reading audience became available to Singer in 1955 when *Satan in Goray* was published in a superb translation by Jacob Sloan. In his review in the *New Republic*, Irving Howe called it "a remarkable book, brilliant, enigmatic, and deserving the attention of anyone interested in modern literature." Six years later Howe still was enthusiastic about Singer and called him a "genius" who had "total command of the imagined world." By virtue of their commitments to Singer, Bellow (as translator) and Howe (as critic) have brought his work into the orbit of the American literary establishment.

Whether Jewish or not, by 1955 many American readers apparently recognized in Singer's East European Jews, and especially in the Hasidim, embodiments of modern man, suffering in exile and denied the endowments and human legacy which rightfully belong to him. Reversing the directions of modern man's own experience, Singer transports his American readers back into a territory where they find themselves totally disoriented, dislocated strangers in a culture which is often incomprehensible.

Singer's narrative strategy requires the presentation of fact without commentary and of experiences which release their own meanings without external explanations. Like God, Singer the artist sees but is not seen. Like God, he speaks through the facts of nature and history, but otherwise remains silent. Singer's fiction therefore derives from a universe of discourse which is foreign to all but a handful of readers; yet he makes no effort to accommodate the needs of his larger audience. And because Singer so often is interested in the nonconformist, the eccentric, the freakish, the solitary sufferer, or the unique hero involved in a unique conjunction of circumstances (especially in his short stories), his hold upon his American audience is overpowering when he is at his best. This is particularly true for the figure in his fiction who appears most frequently: the Jew without roots, cut off from the cultural influences which shaped him, homeless, stranded in an alien world, haunted by memories of the past, living a dream which periodically explodes into nightmare or evaporates into death. Ultimately his fiction concerns itself with the reader's own concern: the emergence and survival of some measure of hope from the most desperate of circumstances. Even Singer's frequent references to demonism are ultimately hopeful, to the extent that through them the remote past makes contact and attempts to mediate with the modern world.

The Magician of Lublin (written in 1958; serialized in the *Forward* in 1959; and published in English translation in 1960) is a novel about Yasha Mazur, prosperous, respected in his community, and decent. He is a man whose personal powers derive initially from traditional piety as well as from the creative energies of the artist, both sources involved for him with the miracles of sexuality. He is an itinerant conjurer: a professional hypnotist, mind reader, escape artist, tightrope walker, charismatic personality, animal trainer, popular entertainer, and wall-climbing exhibitionist. He has private fantasies of the ultimate power—of the Messianic ability to fly anywhere. But violence and desperation lurk beneath the confident surfaces of his life.

The novel takes shape from his relations with five women—his pious and childless wife, his coarse but devoted peasant assistant, his matronly mistress of many years, his recently widowed beloved, and her young daughter. He loves them all, passionately and sensually. But the points on which the novel turns are intricate deceptions and ethical sensibilities. Gradually Yasha loses his power to envision, to believe, and to deceive. This agile and lusty man, this innocent criminal who fails in a clumsy attempt to steal for his beloved, this miracle-working believer in God even when he can no longer believe in himself, injures all the women from whom he draws his energies. The novel therefore dramatizes masculine fantasies—of power and impotence, of sensual pleasure and asceticism, of escape and captivity—and culminates in self-injury, desperation, and self-imposed martyrdom.

Forced by frustration, excruciating pain, and feelings of guilt, Yasha seeks to extricate himself from what he judges to be his sins by imposing upon himself a hermitlike existence in a cell, thereby spiritually preparing himself for his return to his wife. His greatest feat of magic is this quixotic willingness to lock himself into the tightly confined space he has prepared, instead of escaping confinements as his art formerly had required. Prayer, meditation, and introspection occupy him instead, giving him the status of holy man in the unseeing eyes of his neighbors. But through penitential isolation he causes more suffering to his wife—and perhaps needlessly to himself as well—than through all his previous deceptions and escapades. His self-imposed discipline, after all, isolates him from the home and community which in the *shtetl* culture are the ultimate sources of spiritual energy for the individual.

It was skepticism (an element from his maternal endowment) which freed Singer first from Hasidic orthodoxy and then from the dogmas of the Jewish "enlightenment," enabling him in turn to embrace the "old Jewishness," not as an act of worship but as a matter of imaginative and artistic choice. A disbeliever himself in wonder-working rabbis, he is himself a wonder-worker in his fiction, capable of materializing demons and angels, but, most impressively, the past, by evoking the spirit of time lapsed and elapsed.

The Slave (written in 1960; serialized in the *Forward* in 1961; published in English in 1962) is a love story of miraculous redemption. It takes place in the same demon-haunted terrain and time as *Satan in Goray*, and it therefore is infused with the violent medievalism of that masterpiece. The personal drama of Jacob the Jewish slave and Wanda the pagan daughter of his peasant master brings transient moments of loveliness into the brutal world they inhabit. Secretly faithful to the rituals and beliefs of his heritage, Jacob knows he must avoid her to preserve his spiritual integrity. But once they are drawn together sexually by satanic powers, she enables him to fulfill his sacred obligations as a Jew. When unexpectedly redeemed from bondage, he is separated from his beloved and once again lives in a distant *shtetl*. But he returns to Wanda, traveling through the demon-infested landscape separating them, and rescues her from the savagery of her own village.

They end their wanderings in a wretched *shtetl*, living in a hovel. Wanda now is known as Sarah; she lives as a pious Jew without undergoing the formal rituals of conversion and conceals her pagan origins by pretending to be mute. But possessed by demons during painful childbirth, Wanda-Sarah screams and discloses her identity to the astonished townspeople. She dies, but her son survives and becomes eventually a leading scholar in Jerusalem. Jacob, after twenty years of wandering, returns to the *shtetl* and dies in the poorhouse. Miraculously, he is buried beside Sarah's unmarked grave, united with her in death.

Only the brilliantly archaic mode of storytelling—at times bringing biblical simplicity and power to the often nightmarish narrative—enables the novel to rise above melodrama, sentimentality, and conventional romance. As narrative, it complements *Satan in Goray* by adding a personal analogue to that masterly vision of communal crisis.

Of three novels set in America and published in the *Forward*, the only one to appear as a book in English is *Enemies, A Love Story* (1972). The others are "Shadows by the Hudson" (1957) and "A Ship to America" (1958), neither being considered for publication in English. Each deals with Polish Jews in New York City, Jews whose Old World experiences continue to haunt them in America and provide the functional realities in their lives.

Because Singer has been conditioned to use New York primarily as a locale for releasing his own Old World consciousness, the characters in his novels are oblivious to whatever is distinctively American in their experience. As a consequence, the New York of his fiction is scarcely distinguishable from the Warsaw of his memory: the topography is changed; the names of the streets are different; the modes of transportation are more efficient. But the people who interest him—their circumstances, their shared experiences, their cultural roots—are scarcely different from those in the other novels. Warsaw and Manhattan are equivalents for the purposes of Singer's imagination.

Enemies, A Love Story derives from Singer's profound and sustained preoccupation with the Holocaust: he has said with shockingly casual irony, "I did not have the privilege of going through the Hitler Holocaust." The perversely comic undertones to that irony animate *Enemies*, the most ambitious of all his novels because it entails the greatest risks, given its underlying comic tone and circumstances.

Herman Broder, trying frantically to support himself in New York as a ghostwriter for a charlatan rabbi, has spent World War II in a Polish hayloft with Yadwiga, the peasant girl. She has satisfied perfectly and amply his every human need and desire—at a time when, unknown to him, six million Jews were being exterminated. The defining experiences for surviving European Jews—the concentration camps, the terror, the forced labor and death marches, the torment, the abuse, the degradation, the brutalization—all the unspeakable horrors have passed by Herman Broder while he was privileged in his Eden. So far as personal and cultural identity are concerned, he has been deprived of what defines modern Jewishness. Consequently, his life in America becomes a moral equivalent for the war: he creates situations so absurdly painful, so anxiety-ridden, so oppressive, that vicariously he experiences in New York what he has missed in Europe. The comedy is developed through amorous affairs, deceptions, multiple marriages with women survivors of the ordeals he escaped, with fantasies involving demons and other occult forces, with Jews becoming their own enemies, and with every other experience containing for Herman the maximum threat or discomfort. He finally disappears, either by suicide or by finding a hayloft in America. The alternatives seem inconsequential in the context of the novel.

Shosha (1978) is Singer's sharp-edged rendering of circumstances he had dealt with in *The Family Moskat*, where he had used his brother's ponderous techniques. Now cultural disintegration is perceived through the consciousness of Aaron Greidinger, the disoriented writer-narrator who unwittingly participates in the coming-of-the-end while never quite forgetting his Hasidic origins. Wisps of decay swirl undetected around the social comedy, cryptic forecasts of the future. Shosha herself (who appears several times in Singer's own written reminiscences) is the child-woman of the Warsaw ghetto. For Greidinger she embodies all the experiences and values of the culture he had abandoned when he elected chaotic rootlessness and frenzied weariness in modern Warsaw. He himself oscillates between the hopes and despairs of a struggling young artist, and these tragicomical states are complicated by his sexual adventures with sophisticated modern women. But feelings of innocent yet erotic love lead Greidinger back to Krochmalna Street. His first genuinely creative act is his marriage to Shosha. The forces of myth however cannot withstand historical ones: she dies a victim of a death camp march, while he is reported to be surviving in America.

The 1978 award of the Nobel Prize to Singer (after his nomination by Edmund Wilson and Rebecca West) scarcely surprised those who follow the literary politics determining such honors. He is read throughout the world in more than a dozen languages, the author of more than eight major novels, hundreds of extraordinary short stories, four volumes of artful autobiography, a dozen or more volumes for children; he is a sought-after teacher of writing and literature at universities here and abroad, and a lifelong journalist who continues to meet at least two weekly deadlines—his energy alone testifies to the greatness of his career.

The most remarkable aspect of the award itself was his formal lecture at Stockholm. He began by speaking in Yiddish about Yiddish, the language and the culture: "*Der groyser kovad vos di Shwedishe Academie hot mir ongeton is oich an anerkenung fun Yiddish—a loshon fun golus.*" ("The high honor bestowed upon me by the Swedish Academy is also a recognition of the Yiddish language—a language of exile.") He went on to equate the language with the "conduct" of its speakers, and to explain that the "Yiddish mentality" is inherently modest: "it muddles through" by way of surviving "amid the powers of destruction." He characterized the ghetto culture as knowing "no greater joy than the study of man and human relations," and as constituting "a great experiment in peace, in self-discipline, and in humanism." In this, he concluded, Yiddish is figuratively "the wise and humble language of us all, the idiom of frightened and hopeful humanity." Singer's novels have always employed this idiom.

—Edwin Gittleman

Other:

Introduction to I. J. Singer, *Yoshe Kalb*, trans. Maurice Samuel (New York: Harper & Row, 1965);

"Knut Hamsun, Artist of Skepticism," in Knut Hamsun, *Hunger*, trans. Robert Bly (New York: Farrar, Straus & Giroux, 1967);

"The Extreme Jews," *Harper's*, 234 (April 1967): 55-62.

Interviews:

Joel Blocker and Richard Elman, "An Interview

with Isaac Bashevis Singer," *Commentary*, 36 (November 1963): 364-372;

Harold Flender, "The Art of Fiction, XLII," *Paris Review*, 11 (Fall 1968): 53-73;

Paul Rosenblatt and Gene Koppel, *A Certain Bridge: Isaac Bashevis Singer* (Tucson: University of Arizona Press, 1971);

Philip Roth, "Roth and Singer on Bruno Schulz," *New York Times Book Review*, 13 February 1977, pp. 5, 22;

Richard Burgin, "Isaac Bashevis Singer Talks . . . About Everything," *New York Times Magazine*, 26 November 1978, pp. 24-26, 32, 36-38, 42-48;

Burgin, "Isaac Bashevis Singer's Universe," *New York Times Magazine*, 3 December 1978, pp. 38-40, 44-46, 50-52.

References:

Marcia Allentuck, ed., *The Achievement of Isaac Bashevis Singer* (Carbondale: Southern Illinois University Press, 1970);

Irving H. Buchen, *Isaac Bashevis Singer and the Eternal Past* (New York: New York University Press, 1968);

Paul Kresh, *Isaac Bashevis Singer: The Magician of West 86th Street* (New York: Dial, 1979);

Irving Malin, ed., *Critical Views of Isaac Bashevis Singer* (New York: New York University Press, 1969);

Malin, *Isaac Bashevis Singer* (New York: Unger, 1972);

Ben Siegel, *Isaac Bashevis Singer* (Minneapolis: University of Minnesota Press, 1969).

DAVID SLAVITT
(23 March 1935-)

BOOKS: *Suits for the Dead: Poems* in *Poets of Today VIII*, ed. John Hall Wheelock (New York: Scribners, 1961);

The Carnivore (Chapel Hill: University of North Carolina Press, 1965);

Rochelle, Or Virtue Rewarded (London: Chapman & Hall, 1966; New York: Delacorte, 1967);

The Exhibitionist, as Henry Sutton (New York: Geis, 1967; London: Geis, 1968);

Feel Free (New York: Delacorte, 1968; London: Hodder & Stoughton, 1969);

Day Sailing (Chapel Hill: University of North Carolina Press, 1969);

The Voyeur, as Henry Sutton (New York: Geis, 1969; London: Hodder & Stoughton, 1969);

Anagrams (London: Hodder & Stoughton, 1970; Garden City: Doubleday, 1971);

Vector, as Henry Sutton (New York: Geis, 1970; London: Hodder & Stoughton, 1971);

The Eclogues of Virgil (Garden City: Doubleday, 1971);

A B C D (Garden City: Doubleday, 1972);

Child's Play: Poems (Baton Rouge: Louisiana State University Press, 1972);

The Eclogues and The Georgics of Virgil (Garden City: Doubleday, 1972);

The Liberated, as Henry Sutton (Garden City: Doubleday, 1973; London: Allen, 1973);

The Outer Mongolian (Garden City: Doubleday, 1973);

The Killing of the King (Garden City: Doubleday, 1974; London: Allen, 1974);

Vital Signs: New and Selected Poems (Garden City: Doubleday, 1975);

King of Hearts (New York: Arbor House, 1976);

That Golden Woman, as Henry Lazarus (New York: Fawcett, 1976; London: Sphere, 1977);

Jo Stern (New York: Harper & Row, 1978);

Rounding the Horn: Poems (Baton Rouge: Louisiana State University Press, 1978);

The Sacrifice, as Henry Sutton (New York: Grosset & Dunlap, 1978);

The Idol, as David Benjamin (New York: Putnam's, 1979);

The Proposal, as Henry Sutton (New York: Charter, 1980);

Cold Comfort (New York & London: Methuen, 1980).

Although he has written and published seventeen novels in the past fourteen years, David Slavitt considers himself first and foremost a poet, a poet who writes novels to earn some time and money to support his habit of writing poetry. So, in 1967, when he published the popular novel *The Exhibitionist* under the pen name of Henry Sutton and with massive promotion by the publisher (and a certain amount of pure luck), it rose high on the *New York Times* best-seller list and stayed there for months, earning both author and publisher a decent fortune Slavitt had achieved the Walter Mitty dream of almost every poet in America—to write a bona fide, big time best-seller. Slavitt had written one novel, *Rochelle* (1966), under his own name; the clever, witty, intelligent, serious novel appeared, sold a handful of copies and vanished without a trace in a few months. There was, it seemed, no indication

137

"You give yourself more of a chance than you gave the boys at that initiation," Stanley said.

"Maybe."

"Drink the rum," Stanley said.

"No. I don't think I will. And I don't think you're going to shoot me, either. You're bluffing."

"You hope I'm bluffing," Stanley said. ~~But he wondered whether Chelmsford wasn't right. Was he going to shoot the man?~~

would have liked

He ~~didn't mind~~ shooting him. ~~The only thing wrong with it was that it was too easy, too quick.~~ He transferred the gun to his left hand. He went to the fireplace where there was a set of brass fire tongs, brush, and poker in a matching stand. He picked up the poker, hefted it, then reversed it, holding it near the working end so that he could use the handle as a club. He took a few steps toward Chelmsford and stopped.

"Drink that rum or I'll break your leg for you."

"No."

He struck, a sharp blow on a horizontal arc, so that the heavy brass turnings of the poker met Chelmsford's left shin.

Chelmsford let out a shriek of pain, rather higher than Stanley would have expected. And rather more satisfactory too.

"You fucker! You've done it. You've broken my leg."

"Yes. Now, drink the rum or I'll break the other one."

"You're crazy."

"Yes. But so are you. Anybody standing by while a bunch of kids lock a boy in the trunk of a car that way has got to be crazy. Crazy. And crazy people should be put away. Or destroy-

Cold Comfort, *revised typescript*

that he possessed the slightest capacity to develop and to produce a popular best-selling novel. Like most other intellectuals, he had expressed no great respect for the form and genre of the popular novel. It was generally agreed, by successful popular writers and disgruntled intellectuals who had tried the form and failed at it, that in order to succeed one had to *believe in* the form, one had to be sincere. Stupid perhaps, even simpleminded and often enough, as editorial stories seemed to confirm, functionally illiterate, but nevertheless sincere. Slavitt exploded this myth with relish. He wrote *The Exhibitionist* with considerable craft and with no illusions and next to no "sincerity" except to the craft and workmanship of it. As he described the writing of *The Exhibitionist* (and the results of it) in *The Writer's Voice* (1973), it was as much craft as subject matter which made a best-seller: "The next novel was *The Exhibitionist*, which is, you know, big money and all, and you write as though the nineteenth century was still here. You come on straight, flat-footed, and dirty. It sells." That single success story might have earned Slavitt, as the exception to all the rules, a place in the history of the American novel since World War II. But perhaps more remarkable and more significant is the fact that *The Exhibitionist* proved to be only the beginning of a multiple and complex and amazingly productive career. Slavitt wrote and published seven more pseudonymous novels, nine novels under his own name, not to mention five books of poetry, and gives no sign of slowing down. Responding to queries, in a recent letter Slavitt has described with characteristic candor what has happened to him:

> I do understand the success of *The Exhibitionist*. I think that was a lucky conjunction of the stars. The time was perfect, the book was just dirty enough and just sincere enough to wow 'em in 67. (It would have been a yawn in '71.) And Geis was riding high, throwing money around, and promoting things intensively and with flair and vigor. It all came together for me. I'm still living off that, in a way. The money is long gone, but each new publisher I deal with sees me as a possible moneymaker because of that book. That allows me to make a small strenuous living writing almost anything I want to—and this is a situation of convenience to me and considerable luck.

Slavitt may well be unique in the contemporary American literary scene, being able to write "public" and "private" novels (a distinction he now uses instead of the earlier and widely used division between "popular" and "serious" fiction) with apparent ease, with certainly no fall-off of energy, and, at one and the same time, to continue to be one of our most productive and independent poets.

The son of Samuel Saul and Adele Beatrice Rytman Slavitt, David Rytman Slavitt was born in White Plains, New York, in 1935. He attended Phillips Academy in Andover, Massachusetts, where he studied with the celebrated poet and classicist, Dudley Fitts, who had a great and lasting influence on Slavitt. Slavitt wrote his M.A. thesis at Columbia University on Fitts's poetry, and, years later, dedicated his translations of the *Eclogues* and the *Georgics* of Virgil to the memory of Fitts. It was while Slavitt was still at Andover that he published his first literary work, a parody of Whittier's "Snowbound" which Winfield Townley Scott published in the magazine section of the *Providence Journal*. Slavitt entered Yale in 1952 and graduated with a B.A., magna cum laude, in 1956. While he was at Yale, he helped to carry the huge bass drum for the marching band, and he earned the distinction of being named a Scholar of the House. He studied with Cleanth Brooks, Robert Penn Warren, Richard Sewall, and Paul Weiss. He attributes some of his direction and ambition to that time and the examples of the teachers he studied with, especially Warren: "Life isn't always categorizable. A 'man of letters', who plays all the different games, tends to produce duplication of effort. Or to belie the notions of the editors as to what the world is like. . . . I started out, a long time ago, having that kind of 'man of letters' ambition, having studied with Red Warren." From Yale Slavitt went to graduate school at Columbia where he worked under R. W. B. Lewis and took his M.A. in 1957. For one year, 1957-1958, he taught at Georgia Tech. Then he moved to New York to take a job at *Newsweek* where he worked from 1958 to 1965, eventually as associate editor and film critic and often also reviewing books. In the interview with John Graham in *The Writer's Voice* he described the time at *Newsweek* as "a very fortunate kind of training" for keeping his "public" and "private" work apart: "if you put in seven years working for *Newsweek*, you know what writing for millions of people is. And then you go home and you write poems. And you know what writing for dozens of people is. They're different. Faulkner was able to go out to Hollywood and write Howard Hawks' screenplays and come back to Mississippi and write William Faulkner novels. It can be done." It is interesting that Slavitt, with experience as a film critic, was fully aware of the difference of the two generations, that in Faulkner's time, the heyday of

Bernard Gotfryd

the Hollywood studio and of large numbers of employed writers, the analogy to today's popular, or public, novel was the screenplay.

In 1965 Slavitt left *Newsweek* to devote himself to free-lance writing. In recent years he has also done some teaching, first at the University of Maryland and then at Temple University in Philadelphia. He had married Lynn Nita Meyer in 1956 and fathered three children—Evan (now at Harvard Law School), Sarah (a student at Yale), and Joshua (at Andover). This marriage ended by divorce in 1977. In 1978 he married Janet Lee Abrahm, a physician.

The checklists with this essay do not begin to suggest all the writing that David Slavitt has accomplished in a busy career. During the years at *Newsweek* there were literally hundreds of film reviews, book reviews, articles, and interviews. Slavitt earned a considerable reputation as the most savage and witty film critic in the business (John Simon had not yet arrived on the scene). But, unlike many of his contemporaries, Slavitt does not take film criticism, or indeed most journalism, very seriously. In an essay, "Critics and Criticism," for the anthology *Man and the Movies* (1967), Slavitt said: "The critics are a bunch of clowns promoted from covering weddings or shipping news or fires in Brooklyn to this dubious eminence." We know of work published under three pseudonyms—Henry Sutton, David Benjamin, and Henry Lazarus. There may be others. He is said to be the coauthor of the McGraw-Hill textbook, *Understanding Social Life* (1976), and he is believed to have done some successful ghost writing. Thus he brings to his fiction a great deal of practical knowledge of and experience in the craft of writing, ranging from poetry to reportage and made richer and complex by his educational background with its emphasis on the classics. And all this is coupled with the trained reporter's confidence in going after a story and following it through, opening up a wider range of the national (and international) experience of contemporary life to him than is available to many of our writers, whose craft and art have tended, for better and worse, to isolate them somewhat from all but the most general quotidian concerns of life in contemporary America. There are a great many details about the way things work or don't work, about how things are done or not done in business, law, medicine, science, police work, even publishing, which David Slavitt understands well. And he uses them, uses the inherent fascination of and with the factual in all of his novels. Since the death of John O'Hara, there is probably no other contemporary American novelist (except maybe John D. Macdonald) who can match Slavitt's magical enthusiasm and almost pedagogical ability for the communication of the sense and shine of facts, how things work and how things are done. People work in Slavitt novels. They earn livings. Operations are performed, trials take place, trucks are driven, and ditches are dug. And all this is done in such a way that the information does not seem to be grafted onto the narrative, but, instead, appears to arise, naturally and necessarily, from the whole context of the story and from the nature of the characters involved. Fact, in this sense, becomes not only a matter of fascination and of narrative suspense, but also becomes the ritual kindling for the fires and pyrotechnics of the imagination. For, in spite of this profound interest in the factual, and, as well, a brilliant focus on *surface,* on the (yes) superficial aspects of daily life—of brand names, of manners, of subtle degrees and gradients of social status, or the lack of it, Slavitt's fiction is also highly imaginative, often fanciful, though never explicitly fantasy. (The nearest thing to an exception to the rule, so far, is *The Outer Mongolian,* 1973, which predicates an accidental "cure" of mongolism through mega-vitamins, permitting the mongoloid protagonist to become a master of the commodity market and ultimately to direct and control history and events in a way that even David Rockefeller might envy. And there are some supernatural elements in *King of Hearts*, 1976, and *The Sacrifice*, 1978.) Slavitt seems to find the plain facts of our times, subjected to a clear hard light and unrelenting scrutiny, to be purely and simply fantastic. This characteristic is present in all of his novels, both "public" and "private," and in his poems. Not many among the American poets, of his generation at least, would or indeed *could* create solid poems out of and around such things as the isobars on a weather map and black holes in outer space, the behavior and characteristics of cockroaches and of tropical fish, how fish nets are correctly mended and how a catboat is best to be sailed, the effects of the Korsakof Syndrome, the fact that airport rabbits are stone deaf and that some pigs in Poland are carefully clothed in burlap and others are not and why, the results of regularly performing the Royal Canadian Air Force exercises, and, as a final and typical example, the given names of the pet dogs belonging to Wordsworth, Hood, Cowper, Byron, Pope, Landor, Arnold, and Elizabeth Barrett.

His novels from first to latest, from *Rochelle* to *Cold Comfort* (1980), are, then, replete with interesting "information," both broadly general and briskly specific. For example, he deals gracefully with the complexities of transplant surgery (*King of Hearts*), cryptanalysis (*The Sacrifice*), bacteriological warfare experiments (*Vector*, 1970), the making of movies and movie deals (*The Idol*, 1979), bankruptcy (*Feel Free*, 1968), the publishing industry (*Jo Stern*, 1978), and the groves of academe (*Anagrams*, 1970, and *Cold Comfort*). In both the poems and the novels Slavitt is brilliant at the evocation of places, as good at this as Eric Ambler. And, as might be expected where there is considerable connection between the work of an author in separate forms, the language of his prose fiction is careful, graceful, and economical, a blending of the controlled resources of classical rhetoric with the lingo of pop culture and the idiom of the everyday vernacular. Tom Wolfe, whose training and education were somewhat similar, employs the same sort of mixed and shifting rhetoric, though the *style itself*, is somewhat different.

Slavitt's style aims for clarity, apparent transparency. And, as his poems are often the working out of various kinds of formal games ("To do a sestina is deliberately to noodle around and then see if you can overcome the circularities of form and appear to be making a linear statement of any kind at all," he says in *The Writer's Voice*), so there are many kinds and levels of games in the novels. Some are just silly fun. Like the dedication, in French, of his first big "dirty" book, *The Exhibitionist*, to two gentlemen who turn out to be prominent on Cape Cod (where Slavitt lived at the time) for the care and maintenance of cesspools and septic tanks. Or the dedication of his second "blockbuster," *The Voyeur* (1969), "To Sheldon S. Cohen and all the guys down at the office." Cohen was director of the Internal Revenue Service at the time. There are odd little resonances from his pseudonymns. Henry Sutton was the name of a printer's devil known to Walt Whitman. Henry Lazarus (who, by the way, appeared on the literary scene when Henry Sutton was reported to be "dead") seems to be close kin to Bernie Lazarus, protagonist of *Feel Free*, if it is not in fact Bernie himself; David Benjamin, author of *The Idol*, may well be the brother of Waldo Benjamin, the mongoloid hero of *The Outer Mongolian*.

Some of his games are frankly ritualistic, a sort of literary knock on wood. For example, a good many of his novels have at least one cameo appearance by a minor character who is named Mull, this in honor of the Henry James scholar, Donald Mull, and, as well, an allusion to "the Mull Monster" in the movie *Frankenstein Meets The Space Monster*. Similarly the names of friends and enemies appear among the minor characters. Names from history and literature appear, sometimes mildly garbled or placed in odd combinations, like the law firm of Marx, Bronstein and Engles in *The Voyeur*. Sometimes they are anagrams, as in the game which Slavitt greatly enjoys playing. And in the sense of games and gamesmanship *Anagrams* may be his most complex novel so far and, for those who enjoy high-culture fun and foolery, his most entertaining. Certainly it is also one of the finest (and most serious, inwardly) books in contemporary literature about poets and the making of poetry. But both the surface and the structure of the story line are zany and apparently lighthearted. "It's a novel about a guy who comes down, like to a poetry reading," Slavitt says in the interview with Graham, "and it's based roughly on a literary festival that was at Hollins and at the University of Virginia some years ago. During the course of this, the guy is writing a poem, so it's really a novel about the writing of a sonnet." Continuing, here is how he describes a portion of the book in that same interview:

> There are two poets in it, a young poet and a sort of old poet friend, lots of funny things in it, all kinds of games. At one point he loses his poems, and he has to come on to a reading but he doesn't have a poem. He goes to the library

> to steal one. I'm able to settle a lot of scores. There are a lot of poets that are not worth stealing from, he discovers. Finally he steals one from a literary magazine. The poem is an undergraduate poem by D. Martyn Vattlis, which is an anagram on D. Rytman Slavitt. And it's in fact a poem of mine that I wrote and published in the *Yale Lit* that wasn't good enough to keep.There are things wrong with it. So I have my character steal that poem from me, fix it, and then do it fixed at the reading.

At his highest level of gamesmanship Slavitt is Nabokovian, even in the "public" novels. In fact Nabokov and his wife appear, briefly and perfectly in character, in a little hotel on the Italian coast south of Rome: "The other guests of the hotel appeared, arrested in their pursuit of pleasure by the inclement weather: a couple from the Isle of Man; a chic Frenchwoman with two well-groomed poodles of an apricot color; a party of four Germans who never went anywhere, not even from their rooms to the dining room, without cameras hanging from their necks; an elderly Russian couple, citizens of the United States but residents of Switzerland, who played chess and drank tea all afternoon; a Hollander named Mull who talked to no one and seemed very sad."

For all his jests, japes, and pasquils, Slavitt has a serious assessment of his own work, which is confident and not without pride, but quite without arrogance. Responding (in a letter of 21 January 1980) to a series of questions, he writes that:

> I have written a lot of novels, some of which I think may be pretty good, but how the hell do I know? I don't re-read myself much. There are too many good books I haven't read by writers I should know better for me to waste my time reading me. . . . I'm allowed to think myself as good as I need to in order to keep on going, though, and that's the important thing. I think I'm as clever as Updike, and smarter than Barth or Gardner. I don't think I'm as good as Nabokov. Or Bourjaily, or Brophy. But that's okay. I figure that I can plod along like Forty Mad-dogs Hoofer and hit it lucky once or twice (as with Parade's End and the other one).

From the primary interest and first love of poetry, Slavitt seems to have transferred a number of other qualities. One of these is, in effect, the equivalent of the poet's necessary concentration upon one subject or one premise. Both the "public" and the "private" novels are often in the "what-if" category—what if a bacteriological warfare experiment got out of control? (*Vector*); what if the world were suddenly plunged into another honest-to-God depression? (*The Liberated*, 1973); what if a mongoloid child, as a result of an accidental mega-vitamin overdose, proved to be a great genius? (*The Outer Mongolian*); what if a successful businessman went bankrupt and loved it? (*Feel Free*).

In the popular contemporary tradition, now somewhat restricted by recent Supreme Court libel decisions, the novels are loosely based on the examples and lives of well-known celebrities, a kind of shadow biography. Even before the Supreme Court decisions of 1978 and 1979 it was important (and part of the fun and games) to be clear about what the novel was "not" really about. Thus, in *The Writer's Voice*, Slavitt made light of this characteristic: "The next novel was *The Voyeur*, which was like *Son of the Exhibitionist—The Exhibitionist* was not about the Fondas, and *The Voyeur* was not about Hugh Hefner—which is the big difference." Both "private" and "public" novels are built on this sort of narrative premise, also. Thus *The Killing of the King* (1974) is "not" about the late King Farouk of Egypt. *That Golden Woman* (1976) is "not" yet another novel about Jackie Kennedy Onassis. *Jo Stern* is "not" a life of Jacqueline Susann, and *The Idol* is, of course, "not" about Elizabeth Taylor. There is at least a strong hint in these books that Slavitt, the skilled newsman, has, in fact, used *some* key facts, nowhere else widely known, concerning the shadowy figures the novels are "not" about. For example, *The Idol* seems to predicate a new and quite different version of the death of actor Montgomery Clift. Or the books are built upon the foundation of a familiar genre: *A B C D* (1972) is a murder story as is, in a different sense, *King of Hearts*; *The Sacrifice* dabbles in the occult and witchcraft genre while *Cold Comfort*, with an epigraph from Poe, is a classic revenge (and justice) story.

Thus, just as Slavitt the poet is an innovative formalist, who uses all the given forms, but in an innovative, sophisticated fashion, so he as a novelist is interested in working within certain clear and explicit guidelines, using established forms but adding new twists and dimensions. In the brilliant virtuoso exercise of *A B C D* (which is built formally upon the musical structure of Bach's *The Art of the Fugue*), Slavitt mangages to work out the murder mystery so that the wrong man is caught and convicted for the killing, but in such a way that the reader is delighted and recognizes the cosmic justice of this mistake. Or, similarly, in *Anagrams*, poet Jerome Carpenter, recovering from a long period of poetic aridity, manages to compose a first-rate poem (and we watch the compostion of it, step by step) out of the entire experience of the story, only to see, as a result of impeccable plotting by Slavitt, another poet receive the credit for this work of art.

Faced with such a formidable array of Slavitt's titles (and not even allowing for the fact that there may very well be other pseudonymns and novels unknown to us), all of them various and all published within a very short time, one has difficulty, at this stage, speaking of the development of his fiction, or its possible future directions. He is hard to pin down, resisting the conventional critical labels not merely by and through the wide range and variety of his fiction, and the sheer bulk and amount of it, but by the multiplicity of his talents. He is, then, a hard case, harder for the critic to contend with than any of those serious novelists who have established themselves as slow, careful, methodical creators (Joseph Heller, William Styron, and Richard Yates, for example) or others who tend to be deeply obsessional and, in a perfectly neutral sense of the word, predictable like Kurt Vonnegut, Jr., or John Hawkes or John Cheever. He could be vaguely compared, at least in variety of forms and in literary sophistication, to Thomas Berger. In his concept of the "public" and "private" novel (which, by the way, has also been advanced on more than one occasion lately by Nobel laureate Saul Bellow) he is close to novelist R. V. Cassill, who also has written a number of pseudonymous novels. Slavitt's pseudonymous critical piece, purporting to be part of a forthcoming biography, in the *Mill Mountain Review* is, in part, a celebration of a novelist as offbeat as himself and as productive—the late David Stacton. But the critic, coming with the usual kit of tools and responses that seem to work well enough for much, if not most, contemporary fiction, is at a loss. Shrugs critical shoulders. First of all, what is Slavitt—poet, translator, novelist? Which works are "serious" and which are not? How to deal with the commercial success of his "public" novels? It should come as no surprise that except for book reviews of the Sutton ventures (a reviewer cannot very well completely ignore the best-sellers), there has been very little written about Slavitt's fiction.

Perhaps the best guide to his development is to be found in the two novels he has written about the literary world, about writers and critics and publishers, what is called "the quality lit biz." As indicated, *Anagrams* is cheerfully, energetically "private." Though Jerome Carpenter is a battered old poet who has long since shed both ambitions and illusions, and though the book ends with the death of Carpenter's friend and fellow poet, John Royle (who chokes to death on a piece of meat), with the ironic result that Carpenter's good latest poem is attributed to Royle, this is nonetheless a happy, lighthearted story, a "young" book. In *The Writer's Voice* Slavitt describes it as essentially, though not literally, his "first" novel—"*Anagrams* is really my first novel. Or what most novelists do when they're writing their first novel." Although it is a Slavitt, not a Sutton, novel, *Jo Stern* takes the form of a public novel. It shadows closely the life of Jacqueline Susann. And for those who may be indifferent to or ignorant of the analogy, there's an element of "what-if." As the jacket copy says—"What can you say about a foul-mouthed powerhouse of a woman novelist who holds up her publisher for a million-dollar advance on her next book when she's dying of cancer—and knows it?" In style—first person, straightforward, appropriately slick and sophisticated, bright and clever and clear, with a sequence of dramatized scenes and minimal digression and introspection—it is as "public" a novel as can be. And it reaches a surprising sort of "public" conclusion in the sense that it becomes a celebration of the Susann-type novelist and of her work and of her publisher. It is told by a narrator, known only as Henry (Sutton? Lazarus?), who has been hired to write a book about Jo Stern. Beginning with a considerable contempt for everything but her success, he follows her trail and puts together a tale of her life and woe, failing in the end to produce the kind of book he was hired to do—creating, instead, this one, the novel *Jo Stern*. Here, then, the tricky elements of the "private" novel are fused with the "public," and, in effect, the "public" work triumphs.

Between the two novels falls not only almost a decade of hard work and hard personal experience for Slavitt (the latter rather literally alluded to early in *Jo Stern*), but also the experience, joyous for Slavitt, of translating and re-creating Virgil's *Eclogues* and *Georgics*. His central focus was upon the literary allegory of these poems. Thus Virgil guided the modern poet not through the Afterlife, but through (as Slavitt puts it in his preface to the *Eclogues*) "the elegant drawing rooms of Roman literary life" where both he and Virgil "feeling the brittleness, the sophistication, the suffocation of Rome, yearned for something else, something better. . . ."

It seems clear from *Jo Stern* and from the brand-new *Cold Comfort* that, at least for the time being, the "public" novel, skillfully arranged and presented, will be the main thrust of Slavitt's fiction—something he understands and has come to feel better about. Here is what he says about the goals of his novels:

> I think—or maybe hope—I'm a better poet than I am a novelist. But I'm a better novelist than I am an intellectual. I am suspicious of ideas. I like to see how quirky the unfolding of an action can be. The specificity of novels is what keeps them interesting and alive. Their thinginess—which started out a long time ago as a way of reaching a middle class audience but serves a quite different purpose now—of reaching people who are uncomfortable with generalizations of any sort. Things are quite undeniable in their being.

Still, if we turn back to his poetry as a kind of touchstone for all his work, we shall see that one major characteristic of his poetry has not yet appeared in his fiction. And that quality is his profound interest in history, particularly ancient history but not exclusively so. A good number of his poems are built upon and around the facts of real historical events. History has remained a fascination for him from his earliest published poems to his most recent. If one were to indulge in prediction, it would seem almost safe to predict that sooner or later, having refined his "public" novel form, he will try that form within the genre of historical fiction. There have been some rumors of a biographical novel about Lord Byron in the works. That seems an apt possibility and may well, when and if it comes, mark the next turning point in his energetic and unusual career.

—George Garrett

Play:

The Cardinal Sins, New York, Playwright's Unit, 1968.

Other:

"The Ageless Kittens of Cardinal Richelieu," in *The Girl in the Black Raincoat*, ed. George Garrett (New York: Duell, Sloan & Pearce, 1966), pp. 78-91;

"Critics and Criticism," in *Man and the Movies*, ed. W. R. Robinson (Baton Rouge: Louisiana State University Press, 1967), pp. 335-344;

"Sexuality in Film: Reconsiderations after Seeing *Cries and Whispers*," in *Sexuality in the Movies*, ed. Thomas R. Atkins (Bloomington: Indiana University Press, 1975), pp. 233-240.

Periodical Publications:

"Conscience of an Exhibitionist," *Esquire*, 69 (May 1968): 122-125;

"Notes Toward the Destitution of Culture," as Henry Sutton, *Kenyon Review*, 118 (1968): 108-115;

"An Excerpt from *David Stacton: A Life In Fictions*," as Lionel Weems-Horsefall, *Mill Mountain Review*, Special Edition (Summer 1971): 133.

Interviews:

George Garrett and John Graham, "Forms of the Public Novel: Conversations with R. V. Cassill and David Slavitt," *Contempora*, 2 (September-February 1971-1972): 13-16;

Graham, "David Slavitt," in *The Writer's Voice: Conversations with Contemporary Writers*, ed. Graham and Garrett (New York: Morrow, 1973), pp. 248-272.

References:

George Garrett, "An Amoebaean Contest Where Nobody Loses," *Hollins Critic*, 8 (June 1971): 2-14;

John Hall Wheelock, "Man's Struggle to Understand," in *Poets Of Today VIII*, pp. 13-27.

ELIZABETH SPENCER
(19 July 1921-)

BOOKS: *Fire in the Morning* (New York: Dodd, Mead, 1948);

This Crooked Way (New York: Dodd, Mead, 1952; London: Gollancz, 1952);

The Voice at the Back Door (New York: McGraw-Hill, 1956; London: Gollancz, 1957);

The Light in the Piazza (New York: McGraw-Hill, 1960; London: Heinemann, 1961);

Knights and Dragons (New York: McGraw-Hill, 1965; London: Heinemann, 1966);

No Place for an Angel (New York: McGraw-Hill, 1967; London: Weidenfeld & Nicolson, 1968);

Ship Island and Other Stories (New York: McGraw-Hill, 1968; London: Weidenfeld & Nicolson, 1969);

The Snare (New York: McGraw-Hill, 1972);

The Stories of Elizabeth Spencer (Garden City: Doubleday, forthcoming 1981).

Elizabeth Spencer, who started writing fiction in the 1940s, has produced a number of distinguished works marked for their range in subject and style. To date she has written seven novels, the first three set in her native Mississippi, the later ones having national and international settings. One published collection of short stories and a forthcoming second collection give evidence of her mastery of short forms, showing both her considerable versatility in approach and her talent for portraying subtle feelings and evoking sharp impressions. Her stories frequently appear in the *New Yorker*.

Spencer was born in Carrollton, Mississippi, attended public schools, and in 1942 was graduated from Belhaven College, a Presbyterian liberal arts college in Jackson. She attended Vanderbilt University, where she took an M.A. degree in 1943, coming under the tutelage of Donald Davidson. She taught English at Northwest Mississippi Junior College in Senatobia (1943-1944) and at Ward-Belmont in Nashville (1944-1945), before taking a job as a reporter with the *Nashville Tennessean* (1945-1946). After leaving her newspaper job, she worked for the next few years as an instructor at the University of Mississippi, teaching traditional English courses and creative writing. In 1953 she was awarded a Guggenheim Fellowship and left Mississippi to live in Italy and pursue her writing full time. She married John Rusher of Cornwall, England, in 1956, and they have lived in Montreal since 1958.

The themes and techniques of Spencer's fiction are complex and varied. In the early novels she writes both of social conflicts, those within families and between classes, races, and regions, and of inner conflicts, often religious, which take form and direction from a character's place and time. She extends these concerns in later novels and stories, mostly set outside the South, to explore the possibilities and conditions of moral order and ethical action in the mid-twentieth century. Throughout her fiction she shows keen psychological insight into the irrepressible motive for the nonrational, the human need for mystery and awe, the longing for faith. Stylistically, she has employed traditional and experimental modes of narration, including shifting points of view, intricate manipulation of chronology, and vivid, allusive imagery cast in patterns of symbolism.

In her first novel, *Fire in the Morning* (1948), Spencer creates a fictional community, Tarsus, Mississippi, that resembles the Mississippi hill country she knew as a child. Principally the story of Kinloch Armstrong, the son of a respected, unpretentious agrarian family, the novel traces Kinloch's gradual discovery of an evil buried in the past, which has had lasting consequences for his father Daniel and the community. The secret is a familiar American story of ambition and greed in conflict with honor, with the battle fought over ownership of land.

Through the prodding of his own curiosity and self-righteousness, and the information furnished by his cousin Randall Gibson, Kinloch exposes the sordid account of bribery that explains how the upstart Gerrards came to prominence in Tarsus.

The Gerrards' large land holding had once belonged to Kinloch Walston, who at his death bequeathed it to his friends Daniel Armstrong and Felix McKie. But the bequest was undone through the chicanery of Wills and Simon Gerrard. The crux of the mystery for Kinloch Armstrong is why his father did not oppose the Gerrards, whereas McKie, in an act of rage and retribution, set out to kill Wills Gerrard, an act he accomplished only after being himself blinded by an innocent black man caught in the scuffle.

Kinloch Armstrong's own hatred for the Gerrards has built steadily from childhood, aimed chiefly at Simon's son Lance, who is his own age; but Kinloch's wife, Ruth, an outsider who has come to Tarsus as a secretary for a federal agency, becomes friendly with Lance, his wife Elinor, and his sister Justin. The Gerrard family has a destructive influence on Ruth, and one evening she accidentally kills a man and tries to keep her crime secret. The Gerrards know about the accident, however, and when Simon Gerrard presents to Kinloch an affidavit signed by Justin and Lance stating Ruth's complicity in the accident, Kinloch in turn shows Simon the testimony of one Dr. Derryberry, exposing the lie that originally put the Walston land into Gerrard hands. At the novel's conclusion, Kinloch finally comes to realize his own complicity in the web of crimes, but not before his father dies of a heart attack in a violent effort to save Simon Gerrard, who falls to his death before a raging Felix McKie.

Spencer's plot is intricate and well made; the characters are vivid individuals—realistic Mississippians of their time and place and embodiments of universal human circumstance. The novel's themes are chiefly discovery and reversal: a young man finds that the past cannot be separated from the present, that his good intentions are no assurance of good deeds and outcomes, that evil is rarely dramatic and clearly designated. Though a fire at night is the more familiar image of destruction, as the epigraph makes clear, a fire in the morning can be more devastating. Spencer's controlling metaphor is exact: burning in full sunlight, fire, like evil, takes on a stealthy ordinariness, its ambiguity and mediocrity bemusing those in its presence.

Spencer turns again to the hill country people of Mississippi for her next novel, *This Crooked Way* (1952). In fact, the family chronicle of the Dudleys grows out of a brief account in *Fire in the Morning* of Elinor Dudley Gerrard's Mississippi Delta upbringing. Ironically, despite the Gerrards' pride in Lance's marriage to a Delta aristocrat, Elinor's father Amos turns out to have had an impoverished beginning in the hills. But Amos's rise to power and wealth is a story different from that of the Gerrards. Amos got "tangled up with God."

In an interview with Charles Bunting, Spencer commented that the South has "a native tendency to the mythical and to the imaginative and to the primitive." She says, "I think this has something to do with the South's more fundamentalist approach to religion, that the things of religion are to be taken literally, not rationalized, but to be taken instinctively and in an immediate sense." As a sixteen year old, Amos Dudley experiences this sort of direct apprehension of God, which is confirmed for him as he listens in the tabernacle to a sermon on Jacob and, later, when he baptizes himself in the Yocona River.

Thomas Victor

From that moment he moves with certainty, full of assurance that God knows and approves the secrets of his heart, no matter that for him as for every man, Amos thinks, the secret way is "crooked as it goes." True to the tradition of such fictional American characters as Jay Gatsby and Thomas Sutpen, or Flem Snopes, Amos leaves the hills and his family, works like a man obsessed, and soon manages to own a small grocery store.

When he sees Ary Morgan for the first time, he knows immediately that she embodies the completion of his vision. Her patrician manner and her calm, steady control of her thoroughbred mare convince him she is "good enough" and "sure enough" to vouchsafe his entry into the planters' circle and the good life, whatever that turns out to be. Winning Ary becomes for Amos the ultimate test of himself and of God's backing. He says in his matter-of-fact prayer: "I've got to have that land. I've got to have Ary Morgan. You've got to give me the land. I can't get it no other way. You've got to give me Ary. I can't get her no other way either." In Amos's view God makes his sign in the shape of a Chinaman who shows up one day with six hundred acres of Delta land, ready to trade for a grocery store.

In the first section of the book, "The Wandering," Spencer uses a limited omniscient voice to show Amos's setting out. Three "Indictments" narrated in the first person compose the long midsection of the novel. Amos's friend Arney, niece Dolly, and Ary, drawn to Amos for what they see as strength and a sure sense of direction, all discover and bear witness to his use of people to serve his secret and private vision. In the end, thwarted in his desire for a male heir, Amos has to face the messy consequences of his life and the unarguable evidence that people and events cannot be ordered according to desire.

The narrative consciousness of the final section, "The Return," is that of Amos. He returns to the hills, undergoes a ritualized baptism (to replace the earlier self-imposed one), and brings various displaced members of his family home with him to the Delta plantation. The almost comic tone of the family reunion veers sharply from the earlier sections, but the conclusion rightly completes Amos's discovery of—and acquiescence to—the unknowable ways of God and men.

With *The Voice at the Back Door* (1956), Spencer completes what amounts to a cycle of novels that, taken together, portray the social and political circumstance of the rural South during the first half of the twentieth century. In this novel she focuses upon the racial relationships in a small Mississippi town at a time between the end of World War II and the beginning of the civil rights upheavals of the 1960s, a time when peaceable change in the white South's treatment of blacks seemed possible.

Spencer wrote most of the novel while on her Guggenheim grant in Italy in 1953. In an introduction to a Time-Life edition of the novel (1965), she explained that she returned to Mississippi between the first draft and a final revision to find the "precipitate moment had come and gone." In the interval the Supreme Court had ended legal segregation, a scandalous murder of a black man in the state had occurred, and feelings were so inflamed as to make the actions of Duncan Harper, the novel's main character, hopelessly idealistic. Spencer decided, however, not to change Harper, to "stick to [her] story," she said, because it was written originally out of a truth she knew and because the act of honest seeing, especially in a society that refuses to see, "will always seem to be impossible."

Spencer's plot is intricately woven, with a vast number of characters from the fictional town of Lacey, county seat of Winfield County, Mississippi. As in *Fire in the Morning*, the present action of the novel is linked to the preceding generation, and the consequences of the present are clearly to be the shaping influence on Lacey's future. The turning point of the novel is Duncan Harper's decision, in his role as acting sheriff caught up in an election campaign, to protect Beck Dozer, a black man whom the unreasoning white citizenry seems intent upon lynching.

The question of what to do about Duncan Harper becomes the generating force of much of the book's action. Harper, long admired by the town for his college football exploits, faces the opposition and doubts of virtually everyone in town, each having private, unspoken motives: Kerney Woolbright, Harper's friend who is running for office, Woolbright's fiancee Cissy Hunt, and her father Jason, all fearful of Harper's threat to the status quo and their comfortable, predictable place in it; Jimmy Tallant, also a childhood friend, a war hero turned bootlegger who does not want his business hindered by a reform-minded sheriff; Tinker, Duncan's wife, whose childhood has made her cautious and fearful; and a host of others—including the "boys" who slash Harper's tires, ultimately causing his fatal accident—whose racist reactions are automatic and absolute.

Like the characters in Spencer's earlier novels, Harper comes to see human action as ambiguous and problematical. Dozer, who presses Harper and the white community for recognition, and Tallant, who at last exonerates Dozer, are both burdened with the sins of the past. Tallant's father had led a mob that killed Dozer's father and a group of blacks seeking a hearing at the courthouse. The mob committed murder at the very seat of justice, and the memory of the desecration hangs heavily over the present townspeople of Lacey.

The Voice at the Back Door, a phrase explained in the novel as the ever-present voice of some Negro at the door of some white Southerner—perhaps the voice haunting the conscience as well—portrays a society described in rich detail. It succeeds as social criticism and as a portrait of provocative characters caught up in the business of living. The novel was widely reviewed and much praised for its penetrating insights into the motives of human action, as well as for the social realism that Spencer evokes through taut dialogue and fast-paced narrative.

Spencer turned from Mississippi to international settings for her next two books, *The Light in the Piazza* (1960) and *Knights and Dragons* (1965). Critics particularly praised the novella, *The Light in the Piazza*, which received the first McGraw-Hill Fiction Award and also was made into a Hollywood film.

The American-in-Europe theme, as well as the book's concern with subtle motives and introspections, led to many comparisons with Henry James. Even the plot, the courtship and marriage of a blushingly open and innocent American girl to an Italian, suggests a Jamesian influence. But the youthful Clara Johnson is a Daisy Miller with a difference. Kicked in the head by a pony when she was a child, the twenty-six-year-old Clara has the mind of a ten year old, a freakish turn of fortune that her mother, Margaret, has never fully accepted. Mrs. Johnson's decision to encourage the marriage, not telling her plan to her homebound husband, an American businessman who would certainly oppose it, nor telling the truth of Clara's infirmity to the Italian fiance and his family, furnishes the basis of a morality tale that is also a suspenseful psychological study.

In a remarkably straightforward prose style, admirable for its clarity and economy, Spencer fuses setting and action into a symbolic study of life's ambiguities. By the end of the book Margaret Johnson understands precisely what she has done—"played single handed and unadvised a tricky game in a foreign country"—but the question of whether she has violated the moral order or acquiesced to a maternal, natural one hangs in the balance.

Margaret is never certain whether she rationalizes or whether she realizes conditions of life she sees as inexorable. Individual goals and achievements, symbolized in the concluding scene by Cellini's Perseus holding aloft the Medusa's head, are transitory, even peripheral. In constrast stands the regenerating maternal world that values not so much mental power and heroism as fertility and faith, represented by the Holy Mother Church, with its Virgin and Child, and the bridegroom's Italian mother, whose arms "had yearned for some time for Clara and were already beginning to yearn for her children."

In *Knights and Dragons*, Martha Ingram also undergoes a severe inner conflict, but she is less able than Margaret Johnson to mark off the battlefield or delineate the opposing forces. She thinks of herself as "that meeting point of shadow and sun. It is everything there is I need to know, that I am that and that is me."

She meets two Americans who come to Italy with their families on a cultural exchange—Richard Coggins, who presumes to lecture Italians on opera and inexplicably wins over every Italian audience he meets, and Jim Wilbourne, a quarrelsome economist who becomes Martha's lover. George Hartwell, Martha's protective superior and friend, and his wife Grace, together with Coggins's wife and daughter and Wilbourne's wife, complete the main cast of characters. The dramatic presence of these characters who encircle Martha is attenuated, however, by the novel's elusive point of view and shifting center of action, as well as by a slow-motion plot and a complex handling of chronology.

Martha is haunted by a demonic memory of her former husband, Gordon, who never appears—except in one brief scene in which Martha sees or imagines his writing a letter in a post office. Once her teacher, Gordon is something of a philosopher, writing of a "world of clear and open truth, reasonable and calm, a warm untroubled radiance"—which is a seductive, impossible vision, as Martha discovers.

In their separate efforts to enlighten or protect Martha, both Wilbourne and Hartwell play ersatz knights, as Gordon no doubt once had tried to do. But the dragon they slay is Martha's emotional vitality and capacity for wonderment. In the end "she simply did not care very deeply about anything." Like Stephen Crane's narrator of "The Open Boat," however, Martha meets and withstands life's dissolution by interpreting it.

No Place for an Angel (1967) enlarges upon and intensifies Spencer's earlier portraits of displaced Americans who wander haphazardly in and out of foreign countries, relationships, and private dreams of success. Five characters—Charles and Irene Waddell, Jerry and Catherine Sasser, and Barry Day, a young artist who sculpts angels—are at the center of the novel's action. The Waddells live well on life's surface. Irene is generous and easy to please, while Charles brashly manages to live life without giving too much thought to it, except as his job and income are affected. When the loss of a job forces him to face his vulnerability to fate's caprices, he seeks refuge in a sudden trip to Florida to attempt a new start. Not finding a fountain of youth there, he does seek it again later, however, in a visit with his twin sons away at school. The promise of the new generation is purpose enough for Charles. Even Barry Day (or Bernard Desportes before he renamed himself) at last soothes his artist's melancholia and bemusement at the world by making a happy marriage. But the Sassers, Jerry and Catherine, do not float along so well on surfaces.

Catherine perceives the world as everywhere threatening and dissolving. The bomb hangs heavily over all; for most of the Americans, Italy is "used up," and for Catherine, "America is murderous." The intricate, carefully knit web of action—fleeting scenes, shifting time sequences, uncertain memories—conveys a sense of the world vividly concrete but also diaphanous, hallucinatory.

Jerry Sasser, a lawyer, aide to a U.S. Senator, later a middleman in big oil deals, understands power and its uses—the gain of money and women, but chiefly the appeasement of a ravenous appetite for more and ever more power. Reared by a fanatical father whose religious beliefs turned to a blood-drinking cult of the "Messiah's Brotherhood," Jerry has neither faith of the fathers nor, in the contemporary gray world of power brokerage, faith in the fatherland. Finally, his sole hope is his illegitimate daughter, whom he entrusts to a black nurse in Washington, D.C.

To an important degree, Catherine and their son Latham escape the world's corruption. Latham, a naturalist, lamed by polio as a child, finds purpose and mutual sympathy in nature, as, in the end, does Catherine in her modest, routine life in Massachusetts, when, after having been driven almost to destructive madness, she breaks from Jerry and the overly blase Texas-oil, New Frontier world.

Early in the novel Irene Waddell dismisses Barry Day's announcement of his new project, the statue of an angel, with the comment, "Angels never crossed the Atlantic." Spencer shows in this suggestive

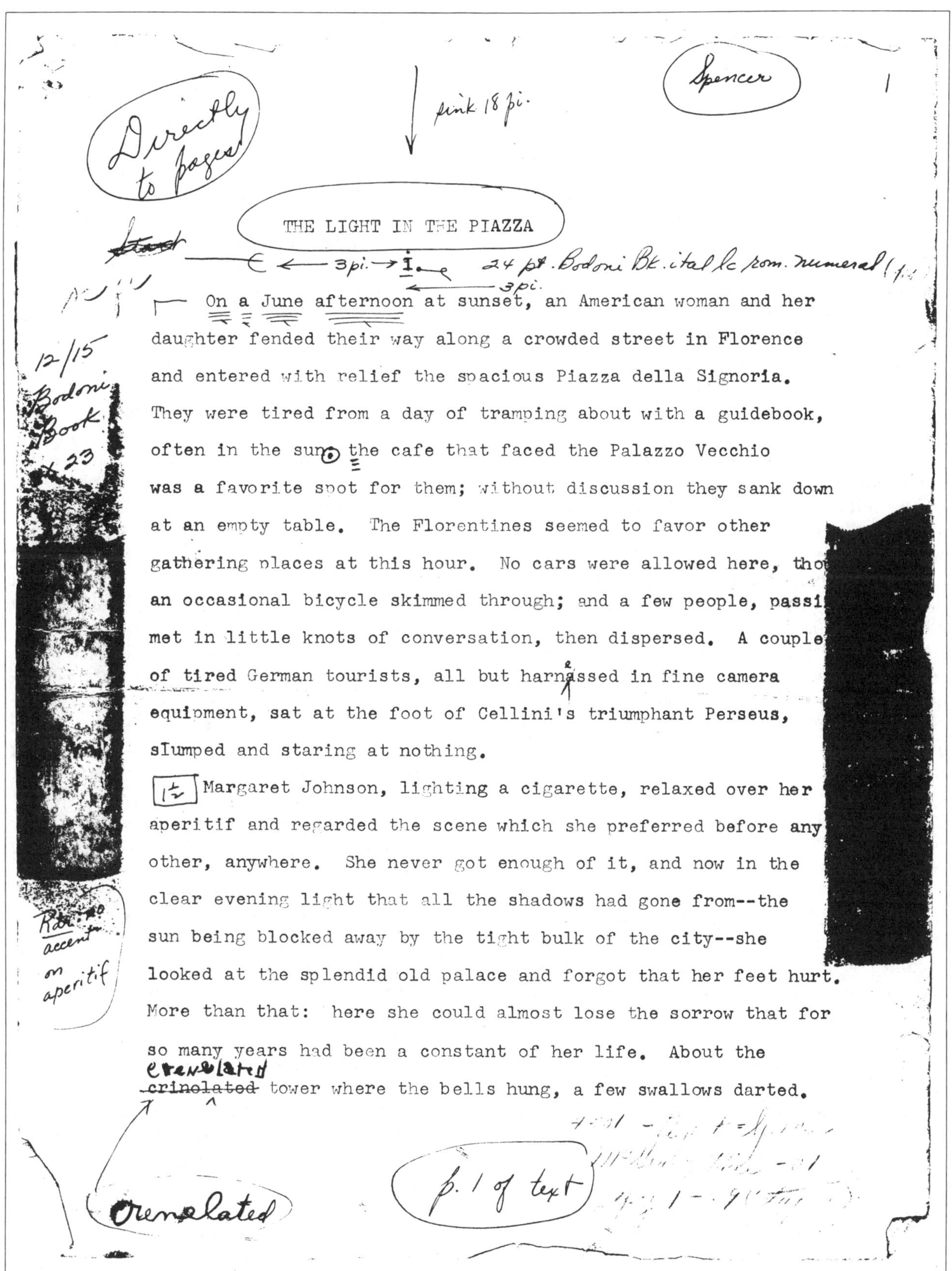

THE LIGHT IN THE PIAZZA

I

On a June afternoon at sunset, an American woman and her daughter fended their way along a crowded street in Florence and entered with relief the spacious Piazza della Signoria. They were tired from a day of tramping about with a guidebook, often in the sun; the cafe that faced the Palazzo Vecchio was a favorite spot for them; without discussion they sank down at an empty table. The Florentines seemed to favor other gathering places at this hour. No cars were allowed here, tho[ugh] an occasional bicycle skimmed through; and a few people, passi[ng,] met in little knots of conversation, then dispersed. A couple of tired German tourists, all but harnessed in fine camera equipment, sat at the foot of Cellini's triumphant Perseus, slumped and staring at nothing.

Margaret Johnson, lighting a cigarette, relaxed over her aperitif and regarded the scene which she preferred before any other, anywhere. She never got enough of it, and now in the clear evening light that all the shadows had gone from--the sun being blocked away by the tight bulk of the city--she looked at the splendid old palace and forgot that her feet hurt. More than that: here she could almost lose the sorrow that for so many years had been a constant of her life. About the crenelated tower where the bells hung, a few swallows darted.

The Light in the Piazza, *setting copy*

novel, filled with insights about Americans and their cultural history, that hospitality for angels has waned everywhere, especially so in the United States, if it ever existed here. Nevertheless, an American like Catherine Sasser is still able to pull back and find sanctuary, even if it is only in a little Massachusetts town with slight connection to earlier, less materialistic times. There are yet, if barely, conditions for living that will sustain soul as well as body.

In *The Snare* (1972) Spencer takes a different direction in her exploration of the possibilities for living in a menacing world. The threat that Julia Garrett faces is not stultifying materialism, or lotus-eating artiness, or even power hunger; it is rather her discovery within herself of an unappeasable appetite for bestiality that matches an appetite for human, civilized life.

The novel's New Orleans setting serves, as does Italy in the earlier novels, as an enlarged symbol of the possibilities for life beyond the conventional margins of most Americans' lives. Boozy chance meetings at late-night parties—rather tame dissolutions—quickly lead to a tempestuous love affair between Julia and Jake Springland, a musician connected obscurely with the underworld.

Julia, who has been reared by a well-to-do aunt and uncle in the ritzy section of the city, continually throws over her chances for a good marriage and a safe, respectable life. First, although she refuses to marry Martin Parham, a Mississippi millionaire who seems as bewitched by Julia as later she is by Springland, she becomes Martin's mistress for a time before his death. Then she meets and finally refuses respectable Joe Delaney, who wants to marry her and live happily ever after in Mobile.

In a series of flashbacks, diary entries, and fragments of memory, Julia is revealed as a woman whose obsessions and sensuality can partly be explained by her childhood. When her mother died, her father gave her over to the Devigny relatives (her mother's sister) and disappeared. Preoccupied with themselves, the Devignys in turn gave her away, in spirit at least, to Maurice Devigny's father, old Dev, who had quarters in the upstairs rooms. What Julia gains from him—love, initiation into unspeakable sex acts, or both—she is never quite able to tell herself or anyone else, but the relationship changes her life.

The novel is filled with action, introspection, and bizarre characters, or those at least who seem bizarre when portrayed in the shadowy New Orleans setting and filtered through Julia's consciousness. For instance, Ted Marnie is a gangster friend of Springland, whose apparent death leads to a sensational murder trial of Springland. Years later it is learned that his "death" was a carefully arranged hoax. He is a demonic underworld character, a conspirator in the drug culture, whose torturous abuse of Julia and Springland ironically pushes them toward salvation, given Julia's view that only by hitting bottom can she begin to remake her life.

At the conclusion Julia is living with her child fathered by Jake, and she is visited from time to time by Tommy Arnold, a newspaper reporter who has become her lover. In Julia, Spencer has created a character who seeks out the "evil challenge" because desire and attraction for evil are also her life source. Contrary to her fears, her reckless search of the depths of soul and city invigorates those who are drawn to her and goads them along on their necessary and private journeys.

In addition to Elizabeth Spencer's impressive productivity and literary achievement with the novel, she has published almost forty short stories, many of which have won prizes and been chosen for inclusion in story anthologies. *Ship Island and Other Stories* (1968) shows her craftsmanship and control in the handling of the form and includes some memorable characters—Nancy Lewis of the title story and Judith Kane—who are marked by the kind of mystery and vitality that characterize Julia Garrett. Like the novels, the stories vary in setting from small Southern towns to Europe, and they show many different stylistic approaches. Reviewing the collection in the *New York Times*, 26 December 1968, Charles Poore praised the clarity and grace of the writing, noting that Spencer manages to achieve depth without murkiness. Scheduled for publication by Doubleday in 1981 is a new collection that will include ten stories from *Ship Island* and *Knights and Dragons* and twenty-two other previously published but uncollected stories.

In the course of her career Spencer has moved from the early Mississippi novels to studies of Americans in Europe and on to an American city novel that probes the underside of urban society and the individual psyche. Starting in the tradition of the Southern Literary Renaissance, compared early, and perhaps too often, with the older luminaries of that tradition—Faulkner, Warren, Welty, and others—Spencer has always written with a distinctive voice and vision.

Her future development, as evidenced in the recent story "I Maureen," is likely to extend in the direction embodied by *The Snare*—thematically, a concern with broad, contemporary experience and, stylistically, a continuation of experimentation with point of view and chronology. In fact, Spencer herself forecast this development in her 1975 interview with Charles Bunting: "I really feel my direction is more toward doing the large American experience, but I'd like to do this as broadly as possible, that is to say, a new novel that brings a good many elements into focus around one theme: a large range of characters caught up in one broad thing, embodying our experience in our time.... I feel more in focus with modern experience as a whole than I used to."

Still midway in a vigorous career, Spencer commands serious critical attention for her achievement in fiction and for her promise of continued productivity and artistic development.

—Peggy Whitman Prenshaw

Other:

"I Maureen," in *76: New Canadian Stories* (Ottawa: Oberon Press, 1976), pp. 70-98.

Periodical Publications:

"Valley Hill," *Delta Review*, 1 (Autumn 1964): 18-23;

"On Writing Fiction," *Notes on Mississippi Writers*, 3 (Fall 1970): 71-72;

"State of Grace," *Weekend Magazine*, 12 August 1978, pp. 18-21.

Interviews:

Josephine Haley, "An Interview with Elizabeth Spencer," *Notes on Mississippi Writers*, 1 (Fall 1968): 42-53;

Hunter McKelva Cole, "Elizabeth Spencer at Sycamore Fair," *Notes on Mississippi Writers*, 6 (Winter 1974): 81-86;

Charles Bunting, " 'In That Time and at That Place': The Literary World of Elizabeth Spencer," *Mississippi Quarterly*, 28 (Fall 1975): 435-460.

References:

Laura Barge, "An Elizabeth Spencer Checklist, 1948 to 1976," *Mississippi Quarterly*, 29 (Fall 1976): 569-590;

Nash K. Burger, "Elizabeth Spencer's Three Mississippi Novels," *South Atlantic Quarterly*, 63 (Summer 1964): 351-362;

D. G. Pugh, "*The Voice at the Back Door*: Elizabeth Spencer Looks into Mississippi," in *The Fifties: Fiction, Poetry, Drama*, ed. Warren C. French (Deland, Fla.: Everett/Edwards, 1970), pp. 291-304.

Papers:

The repository for Spencer's manuscripts and papers is the University of Kentucky Library in Lexington.

MARK STEADMAN

(2 July 1930-)

BOOKS: *McAfee County: A Chronicle* (New York: Holt, Rinehart & Winston, 1971; London: Secker & Warburg, 1972);

A Lion's Share (New York: Holt, Rinehart & Winston, 1975).

Mark Steadman is a patient craftsman whose two volumes of fiction have identified him as an important, if not yet major, Southern voice. His collection of twelve Gothic stories, *McAfee County: A Chronicle* (1971), received outstanding notices in this country, its most perceptive reviewer calling it an "exceptional first work of fiction" and "an excellent harbinger of the career of a talented writer." The British edition went largely unreviewed; but a French translation, *Quoi de Neuf en Georgie?* (1974), and a German translation, *Schwarze Chronik* (1975), were both notable successes. His novel, *A Lion's Share* (1975), was well received and became an Avon paperback (1977) that continues in print.

Steadman was born in Statesboro, Georgia, to Mark Steadman, Sr., and Marie Hopkins Steadman. He attended the Georgia public schools and then took his B.A. in English from Emory University in 1951. He did a tour of duty with the U.S. Navy (1951-1953) before beginning graduate work in American literature. He completed his M.A. in 1956 and his Ph.D. in 1963, both at Florida State University.

Steadman married Joan Anderson of Savannah, Georgia, on 29 March 1952. They have three sons: Clayton D. (born 30 December 1954), Todd A. (born 4 March 1957), and Wade H. (born 23 December 1959). The family lives in rural Pickens County, a few miles from Clemson, South Carolina, where Steadman has been a member of the English faculty at Clemson University since 1957. In 1968 he took a year's leave of absence to be a visiting associate professor of American literature at the American University in Cairo. Currently, he is a professor of English at

Clemson University, teaching courses in the American novel, American humor, and fiction writing.

In the notes that conclude *McAfee County*, Steadman says that the setting for the stories is "an imaginary coastal county of the state of Georgia." It has five communities: Kose, Two-Oaks, Rainbow, Willie, and Fork Shoal. They are, as he puts it, "pretty much the kind of a place they sound like they would be, though the people in them have their good times too." Steadman sums up their vocations and avocations, as well as the terrain, with these statistics: "The average adult male consumes 1.8 cartons of shotgun shells per year, 21 pounds of twelvepenny nails, 149 inches of galvanized chain, 1/3 of a shovel, and 1/16 of a submersible pump."

Generally the rednecks of this swamp seem to be frightened—of themselves, of each other, of the world around them. And their responses are often depraved. There is incest in "Daddy's Girl," castration and murder in "After John Henry," miscegenation in "Annie's Love Child," and voodoo in "Anse Starkey at Rest." But these are not just grim sketches; they are complete tales that, even at their darkest, come to some kind of just finish. The father of "Daddy's Girl" suffers miserably for his crime; John Henry, bleeding to death after his mutilation on a church picnic table inscribed with the Beatitudes, gets revenge on one of his torturers; and Anse Starkey, the meanest man in the county, stumbles and falls as he tries to carry away his own tombstone.

If the Gothic elements of these tales seem heavy-handed at times, they are always undercut by Steadman's marvelous sense of the comic. McAfee County can be grim; but the way is lightened when, for instance, Anse, Dee Witt, and Lee Jay visit the beach in "Lee Jay's Chinese-Box Mystery." These boys are curious about the anatomy of Oriental females, so they rape an Oriental burlesque dancer and whore, only to be arrested and fined her usual fee. John Fletcher, in "John Fletcher's Night of Love," tries to add class to his appointment with the hooker, Nettie Oatley. He fixes up his shack in all the elegance he knows; he buys TV dinners (Salisbury steaks, for their foreign flavor), English Ovals, copies of *National Geographic*, the Atlanta newspaper, and Frank Slaughter's *Sangaree*. His grandest touch is a bottle of Roma burgundy and a box of chocolate-covered cherries.

Steadman has another sure gift, too, and that is a compassion for these characters who are so funny in their deadpan seriousness. He allows them a dignity that is emphasized by the first and the last stories of

Wally Bowen

Mark Steadman

the collection. In "Mr. McAllister's Cigarette Holder," Mr. McAllister is determined to be an individual set apart from the riffraff of his world. He is a common laborer on a highway gang, scratching the rough spots from the roadbed. But he takes his work seriously. He calls his fellow workers "Mister" and insists on the same from them. Moreover, his good posture and a red cigarette holder that he dug out of the road set him apart from the other laborers. But one of these claims to individuality is shattered when he discovers a box of red cigarette holders on a store counter. His wife, however, buys the entire box of holders, and the couple break each of them in half as they ride the bus home. Mr. McAllister may not know that he should cherish his wife more than his cigarette holder, but the story is nonetheless as touching as it is funny.

The last story in the collection, "A Worker of Miracles," has a similar touch. Brother Garnet Frisco, saved at a tent meeting, joins the Two-Oak Missionary Baptist Church. And when the preacher, Brother Campbell, "left to go back full time in the mobile-home business in Brunswick," Brother Frisco takes over. In a fit of zeal, he promises a miracle: he will walk across Kallisaw Sound. Selling all of his worldly goods for a dollar, he stakes everything on his genuine belief that he can walk on water. But he fails miserably, before TV cameras and a huge crowd, and wanders off to Rainbow Pool where Della finds him at sunset and assures him, "It'll be all right. I didn't never take you for no liar." Thus Della retrieves her husband from God and brings *McAfee County*—a book remarkable for its fresh handling of Gothic familiarities, for its comedy, and for its compassion—to its close.

Steadman's novel, *A Lion's Share,* is often as funny as *McAfee County*; but most of the Gothic cast is gone and with it some of the author's hope for his characters. Donald Greiner is correct when he says that the characters of this book have to *"create* significance for their lives." The hero, Jack Curran, gets his meaning from one winning football season, perhaps from just one high-school game. All to follow fails for Jack, and he is dead at twenty-six, the victim of a meaningless accident. Jack, however, is no athlete dying young; for in spite of his age, he had long outlived his fame and his reason for being alive: "What he wanted, deep in his heart, was for someone to offer to pay him for being a wonderful fellow, without any strings attached. Just to be himself and do things that were free and good." No one is quite that eager to have Jack on hand. But the saddest irony of *A Lion's Share* is that any number of Jack's acquaintances attach themselves to the hero, trying to gather a bit of light for their own lives from the brief flash that was Jack's.

The novel begins with the responses of several of these characters to Jack's death. Old Johnny Curran, Jack's father, divorced from Jack's mother, is drunk in the streets of Savannah. A cat, hit by a car, growls in the gutter and scratches Johnny when he tries to pick it up. In his anger, the old drunk pounds the cat to death on the curb. Charlie Carne, the mortician, is up late worried about the several funerals, including Jack's, that he must take care of the next day. George Bogger, an epileptic who is Jack's greatest admirer, makes a small cross out of bird feathers as he listens to Jack's radio obituary. Feeb, one of Jack's old teammates, goes through the business of evaluating Jack as high-school football player. Mary, Jack's divorced wife, has to explain to her husband why she, a Protestant, can go to a Catholic funeral. And Mackey, Jack's mistress, gets drunk in bed alone—not much drama, obviously, but as much as these lives can generate.

Then the narrative turns back to Jack's life. St. Boniface High has a miserable football team. The players are fat and timid, led by Chicken Garfield, a coach who later finds his true calling in selling life insurance. All are content to lose provided they do not get hurt. But Jack changes everything when he comes to Boniface in his senior year. He is a huge and aggressive center who pulls the team together and leads them to an undefeated season.

This section of the novel gives Steadman much room for his talent for comedy. Before Jack arrives, the Boniface team needs nothing more than an organ grinder. The quarterback will not carry out fakes for fear of being hit. And when Chicken Garfield gives one of his famous speeches, "Wellllll . . . I feel pretty . . . good about the team . . . ," the only response he gets is from Frog Finnechairo who says, "You do?" But with Jack they are winners, and they have their best and funniest moment, when, high on Dexedrine, they beat their major rival Oglethorpe, 63 to 13 on Thanksgiving Day.

College scholarships follow for several players, and Jack goes to Georgia Tech, to become a failure. He is homesick for his love, Mary O'dell, and he flunks his courses with some deliberateness. He returns to Savannah to drive a beer truck and marry Mary. This rather melancholy section of the book contains Steadman's best writing. Jack, the idolized, needs an idol of his own, and he turns to Mary, whom he sees as being sacred. He even makes a confession to her as if she were a priestess. Such idolizing, needless to say, does not make for much of a marriage. Jack simply cannot think of Mary in sexual terms, and the marriage sours as they sleep apart. Then Mary's brave and rather vulgar attempts to activate their sex lives destroy Jack's vision of her, and the marriage collapses.

Jack tries to enlist for the Korean War but is too tall for the service, so he turns to hustling pool until his drinking leaves him too unsteady to shoot. He dries out to take up professional wrestling as well as a friendship with George Bogger, the reclusive epileptic and frog hunter who becomes Jack's foil. One character has small fame; the other lives in oblivion. But one comes to be as insignificant as the other as they both fail in careers and in romance before they die meaninglessly.

Jack ends up working for the fire department. As Steadman says, "There was always room for one more mick at the fire department—the next thing to a retirement home." The hero dies in his first major fire, and the death scene says everything about his life:

> There was a split second as the wall opened up, just before it began to fall outward, when the fire lit up Hull Street, and they could see

> Jack moving with the hose in his hands like a lance. In the bright glare of the light from the flames, the polished brass nozzle was gleaming like a jewel. He looked dwarfed in the glare—only his shadow loomed large, gliding on the fronts of the houses. Just for a second. Then the wall of bricks came down on top of him with a long, angry boom, breaking like a wave and rolling dust up onto the fronts of the Hull Street houses, and making the earth shake. Afterward, those who saw it happen would only be able to gauge him by his house-tall shadow. They were the ones who passed the word, making a parable of his death.

So this carefully structured story returns the reader to its beginning, to Jack's funeral in Savannah.

This is a powerful book that gains momentum as it moves from comedy to genuine tragedy—Steadman's particular strength. He says that comedy comes to him with some ease but that he intends to be a serious writer. The point, then, concerns his bringing together the opposites. *McAfee County* treats characters who are funny without ever denying them their humanity, without ever holding them up for ridicule. Such seems to be a major concern of the author, at times perhaps even a self-conscious concern. *A Lion's Share* may be a stronger book because here Steadman does not seem to be preoccupied with preventing the comedy's violation of humanity; he is more comfortable with his skill at comedy. In *McAfee County,* he tells good and amusing stories which always include his reminders that his people are human. In *A Lion's Share,* he tells a familiar tale well, allowing the characters, and life itself, to be amusing and sad as they will.

So the progression in Steadman's work involves his move from a writer who handles comedy as well as nearly anyone to a writer who can subtly use comedy to further serious statements on reality. He has mastered one craft and is now at the business of making that craft part of a larger talent. He is at work on a book tentatively called "The Broken Door: An Autobiographical Fiction." The novel examines the racial attitudes of the author's father, who died in 1946, and attempts to reconcile those views with those of the author himself. The work, supported by a National Endowment of the Arts Creative Writing Fellowship, promises to show Steadman at his most serious, to show a third step in his move from first-rate comedy to more reflective views of the human condition.

—William Koon

Periodical Publications:

"Annie's Love Child," *Red Clay Reader,* 6 (1969): 107-116;

"A Worker of Miracles," *Works in Progress,* 3 (1971): 181-208;

"Anse Starkey at Rest," *Works in Progress,* 4 (1971): 253-288;

"Daddy's Girl," *Nova,* February 1972, pp. 62-70;

"Nuzzle a Salamander With Care," *Sandlapper,* 5 (February 1972): 26-27;

"Kate," *South Carolina Review,* 7 (November 1974): 71-84;

"The Broken Door," *South Carolina Review,* 9 (November 1976): 74-114;

"Savannah," *Sandlapper,* 10 (December 1977): 54-58;

"Cast on the Waters and Raised on High," *South Carolina Review,* 10 (April 1978): 33-46.

References:

Donald J. Greiner, "The Southern Fiction of Mark Steadman," *South Carolina Review,* 9 (November 1976): 5-11;

Cathy Hill, Review of *McAfee County, Studies in Short Fiction,* 9 (Summer 1972): 283-285;

Martin Levin, Review of *A Lion's Share, New York Times Book Review,* 21 March 1976, p. 32.

HOLLIS SUMMERS
(21 June 1916-)

BOOKS: *City Limit* (Boston: Houghton Mifflin, 1948);

Brighten the Corner (Garden City: Doubleday, 1952);

Teach You a Lesson, by Summers and James F. Rourke, as Jim Hollis (New York: Harper, 1955; London: W. Foulsham, 1956); republished as *The Case of the Bludgeoned Teacher* (New York: Avon, 1955);

The Weather of February (New York: Harper, 1957);

The Walk Near Athens (New York: Harper, 1959);

Someone Else: Sixteen Poems About Other Children (Philadelphia: Lippincott, 1962);

Seven Occasions (New Brunswick, N.J.: Rutgers University Press, 1964);

The Peddler and Other Domestic Matters (New Brunswick, N.J.: Rutgers University Press, 1967);

The Day After Sunday (New York, Evanston & London: Harper, 1968);
Sit Opposite Each Other (New Brunswick, N.J.: Rutgers University Press, 1970);
Start from Home (New Brunswick, N.J.: Rutgers University Press, 1972);
The Garden (New York, Evanston, San Francisco & London: Harper, 1972);
How They Chose the Dead (Baton Rouge: Louisiana State University Press, 1973);
Occupant Please Forward (New Brunswick, N.J.: Rutgers University Press, 1976).

Characterizing his and his wife's habit of neighborliness as "cupcakes for the wounded," Hollis Spurgeon Summers, Jr., reveals his charming, self-effacing humor. Born in Eminence, Kentucky, to Hollis Spurgeon and Hazel Holmes Summers, Hollis Summers spent his youth living in Baptist parsonages in Louisville, Campbellsville, and Madisonville. As the older brother in a family where grandfather, father, and uncle were all preachers, Summers was expected to accept the ministry as his vocation. The tradition was, in fact, so virtually absolute that his grandmother insisted he kneel before his grandfather's casket and promise he would accept his inheritance by becoming a minister. Twenty years old at the time, Summers refused to make the promise.

Summers did, however, follow the example of his father's family by graduating from Georgetown College in Georgetown, Kentucky. He received an A.B. in English in 1937. During college and afterward as a high-school teacher in Covington, Kentucky (1937-1944), Summers experimented with sketches and poems he says now are "too horrible to remember"; he was nevertheless encouraged to develop his writing skills by Ellene Ransom, sister of John Crowe Ransom. During this same period, Summers declared himself a conscientious objector, and unlike his brother Joseph who was assigned to a conscientious objector camp in New England, he was permitted to continue teaching in order to support his parents after his father suffered a massive stroke. Through the auspices of Ellene Ransom, Summers received fellowships to attend Bread Loaf at Middlebury College, where he studied with John Crowe Ransom in the summers of 1941 and 1942. Summers submitted stories to church magazines recommended by Ellene Ransom, and his first work to be published was a short story which he sold for twenty-five dollars to a Methodist publication. In June 1943 he married Laura Vimont Clarke, a fellow Georgetown alumnus and a third-grade teacher. Still supporting his family, newly married, and finally published, Summers returned to Middlebury and completed his M.A. in 1943.

Summers returned in 1944 to Georgetown as a faculty member, where he began writing in earnest. He was encouraged to continue formal studies, mainly during the summers, at the State University of Iowa, where he specialized in seventeenth-century poetry. Surrounded by young scholars writing traditional dissertations, Summers submitted, under the direction of Andrew Lytle and Paul Engel, a creative thesis, the novel *City Limit*, which was published in 1948 just before he was awarded the Ph.D. in 1949.

Summers was appointed to the faculty of the University of Kentucky in 1949. In 1952 was published *Brighten the Corner*, chapters of which had earlier appeared in *Everywoman's* magazine and *Woman's Home Companion*. Summers was also writing and having published a number of short stories and critical essays in the early 1950s. When he was already in his mid-thirties and rapidly acquiring recognition as a fiction writer, Summers began his second artistic career, as a poet. After the publication of nearly one hundred poems in small magazines and literary journals during the 1950s, Summers was named "Distinguished Professor of the Year" by his colleagues at the University of Kentucky in 1959. By that time, Summers had published two more novels, *Teach You a Lesson* (1955) and *The Weather of February* (1957), and numerous poems and short stories, had edited a collection of short fiction by Kentuckians, *Kentucky Story* (1954), and had embarked on the first of several extended leaves in foreign countries which would greatly influence his later work.

Indeed, the contrapuntal rhythms of people leaving and returning home are integral to much of Summers's poetry and fiction. Isolated and often despairing, Summers's fictional characters frequently develop acute awareness as they travel away from familiar, orderly, and comfortable surroundings. They are tested and test themselves in Mexico or Malta; but the crucial tests ultimately occur in the most mundane settings: a quiet Ohio living room, a Kentucky bedroom. The titles of two of Summers's books of poems, *The Peddler and Other Domestic Matters* (1967) and *Start from Home* (1972), emphasize the movement back and forth between the exotic and the ordinary and the centrality of the domestic to Summers's work. The Summerses' own unpretentious life-style reflects the values and understatement found in his work.

In 1959, moving away from his native Kentucky for the first time, Summers brought his wife Laura and their two sons, Hollis Spurgeon III and David Clarke, to Ohio University in Athens where he still teaches and writes. He continued to write both poetry and fiction during the 1960s and 1970s. He notes that some things "come as a poem or a story or a novel. And sometimes they lie to me." Summers recalls how this was precisely the case with the long poem, "Brother Clark," published in the Spring 1980 issue of *Ohio Review*. Working for years on a short story version, Summers suddenly transformed "Brother Clark" into a poem; only then did the work come to fruition.

Teaching and receiving a number of grants for writing and travel, Summers has, in the last twenty years, published *The Day After Sunday* (1968) and *The Garden* (1972), a superb collection of short stories, *How They Chose the Dead* (1973), eight volumes of poetry, and numerous essays and individual pieces in various magazines and journals. He has been honored by his colleagues, receiving an honorary doctorate from Georgetown in 1965 as well as being named Distinguished Professor at Ohio University in 1964. He has taught at many writers workshops and conferences at such places as Bread Loaf; Antioch, Ohio; and Morehead, Kentucky. Summers has served at various times as a Danforth lecturer, and as a Fulbright lecturer in 1978 in New Zealand. He received a poetry award from *Saturday Review* for "Mexico Picnic" in 1957 and the Ohioana Book Award in 1968 for *The Peddler and Other Domestic Matters*; he was a National Endowment for the Arts fellow in 1974.

At the age of sixty-four, Summers is currently finishing a novel tentatively titled "Family Sayings." When asked if it is his best, Summers replies: "A book is always as good as you can do at the time. But yes, perhaps it is richer." When asked in what direction he sees himself moving artistically, Summers says he has "no sense of it" except to characterize his latest manuscript as "more naked, more despairing."

At the same time that he asks rhetorically, "Isn't everything autobiographical?," Summers claims: "You can't tell anything the way it is." This apparent contradiction is manifest in Summers's early novels, particularly *City Limit* and *Brighten the Corner*. Having written much of the latter novel first, but told by an imperceptive editor "that sounds like a second book," Summers revised his work schedule and produced *City Limit*. While it could easily be argued that the apparently autobiographical *Brighten the Corner* is a novel in which the artist exorcises ubiquitous family ghosts, *City Limit* is not autobiographical, although it was clearly influenced by Summers's experience as a high-school teacher in Covington. In her review of the novel for the *New York Times*, Eudora Welty called it "a psychological novel, but it is the reviewer's glad impression that the story was written not following after Freud no matter where, but out of observation and intuition and study of behavior down to its smallest manifestations, and a conception of it on the general scale."

In *City Limit* two young high-school students fall in love in an environment which inadvertently forces sexual confrontation and acknowledgment even while it ostensibly fosters abstinence and morality. While *City Limit* is told in third person, chapters present selective viewpoints and adapt language, perception, and imagery to the singular consciousness being explored. We see the story alternately through the eyes of the lovers, Harriet and Ed, and through the distorted view of Miss Trudy Bates, a perverse dean of girls who represents a dying Southern ersatz aristocratic class much as Blanche du Bois of *Streetcar Named Desire* does. Harriet is a young woman enamoured of poetry and obsessed by her father's suicide, and Ed, inarticulate but sensitive, seems to be a typical jock. But he nevertheless dreams of emulating Gershwin and is drawn to the finer instincts of Harriet. After the two students spend an idyllic day of hooky together, they are ultimately pressured into a premature marriage by a society whose Cerberus, Miss Bates, judges them morally reprehensible and tries to punish them by forcing a wedding, which the two ironically desire. In addition to being inevitably humiliated by the ingenuousness of Harriet in the penultimate scene of the novel, Miss Bates continues to dream of marriage with the new minister in town. She invents social scenarios in which her brilliance and grace will aggrandize them both, even while no genuine emotional or sexual union is fantasized. Miss Bates's brand of refinement represents a spiritual starvation, a repressed sexuality which is not only reflected in her name but in the masturbatory ablutions she ritualistically performs after she has sealed the fate of Harriet and Ed. At the end of the novel Harriet and Ed's temporary triumph over Trudy Bates and society is tempered by the reader's recognition that the lovers are hopelessly young and must return to the bridegroom's home, where they will live out their lives in a society whose scope is defined and restricted by the "city limit."

At a Creative Writing Institute held at Marshall University in 1966, Summers described the importance of controlled narrative perspective to his students. Using an anecdote to illustrate, Summers quoted his grandmother's incessant question: "Aren't you ever going to learn to control your voice?" This, he said, is the central problem of the writer. Corollaries of this problem are: "Where does a writer stand to speak from? Whom does he call? With what words and silences does he call?" This concentration on voice, distance, language, and even silence is evident in the structure and narration of Summers's fiction.

Moving from the multiple points of view he employed in *City Limit,* Summers uses first-person narrative in *Brighten the Corner,* creating a masterful novel from the point of view of a shy but perceptive boy. Inseparable from his younger and far more assertive brother Joseph, Albert (usually called Brother) observes the world of his parents' first parsonage and ministry. As the embryonic artistic consciousness, Albert instinctively perceives hypocrisy, discerns values far beyond his conscious ethical development, and senses emotionally charged situations the implications of which he cannot possibly understand.

While the novel dramatizes a year in the life of a minister and his family, the outstanding scenes in the novel explore the most elemental and mystifying of human problems. The long central chapter introduces the boys' first awareness of death when the elderly mother of a parishioner "slips away." The euphemisms of adult reference are taken literally by the boys who are excited by the funereal "marching" and flowers. This experience forms the symbolic context in which their initial awareness of the relationship between life and death is developed. Shortly after the funeral of Miss Elizabeth's mother, Joseph and Albert decide they want a sister. A hilarious series of questions answered by adult evasions regarding the source of babies, however, confuses the boys altogether. Rejoicing in the discovery that their mother, Hazel, is pregnant, the boys await little Lela, the "gift from God," and cannot understand the painful adult drama which ensues when Hazel prematurely delivers a stillborn child and is herself in serious physical danger. Because no one will explain the meaning of these events, the boys are left speculating, being angry at God, and assuming that an unnatural act has occurred. Responding by instinct, the boys ultimately recognize the importance of their mother to them in the concluding scene of the chapter. The novel ends as the family is called to another, larger parish. Albert, who has waited in vain for a manifestation of the God his father promises exists, finally has a vision in which he sees God "cool like the wind. He mounted the church steps and sailed through the great wooden doors."

Dedicated to Hazel Holmes, *Brighten the Corner* is ultimately the gift of a son to his mother. It is finally a book about the sacrifices and joys of a family whose often painful dedication to the ministry creates a moral order in which the random suffering of humankind is frequently explained away in simple religious terms or evasions. This order nevertheless creates an environment in which the boy Albert finds comfort, meaning, and sustenance.

Summers's next fictional publication was something of a lark. Collaborating with James Rourke, a newspaperman, the two created a potboiler murder mystery set in a high school. *Teach You a Lesson* was published in New York in 1955, in London in 1956, and, retitled *The Case of the Bludgeoned Teacher,* was published by Avon in paperback in 1955. While exhibiting little serious literary merit, the novel is interesting and successful as an exercise in structuring and point of view. A young femme fatale French teacher, who unscrupulously uses sex to advance her status, is brutally murdered and stuffed in a pupil's locker. Since virtually all the men and many of the women at the school and in the small town have been in some way negatively affected by her, everyone has a motive and the multiple possibilities provide the opportunity for suspense and narrative experimentation. After developing the plot together, Summers and Rourke each created five of ten chapters with each chapter from the perspective of a different character.

At the same time *Teach You a Lesson* was being published in the United States and England, the University of Kentucky granted Summers a sabbatical leave to devote full time to writing. Traveling extensively in Mexico in 1955 and 1956, the Summerses experienced their first extended absence from Kentucky. Profoundly affected by the ambience of Mexico and convinced that the geographical separation from home creates psychological and spiritual distances, not only from comfortable routine but also from the protective illusions created in safe and familiar environments, Summers chose for the first time an exotic landscape for a major fictional work.

The Weather of February is told exclusively from the point of view of a feisty female narrator. This fourth novel explores the somewhat bruised but ultimately healthy psyche of an "ordinary" woman who gradually acquires self-knowledge through the artistic process of re-creating her own story. Never revealing her given name, she calls herself Sister. Like an onion being carefully peeled one layer at a time, the story of Sister (also referred to by her surnames from various marriages) is conveyed to the reader through a series of revelations organized around "some variations on the theme of love." Temporarily immobilized in an apartment in Mexico City by an automobile "accident" her spiteful and pretentious current lover, Andy, causes, Sister is left to assess her life, to wrench meaning from its disorder and make decisions that she does not realize at the time will determine her future. She spends the depressing month of February (noting its numerous holidays and gloomy atmosphere as she goes along) re-creating her life's story and gradually recognizing its meaning for her. Having recently reached the age of forty (and acutely aware of the implications of that event), Sister initially has modest expectations of her book in which she will "try to write out what is the truth." Her descriptions of her conventional and sheltered youth in a Kentucky parsonage and of her first picture-book romance and subsequent marriage to a young college professor foreshadow the suffering she will experience before she becomes the lonely woman who tells her story. Sister recounts her two traumatic marriages to men whose only common characteristic was their unwillingness to recognize her separate identity. She dramatizes the spiritual and psychological suffering which accompanies the knowledge that she cannot bear children (she goes through two miscarriages and the pathetic experience of bearing a child who lives five days); she gradually discovers she no longer reflects the traditional values of her family as she willingly engages in several affairs. She also comes to discover how her attempt to recapture youthful extravagance and enthusiasm by running away to Mexico with Andy Elmendorf, a plumbing fixtures heir, fails to offer fulfillment. Sister finally begins to recognize that repudiating one's past and home ultimately resolves nothing. Her quiet victory comes as she rejects the opportunity to become involved in another transitory love relationship to "pass the time." She will return to Lexington, Kentucky, without unrealistic expectations.

Devoting his creative energy primarily to poetry, Summers did not publish another novel for eleven years. *The Day After Sunday* is perhaps Summers's finest novel to date. Jessamyn West wrote to Summers's editor: "If any word of mine can bring the pleasures of this book to other readers, I'll be glad to shout them." Returning to a Lexington, Kentucky, setting Summers creates a totally controlled, brilliantly structured novel about an ordinary family whose daily lives—mundane, pleasant, and comfortable on the surface—mask emotional trauma, psychological imbalance, and spiritual despair. As reviewer Warren French wrote: "Hollis Summers, who knows this country like Antonioni knows Rome, has captured the feeling of emotional starvation in a land of physical plenty with a skill that leaves a critic at a loss for words."

The main action of the novel takes place over approximately nine months and is revealed to the reader through three main sections, each occurring on a Monday in three distinct seasons. *The Day After Sunday* focuses upon the conception, gestation, birth, and "adoption" of the Wattses' illegitimate grandson. A thirty-five-year-old Christian spinster and boarder at the Wattses', Beulah Thomas, becomes pregnant when, in a moment of weakness, she receives the drunken seventeen-year-old Joe Bill Watts into her bed. David Watts, Joe Bill's father, is the only person who even remotely suspects Beulah's condition and its perpetrator, so life simply goes on in the Wattses' household until the baby's birth and Beulah's "adoption" of Mark Malcolm Thomas.

Summers's skill at configuring highly individualized points of view is evident when the story, told in the third person, nevertheless unfolds through the very distinct perspectives of five main characters: the points of view of David, Joe Bill, and Beulah are alternated with the consciousnesses of Maribeth Watts and her father, Daddy Joe Allendon. The perceptions of Maribeth and Daddy Joe create the regional and social frameworks within which the primary drama of the novel takes place. Both living in the genteel past symbolized by the "best house in Lexington" and increasingly vivid memories of Maribeth's mother, Muneen, the daughter and nearly deaf father literally and figuratively repress the complexities of the modern world and suppress the evidence of the basic human drives and needs which propel and consume Beulah, David, and Joe Bill.

Despite the sterile environment they inhabit, however, Joe Bill, Beulah, and David strive to create meaning for their lives. Rationalizing his impulsive sexual act with Beulah by remembering it as a dream, Joe Bill is struggling to understand his own sexual nature, is awkwardly seeking love and commitment, and desires some recognizable human, adult ties with his family. At the same time Maribeth treats him as a child, inadvertently humiliating him before family and friends, David is unable to communicate with him at all until the very end of the novel.

Though Beulah thinks she loves Joe Bill, her fundamentalist religiosity at first transforms the fact of her pregnancy into an immaculate conception. The strength she finally musters to deal with the reality, her refusal to share the knowledge of the child's parentage with Joe Bill or any of his family, and her determination to raise the child as her adopted son are all private and painful decisions which elevate her substantially above those who would condemn her. While Beulah and Joe Bill are effective characters, David's consciousness is at the spiritual heart of *The Day After Sunday*. Denied sexual intimacy by Maribeth, sleeping and drinking through a routine professional life as an accountant, denied respect by either son or father-in-law, David Watts is a striking modern antihero. The man feels despair at the spiritual impotence which characterizes his world and his life.

At the end of the novel, Beulah leaves to raise her son in her family's poor country home. Her departure precipitates a delicate confrontation between Joe Bill and David (who is gradually succumbing to alcoholism) as they share the knowledge of the child's parentage, creating between them, perhaps for the first time, an emotional bond.

While this moment of sharing is tenuous indeed, it offers promise of renewal, much as the Christmas story (whose words haunt David throughout and whose language is beautifully parodied by Summers in his description of Beulah's preparations for the adoption) often does in Summers's work. Summers uses the birth of a child, and the human commitments made as a result, to soften the effects of individual despair.

The Garden, published in 1972, seems initially to defy symbolic interpretations. However, the novel's central metaphor, the garden, transforms the simple story into a phantasmagorical experience. Like Summers's superb short story "How They Chose the Dead," *The Garden* places ordinary people who cannot cope successfully with anguish, inadequacy, and loss in a richly symbolic setting.

Spending their vacation in Malta, Tom and Caroline Hutton and Lewis, Tom's son by his first wife, Marie, seem to be enjoying their first extended time together away from Athens, Ohio. A sometimes frumpy organizer, Tom establishes their itinerary, finds a house, and generally directs activities. Caroline, another of Summers's female characters whose fundamental need appears to be satisfying her man, is learning to love the sweetly precocious Lewis, come to terms with marital intimacy, exorcise the ghost of Marie, and deal with her own recent miscarriage. Because the unfamiliar environment of Malta seems to free her from the mundane tasks of home which would normally obscure these complex emotional problems, the holiday provides her with insight.

Exploring the island with Lewis, Caroline discovers a park where she makes friends with a crass, aggressive, lusty but affectionate woman named Clar Tate and her children. Surprised that she is so deeply, almost obsessively, attracted to Clar, Caroline frequently returns to the park with Lewis and consciously chooses not to share this experience with Tom. Once Caroline is inside the park and reunited with Clar, who does not seem real to her, Caroline symbolically enters another world. The archetypal garden is a timeless, primordial natural place where Clar (Caroline's alter ego) encourages Caroline to share her experiences, anxieties, and deepest feelings.

Unwilling to tell Clar that she will be returning home shortly, Caroline visits the garden for the last time. Preternatural quiet envelops the two women and their children: no guard is there to admit them; the weather is perfect; the flowers "were lasting forever." Suddenly the idyllic scene becomes threatening: "One tricycle stood beside the green pond." Caroline rushes to the pond, unsure of which child she will find and, dragging Becky, Clar's young daughter (whose face was an old woman's), administers mouth to mouth resuscitation: "She kissed Becky. She opened her mouth and breathed. She lifted her head. She breathed. Lifted. Breathed. Out. In. Out. In. Out. . . . I have not loved enough, she thought, not knowing what she meant." Literally breathing life into the child, Caroline "walked away from Clar and the fetus." Casting out the subconscious guilt she feels over the miscarriage, Caroline simultaneously frees herself from the hidden need to destroy Tom's past and its issue: "She had not killed Lewis. . . . She had not killed anybody, any more than everybody killed everybody."

While Caroline undergoes her symbolic trial and purgation, Tom experiences his own. Refusing to be seduced by a sophisticated Englishwoman who cynically toys with his ingenuousness, Tom observes a Maltese funeral and a mourning young woman whose haunted face triggers in him discomfort and awareness: "He didn't think about dying, exactly, but he kept thinking the word *death*." Normally smug and self-satisfied, even Tom is forced in the unfamiliar surroundings of Malta to examine the more profound experiences of human existence. While Tom and Caroline do not explicitly share these experiences with each other, their relationship shows signs of deepening as they return to familiar surroundings.

While Summers's novels have each received

positive reviews (particularly *The Weather of February* and *The Day After Sunday*), no full-length studies of his fiction have yet been undertaken. While he has established a solid reputation as a poet, his failure to achieve broad recognition as a major novelist has not dampened his enthusiasm for fictional writing.

Summers has written one novel since *The Garden*. Not at all satisfied with the book, he plans to revise it dramatically sometime in the future. Never abandoning his understated, sparse, and muscular prose, Summers continues to hone what he calls his "de-dramatized" style. As his current project, "Family Sayings," is nearing completion, he tantalizes the prospective reader with the possibilities: "At the end the man says he would like for every book to end with a hallelujah chorus for King George . . . but he hangs onto what he has—the family things—sensitivity and love and annoyance and horror." These are perhaps the very things for which we will ultimately remember Hollis Summers.

—*Carol C. Harter*

Other:

Kentucky Story, A Collection of Short Stories, edited by Summers (Lexington: University of Kentucky Press, 1954);

Literature: An Introduction, edited by Summers and Edgar Whan (New York: McGraw-Hill, 1960);

Discussions of the Short Story, edited by Summers (Boston: Heath, 1963).

Periodical Publications:

POETRY:

"The Flicker," *Beloit Poetry Journal*, 5 (Spring 1955): 117;

"Committee Meeting," *Sewanee Review*, 64 (Autumn 1956): 606;

"Mexico Picnic, October 31," *Saturday Review*, 40 (12 January 1957): 54;

"Lexington, Kentucky," *American Weave*, 100 (Spring 1961): 4-6;

"Seven Occasions for Song," *Hudson Review*, 15 (Spring 1962): 86-87;

"Title: To Be Supplied," *Western Humanities Review*, 17 (Winter 1963): 64;

"Waiting Bench with Figure," *Midwest Quarterly*, 7 (Autumn 1964): 96;

"The Gift," *New Mexico Quarterly*, 25 (Summer 1965): 137;

"Snapshots of the Four Grandchildren," *Atlantic*, 217 (May 1966): 113;

"Mercy," *English Record*, 19 (February 1969): 28;

"Grace Before Calling the Nursing Home and the Jail," *Southern Poetry Review*, 16 (1977): 83.

FICTION:

"Mister Joseph Potts," *Paris Review*, 8 (Spring 1955): 107-121;

"The Prayer Meeting," *Sewanee Review*, 64 (Winter 1956): 110-122;

"Cafe Nore," *Epoch*, 8 (Fall 1957): 153-166;

"If You Don't Go Out the Way You Came In," *Colorado Quarterly*, 9 (Summer 1960): 69-83;

"The Third Ocean," *Hudson Review*, 22 (Summer 1969): 232-252.

NONFICTION:

"Rejections and Acceptances from Editors and Other Readers: Jesse Stuart's 'Dawn of a Remembered Spring' Remembered," *Focus: Teaching English Language Arts*, 3 (Spring 1977): 1-5.

Papers:

Various holographs, typescripts, and galley proofs, as well as miscellaneous papers, are collected at the State University of Iowa, the University of Kentucky, and Ohio University.

ANNE TYLER

(25 October 1941-)

BOOKS: *If Morning Ever Comes* (New York: Knopf, 1964; London: Chatto & Windus, 1965);

The Tin Can Tree (New York: Knopf, 1965; London: Macmillan, 1966);

A Slipping-Down Life (New York: Knopf, 1970);

The Clock Winder (New York: Knopf, 1972; London: Chatto & Windus, 1973);

Celestial Navigation (New York: Knopf, 1974; London: Chatto & Windus, 1975);

Searching for Caleb (New York: Knopf, 1976; London: Chatto & Windus, 1976);

Earthly Possessions (New York: Knopf, 1977; London: Chatto & Windus, 1977);

Morgan's Passing (New York: Knopf, 1980).

Anne Tyler has been steadily gaining well-deserved critical and popular attention for the eight novels and numerous short stories she has produced over the past seventeen years. Her work is as remarkable for its originality of plot as for its ingeniously conceived characters and polished prose. Tyler has not yet been the subject of close academic analysis, but there is widespread appreciation of her talent and recognition of her importance in contemporary literature.

Tyler was born in Minneapolis, Minnesota, on 25 October 1941 to Lloyd Parry Tyler, a chemist, and Phyllis Mahon Tyler. She has spent most of her life in the South, particularly in North Carolina and Maryland, which also provide the settings for her novels. Until age eleven she was raised in a series of communes, an experience which she believes made her look "at the normal world with a certain amount of distance and surprise, which can sometimes be helpful to a writer." Yet Tyler states that in her works "there is nothing at all autobiographical, since the purpose of my writing (for me) is to live lives other than my own."

After receiving a B.A. from Duke University in 1961, Tyler attended Columbia University for a year continuing her studies in Russian. She returned to Duke, where she worked in the library as the Russian bibliographer from 1962 to 1963, then moved to Montreal where she was assistant to the librarian at McGill University from 1964 to 1965. She married Taghi Modarressi, a psychiatrist, on 3 May 1963, and in 1965 they had a daughter, Tezh. Another daughter, Mitra, was born in 1967.

Tyler, who says that she never actually intended to become a writer, would have liked to be an artist and still entertains the fantasy that she might become a book illustrator. Her attention to graphic detail is evident in her careful descriptions, which may gain some lucidity from her habit of doodling portraits of her intended characters before she starts writing. Tyler's skill in presenting the visual might also be a reflection of her admiration for the work of Eudora Welty, who influenced especially her early writings.

Tyler began her writing career with a deluge of short stories of which only one or two were published and "a novel which was turned down everywhere." Reynolds Price recognized Tyler's promising talents and, while she was still a senior at Duke, referred her to his agent, Diarmuid Russell.

Overall, Tyler has lived a rather quiet life, almost as uneventful in the dramatic sense as the lives of some of her characters. In response to the question of how her life developed as her writing developed, she replied, "maybe what's most significant is that it *didn't* develop much at least in any visible way to the naked eye. I often feel that my imagination is freest when I am most confined; also that suddenly having to stay put, having to deal with the discouragements and rewards of family life without any means of escape, has somehow made my inner world richer and deeper."

The humor that characterizes Tyler's work is achieved primarily through understatement and irony. Her characters are eccentrics who stop just short of being the usual southern grotesques but who nonetheless evoke the reader's sympathy. Pathos always follows closely on the heels of her comedy as she combines dramatic tension and wit so that serious situations often become funny because unexpected details emerge to alleviate the dramatic strain. Tyler's major theme is the obstinate endurance of the human spirit, reflected in every character's acceptance or rejection of his fate and in how that attitude affects his day-to-day life. She uses the family unit as a vehicle for portraying "how people manage to endure together—how they grate against each other, adjust, intrude and protect themselves from intrusions, give up, and start all over again in the morning." Her characters react to the inevitable births, marriages, illnesses, and deaths of family members, and in every novel, at least one character succumbs to the urge to escape from the strains of family ties, but in almost every instance the running away proves to be only a temporary and ineffectual means of dealing with reality.

If Morning Ever Comes (1964), which she now disowns, was written during the first six months of her marriage when she was unemployed and "had nothing else to do," she says. It is a straightforward narrative centering on the Hawkes family, particularly on Ben Joe, the only male in a family of six women, who feels responsible for the family's well-being now that his father is dead. His familial position dominates every aspect of Ben Joe's life; he even chose to go to law school, not because he liked law, but because it was practical "and practicality was a good thing when you headed up a family of six women." The novel covers only about a week's time during which Ben Joe leaves Columbia Law School in order to go home to North Carolina to solve a minor family crisis and comes to grips with his false sense of responsibility to his family. He has had a long and turbulent adjustment period in trying to understand his father's behavior, especially his actions in a bizarre, public extramarital affair. Yet his biggest problem is admitting that he is just as dispensible to his family as his father was. Near the end of his visit home, he finally begins to think honestly about his family relationships and how even as he would be heading back to New York, this "unchanging world of women" would continue to "exist solid and untouched no matter where he was."

The characters in *If Morning Ever Comes* are for the most part developed only superficially. All of the girls except Ben Joe's sister Joanne, who has precipitated most of the novel's action by running away from her husband, are nearly indistinguishable, and Joanne's reasons for leaving her husband are too inadequately explored to allow the reader to sympathize with her. Rather, when her husband does arrive to retrieve her and their daughter, he is so likable that the reader feels that Joanne's action was entirely unjustified.

In *If Morning Ever Comes* Tyler employs a layering technique in which an accumulation of rich detail from the past merges with the present to explain it. All of her characters have strong nostalgic urges to re-create the past so that the "flat and impersonal" present may be ignored. The novel received enthusiastic reviews, but Tyler herself now expresses a strong dislike for it. What impressed most reviewers was the fact that the author was only twenty-two years old and yet had such a mature command of the novel form. Negative remarks concerned the slowness of the plot and the lack of meaningful character development.

Tyler's second novel was, like her first, the result of a desire to keep busy rather than from "any pressing need to tell the stories." *The Tin Can Tree* describes the reactions of relatives and friends to the death of Janie Rose Pike, a six-year-old child who was killed in a tractor accident. The novel begins as Janie Rose's funeral concludes and focuses immediately upon her only brother Simon, who must not only confront his own grief and shock but must also suffer because of his mother's inability to cope with Janie Rose's death. Throughout the novel Mrs. Pike's total immersion in her grief is the constant concern of all the other characters. While Simon voices some typically childlike ideas about the nature of death, he also shows a more mature understanding and acceptance of death than his mother does. Throughout the novel, Simon endures an existence in which he is almost completely ignored by both of his parents, especially by his mother. Finally he runs away, and his parents are brought back to the reality that they must go on with their lives and resume their relationship with Simon.

Most of the action of *The Tin Can Tree* revolves around the Pike family, which also includes Joan, a quiet niece who takes care of the domestic chores and who becomes the major impetus in getting the family back together. She is engaged to James Green, a photographer and part-time tobacco worker who, with his brother Ansel, lives in another part of the same three-family dwelling as the Pikes. Ansel, a full-time hypochondriac who thoroughly enjoys his invalid role but occasionally musters the strength to go out and get drunk, serves as a choruslike character who constantly keeps Janie Rose's death in the forefront of everyone's thoughts.

In the course of the novel, Joan painfully realizes that Ansel will always be an impediment to James's marrying, and she finally decides to return to her hometown to avoid the long engagement that would finally become the "town's fondest joke." She tries to leave quietly, but Simon, the most dependent on Joan, overhears her plans, and after failing to convince her to stay, he runs away on the same afternoon. James guesses correctly that Simon, intrigued by Ansel's romantic memories of his own boyhood, has gone to their father's home in nearby Caraway, and he retrieves Simon from his family. Meanwhile Joan changes her mind in the middle of her bus trip home and returns to the Pikes where she finds everyone celebrating Simon's being found. Her departure has gone entirely unnoticed except by Ansel, who shrewdly tells Joan that he saw her leaving but did not tell anyone, meaning of course that her absense was of no importance.

The Tin Can Tree is another novel that Tyler does not care to claim. The work did not receive widespread critical attention and was criticized for a lack of development. *The Tin Can Tree* moves slowly as Tyler painstakingly presents details which make each character's movements appear to be documentaries in slow motion. Such a method is appropriate, given the plot: the characters are more or less waiting for time to mitigate Mrs. Pike's unabated sorrow, and they are unsure of how to hasten that end.

By the time she was working on her third novel, *A Slipping-Down Life* (1970), Tyler's personal life had altered dramatically as she was "tied down by two infants, trying to work in snatched moments at night." The novel tells the story of a young high-school girl who carves the name of a local, third-rate rock singer onto her forehead with fingernail scissors. Evie Decker seems initially to be a sensible, drab, overweight girl bored with the loneliness of her life. Yet she is propelled into her dramatic action by nothing more than her desire to gain the attention of Drumstrings Casey, a semiliterate guitar player in a two-man band.

Tyler gives the reader little preparation for Evie's self-defacement, which occurs early in the novel. Evie is a rather passive girl, who has lived a thoroughly eventless life with her father, a gentle,

CELESTIAL NAVIGATION

1960: Amanda 

My brother Jeremy is a thirty-eight year old bachelor who never did leave home. Long ago we gave up expecting very much of him, but still he is the last man in our family and you would think that in time of tragedy he might pull himself together and take over a few of the responsibilities. Well, he didn't. He telephoned my sister and me in Richmond, where we have a little apartment together. If memory serves me it was the first time in his life he had ever placed a call to us; can you imagine? Ordinarily we phoned Mother every Sunday evening when the rates were down and then she would put Jeremy on the line to say hello. Which was about all he did say: "Hello," and "Fine, thank you," and then a long breathing pause and, "Well, goodbye now." So when I heard his voice that night I had trouble placing it for a moment. "Amanda?" he said, and I said, "Yes? Who is it?"

"I wanted to tell you about Mama," Jeremy said.

That's what he calls her still: Mama. Laura and I switched to Mother when we were grown but Jeremy didn't.

Celestial Navigation, *manuscript*

quiet, high-school math teacher generally underestimated by Evie and her best friend, Violet. Even surprised herself after she has mutilated her forehead, Evie boasts that her action was spur of the moment, saying, " 'Why not?' I thought, and did it... Impulse was the clue." She is unable to explain her actions to her father, the doctor, or the newspaper man. But to Violet she says, "I believe this is the best thing I've ever done . . . something out of character. Definite." Ironically, because she was looking in a mirror and did not stop to think how mirrors reverse images, she has carved Casey's name backwards. Evie recognizes her passive personality, but while she wants to change it she does not know how. She is proud of "Taking something in my own hands for once . . . if I had started acting like this a long time ago my whole life might've been different." Later, acting without thinking about the consequences becomes a way of life for Evie. She accepts Casey's casual, almost indifferent proposal of marriage immediately, saying "Oh, why not." Her cutting her forehead is a superficial manifestation of her frustration with her empty life. It is a surface wound, finally, and one which can be covered up by a change of hairstyle or removed by plastic surgery. Evie's main concern is with her classmates' reaction to the cutting, and she is disappointed to find that they accept it with little more than curiosity. Later her self-sacrifice becomes even more meaningless as she admits that she no longer notices the letters now when looking in the mirror.

Casey is just as frustrated as Evie, but he expresses it in a different manner. His lack of direction even shows up in his songs. At age nineteen he already detects the deterioration of his own life and his lack of control over it. Evie has thought Casey's talent would make him famous, but even in their small town he is unable to make any progress in his career.

Throughout the novel Evie is confused by people and constantly misjudges them. Until the conclusion of the novel, after she has returned home from making arrangements for her father's funeral and found Casey in bed with her friend Fay-Jean, it is as though she sees people and situations backwards, like the letters on her forehead. Pregnant, she returns to live in her father's house alone, with no more control over her life than before. The inconclusive ending of the novel further underscores the passivity and shallowness of Evie's and Casey's lives. After their experiences, they remain virtually unchanged; and both return to where they were at the beginning of the novel: Casey playing nights at the Unicorn roadhouse and Evie sitting alone in her father's house, now waiting for her baby's birth.

A Slipping-Down Life received only a modest number of reviews, probably because the book was classified as a novel for young adults. Yet the novel is an accurate depiction of loneliness, failure to communicate, and regrets over decisions that are irreversible—problems with which any age group can identify. Tyler, who describes *A Slipping-Down Life* as one of her most bizarre works, believes that the novel "is flawed, but represents, for me, a certain brave stepping forth."

The Clock Winder (1972), a novel that Tyler now bluntly dismisses as boring, also deals with the problems of growing up, presented through the eyes of Elizabeth Abbot who fears that "life might be a triangle, with adulthood at its apex; or worse yet, a cycle of seasons, with childhood recurring over and over like that cold rainy period in February." She drifts into becoming a live-in handyman for the recently widowed Mrs. Emerson, a helpless woman looking for someone to take care of her and her possessions.

Two of Mrs. Emerson's seven grown children, Matthew and Timothy, decide after a short acquaintance with Elizabeth that they love her. Elizabeth seems to have a preference for Matthew, and when Timothy tries to persuade Elizabeth to go on a trip with him, he finds that he has no control over her and shoots himself as she tries to wrest a gun away from him. Elizabeth blames herself for Timothy's death and decides to return to her parents' home in North Carolina.

While there, she receives numerous letters from the Emersons, especially from Matthew, who claims he still loves her and wants to marry her. Elizabeth, however, is unable to come to grips with her guilt and tries to ignore the letters from the Emersons and to gain a new control over her life. Her father, a Baptist preacher, encourages Elizabeth to take a job as companion to an old bedridden man whom Elizabeth comes to love and whose influence helps her to mature. However, upon learning that Mrs. Emerson has had a serious stroke and wants her to take care of her, Elizabeth is finally persuaded to go to Mrs. Emerson on a temporary basis. Suddenly, more time has passed and Elizabeth and Matthew are married and living with their two children, Mrs. Emerson, and Timothy's twin brother, Andrew.

In *The Clock Winder* Tyler establishes a dominant image at the outset and sustains it throughout the novel. The idea of hiring a clock winder comes to Mrs. Emerson initially as she confronts her dead husband's collection of clocks whose ticking and striking seem to be so carefully synchronized. Mrs. Emerson wishes to establish a continuity between the past and the present by keeping her husband's clocks running in perfect order, but because she has always been pampered and protected, she has become so passive that the simple task of rewinding the clocks bewilders her. The concept of the clock winder, or systematic source of energy, becomes embodied in Elizabeth with her ability to fix things and people in both the physical and spiritual sense. Lives constantly wind down and then gain new momentum from Elizabeth's influence.

Tyler explores the complexities of family relationships in two very different families in *The Clock Winder.* Obvious contrasts exist in the socio-economic levels of the wealthy Emersons and the Abbots, but it is clear that beneath these trappings the families are almost identical in their basic relationships involving sibling rivalries and parent-child conflicts. Elizabeth forms the bridge between the two families, although she is compelled to run away temporarily from both in order to establish an independence necessary for complete maturity.

Critics responded favorably to Tyler's fourth novel. The fiction itself is credible, the characters are more fully developed, and the pace fast-moving in comparison to the earlier works. In order to propel the action, Tyler established a strong central character whose independence and sensitivity are appealing. Following the vicissitudes of Elizabeth's life, the reader shares her tensions and conflicts, which only time can resolve. Overall, the novel is successful.

As Tyler began her most difficult novel, *Celestial Navigation* (1974), she was "fighting the urge to remain in retreat even though the children had started school." The main character of the novel, Jeremy, is the only character in any of her novels with whom Tyler strongly identifies, "particularly with his dread of making telephone calls." But more important, she believes that creating Jeremy was a way of investigating her own "tendency to turn more and more inward." Jeremy Paulding is an artist who specializes in making collages from fragments and scraps lifted from other people's lives. His observations and memories of people are based on colors and textures like the bits and pieces of his art, which together form teeming miniatures that depict the disorder and passivity of the various stages of his life.

Jeremy is the focus of the narration from the beginning when his older sister Amanda takes the occasion of their mother's funeral to describe Jeremy and his many inadequacies. On her way home from the funeral, Amanda thinks of her mother, Jeremy, and their deteriorating boardinghouse as reflections of each other and of a deeper moral disorder. She sees only stagnation in her mother's and Jeremy's meaningless lives. Amanda, who disappears from the novel after the first chapter, introduces her family members and boarders with succinct and pointed descriptions that reveal her disdain for anything and anybody weak and vulnerable to time and emotions. The rest of the novel, which spans approximately thirteen years, shows how everyone copes with that universal vulnerability.

Jeremy is completely disoriented. Flashbacks reveal that he had never in his life showed an awareness of time; he had always been protected by a succession of sympathetic women, starting with his mother, sisters, then his wife, and finally one of the boarders. Tyler uses sea imagery subtly throughout the novel as a metaphor for the timelessness that engulfs Jeremy. Sitting in the dark television room with the other boarders, he is "conscious of particles of dark floating between people, some deep substance in which they all swam, intent upon keeping their heads free, their chins straining upward." Suffering from acute agoraphobia, he sees his house as an island of refuge, and another character thinks about the way Jeremy gets through his uncertain life guided only by celestial nagivation. When at the end of the novel Jeremy finally overcomes his fear, leaving the house to find his wife and six children, who have abandoned him, it is a journey that takes him to a real island where he experiences a sea change. After a lifetime of incompetence and impracticality, Jeremy gathers the strength to take control of his life, but the reward for his success is that he loses his wife and children. As he rows away from them as they stand on the shore, he "pretended they were gone. For him they were gone."

Mary enters Jeremy's life as a boarder—who has just left a note on the refrigerator door for her husband, saying that she and her baby were leaving. Mary's honest description of herself is based on her simple precept: "Motherhood is what I was made for, and pregnancy is my natural state." Ten years and five children after that statement, Mary remains true to her convictions saying that "all events, except childbirth, can be reduced to a heap of trivia in the end." Mary's salient characteristic is self-sufficiency. Her ability to take control of situations and of other people's lives allows her the freedom to walk away from people when they no longer suit her. Later as she reflects on her actions she realizes that while she had been trying to avoid leading a "single narrow life" like her parents', her life is still a predictable pattern "involving elopements and love children, and men stretching in a nearly unbroken series."

Celestial Navigation deals essentially with two character extremes: Jeremy, totally dependent on any woman who will take care of him, and Mary, independent and self-sufficient to such an extent that she dwarfs the men who try to contain her. After years of interaction each is changed slightly by the influence of the other. Yet despite their experiences together, in the end each returns to his separate life, each still dominated by his innate driving characteristic. Jeremy returns to his life as a reclusive artist in a crumbling dark house while Mary prepares for winter in a run-down shack, knowing that another man will eventually provide for her and her children when her resources run out.

Tyler effectively develops her characters through flashbacks and through revelations of their day-dreams and fantasies. The flashbacks permit the reader to understand how past events shape the thinking and reactions of the various characters. On the other hand, the fantasies serve a dual purpose in showing repeatedly the contrast between what people's perceptions lead them to predict and what actually happens in reality where the variables are entirely unpredictable. For instance, Jeremy's favorite fantasy is to act on impulse, to drive forever, and perhaps to settle down in a "small, bare, whitewashed cubicle possibly in a desert"; he would be completely alone, his art would be altogether different. The reality is that his wife and children leave him suddenly, and he reacts by retreating into the silent dustiness of his cluttered studio and continuing his art while a surrogate mother brings him cocoa and takes care of him in his decline.

Tyler says that she is "very, very fond of *Celestial Navigation,* although it was hardest to write"; and critical opinion concurs that this is Tyler's best novel. The overall superiority is a result of the right combination of plot and character development supplemented with a rich accretion of meaningful detail. Tyler has created a series of intricate past lives and present fantasies that allow the reader insight into the characters' personalities. Jeremy's very nature sets him at the center of a universe which is composed almost entirely of the women who must constantly take care of him. Consequently there is an overall feminine quality to the shifting points of view. The novel is progressively embellished with the repetition of the same incidents presented from different characters' points of view, thus continually forcing the reader to reevaluate opinions and ultimately to define for himself the reality of this richly complicated novel.

Tyler recalls that *Searching for Caleb* (1976) "was the most pure fun to write" and kept her "happy for the duration." Daniel Peck, the grandfather in the novel, is similar in some aspects to Tyler's Grandfather Tyler, and Tyler bestowed upon Daniel Peck a full set of perfect teeth as a gift to her grand-father "since in real life he had suffered the loss of most of his teeth and complained continually about having to live on applesauce." The novel explores the complexities of the large, clannish Peck family of Baltimore. Since 1912, when his half-brother Caleb disappeared from their Roland Park home, Daniel, who was partly responsible for his leaving, has been looking for him. His granddaughter Justine accompanies Daniel on all of his searching expeditions, but other family members believe Caleb to be dead and speak of him only as a legend. The dominating feature of the Peck family is their desire to exclude from their lives anything foreign to their established traditions. It was Caleb's shocking announcement to his father that he wanted to be a musician instead of taking over the lucrative family shipping business that precipitated his father's stroke and ultimately caused his death. Unorthodox decisions historically throw the family into turmoil: Justine's marriage to her unconventional first cousin Duncan causes a family feud that results in her father's having a fatal stroke and her mother's subsequently committing suicide.

Despite all the pressures to conform to the family's expectations, there is a history of family members running away. Subtle similarities between Duncan and Caleb appear throughout the novel; as Justine searches for Caleb in a physical sense, she is simultaneously searching for Duncan in a meta-phorical sense. Both Caleb and Duncan are at odds with their family traditions and are unable to cope with the situation except by running away. Yet neither abandons the Pecks completely. Both leave clues when they leave the family, but no one finds Caleb's clue. Duncan is obsessed with love of mechanical gadgets in the same way that Caleb is obsessed with anything musical, but neither seems to be capable of using his talents to achieve success.

Justine and Duncan's married life contrasts sharply with their upbringing. Tyler's use of details effectively emphasizes the discrepancy between their youths spent in comfortable homes furnished with fine antiques and their married life together in dilapidated low-rent dwellings equipped with free mugs from the gas station, plastic picnic forks, and homemade yellow pine beds. Justine makes instant coffee and stirs it with a screwdriver. Their daughter, Meg, values everything that they have sought to leave behind. They want rootless freedom and she wants security and continuity. Meg clearly is a true Peck who is tormented and embarrassed by her parents' unorthodox life-style. She is forced into eloping because Duncan refuses to cooperate with her plans to marry a very conventional young man, saying essentially the same things Justine's father had said to her about her choice for a husband. Duncan's negative response to Meg and her fiance reveals that he has become as narrow-minded as the Pecks he ran away from.

Caleb appears late in the novel after a professional detective finds him in a county old age home in Louisiana, still holding on to his musical dreams, but with little success. Daniel dies shortly after finding out that Caleb is in the home and is never reunited with his brother. Consequently, Caleb goes to live with Justine and Duncan, but after a short visit with them, he runs away again leaving only a brief, conventional thank-you note, written as all the Peck children were taught to write them, suggesting that certain family traits and habits are too thoroughly ingrained ever to be erased. At the end of the novel, Duncan is also running away again, to try yet another job, this time as a mechanic for a traveling circus.

Critical attention to *Searching for Caleb* revealed a decided growth in appreciation for Tyler's work. Her sixth novel was widely reviewed and accepted as another indication that she was becoming an increasingly skillful novelist. *Searching for Caleb* received praise for the artistic handling of its plot as well as for the wide range of believable characters. In this novel Tyler masterfully displays her inventive abilities with the narrative line as well as her considerable skill in investing even satellite characters with a positive sense of reality and endowing them all with interesting individual stories succinctly told and interwoven with each other. *Searching for Caleb* is a compelling depiction of the Peck family from its promising beginning four generations back through to its ultimate, disappointing demise as a unified group.

Tyler says of *Earthly Possessions* (1977), which she believes is often misunderstood, that it strikes her now "as the work of somebody entering middle age, beginning to notice how the bags and baggage of the past are weighing her down, and how much she values them." The novel represents a structural departure from Tyler's earlier novels. It is narrated entirely in the first person by Charlotte Emory, who in the first chapter becomes a hostage in an amateurish bank robbery. After setting up the hopelessness of the situation, Tyler allots every other chapter to Charlotte's flashbacks, which demonstrate that her actions as a hostage are completely in keeping with her past behavior. As Charlotte looks back on the events that have formed her, both she and the reader gain an understanding of her life and its meaning. In the conclusion, Charlotte is still the same person, but she has made the adjustments necessary for coping with her existence.

The plot may be summarized in a few words: a woman who is planning to leave her husband is kidnapped in a small-town bank robbery and remains the robber's hostage through their flight from Maryland to Florida, where she finally walks away from the robber as he threatens to shoot her. The complications of the novel are achieved in Charlotte's flashbacks, which are arranged chronologically, starting with her birth and taking her through school, marriage, and motherhood, with stops in between for a brief affair with her brother-in-law, and the sicknesses and deaths of her father and mother. The kidnapping allows Charlotte the distance to look at her life objectively and to make judgments about her situation and her relationship with her family.

Charlotte's birth was an anticlimactic affair, since her mother never even realized that she was pregnant, thinking instead that she was suffering from an ever increasing tumor. During her childhood Charlotte suffers constant embarrassment because of her parents' eccentricities, and she is firmly convinced that she is not the true daughter of her middle-aged parents, but instead someone else's child mistakenly identified due to a mix-up at the hospital. She is also obsessed with the fear that she is hopelessly trapped, stating her two main childhood worries as, "One, that I was not their true daughter, and would be sent away. The other was that I *was* their true daughter and would never, ever manage to escape to the outside world." Charlotte's desire to escape from her captors in the present repeats the need for freedom she has experienced in the past. Charlotte's captors also fear entrapment. Jake has taken his girl friend Mindy out of a Florida home for unwed mothers because she does not want to have her baby in a prison. Their controlled but nearly claustrophobic fears add tension to the novel. The urge to escape manifests itself even in the peripheral character, Alberta, Charlotte's much-admired neighbor who elopes with her own father-in-law.

Passivity, Charlotte's salient characteristic, is a major theme in the novel. Psychologically, she is a perfect hostage; she remembers that "As a child I nearly drowned once, sinking in a panic beneath the lifeguard's eyes with my lips clamped tightly together. I would rather die than make any sort of disturbance." Her voluntary and automatic acceptance of whatever occurs becomes the reaction the other characters and the reader expect from her. Charlotte establishes her pattern of passivity early in her life, remains true to that pattern throughout her youth, through her marriage, and through the casual adoption of an abandoned child, right until the point at which she walks away from her armed captor.

Earthly Possessions was widely reviewed, and received some negative critical responses, although most critics conceded that there are exceptional episodes in the novel. Tyler herself believes that the novel is generally misunderstood to be "another Unhappy Housewife Leaves Home book, which was the last thought in my mind."

Tyler describes her recently completed eighth novel, *Morgan's Passing* (1980), as one that "deals with a situation I've been fascinated by for most of my life, and one which probably is not unrelated to being a writer: the inveterate imposter, who is unable to stop himself from stepping into other people's worlds." The main character, Morgan Gower, is a fraud from the beginning of the novel (when he pretends to be a doctor and ends up delivering a baby in the back seat of his car) until the end of the novel (when his wife publishes his premature obituary in the newspaper).

A character reverse of Jeremy Paulding, the agoraphobic artist in *Celestial Navigation*, Morgan is an expansive individual who needs to be, as his wife says, "more narrowed in." He cannot contain himself; he spills over and becomes, with the aid of costuming, other characters such as a street priest, a French immigrant, a doctor, an artist, and innumerable others. He observes that the more outrageous the lies he produces are, the more people tend to believe him. He even fools himself most of the time. Morgan becomes entangled with Emily and Leon Meredith, the puppeteers whose baby he delivers, and gradually yearns to take Leon's place. He finally accomplishes this, even to the extent of taking Leon's name and job, abandoning his own household full of children, grandchildren, a wife, a senile mother, and an unbalanced sister.

Morgan can easily be criticized for his self-centered attitudes; several characters including Bonny, his wife, and Emily who eventually marries him, can recite litanies of his faults. Yet he can also elicit sympathy when he displays his vulnerability to the real world and to the few people who know his true place in it as a middle-aged, paunchy, hardware store operator. In *Morgan's Passing*, as in all of Tyler's novels, there are characters who attempt to cope with their problems by running away.

Emily and Leon's puppet shows attract Morgan into their world in the beginning of the novel, and the variations on the puppet fantasy are integrated skillfully into the real lives of the characters. As Leon and Emily's marriage slowly disintegrates, the puppet shows reflect their unhappy situation until finally the puppet shows become unsynchronized and fragmented like their own lives. The fairy tales of the puppet shows are an integral part of *Morgan's Passing*, forming a vital continuity of theme, imagery, and character development. More subtle, however, is the manner in which Tyler incorporates the concept of Emily and Leon as manipulators of their real and imaginary universes so that their lives do have a fairy tale quality.

Critical response to *Morgan's Passing* has been favorable, though some critics have expressed reservations about Morgan's almost meaningless existence. But this is in itself a theme, almost a trademark of Tyler's fiction, which glorifies the ordinary man who accomplishes something if he only manages to cope with his frustrating circumstances.

Tyler's work has evolved from the simple story-telling of the early novels into the carefully crafted, eloquent novels of her later career. The increased sophistication of her work, although gradual, becomes noticeable with the intricate design of *Celestial Navigation*, which marks a turning point in her stylistic maturity. Much of the strength of Tyler's prose comes from the refinement of her narrative technique and the reiteration of the common themes that merge finally into a solid coherence of vision. Morals, abstractions, and value judgments are almost nonexistent in Tyler's works, which only focus on the particulars of a time and place. Tyler's accomplishments have earned her the respect and admiration of the popular audience as well as of the critics. That her international literary reputation is growing is evidenced by recent translations into Swedish, German, and French. The potential shown in Tyler's early novels has been fulfilled in her later works where the development is both apparent and satisfying.

—*Mary Ellen Brooks*

Periodical Publications:

"Dry Waters," *Southern Review*, new series,1 (April 1965): 259-291;

"I'm Not Going to Ask You Again," *Harper's*, 231 (September 1965): 88-98;

"The Saints in Caesar's Household," *Archive*, 79 (September 1966): 18-21;

"As the Earth Gets Old," *New Yorker*, 42 (29 October 1966): 60-64;

"Two People and a Clock on the Wall," *New Yorker*, 42 (19 November 1966): 207-208, 210, 212, 214, 217;

"The Genuine Fur Eyelashes," *Mademoiselle*, 69 (January 1967): 102-103, 136-138;

"The Tea-Machine," *Southern Review*, new series,3 (January 1967): 171-179;

"The Feather Behind the Rock," *New Yorker*, 43 (12 August 1967): 26-30;

"Who Would Want a Little Boy?" *Ladies Home Journal*, 85 (May 1968): 132-133, 156-158;

"The Common Courtesies," *McCall's*, 95 (June 1968): 62-63, 115-116;

"A Knack for Languages," *New Yorker*, 50 (13 January 1975): 32-37;

"The Geologist's Maid," *New Yorker*, 51 (28 July 1975): 29-33;

"Your Place Is Empty," *New Yorker*, 52 (22 November 1976): 45-54;

"Holding Things Together," *New Yorker*, 52 (24 January 1977): 30-35;

"Average Waves in Unprotected Waters," *New Yorker*, 53 (28 February 1977): 32-36.

GORE VIDAL

(3 October 1925-)

BOOKS: *Williwaw* (New York: Dutton, 1946; London: Panther, 1965);

In a Yellow Wood (New York: Dutton, 1947; London: New English Library, 1967);

The City and the Pillar (New York: Dutton, 1948; London: Lehmann, 1949; revised and enlarged edition, New York: Dutton, 1965; London: Heinemann, 1965);

The Season of Comfort (New York: Dutton, 1949);

A Search for the King (New York: Dutton, 1950; London: New English Library, 1967);

Dark Green, Bright Red (New York: Dutton, 1950; London: Lehmann, 1950; revised edition, New York: Signet / New American Library, 1968; London: New English Library, 1968);

Death in the Fifth Position, as Edgar Box (New York: Dutton, 1952; London: Heinemann, 1954);

The Judgment of Paris (New York: Dutton, 1952; London: Heinemann, 1953; revised and abridged edition, New York: Ballantine, 1961; revised edition, Boston & Toronto: Little, Brown, 1965; London: Heinemann, 1966);

Death Before Bedtime . . ., as Edgar Box (New York: Dutton, 1953; London: Heinemann, 1954);

Death Likes It Hot, as Edgar Box (New York: Dutton, 1954; London: Heinemann, 1955);

Messiah (New York: Dutton, 1954; London: Heinemann, 1955; revised edition, Boston & Toronto: Little, Brown, 1965; London: Heinemann, 1968);

A Thirsty Evil: Seven Short Stories (New York: Zero Press, 1956; London: Heinemann, 1958; enlarged edition, London: New English Library, 1967);

Visit to a Small Planet and Other Television Plays (Boston & Toronto: Little, Brown, 1956);

Visit to a Small Planet: A Comedy Akin to a Vaudeville (Boston & Toronto: Little, Brown, 1957);

The Best Man: A Play about Politics (Boston & Toronto: Little, Brown, 1960);

Three Plays (London, Melbourne & Toronto: Heinemann, 1962);

Rocking the Boat (Boston & Toronto: Little, Brown, 1962; London: Heinemann, 1963);

Romulus, adapted from a play by Friedrich Duerrenmatt (New York: Dramatists Play Service, 1962; New York: Grove, 1966);

Julian (Boston & Toronto: Little, Brown, 1964; London: Heinemann, 1964);

Washington, D.C. (Boston & Toronto: Little, Brown, 1967; London: Heinemann, 1967);

Myra Breckinridge (Boston & Toronto: Little, Brown, 1968; bowdlerized edition, London: Blond, 1968);

Sex, Death and Money (Toronto, New York & London: Bantam, 1968);

Weekend (New York: Dramatists Play Service, 1968);

Reflections Upon a Sinking Ship (Boston & Toronto: Little, Brown, 1969; London: Heinemann, 1969);

Two Sisters: A Memoir in the Form of a Novel (Boston & Toronto: Little, Brown, 1970);

An Evening with Richard Nixon (New York: Random House, 1972);

Homage to Daniel Shays: Collected Essays, 1952-1972 (New York: Random House, 1972); republished as *Collected Essays, 1952-1972* (London: Heinemann, 1974); republished as *On Our Own Now* (St. Albans, U.K.: Panther, 1976);

Burr (New York: Random House, 1973; London: Heinemann, 1974);

Myron (New York: Random House, 1974; London: Heinemann, 1975);

1876 (New York: Random House, 1976; London:

Heinemann, 1976);
Matters of Fact and of Fiction: Essays 1973-1976 (New York: Random House, 1977);
Kalki (New York: Random House, 1978; London: Heinemann, 1978).

Eugene Luther Vidal was born in West Point, New York, where his father was an army instructor of aeronautics. He later took the name, Gore, from his mother, Nina Gore. As a prolific novelist, Vidal is famous for his controversial (some might say bizarre) subjects and his historical novels. But Vidal's versatility extends beyond the world of the novel, as he has also achieved fame as playwright, critic, essayist, mystery writer, screenwriter, and almost, politician. Despite his many abilities Vidal may be best known as a successful, flamboyant, and eccentric talk-show guest who exhibits an irrepressible urge to debate. Vidal *has* managed to endure, both as "public figure" and "artist"; an examination of his life and works will indicate that his artistic achievements and commercial successes are compatible, for he has shown from the beginning of his career an insight into contemporary themes and an ability to construct novels in effective ways.

During his childhood there were periods of sadness, but at the same time there was the exhilaration of an active young mind maturing near an exciting cultural center, Washington, D.C. His father, a successful businessman, was divorced from his mother in 1935. As a result of the discord between his parents, Vidal was more influenced by his grandfather, Thomas P. Gore, Oklahoma's first U.S. Senator; he spent many hours in Gore's extensive library and, through his grandfather, met the personalities of Washington. Vidal experienced a stimulating tour of pre-World War II Europe at fourteen and was educated at Phillips Exeter Academy, where he published his first writing.

After graduating and enlisting in the army in 1943, Vidal was trained as an engineer in Virginia, was sent to the Army Air Corps, and was then assigned to the Army Transportation Corps as a maritime warrant officer. To relieve the boredom of his service responsibilities, he began his first novel, *Williwaw*.

Following the war he continued to write, worked in publishing, traveled extensively, and finally settled near West Point, badly in need of money. The solution was what he called his "five-year plan: an all-out raid on television, which could make me enough money to live the rest of my life." He became an important figure in television drama of the 1950s, the heyday of "meaningful" television theatre, writing well and writing enough to achieve financial success.

By the end of his "plan" he had gained enough confidence to enter the political arena, first as essayist and spokesman, eventually as candidate. He ran for Congress in 1960 as a liberal Democrat, and while he was not victorious, neither was his race a disaster; the writer had shown that he possessed the political acumen and the persuasive skills necessary to collect votes. He continues to make his position clear in political matters (his television debate with William F. Buckley during the 1968 presidential campaign is now legendary). As politician and citizen, he firmly supports the democratic system while rejecting any attempt to label his philosophy: "I am a correctionist. If something is wrong in society, it must be fixed," he has said; and "in actual fact, I have always been a conservative cross borne sadly by liberal friends. . . . Temperamentally, I am suspicious of belonging to anything."

As an essayist, Vidal argues just as emphatically for his beliefs as he does to reject a political tag. He can be an articulate and vigorous commentator against, for example, such a topic as the horrors of television advertising, for something as grand as governmental responsibility, and most forcibly for a more humane, realistic, and finally liberating attitude on the subject of sexuality in Western civilization. Since the publication of *The City and the Pillar* in 1948 and the accompanying public and critical clamor over its depiction of homosexual behavior, Vidal has steadfastly defended his thesis that in no other aspect of modern life does civilization more blatantly illustrate its narrow-mindedness. Yet one does not get the impression that this is just a "liberal cause" for Vidal. His arguments are based on what is ethical, what should be legal, and they are supported by a wealth of historical background.

Vidal has also proven to be a perceptive interviewer, reviewer, and critic. Whether trying to extract information from Barry Goldwater, dealing with the mythic proportions of the Kennedy clan, comparing himself to Norman Mailer, or analyzing the literature of another era, the same versatility, preparation, wit, and style are apparent. His is a polished and convincing rhetoric, rarely overtly crude or insulting, but devastating in its results; the wealth of his reading background and his tendency to embrace the classical approach (which applies also to his fiction) have prepared him well to comment, most eloquently, on a variety of public and literary topics.

This preparation is also noticeable in the scope

of his literary productions. A belief that appears to dominate his career is that the artist must not only comment on and participate in the affairs of "the world," but also be flexible enough to insure that this approach is successful. One need not search far to see that Vidal meets the standards he has set for himself. His *Visit to a Small Planet* was a television favorite of the 1950s, and his political drama, *The Best Man*, a slick, tense depiction of political maneuvering, was not only a hit with critics, but also received public acceptance. Furthermore, during the early 1950s, Vidal achieved success as a mystery writer under the pseudonym Edgar Box, composing sophisticated detective fiction about the Washington political scene and Eastern social circles. Finally, his dramatic adaptations indicated that he can popularize a work without sacrificing or compromising the merits of the original.

But it is the novel that captivates and inspires Vidal; some of his pronouncements on the subject appear classically inspired, for he sees his task as embodying what is at once entertaining and instructive. Writing in the introduction to a collection of his essays, *Rocking the Boat* (1962), he complains that, contrary to popular opinion, he is not a social or moral pedant, but admits that maturation has made him more "relevant":

> When I was younger literature in itself and for itself seemed to me to be quite enough. At moments in this book I sound like a dogged social realist and moralist pregnant with an extremely long and dispirited novel about the effect of the New York milk marketing order on the financial structure of a village in Scoharie County. For those who do not know my novels, I am not really that sort of writer. I invent rather than record. Nor do I demand that the novel, necessarily, have a social purpose. Perhaps what I am trying to say is that in a difficult age each of us, artist or not, must have some sense not only of social purpose but of moral priority. My adventures in practical politics . . . convinced me of the need, simply and unpietistically, for right action.

Later in the same volume, Vidal comments on the charge that he has theorized the death of the novel. Not so, he responds. Certainly the audience has changed, diminished, due largely to dominance of the electronic media, and the public image of the author has changed, making him more human, less mythic. But the novel survives, even can flourish in such an environment. "As an art form the novel goes right on and in many ways it is healthier than ever. . . . How could the novel be dead and the audience gone when young men are still writing novels with such hope and ferocity?" Vidal asks. He concludes simply and hopefully that "it is still enormously worthwhile to make something good, and there will always be those happy few who appreciate prose."

Matthew Rolston

Gore Vidal

In a less optimistic sequence of essays, *Reflections Upon a Sinking Ship*, Vidal is noticeably more despairing about the world and the audience for fiction; but he remains convinced of the possibilities of the novel, albeit a novel dissimilar to the accepted definition:

> Our lovely vulgar and most human art is at an end, if not the end. Yet that is no reason not to want to practice it, or even to read it. In any case, rather like priests who have forgotten the meaning of the prayers they chant, we shall go on for quite a long time talking of books and writing books, pretending all the while not to notice that the church is empty and the parishioners have gone elsewhere to attend other gods, perhaps in silence or with new words.

Vidal wrote his first novel, *Williwaw* (1946), when he was serving as first mate on a ship for the Army Transport Corps near the Aleutian Islands. Published after his tour of duty, *Williwaw* is a reflection upon the war experience no doubt recognizable to a majority of veterans. War for the crew of this transport vessel in the Aleutian Islands is a tedious, mind-benumbing exercise in which the indefinable enemies are the violence of nature and the distasteful constant presence of one's comrades; yet the results can be as devastating as the most brutal combat mission.

The plot of the story is not complex. An ambitious and arrogant officer commandeers a transport ship to deliver official messages to his superiors because foul weather limits normal lines of communication. During the run, the ship encounters a terrific storm (a williwaw) that tests the courage of its commander, a competent seaman who is dissatisfied with his assignment and disliked by his crew. The other major action of *Williwaw* concerns two minor characters, Duval and Bervick, who are competing for the affections of a Norwegian prostitute. Their seemingly innocent confrontation erupts into violence when Duval accidentally goes overboard during a childish struggle about her. Bervick recognizes that no one has witnessed the events and covers up the incident, a course of action that the rest of the crew accepts, despite their suspicions of Bervick. This failure to "become involved" in another person's tragedy is Vidal's theme: survival, personal gain, selfishness are primary motives for man's actions, especially in a wartime setting.

What is most important for the reader to recognize is that *Williwaw* was written by Vidal at age 21, and that its tone, setting, rhythm, and character development are distinctly achieved by the young artist. Written in a spare but evocative style that faintly resembles the patterns of Hemingway (Vidal also names Crane as an inspiration), *Williwaw* remains for many readers one of Vidal's most convincing and capable efforts.

Vidal continues to reflect on war in *In a Yellow Wood* (1947), this time by illustrating the post-World War II life-style of a veteran, Robert Holton, who has become an employee of a prestigious New York firm. Holton seems to have been broken spiritually by the war (his ritualized and careful actions of the day are similar to those of Nick in "Big Two-Hearted River"); during the course of a single day, as he goes about his personal and professional duties, he banters with a lovelorn coffee shop waitress, meets with a carefree friend of his past, and attends a company party where he meets Carla, a lovely woman with whom he shared a wartime affair. Carla, still fond of Robert, offers him affection and an exciting way out of his present existence, but he seems to have lost his imagination; he accepts a promotion within his company. His decision made, past rejected, future confirmed, Robert's last thoughts are of his newfound, dignified security and of the financial rewards implicit in his decision. The conclusions, not optimistic, are nevertheless convincing, both artistically and psychologically.

Both *Williwaw* and *In a Yellow Wood* provided evidence that Vidal was an American novelist who possessed generous measures of psychological insight and literary flair. But neither novel captured attention as vividly as his third, *The City and the Pillar*, for here Vidal adds a third ingredient, risk, by writing about homosexual life. In an afterword to the revised edition of *The City and the Pillar* (1965), Vidal comments on his decision to deal with this controversial subject: "I was twenty-one when I wrote *The City and the Pillar*. Although I had already published two novels, . . . my talent was not precocious. I knew how to do a few things well, and I did them all in *Williwaw*. By the time I came to write *The City and the Pillar*, I was bored with playing it safe. I wanted to take risks, to try something no American had done before. I decided to examine the homosexual underworld. . . ."

Jim Willard, the protagonist, reflects at the beginning of the novel on the events that have led him at age twenty-five to be a somewhat confused and bitter man. When he was seventeen, Jim, a skilled athlete but by no means remarkable socially or intellectually, had experienced a frantic and entirely surprising and innocent moment of passion with his friend Bob, who is bound for college. Jim leaves home, begins to recognize that he is not attracted to women, and eventually, through contacts made because of his job as a tennis coach in Hollywood, is noticed by Ronald Shaw, a screen star who regularly "keeps" young men in his mansion. Jim begins to accept his own behavior while at the same time observing with some contempt the life-style around him. He and Shaw quarrel; Jim meets another lover, this time a writer. After serving in the army during World War II, Jim learns Bob is going to marry. Finally the long-awaited confrontation with the memory of his first encounter arrives; Jim and Bob meet in a New York hotel room; Jim flies into a rage when thwarted in his advances and strangles Bob.

The critical debates over *The City and the Pillar* were many, from outrage over the explicit treatment of a sensitive subject to more academic and perhaps accurate complaints about "preachiness." A focal point for discussion of the novel is the logic of the ending, if the murder is consistent with the development of Jim's character. Evidently Vidal agreed with some of these criticisms, for in 1965 he published *The City and the Pillar Revised*; in this version he corrects what he considers examples of an immature style, and most significantly, creates a final scene in which Jim forces Bob to make love and Jim then leaves, the past rearranged, the future a bit more clear.

Vidal's apprenticeship as a novelist served, he moved to new ground. His next book, *The Season of Comfort* (1949), is autobiographical, the story of his early life, as told through the character Bill Giraud. Vidal uses this work not only to reminisce but to experiment with style, seeking to create a more modernistic novel while at the same time finding a more distinct authorial voice. Next, in *A Search for the King* (1950) Vidal describes, with much imagination and insight, the legendary search of Blondel de Neel for Richard the Lion-Hearted, who was captured by Leopold of Austria after the third crusade. In this book Vidal again exhibits his facility for plot and rich description, and now, imbues fascinating historical characters with the stuff of humanity, verity. It is a talent that Vidal would employ effectively in future works.

Vidal continued to develop a more elaborate, distinctive writing style in his sixth novel, *Dark Green, Bright Red* (1950). Set in an unnamed country of Central America, this story contains elements of satire and comedy as it details the various exploits of an American mercenary soldier, a general returning to his country after a long exile, and numerous other conspirators, politicos, and other characters readily identified by those familiar with stock descriptions of "banana republic" intrigue. Though not popular or financially successful, this novel is important as a stylistic precursor to his next two productions.

Written at a New York mansion that he purchased to seclude himself from the world after the intense traveling and writing of his early twenties, *The Judgment of Paris* (1952) and *Messiah* (1954) convinced many that Vidal was an important literary talent, for they reflect not only his confidence in his newly found style but also a philosophical depth that many found lacking in earlier works. Ray Lewis White expresses these sentiments when he writes "in the two novels that Vidal wrote at 'Edgewater'—*The Judgment of Paris* and *Messiah*—he demonstrated the firm control of his medium that had been present in promise more than in execution in his earlier work," and Bernard Dick implies that the explosion of "philosophy" (my word) contained in these two novels can be ascribed to the enormous reading schedule that Vidal imposed upon himself at his new home, a sort of "crash major in English Lit." Vidal himself concurs with critical evaluation of these works, finding them satisfying and worthy.

In *The Judgment of Paris* Vidal describes the adventures of an American wanderer who tours Europe prefatory to a commitment to a reasonable life of some purpose. The framework for the story is mythical, a reconstruction of the myth of Paris and Helen. In Vidal's version, Philip Warren meets three women who tempt and flatter him with offers for his future. Philip finally rejects wealth and power and intellect in favor of consummate love, a decision that the narrator treats with a goodly amount of sophisticated, satirical humor, plus a fair amount of ambiguity.

Vidal again deals with myth but of a different kind, in *Messiah*, in order to enter into a many-layered discussion of man's most honored institution, his religion, and by connection, whether life or death is a more satisfactory condition. The high priest of a new religion, John Cave, professes knowledge of the beneficence of death. Eugene Luther, the narrator, becomes involved in this new religious movement (Cavesword) that sweeps the country, both as believer and mass marketer. But eventually Eugene and other "disciples" recognize the necessity of Cave's death if "Cavesway" is to survive; the industry that his religion has become now needs its martyr. Cave is murdered, the survivors split, Eugene Luther rebels, arguing a more humanistic interpretation of Cavesway dogma, and is exiled to Egypt as his name becomes associated with heresy. *Messiah* ends with Luther struggling to cling to life, recognizing that he could have been the messiah of a better, truer world religion. Vidal has not written a more entertaining novel than *Messiah*. In it he speculates, criticizes, records his version of contemporary religious behavior, and prophesies with the skill and design of a master writer.

For ten years after *Messiah* Vidal pursued his quest for financial independence by writing stage and television plays. He had, by a relatively young age, written with increasing confidence eight novels on a variety of subjects. When he resumed writing fiction in the early 1960s, he showed the same tendencies to redefine history, to examine the political world, and to alarm the "public." For many readers, his later novels are less satisfying.

Julian (1964) and *Washington, D.C.* (1967) are Vidal's renderings of the worlds of politics and power, one of which is about an era (fourth century Rome) that he assiduously studied, and the other is about an environment (Washington, D.C.) that he intimately knew. In *Julian*, Vidal creates a fascinating scenario of a crucial epoch in the development of our civilization and asks the reader to consider the fate of the world had Julian, a brilliant leader, survived to enforce his liberal acceptance of variant (non-Christian) religions. *Washington, D.C.* is an examination of a political world familiar to the reader and more secular in its thematic implications. The characters are many, as are the descriptions of political infighting, greedy maneuvering, and social dalliance that pervade the capital city. It is a story with which Vidal is fascinated and he tells it with scathing affection. *Washington, D.C.* is the first volume of what could be called Vidal's "American Trilogy." In the next two, *Burr* (1973) and *1876* (1976), as he had in the first, Vidal shows that he relishes portraying the American political scene. Aaron Burr has, of course, a somewhat vague reputation in America as master but renegade politician who nearly became president and who killed Alexander Hamilton in a duel. Vidal, through the narrator Charles Schuyler, a biographer of and unacknowledged son of Burr, eloquently gives Burr a human, believable personality, often at the expense of more honored American revolutionary heroes, and at the same time chips away at traditional, often chauvinistic, beliefs about the American Republic. In *1876* Vidal brings an aging Schuyler back from Europe to spin another tale of historical fiction. The characters are perhaps not as appealing as the legendary names mentioned in *Burr*, but the descriptions of New York and Washington, D.C., are delightful, and his version of American history is, as usual, provocative and controversial.

There can be little doubt that most of Gore Vidal's recent fame can be attributed to *Myra Breckinridge* (1968), which, for the average American, bears the standard for sexual revolution, with its confusion and concurrent aggregation of sex roles. Unfortunately for Vidal and other modern authors, there is a similar tendency for the public to confuse novels and their movie adaptations. The artless, vacuous movie version of *Myra Breckinridge* was a major disappointment to audiences who expected a different kind of pornography and critics who hoped for a degree of classiness; Vidal bore the brunt of public and critical fury. His novel certainly must be judged without thoughts of Raquel Welch and Rex Reed to clutter the mind. He is clearly having fun here, but not without some serious shots at contemporary art and life. He continued in this vein with a sequel, *Myron* (1974).

Vidal's remaining published novels are *Two Sisters: A Memoir in the Form of a Novel* (1970) and *Kalki* (1978). In the former he uses the diary of a screenwriter and excerpts from a screenplay about two sisters of the third century B.C. as an excuse to write essays about a variety of subjects. *Two Sisters* is weak and uninspiring, whether or not it is judged as a novel. There is little doubt about *Kalki*'s genre; it is pure fiction with an absurdly fantastic plot about a Vietnam war veteran who sees himself as the Hindu god whose return to earth will signal the end of the world. Narrated by a bisexual aviatrix, *Kalki* takes contemporary mores and blends them with appropriate idiom and character types. After reading this book one can assert with confidence that Vidal has settled on a formula for success—an intriguing plot, plenty of wit and style for the reviews, and some sex and cynicism for the public. It will be interesting to discover what Gore Vidal has planned for the remainder of his literary career, a career that so far is remarkable for its versatility, prolificity, and often, controversy.

—Robert Graalman

References:

John W. Aldridge, *After the Lost Generation: A Critical Study of the Writers of Two Wars* (New York: McGraw-Hill, 1951);

Bernard F. Dick, *The Apostate Angel: A Critical Study of Gore Vidal* (New York: Random House, 1974);

Ray Lewis White, *Gore Vidal* (New York: Twayne, 1968).

ALICE WALKER
(9 February 1944-)

BOOKS: *Once: Poems* (New York: Harcourt, Brace & World, 1968);

The Third Life of Grange Copeland (New York: Harcourt Brace Jovanovich, 1970);

Revolutionary Petunias & Other Poems (New York: Harcourt Brace Jovanovich, 1973);

In Love & Trouble: Stories of Black Women (New York: Harcourt Brace Jovanovich, 1973);

Langston Hughes, American Poet (New York: Crowell, 1974);

Meridian (New York & London: Harcourt Brace Jovanovich, 1976);

Goodnight, Willie Lee, I'll See You in the Morning: Poems (New York: Dial, 1979).

Alice Walker is a talented, versatile writer from the modern South. Since the appearance of her first book in 1968, she has published poetry, fiction, and criticism, all of which have advanced her literary reputation. During the short span of her career, Walker has become a major voice among black and women artists, not only because of her creative writing, but also because of her articulation of the role of art and the artist in a complex society. In both her personal essays and her own art, she has sought a unity of social, moral, and aesthetic purpose. All of her work relies upon her roots in rural Georgia, her experiences as a black woman, and the political ferment of the 1960s and 1970s.

Born into a sharefarming family in Eatonton, Georgia, Walker is the youngest of five boys and three girls. Her parents, Willie Lee and Minnie Tallulah Grant Walker, worked in cotton fields for a living. At eight years old, she received a facial scar that caused her to become solitary and timid. Ashamed of her disfiguration, she daydreamed of "falling on swords, of putting guns to [her] heart or head, of slashing [her] wrists with a razor." Walker envisioned herself as a prematurely aged outcast, rather than as a little girl in a large family, but her conception was not completely debilitating. She became more observant of people in their interactions and learned patience in caring about what happened to others. In her solitude, she discovered the pleasure of reading stories. At the same time, she began to write poems.

After finishing first in her high school class, Walker, like her eldest sister, Molly, left the rural South to attend college. With the aid of scholarships and seventy-five dollars collected by her neighbors, she attended Atlanta's Spelman College for women. Her two years there (1961-1963) were marked by an awakening to intellectual and social issues, an awakening motivated by the civil rights movement that brought Walker and a generation of students to a sense of individual power and to the truth of their collective past. She remembers herself and the other participants in Atlanta as "young and bursting with fear and determination to change our world," and as "thinking, beyond our fervid singing, of death." In a sense, the students were thrown back upon their most private resources of self in the middle of group endeavor. Years later Walker incorporated this condition into her portraits of Meridian Hill and the students of Saxon College, her fictionalized Spelman. The struggle in the South caused Walker to comprehend wholeness and change. As she reveals in *Revolutionary Petunias* (1973), her second collection of poems and National Book Award nominee, the movement became an agent for freeing individuals from a spiritually deadening lethargy, but the freedom carried with it isolation and loneliness.

In 1963 Walker transferred to Sarah Lawrence College in Bronxville, New York, where she broadened her knowledge of the world beyond the South. She even traveled to Africa as a part of her education. A traumatic pregnancy during her senior year caused Walker again to contemplate suicide and "to understand how alone woman is, because of her body." Emotionally and physically exhausted, she practiced how to slice her wrists with a razor blade kept under her pillow. Fortunately, the act proved unnecessary because a college friend located an abortionist. The experience of waiting suspended between life and death led directly to the poems in her first book, *Once* (1968). She shared her poetry with Muriel Rukeyser, then writer in residence at Sarah Lawrence, who was instrumental in bringing the work to an editor's attention. Walker wrote the poems out of a new awareness of herself, her love for being alive; she has since stated, "Writing poetry is my way of celebrating with the world that I have not committed suicide the evening before."

Although, as a youth, Walker enjoyed happier times with her family and school friends, her experiences—as a scarred child, as a civil rights demonstrator, as a pregnant college senior—appear to be central in shaping her particular vision of herself as a writer and in establishing her commitment to black and feminist concerns. These experiences, that pit the fragility of the lonely human being against the strength of spiritual survival, also seem to have influenced Walker's belief in a moral function of art: saving lives. They may account as well for the maturity and wisdom evident in even her earliest works.

By the time she completed her degree at Sarah Lawrence in 1965, Walker had resolved to become a writer. In 1966, she had her first publication, "The Civil Rights Movement: How Good Was It?," which won *The American Scholar* essay contest. That year she attended the Bread Loaf Writers' Conference. After her marriage in 1967 to Melvyn Leventhal, a civil rights lawyer and conscientious objector to the Vietnam War, she moved to Mississippi, where she worked with voter registration drives and black studies programs while beginning her first novel, *The Third Life of Grange Copeland* (1970), which was supported by a National Endowment for the Arts Grant. Her daughter, Rebecca Grant, was born during this active period. Walker's return to the South coincides with her turning to the people, land, and customs of her childhood for the raw materials of her art. Her parents, family, and older residents of her community provide her with the starting point of her narratives, which are shaped by the rural Georgia of her youth: cotton fields, hogwire fences, sharecroppers' shacks, red clay gullies. Despite a strong sense of place, Walker's fiction is neither provincial nor dependent upon local color for significance. She evokes concrete scenes as a means of communicating the richness of a folk heritage and the presence of a tenacious will to survive.

Walker writes best of the social and personal drama in the lives of familiar people who struggle for survival of self in hostile environments. She has expressed a special concern with "exploring the oppressions, the insanities, the loyalties and the triumph of black women," and with portraying old people "who persist in their beauty in spite of everything." Walker shows an enormous respect for the lives and emotions of her people, but she does not flinch from exposing the damage done by bondage and oppression. She draws Southern blacks, women in particular, without stereotyping or idealizing, but with a perception of their being lonely people who suffer physical or psychic injury in defining and asserting their identities. The stories of *In Love and Trouble*, published in 1973, reflect her precision in rendering the psychological states of women characters who are, however, frequently grotesques—maimed, inarticulate individuals. Walker describes them as "mad, raging, loving, resentful, hateful, strong, ugly, weak, pitiful, and magnificent" women who "try to live with the loyalty to black men that characterizes all of their lives." She portrays these troubled personalities as products of a dehumanizing culture, as victims of sexual and racial oppression. Even though her characters may recognize the detrimental effects of their environment, they often kill or do violence to themselves and others, such as the frustrated housewife in " 'Really Doesn't Crime Pay?' " who attempts to murder her husband because her lover absconds with her notebooks and publishes her work as his own. Other characters sacrifice a basic part of themselves in an attempt for a better life. The bride, mother of three children, in "Roselily" places her hopes for the future in a man she neither knows nor loves. Without shame or apology, Walker presents her characters and celebrates their efforts to be themselves. Her approach to characterization reflects a preoccupation with what she terms, "spiritual survival, the survival *whole* of my people." *In Love and Trouble* won the Rosenthal Award of the National Institute of Arts and Letters in 1974; included in *Best American Short Stories* were "Everyday Use" (1973) and "The Revenge of Hannah Kemhuff" (1974).

At the center of Walker's fictional creations is a vision of the isolated condition, but intrinsic value, of human beings. She maintains in the essay "Saving the Life That Is Your Own" that the artist must acquire "a sense of essence, of timelessness and vision." Walker has succeeded in so doing; however, her recognition leads to a personal sadness that is neither melancholy nor nostalgia, but rather grief for what human beings do to others and to themselves. For example, in her autobiographical poem, "For My Sister Molly Who In the Fifties," she mourns the irreparable separation of kin because their lives have followed different courses, one leading to participation in the larger geographical world and the other to a clear perception of place in a contained community.

Walker's singular vision emerges out of her individual and collective experiences. She affirms a struggle to survive whole that presupposes loneliness and grief at the core of existence. She asserts that "the gift of loneliness is sometimes a radical vision of society or one's people that has not previously been taken into account." Not only does Walker take loneliness into account, but she also celebrates its giftlike coming, particularly in her theme of revolution. Although one of her characters, Truman Held in *Meridian* (1976), dismisses revolution as "the theme of the sixties," Walker continues to explore that theme with love and precision. She uses her personal memories and the historical consciousness of her people to communicate the confusion and loss that come from the passing of the old ways. What will replace the certainty of the past is not evident. Walker offers no solutions, but she does suggest that people, young and old, who act alone out of a knowledge of self and the past will emerge whole. Their moral and physical struggle is revolution for a larger freedom, one not sustained by any community.

Although she left the South after receiving a Radcliff Institute fellowship (1971-1973), Walker's understanding of the history and culture of the South informs her stories of survival with a way of seeing the contemporary world and a context for expressing the accumulated meaning of life. She believes that nothing is ever "a product of the immediate present." As a result, she uses Southern history—past and recent—in order to achieve a wholeness in her fictional creations, a wholeness which she finds elusive in the private and public lives of black people. For instance, the father in *Meridian* attempts to reclaim the connections between earlier generations of blacks and American Indians by returning his farm, the site of a burial mound, to its rightful owners, but Sacred Serpent Park becomes a tourist attraction with admission denied blacks. In her essay, "Beyond the Peacock:

The Reconstruction of Flannery O'Connor," Walker responds to her mother's question: "When you make these trips back South . . . what is it exactly that you're looking for?" by stating, "A wholeness." In her personal life and in her art, Walker insists upon searching through both cultural and psychological pasts, through the pain of slavery and segregation, for a meaningful synthesis. The South is inextricably a part of that search.

Walker's stance in her writing is one of patiently looking back to discover meaning. Themes of individual freedom, endurance, and continuity recur as overt statements and as hidden parables throughout her works. Her narrative style is lyrical and infused with a poetry of sadness, longing, and isolation, seen most effectively in her novel *Meridian*. Her tone is elegiac, though often it includes anxiety, confusion, and rage, especially in the relationships between fathers and daughters. When she comments upon the genesis of "The Revenge of Hannah Kemhuff," she provides a summary of her primary themes and her method: "I gathered up the historical and psychological threads of the life my ancestors lived, and in the writing . . . felt joy and strength and my own continuity."

While ancestors may give Walker what she calls "the joy of their presence" and reassure her that she is "not alone," her characters are very much alone in their searches, and their sorrows outweigh joy. John's mother, the revolutionary poet in "Entertaining God," leaves miserably alone after her poetry readings in which she establishes her identity as a black woman and fosters a spirit of community among her listeners. An attempt to overcome being alone characterizes Walker's protagonists; few succeed, and their success is always spiritual. Feather Mae, Meridian's great-grandmother, experiences a "strange spiritual intoxication" on sacred ground which connects her to other lives, but thereafter is excluded from her community for her "harmless madness." Walker's message is relentless: comfort or uplift emanates only from within, from an inexplicable internal spirituality which must be acknowledged. Denial of one's spiritual essence signals failure and fragmentation in her world. How some individuals manage to sustain their inner resources is part of life's mystery. Walker has remarked, "One thing I try to have in my life and in my fiction is an awareness of and openness to mystery, which to me is deeper than any politics, race, or geographical location." Because she responds to mystery, her early poetry is influenced by Zen epigrams and Japanese haiku, and her fiction affected by authors such as Zora Neale Hurston, Jean Toomer, and Flannery O'Connor, whose lives and works reflect a sense of mystery. In "To Hell With Dying," the final story in *In Love and Trouble*, her young heroine, apparently based upon Walker herself, believes that she has the power to bring an elderly neighbor, Mr. Sweet, back from death, and through her love she does so several times. The story illustrates the presence of mystery in everyday life.

A recurring image in Walker's work is that of the individual who loves flowers and cultivates them even in the poorest soil. The growing of flowers under adverse conditions becomes symbolic of the mysterious transformations possible in human beings. The image is Walker's emblem for growing and living in spiritual beauty. She incorporates it into her poems, novels, and essays, especially in the essay "In Search of Our Mothers' Gardens." There, as she does generally, Walker traces the imagery back to her own mother who, no matter where she lived or how great her responsibilities, cultivated magnificent flower gardens. She calls those varied gardens her mother's "art," "her ability to hold on, even in very simple ways." Alice Walker's special value as a novelist lies in her illumination of art in society, of the artist in ordinary people—artists who only grow flowers, poets who never write poems. More than any other contemporary black writer, she combines a consciousness of self as artist with a recognition of art in "little people."

Walker's novel *The Third Life of Grange Copeland* explores the psychological terrain of "little people" in need of cultivation for internal flowering. It develops the inner realities of a black family living within a restrictive environment. The book begins in 1920 when Grange Copeland, the thirty-five-year-old patriarch, is already aged from a life of subjugation as a sharecropper; it concludes in 1960 with his death and the arrival of new field workers for civil rights. In rendering the forty-year history of three generations of Copelands, Walker has written her most effective novel.

The structure juxtaposes the responses of Grange and his son Brownfield to their lives. Grange's life reverberates in his son's. Their physical and spiritual bondage is symmetrical, though it does not occur simultaneously. As tenant farmers, they are aware of an oppressive system keeping them in despair, because "cotton production was all that mattered in their world." Because they expect no relief from the poverty limiting their existences, both turn to alcohol to escape degradation. Yet the Copeland men are as entrapped by their own psyches as they are by the system. Incapable of expressing love or deflecting rage away from their families, they

Dana Durst

Alice Walker

are isolated in self-hatred and guilt. Grange feels guilty for sentencing his son to "a familiar death," and Brownfield for not providing for his daughters. Yet both abuse their offspring—Grange by ignoring his and Brownfield by cursing or beating Daphne, Ornette, and Ruth. Instead of sharing their concerns with their families, they alienate those around them by their inability to communicate. Grange mistakenly believes that he does not need to tell his wife Margaret that she "had married not into ecstasy, but into dread. Not into freedom, but into bondage; not into perpetual love, but into deepening despair." Brownfield cannot communicate his desperation to his wife, Mem, because "he did not know the words she knew, and even if he could learn them he had no faith that they would fit the emotions he had." As a result of internal confusion as well as economic realities, Grange and Brownfield are responsible for the destruction of their wives and children. Margaret kills herself and her baby after Grange deserts them; Brownfield brutally murders Mem.

Walker skillfully controls the contrapuntal development. The tone remains objective and unpatronizing, but the terse language, only occasionally marred by rhetorical questions, evokes the narrow confines of the Copelands' experience. The narrative perspective is compelling in its frankness and caring. However, a weakness in the parallel pattern of Grange's and Brownfield's existence is that they never acknowledge the extent of their bond, though Grange does admit, "We both jumped our responsibility and without facing up to at least *some* of his wrong a man loses his muscle." Perhaps the omission is deliberate; Walker may well intend to emphasize the extent of the dehumanization suffered by this family, but her strategy undermines Grange's wise humanity in his old age.

After years of living in the North, Grange returns to Baker County, Georgia, and starts his third life as the guardian of Brownfield's daughter Ruth. Although he dismisses his son as "a member of the living dead, one of the many who had lost their souls in the American wilderness," he acknowledges Ruth's humanity, and thereby his own. He protects her from the social and economic hardships of their world and, more importantly, nurtures her dreams. Grange wants "in her living . . . joy, laughter, contentment in being a woman"; he prepares her to safeguard her "purity and openeyedness and humor and compassion." He cherishes in Ruth all of the qualities he has destroyed in his own son and the submissive women from his first two lives. In his last years, Grange believes, "Survival was not everything. *He* had survived. But to survive *whole* was what he wanted for Ruth."

Grange articulates the vision of survival that is Walker's major theme. At whatever costs, human beings have the capacity to live in spiritual health and beauty; they may be poor, black, and uneducated, but their inner selves can blossom as do Mem's remarkable flowers and as Ruth herself does. Grange's insight is partly the consequence of his attention to Ruth's innocence, honesty, and inquisitiveness. In addition, his perception results from his cumulative experiences as a black man. However, Grange's moral awareness of the potential for living in the world is possible because he learns to be introspective and to value being alone. Grange becomes more reflective in his old age and examines himself in the context of his society. He states, "one day I had to look back on my life and see where *I* went wrong." He takes a political stance, which imparts a fighting spirit as well as a personal confidence, missing in his former lives. Grange understands the role of whites in his suffering, but he is convinced that *"you got to hold tight a place in you where they can't come."* His return home marks his resolve to assume control over his own being by securing "independence from whites, complete and unrestricted, and obscurity from those parts of the world he chose."

Grange represents the individual values that Walker most esteems. He stands alone, introspective and analytical. Whereas his son Brownfield fears self-analysis as a process of disintegration ("The least deep thinking and he was sure he would be lost. . . . He had a great fear of being alone."), Grange welcomes introspection as an opportunity for synthesis. Without self-examination Brownfield becomes as brutal as the society in which he lives. Grange, on the other hand, transcends his environment as he examines himself.

Grange's vision is his legacy to Ruth. His final bequest is more than temporary protection from brutality and restriction; he leaves Ruth with the resources for flowering, for living whole. In the last chapter, Ruth is alone; Grange has killed his son and lies dying in a field. But all along Grange has taught Ruth how to live alone and independently. By building her a separate house, a cabin "playhouse," he has helped Ruth to experience freedom and understand it, not as an abstraction, but as a practical, necessary condition. Constructed in love and hope, Ruth's house is symbolic of the intricate bond between individuals. It is an expression of personal need, fulfillment, and continuity. Heritage may trap and ensnare, yet it also becomes the means by which the young may flower in the world. Ruth survives alone, but she is an individual who is certain of herself and her own value.

It is appropriate that Ruth, the one person in three generations of Copelands with a chance for "survival whole," is female, because the Copeland women have suffered the most from their environment and their men. Margaret, Ruth's grandmother, dominates the first chapters of the novel, though her life is seen through the eyes of her child Brownfield. She is "kind, submissive, smelling faintly of milk," but forced to dig baits and endure Grange's abusive moods. Margaret longs for a better life with Grange as a faithful, responsible husband. Ultimately out of deprivation and weariness, she loses herself in despair, drink, and other men. Her suicide is a final submission to Grange's will. Mem, Ruth's mother, fills the central sections of the book with her "warm life-giving" presence. Intelligent and sensitive, she has worked to become a teacher. But gradually, her husband (the most debased character in Walker's entire canon) strips her of her books, speech, health, gentleness, spirit, and then shoots off her face. The portrait of Mem's destruction is graphic and shocking, because it records, without sentimentality, the unrelenting cruelty of a man toward a woman who embodies the essence of humanity.

Ruth has the sensitivity and love evident in the lives of her mother and grandmother, but she has more. She has a distinct conception of herself: "I'm not just a pitcher to be filled by someone else. I have a mind, I have a memory." The destructive psychological attitude of the males toward their women has lessened, as Grange's treatment of Ruth suggests. And the segregated world is on the threshold of change, announced by the appearance of the civil rights activists who believe that "if you fight with all you got, you don't have to *be* bitter." Ruth's existence will combine the old and the new. She may join the public movement of young blacks and whites who work for the social and political justice denied her ancestors, or she may remain apart. But, unlike Mem and Margaret, she will have a moral courage and social consciousness to fight abuse on her own terms.

In spite of the affirmation of Ruth's survival, Walker delivers a bleak message. The traditional family disintegrates primarily from the attitudes and actions of its members. The family offers neither solace nor strength; it assures nothing. The Copelands fail as a family because they forget that against the chaos of the world, they have only themselves and one another. Although individuals survive, Walker does not extend survival to the group.

The Third Life of Grange Copeland has received little critical attention. When first published it was reviewed sparsely but called a powerful, compassionate view of black family life. Since then the work has elicited praise for its authentic treatment of women, but also concern about its excessive violence. Walker's novel deserves thorough consideration, because it is a multilayered fictional experience that eloquently communicates the vital struggle of ordinary people to preserve their humanity.

Alice Walker's second novel, *Meridian*, begins at the historical moment at which *The Third Life of Grange Copeland* concludes. The civil rights movement and its effects form the backdrop for the narrative, which is diffused through the consciousness of two participants, Meridian Hill and Truman Held. Divided into three parts, "Meridian," "Truman Held," and "Ending," the novel forgoes chronological development for an associative pattern interweaving actions in the present with memories from the past. Narrative dislocations emphasize the fractured lives of the characters and intensify their search for meaning. The strategy relies upon the technical innovations of modern fiction, such as interior and narrated monologue. The style is poetic; isolated events, impressionistic portraits, and recurring images form clusters of information necessary for understanding the subject:

the mysterious truth and reality of how and why individuals survive.

Meridian Hill, a solitary woman who embodies the mystery of human existence in the novel, is one of the most unusual contemporary heroines. Essentially an ascetic, she renounces all of her worldly possessions to live among and serve her people, rural Southern blacks. Meridian radiates spirituality; however, her personality defies simple definition. Ostensibly, she is "weak, penniless, a little crazy and without power," yet she possesses a "resolute and relatively fearless" quality "which, sufficient in its calm acceptance of its own purpose, could bring the mightiest nation to its knees." Her progress toward her state of being, revealed by narrative sequences circling backward into the intertwined lives of Meridian and Truman, provides the central focus.

Truman's pilgrimage to Meridian in the small town, Chicokema, where she carries out her work, initiates both the action in the present and the reflections upon the past. His trip from New York, where he is an artist, back to the South, where he has been a student and political activist, establishes the major motifs of journeys and quests. These motifs include actual, spiritual, and imaginary journeys which operate in conjunction with themes of personal transformation and societal change that are linked on a literal level to the civil rights movement and on a symbolic level to Meridian. Truman's recurrent visits to Meridian are part of his search for meaning in his own life and for an understanding of hers. His uncanny ability to locate her exact whereabouts surprises neither character, even though Meridian's lonely mission keeps her moving throughout the South. Truman's more difficult effort is discovering who Meridian is.

A "woman who has tried, however encumbered by guilt and fears and remorse, to claim her own life," Meridian is, like Truman, a veteran of the early civil rights movement. But, unlike his, her background lies in the rural South and is a source of her shame. She is the daughter of a contemplative father, whose efforts to restore sacred land to native Americans cause his great suffering, and of an uncomplaining mother whose life is sacrifice ("blind, enduring, stumbling . . . with dignity . . . through life"). Her father gives her a historical vision and a sense of continuity in all things, while her mother burdens Meridian's childhood with feelings of guilt. Married as a teenager, Meridian has a son whose birth kills her "dreams of happy endings" and replaces them with nightmares of murdering her child and committing suicide. However in mid-April 1960, she awakens to new possibilities for her own life when civil rights workers, one of whom is Truman Held, expose her insulated community to an awareness of "the past and present of the larger world." Meridian joins them as a tireless volunteer; for her efforts, she receives not only a stronger sense of her potential, but also a college scholarship to further her development. The cost is giving away her son.

Walker skillfully filters Meridian's biography through an intensely personal consciousness. She threads the subjective examination of Meridian's formative years into an ongoing discussion of moral philosophies and political theories affecting one's strategies for living fully. But her concrete details of everyday life and precise rendering of ordinary speech prevent the narrative from becoming too abstract.

Walker's primary concern is with Meridian's life as a modern parable of spiritual rebirth and survival. Despair leads invariably to soul-searching, then to regeneration. The major sections of the novel, set in Atlanta during Meridian's college years, reveal the pivotal stages of her personal development and connect her to the historical conditions of black women. Disillusioned with Truman who rejects her for a white civil rights worker, with Saxon College for refusing burial to an orphaned black girl, and with the radical rhetoric of the movement, Meridian becomes more estranged from her world. Her one source of comfort and peace, the ancient Sojourner Tree, alleged to have grown from the severed tongue of a slave woman and a symbol for the music in one's soul, is destroyed during a night of campus riots. Meridian begins to have a peculiar illness which subjects her to periods of paralysis and unconsciousness. The illness coincides with her withdrawal into questioning her values and her heritage, particularly her attitudes toward her mother and the traditional black church.

An important catalyst for her self-examination is the change within the civil rights movement. Walker establishes the impetus for change by recording the physical abuse suffered by nonviolent demonstrators and by interspersing elegies for the violent deaths during the 1960s throughout her chapters. The ideological split between violent and nonviolent tactics for revolution separates Meridian from her more radical friends, who expect her to say that she will kill for freedom. She cannot make the statement because she recognizes a conflict within herself between rhetorical constructions and emotional responses. She sees in the black militants a rupture with the past and a confusion about the future that results in lost continuity and individual fragmentation. She holds on "to something the others had let go. If not completely, then partially—by their words today, their deeds tomorrow." At the end of the 1960s, Meridian alone "felt herself to be, not holding on to something from the past, but *held* by something in the past." Consequently, she returns to the South and, contrary to current theories of political action, assumes her solitary role of atonement and reconciliation. But she carries with her the question of killing for the revolution which becomes a major source of her personal anguish.

Walker's treatment of the role of the civil rights movement in Meridian's personal transformation is perhaps her greatest achievement in this novel. She astutely conveys its dynamic effect upon the lives of participants, and she does so without simplistic reductions. She is less successful, however, in her attempt to link the movement to religious convictions, because the associations drawn by her characters, especially Meridian, remain ambiguous and the symbolism seems overextended (for example, a roommate Anne-Marion sees a soft light glowing around Meridian's head, then becomes annoyed for "thinking of Meridian in a religious context"). Nonetheless, Walker's handling of Meridian's survival as a spiritual effort is effective.

Meridian, who has been gravely ill and near death throughout the narrative present, restores herself to health when she finally admits that her vital work is not in the political revolution, but in sustaining older values of black experience. She will function alone as a reminder that "it is the song of the people transformed by the experiences of each generation, that holds them together, and if any part of it is lost the people suffer and are without soul." Her rebirth, symbolized by a new growth of hair on her once bald head, marks a beginning, a clarification of her mission and a healing of guilt and shame—her own and that of others.

After Meridian embarks on another phase of her work, Truman, who has nursed her, reads her two poems; the last lines of one ("and we, cast out alone / to heal / and re-create / ourselves") bring him to a full understanding of Meridian's meaning in his life. He curls himself into her sleeping bag and begins again the cycle of renewal, which will spread to Lynn, his Jewish wife who cannot belong to the black world and abhors the white one, and to Anne-Marion, their militant friend who has become a middle-class poet celebrating a lake on her property. In effect, personal transformation occurs even as society changes. The symbol of music in the soul shall not die, as a photograph of a tiny bit of growth from the Sojourner Tree stump illustrates. The photograph from Anne-Marion and Truman's assumption of Meridian's place are harbingers of what is yet to come. Truman intimates as much in the concluding sentence of the novel: "He had a vision of Anne-Marion herself arriving, lost, someday, at the door, which would remain open, and wondered if Meridian knew that the sentence of bearing the conflict in her own soul which she had imposed on herself—and lived through—must now be born in terror by all the rest of them."

Meridian represents the possibility for new life, for catharsis, redemption, and hope. Her particular value, as she reminds Truman, is being always alone. Her emergence in health is a miraculous affirmation of individual transcendence over suffering and confusion, but because she has also deeply touched the lives of others, her experience will not be an isolated incident. This message is Walker's most optimistic thus far.

Meridian has received more widespread attention than Walker's first novel. Critics, such as Marge Piercy and Margo Jefferson, have praised the work for its ambitious and sharp exploration of the civil rights movement. Some have remarked Walker's gift for storytelling and her talent in creating subtle, yet compelling, characters. Others, Greil Marcus for example, have observed that the symbolism is both pretentious and one-dimensional, but the scenes are powerful. Feminist critics have commented on Walker's strong portrait of an emergent woman. What is most apparent in the critical response to *Meridian* is that Walker is being taken seriously as a mature and important writer. *Meridian* is both her elegy for the 1960s and her proclamation of her work ahead.

Walker was divorced in 1976. She received a Guggenheim Fellowship (1977-1978) to assist her writing of fiction. However, since the mid-1970s much of Walker's work has concentrated on feminist concerns. As an editor of *Ms.* magazine, she regularly contributes essays and reviews that confront issues affecting women. These articles have led to her popularity among feminists. Her general readership is growing, however, because of her attention and patience in listening—to the sounds of women in today's world, to the voices of Southern blacks, to the messages from a cultural past, to the expressions of earlier artists, to the cries of all humanity, and most importantly, to the utterances of her own inner self. Because she listens well, Walker should continue to produce fiction of honesty and wisdom.

—*Thadious M. Davis*

Other:

I Love Myself When I Am Laughing . . . and Then Again When I Am Looking Mean and Impressive: A Zora Neale Hurston Reader, edited by Walker (Old Westbury, N.Y.: Feminist Press,1979);

"Saving the Life That Is Your Own: The Importance of Modes in the Artist's Life," in *The Third Woman: Minority Women Writers of the United States*, ed. Dexter Fisher (Boston: Houghton Mifflin, 1980), pp. 151-158.

Periodical Publications:

"But Yet and Still, the Cotton Gin Kept on Working," *Black Scholar*, 1 (January / February 1970): 17-21;

"The Black Writer and the Southern Experience," *New South*, 25 (Fall 1970): 23-26;

"Eudora Welty: An Interview," *Harvard Advocate*, 106 (Winter 1973): 68-72;

"In Search of Our Mothers' Gardens: The Creativity of Black Women in the South," *Ms.*, 2 (May 1974): 64-70, 105;

"In Search of Zora Neale Hurston," *Ms.*, 3 (March 1975): 74-79, 85-89;

"Beyond the Peacock: The Reconstruction of Flannery O'Connor," *Ms.*, 3 (December 1975): 77-79, 102-106;

"My Father's Country is the Poor," *New York Times*, 21 March 1977, p. 27;

"One Child of One's Own," *Ms.*, 7 (August 1979): 47-50, 72-75.

References:

John Callahan, "The Higher Ground of Alice Walker," *New Republic*, 171 (14 September 1974): 21-22;

Robert Coles, "To Try Men's Souls," *New Yorker*, 47 (27 February 1971): 104-106;

Peter Erickson, " 'Cast Out Alone / to Heal and Recreate / Ourselves': Family-Based Identity in the Work of Alice Walker," *College Language Association Journal*, 23 (September 1979): 71-94;

Chester J. Fontenot, "Alice Walker: 'The Diary of an African Nun' and DuBois' Double Consciousness," in *Sturdy Black Bridges: Visions of Black Women in Literature*, ed. Roseann P. Bell, Bettye J. Parker, and Beverly Guy-Sheftall (Garden City: Doubleday, 1979), pp. 150-156;

Loyle Hairston, "Work of Rare Beauty and Power," *Freedomways*, 14 (First Quarter 1971): 170-177;

Trudier Harris, "Folklore in the Fiction of Alice Walker: A Perpetuation of Historical and Literary Traditions," *Black American Literature Forum*, 2 (Spring 1977): 3-8;

Harris, "Violence in *The Third Life of Grange Copeland*," *College Language Association Journal*, 19 (December 1975): 238-247;

Greil Marcus, Review of *Meridian*, *New Yorker*, 52 (7 June 1976): 133-136;

John O'Brien, "Alice Walker," in *Interviews with Black Writers* (New York: Liveright, 1973), pp. 185-211;

Barbara Smith, "The Souls of Black Women," *Ms.*, 2 (February 1974): 42-43, 78;

Cam Walker, Essay-Review of *The Third Life of Grange Copeland* and *Meridian*, *Southern Exposure*, 5 (Spring 1977): 102-103;

Mary Helen Washington, "Black Women: Myth and Image Makers," *Black World*, 23 (August 1974): 10-18;

Washington, "An Essay on Alice Walker," in *Sturdy Black Bridges*, pp. 133-149.

JOSEPH WAMBAUGH

(22 January 1937-)

BOOKS: *The New Centurions* (Boston: Atlantic / Little, Brown, 1970; London: Joseph, 1971);

The Blue Knight (Boston & Toronto: Atlantic / Little, Brown, 1972; London: Joseph, 1973);

The Onion Field (New York: Delacorte, 1973; London: Weidenfeld & Nicolson, 1974);

The Choirboys (New York: Delacorte, 1975; London: Weidenfeld & Nicolson, 1976);

The Black Marble (New York: Delacorte, 1978; London: Weidenfeld & Nicolson, 1978).

A former detective sergeant in the Los Angeles Police Department, Joseph Wambaugh is the author of five best-selling novels about cops. Wambaugh's first three books, written while he was a policeman, are serious, straightforward, and realistic accounts of police work; the third is a nonfiction novel modeled on Truman Capote's *In Cold Blood* (1965). Wambaugh's last two books, written after his retirement from the LAPD, continue to portray police work realistically, but Wambaugh brings to these books a dark and comic vision. Each of Wambaugh's novels portrays not only the action of police work, but also the psychological toll such work takes on policemen.

Wambaugh was born in East Pittsburgh, Pennsylvania, the only child in an Irish Catholic family; his father was a small-town police chief and, later, a steelworker. The family moved to California in 1951, when Wambaugh was fourteen; and three years later he joined the U.S. Marine Corps, serving for three years and also attending college in night school. While a Marine, he married his high school sweetheart, Dee Allsup, and the couple settled in Ontario, California, upon his discharge in 1957. He took a job at nearby Kaiser Steel Mill and continued to attend college part-time, majoring in literature, "the only courses I was any good in," he says. He hoped to become an English teacher but decided against it while in his senior year. Instead, in 1960 he joined the Los Angeles Police Department. He did manage to continue his formal education, however, eventually earning both a B.A. and an M.A. in English from California State College, Los Angeles.

Wambaugh joined the police force, he claimed, because he had "nothing better to do." As he told Steven V. Roberts, "I needed a job. And the pay was pretty good. Also, I strongly suspect there was something in me from the time I was a child, admiring my father's badge and so forth." Whatever his reasons, he enjoyed police work. "I could live life more intensely as a cop," he said. "In a single night I sometimes learned things that a man could not expect to learn in a month, or a year. About mankind. About myself." Wambaugh also had several reasons for beginning to write. "All the Irish are storytellers," and all English majors want to write, he claimed. More seriously, he said, "After the Watts riot, when the most turbulent decade in modern American history was drawing to a close, I felt I wanted to say something about it. What it was like for young men, young policemen, to grow up, on the streets, in that dreadful but fascinating era." He began with short stories, but they were rejected everywhere he sent them. An editor at *Atlantic Monthly* suggested that he try a novel, and Wambaugh, encouraged, wrote *The New Centurions* (1970).

That novel sketches the careers of three patrolmen, Sergio Duran, Gus Plebesly, and Roy Fehler, from their entrance into the Los Angeles police academy in 1960 through the Watts riot of 1965. Dividing the book into six large segments by years, Wambaugh uses a series of vignettes about the three patrolmen to indicate the maturation of each as a result of his experiences on the street. The episodic nature of the novel also enables Wambaugh to focus attention on various aspects of police work: for example, by assigning Gus to a juvenile unit and Roy to the vice squad, Wambaugh chronicles the nature of work in both areas. The book ends with the brief reunion of the three men during the Watts riot, symbol of the barbarous anarchy which challenges the legal order these new centurions believe they represent. The novel was a Book-of-the-Month Club selection and on best-seller lists for eight months. A movie version of it starred George C. Scott and Stacy Keach. According to *Time* magazine, the novel prompted the deluge of police stories in the 1970s. Certainly, it prompted the television series, *Police Story*, for which Wambaugh served as consultant.

Wambaugh followed his first success with *The Blue Knight* (1972), which focuses on three days in the life of Bumper Morgan, a policeman approaching retirement after twenty years in the department. Bumper, a fallible human being, fat, crude, and stubborn, has been a cop for so long he now believes he *is* the law. He believes, too, that the legal system often corrupts and thwarts justice; he therefore "bends the law" to ensure that criminals do not go unpunished. The book is an effective study of the ways in which police work can corrupt and change policemen. Yet Wambaugh manages to make Bumper a sympathetic figure in spite of his flaws. The novel reveals, perhaps unexpectedly, that Wambaugh is capable of fairly subtle characterization, very much aware of the failings of his characters and the reasons for those failings. Another best-seller, the novel was adapted first for a television "mini-series" starring William Holden and then a regular series with George Kennedy in the title role.

His "apprenticeship" novels behind him, Wambaugh set to work on the story that had driven him to become a writer, the kidnapping of two of his fellow Los Angeles policemen, Ian Campbell and Karl Hettinger, who were driven to an onion field where Campbell was murdered while Hettinger managed to escape. That story did not come easily; and in order to complete it, he took a six-month leave of absence from the LAPD, returning to that job in 1973, after he had completed *The Onion Field* (1973). The nonfiction novel tells the story of four men, two policemen and two criminals. The first half of the work chronicles their lives up to the night of 9 March 1963 when Hettinger and Campbell stopped the car in which Gregory Powell and Jimmy Smith were cruising, looking for a liquor store to rob. Powell and Smith surprised and overpowered the policemen, forced them to drive to an onion field near

Bakersfield, and there shot Campbell five times while Hettinger escaped in the dark. The last half of the book depicts the trials of Powell and Smith and describes the effects of the murder on Hettinger. Hettinger blamed himself for Campbell's death, for both he and his department held to a "dynamic man concept"; that is, as Wambaugh states, policemen believe that "no man-caused calamity happens by chance, that there is always a step that should have been taken, would have been taken if the sufferer had been alert, cautious, brave, aggressive—in short, if he'd been like a prototype policeman . . . the most dynamic of men . . . who could take positive action in any of life's bizarre and paralyzing moments." By this measure, Hettinger was a failure, who shared responsibility for the murder of Campbell just as surely as did Powell and Smith. As a result, Hettinger suffered continually from nightmares; he lost weight and an inch of height; he became both sexually impotent and a kleptomaniac. The psychiatrists who eventually examined him three years after the murder attributed all of these results to the fear and shame caused by the event. Allowed to resign from the department after he was caught shoplifting, Hettinger did not recover psychologically until the 1970s, when the trials of Powell and Smith were at last completed. They were first convicted of murder on 4 September 1963; their penalty trial concluded on 12 September with a verdict of death to both defendants; they were officially sentenced on 13 November. While Powell and Smith were in San Quentin on death row, the

Larry B. Stevenson

U.S. Supreme Court handed down the Escobedo decision (1964) and the Miranda decision (1966). As a result, Powell and Smith were granted new trials, and their retrials dragged on until November 1969, when they were again convicted. Powell was again sentenced to death, but Smith was given life imprisonment. In 1972, however, the California Supreme Court declared capital punishment cruel and unusual, and Powell escaped the gas chamber forever.

Wambaugh's juxtaposition of Hettinger's psychic torment with the legal maneuverings of the murderers' attorneys effectively suggests Wambaugh's belief that the law favors offenders more than policemen. Certainly, Wambaugh provides in this book an affecting study of the guilt-ridden Hettinger, who comes to seem as much the murderers' victim as Campbell. The book was another best-seller. Wambaugh's continuing interest in the story is indicated by the fact that he turned his attention to it again several years later, writing the film script and coproducing its movie version, which was released in 1979.

Wambaugh resigned from the LAPD on 8 March 1974, citing his celebrity as a writer as the reason for his resignation: "So many people knew who I was, so many came to the station trying to see me. There were so many telephone calls that the other detectives had to screen them for me. That made them my secretaries. I had to stop it all. I have often thought that power and fame are perverted bedfellows. For the past three years, they have hounded me. The first could never catch me, but the second has run me to earth." Yet, if his resignation saddened him personally, it also seems to have had a liberating effect on his writing. For *The Choirboys*, published a year later, is a darkly comic work in which Wambaugh insults the stupidity of every police officer holding a rank above that of sergeant (his own rank when he retired), while at the same time portraying the ten patrolmen who are the novel's protagonists as rather less than the "dynamic men" they would hope to be. In fact, their number includes an alcoholic, a sadist, and a masochist. In an episodic form reminiscent of Joseph Heller's *Catch-22* (1961), Wambaugh chronicles the increasingly awful events which lead the patrolmen to conduct "choir practice." As Wambaugh defines it, "choir practice . . . was merely an off-duty meeting, usually in a secluded hide-away, for policemen who, having just finished their tour of duty, were too tense or stimulated or electrified to go to a silent sleeping house and lie down like ordinary people while nerve ends sparked." The manic hilarity and drunkenness at their meetings serve the choirboys as defense mechanisms against full consciousness of the fact that the ordinary people they protect are, by and large, barbaric savages, capable of any horror.

The Choirboys, Wambaugh's favorite among his books, is also his best work to date, a fine study of what he calls the "emotional violence" of police work. The book earned widespread rave reviews in such places as the *New York Times* and *Los Angeles Times* and was another best-seller. Wambaugh wrote a script for the film version, but he was so upset by the director's many changes in that script that he sued to have his name removed from the picture credits and won his case. He has called the film "sleazy" and "insidious," and most movie reviewers agreed with him.

His latest work, *The Black Marble* (1978), differs from his earlier books in that it offers a love story combined with a police procedural story. Like his earlier books, however, it also studies the psychic effects of police work, this time on a Russian detective sergeant and alcoholic, Valnikov, who attempts to solve the dognapping of a champion miniature schnauzer being held for ransom by its former trainer. The novel traces Valnikov's growing love for Natalie Zimmerman, his partner in the burglary division, who thinks (not without reason) that Valnikov is unstable, while at the same time it depicts Valnikov's attempt to come to terms with the nightmares which he tries to obliterate with vodka—nightmares which are his legacy from many years in the homicide division. Again, Wambaugh attacks the stupidity of police administrators; but he adds here some sharp satire of the California wealthy, particularly those with show dogs, and of the mentality of the amateur criminal. The book was another best-seller, and Wambaugh wrote the film script and coproduced its film version, released in March 1980.

The constant focus of Wambaugh's novels has been the negative psychological effect of police work on the cops themselves and their cynicism and outrage with the barbarity of humankind. The grim earnestness of his first three novels has given way to a dark comedy which intensifies the message in his last two books. Wambaugh's reputation as an artistically and financially successful "cop-novelist" is certainly secure. Moreover, *The Black Marble* suggests that he may be equally successful with a broader range of subjects in future novels.

—David K. Jeffrey

Screenplays:

The Onion Field, Black Marble Productions, 1979;
The Black Marble, Black Marble Productions, 1980.

Interviews:

John Brady, "Joe Wambaugh cops from experience," *Writer's Digest,* 53 (December 1973): 16-25;
"Playboy Interview: Joseph Wambaugh," *Playboy,* 26 (July 1979): 69-86, 112, 220, 223.

References:

David K. Jeffrey, "Wambaugh's Police Stories," *Midwest Quarterly* (Forthcoming, Summer 1980);
Steven V. Roberts, "Cop of the Year," *Esquire,* 80 (December 1973): 150-153, 310-314.

JESSAMYN WEST
(18 July 1902-)

SELECTED BOOKS: *The Friendly Persuasion* (New York: Harcourt, Brace, 1945; London: Hodder & Stoughton, 1946);
A Mirror for the Sky (New York: Harcourt, Brace, 1948);
The Witch Diggers (New York: Harcourt, Brace, 1951; London: Heinemann, 1952);
Cress Delahanty (New York: Harcourt, Brace, 1953; London: Hodder & Stoughton, 1954);
Love, Death, and the Ladies' Drill Team (New York: Harcourt, Brace, 1955); republished as *Learn to Say Good-bye* (London: Hodder & Stoughton, 1957);
To See the Dream (New York: Harcourt, Brace, 1957; London: Hodder & Stoughton, 1958);
Love Is Not What You Think (New York: Harcourt, Brace, 1959); republished as *A Woman's Love* (London: Hodder & Stoughton, 1960);
South of the Angels (New York: Harcourt, Brace, 1960; London: Hodder & Stoughton, 1961);
A Matter of Time (New York: Harcourt, Brace & World, 1966; London: Macmillan, 1967);
Leafy Rivers (New York: Harcourt, Brace & World, 1967; London: Macmillan, 1968);
Except for Me and Thee (New York: Harcourt, Brace & World, 1967; London: Macmillan, 1969);
Crimson Ramblers of the World, Farewell (New York: Harcourt Brace Jovanovich, 1970; London: Macmillan, 1971);
Hide and Seek (New York: Harcourt Brace Jovanovich, 1973; London: Macmillan, 1973);
The Massacre at Fall Creek (New York & London: Harcourt Brace Jovanovich, 1975; London: Macmillan, 1976);
The Woman Said Yes (New York & London: Harcourt Brace Jovanovich, 1976);
The Life I Really Lived (New York & London: Harcourt Brace Jovanovich, 1979).

Jessamyn West is a notably successful popular writer. She has published short stories, novels, poetry, journals, autobiography, and an operetta. She has also written screenplays, and she served as technical adviser on the film *Friendly Persuasion* (1955), adapted from her first novel. Almost all West's books have been well received, even acclaimed, by reviewers; but despite this reception (or perhaps because of it) her work has been mostly neglected by academic critics. This is especially surprising in view of West's vivid, vigorous, and eloquent style and the compassion and humanity with which she treats the serious themes of her work.

Born in 1902 in Indiana to Eldo and Grace Milhous West, Jessamyn West is a birthright Quaker, descended from a long line of Quaker ministers. In 1909 the family (including two other children) moved to California and eventually settled at Yorba Linda. West attended Fullerton High School and made a name for herself with her English compositions; eventually she graduated from Whittier College (in 1923) with a major in English. The summer after her graduation, she married Harry Maxwell McPherson. The couple presently lives in Napa, California.

During her school years, West had a desire to write, but nothing came of it at that time. She began her career as a school secretary and then taught for four years before returning to graduate school, attending Oxford University and then the University of California at Berkeley. Just before taking her doctoral orals, she discovered that she had an advanced case of tuberculosis and in 1931 entered a sanitorium for a two-year stay, beginning a long period of convalescence that did not end until 1945. Her condition was so serious that sanitorium doctors did not expect her to survive.

But West did survive, thanks primarily to the help and influence of her mother; and in this long period of enforced physical inactivity she began at last to write the stories which she had waited so long to tell, beginning probably around 1933 after she had rejoined her husband in Yuba City. The first of these stories, "99.6," was not published until 1939 when West, at her husband's insistence, finally began submitting her work for publication.

A number of West's early short stories reflected her Quaker ancestry, describing the life of the fictional Millhouse family in nineteenth-century Indiana. These stories were not intended to be in any way biographical, but they were based to some extent on stories of West's great-grandparents as she heard them from her mother. In 1945 these stories were collected and published in book form (the Millhouse name being changed to "Birdwell") as *The Friendly Persuasion*. Because the stories all deal with the Birdwell family, appear in chronological order, and are united by their themes, the book has the effect of a novel and is in fact often referred to as such. The themes with which it deals are those which are sometimes called traditional: life, death, love, courage, and joy. These are themes with which West has continued to work in her subsequent books.

Jess Birdwell, Eliza (his Quaker minister bride), and their children live on the banks of the Muscatatuck River, where Jess operates a nursery. Various stories tell of their experiences as the children learn about such things as life ("Shivaree Before Breakfast") and conscience ("The Battle of Finney's Ford"), while the parents learn about each other ("The Vase") and themselves ("First Day Finish"). The stories carry the family from the ten years preceding the Civil War to Jess's old age, around the turn of the century. A remarkable feeling of familial love and understanding permeates the book, which is also notable for its warmth and humor. The novel was an immediate success.

The Witch Diggers (1951) is a very different kind of story. It tells of Christie Fraser and his courting of Cate Conboy, whose father, Link Conboy, runs a county poor farm. The book is a record of failure, as all the characters lose in their search for happiness, a search as futile as that of the witch diggers, who continually dig in the earth for Truth, which they believe has been buried there by the Devil. The greatest failure is that of Cate, who cannot allow herself to respond to Christie's love because she equates passion with evil, an idea instilled in her by her mother. Cate settles instead for marriage with the bloodless Ferris Thompson, dooming herself to unhappiness. This theme of "sense and sensibility" is one that West develops in later novels and addresses directly in the nonfictional *Love Is Not What You Think* (1959).

Cress Delahanty (1953) is another collection of stories, originally about a number of different girls, but revised to have the same central character, Crescent Delahanty. As with *The Friendly Persuasion,* the effect is novelistic. The book takes Cress from the ages of twelve to sixteen through a series of initiatory experiences. Each episode is filled with wisdom and humor, as well as the pain of growing up; and the book achieved a well-deserved popular success. It is one of West's best books, and it remains one of her most popular.

In 1955, another collection of stories appeared under the title of *Love, Death, and the Ladies' Drill Team*. In this collection, though many of the stories deal with love and death, there is no unifying character or theme. In the title story, one of the best in the book, Emily Cooper and the rest of her exercise class composed of other women of her age and status watch through a window as another woman meets her lover in an episode indicative of what the lives of the watchers lack.

Several years after the appearance of *Cress Delahanty,* West published *To See the Dream* (1957), which purports to be a journal of her experiences while working as technical adviser for the movie version of *The Friendly Persuasion*. Whether the book is an actual journal or not, it gives an excellent picture of the filmmaking process from a writer's point of view. West understood that film and print are different media and have different requirements, yet she constantly resisted changes in the plot of her book that would violate its integrity. Her reports of discussions with William Wyler, the director, about the character of Jess Birdwell (portrayed by Gary Cooper) are especially enlightening. Far from being embittered by her experience in Hollywood, as many writers profess to be, West appears to have turned the episode to her benefit. She later worked with Wyler again when she did the script of *The Big Country* (1958).

South of the Angels (1960) is West's second novel in the strict sense of the term. It is a long, hugely populated book, difficult to summarize. It deals mainly with a number of families living on the Tract, south of Los Angeles, around 1925. Their establishment of permanent homes and a permanent settlement on the Tract, their battles over water rights, and their mingled lives and loves form the basis of the story. One critic, Alfred S. Shivers, notes that the book is also unified by its use of the cycle of love, death, and rebirth. The seasonal scheme may also be noted in other of West's books, such as *The*

Jessamyn West and her husband, H. M. McPherson

Friendly Persuasion and *Cress Delahanty*. Despite its intricacy of plot and theme, *South of the Angels* was not as highly praised by reviewers as West's earlier books. Nevertheless, it is a distinguished work which deserves more attention.

A Matter of Time (1966) is among West's most openly autobiographical novels; the experience that it treats is dealt with even more openly in *The Woman Said Yes* (1976), which gives a nonfiction account of some of the episodes described in the novel, particularly the death by cancer of West's sister, Carmen. Basically, *A Matter of Time* is the story of Blix Murphy, who is dying of cancer, of her sister Tassie, and of their conspiracy to see that Blix dies before her suffering becomes unbearable. Much of the novel is told in the form of flashbacks. In this way it becomes a story of the two women's lives—their sexual adventures, their families, their shared experiences—all the things that have led them to this crucial moment in their lives. The nature of Blix's death is controversial, especially as Tassie, the narrator, praises her sister's courage in acquiescing to the mercy killing. Tassie expresses not the least regret for the course of action she and Blix have pursued, a fact that naturally makes the book unacceptable to some, though again the book is filled with the same warm feeling of familial love that pervades a number of West's other, more cheerful, books.

With *Leafy Rivers* (1967) West returned to a more old-fashioned kind of novel, really a love story in the sense that the title character, Mary Pratt (Leafy) Rivers, through her experiences with different kinds of men, comes to a kind of knowledge of herself and an acceptance of her life. The story actually takes place as Leafy struggles to give birth to her first child at her parents' Indiana farmhouse early in the nineteenth century. During her labor, the major events of the story are related through flashbacks. These events include Leafy's marriage to her teacher, their move from home, Leafy's encounter with the virile Simon Yanders, her driving of her pigs to market, and her liaison with Cashie Wade. A major subplot develops around Leafy's brother, Chancelor Converse, his courting of Venese Lucey, and his decision to become a preacher. The varied threads of the story are skillfully interwoven, and the cast of major characters is carefully delineated. The novel's clear-cut resolution leaves little doubt as to the changed lives and future prospects of all those involved in Leafy's life and the birth of her child.

With her next book, *Except for Me and Thee* (1967), West returned to the subject matter and form that had been so successful in *The Friendly Persuasion*. Once more she takes up the story of the Birdwell family in a series of self-contained episodes which delve further into their lives. The stories do not simply begin where the earlier book left off; instead, West has chosen to cover approximately the same time span but to provide new information about certain events alluded to or implicit in *The Friendly Persuasion*, events such as Jess and Eliza's courtship, their decision to begin their own life in Indiana (free of Jess's family), the death of their daughter Sarah, their deep involvement in an antislavery episode, and Jess's love of fast horses. While perhaps a more unified collection than its predecessor, possibly as a result of West's having written many of the stories especially for the volume, *Except for Me and Thee* is a somewhat less powerful book, though it maintains some of the emotional force of *The Friendly Persuasion*. It was also successful, selling around four hundred thousand copies in hardcover alone.

In 1970 appeared *Crimson Ramblers of the World, Farewell*, another collection of short stories. It contains "99.6," her first published story, as well as the excellent title story in which Elizabeth Prescott refuses to be tempted from her mother's teachings by the attractive Crimson Rambler. This latter character's real name is Clarence Rice; and he is very similar to Clarence Rambo, who appears as the Crimson Rambler character in *Cress Delahanty*. Another fine story is "Like Visitant of Air," in which West fictionalizes a brief moment in the lives of two of her favorite writers, Henry David Thoreau and Emily Brontë, whose work she refers to again and again in her nonfiction books. Although these two of course never met, West speculates imaginatively on the way their lives might have touched. "Up a Tree" is a gruesome mystery story, particularly effective in its use of a first-person narration which allows West to reveal gradually the truly disturbed state of the youthful narrator's mind and her involvement in the murder of her mother. Overall, this is a collection of high quality, which along with *Love, Death, and the Ladies' Drill Team*, proves West's mastery of the short story.

With her next book, West returned to nonfiction. *Hide and Seek* (1973) is the record of the three months she spent alone in a travel trailer in a remote area on the bank of the Colorado River. Past and present mingle as the author reminisces about her childhood and tells of her everyday experiences while living in the desert. The book reminds one strongly of Thoreau, especially in its celebration of solitude, but it is in no sense an attempt to imitate *Walden*. West has been a seeker of privacy from childhood, but like Thoreau she is never really alone in her trailer. She has her neighbors, her thoughts, and her memories; so the book teems with life and reflection. The subtitle, *A Continuing Journey*, implies that like Thoreau's sojourn at Walden Pond, her stay in the trailer is an experiment in living which gives her time to reflect and renew herself. West expresses her thoughts on a wide range of topics, from youth to maturity, from love to fear, with both seriousness and humor. The joy of living, always present in her best work, is the book's constant theme.

After her return to society, West soon published another novel. An obscure historical incident which occurred in Indiana in 1824—the premeditated killing of nine Indians by five white men—forms the basis of *The Massacre at Fall Creek* (1975). Four of the white men were brought to trial; and as far as West was able to discover, this was the first time in the history of the United States that whites were tried, convicted, and executed for the murder of native Americans. Most of the facts of the event are now lost or obscure, and West does not attempt to give a factual account. Instead, while basing her fiction on the records that do exist, she creates her own story about what the people involved might have been like and what motives the killers might have had for slaughtering the two braves, three squaws, and four children. In doing so, West gives an honest account of a cultural conflict that was repeated in a multiplicity of ways during the westward movement. At the same time she is able to tell a story of religious faith, love, and courage through the character of Lute Bemis, one of the killers, and to raise the questions of justice and retribution. Perhaps the novel's one flaw is the intrusive love story involving young Hannah Cape and Charlie Fort, one of the defense lawyers. Although off the subject, it does, however, give West another opportunity to develop one of her favorite themes, that of sense and sensibility, as Hannah almost makes the mistake of giving up Fort for the priggish Oscar Dilk; and it does provide some romantic relief from the harsh realities of life and death with which the rest of the story deals. On the whole, the book is a powerful and effective treatment of an affecting human drama that has a resonance and relevance for contemporary readers.

West turned once more to autobiography in *The Woman Said Yes,* which grapples with the questions of life and of death. This book is a celebration of West's mother, whose role as "life enhancer" affected so profoundly the lives of her daughters: Jessamyn during her bout with tuberculosis and her sister Carmen during her struggle with terminal cancer. The memories the two women had of their mother naturally entered into their discussions of Carmen's illness and approach to death. Having dealt with her sister's death as fiction in *A Matter of Time* and now as autobiography in this book, West is able to describe clearly the effect that it has had on her life. In saying yes to death, Carmen also said yes to life, just as her sister does in this and all her other books. Though for many readers West's complicity in her sister's suicide will seem the center of the story, the life enhancement theme should not be ignored; and though many readers may doubt the morality of the sister's final decision for euthanasia, it is an unforgettable statement.

West's most recent book is *The Life I Really Lived* (1979). Although the title sounds autobiographical, although the central character is a novelist whose life span approximates that of Jessamyn West, and although some of the incidents seem based on those from West's own life, the book is a novel. One of its epigraphs is taken from Oscar Wilde: "One's real life is the life one does not lead." In this sense, the title relates, the author's books may be her "real" life, and indeed many of the events in this story of Orpha Chase mirror those in earlier works. *The Life I Really Lived* is an excellent novel, and its theme is typically basic and universal: love sanctifies. Orpha Chase, a writer, discovers this fact through her own life and that of her brother, Joe, who has become a faith-healing minister. The story follows Orpha from her birthplace in Kentucky to Los Angeles to Maui; through three marriages and one love affair; through her experiences with rape, incest, suicide, and murder; through her brother's trial for manslaughter and his death from tuberculosis. And through all of it, Orpha Chase endures. She gets her work done, and she tells of her life with gusto and humor.

The works of Jessamyn West provide the literary record of a remarkable career, capped with what is perhaps her finest achievement at this point: *The Life I Really Lived.* She has written fine books about the American past in *The Friendly Persuasion* and *The Massacre at Fall Creek.* She has dealt as well as any writer with the pains and pleasures of adolescence in *Cress Delahanty.* She has written thoughtful and stimulating autobiography. Owing to her talents as a storyteller, she has achieved a large popular success. It is possible that acceptance by academic critics may be forthcoming, particularly if any study is devoted to *The Life I Really Lived,* a book which should prove of particular interest to feminist critics and to those exploring the relationship between literature and biography. West's career has been long and distinguished, and one expects from her more works of high merit.

—Bill Crider

Screenplays:

The Big Country, United Artists, 1958;
Stolen Hours, United Artists, 1963.

Operetta:

A Mirror for the Sky, 23-24 May 1958, University of Oregon.

Other:

The Quaker Reader, edited by West (New York: Viking, 1962).

References:

Jane S. Bakerman, "Jessamyn West: A Wish to Put Something into Words," *Writer's Digest,* 56 (January 1976): 28-29;

Barbara Bannon, "Authors & Editors," *Publishers Weekly,* 195 (28 April 1969): 31-32;

Lee Graham, "An Interview with Jessamyn West," *Writer's Digest,* 47 (May 1967): 24-27;

Brenda King, "Jessamyn West," *Saturday Review,* 40 (21 September 1957): 14;

Elizabeth Poe, "Credits and Oscars," *Nation,* 184 (30 March 1957): 267-269;

Alfred S. Shivers, *Jessamyn West* (New York: Twayne, 1972).

JOAN WILLIAMS

(26 September 1928-)

BOOKS: *The Morning and the Evening* (New York: Atheneum, 1961; London: Joseph, 1962);

Old Powder Man (New York: Harcourt, Brace & World, 1966);

The Wintering (New York: Harcourt Brace Jovanovich, 1971).

Joan Williams's first two novels were heralded by critics and fellow authors alike. Among the distinguished voices raised in praise were those of Robert Penn Warren, William Styron, and Fred Chappell. Quiet yet compelling in style, poignant in their depiction of characters isolated and alienated from their communities and themselves, Williams's works are set in the hill country of northwest Mississippi and follow in the tradition of the two writers who she acknowledges exerted the greatest influence on her writing: Eudora Welty and Katherine Anne Porter. Williams's third novel is a thinly veiled account of her love affair with William Faulkner.

Born in Memphis, Tennessee, to Priestly H. and Maude Moore Williams, Joan Williams attended public schools through the eighth grade. Summers were frequently spent with her mother's family in Arkabutla, Mississippi. By the time Williams graduated from Miss Hutchinson's School for Girls in Memphis, she had determined to become a writer, despite considerable opposition from her family, who were skeptical of her ability to do anything substantial with her writing. Before she attended college, the loneliness and rebelliousness of her youth culminated in her elopement at the age of seventeen. Her parents immediately annulled this marriage. Williams attended college for one year at Southwestern at Memphis, then transferred for another year to Chevy Chase Junior College. She graduated in June 1950 from Bard College in Annandale-on-Hudson, New York. Her first published story, "Rain Later," was written during her junior year at Bard and appeared in the August 1949 issue of *Mademoiselle,* one of two winners of the magazine's College Fiction Contest.

Impelled both by her own desire to become a writer as well as by her moving experience of reading *The Sound and the Fury* (1929), that same August the nearly twenty-one-year-old Williams secured an invitation from her cousin to visit Oxford, Mississippi, for the express purpose of meeting William Faulkner. The meeting itself was not auspicious; Faulkner said virtually nothing to her, but back home in Memphis, Williams initiated a correspondence with him. Captivated by her youthful enthusiasm and sufficiently impressed by her inquiries about the role of the artist, Faulkner procured a copy of Williams's *Mademoiselle* story and corresponded with her about the writer's need for sacrifice, fortitude, and endurance. In February 1950 Faulkner invited her to collaborate on his play, *Requiem for a Nun* (1951); he specified certain scenes and methods of treatment for her to use. The attempt to collaborate on the play was, however, unsuccessful; and Williams affirms that nothing she wrote was ever incorporated into it.

In a pattern perhaps imitative of Faulkner's apprentice years, Williams lived three months in New Orleans (following her graduation from Bard in June 1950), where she worked for the Doubleday Bookshop on Canal Street in the French Quarter. Returning to New York, she worked briefly in the admissions office at Bard and then accepted a position answering letters to the editor of *Look* magazine in New York City, where she lived in Greenwich Village.

She was more successful collaborating with Faulkner when he suggested she work with him to provide ideas and plots for television scripts for James J. Geller. But although their script entitled "The Graduation Dress" (1952) was completed and telecast, Faulkner criticized the story because it did not "move" and urged her to write from the "outside" rather than the "inside"; but as frequently happened, the only way he could assist her was by rewriting her material so that the script ultimately remained hers only insofar as the initial idea was concerned.

Williams did, however, continue to send Faulkner stories for evaluation and criticism. But just as Faulkner's own masters (Housman, Eliot, Dostoevski, Cervantes, and the other authors he urged her to read) seemed not to speak to Williams as they had to him during his own apprenticeship, so too Faulkner's voice, his revisions and rewritings of her material, was not hers. Nevertheless, Williams continued to ask searching questions about the artist and his role, and in May 1952 she wrote him questioning the worth of her own suffering if she could make no use of it in her writing. Meanwhile, their personal relationship intensified. For a brief time, they were lovers. During this time, Faulkner gave her the manuscript of *The Sound and the Fury,* the novel that had brought them together.

During the summer of 1952, Williams worked on her second short story, "The Morning and the Evening." In a meeting parallel to that between Amy and Almoner in *The Wintering* (1971), Williams showed it to Faulkner only after it was completed. Beyond giving the story its title, Faulkner made no revision except to add a dependent clause in parentheses, which Williams later shortened, to the first sentence. Sufficiently impressed by the story, which would become the first chapter in *The Morning and the Evening* (1961), Faulkner sent the story to *Harper's*. When it was rejected, he sent it to his agent, Harold Ober, a gesture which in retrospect Williams views as the most valuable service Faulkner rendered to her as a writer. The story was published in the January 1953 issue of *Atlantic Monthly*.

Williams's marriage to Ezra Drinker Bowen, son of biographer Catherine Drinker Bowen, and then a writer for *Sports Illustrated*, occurred shortly thereafter. A period of relative literary inactivity followed, although *Mademoiselle* purchased a story entitled "The Sound of Silence." Never published, this story became the third chapter of *The Morning and the Evening*. Divorced in March 1970, Williams had two sons by her first husband: Ezra Drinker and Matthew Williams Bowen. In October 1970 she married John Fargason of Memphis and Clover Hill Plantation in Coahoma County, Mississippi. Their permanent residence is now in Westport, Connecticut, where Williams has just completed her fourth novel. Entitled "County Woman," this novel draws, for setting and characters, upon "Spring is Now," a story published in the Autumn 1968 issue of the *Virginia Quarterly Review*. Using the 1962 integration of the University of Mississippi by James Meredith as a catalyst, the novel traces the efforts of a middle-aged woman to enlarge her own life. In the May 1980 issue of the *Atlantic* is a reminiscence entitled "Twenty Will Not Come Again" about her initial meeting with Faulkner.

The Morning and the Evening was enthusiastically received by reviewers, who greeted Williams as a fine new talent from the South. The novel won the John P. Marquand Award of $10,000, sponsored by the Book-of-the-Month Club and awarded to an American or Canadian author for the most distinguished first novel. Robert Penn Warren praised her subtlety of psychological insight and the emotional impact of the novel; William Styron compared her evocation of the Southern setting of northwest Mississippi to the simplicity and sensuous reality of Flaubert's Normandy. She was also awarded a National Institute of Arts and Letters grant in 1962.

Tightly controlled in tone, the tale is a moving one. In simple, dispassionate language, Williams tells the story of a mute, Jake Darby, a "loony" insofar as his community is concerned. Jake's ability to fend for himself, after the death of his mother and his abandonment by his brother, is kindly but inaccurately judged to be inadequate by the community. Thus Jake becomes the community's albatross, a test of their sensitivity, generosity, and forbearance; the community fails that test not out of maliciousness but because of its own selfishness. Insensitive to Jake's ability to learn the rudimentary skills necessary for relative self-sufficiency, begrudging the charity and kindness extended him by several of the women in the town, and fearful of Jake's unconventional (although perfectly harmless) behavior, the community tries to evade its collective responsibility by putting him in an institution. The effect of the "Strange places and strange ways" on Jake is tragic: "Something that had been alive in Jake, that made him go, had gone out of him." One of the characters who goes to visit him and bring him home remarks, "when your heart's broke, it don't ever heal." Ironically, the institution rejects Jake as well; he is not insane and therefore is as much out of place there as in the community itself. For Jake, however, home can never be the same again, for he senses the community's repudiation of him: "Sometimes now his loneliness tugged him toward town, but a stronger instinct kept him away." His accidental death by fire is, finally, a release from his isolation and alienation, and the blackened chimney of his cabin is a lasting reminder to the community of its collective guilt in rejecting him.

While the novel displays some plot similarities to Carson McCullers's *The Heart is a Lonely Hunter* (1940) and resembles her *Ballad of the Sad Cafe* (1951) in its handling of point of view and in its final evocation of atmosphere through descriptions of the weather and the snow, its ties to Faulkner's *The Sound and the Fury* are obvious. Faulkner and Williams frequently spoke about Benjy and Jake together; both characters are misinterpreted by their respective communities which ultimately cannot tolerate their unconventional behavior. Equally striking is the similarity of Jake to Ike Snopes in *The Hamlet* (1940). Although Williams had read this novel approximately four years before composing "The Morning and the Evening," she denied consciously remembering it during the writing of her story. In retrospect, for Williams, Jake was an alter ego: "He was indeed myself; all the locked-in terrible years of my silence and fears which Faulkner wished to break through and never could."

Equally effective in its portrayal of its protagonist's loneliness, but considerably more mature, is Williams's second novel, *Old Powder*

Robert Satter

Joan Williams

Man (1966). Where her first novel had drawn heavily on the town where her mother grew up for its setting and for the prototype of Jake in a retarded man named Buck, her second novel grew out of Williams's sense of the sadness of her father's life and of her relationship with him. Frank "Son" Wynn and his daughter Laurel are based on Williams's father and herself. To depict the business of levee building she interviewed her father's co-workers long after he was dead, and traveled through Tennessee, Mississippi, and Arkansas along the same dusty roads he had known. Williams also researched the dynamiting business in books obtained from the Dupont Company and the U.S. Army Corps of Engineers. Thus, although none of the reviewers commented on the fact, for Williams what is particularly significant about the novel is its re-creation of the particular historical context of the levee-building era, which was "a part of Americana that will never happen again."

Submitted to Hiram Haydn, former editor at Atheneum who had accepted *The Morning and the Evening* and had since joined Harcourt, Brace, *Old Powder Man* underwent one complete rewriting. Commenting that he did not understand what the novel was about, Haydn returned the very rough first draft to Williams. She began again, "with one single thought in mind: the book is about the man's desire to achieve." As rewritten, the novel is "the story of a salesman's life," Williams notes, "the things he neglects in order to achieve success and his sad realization of it, too late." The novel begins in the small town of Mill's Landing and rapidly but dexterously recapitulates the nomadic life of Son's parents as they move from one temporary job to another. Against this background of poverty and poor education, the obsession of the handsome, energetic Son to better himself emerges: "he sat up, crying out . . . to the whole vast dark Goddamned world: 'Listen! There's got to be a place in the world for a man as willing to work as me.' " Moving to the larger city of Delton (very much like Memphis), Son discovers that the dynamiting business can fulfill that need.

However, Son's single-minded dedication to success sends him on a journey that lasts thirty years as he markets dynamite and does blasting for the levee. Hard-drinking, hard-working, and hard-loving, as his material wealth increases, he blindly permits his personal life to deteriorate. His first wife has an affair and ultimately leaves him; his second wife turns to alcohol for solace; his daughter Laurel becomes a stranger to him. Only as an old man, the levees completed and the demand for dynamite declining as irrevocably as his health, does Son begin to perceive that his triumph is an empty one. Material prosperity does not insulate him from loneliness, and his fame as a dynamiter fades away with the deaths of those who knew him and worked with him. Hesitantly, he turns to the daughter he had ignored, and after an initial false start in which he tries to force her to take an interest in his company, he begins to discover her on her own terms. Thus, in the closing seventy pages of the novel, Laurel emerges as an increasingly important character as she gropes toward an understanding and appreciation of the father whose emphysema finally kills him just as their new friendship is emerging. " 'I've learned a lot too late, too,' Laurel said, thinking no one was without regrets."

Williams's third novel, *The Wintering*, did not meet with the favorable reception granted its two predecessors. One reviewer complained about its unbelievable incidents, its unclearly motivated characters, its ragged style, and the confusing shifts in points of view; but he failed to take into consideration that these problems arose logically enough out of Williams's attempt to write a "fictionalized" account of her love affair with William Faulkner. Jeffrey Almoner is Faulkner; Amy Howard is Joan Williams; and it is in the creation of the character of Almoner, who remains a two-dimensional figure, rather than in Amy's portrait, that Williams is least successful. Faulkner had once urged Williams to write a book about their relationship; he had even named the two characters Almoner and Laurel Wynn, although Williams used the latter name in her second novel. Further, he had suggested that the novel employ an epistolary form, a method which Williams ultimately rejected although a number of letters, some entirely fictional, others taken almost verbatim from her correspondence with Faulkner, were incorporated in *The Wintering*.

The novel includes segments that are heavily autobiographical, such as Amy's first meeting with Almoner and their encounter in the woods, where she shows him her story; other episodes, such as the interlude in Greenwich Village, are more thoroughly fictitious. Several characters are also autobiographical; the publisher who loans Almoner his apartment is a composite of editors Albert Erskine and Robert Linscott, for instance. Other characters, such as Inga, Almoner's Swiss-born wife, are fictitious. The Southern setting, although clearly Mississippi and Tennessee, is never precisely named. Thus, while some details are recognizable representations of reality, others are obviously added to disguise the truth so that the novel is a work torn between two genres, neither fact nor fiction. Instead, it hovers uneasily somewhere in between.

Ultimately, however, the novel is Amy's story rather than Almoner's and sets forth not only her personal relationship with him but also her struggle to emerge as a writer. Torn between her sense of guilt at her inability to reciprocate the depth of Almoner's love for her and her fear that "in trying to help her, Jeff was about to take over what had belonged to her," only by distancing herself from Almoner professionally as well as emotionally is Amy able to embark successfully on a writing career. After rejecting Almoner and finding a subsequent love affair unsatisfactory, Amy decides to return to the safety of Almoner's love. Ironically, although he had not planned to meet her on her return and accept what is in effect her withdrawal from life, Almoner dies shortly before Amy arrives. She understands that his death is opportune because it prevents her retreat: "She had, for too long, run away from everything, and alienation of the spirit was bad. She had to have the courage to be, which meant not to fear emotions. She wanted to take hold of life and shake it as a terrier shakes a rat; everything, everything, she thought, must be gotten out of it." Even in death, Almoner renders her a selfless and valuable service by releasing the emotions she had repressed for so long by eliciting her intense grief for him. No longer afraid of emotion, Amy is thereby freed to write, and in fact, the novel closes with her sitting by a window in the spring sun doing just that.

Neglected today, Williams's novels are limited in range; but within that range, the best of them are noteworthy in their re-creation of Southern settings and in their depiction of characters alienated from themselves and others in their loneliness. They deserve attention more serious than has been accorded them thus far.

—Gail M. Morrison

Teleplay:

"The Graduation Dress," by Williams and William Faulkner, "General Electric Theatre," CBS, 30 October 1960.

Periodical Publications:

FICTION:

"Rain Later," *Mademoiselle,* 29 (August 1949): 229, 331-338;

"The Morning and the Evening," *Atlantic Monthly,* 191 (January 1953): 65-69;

"No Love for the Lonely," *Saturday Evening Post,* 236 (19 January 1963): 48-51;

"Going Ahead," *Saturday Evening Post,* 237 (12 December 1964): 58-60;

"Pariah," *McCall's,* 94 (August 1967): 80-81, 123-126;

"Spring is Now," *Virginia Quarterly Review,* 44 (Autumn 1968): 626-640;

"Jesse," *Esquire,* 72 (November 1969): 164-165, 249-257.

NONFICTION:

" 'You-Are-Thereness' in Fiction," *Writer,* 80 (April 1967): 20-21, 72-73;

"Twenty Will Not Come Again," *Atlantic Monthly,* 245 (May 1980): 58-65.

References:

Joseph Blotner, *Faulkner: A Biography* (New York: Random House, 1974), pp. 1291-1293, 1301-1303, 1429-1435;

Blotner, ed., *Selected Letters of William Faulkner* (New York: Random House, 1977), pp. 296-301, 336-339, 348-352;

Beverly Scafidel, "Biographical Sketch of Joan Williams," *Mississippi Writers Project,* ed. James B. Lloyd (Oxford: University Press of Mississippi, forthcoming 1981).

JOHN E. WILLIAMS
(29 August 1922-)

BOOKS: *Nothing But the Night* (Denver: Swallow, 1948);
The Broken Landscape (Denver: Swallow, 1949);
Butcher's Crossing (New York: Macmillan, 1960; London: Gollancz, 1960);
Stoner (New York: Viking, 1965; London: Allen Lane, 1973);
The Necessary Lie (Denver: Verb Publications, 1965);
Augustus (New York: Viking, 1972; London: Allen Lane, 1973).

John E. Williams's literary reputation rests largely on his treatment of the tension between public duty and private desire as depicted in *Stoner* (1965) and *Augustus* (1972). A polished but rarely flamboyant craftsman, Williams dwells, as he put it in *Stoner*, on "legends that grew more detailed and elaborate year by year, progressing like myth from personal fact to ritual truth." These legends as often concern little individuals such as William Stoner as they do world rulers; in either case the resulting "truth" is the same: that man can construct only momentary stays against chaos. Since *Augustus* shared the National Book Award for fiction in 1973, Williams's vision has begun to attract attention outside the Rocky Mountain region where he has worked throughout his career.

Born in Clarksville, Texas, John Edward Williams began his lengthy association with the University of Denver following what he has called his "somewhat reluctant" service in the U.S. Army Air Force during World War II. After receiving both his B.A. (1949) and M.A. (1950) degrees from Denver, Williams moved to the University of Missouri where he earned his Ph.D. in English in 1954. In the same year, he joined the faculty at the University of Denver, an association he has retained, rising from the rank of assistant professor to his current position as Laurence Phipps Professor of Humanities, a position he has held since 1976.

Beginning with his undergraduate days, Williams has been closely associated with efforts to encourage literary activity in the Rocky Mountain region. His first novel, *Nothing But the Night* (1948), and volume of poetry, *The Broken Landscape* (1949), were published by Alan Swallow's small Denver publishing house. His 1965 volume of poetry, *The Necessary Lie*, was published by the Denver-based Verb Publications. Following his return to Denver from Missouri, Williams became director of the creative writing program at the University of Denver, a post he kept until 1974. In 1966 he founded and served as the first editor of the *University of Denver Quarterly*, a periodical that has helped solidify Williams's regional prominence. Outside the Rocky Mountain region, Williams has been writer in residence at Wisconsin State University, Smith College, and Brandeis University and served on the staff of the Bread Loaf Writers' Conference in Vermont from 1966 to 1972.

While his regional base and personal experience provide the settings for *Butcher's Crossing* (Colorado) and *Stoner* (Missouri), Williams is in no sense a regional or an autobiographical writer. His primary interest is in the examination of the ways in which characters adapt their private beings to the pressures of the public world, whether represented by family, faculty colleagues, or political rivals. Striving "not to repeat myself from novel to novel," he develops this concern from varied perspectives. Gradually he has shifted the focus of his novels from the private to the public world. His early protagonists, Arthur Maxley of *Nothing But the Night* and Will Andrews of *Butcher's Crossing* (1960), are variations on the familiar naive youth of the Bildungsroman tradition. Williams focuses narrowly on their individual responses to pressure, placing the public world in the background. *Stoner*, providing a view of fifty years in the life of its protagonist, emphasizes the shifts in the way the private self adapts to external circumstances. In *Augustus* Williams shifts dramatically from his focus on the "unknown" men whose "wars and defeats and victories . . . are not recorded in the annals of history" to Augustus Caesar, a man central to those annals. While *Augustus* is the first of Williams's works written in a fragmented modernist mode, it is also a variation on the epistolary novel. The apparent technical shift masks his continuing concern with the theme of the private individual's struggle against chaos.

Nothing But the Night, which has remained almost totally unknown since its publication in 1948, is essentially a Freudian family drama that, Williams has observed, totally ignores the public events of World War II. The alienated protagonist, Arthur Maxley, who describes himself as a "parasite," encounters a stream of bohemian friends, women, and (most importantly) his father, Hollis, whom he has not seen for three years. Williams uses these encounters to strip away the layers of Arthur's protective withdrawal, leading to his confrontation, during a Bergsonian duration of thoughts triggered by the dancing of a nightclub performer, with the memory of his mother's suicide. The thematic structure of the novel revolves around Arthur's progress toward and reaction to this confrontation.

One of Williams's observations concerns Arthur's futile attempts to avoid the confrontation entirely and to cling to the memory of an Edenic past, a time of "ageless and impossible beauty." The novel opens with an image of Arthur floating in a womb from which he cannot escape so long as his memory of his mother's death remains repressed. Both Arthur and his father attempt to create substitutes for the dead mother; their only moment of communication is shattered by the arrival of Hollis's mistress, Ellen Phillips, who closely resembles his dead wife and whose presence revives the oedipal tension between father and son. Later, when the nightclub dancer leads him to a near recognition of the sexual nature of his love for his mother, Arthur attempts to repress the realization by acting out his repressed desires on the body of Claire Hegsic, a woman he has picked up at the club. The attempt inevitably fails, and unable to achieve maturity, Arthur passively accepts a beating from a surrogate father who assumes Hollis's role in the "ancient impending ritual."

The Freudian elements of the novel remain somewhat programmatic in execution and contribute to an overly portentous atmosphere. By holding the focus tightly on Arthur, Williams continually emphasizes the presence of the large inchoate forces that Arthur associates with darkness, night, and an encompassing fate. Arthur believes in "some fortuitous intelligence, some obscure power which controlled both their destinies [which] had willed this thing to happen." Against such a force, humanity is reduced to a mass of "dumb puppets manipulated by unseen hands." The Freudian pattern simply provides the pattern for the puppeteer.

Particularly in the early sections of *Nothing But the Night*, Williams intimates that the novel will consider the relationship of this fate to the creative imagination of the protagonist. The opening scenes portray Arthur as "the tool of a dark prankster, a grim little joker who creates worlds within world, lives within life, brains within brain. All of his illusionary power comes from this gleeful scenarist whose whim it is to bestow and withdraw." But the echoes of Samuel Beckett and self-reflexive resonances of the passage go largely undeveloped, and not until *Augustus* does Williams deal effectively with the theme of creativity.

Will Andrews, the protagonist of *Butcher's Crossing*, shares some of Arthur Maxley's alienated feelings but leaves his father in Boston and goes west. A former Harvard student, Andrews feels, when he first reaches the buffalo-skin-trading town of Butcher's Crossing, Kansas, that he, like Arthur, is "blind, suspended in nowhere, unmoving" and that "all proceeded from his own head." Rather than abandoning himself to solipsism, however, Andrews pursues "the wilderness and freedom that his instinct sought" in an environment that makes it clear that the individual does not possess the ultimate power of creating his surroundings. During the course of a buffalo-hunting expedition to a hidden Colorado mountain valley, Andrews observes the one-handed cook Charley Hoge, the animal skinner Fred Schneider, and the obsessed leader of the party, an old mountain man named Miller, as they react to a variety of adversities: an early snow which seals them in the valley for the winter, a catastrophic accident while fording a river, and the final collapse of the buffalo-hunting industry.

On the surface, *Butcher's Crossing* concerns the exploitative buffalo industry, which provides an outlet for human rapacity. But this social critique also contributes to the complex revaluation of the American transcendental tradition that unites the strands of the book. To be sure, Williams portrays the hide buyer J. D. McDonald, an old friend of Andrews's father, as a man totally obsessed with possession. Even after the industry has collapsed, transforming exploiter into exploited, McDonald reflects on the skins: "It's not that they were worth anything. But they were mine." The hunter Miller's obsession with the destruction of the buffalo herd in the valley, however, is not simply parallel to McDonald's greed. Williams stresses that Andrews "came to see Miller's destruction of the buffalo not as a lust for blood or a lust for the hides or a lust for what the hides would bring, or even at last the blind lust of fury that toiled darkly within him—he came to see the destruction as a cold, mindless response to the life in which Miller had immersed himself." This obsession intimates the metaphysical resonances that underlie Williams's treatment of the buffalo hunt as social ritual.

Williams establishes one point of reference for the metaphysical discussion when Andrews remembers Emerson's image of the transparent eyeball and meditates on his own relationship with nature: "in a way that he could not feel in King's Chapel, in the college rooms, or on the Cambridge streets, he was a part and parcel of God, free and uncontained. Through the trees and across the rolling landscape, he had been able to see a hint of the distant horizon to the west; and there, for an instant, he had beheld somewhat as beautiful as his own undiscovered nature." But if Andrews believes that his "undiscovered" nature is pure and beautiful or that his confrontation with nature in the West will be as liberating as Emerson's walk through Boston, he is soon disabused of the idea. For nature as manifested in the parched plains and snow-covered mountains of Colorado is far from a benevolent force. Nature in *Butcher's Crossing* has a great deal in common with the malevolent force in Jack London or the impenetrable ciphers in *Moby-Dick* and Poe's *The Narrative of Arthur Gordon Pym.* In fact, images of encompassing whiteness, so ambivalently symbolic

in these earlier novels, recur throughout Williams's book, from the prairie covered with buffalo bones to the snow that blinds Andrews, threatening his life. Rather than liberating man's internal glory, the Rocky Mountains press in about Andrews until he feels himself and his companions "circling around and around in a circle that gradually decreased, until they were spinning furiously upon a single point." Nature in this brutally un-Emersonian guise circumscribes rather than releases human potential.

Williams portrays a wide range of responses to the indifference or malevolence (as the men affected see it) of nature. Charley Hoge retreats to his Bible, which is ironically covered with buffalo blood and then lost in the snow; Schneider adopts a stoic attitude, demanding his monthly wage every thirty days throughout the long winter; Miller strikes out blindly against all life, asserting his own power against the universe; Andrews, an Ishmael to Miller's Ahab, silently observes. Recognizing that he has left behind absolutist rules and boundaries, he feels that he must create his own social, moral, and psychological structures as he moves on. His surroundings become to him an existential landscape, contrasting sharply with the Emersonian manifestation of the oversoul: "his very gaze shaped what he saw, and in turn gave his own existence form and place." On his return to Butcher's Crossing, Andrews carries with him a knowledge of the "nothingness" that marks the faces of everyone in the West. Although he remains unable to articulate the lessons of the journey, Andrews rejects the East and commits himself to the "wilderness in which he had thought to find a truer shape of himself." He moves from an Emersonian to an existential outlook. The development of the ramifications of this outlook comes to fruition in Williams's two mature novels.

A deceptively simple novel, *Stoner* tells the story of an outwardly undistinguished assistant professor of English at the University of Missouri. The central interest in the novel lies not in the plot but in Stoner's attempts to erect intellectual and emotional orders to restrain his sense of the meaninglessness of life. These attempts result in an extreme tension between his public duties and private desires, a tension which is the keynote of Williams's mature work. Stoner's attempt to defend his intellectual ideals leads inexorably to the collapse of his personal happiness, which revolves around his love affair with a former student, Katherine Driscoll.

Williams establishes the tone and one of the major thematic issues of the novel when the young Stoner listens to his mentor, Archer Sloane, read Shakespeare's Sonnet 73 in a sophomore literature class. Throughout the novel, Stoner looks on landscapes that, like those of the sonnet, with its "Bare ruined choirs where late the sweet birds sang," reflect both an inner and an outer barrenness. Against this existential wasteland, Stoner, like the persona of the sonnet, can resolve only "To love that well which thou must leave ere long." He realizes that his attempts to construct order in his environment are simultaneously attempts to restructure his interior life: "as he repaired his furniture and arranged it in the room, it was himself that he was slowly shaping, it was himself that he was putting into a kind of order, it was himself that he was making possible." Struggling in almost total obscurity, Stoner attempts both to maintain the university as a place apart from the world, which he sees torn by two world wars, and to realize his human potential through his love for Katherine. Both orders collapse, but there remains a strong sense that Stoner has nonetheless succeeded in making himself possible.

Stoner supports the university as a bastion against the indulgence of mankind's imperfections. Holding no illusions concerning the *actual* purity of the institution, he still commits himself to the ideal of the teacher as "a man to whom his book [that which he is teaching] is true, to whom is given a dignity of art that has little to do with his foolishness or weakness or inadequacy as a man." Stoner's friend David Masters, killed in World War I, once commented that Stoner is "the dreamer, the madman in a madder world, our own midwestern Don Quixote without his Sancho," a visionary who loves the university because he believes "there's something *here*, something to find." Williams demonstrates that in fact the university provides no release from external pressure for Stoner who, like Don Quixote, sometimes appears absurd in his commitment to an impossible and obsolete ideal. When explaining to another old friend why he is determined to resist a charlatan student despite the great political and personal cost to himself, Stoner recalls Masters's words: "he said—something about the University being an asylum, a refuge from the world, for the dispossessed, the crippled. But he didn't mean Walker [the student]. Dave would have thought of Walker as—as the world. And we can't let him in. For if we do, we become the world, just as unreal." This rich tension between varieties of "unreality" provides one of the novel's best realized thematic explorations.

Ultimately what shelter Stoner finds comes through his love for Katherine, which he sees as "a human act of becoming, a condition that was invented and modified moment by moment and day by day, by the will and the intelligence and the heart." The emotional intensity of the affair contrasts sharply with Stoner's failed marriage to Edith, who periodically declares silent war on his delicately constructed orders, including his growing love for their daughter Grace. But even Stoner's love for Katherine cannot stand up against the pressures of the external world. As the public world of university politics begins to press in on the lovers, they find "Their lives were sharply divided between the two worlds, and it seemed to them natural that they should live so divided." Stoner's retreat to Katherine's "world" is one of the few times in Williams's work when a character can even momentarily find escape from the public-private split through contact with another human being. But, as in Sonnet 73 which concludes with the admonition "To love that well which thou must leave ere long," the experience is temporary, leaving Stoner with an intense feeling of failure. Still, the quiet, almost dispassionate tone of the novel's final scene tempers the sense of failure. While Stoner has been unable to transcend his circumstances, he has lived an honorable and compassionate life. Williams's encompassing sympathy for the noble failure makes *Stoner* a small masterpiece of moral literature.

Augustus, despite its fragmented epistolary style, resembles *Stoner* in its concern with a sensitive man attempting to resist social and personal disintegration. The protagonist is referred to more frequently in the novel by his given name, Octavius, than by his honorary title, Augustus, thereby stressing the disjunction between the public entity and the private man. Williams's use of the numerous voices implies that only a combination of perspectives can apprehend Augustus's full human reality. These voices, which are transmitted through journals, published works, letters, and documents, fall into two main groupings: those of active political and military figures, and those of observers, including writers like Cicero, Livy, and Horace. The groupings are of both technical and thematic significance since Augustus insists that the poet, like the politician, "contemplates the chaos of experience" in order to discover or invent "some small principle of harmony and order that may be isolated from that disorder which obscures it." Although Augustus envies the poet his "freedom," it is apparent that he, like Stoner, is engaged in an attempt to create a structure that will resist the incursion of an overpowering external force, which Augustus identifies with "the barbarian."

Structurally, *Augustus* is divided into three books. The first focuses on Augustus's rise to and consolidation of power following the death of Julius Caesar. Williams establishes two time frames for the book's voices, one concurrent with the events (45-32 B.C.) and one revolving around the historian Livy's attempts to research those events several decades later (13-12 B.C.). Similarly, book two, which tells of Augustus's maneuvers for stability during and after his consolidation of power, is split between the "current" events of 39-2 B.C. and the retrospective

And yet, among those who came in out of the weather, and among others who did not, there would be a few possessed of that odd quirk of seeing, that knack of accession, who in the presence of that which was ~~authentic~~ distinguished in its authenticity and grace would ~~be able to~~ perform [undergo] a kind of transmigration, a passage from the self into the painting; where one did not possess but became contour and line and form and color, when one did not have but was the feeling and spirit and soul of what one had lately seen. It was a gift, Mathews knew, that did not come to many, and its coming could not be foreseen [predicted] or willed [forced by the will]. Learning had something to do with it, but learning alone was ~~not~~ enough; it was perhaps the occasion of the gift rather than the cause. To many with much learning the gift had ~~never~~ [not] come and might never, as a vision of God might never come to the theologian, however devout and learned he might be, nor the [grace] of love to the suitor, however he might wish to become ~~one with~~ the otherness of the beloved. To some it came suddenly, if it came, as if an inward shifting had allowed light to enter consciousness in a way that it had not done before, so that vision itself became a means of transport from the inanimate self to the animate object of art; to others it came slowly, as if instilled by a long accretion of seeing, so that it arrived ~~almost~~ beyond the awareness of the recipient, who might never fully apprehend the nature and rarity of his gift.

William Mathews was one of those to whom the gift had come suddenly, and it had come relatively late in his life, so that he knew always the change that it had made in him. It was during his first year of graduate work at the University of California. He was twenty-eight years old. A now barely remembered professor of Art History—an indifferent teacher, as Mathews recalled—had ~~given~~ [assigned] the class of which Mathews was a member ~~an assignment~~ a paper that was to examine

Novel-in-progress, manuscript

journal of Augustus's exiled daughter Julia, written in 4 A.D. The final book is composed entirely of an introspective letter written by Augustus shortly before his death in 14 A.D.

Augustus decides to pursue a public life in a cynical, amoral Rome, which most critics believe is intended as a reflection of contemporary America. Julius Caesar, who will soon become its victim, refers to the "Roman lie" that justifies "murder, theft, and pillage in the name of the Republic." Maecenus echoes the thought when writing to Livy three decades later: "the ideals which supported the old Republic had no correspondence to the fact of the old Republic." While the chaos is more controlled under Augustus than under Julius Caesar, Ovid comments that even then "those old 'virtues,' of which the Roman professes himself to be so proud, and upon which, he insists, the greatness of the Empire is founded—it seems to me more and more that those 'virtues' of rank, prestige, honor, duty, and piety have simply denuded man of his humanity."

In attempting to establish an order against this chaotic background, Augustus at times invokes these very principles, but his attitude toward them resembles Stoner's toward the university. While he is willing to support their symbolic importance, Augustus backs them up with a mixture of public relations, brutal suppression of dissent, and generosity toward vanquished foes. He understands the inevitable disillusionment of the idealist and is willing to fight with and against both Brutus and Marcus Antonius when the situation demands. His primary and perhaps his only concern is to avoid further civil war in Rome. Somewhat sadly, he admits that he has frequently been "guided by the desires of my countrymen, so that I might control them," even when such guidance meant the indulgence of amoral or brutal desires directed against outsiders.

The cost of this control, which provides the basis for the *Pax Augustana*, is Augustus's personal life. He withdraws from his friends, uses his daughter, whom he refers to as his "Little Rome," as a pawn in a series of politically motivated marriages, and finally sends her into exile. The Syrian scholar Nicolaus sounds a major theme when he observes that "Octavius Caesar is Rome; and that, perhaps, is the tragedy of his life." The extent of the tragedy is clear when Augustus foresees the fragility of the order that he has established, telling Nicolaus that "we both must have reached the age when we can take some ironic pleasure in the knowledge of the triviality into which our lives have finally descended." All of Augustus's private sacrifice and public effort come to very little in the end. Envisioning himself as a sacrificial ox, Augustus hopes despairingly for a new religion based on "the ideal of love." But he rejects Nicolaus's benevolent monotheism and says that if one god rules the universe, "He is Accident, and his priest is man, and that priest's only victim must be at last himself, his poor divided self." The "Epilog of Augustus," which ironically hails Nero as the emperor who will fulfill Augustus's hopes for Rome, makes it clear that the public Augustus, like the private Stoner, has been able to forge only a momentary stay against chaos.

The fragmented style of *Augustus*, which has won nearly unanimous critical praise for the air of authenticity it lends its historical materials, also contributes to one of Williams's major themes: that the truth cannot, ultimately, be told. Augustus, the one character in the novel whose temperament allows him to understand both the world of the poet and that of the politician, writes that his "words must conceal at least as much truth as they display." Similarly, Julia recognizes the futility of her journal and vows "I shall write no more." Nicolaus expresses the frustration implicit in the struggles of each character to communicate a vision of reality most cogently when he reluctantly admits the limitations of the classical modes of discourse: "There is so much that is not said. I almost believe that the form has not been devised that will let me say what I need to say." The achievement of *Augustus* lies in Williams's largely successful struggle to generate a form that will transcend this limitation, and express both the private and public reality of Octavius/Augustus.

Perhaps the development of Williams's vision may best be summed up through the thoughts of Stoner as he contemplates the carnage of World War II: "It was the force of a public tragedy he felt, a horror and a woe so allpervasive that private tragedies and personal misfortunes were removed to another state of being, yet were intensified by the very vastness in which they took place, as the poignancy of a lone grave might be intensified by a great desert surrounding it." Increasingly, Williams has concentrated on the poignancy derived from the juxtaposition of public and private misfortunes and struggles. Where his early work occasionally suffered from too narrow a focus on the private agony, his mature novels express both aspects of the problem, employing increasingly complex, but always lucid and accessible, techniques. Williams seems assured of continued popular and critical attention following the success of *Augustus*. His ultimate critical reputation will be determined by how highly future commentators value the quiet craftsmanship and moral intensity of his work.

—Craig Werner

Other:

English Renaissance Poetry: A Collection of Shorter Poems from Skelton to Jonson, edited by Williams (Garden City: Doubleday, 1963).

Periodical Publications:

"Henry Miller: The Success of Failure," *Virginia Quarterly Review,* 44 (Spring 1968): 225-245;

"Fact in Fiction: Problems for the Historical Novelist," *University of Denver Quarterly,* 7 (Winter 1973): 1-12;

"The World and God: Fulke Greville," *University of Denver Quarterly,* 9 (Summer 1975): 24-36.

References:

Jack Brenner, *"Butcher's Crossing*: The Husks and Shells of Exploitation," *Western American Literature,* 7 (February 1973): 243-259;

Julian N. Hartt, "Two Historical Novels," *Virginia Quarterly Review,* 49 (Summer 1973): 45-58;

Robert B. Heilman, "The Western Theme: Exploiters and Explorers," *Partisan Review,* 28 (March-April 1961): 286-297;

Robert Nelson, "Accounts of Mutual Acquaintances to a Group of Friends: the Fiction of John Williams," *University of Denver Quarterly,* 7 (Winter 1973): 13-36;

Rexford Stamper, "John Williams: An Introduction to the Major Novels," *Mississippi Review,* 3 (1974): 89-98.

WIRT WILLIAMS
(21 August 1921-)

SELECTED BOOKS: *The Enemy* (Boston: Houghton Mifflin, 1951; London: Harborough, 1957);

Love in a Windy Space (New York: Reynal, 1957; London: Avon, 1958);

Ada Dallas (New York: McGraw-Hill, 1959; London: Muller, 1960);

A Passage of Hawks (New York: McGraw-Hill, 1963; London: Muller, 1964);

The Trojans (Boston: Little, Brown, 1966; London: Barrie & Rockliff, 1967);

The Far Side (New York: Horizon, 1972).

Although Wirt Alfred Williams, Jr., is a writer unknown to some critics and many readers, he has received more critical recognition than many established writers. Of his six novels, three—*The Enemy* (1951), *Ada Dallas* (1959), and *The Far Side* (1972)—have been nominated for Pulitzer Prizes.

Williams was born in Goodman, Mississippi, and raised in Cleveland, Mississippi. After graduating from Cleveland High School at age fifteen, he attended Delta State University, where he occasionally taught history classes for his father, who was head of the social studies department, and received a B.A. degree in English and American literature there in 1940 at the age of eighteen. Williams then entered graduate school at Louisiana State University and studied under Robert Penn Warren and Cleanth Brooks. He received an M.A. in journalism in 1941 and joined the navy the following year.

After the war, Williams returned to Louisiana and worked briefly as a reporter for the *Shreveport Times*. Later, he distinguished himself as a reporter, feature writer, researcher, and city editor with the *New Orleans Item* (1946-1949), where he helped expose corruption and illegal practices within the state. To gather information for one story, Williams worked for weeks as a ward attendant in the East Louisiana Hospital for the Insane at Jackson, Louisiana; his reporting of the situation there brought before the public inefficiency and corruption in the hospital operations. Another time he lived in a leper colony for a week in order to gather material for a story. For his journalism Williams won the Heyward Broun Newspaper Guild Award and the ABC Award in 1949, and was nominated for a Pulitzer Prize.

Even though Williams was highly successful as a journalist, he turned to an academic career. He received a doctorate in English from the University of Iowa in 1953 and then became a member of the English department of California State University at Los Angeles, where he teaches creative writing and seminars on tragedy and Hemingway. He is currently working on a new novel and is in the process of revising a book-length study of Hemingway's fiction.

Williams became interested in writing at an early age, when he thought writing fiction would be

Richard W. Purdie

glamorous, exciting, profitable, and easy. This interest in writing, according to Williams, "fused with my desire to be a reporter." However, it was not until he was eighteen, when he read Ernest Hemingway's collection of short stories *In Our Time* (1925), that "the impulse underwent the sure change and became a desire to write seriously. . . . I got the same feeling from reading the Robinson Jeffers poems a little later, but this was after I was hooked. . . ."

From these readings during his formative years, Williams moved on to other influences, especially the Imagist poets, Flaubert, Conrad, Faulkner, Warren, and Sartre. It was Hemingway, however, who proved to be the overwhelming influence. Like Hemingway's, Williams's writing is never obscure. His prose is tight and terse, yet descriptive and informative. Critic and novelist James B. Hall praises Williams's brief descriptive passages which create "a pervasive atmosphere" so strong "that a delicately controlled atmosphere may become an important protagonist in the story."

Another important influence on Williams is Jean-Paul Sartre's existentialist writings. Williams's first novel, *The Enemy,* has been called an existentialist novel, even though it was written before Williams formally studied existentialism or Sartre's work. *A Passage of Hawks* (1963) and *The Trojans* (1966) are, however, consciously existential. In *A Passage of Hawks* Ginch Lorraine is characterized as an existentialist who is completely evil and amoral. According to Williams, Ginch "was intended to demonstrate that any formally coded philosophy carried to its ultimate lengths becomes ridiculous." In *The Trojans* Williams uses Sartre's philosophy as "a formal equation to define the life thrust of each character. . . ."

While Williams's novels are rich in thematic expression, the themes are not wholly original. In addition to existentialism, Williams relies upon such resources as myth, Jacobean drama, tragedy, and the South. His writing reveals broad patterns or designs; and his characters, who are occasionally larger than life, act consistently with the patterns imposed upon the novels. For example, three of his novels—*Love in a Windy Space* (1957), *Ada Dallas,* and *A Passage of Hawks*—follow a tragic pattern in which his heroines possess the traditionally defined tragic elements in varying degrees of effectiveness.

The Enemy grew from Williams's experiences in the navy. He began the book in the South Pacific after the Medium Landing Ship he commanded ran aground during a typhoon. He finished the book six years later at the University of Iowa. According to Williams, he had difficulty in shaping the novel. A newspaper friend and novelist, Flannery Lewis, helped him with the first version. More formal instruction and advice came from Paul Engle, head of the University of Iowa's Writers Workshop.

What further helped Williams focus the novel was his friend Raymond Weaver's introduction to an edition of *Moby-Dick.* Like Melville's novel, *The Enemy* in its final form is a narrative of action that symbolizes a conflict between man and unseen evil: a destroyer on a search-and-destroy mission combs the North Atlantic for German submarines it never sees. Williams gives an accurate, detailed description of submarine-searching procedures and the routines of naval life and, by doing so, illustrates the tedium of sea duty. A subplot in *The Enemy* deals with a pretentious officer who is disliked by his fellow officers and crew because of his condescending attitude and ineptitude in performing duties.

Williams's second novel, *Love in a Windy Space,* is also the result of personal experience and has several autobiographical sources. The male protagonist is a one-time Southern gentleman and ex-navy man who has become a public relations man in New Orleans; the female protagonist is a member of the Southern aristocracy who sees in him an answer to her need for men. These two products of a quiet, orderly, agrarian South are lost in a chaotic world that bares their insecurities and weaknesses. Although *Love in a Windy Space* received favorable reviews when it was published, Williams had difficulty finding a publisher, for the novel was not considered "commercial" enough. It was only after four revisions and twenty-five submissions to various publishers that the novel was finally accepted by Reynal.

Ada Dallas, one of Williams's most popular novels, was a best-seller for more than three months. Joseph Blotner considers it one of the best written recent political novels dealing with the role of women in politics. Based on the brand of Louisiana politics Robert Penn Warren had written about in *All the King's Men* (1946), *Ada Dallas* traces the political advancement of Ada from call girl to governor of the state from the points of view of the man who loves her, the man who is her partner in crime, and the man whom she replaces as governor. The use of multiple points of view helps distance the reader from Ada and presents an ambivalent picture of her: both cold and loving, then opportunistic and fragile.

The novel stems from Williams's experiences as a Louisiana political reporter and was partly inspired by a cover story on Eva Perón in *Time* magazine. Williams spent five years on *Ada Dallas*; and when the novel finally appeared, it received much attention from the media. Indeed, one of the characters in the novel, Tommy Dallas, bears a strong resemblance to Jimmie Davis, the colorful country singer who became governor of Louisiana in the 1950s. In 1961 MGM released a movie version.

Unlike some of the factually based incidents and characters in *Love in a Windy Space* and *Ada Dallas,* the Mississippi Delta setting is the only nonfictional ingredient of *A Passage of Hawks.* Williams notes that the novel is a "deliberately Jacobean story of murder and wickedness . . . suggested by T. S. Eliot's examination of Thomas Middleton's *The Changeling.* . . ." The novel presents sex, murder, and blackmail within a framework of tragedy. A young woman comes to town and soon begins a love affair with the husband of one of the richest and most beautiful women in the Delta. The lovers scheme to blackmail the wife into giving him a divorce, but the plan backfires when the wife is murdered and the young woman is blackmailed. Critically, this novel is perhaps Williams's least successful; the series of incidents merely reduces the story to the level of a potboiler—an incredible tale of sex and violence.

Williams's next novel was even more popular than *Ada Dallas. The Trojans* sold more than a million copies and was on the best-seller list in England as well as America. Its subject is the motion picture industry. The beautiful blonde star of a movie being filmed on location mysteriously disappears. As the production costs run into millions of dollars, the star's past is revealed through the flashbacks of several people: her author-husband, her producer, the president of the movie company, her mother, her agent, her male co-star. The reasons each of them wants her found and the movie completed are varied. *The Trojans* signals Williams's growing preoccupation with the problems of the artist. He uses the actress as artist to explore the various aspects of the creative process, the relationship of intuitive expression to book learning, and the artist's relationship to the world.

Williams's latest novel, *The Far Side,* is perhaps his most sophisticated in terms of theme and idea. Like *The Trojans,* this novel deals with the relationship between the artist and his world. In *The Far Side* John Slade enters a writer's workshop to hammer out a novel. The retreat is run by Karen Munday, an unsuccessful writer who receives from the workshop members' literary successes some compensation for her own failure as a writer. With her help, Slade finishes his novel, and it becomes a best-seller. Later, he is hired by a movie studio to write the screenplay. When he begins his second novel, he realizes he cannot write without the guiding hand of Karen Munday, so he returns to the workshop. This time they become lovers, but Karen's control over him as a mother figure and the primary motivating force begins to smother Slade until he finally escapes.

Williams approached seventeen publishers before Horizon Press agreed to publish *The Far Side,* and while it was critically well received, it was his poorest seller. Says Williams: "It is interesting to note that the novel about the actress-sex symbol as artist sold more than a million copies; the one about the *writer* as same barely broke even. If one needed an example about the public's interest in writers as compared to movie stars, this is as good as any."

Williams is a slow, careful writer, often spending years writing a novel. He considers himself "an extremely self-conscious writer: I can never quite forget technical principles of the art of fiction that I learned, or at least had explained to me, in the classroom. . . ." Indeed, Williams recognizes his debt to such teachers as Ray B. West, Jr., Hansford

Martin, and especially Paul Engle for giving him an understanding of the form, structure, and aesthetics of the novel. Williams realizes the problems of any writer who attempts to present comments or observations on life and who also wishes at the same time to make his writing absorbing and appealing. Williams says, "If a novelist is to be heard . . . he must offer one level of appeal—among all his levels of statement—to a large and completely non-literary audience. I have accepted the condition and find it just: there are many fine things a novelist can do, but the finest of all is to tell a wonderful story." To be sure, his novels are stories which attract and beguile the reader, but Williams does more. He reveals an artist's preoccupation with structure, theme, and technique; and while his novels do entertain, they also possess moral and ethical significance. This complexity is what gives his novels their richness.

—*Sung Gay Chow*

Other:

Heinrich Mann, *Professor Unrat,* translated by Williams (New York: New American Library, 1959).

Reference:

Joseph Blotner, *The Modern American Political Novel, 1900-1960* (Austin: University of Texas Press, 1966), pp. 180-185, 189.

DONALD WINDHAM
(2 July 1920-)

BOOKS: *You Touched Me: A Romantic Comedy in Three Acts,* by Windham and Tennessee Williams (New York: French, 1947);

The Dog Star (Garden City: Doubleday, 1950; London: Hart-Davis, 1951);

The Hitchhiker (Florence: Privately printed, 1950);

Servants with Torches (New York: Privately printed, (1955);

The Kelly Boys (New York: Privately printed, 1957);

The Hero Continues (New York: Crowell, 1960; London: Hart-Davis, 1960);

The Warm Country (London: Hart-Davis, 1960; New York: Scribners, 1962);

Emblems of Conduct (New York: Scribners, 1964);

Two People (New York: Coward McCann, 1965; London: Joseph, 1966);

Tanaquil (Verona: Stamperia Valdonega, 1972; revised edition, New York: Holt, Rinehart & Winston, 1977).

Donald Windham's literary contributions have been many and varied. He has been playwright, editor, novelist, short-story writer, and memoirist. Born to Fred and Louise Donaldson Windham in Atlanta, Windham's early life revolved around his mother, his brother, and his maternal grandparents' rambling Victorian house on Peachtree Street, where they lived after his parents' divorce when Windham was six. His childhood, through his graduation from Boys' High School at seventeen and his decision to leave for New York at nineteen, is chronicled in Windham's autobiography, *Emblems of Conduct* (1964), whose chapters, titled with the names of everyday objects, "The Chifforobe," "The Bath Tub," "The Blond Bed," "A Coin with a Hole in It," record the struggles of the family in the Depression years. *Emblems of Conduct* is not simply reminiscence, however. As Ralph McGill wrote in the *New York Times Book Review*: "It is a moving and rewarding piece of creative writing about a childhood which became, finally, an exit of escape into that mysterious, unknown something for which the child had yearned."

Windham's influences are much more Proustian than Faulknerian or Southern Gothic, and *Emblems of Conduct* is less an autobiography of his childhood than a chronicle of the developing instincts of a young American artist, who voraciously read Saroyan, Huxley, Proust, Stein, and Joyce. Windham remembers that "The books that I liked in my teens were books in which the author is also the hero," and after commenting that he reread Proust's *Swann's Way* (1928) three times, he adds, "Ultimately, I liked books that I wanted to reread, even more than I wanted to reread books that I liked." Despite Windham's early preference for the author as hero, David Jackson, reviewing *Emblems of Conduct* for *Village Voice,* lauds the absence of "that noisy and finally irritating 'I' which has infiltrated American prose (and poetry) leaving a grit of personality on the page and the author's photo on the back flap. Windham sets a standard for first-person narration." Although Jackson praises Windham's simple language, it is Windham's simplicity that has kept far too many critics from examining his works carefully.

In *Emblems of Conduct* Windham reviews the faded family fortunes' disintegrating into poverty and his underlying loneliness and isolation that inevitably ensued sensitively but without sentimentality or nostalgia. His memories are word photographs, images caught with the camera-pen in its sharpest focus to record the minutest detail of such things as the blocks he was given one Christmas:

> I can still see, feel, smell, taste, and hear those colored blocks. They were inch-and-a-quarter cubes, their surfaces solid squares of the primary colors and black, or divided into two contrasting triangles. They smelled like paint, and if you put your tongue on one there was a faint taste of colored paper. Their lacquer was as smooth as china. They clicked against one another when you shook their box.

Windham refers to these blocks again in his paragraph on Proust in the "Blocks and Books" chapter of *Emblems of Conduct*: "There was no more reason to go on [reading the volumes of *Remembrance of Things Past* that followed *Swann's Way*] than there would have been, in the past, to get a new set of blocks when I still had the old ones." And he brings together his descriptive abilities with his own creative instincts: "As far back as I remember, I liked objects that did not do anything, but that I did something with, pieces of wood, glass, paper." One can also place in this category Windham's own novels, all so seemingly simple, yet filled with meaning and impact if the reader is receptive to them.

After graduating from high school Windham went to work for the Coca-Cola Company in its barrel factory. This job was, for his family, to be a stepping stone to an eventual position in the company's office, where his mother already worked. However, as he has commented in a recent interview, "During my adolescence, I had come to dislike the possibilities of myself that I saw reflected around me in Atlanta." He elaborates, "The Coca-Cola office was the last place in the world that I wanted to be. I had to get away from Georgia, in part, because of everything that was planned for me here." Thus, just turned nineteen, on his first week off from the barrel factory, Windham boarded a Greyhound bus bound for New York, to return to Atlanta only for visits since that day.

"New York," in Windham's words, "bestowed upon me a longed-for anonymity," but the profession of writing for him was still mainly an ambition. Ironically, his first "joyous but impecunious months" in New York in 1940 forced him once more to work for the Coca-Cola Company, this time at a drink stand at the World's Fair. His chosen profession was and is something that Windham's family does not comprehend: "They react to my being a writer by assuming that I don't do anything for a living," he related in a conversation while on a visit to Georgia in 1979. "One of my brother's sons didn't know I was a writer until he came across a short story of mine that was being studied in his college English class and brought it home and asked if it wasn't by his uncle." Windham had written in Atlanta before he left for New York, but it was in New York that he began to understand the complexities and commitments necessary for writing. During his first year there he met Tennessee Williams, as Windham has said, "The first person I ever encountered who felt that writing was the most important thing anyone could do, the first person I knew who was willing to sacrifice everything for his writing. He influenced me very much in that way."

During 1942 and 1943 Windham and Williams wrote a play, *You Touched Me* (1947), based on the D. H. Lawrence short story of the same title. A romantic comedy set in England, it centers on the revitalization of an old sea captain when his adopted son returns home from the war and the two of them rescue the sea captain's daughter from the sterile domination of her old maid aunt. The two authors hoped to make enough money from the play to concentrate on their writing; but although *You Touched Me* was tried out in Cleveland and Pasadena, it was not produced on Broadway until September 1945 after Williams's success with *The Glass Menagerie* (1945). Following the Broadway production, Windham had enough money to quit his job as editor of the small magazine, *Dance Index*, which had offices at the School of American Ballet, a position he had held since 1943, and to finish the novel he had begun.

This novel, which would become *The Dog Star*, was completed on his first trip to Italy in 1948. Windham looked unsuccessfully for a publisher for nine months after his return to New York, and the book did not come out until the spring of 1950. Blackie Pride, the protagonist of *The Dog Star*, longs for "strength and courage and indifference." He is guided by this ideal, but he cannot apply it to his everyday life: he fails to accept the aspects of his own character that would bind him to other people, and in losing his identity, he loses his life. The book opens with Blackie, at the age of fifteen, leaving the County Farm School, a juvenile detention center, with all-consuming memories of Whitey Maddox, a youthful suicide, who for Blackie is the symbol of the greatness for which he strives.

Ultimately one of the most self-destructive characters in modern literature, Blackie stalks the

Donald Windham

streets of Atlanta in much the same manner that Pinkie stalks the streets of the British seaside resort in Graham Greene's *Brighton Rock* (1938). Blackie grows from a contempt for weakness, human frailty, and dependence to a contempt for life itself. In his affair with Mabel, the older woman he takes on as a companion, he tests love against his ideal of it as "something great and strong" and finds that only anger is left after desire is gone. In the face of his mother's coarseness he becomes crude and revels in his ability to shock. Only with older sister Pearl and younger brother Caleb does he retain the capability to drop his facade of toughness and again be a boy of fifteen.

In England, where the novel was published in 1951, the *Times Literary Supplement* said: "The atmosphere of *The Dog Star* seems unimpeachably authentic; the family for whom Blackie feels mingled affection and repulsion, the neighborhood boys who seem to him pathetically feeble compared with the dead hero, the girl to whom he behaves with savage and unmeaning violence." It is this atmosphere that dominates the tone of the work. For Blackie, life was not the city park's golfing green with "the odor of warm newly cut grass" but its playground, the "dry earth littered with chewing gum and candy bar wrappers, ice cream cups and wooden spoons, cigarette and contraceptive packages, bits of torn newspaper, dry leaves, pebbles and broken glass." Windham's imagery drives forth the sterility and fragmentation reflected in Blackie's own existence.

In the last chapter, at the studio of a homosexual photographer, Blackie's longing to be "strong and alone, alone and strong" comes to its inevitable conclusion:

> With a final disdain and determination he turned and walked out of the room, the determination and disdain in him turning to joy. He was ravished out of himself. He was converted into the prey which he pursued. . . . He saw only himself, companionless as the last cloud of an expiring storm whose thunder is its knell; and descending the steps to the sidewalk he walked to the curb and straight across the street, his movements stiff and stark, his arms held out from his sides.

The reader learns of Blackie's death when his young brother approaches their sister's house to rendezvous with Blackie and hears a rain-drenched cigar-smoking man say, "Some damned fool just shot himself through the head."

Thomas Mann, interviewed on his seventy-fifth birthday in 1950, singled out *The Dog Star* as the one American novel of the year he wished to praise, describing it as "simple, natural, and strong"; and Tennessee Williams contributed a blurb filled with typical Williamsian enthusiasm:

> I think it marks the advent of probably the most distinguished new talent to appear in the last decade. Its theme is of profound relevance to a tragedy of modern youth. The writing is utterly pure without the affectation of purity. It is the creation of an unadulterated artist.

The 1950s were, however, for Windham not a time of great successes. Though *The Dog Star* received praise, it was for the most part passed over. Windham's endeavors in this period were generally both frustrating and unprofitable. His play *The*

Starless Air (in 1953) received a trial run in Houston, where it was directed by Tennessee Williams, and was optioned by the Theatre Guild but never produced in New York. His short stories, some of which he had begun a decade earlier, were ignored by American magazines, although they were appearing in *Horizon, Paris Review,* and *Botteghe Oscure* in Europe. Then, at the end of 1959, William Maxwell of the *New Yorker* accepted several of Windham's sketches, which, with Maxwell's encouragement, eventually developed into *Emblems of Conduct.* Nineteen sixty saw a progressive rise in Windham's fortunes with the publication in America and England of his second novel, *The Hero Continues,* and the publication in England of his collection of short stories *The Warm Country* (not published in America until 1962). The same year he received a Guggenheim Fellowship for creative writing in fiction and set off for a year-and-a-half stay in Europe.

The Hero Continues, centered like *The Dog Star* upon alienation and the hostility of the world, shows not only a maturer central character in Denis Freeman, but also an author surer of himself and more adept at his craft. This work is, however, perhaps even less easy for readers to empathize with. Part of the reason is Freeman himself, whose almost paranoid response to occurrences and individuals surrounding his rapid rise to fame makes him an even less endearing and more pathetic protagonist than Blackie Pride. Yet this same paranoia heightens the fascination of the novel.

The novel is dedicated to Tennessee Williams and its main character has much in common with him. But to say that the book is veiled biography is to mistake Windham's literary method. Windham does utilize the things and people of his life as points of departure for fiction, and certainly his friendship and association with Williams was one of long standing; but in Freeman, Windham, dominated by his theme, has created a character more believable and less a caricature than Williams himself.

This novel *is* Denis Freeman. Unlike *The Dog Star,* where environment and locale are important, all but Freeman is incidental. Self-centered, brusquely egocentric, Freeman concentrates on his work (or ambition), friends and relationships be damned. Freeman is, for all that, possessed of a sensitivity and a need for people but is unable to give this need priority in a rational or even realistic way. One might say of him what Gide said of a certain French writer: "He is a sort of Bernard Palissy who throws his friendships into the fire to keep his oven going." Whether it be his self-serving use and abuse of his friend Morgan or his inability to separate his aesthetic from his personal existence, Freeman struggles with subdued violence for his goal. But achieving it separates him even further from other people. In the last chapter, after Morgan's death relieves the novel's hero of his temporary sterility, Windham notes, "Like a man reprieved, separated from and attracted to everything, he did what was necessary."

The Hero Continues is about Denis Freeman's drive for success, but it is also about the sources of creativity. In the penultimate scene at a restaurant opposite the catacomb of San Callisto outside Rome, Freeman is annoyed by another character's suggestion

> that one could write a play at someone else's suggestion. At such moments he almost felt that he could confide in her the secret concealed beneath his carefully-husbanded calm, but the feeling vanished as quickly as it had come and he merely said that the idea was too corny.
>
> —But you haven't written anything since I met you.
>
> —I've successfully learned to avoid the disasters which make writing necessary.

Freeman is left alone with his "continuing," his ambivalent attraction to and fear of death and the realization that his creativity, like a malformed phoenix, can only rise from the ashes of sacrificed lives, maimed personalities, cruelty, and self-deception.

Windham's short-story collection, *The Warm Country,* contains an introduction by E. M. Forster that is both laudatory and perceptive. Forster comments that the stories "are simply written, they do not shout or fuss, they do not contain too much alcohol, and above all they are completely free from the slickness that comes from attending courses in Creative Literature." *The Warm Country* ranges in places from Georgia to Venice and stays in no fixed stratum of society. Its characters are an old maid schoolteacher, a Negro motorcycle delivery boy, an Italian carabiniere, and an American sailor. They suffer from battle depression, isolation, fear, and malaise. They struggle to attain "warmth," to be not statues but, as Forster says, "flesh and blood and a heart," for they must "contact one another or they will decay."

After the memoir, *Emblems of Conduct,* appeared in book form in 1964, Windham's third novel, *Two People* (1965), was published. Its critical reception, like that of his earlier books, was more enthusiastic in England than in America. The jacket blurbs from E.M. Forster, Truman Capote, Luigi

Your new writing is better
old arrangement is better

3 3

works unless they are hugh crazy negros like George. [The white men make him self-conscious]

"You'll be having a big week end," answered George. He wiped the sweat from around his eyes and laughed, swinging ~~his~~ body ~~and~~ glistening all over.

"Might get a pint to take home. Got to save some. The way Scarrett hates to see a penny of the companyés money go as bad as if it were his own, I bet he's as mad as hell."

"Yes sir, Mis'er Williams." George was still smiling and he said carefully, "If you going to put some of h that away, I ~~sure~~ sho's could use a little till next week. I ain't lying, Mis'er Williams, and I'll tell you the truth of what I want it for. I's buying me a second hand automobile to ride to work in, and take my wife out riding on Sundays, and if you lets me borrow three dollars to make the payment this week I'll give it back to you next Friday."

"Yeah," said Williams, " how the hell are you going to have more money next week than this?" (action description) why here?

"I just got to pay my doctor bill ~~this week~~, Mister Williams, Last month when I was sick at work with the piles Mis'er Scarrett took me to his doctor instead of the companyés. I didn't know nothing about it and now I got to pay him this week or he's going to sue me."

Williams leaned over the iron backbar of George's machine. "Why don't you borrow it from Scarrett. He's got pleanty of money. I haven't."

"He wont lend it to me. I asked him, and told him

The Warm Country, *revised typescript (1940), with additional notes by Tennessee Williams*

Barzini, and Tennessee Williams are impressive enough, but American critics immediately launched into the novel's low-key nature. Eliot Fremont-Smith called it "a vapid boy-meets-boy affair . . . less passionate or painful than just pretentious—a simply written tale, so devoid of relevancy that it may, to some, seem art."

Through his cynicism about Windham's book Fremont-Smith may have found the essence of *Two People*. Unlike most 1960s writing, it does not shout, it whispers. The shout may attract immediate attention, but the whisper is more provocative and lingering. Michael Ratcliffe in the London *Sunday Times* says that here "Something is being said about the absence of strong love and affection, and the sense of uncompleted gestures, of risking half-truths is marvelously done; but the real pleasure of the book lies in the writing itself. Mr. Windham deploys a fairly simple Latinate vocabulary in sentences of an almost baroque complexity, the best of which is precisely calculated as to the exact moral and syntactical weight that each word has to bear." Homosexuality (or, more accurately, bisexuality), briefly present in Windham's first two novels, becomes an integral theme in *Two People*. Forrest, the middle-aged, middle-class American, and Marcello, the young patriarchially dominated Italian boy fall more into self-awareness than into love. The American's travel agent friend tells him that "promiscuous encounters are to Italian boys what ice cream sodas at the corner drugstore are to their American counterparts." Yet both Forrest and Marcello almost cry out for this interlude. Their experience of each other, although neither momentous nor enduring, is necessary. As a reviewer in the *Times Literary Supplement* points out, their casual affair "grows into a fruitful and rewarding relationship" that not only contributes to Marcello's increasing maturity but also helps to reunite Forrest and his estranged wife.

What Windham presents the reader is a story of seemingly little dramatic intensity, for its climax is disaster avoided. Eleanor Perry's comment that "it is unavoidable that this small pebble of a meeting and a parting will make a very small ripple on the reader's consciousness" missed the major point Windham expresses about the human condition. Distasteful or not, and genuinely ego-deflating, Windham's work perceptively relays his belief that the ripples, not the splashes, determine the texture of life, that life's obscure complexities and possibilities, and their sudden illuminations, mean most in personal relationships.

For Forrest his encounter is twofold—with Marcello and with Rome, both alluring and promiscuous. It is experience, denied him by his wife, not of sex or place alone, but of life itself. Forrest's return to America is inevitable, but his last walk through Rome presents a farewell to the city and the boy, as well as the writer's revelation of his purpose:

> All around him as he walked, he sensed the physical complexity of the earth present beneath the streets and buildings. In the air there was an atmosphere of Paradise, not of perfection but of all things being possible. He was trying to go in a more or less straight line, rather than through the larger and more frequented streets, and he became lost in an obscure byway. He could find neither light nor people, nor an open space. Then suddenly, he came out into a small, dark, deserted square, in the center of which, lit by a spotlight, was the fountain of the tortoises. By some chance, he had never seen it before.

Windham's fourth novel *Tanaquil* first appeared in a limited edition printed in Verona in 1972. Its commercial publication in somewhat revised form was in 1977. This novel once again has perhaps not received the critical examination due it. Like *The Hero Continues*, it is a novel centered in New York, the business world of art, and the artists who live there. But most of all it is a novel of two people, Tanaquil and Frankie, both idealists and isolated. In their chance meeting at the Silver Dollar Bar, these two displaced persons begin to find themselves in each other. They share love; they share sex; they are continually amazed at the significance of their bond.

Katha Pollitt in the *New York Times Book Review* dismisses them as "little more than labels for narrative pawns" and ridicules the "simplicity of the sexual feelings of [Windham's] characters." Yet, on the contrary, they are two ordinary people, perplexed, certain of little but their intrinsic feelings, unable always to comprehend, in turn swept along with events and emotions. In Windham's characters there is seldom a vastly moving spiritual growth or a particular point of enlightenment, but rather human vacillations, indecisions becoming decisions, realization that the clenched fist is futility, and the gradual opening of the hand to let palm touch palm. Tanaquil and Frankie are not exceptional, but they are real. They reveal themselves in the simplicity of daily life and shared experience. We can recognize their truths in the tenuous balance of their love. *Tanaquil* closes with a sense of resolution and enlightenment:

> When his hand touched her bare hip, he breathed a sigh that released all the regret that remained in him. Gently, he placed his face against the soft warm flesh of her neck. In the past he had never understood what she meant when she told him that he smelled wonderful. Now he did. Enclosed in the odor of her body, he felt as the bees he had seen in his childhood must have felt enclosed in the fragrant blossoms of the flowering apple trees. Half asleep, he breathed in the perfume of her hair. His face pressed against her neck, confusing scent and touch, he exhaled. Slowly, aware of the sound of his breath as a part of the warmth and odor, he went to sleep, lost somewhere between flesh and flowers.

Between the two versions of *Tanaquil*, Windham edited E. M. Forster's letters to him (published in a limited edition at Verona in 1975). This in part led to Windham's publication of *Tennessee Williams's Letters to Donald Windham 1940-1965* (1977), first printed as a limited edition in 1976 in Verona. These letters chronicle the friendship of Williams and Windham, their literary acquaintances, and the gradual deterioration of their closeness. They also present detailed insight into the characters of both correspondent and recipient. Windham comments that Williams gave permission to reprint his letters having already brought out his *Memoirs*, which was "very frank, even indiscreet. After that book there was nothing in his letters that could be indiscreet about him, but there was a good deal that was indiscreet about me. So I had to think it over for a while. Then I decided that we'll all be dead soon anyway, so I'd just pretend we are dead now and be just as frank."

Windham's current work-in-progress is a novel tentatively titled "The Stone in the Hourglass." The author describes it as "a story of the 1970s, set half in New York, half in Verona." Centered upon the art world, Windham considers it "more about the state of the world than about love."

Reading Windham's fiction makes it apparent that the author maintains a deep sense of place. Although rooted in his Southern heritage, his writing is not limited there geographically. For Windham it was in leaving a particular place that it became more real to him:

> I started writing about Atlanta when I moved to New York. I could never write about New York until I was in Europe. I always write about places very strongly. One place can suggest another. It is emotion that makes you leave and nostalgia that makes you write.

Although long a resident of New York City, Windham recently has stated, "I think of myself as a Southern writer, a Georgia writer. Other people don't see me that way, I suppose, because I don't write what they consider the appropriate Southern Gothic," and he disagrees "with the advice 'write about what you know'; write about what you *need* to know, in an effort to understand." He elaborates, "I think the minute someone believes that he knows something he becomes a bore. You should always want to go further. I write because I'm upset about something I can't figure out."

Windham and his writing maintain that quality. There is no smugness or pretense in the man or his art. His prose is unadorned and precise, melodious and evocative, a capturing of a slice of the real in unfaced and untarnished words. As one of his characters in the short story "Life of Georgia" remarked, "for in the end all reality was related to the reality which cannot be borne, the reality of life as it is, rather than as it should be, or at least as they had always heard that it should be."

—Robert M. Willingham, Jr.

Plays:

You Touched Me, New York, Booth Theatre, 1945;
The Starless Air, Houston, Playhouse Theatre, 1953.

Other:

E. M. Forster's Letters to Donald Windham; with Comments by the Recipient, edited by Windham (Verona: Stamperia Valdonega, 1975);

Tennessee Williams's Letters to Donald Windham 1940-1965, edited by Windham (Verona: Stamperia Valdonega, 1976; New York: Holt, Rinehart & Winston, 1977).

Papers:

Donald Windham's papers are housed in Special Collections, University of Georgia Libraries.

LARRY WOIWODE

(30 October 1941-)

BOOKS: *What I'm Going to Do, I Think* (New York: Farrar, Straus & Giroux, 1969; London: Weidenfeld & Nicolson, 1970);

Beyond the Bedroom Wall: A Family Album (New York: Farrar, Straus & Giroux, 1975);

Even Tide (New York: Farrar, Straus & Giroux, 1977).

With two finely crafted, award-winning novels, Larry Woiwode has attracted both popular and critical attention. Writing in a deliberately mannered, traditional, realistic style, he evokes to a degree unusual in modern fiction an emotional response from his readers. His fiction is tinged with personal reminiscence and seemingly autobiographical details, but he has also proved adept at projecting himself into the consciousnesses of a wide variety of characters of both sexes. His second novel, *Beyond the Bedroom Wall* (1975), merits special attention as a revival of the family chronicle, a revered though out-of-fashion form, and for its montage format with diverse characters and settings, a shifting point of view and temporal structure, a variety of narrative forms, and a complex, episodic plot. About one-third of its chapters appeared originally as short stories, but Woiwode skillfully weaves them into a unified whole. His fiction is religious and intellectual in the broadest sense, with recurrent emphasis on the meaning and impact of death and the intricate negotiations between one's psyche and personal moral code and the demands of family and society. He achieves a powerful psychological realism and depth of insight in an intensely imagined, lyrical style remarkable for its clarity and precision.

Woiwode's birthplace is Carrington, North Dakota, the closest hospital to his home in Sykeston, a predominately German settlement of a few hundred people. The harsh climate, stark beauty, and pervasive loneliness of this remote corner of rural America and its dignified, somewhat fatalistic Northern European populace provide the inspiration and much of the material for his fiction and poetry. His only substantial nonfiction, an article entitled "Guns" in *Esquire* (December 1975), records an undercurrent of violence in life "near the edge of the West" which is especially marked by a "fetish for guns, not to say pride in it" and an acute fascination with death, both of which become prominent themes in his writing.

When he was ten, Woiwode's family moved to Manito, Illinois. As a student for five years at the University of Illinois, his interests ranged throughout the curriculum, but he did not complete a bachelor's degree. Upon leaving in 1964, he was awarded an A.A. degree in rhetoric. He has since worked exclusively as a free-lance writer. In addition to the novels, numerous poems and short stories have been published in an assortment of periodicals: *Partisan Review, McCall's, New Yorker, Audience, Atlantic, Mademoiselle, New American Review*, and *Harper's*.

Beyond the Bedroom Wall is, in a sense, his first novel, since it was conceived first and its chapters began to appear as short stories in 1965. Over a ten-year period, twenty stories were published, most frequently in the *New Yorker*. With few exceptions, the stories focus on the childhood experiences of three characters—Jerome, Charles, and Tim Neumiller, the last generation of the family chronicled in the novel. The chapters were considerably revised from the original draft of the novel to fit the demands of the short-story form. In the novel, the syntax is more complex and the descriptions fuller and more evocative; isolated incidents are expanded and interwoven by adding details about the characters and parallel incidents from their pasts, and deeper psychological development is accomplished by modifying point of view. In most cases, the first published version eliminated or changed names, even to the point of giving a character different names in different stories, so that a casual reader of the series would not immediately recognize the continuities of a novel-in-progress.

As he had published parts of what was to become his second novel, Woiwode completed his first, *What I'm Going to Do, I Think*, in 1969. It also appeared piecemeal in the *New Yorker* (1966-1968) in four segments shortened but not otherwise very different from the novel. The novel was an immediate critical success, with several reviewers calling Woiwode a new Hemingway; it was heavily promoted, with full-page advertisements in major newspapers and book review magazines. The William Faulkner Foundation designated it the year's best first novel. Accompanying these accolades were tokens of admission into the literary establishment: he received a Guggenheim Fellowship for 1971-1972; served as a judge for the National Book Awards in 1972; became writer in residence at the University of Wisconsin in 1973-1974; and lectured, read, and conducted workshops at other major universities. The novel has been translated into eight

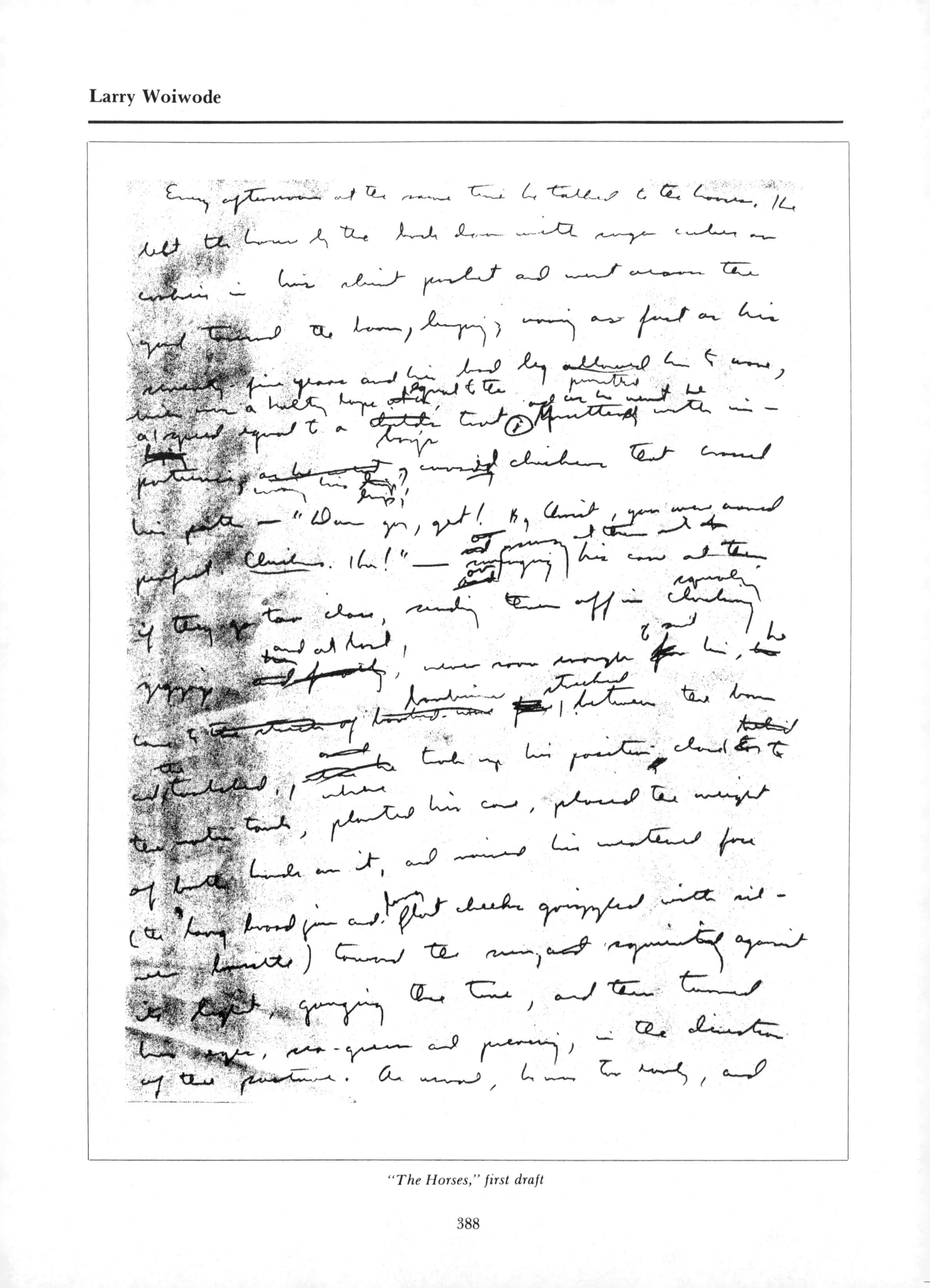

"The Horses," first draft

foreign languages, including Czechoslovak and Japanese.

Through the early 1970s, Woiwode continued to publish poems and individual chapters of *Beyond the Bedroom Wall,* which appeared in 1975. The novel generated critical enthusiasm in the popular and academic press and, because of its serious themes and intimate portrayal of Catholicism, also in religious periodicals such as *America, Christian Century,* and *Commonweal.* More honors followed: nominations for the National Book Award and the National Book Critics Circle Award, the fiction award from the Friends of American Writers, an honorary Doctor of Letters degree from North Dakota State University (1977), and an award in fiction from the National Institute of Arts and Letters (1980).

Woiwode has continued to write poetry and in 1977 his first collection of poems, entitled *Even Tide,* was published. After living for some years in Hager City, Wisconsin, and New York City and traveling extensively to find a place "quiet enough to work with some permanence," he has recently moved to a farm in the southwestern corner of his native North Dakota.

What I'm Going to Do, I Think is a penetrating character study of two newly married young people, struggling to adjust to each other and the adult responsibility brought on by an unwanted pregnancy. Chris Van Eenanam, the protagonist, is a graduate student in mathematics who, despite his political apathy, faithfully portrays through his painful self-awareness and self-righteousness the restless generation of the 1960s. His pregnant bride, Ellen Strohe, is an intelligent but abnormally subdued woman whose identity has been nearly obliterated by the doting but psychologically domineering grandparents who raised her. The novel focuses on their wedding, a near-comic interlude with a naive minister, and their lengthy honeymoon at her grandparents' cabin on Lake Michigan, a soured idyll which portends disaster for the relationship.

The nature of the relationship is, on the whole, puzzling: beyond cliches (not mentioned in the book) about the attraction of opposites, there seems little rationale for their coming together. Moreover, though the novel sketches, in flashbacks about Ellen's grandparents, sufficient details to make her character plausible, Chris remains an enigma despite detailed development of his thoughts and perceptions. His motivation is obscured by self-doubt which derives from some unrevealed, perhaps unknowable, source. He may suffer from an overdeveloped machismo or a deep-seated neurosis; perhaps he is merely selfish and immature. He proves to be a sullen, sometimes humorless, finally rather unpleasant character who moves through the novel always on the verge of anger. Periodically, he lashes out almost predaceously at his wife—at a pivotal moment he appears to contemplate shooting her—and exploits her vulnerabilities in ways unlikely to win the sympathy of most readers. Also, he often broods rather than thinks; his musings expose him as intellectually immature and morally uncentered. He resents bitterly, for example, Ellen's premarital affairs but is obsessed by one of his own, and shows himself to be susceptible to the charms of other women even after the wedding. Also, despite years of academic discipline his thoughts and actions lack, as the title suggests, a clear sense of purpose.

Woiwode compensates for this unfinished, frustrating conception of character with a stylistic polish and tonal control unusual for a first novel. Nothing exhibits his mastery of style better than the presentation of setting. The action is set largely at the Strohes' lodge on Lake Michigan, which provides the opportunity to depict nature in many moods and guises. With a nod towards Hemingway's Nick Adams stories, place is rendered in carefully measured observations whose very austerity becomes lyrical: "The bronze channel on the lake widened as the sun went down. She put her arm around his waist and led him closer to the edge of the bluff. He looked down. . . . A gust of wind, guided up the wash, swept over the bluff and took the hair back from his forehead and stung his eyes, and the leaves of the silver maples took orange on their undersides from the sun." The lake, the countryside, and the local fauna become the dominant reality in the narrative and serve as metaphors for Chris and Ellen's dilemma. The vast, misty lake mirrors their changing moods and reminds them constantly of the unknowable future stretched before them. The countryside becomes the focal point of Chris's insecurity about himself, his work, and his new role; so simple an act as mowing the lawn becomes a fierce struggle to impose order on his environment. Only once does he achieve genuine communion with the natural world, when, in the novel's best sequence and only scene of concentrated action, he exhausts himself baling hay with a local farmer. However, his sense of purpose is short-lived; for the most part, he wanders aimlessly through the woods and on the beach or clambers up the bluff in parodic explorations. Finally, he buys a rifle and fires endlessly at birds and small animals, an action which combines boredom, his need to reaffirm his manhood, and, more symbolically, his half-formed desire to destroy Ellen's child, thus evading parental responsibility. In a tense epilogue, placed several years later, we learn that Ellen has miscarried and that Chris's ennui has grown. He wanders down to the beach, apparently contemplating suicide, but at the last minute—confronted again by the void of the lake and the well-oiled, power-conferring rifle—he appears to make a positive decision, sending his final round of ammunition "out over the open lake."

Although *What I'm Going to Do, I Think* seemed to capture the mood of its time and was widely admired, it proved controversial among reviewers. The vehemence of both positive and negative criticism attests to Woiwode's ability to evoke reader response. Not surprisingly, some reviewers found Chris's character unsatisfactory, terming him dense, needlessly obscure, or, more tellingly, insensitive, a "moral thug." Others objected to the novel's excess of emotions and lack of purposeful action. The usual search for antecedents and influences turned up—along with Hemingway—Fitzgerald and, interestingly, D. H. Lawrence, especially with reference to Woiwode's presentation of sensuality and of natural imagery as indexes of feelings. Many reviewers also commented on the novel's poetic language and its symbolism, with special attention to Chris's rifle (which is depicted on the dust jacket). Finally, some commentators were troubled by the writer's apparent close identification with his hero; for them, the novel projects experience so intensely that it appears to be confessional or even a form of therapy. Such an interpretation anticipates a central theme of Woiwode's second novel.

Thomas Victor

Beyond the Bedroom Wall: A Family Album is more experimental in conception and more satisfying in execution than Woiwode's first novel. In essence, it is a series of tightly interwoven situations and soliloquies rendered so vividly and with so palpable a sense of emotional involvement that it suggests autobiography. The novel traces the fortunes of the Neumiller family, loosely based upon Woiwode's own, from the first immigrant to North Dakota in 1881 to its scattering throughout the nation ninety years and three generations later. The narrative concentrates on the third and fourth generations, which are represented by Martin, a schoolteacher who sacrifices his ambition to his family's needs and his own powerful moral instincts, and his wife Alpha, whose quiet strength, deep sensibility, and tragic early death exert a decisive influence on her entire family, and by their four oldest children: Jerome, Charles, Timothy, and Marie.

The novel opens with a moving recollection by Tim (the character who best exemplifies Woiwode's poetic gift) of his boyhood in the hamlet of Hyatt, North Dakota. The prologue sets the stage for the narrative and establishes its tone and strategy of development. Other retrospectives are interspersed with the central chronological narrative, which is itself an elaborate pattern using seven centers of consciousness (Martin's family plus his father). Other narrative forms complete the montage: several letters, Martin's resume, Tim's poems, objective descriptions of photographs and photographic vignettes to fill out the "Family Album" motif, and, the most moving segment, pages from Alpha's diary.

As with any chronicle, the interplay of themes and motifs is of more enduring interest than the sequence of events. The organizing reality and central motif is death, especially that of four characters: Otto, the original Neumiller, whose passing in 1935 opens the central narrative; Alpha, around whose death in 1951 all events radiate; Martin's father, Charles, in 1962; and Laura, Martin's second wife, in the late 1960s. Each death provokes others into character-revealing action which brings the family together to interact, and, most important, becomes an important event in the major characters' emotional and psychological history. The collective interpretation of those histories and the distinctive habits of perception which create them become, finally, the novel's central concern.

Chapter 37 begins, "The dream is very much in season," a statement that could serve to introduce the novel as well as Woiwode's epigraph from Erik Erikson: " 'Reality,' of course, is man's most powerful illusion; but while he attends to this world, it must outbalance the total enigma of being in it at all." Dreams and dreamlike visions merge repeatedly with hard-edged realism; characters are frequently caught at the threshold of sleep, reconstituting half-remembered events or sifting through a day's events to forge from them a sensible pattern. One's life story is shown to be a fiction as ephemeral as the dream itself, but in a deeper sense, it is also one's nearest approach to reality. Woiwode's purpose is to create a unified family history out of individual, but not isolated, perceptions. Separate versions of the family history reinforce rather than contradict one another, with each member supplying the events crucial to him or her and contributing to an outpouring of emotional responses which, taken together, identify the Neumiller family as a vital unit which confers values and molds consciousness.

In this novel, Woiwode's style moves decisively toward precision and intricacy. His revisions in the previously published chapters suggest this shift. For example, the original text of chapter 34, "Burning the Couch" (1970), begins: "Blue flames burn low over cotton wadding, and black whorls of smoke ascend from the cushions and climb above their heads into the light blue sky of June." In the novel, the flames "scrumble" and "yellowish columns" ascend into "the misty-blue, cerulescent sky of June, which the sun, a silver disk, clings to and hovers behind." Such reworkings represent a radical rethinking of the more objective style of the stories and *What I'm Going to Do, I Think*. Though occasionally (as in this example) the language seems overworked and has the effect of distancing the reader, the style also serves to support the poetic, dreamlike quality of observation and reflection in the novel. Language becomes a complex medium of thought rather than action, a way of creating sensibility rather than simply describing what is done or observed.

Reviewers were generally more receptive to this novel than to his first. Even those put off by its length (620 pages), its metaphoric style, and what they saw as an overt sentimentality recognized Woiwode's skill as a storyteller and, often comparing him to Proust, his serious commitment to understanding the modes of recollection as a central concern of fiction. An especially perceptive commentary is John Gardner's lead review in the *New York Times Book Review* (28 September 1975). Gardner sees the novel as a successful response to the Jamesian bias against episodic fictional structures and as an alternative to the self-conscious mode popularized by Barth and Pynchon. He notes also the cultural significance of a serious presentation of the "link of love, fragmentary shared experience, and faith" to the postwar generation, which has downplayed or dismissed entirely any unifying force.

Larry Woiwode's two novels thus far have established his reputation as a serious thinker and writer; moreover, they have exhibited his capacity for growth, and his best work may yet lie ahead. His independent course—stressing realism, traditional values, and the unity rather than the fragmentation of human experience—runs counter to contemporary critical canons, but his control of language and his instinct for a good story would be regarded as assets in any era. The highly personal flavor of his fiction and his apparent insistence that one experience a novel (at least psychologically) before writing it could restrict his output, although *Beyond the Bedroom Wall* shows considerable ability to depict the world view of disparate characters. Whether his work will prove influential enough to herald a return to the novel of sensibility remains to be seen, but he has already demonstrated that a writer of intelligence and discipline can revitalize traditional forms.

—*Michael E. Connaughton*

Periodical Publications:

"The Horses," *New Yorker*, 44 (28 December 1968): 24-26;

"Owen's Father," *Partisan Review*, 37, no. 3 (1970): 359-377;

"Guns," *Esquire*, 84 (December 1975): 94-95, 210.

Contributors

Martha Adams	*Northeast Louisiana University*
Dorothy Jewell Altman	*Bergen College*
John Alvis	*University of Dallas*
Edwin T. Arnold	*Appalachian State University*
John Auchard	*University of North Carolina*
Joseph J. Branin	*University of Georgia Libraries*
Mary Ellen Brooks	*University of Georgia Libraries*
Charles Harmon Cagle	*Pittsburg State University*
Alan Cheuse	*Knoxville, Tennessee*
Sung Gay Chow	*University of Alabama*
John L. Cobbs	*Elizabeth City State University*
Michael E. Connaughton	*Pittsburg State University*
Dianne L. Cox	*University of South Carolina*
Bill Crider	*Howard Payne University*
Thomas E. Dasher	*Georgia Southern College*
Thadious M. Davis	*University of North Carolina*
A. Grove Day	*University of Hawaii*
Frank Day	*Clemson University*
L. W. Denton	*Auburn University*
Richard Fine	*Virginia Commonwealth University*
Joseph M. Flora	*University of North Carolina*
George Garrett	*Bennington College*
Sam B. Girgus	*University of New Mexico*
Edwin Gittleman	*University of Massachusetts, Boston*
Robert Graalman	*Illinois State University*
William E. Grant	*Bowling Green State University*
Donald J. Greiner	*University of South Carolina*
James B. Hall	*Santa Cruz, California*
Nancy Duvall Hargrove	*Mississippi State University*
James A. Hart	*University of British Columbia*
Carol C. Harter	*Ohio University*
William R. Higgins	*Western Carolina University*
Glenda Hobbs	*Los Angeles, California*
Charles Israel	*South Carolina State College*
David K. Jeffrey	*Auburn University*
Nancy Carol Joyner	*Western Carolina University*
James E. Kibler, Jr.	*University of Georgia*
James Kilgo	*University of Georgia*
William Koon	*Clemson University*
Thomas Landess	*University of Dallas*
James W. Lee	*North Texas State University*
Stanley W. Lindberg	*University of Georgia*
George C. Longest	*Virginia Commonwealth University*
Patricia Jewell McAlexander	*University of Georgia*
Gail M. Morrison	*Midlands Technical College*
Elisabeth Muhlenfeld	*Florida State University*
Robert M. Nelson	*University of Richmond*

Contributors

Peggy Whitman Prenshaw	*University of Southern Mississippi*
David Paul Ragan	*University of South Carolina*
Martha Ragland	*Virginia Commonwealth University*
Bin Ramke	*Columbus College*
Carl Rapp	*University of Georgia*
Walter W. Ross III	*Columbia, South Carolina*
Hugh M. Ruppersburg	*University of Georgia*
Allen Shepherd	*University of Vermont*
Lawrence D. Stewart	*California State University*
Gary Tolliver	*Ohio University*
Ben Merchant Vorpahl	*University of Georgia*
James R. Waddell	*Crystal Springs, Mississippi*
Carl Solana Weeks	*University of Georgia*
Craig Werner	*University of Mississippi*
Robert M. Willingham, Jr.	*University of Georgia Libraries*
James D. Wilson	*Georgia State University*

ISBN 0-8103-0908-4
90000
9 780810 309081

There were two American dream
both cruel/ ~~apparently~~
frontier, ~~savage~~ and innocent, and/

a fortune

There were two Am

rhapsody
of the frontier, wh
both
and was
boundless in beauty,
made men, and search
or stuffed them. The oth
equally
to seize the day
If you
a fortune involved
a craving for the inve
expending of mar
always new settlem
ed Mass production instead of
everybody happy

CELESTIAL NAVIGATION

1960: ~~AMANDA PAULDING~~ Amanda

My brother Jeremy is a thirty-eight year old bachelor who never did leave home. Long ago we gave up expecting very much of him, but still he is the last man in our family and you would think that in time of tragedy he might pull himself together and take over a few of the responsibilities. Well, he didn't. He telephoned my sister and me in Richmond, where we have a little apartment together. If memory serves me it was the first time in his life he had ever placed a call to us; can you imagine? Ordinarily we phoned Mother every Sunday evening when the rates were down and then she would put Jeremy on the line to say hello. Which was about all he did say: "Hello," and "Fine, thank you," and then a long breathing pause and, "Well, goodbye now." So when I heard his voice that night I had trouble placing it for a moment. "Amanda?" he said, and I said, "Yes? Who is it?"

"I wanted to tell you about Mama," Jeremy said.

That's what he calls her still: Mama. Laura and I switched to Mother when we were grown but Jeremy didn't.